University of Essex Library

Date Due Back

Books may be renewed online (or telephone 01206 873187)
Unless they have been recalled.

Form No. L.43 April 2004

THE IDEA OF MUSIC

Early Drama, Art, and Music
Monograph Series, 9

THE IDEA OF MUSIC

*An Introduction to Musical Aesthetics
in Antiquity and the Middle Ages*

by Herbert M. Schueller

Early Drama, Art, and Music
Monograph Series, 9

Medieval Institute Publications
Western Michigan University
Kalamazoo, MI 49008-3851
1988

ISBN 0-918720-87-7 hardbound
ISBN 0-918720-88-5 paperbound

Printed in the United States of America

Cover Design by Pamela Rups

Contents

To My Wife

Preface

While I have written this book in part to satisfy my own curiosity, I have also for a long time wanted to see an orderly presentation of works which furnish an outline of the *idea* of music prior to the Renaissance in the West, especially as this idea pertains to the larger study of aesthetics. Aestheticians frequently ignore music and concentrate instead on the visual arts and literature, though in fact the aesthetics of music may be more important historically for an understanding of the artistic experience. I have been interested in how the idea took root in classical antiquity and in how it was transmitted and transformed from the recorded beginning through the centuries called medieval. Quite well known are the Platonic notion that music can change human character and disposition and the Aristotelian agreement with this position. But music functions in a tradition. It is not something static and fixed but alive and moving within a cultural matrix. Hence in undertaking this book I have attempted to write principally for the scholar who is a non-specialist in early music theory and especially for the aesthetician, though I have also had in mind medieval scholars in various fields (and even the general reader) who would find the concentrated method of the encyclopedist confusing or the treatises of the specialized researcher too distracting and opaque.

Keeping in mind such an audience for this book, I have made a deliberate effort not to treat technical theory in elaborate and final detail. Nevertheless, I have had of course to pursue technical aspects of music theory to some degree, though I recognize that my presentation will of necessity be less than satisfying to the technical theorist who up until now has been the chief exponent of the works considered here. While the expert may consider my approach to be superficial in the treatment of his specialty, I would submit that he has been superficial in other ways. His approach has been professional and has thus been indifferent to the context in which his subject appears as well as to the aesthetic considerations that are central to my concerns. In contrast to his positivist-historical approach, mine has essentially been humanistic.

Thus I have written a chronological account in discussion of certain documents, what they contain, and how they are related to one another. I treat each writer in turn, outline his music theory, and describe his intellectual interrelations with others. My method is to pursue individual ideas not as separate entities throughout the periods under discussion--ideas like truth, beauty, progress, and so forth--but as elements in a complex of a writer's theories of music as a whole. Individual ideas--number, pitch, mode, or poetic theory--are sub-ideas in a thinker's complete music theory, however limited or extensive.

Whenever possible I have quoted from readily available texts in English translation, though in some instances where such texts are not available the translations from German or Latin are necessarily my own. I have found it prudent in general to stay with the normal English forms for terms and not to follow Schäfke's practice of employing the original Greek terminology, with which few of my readers will likely be acquainted. On the whole the writers treated in my study attempted to state (supposed) facts about music in a sober prose and thus were concerned to present such facts in rational and clear ways. For this reason, I trust that readers will not object to my use throughout of translations in place of the original texts, since my purpose has likewise been to achieve a narrative characterized with as much clarity as possible.

As I have indicated above, I have concentrated on the idea of music in the West. This may seem to some to be a limitation, but my study has revealed further and probably more serious limitations in other scholarship. For example, music is seldom mentioned in the existing mass of scholarly writings about the Greek lyric, the epic, or the theater. If translators have involuntarily distorted ancient works, commentators have done so to an even greater extent. They have ignored the fact that lyric and epic poets and dramatists were practicing musicians and have silently treated them as exclusively literary men. We know that in the ancient world the word 'music' was associated with all the Muses and that it stood for a blend of music, literature, and the dance. Yet many literary scholars are loath to recognize this fact, and when they see Aeschylus, Sophocles, and Euripides as purely literary figures or wear blinders against Platonic and Aristotelian theories of music, they are unconsciously altering the facts. If I am accused of doing the same thing, but in reverse, I am at least only trying to redress the balance, as it were, and to correct mistaken interpretations, scholarly and historical, no matter how elegant and aristocratic their origins.

In choosing to organize this book around the *idea* of music rather than to write a *history* of the aesthetics of music, I realize that I run the risk of encountering some problems, not the least of which concerns the relationship of music to the Platonic Ideas or Forms. I made this choice because I am aware of the lack of agreement which exists concerning the term 'aesthetics,' even after two and one-half centuries of use. I have not, of course, avoided the use of this term, but it will be noticed that I have not applied it in the strict, narrow, and "pure" sense used for the examination of musical structure as written and transferred to the ear and mind. Aesthetic theory as such is a development out of the eighteenth century and serves to give rational support for an "instinctive" attitude, a "response," and even an area of knowledge and judgment which are not restricted to one's time, place, or social position. At the same time, another term, 'criticism,' seemed to me to be too broad, and it applies in any case chiefly to the analysis and judgment of individual works, which are not mentioned at all in Greek musical speculation and in the Middle Ages only at their end. So I decided that the term 'idea' was more useful, in spite of the potential confusion mentioned at the opening of this paragraph. An Idea is *a priori* and an idea *a posteriori*. I wanted to take the low *a posteriori* road even in the face of possible evidences that an Idea of music does indeed exist.

In essence I wanted to see in perspective the history of what music was thought to be, how it received its name, what it at different times was, and what it was expected to be. I asked certain questions. What is the function of music? What is the extent of its appeal? What classes of society cherish it--or is its application universal? What are its characteristic attractions for an educated man--or for an uneducated one? And so forth. As will be obvious, I still had to touch upon important matters of structure as well as on mathematical, social, and biological phenomena. But because from an early point in the history of thought, music was deemed a concern of the educated man--not the professional engineer, let us say, not the technician, but the cultivated, mature citizen, and also not the craftsman, but instead the man of leisure looking toward philosophy--I found that I could indeed focus my study in a way appropriate to the treatment of a cultural phenomenon having psychological, social, religious, and moral implications, for music was also regarded as a science that could be tested by its influence on human life.

For my good fortune at the beginning of my work on the present book I must thank the officers of the American Council of Learned Societies and, at its end, President Diether Haenicke of Western Michigan University. In the absence of research assistants and devoted secretaries, I was richly helped by the former, but my gratitude extends equally to the latter for his personal interest in my scholarship. I also thank for their comments and opinions the various readers, chiefly anonymous, who expressed themselves, often pleasantly, so that I could continue my work on this book with renewed courage. A number of individuals, whom I cannot name, helped me to receive materials through the interlibrary loan systems of the libraries of Brandeis University, Kalamazoo College, the University of Akron, the University of Detroit, the State University of Wisconsin at Stevens Point, the University of California at Berkeley, the University of Illinois, the University of Oregon, the University of Michigan, and others. I must express special gratitude also to the professionals in the library of the Detroit Institute of Arts, in the Detroit Public Library, in the libraries of Wayne State University, and in the library of St. John's Seminary in Plymouth, Michigan. Together these libraries proved to house depositories, unexpected and comprehensive, of works germane to my subject. It would be brave of me to mention the many persons in these libraries who have been generous with their help, brave and risky, for fear of overlooking someone who has always been courteous, friendly, and helpful.

But there are people whom I can and must name: James Toy for his bibliographical assistance, Ralph Nash for his help in translating Latin, and Audrey Davidson for her material contributions to the substance of my discourse. Above all, I must thank my editor, Clifford Davidson, for saving me from making innumerable gaffes resulting from my devotion to the *idea* I was pursuing and from my consequent treatment of editorial details in cavalier fashion. I must also thank Verne Emlaw for her careful typing of my hobby, as she thought of it, and Juleen Audrey Eichinger for her meticulous preparation of the computer disks for the typesetter. But my gratitude must go especially to my wife, who contributed her considerable skills to my project and was regretful that I could not take more advantage of what she had to offer.

PART I

THE IDEA OF MUSIC IN ANCIENT EUROPE

I
From Apollo to Damon

Greek legend tells us that Harmonia, a goddess of Boeotia, the ancient home of mysteries and divination, personified harmony and order. Daughter to Aphrodite, the goddess of love, and Ares, the god of war, she married Cadmus, the founder of Thebes, the bringer of the alphabet out of Phoenicia into Greece, and therefore the founder of civilized life. Theirs supposedly was the first wedding involving a mortal attended by the Olympians. As gifts, Athena gave Harmonia a golden robe which conferred divine dignity on its wearer--and a set of *auloi*. The Muses played the *auloi* and also sang. Apollo, the inventor of music, played his cithara or lyre. Thus, universal love and war as opposites were united to produce in Harmonia a cosmological and earthly harmony symbolized by the music of the aulos and the lyre, the traditional musical instruments of Greece. Mount Olympus and the lower earth were brought together through Harmonia, who was named for the aesthetic principle inherent not only in the universe, but also in the mind of man and its creations. If an aesthetics of music, unacknowledged, tacit, and unrecognized, began at any discernible time, it must have been in this mythological past when men and gods felt the balancing and the ordering effects of music. The aulos and the lyre celebrated the wedding of concord with the symbol of language, which is the alphabet; it celebrated the union of music with poetry. And with music and poetry had been associated, from time immemorial, the dance, also a part of this wedding ceremony. All three--music, poetry, and dance--were as one in an aesthetic state of harmony, the first principle of universal law.

In another version of the myth, Harmonia was the daughter of Zeus and the Atalantide Elektra, and she was the mother of the Muses, who were usually assigned to Zeus and Mnemosyne (or memory). She was also therefore allied with Euterpe, or music, one of the seven Muses, and also with Orpheus, the founder of the Orphic mysteries, whose music, according to legend, was so beautiful that it charmed beasts, trees, and rocks, and even the gods of the underworld. He was a predecessor to Amphion, said to have invented the lyre and to have at will moved stones with the sound of his instrument.

Orpheus was sometimes thought to be bard-servant to Apollo and the son of a Muse; and sometimes he was reputed to be the son of Calliope and Apollo himself. He was both creator and performer, both poet and musician. He and his instrument, both representatives of the ancient art of

1

eloquence, were destroyed by Thracian Maenads, whose fury was aroused when he scorned their attempts to seduce him. As man-god and artist, he was later thought to be the supreme pagan poet. For the Greeks, he was the sweet singer, and sometimes he was the originator of the lineage of Homer. He was also the great physician, and in the temple he was the object of intense religious devotion. He used music for its therapeutic and religious effects, which were not necessarily or always separate. He had a pupil or, as was sometimes claimed, a son called Musaeus, who, according to Aristophanes, was a physician of the soul and whose music was a treasury of joy and delight. Musaeus himself, according to Aristotle (*Pol.* 1339b), said that music is "to mortals of all things the sweetest."

Orpheus made music the basic feature of the Mysteries. As a representative of the Olympian gods, he was not only an idealized human being who could communicate in realms far above the human but also one who was the center of a secret cult of his own. His favorite instrument was the cithara. Dionysius, the center of another well-known cult, preferred the aulos and was sometimes identified with Bacchus because he represented the mystery gods accessible to human beings when they were in a state of emotional ecstasy or frenzy, or when they indulged in food and drink. Bacchus himself was a Thracian god, but there also were cults of Cybele, the mother-goddess of nature and a Phrygian deity, and of many other gods and goddesses for whom music was a stimulating force. There was even a later cult of Pythagoras, who shared with Orpheus the aim of bringing the human soul into a state of harmony. The two cults most dramatically contrasted by the early Greeks (and also, in modern times, by Nietzsche) were the Apollonian, representing clarity, temperance, and moderation, in keeping with the music of the cithara, and the Dionysian, representing the excessive, the unrestrained, the fantastic, the irrational, and the orgiastic, in keeping with the abrasive music of the aulos.

Thought to be immortal, the Greek gods were conceived anthropomorphically. Euhemerus, a Greek mythologer of the late fourth century B.C., called them and the myths about them distortions of human heroes and warriors of the long-ago past. They differed from men only to the extent that they possessed knowledge and power. They too were subject to the laws of the cosmos and nature. Not omniscient or omnipotent like the later God of Christianity, they were yet superior to human beings, who in turn were subject to them. Apollo, though strictly speaking only one of the minor gods, was nevertheless worshipped intensely, and in human imagination he played many roles. He was thought, for example, to be a predecessor of Aesculapius, the "blameless physician" of Homer, the two of them combining music and medicine.[1] Of all the ancient gods, it was they who were the most frequently mentioned in musico-medical terms, Apollo being thought by far the more versatile. Also frequently invoked as the earth god, he governed agriculture, vegetation, cattle, and the meadows and pastures which nourished them. He was also god of music, dancing, and poetry, and in another transformation served as a symbol of sunlight, as the giver of life and all its blessings. A physician of the body, he was an archaic--psychophysicist who could purge men of their guilts. If life is indeed harmony, both physical and mental disturbances could destroy it. And Apollo, however related to Harmonia, could dispel physical and mental disturbances: through mere rythmical movement alone, he could restore universal harmony, measure, and beauty.

In the dimmest of pasts, therefore, music was allied with the religious cults in a blend with poetry and dance to form the "triune *choreia*" (words, gesture, and music). There were songs of praise for Apollo, dithyrambic songs performed by choirs in the spring in praise of Dionysius (the dithyramb from which Aristotle in the *Poetics* [1449a] said tragedy sprang), and syllabic chants accompanying processions. These made up the dominant expressive art in religion and in ancient civic life. Music was the special gift of the gods, it was thought, and it has magical powers enabling it even to tear the soul out of the flesh.

Like the Muses, who were goddesses of knowledge, it would seem that Harmonia should rightly have been the daughter of Mnemosyne rather than of Aphrodite and Ares, as in the primary version of her myth. To be sure, her heritage allowed her to symbolize opposites, not only of parents male and female, but also the contraries of love and war; she was both harmony and harmony-in-disagreement. Empedocles called her serious of mien,[2] which is sometimes translated as "grave-eyed" and implies the alliance of two opposing fates or spirits. Plutarch celebrates her when he writes about tranquillity of mind (*Moralia*, "On Tranquillity of Mind" 474), and Horace (*Ep*. 1.12.27-28) speaks of the discordant union which binds together the world and regulates the heavenly spheres. But to be grasped by the mind she calls for the capacity of memory.

What would poetry and music be without harmony or memory? Harmonia mediates between pitch and rhythm--or pitch, rhythm, and words--and represents order, proportion, or symmetry. To be truly per-ceived, therefore, she demands the presence of memory, which allows one to observe the perceptual order. She is essentially a subjectively arrived-at aesthetic realization. The individual mind must have the ability to remem-ber the parts and recognize their compatibility--or their lack of order (in which case Harmonia is absent). Socrates in Plato (*Phaedr*. 275) seems to think that the invention of writing destroys memory and encourages forgetfulness. (What would he have thought of the effects of printing, the late medieval Renaissance invention to which we shall come around at the end of the lengthy study which is this book?) Memory and perception by themselves can produce true opinions and propositions (*Philebus* 39). The stream of successive impressions from the outside world is perceived only to be stored in memory, organized by intellect, and declared by judgment to be harmonious or inharmonious.

As a general and probably universal goddess, Harmonia, according to report, governed the best music of Greece. One would expect this music with its celebrated powers, like tragedies, pieces of sculpture, and architectural monuments, still to survive as our inheritance from one of the great ages of the civilized world, as an unexcelled example of practical music in the "grand" tradition. Unfortunately, only glimpses of this music exist in fragments which cannot give us an adequate view of all the musical practices involved. The musical notation has been studied, and attempts at reconstruction of the sounds have been attempted.[3] Yet theory about this music, about how it was made, how it was organized and how it sounded, or how its actual effects were produced--all of this is in large part a matter of written record. It may be true that aesthetic theory is empty unless it is based on concrete instances in nature and art. Significant as the few extant fragments of ancient Greek music are, it must be admitted that most concrete instances of such music have in fact disappeared, while at least a larger selection of the poetry and drama it accompanied remains, small as that selection is when compared with the entire body of poetry and drama which must once have existed. Poet and musician, dramatist and musician, were usually identical; but the preservation of musical works required that they be written down in notation (which, apparently was not usually the case) and that these written records might survive into modern times. The musical side of performance, often extemporized, was usually, it would seem, not preserved in a musical score of any kind. Yet written theory and speculation remain: they "float up there," as it were, and tell us more about what was thought about music--what was the idea of it--than of what it concretely was. The idea existed in a context of legends about gods who embraced ideals of concord in everything, in good and evil, in love and war, in godliness and morality, in music and dance, in musical poetry all--in a combination which was cosmological, cultural, political, psychological, and artistic in activity (*technē*).

Everything in connection with the Greek idea of music, therefore, is based on assumptions in outline unclear, in details hazy, and, in modern terms, unscientific. There is, first, a world view based on a theory that the cosmos is characterized by an order assumed but not observed, an order which includes everything as an All. There is a fundamental law, or a principle of organization, including metaphorically high and low planes-- the Great Chain of Being--according to which everything higher and lower exists in a necessary coherence, in a necessary aesthetic state of harmony. Human beings are subject to the same principles as the material elements of the universe, and so too are animals and plants. Furthermore, everything is governed by the basic principle of rhythm, which in cosmology historically precedes sound. (It was also the first predominating element in the history of music.) In addition, there are opposites in the universe--light and dark, cold and wet, day and night; these are analogically in permanent oscillation; they are like flowering and death, the rhythms of plant and animal life and of human existence, of pain and pleasure, of happiness and misfortune, and so forth. Their beauty is in their "reconciliation." The ancient philosopher, who sometimes thought of geometrical spheres as representatives of the universe as a whole and as symbols of the levels and planes on which all creatures in the cosmos abide, was supposedly the observer of and the instructor about the vast universe of relationships from the divine top to the inanimate bottom. Somewhere in the middle of the ontological mixture was music, a phenomenon of transmission, as it were, which in partaking of the universal organization, and in exemplifying it, profoundly affected the lives and actions of human beings.

It derived its name from *mousikē*, an untranslatable term modelled after the name of the Muses. At first it meant an activity, an art, or a craft (*technē*) over which the Muses presided.[4] It was the only art whose name was not separate and individual. Originally it was not confined to the art of pure sound we recognize today, or even to singing and playing as we know them. Instead, it shared in whatever governs knowledge and ability or capacity. Suggested is everything except gymnastics--that is, the mental, as compared with the physical man. It was thought that a person guided by the Muses was favored by them with a certain capacity which allowed him to pursue his own characteristic activities and skills. As god and leader, Apollo would transmit the gift of music to human beings. Homer and Hesiod, as they themselves remind us, were granted their priestly domain, functions, and gifts by the Muses, upon whom they not infrequently called for help in the course of their works. The musician created an aesthetic union of "music proper" with poetry, epic, or lyric, or with drama and dance, or with all together, to form a single harmonic structure whose determining factor was words. Tragedy as Aristotle was to define it (*Poet.* 1449b) was made up of language, but it had added pleasurable accessories, all being introduced separately in various parts of a work: choric song or hymn (which had been the original nucleus of drama as a type), the lesser music of instruments, and dance with gesture took their places in the whole. All such combinations were judged to be art or skillful production, like crafts such as carpentry and weaving, which were created by man in contradistinction to nature.

Art did indeed include the fine arts of modern times, but it was not confined to them. All the arts, all the crafts, all based on knowledge and skill, were "fine." But music in the most philosophical sense was not so restricted: it was "free" because as a universal phenomenon it was intellectual and did not require manual work. Its contraries were vulgar and servile arts like sculpture and architecture, which pursue practical ends. As an intellectual preoccupation, as a matter of theory, music was indeed "free." If it demanded handwork, however, it was no more free than the job of sailing a boat or leading an army. *Auletics* was the art of playing the aulos, and *citharoetics* was the art of playing the cithara. Both were professional and practical; neither was free. For to the Greeks, terms like *poiētēs* and *mousikē* had more practical meanings than they have for us. When *mousikē* was a practical art, it included every activity encouraged by the Muses. Because of its inclusive character, it was taken as a category whose guiding Muse was Euterpe and whose characteristic and name meant harmony (Harmonia). Allied with mathematics and gymnastics (or athletics), it meant education for the complete man of high social rank and of course also for philosophers. It represented a cluster of skills and knowledges judged in our day not to be even remotely related. And its effects were held to be social, psychological, and ethical or moral. Its aim was benefit for both the individual soul and the total social unit. Society being male-oriented and cherishing the accepted masculine occupations of males with war and civic or political activity, it was an art which in its preferred results was directed towards masculine or manly qualities as illustrated, for example, in two of the staples of education, the *Iliad* and the *Odyssey*.

Despite the paucity of known examples of the Greek art of music, however, Greek music theory held first place in the minds of learned men for many centuries and for at least two millennia. Both Greek aesthetic theory--not so termed, of course--and the Greek idea of music--also not so termed--exerted a profound intellectual influence on later ages along with other recorded aspects of Greek life and thought. The Greek term *aisthēsis* meant mental as opposed to physical feeling, and, as a corollary, the term 'music' in the theoretical sense embodied ideals which stood for intellectual and permanently valid principles. The idea of music was part of a tradition, and was itself a tradition which earned respect through Roman times up to the seventeenth century. Occasionally revived even today, the idea of music remains in many respects obscure, and it has often been misunderstood and misinterpreted by every age according to its own preconceptions. Some-times men have simply tried to clarify the theory, and in nearly every century in Western thought--and no less in the centuries called medieval--the musical philosophy of Greece has been almost a tyrannical or obsessive passion, so much so that even the unavailable music itself has constantly been held up as a model (as a correlate with Greek poetry, drama, and thought) for "revivals," imitations, and approximations. Even the modern age, musically and culturally complex, has repeatedly tried to return to the pristine simplicity of Greek music, though it must surely be true that Greek rhythms--microrhythms, actually--were more complex than ours. Besides their ideal and much imitated simplicity, however, there is also the exotic. The Greeks themselves admitted to a reliance on Egyptian, Assyrian, Phoenician, and other influences from Asia Minor. They called two of their modes Phrygian and Lydian, said that Egypt was the source of their musico-pedagogic ideas, and sometimes attributed the existence of their own music to Olympus, the son of Marsyas the Phrygian.

I

Music as Epic and Didactic Poetry, Public Pronouncement, and Lyric Poetry. To the modern mind, which has difficulty in locating early Greek poets in time, Homer (eighth century B.C. or earlier) represents time immemorial. In the eyes of the Greeks, never strong on chronology, he recorded their early history in the siege of Troy. In his traditional wisdom, he knew that people sang and played instruments for pleasure and for the purpose of intensifying a message or making it exciting and sometimes only palatable. Whether man, woman (according to Samuel Butler), or committee, Homer in the Odyssey (8.63ff)[5] describes the blind bard Demodocus, to whom the Muses gave "strains divine"; he sings to the satisfaction of Agamemnon about the conflicts between Achilles and Odysseus at the gates of Troy. In the ancient world, such blindness as his was associated with poetry, music, and prophecy. Inspired by Apollo, he sang so feelingly of that terrible time of war that his audience was delighted, and Odysseus himself was transported and moved to tears. Homer (whatever his identity) was of course both poet and musician, and it may have seemed to him more literally than figuratively (and fictionally) true that the nine Muses did indeed sing alternating songs at the funeral of Achilles (*Od.* 24.63ff) and, to the accompaniment of Apollo's lyre, before the gods (*Iliad* 1.603ff). Thus also the Sirens (*Od.* 12.40, 160) had employed the luring and seductive aspects of music, and the sons of Autolycus (*Od.* 19.457ff) had bound up Odysseus' wound to stay "the black blood with a song of healing"--in doing which they may have acted much like the reciting poet whose sounds in concordant rhythm or meter accompanied by instrumental "melody" only existed to make the words more recollectable. The Greeks, Homer says, stopped a pestilence with music (*Iliad* 1.472). Besides, music gives sober sense to those lacking it, incites cowards to courage, and calms those burning with rage. Achilles loved music, played the harp (*Iliad* 9.180ff), and sang of the deeds of heroes.

These heroes sometimes assigned musicians as the best guardians of the wives they left behind them: Clytemnestra had at hand a minstrel given to her as a companion by Agamemnon when he left Troy (*Od.* 3.270ff); this man sang to her in anapests in order to control her amorous passion for Aegisthus. Odysseus (*Od.* 9.7ff) praised the use of music with bread, meat, and wine at banqueting--in short, as crowning the festive board (*Od.* 1.150-52)--and thereby encouraged a practice which almost became a tradition in later aristocratic times. Singers, along with craftsmen, prophets, healers, or workers in wood, were everywhere invited into a noble's house (*Od.* 17.382-85). Agamemnon hears with dismay the *auloi* and fifes of the Phrygians (*Iliad* 10.13), and the famous bard Phemius sings to Penelope's suitors (*Od.* 1.152ff, 323). When Penelope asks him to stop singing about the bitter homecoming of the Achaeans, her son Telemachus reminds her that "Men like best/ a song that rings like morning on the ear" (1.351-52). At the banquet of the gods in the Iliad, Apollo himself plays the "flawless harp" (1.601), Achilles' wrath against Agamemnon is allayed by the music he learned from the sage Chiron (*Iliad* 11.832), and Eumaeus the swineherd says that a minstrel is taught by heaven to touch the hearts of men (*Od.* 17.520ff). Odysseus himself says that all men owe honor and respect to poets, the darlings of the Muse, who "puts upon their lips the ways of life" (*Od.* 8.479). Of all uses of music, however, the best is in the praise of the gods.

Did music have the heroic effects which Homer claimed for it? If Homer was indeed the realistic artist-bard he is often said to have been, the answer must be in the affirmative. Music in ancient, even pre-classical, times had its major place at banquets, at assemblies, at the announcements of old or new laws or of royal decisions, and at bardic recitals. By virtue of its moral message, it could restrain Clytemnestra and Penelope; the latter's amorous propensities could indeed have been modified by the chanted words of Phemius. And Achilles could indeed pass the time in "musical" thought, which, one may conjecture, was probably a song-like chanting not confined to precise pitches and pitch relationships. There were repetitions of euphonious names of men lost before the gates of Troy (*Iliad* 2.24-37, 66-77) and often of identical passages. What quality of voice was used none can say. All was probably traditional or occasionally improvised, and sung in the courts of petty kings and in small towns, at first, it may be, in Ionia, often called the cradle of Western philosophy and culture.

Homer was the model disseminator of an inherited background or tradition. His themes were actions, not ideas. His audience knew he was retelling old stories with poetic elaborations. We know that his art was composed of words declaimed in a special type of melody, rhythm, and (successive) harmony, all in a unified blend. The melody had no or little connection with modern melody based on artificially predetermined pitches in predetermined relationships to one another. It was probably an expressive declamation extending in pitch and quality of pitch from a low hum-like whisper to a high-pitched howl, with infinite possibilities and gradations in between. The rhythm was literary and based on the hexameter. The harmony was a binding of elements into a unity--by the listener, through memory--of sound-elements appearing successively. It was the art not alone of melody, but of *melopoeia*.

Attempts to approximate Homer's chant or declamation in our time often lead to the uninteresting, rambling, and dull. Comparison is impossible. Are we allowed to imagine that Schoenbergian *Sprechstimme* is something like it? Yet the Homeric utterances about musical effects cannot be ignored in a history of the idea of music: they ultimately took on the certainty of transmitted truth. From the sixth century B.C. onward, Homer was part of education and the *Iliad* and *Odyssey* were textbooks.

To think back to Homer's time and to imagine its music is a process of imagination through deletion: it is a mental act essential to the probable understanding of music (and of all the other arts) long antedating the present. It is a process of anti-memory, of a forgetting, which must be almost complete. We must imagine a singer-composer-bard "singing" in a language whose sounds are now unknown, in intricate Greek hexameters, and in rhythmical lines made up of metrical units, not of accents, but of lengths (of quantities of long and short syllables). He sings about human beings, their loves, hates, deceptions, wars, and fates as crystallized in old plots frequently revived or embellished in new and improvised creations--all done in memorized formulae or in forms improvised on the spot. Chanted lines flexible and irregular in cast are punctuated by frequent repetitions of stock phrases ("the rosy-fingered dawn," "sea-girt Ithaca," "owl-eyed Athena") which held symbolic meanings for Homer's audience, as they still do for us. The bard probably uses gestures if he can and accompanies himself on a string instrument called the *phorminx*, used for beating rhythms and for filling in time when he wants to catch his breath, to take a "break," or to think of what he will sing next. Basic, however, is the cast of characters of the recitation--traditional gods, goddesses, and mortals of high social cast (heroes), all protagonists of actions either moral or immoral.

As a creator of actions through words, the bard is a veritable magus indeed. His insights allow him to sing of social and family life, of eating and drinking, of king and commoner, or of the nature of swineherding, animal-butchering, or agriculture. He names the names, the actions, the virtues and the vices, the loves and hates, and the genealogies of heroes already well known. And then thereafter the speeches of the heroes appearing at frequent intervals are examples of rhetoric intended to inspire and counsel.

Didactic Poetry. Hesiod probably lived a century later than Homer. He was the creator, or organizer, of the pantheon of Greek gods. As historian, he divided the past into five ages of man--gold, silver, bronze, heroic, and iron. According to tradition, he was also the father of Greek didactic poetry. The first person on record to attack Homer as a writer of epics inimical to the truth, he confessed that the Muses appeared to him as he fed his father's flocks, called him prophet and poet, gave him the staff of the rhapsode to signify his wisdom as a singer, and said to him, "We know how to tell many falsehoods that sound like truth;/ But we also know how to utter the truth when we choose" (*Theogony* 27-28). Thus Homer helped him "imitate" and create through falsification, and the Muses were firmly identified for him with fiction. Hesiod was not, however, alone in declaring that art is a matter of illusion or fiction. Later, Pindar spoke of "tales told and overlaid with elaboration of lies"(*Olympia* 1.26-27).

Both Homer and Hesiod fostered their own dignity, superiority, and reliability by declaring that their gift was attributable to divine origin and inspiration. Similarly, the bard Phemius in the *Odyssey* (17.520-21) was "taught by heaven" and possessed a heart in which the gods had planted songs of all kinds. These bards, as they recorded the deeds of their superhuman gods, even then serving as symbols, and of their all-too-human heroes, took on the robes of the *vates*, of the historian, and of the moral teacher. Everything they did served an educative or moral function, and for their audiences the powerful effect of their "music" with its fictional heroes was informative, inspirational, exciting, healthful, and pleasant.

Public Announcement. Among the more mysterious of the early critics of Homer was the Athenian Solon (c.638-557 B.C.), one of the Seven Sages, a law-giver, and the first poet of Athens. In political poems he lamented the inequality of gods and men. He was also perhaps one of the first to think that music should promote morality and strengthen the state so that men can be independent of the gods. For him, immanent laws governed every community, each citizen was a moral agent fulfilling social duties,[6] and music was a social, educational, and law-transmitting force, concretely striking a balance between gymnastics and letters. Through Solon, therefore (who may have been first in propounding the doctrine of the mean), music, however defined, comes into the history of ideas and is said to exert an influence suggested by Homer, but described in detail only by the Pythagoreans, Plato, and Aristotle.

Lyric Poetry. It is probable that lyric poetry as a genre arose during the century when Hesiod was listing, classifying, and describing the gods. Among the earliest poet-musicians was Archilochus (fl. seventh century B.C.), a singer of songs when, it is conjectured, all poetry was sung or chanted. Called the "scurrilous or licentious," he is said to have added instrumental accompaniment to his lyric poetry. Because of the principle of *symphonia*--of the concordance of sounds as opposed to diaphony--the instruments sounded in unison with the voice in both melody and rhythm. It is claimed that he invented iambic poetry, enlivened Greek music by employing tempos faster than had been customary, and introduced unfamiliar rhythmic patterns; and thus he seems to have rebelled against the established *nomoi* or poetic-musical laws of his time. It is probably for this reason that he was sometimes termed a degenerate.

If Orpheus, Amphion, and Linus the Theban were variously declared to be the mythical founders of music, Terpander of Sparta, who either preceded or followed Archilochus (so indefinite is the dating for these early musician-poets), is often thought to be its earthly father as well as the founder of lyric poetry. He is reputed to have constructed *nomoi* or "airs" which became models in hexameters for the use of other poets. His *nomoi* were designed for the cithara, as Olympus is said to have constructed them for the aulos. He increased the number of strings on the cithara or lyre from four to seven--ostensibly a revolutionary innovation since, as Pseudo-Plutarch (?first century A.D.) reports (1144), in Argos the number 4 was held so rigidly that people were fined if the strings of their instruments exceeded it. The seven-string lyre or heptachord, for which Terpander wrote the first *nomos*, was basic, it was thought, to the (*technē*), or the knowledge and skill of all music, and Terpander's melody in seven parts was essentially an outline for the setting of various texts. Each *nomos* as devised by Terpander (and others) became a binding, unwritten rule. In time it of course changed, but the assumption that it was necessary and valid did not. Here is an archaic example of the extent to which rules in art are held to be permanent and, indeed, sacred. Composer-poets like Terpander and his poetic followers for centuries were restricted to rational, objective, and therefore prescribed norms which were theoretically based on the principle of measure in all things.

Terpander's chief successor is said to have been Thales (or Thaletas) of Crete (fl. c.670 B.C.), reputed artificially to have added melodic modes and rhythmic elements to Terpander's *nomoi*. Legend has it that his school of music at Sparta superseded Terpander's (Pseudo-Plutarch, *On Music* 1134c). He arranged choruses for the Dorian festivals and supposedly introduced to Sparta the kind of music and poetry which was indigenous to Crete--calm and solemn paeans in worship of Apollo and also several types of songs and dances. Did he use both the aulos and the lyre? It is said he did. He is classified as a lyric poet, though none of his work remains. It is probable that he followed a double course, however--as a lyric poet and as political moralist and information-giver. Plutarch in his life of Lycurgus (*Lives* 1.212) writes that Thales at first "seemed to be no other than a lyric poet," though "in reality he performed the part of the ablest lawgivers [that is, announcers] of the world." His songs were "exhortations to obedience and concord," their very verse measures and cadences "conveying impressions of order and tranquillity"; the minds of the hearers were so influenced that they were "insensibly softened and civilized"; they "renounced their private feuds and animosities, and were reunited in a common admiration of virtue." Thus, Plutarch adds, it can "truly be said that Thales prepared the way for the discipline introduced by Lycurgus," who, as Quintilian the Roman rhetorician later remarked (1.10.15), allowed music in the presentation of his laws.

Probably the greatest of the musico-poetic innovators was Pindar (c.518-430 B.C.), whose teacher, Lasos of Hermione (fl. c.500 B.C.), was said by Suidas, the lexicographer of Constantinople in the late tenth century A.D., to have written the first treatise on music. Lasos taught *mousikē* in Athens, where he introduced the study and theory of verbal euphony, the predominant element in Greek poetry. He stressed timbre, intonation, and quantity, and discouraged the use of the letter S as representing a disagreeable sound. He was also an experimenter in the speed of vibrations of a string as it sounded a tone and in rhythm, harmony, and tempo (especially in dithyrambic song).[7]

His pupil Pindar is credited with being the greatest lyric poet of ancient Greece, a master of the choral lyric, and the discoverer of vibration as the cause of sound. The originator of the type of ode named after himself, he tried to refute the religious views of the philosophers: the same mother, he said, nurtured both gods and men, the former only being more privileged than the latter. Men should not ape the gods, he thought, because "mortal things befit a mortal." For him, poetry derives from genius rather than from art (*technē*)--a rare opinion in his day. Yet he too like Hesiod ascribed poetry to a source and an inspiration which were divine; in his twelfth Pythian ode he says that the maiden goddess Pallas Athene "discovered the polyphonal music of flutes [*auloi*],/ with instruments to mimic the wailing clamor/ that grew from the mouthing jaws of Euryala [one of the Gorgons]. . . ./ The goddess gave it to mortals to use . . ." (Pindar, p. 93).[8] Like his predecessors, and especially like Homer and

Hesiod, Pindar had a lofty conception of his calling.

But Archilochus, Terpander, and the poetic Thales were not alone in the seventh century B.C., when most poets wrote in Ionic Greek. There was, for example, Alcman, who furnishes the earliest example we have of the choral lyric. He did not invent it, but it may symbolize for us the intensity of community activity in ancient times. His *Parthenion,* or *Maiden Song,* seems to be a work for competing girls' choruses sung before dawn at a religious festival. Another seventh-century poet was Alcaeus of Mytilene, a friend of Sappho, herself a great love-poet who, sometimes ranked with Homer in her day, was later called the tenth Muse by Plato. Alcaeus wrote Aeolic dialect hymns, drinking and love songs, and political odes denouncing tyrants; and he too invented a meter named after himself. Later by half a century came Anacreon, whose favorite verse form, quatrains in trochaic tetrameter, inspired the name of anacreontics. His subject-matter of healthy gaiety, love, and wine (but not the more traditional politics or war), expressed with a clear-sighted and uncomplaining realism, was admired and imitated in almost all later ages in all countries of the Western world. While Alcman wrote choral poetry, Alcaeus and Anacreon wrote for monodic presentation. When Plato (*Phaedr.* 235) called Sappho, who likewise was a monodic singer, the "fair," he also called Anacreon the "wise."

These early bards, then, writers of epics, philosophers, and creators and performers of political lyric as well as of dramatic poetry, sometimes practical "musicians" according to the understanding of their times, implicitly and occasionally explicitly anticipated an aesthetics of music which in its most general form can be called the idea of it. True, they did not describe or espouse theory; but what is most important, a basic assumption, is often not expressed. And it can only be a matter of wonder that the outlines of ancient ideas about music should have been so well preserved as they have. Very few observations, except those of the philosophers, were written down even for personal reference, and many of the fragments now remaining were probably recorded many years after they were thought and stated--recorded by others so that they could preserve what had been transmitted chiefly by word of mouth. Homer, whose works were orally spread abroad for at least two centuries, along with others more than implied that music could inspire people, contribute to their health, support their religious aspirations, contribute to their educational pursuits, help control their civic states of mind and actions, and also add an innocent pleasure to life. That it was divinely based was another matter, to be scientifically--that is, mathematically and rationally--explained by the Pythagoreans.

II

The Pythagoreans. The vaguest figure in the entire history of music aesthetics and one of the most seminal and influential is Pythagoras of

Samos, who flourished c.530 B.C.[9] He is said to have coined the word philosophy and to have been the father of philosophy in Greece. Remembered for his belief in the transmigration of souls, he is also reported, to the amusement of modern philosophers, to have been the leader of a strict religious group living under such negative rules as that one should not eat beans, pick up what has fallen, touch a white cock, break bread, sit on a quart measure, or do other acts that fall within this novel system of taboos. He was priest, ascetic, mathematician, and healer. He was also said to have been the son of Apollo and the pupil of Thales, the Greek philosopher and scientist of Miletus. The Persians thought of him as the patriarch of all scholarly music. Because of the purity of his life, he was thought to have been able to hear the music of the spheres. Both mystic and scientist, he is nevertheless a shadowy figure known chiefly by what is reported of him and his followers. His patron god was indeed Apollo, and his school was probably an attempt to reform Orphism, which held to a basic hierarchy of gods (as in Hesiod). His followers set the tone of Greek philosophical thought, however, by banishing the gods and by asking for a life of intellectual contemplation not confined to the human body, but rather through the highest of human activities pursuing the perfect truth which in essence is divine.

With his followers, the Pythagoreans, music was for the first time analyzed scientifically.[10] Everything in the universe was said to be number, sound being no less and probably more so than anything else. Tones and their relations were analyzed and concretized on instruments like the monochord, for which there were no counterparts for the measuring of light and color or heat and cold. Sound is taken in by sense, but is perceived and judged by the mind, the ultimate human faculty. The use to which sound can be put was of course another matter, and the craft of sound called music was understood in terms of a peculiar amalgam of mathematics and mysticism.

The Pythagoreans, or followers of Pythagoras in the sixth and fifth centuries B.C., are today known through only a few writings, mostly incomplete. It was with them that Harmonia first came into her own; they used the terms 'harmony' (which in the Greek language meant, to begin with, a working together, then a tuning, and, later, the scale), 'symmetry,' and 'eurythmy' (this last was applied to oratory). All were terms designating objectivities and permanencies: harmony is the basis of both science and religion; it penetrates the entire cosmos and is therefore a universal property (Aristotle, *Metaph.* 986a). An objective factor, it also is beauty. It is the unifying of elements originally mixed and disparate: it is both unity and concord in the abstract and the organic unity of the cosmos, or cosmic unity in multeity, in the concrete. The aesthetic theory of harmony was thus based on a paradox: that objects of the universe could be unified--and uniform--in their multiplicity and variety. The term 'cosmos' itself meant an order, a proportion, a harmony, which embraced another paradox, that the complex of things and objects which, besides being beautiful and abstract, are also useful. What lacks proportion is ugly and useless.

The Pythagoreans found the ultimate reality and order of the cosmos in the harmony of the spheres. Later, Aristotle spoke of their "theory that the movement of the stars produces harmony, i.e., that the sounds they make are concordant. . . . Starting from this argument and from the description that their speeds, as measured by their distances, are in the same ratios as musical concordances, they assert that the sound given forth by the circular movement of the stars is a harmony" (*On the Heavens* 290b). All examples among the Pythagoreans of the source of Harmonia indicate that many things or cases are really one. There were four harmonies: (1) of strings ("chords"), (2) of body and soul, (3) of the state, and (4) of the starry sky (the true original). The whole universe is a harmony of the spheres which man cannot hear, his senses being inadequate for such perception, though the harmony sounds continuously. As the songs of the stars and the dance of the planets, the harmony of the spheres is a permanent analogical synthesis or a synaesthesia: everything is held together in a form which is aesthetic, mathematical, and abstract. For the Pythagoreans, the stars and planets making primeval and original sounds were endowed with souls and intelligences. At night they could be seen, and by synaesthetic transfer someone like Pythagoras could hear them. Pythagoras himself is supposed to have had a cosmic lyre, a heptachord of seven strings in imitation of the seven spheres and therefore the primordial instrument revealing to him the music few men could hear.

Accompanying the cosmic organization and intrinsic to it was a number-system, a number-philosophy, derived, the great Syrian Neo-platonist Iamblichus of Chalcis (d. c.333 A.D.) much later said, from the disciples of Orpheus and adopted in terms of itself, an ideal system purely objective in nature and not concerned with things. It was an order of musical-astronomical substance anterior to sound. In its full potentialities it was expected to reveal the physical world as something quite akin to, if not identical with, music, whose superior and unique place in the universe is denied to all the other arts of the Muses. Like mathematics, music is an abstraction; but it resides in both the sensuous, physical world and the ideal, imaginary, or mathematical one. There is no hiatus between the two worlds, and no nexus: the connections between numbers and music need not be bridged; they interpenetrate or even exist in an identity. The result is, of course, a paradox: the acoustical effects of music, less a human construct than a reflection of nature, are coincidental with and a reflection of divine harmony and concord. Things are numbers, or at least all things are similar to numbers, and thus the real beauty of music is independent of the melody which strikes the ear. Through such observations, the Pythagoreans created a model for the "universal" application of number by Vitruvius to architecture, by Leonardo da Vinci to the human figure, and by St. Augustine to poetic and musical rhythm. They also laid the groundwork for the discovery of the "divine proportion" called the Golden Section.

The idea that number is aesthetic may suggest why ancient Greeks like Plato thought arithmetic had no necessary connection with practical matters; it was chiefly a philosophical study and an independent, free science of the mind or intellect. It was something for students aspiring to philosophical understanding, not an elementary study for children. In general, it appeared: (1) in discussions of the properties of numbers and of matters of proof and demonstration involving them, and (2) in a mystical treatment of them as having magical properties and powers and even certain vital characteristics. The second, the mystico-symbolic treatment, called arithmology, is probably oriental, and especially Babylonian, in origin. According to John Burnet, it must be remembered that "at Babylon a number was a different thing from a figure. Just as in ancient times, and, above all, in Egypt, the name had magical power, and ceremonial words formed an irresistible incantation, so here the number possesses an active force, the number is a symbol, and its properties are sacred attributes."[11] According to one aspect of this ancient theory, the motions of the planets produce sounds, and each planetary sound is labelled with one of the seven vowels. The vowels may therefore symbolize the planets. Also, the letters of the Greek alphabet and numbers are identical; in the absence of ciphers, the seven Ionian vowels[12] correspond with the seven planets, both series being a manifestation of the sound of the holy figure 7. Numbers were numinous, co-eternal with the universe, not invented by men or their minds. They were themselves alone, though they also represented archetypes. Divine number was therefore superior to material number, which can be "perceived."

Both arithmetic and arithmology were allied with music, and arithmetic and music were allied with geometry and astronomy. (Of these sciences, geometry was the special contribution of Greece.) As an intellectual enterprise, music involved ratios and was an arithmetical subject in the scientific sense of the term. Having discovered that the pitch of a note depends on the string producing it and (supposedly) having invented the theory that musical intervals found on the calibrated string of the monochord (or canon) can be expressed in numerical ratios, the Pythagoreans established a hierarchy of values among such intervals, the lower the number-ratios being the better. Pythagoras himself is said to have discovered that the most consonant or concordant intervals had the lowest ratios, the octave, the consonance which itself was called harmonia, being 1:2, the fifth 2:3, and the fourth 3:4.[13] (The intervals of the third and sixth were therefore discords. Only during the late Middle Ages did they achieve concordal status.) The "tetrad" or four numbers (the first 4 among 10) became the cornerstone of musical theory, the number of consonance was fixed, and the idea of concord stood for tones appearing successively, not simultaneously. The choice of number determined the interval a priori.[14] Similarly, another Pythagorean series of numbers was 1 for mind, 2 for opinion, 3 for the whole (beginning, middle, and end), 4 for justice (equal times equal), 5 for marriage (the first combination of odd and even: male and female), 7 for opportunity, and 10 for perfection (the whole nature of number and the structure of the universe) (Aristotle, *Metaph*. 985b-986a). And all were allied with the heavenly musical scale.

But the justification of this musical system went deeper, for, to take first things first, the doctrine of numbers was the science of all existence and therefore of unchangeable substance. It was posited upon the existence of a reality beyond physical nature, an eternal reality always being and never becoming, a reality intelligible or spiritual which could be known only through intelligence or mind. According to the Pythagorean Philolaus, it is even impossible to grasp any thing if mind is absent or to recognize it if number is wanting (*Ancilla*, p. 74). Numbers and their harmonious arrangements are true, beautiful, and good, and, as aspects of pure knowledge, they are the means of both ontological and epistemological inquiry. They have a mystical-magical significance and, intellectually, speaking, perform a divine dance.

To begin with, there is the number 1, which is and means identity, the unvaried, the invariable--a mystical reality of oneness. It is less a number than the principle of being. Like the real world itself, however, numbers arise out of a fundamental duality--out of the opposition of *monas* and *dyas*, a monad and a dyad, a 1 and a 2; and then 3, which follows, denotes many.

> 1--the monad (sometimes called the father of number) is the principle and element of number itself; it is unmoved and immovable, equal only to itself, indivisible; not the result of a process of combining, it is incomparable, continuous without end, nonphysical, and located purely in the intellectual world. In geometry its correspondent is the point.
>
> 2--the dyad (sometimes called the mother of number) is the first true number, changeable, unlimited, divisible, composite, comparable, and disjunct; it embraces the multiplicity of the physical world. Its correspondent is the line or longitudinality.
>
> 3--(sometimes called the first real number) is the addition of the dimension of breadth, of superfices, of the plane surface.
>
> 4--achieves the mass (solidity) of bodies and the third dimension of depth. Here is the cube or the first solid.[15]

While the four numbers represent the four possibilities of physical extension, the first harmonic series is made up of additions of 1:

$$1 \quad 2 \quad 3 \quad 4 \quad (1 + 2 + 3 + 4 = 10)$$

For the Pythagoreans 10 was the perfect number underlying the decimal basis of counting, illustrated thus in the "perfect triangle" or pyramid:

```
   •                    1
  •  •                  2
 •  •  •                3
•  •  •  •              4
                      ——
                       10
```

This arrangement was called the *tetractys*, thought to be perfect and harmonious, to be found in the heavens, to embrace all nature, and to be the source and root of eternal being. It was identical with Pythagoras' divisions of the strings of the lyre.

The second harmonic series results from multiplication:

by 2: 1 2 4 8   (2 x 1 = 2; 2 x 2 = 4; etc.)
by 3: 1 3 9 27   (3 x 1 = 3; 3 x 3 = 9; etc.)

The physical number now finally arrived at with the completion of the tetractys--and therefore of all life--is the number 27, or the physical expressed in the quadrant or square, 27 being the cube of 3 as the number of the plane. And if the numbers of both subtype-species of the second class (which of course develop from the first) are combined in a series, the result is a comprehensive complete series:

$$1 \quad 2 \quad 3 \quad 4 \quad 8 \quad 9 \quad 27$$

in which the sum of the first six (1 + 2 + 3 + 4 + 8 + 9) equals 27. It is on this calculation that Plato later in his *Timaeus* (35-36) bases the (musical) structure of the soul.

It must be clear that musical numbers had to do with relations of whole numbers (or multitudes). The numbers expressed ratios, some of which were concordant while others were inharmonious or dissonant. The *tetractys* included all musical consonances and in addition the non-consonance, the whole tone of the ratio of 8:9. How can this be so? If two strings of the same material and thickness are stretched by the same weight first in a relation of 2 to 3 (the fifth) and then of 3 to 4 (the fourth), two perfect intervals occur. If sound moves from the lower to the higher pitch of the perfect fourth, the ear is satisfied; if it moves from the higher to the lower pitch of the perfect fifth, the ear is satisfied. These (with the addition of 1:2, the octave ratio) are the only intervals producing a sense of rest. If the first (lower) pitch of the one string when the relation is a perfect fourth is added to the second pitch of the second string when the relation is a perfect fifth, one has an octave (there are three tones in all, and the bottom of the perfect fourth and the top of the perfect fifth are "identical"). The ratios of the string lengths are 4:3 and 3:2 = 2:1,[16] and the higher pitch seems to repeat the lower as the lower does the higher. The octave too gives a sense of rest. Thus, musical consonances are now set and the nature of consonance itself revealed. They can be tested on the monochord, whose tones represent not what is perceived sensuously but a path to the ideal view of numbers. (Greek verse-rhythms had the same ratios as Greek musical intervals. Lengths of feet in their places were calculated to be 1:1, 2:1, 3:2, and 4:3 and were called *isa, diplasis, hemiolia, epitrita*.) The overall harmony in the intervals of the scale and in the structure of the scale itself is identical with balance and order; it is the law of the astronomical world in principle.

Pythagoras is supposed to have learned the *tetractys* in Egypt. It is also mentioned in the literature of China of 500 B.C. A bringing together of all inwardly homogeneous characteristics, it is a definitive expression or concrete proof of the unity of the world. It is music intellectualized. It symbolizes cosmic unity, it is a mathematical musical identity, the germ of the harmony of the whole world and all of its parts--and (so it was thought) the epitome of Pythagorean wisdom.

Thus the numbers of the tonal system were precisely those of the *tetractys*. But the problem was how to fill the octave of two tetrachords so that a system or scale could be found. The fourth and the fifth were already there. Between them was created an interval called a tone, which the Greeks also treated as fundamental. It can be reached by dividing the ratio of the string length of 3:2 by 2:3; the result is 9:8. From the lower pitch of a fourth were now carved out two pitches at the interval of a tone each. Something was still left over, however, and it, the *lemma* or 256:243, or *approximately a semitone* (half-step), was the result of the fourth divided by 9:8. The end result was the basic tetrachord ("fourstrings") of the diatonic scheme made up of two tones and a semitone (three intervals of two steps and a half-step, the tones representing points, or steps and half-steps, metaphorically representing space):

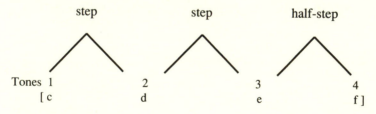

One could complete the octave scale by placing one tetrachord "above" the other, the lowest tone of the "upper" one being identical with the top tone of the "lower" one; or the upper tetrachord could begin a step above the lower one. (The Greek method was probably the reverse.) Since the order of steps and half-steps (tones and semitones) could be different from that illustrated above (half-step, step, step; or step, half-step, step), there were other "solutions" to the scale problem, and two of them (in addition to the diatonic [*diatonikos*]) were called the chromatic and the enharmonic [*enharmonikos* = accordant, fitting], in which even microsteps were used).

Though their own sound system was based on interval perception and though pitch frequencies are perceptible events determined by wave lengths, the Greeks never discovered the overtone series.

Pythagorean numerology was an objective analysis of the integrality of the cosmos, of the organic whole in which music was a dominant element, indeed, the symbol of universal order. The very planets themselves were in musical numerical relations. Consequently, it was supposed that music must have a high significance in human affairs because it serves both metaphorical and physical-social aims. Since the human soul and body contain the divine spark of the world-soul, numerology could be rationally applied equally to bodies and to souls. Harmonically constructed, souls are originally perfect, because they have a proper proportion of parts. Now, the natural man of body and soul was always the measure of Greek religion and philosophy. Health itself was in a ratio of numbers. If an embryo is to be healthy[17] and to grow properly, its numbers must be correct; the harmonic intervals of the fourth, fifth, and octave are required; otherwise, physical deficiencies result. (All odd numbers are important, too. When 9 is decisive as such a number, for example, eight-months children often do not live because of their numerical imperfection.) The psychical and the physical were different elements of different balance in the human unity, and philosophers, like medical scientists, constantly looked for psycho-physical as well as for ethical relations. Because he supposedly brought these together, Pythagoras has been called the father of psycho-therapeutics. Man's soul is a harp whose highest manifestation is its virtue and, in addition, its mental and physical health. The order, proportion, and measure implicit in music can contribute to and control both health[18] and ethical behavior. Singing and playing daily, for instance, are effective for cleansing the soul.

Since it was thought that medicine can be administered with the help of music, music should be part of education for its therapeutic effect on body and soul. Theon of Smyrna, a Neoplatonist of the second century A.D., reports that the Pythagoreans called music a harmonizing of opposites, of separate and disparate elements at war among themselves--but reconciled. Sickness was made up of such opposites, health of their reconciliation. Upon music, with its aim of unity and harmony, depended not only rhythm and melody, but the whole system of the world. God harmonizes the warring elements and through music and medicine brings them together. Theon names three realms in which music achieves the most marked agreements: the universe itself, the state, and the home. But there were four spheres (like the *tetractys*) in which the Pythagoreans saw the effects and application of music; those of the soul, the body, the state, and the home. Strabo (c.63 B.C.-24 A.D.), the Greek geographer, summarized the matter: before Plato's time the Pythagoreans called philosophy music: and they say that the universe is constituted in accordance with harmony, assuming that every form of music is the work of the gods (*Geography* 10.3.10). It could not be otherwise: the stars and planets had to influence everything, and in this sense music, astrology, magic, religion, and medicine were inextricably joined in a beautiful organization called the cosmos or the universe--and inevitably in the secondary cosmos of man and his world.

Iamblichus said of Pythagoras (who sometimes seems to have foreshadowed not only Plato but also Christ) that he had declared the Muses to have a name in common because they all subsist in connection with one another and because among or in themselves they comprehend "symphony, harmony, and rhythm, and all things which procure concord" (*Life of Pythag..* 9, p. 21). In assessing music, Pythagoras began with the perception of beautiful forms, rhythms, or melodies and then maintained that "the first erudition subsists through music": certain melodies supply remedies for human manners and passions and also return the harmonies to the power of the soul which it possessed from the first.[19] Pythagoras mixed diatonic, chromatic, and enharmonic melodies in various ways willfully to turn souls around after they had proceeded in an "irrational and clandestine manner" and to correct sorrow, rage, pity, and so forth, which could be tempered by appropriate melodies. But Pythagoras achieved these changes not by means of voice or instrument alone, but through "a certain ineffable divinity"-- through a "universal harmony and consonance of the spheres" which enabled him to produce a melody more intense "than anything effected by mortal sounds" (ibid. 15, pp. 43-44).[20] Here, clearly, melody means something not terrestrial but transcendental, mystical, and superhuman, and music is again allied with religion and magic. Music *is* sounds of necessity in the cosmos, created to make a certain order permanent on earth.

What practices did the Pythagoreans adopt with respect to music and health? Employing music as medicine, they used magical incantations to cure certain illnesses because, as they thought, music properly used could influence health (ibid. 21, p. 71), just as Homer and Hesiod could repair the soul (ibid. 25, p. 81). It was a tenet of Orphism that music can turn the soul to wholeness through purification, which is the highest aim of man. And purification meant a re-entry into the universal whole or unity. The result could be equally ethical and religious (in modern terms it could be both physical and psycho-physical). Musical science and religion are one, their effect is a catharsis and purification, and the result is an inner balance of soul.

Employing both medicine and music to purge the body and music to purify the soul, therefore, the Pythagoreans were probably the originators of the theory of the ethical effect of music. The "triune choreia," according to Aristides Quintilianus (second century A.D. or later), acted on both dancer and singer on the one hand, and on the spectator or listener on the other--on the performer and the observer. The explanation, which became standard in later musical discussions, was that sounds echo in the soul just as the strings of two lyres vibrate in harmony with one another. Good music can therefore act upon the soul to improve it, and bad music can corrupt it. Souls can be guided (*psychologia*) into a good or bad state of mind (*ethos*). Just as *nomoi* were rigid rules for art, so ethical theory assumed the existence of rules for music which denied its absolute freedom. Examining the effects of music, the Pythagoreans declared that everyone should cultivate music throughout his lifetime because certain fixed melodies, serving either as amusement or for public ceremonies, were operable as laws.[21]

In asserting that the power of music includes an influence on health-- we are here not in the presence of pure medicine, but of the priestly-magical arts--the Pythagoreans were behaving as members of the Orphic cult according to which the human soul is in the condition of a fallen god: only in a kind of transport can it reveal its true nature, which it regains through purification and sacrifice. Because music expresses the soul, its nature, and its ethos, it can alter an individual's character through transfer. It acts on the will and aims not only at pleasure but also at the formation of moral quality: when a soul defective in harmony and rhythm gives itself "as an auditor of divine harmony" to the body and embraces the melodies which preserve the vestiges of harmony, it "recollects divine harmony," tends toward union with it, and participates in it as much as possible (Iamblichus, *Mysteries* 3.9). A catharsis then being effected, the soul is freed from its fallen condition--that is, from the accidental aspects of earthly life. (Its parallel, it is evident, is the redemption of the Christian soul from sin.) The uniqueness of music derives, then, not only from its amalgamating influence on poetry, gesture, and dance, but also and especially from its superiority as an agent of effects it alone of all the arts can produce. Just as the word 'harmony' was used to identify cosmic characteristics and was later applied to music as a structure, and just as the goddess Harmonia symbolized music in both of these senses, so musical theory as devised by the Pythagoreans provided a method for judging harmony through arithmetic. True, arithmetic had to be "perceived" through tones in sequence and then brought into a synthesis as a whole, but once in the mind, harmony was non- or even anti-sensuous because the mind "knew" arithmetical number. Their abstract use of number earned the Pythagoreans the name of canonists in music, a term first fixed by Euclid (c.300 B.C.), who, in his *Division of the Monochord, or Section of the Canon*, described the "Perfect System" of harmony and brought number and physical tone into relation. Even before Euclid, the idea of canonic law was all pervading. Even before he summarized the musical canon (the unreliability of manuscript datings being considered) and approximately a hundred years after Pythagoras, there appeared the first datable work on sculpture, also called *The Canon*. It was a study, a model for many later works like it, of the proportions of the human body, and its author was Polyclitus (fifth century B.C.). In the same century, Empedocles described the painter's mixture of colors as harmony (*Ancilla*, p. 55), which was another attempt to find basic law in another artistic world of the senses.

Pythagoras is said to have taught at Crotona, a Greek settlement in southern Italy on the Gulf of Tarentum. Two of his best-known followers, Philolaus and Archytas, came from Tarentum itself. The work of Philolaus (fl. latter half of the fifth century B.C.) may be of doubtful authenticity, but what is recorded as belonging to him--it appeared a full century after the lifetime of Pythagoras--is clearly Pythagorean: he combined harmony, number, and intellectual comprehension. For him, harmony is the unity of many mixed elements, an agreement among disagreeing elements; it is symbolized by the octave. Number and its working power are supernatural and divine, but are also included in all human activities, both in words and in music.   Things unlike and unrelated need harmony, and harmony, necessarily fixing them together, destines them "to endure in the universe." And Philolaus rings on chimes which have echoed through the centuries: "The nature of number and harmony admits of no falsehood" (*Ancilla*, pp. 74-75).[22]

Of all the Pythagoreans, the one apparently best versed in music as such was Archytus. Probably a pupil of Philolaus, he lived during the first half of the fourth century B.C., late enough to have been Plato's contemporary. Writing in literary Doric, and making certain metaphysical and physical assumptions, he spoke of music as one of the four types of mathematics (arithmetic, geometry, and spherics are the others).   Like Philolaus, he called the octave *harmonia* and used the cube to demonstrate harmonic proportions or ratios.   He thought music deals with ratios according to three means: "one is the arithmetic, the second is the geometric, and the third is the subcontrary, which they call 'harmonic.' The arithmetic mean is when there are three terms showing successively the same excess [6, 4, 2]: the second exceeds the third by the same amount as the first exceeds the second.   In this proportion the ratio of the larger numbers is less, that of the smaller numbers greater. The geometric mean [2, 4, 8] is when the second is to the third as the first is to the second; in this mean, the greater numbers have the same ratio as the smaller numbers. The subcontrary, which we call harmonic, is as follows: by whatever part of itself the first term exceeds the second, the middle term exceeds the third by the same part of the third [6, 4, 3].[23] In this proportion the ratio of the larger numbers is larger, and of the lower numbers less" (*Ancilla*, pp. 79-80). These three means describe harmony, the ratios--those of the octave, the fifth, and the fourth--being so adjusted to one another that they too produce harmony; related to all is, of course, the harmony of the celestial spheres, which are separated by intervals corresponding with the relative lengths of strings producing harmonious tones; as the spheres vibrate--as the spheres on which the stars and planets move--they create music. There is clearly an inner affinity of whole-number arithmetic and music through motion.

It is difficult to determine the importance which motion implies in this passage. Aristotle (*On the Soul* 405a) reports that Alcmaeon, a Pythagorean of the sixth century B.C., thought the soul's "immortality belongs to it in virtue of its ceaseless movement": for all things divine, the moon, the sun, the planets--the whole heavens--are in perpetual motion. In some respects, therefore, Archytas was both a Pythagorean and an anticipator of Aristotle. His achievement was to bring music down to earth, as it were. As well known in his time for his civic as for his scientific accomplishments, he was said to be a moral teacher; yet he paid more attention to the physical nature of sound than did his fellow Pythagoreans, and thus he pointed the way to the science of acoustics. Sound, which results from moving air (vibration), is impossible, he thought, "unless there occurs a striking of objects against one another" (*Ancilla*, p. 78). Yet there are sounds which "cannot be recognized by our nature, some because of the faintness of the sound, others because of their great distance from us, and some even because of their excessive loudness . . ." (ibid.). There are also differences in pitch. What causes them? Impinging on our perception, those sounds "which reach us quickly and powerfully from [their] source . . . seem high-pitched, while those which reach us slowly and feebly seem low-pitched" (ibid., p. 79). Speed of impact is obviously the source of pitch.[24] Archytas illustrates this principle in terms of the voice, the throwing of missiles, the sound production of the aulos, the whirlers (instruments whirled around on a string at the Mysteries), and the blowing of reeds (ibid.). Pitches of swift motion are high, those of slow are low; such empirical acoustical observable facts were in tandem with numerical calculations. Archytas worked out musical ratios corresponding to the intervals between the notes of the tetrachord for the enharmonic, chromatic, and diatonic scales. And he is even thought to have invented notation. Unlike his contemporaries, he thought that in education literature should be subordinate to music, the rational attributes of number and harmony of music as a science being sufficiently wonderful in themselves.[25]

Euclid in his *Section of the Canon* agreed with Archytas that sound is caused by motion and also that pitch is related to frequency of vibration. It has been said that, like his *Elements*, Euclid's *Section of the Canon* dates back further than is usually supposed. Both are remarkable for consisting of mathematics almost bare, stripped of its mystical and cosmological accretions. Archytas is thought to have been Euclid's source for both, and especially for the "harmonic books" (7-9) of the *Elements*. The *Section of the Canon* is the earliest preserved account of the complete system of Pythagorean harmonics. Widely influential in succeeding centuries--the Neoplatonist Porphyry and the Roman Boethius both discuss it--it contains no accounts of actual works of music. Explaining consonances as ratios, Euclid describes them as a uniting, mixing, or blending. He therefore implies that numbers express what is actually heard. But he also implies the familiar Pythagorean tenet that numbers are everything and that all musical reality is exclusively mental or intellectual.[26]

Pythagoreanism, then, is the name for the first memorable scientific world-system, whole, complete, universal, unalterable, and permanent, to be devised in the Western world. A model for all other systems, it embraces an absolutism of truths beyond perception and empirical investigation. It is both a science and a religion. It takes a mystical view of human experience according to which the latter cannot penetrate, except symbolically through action and meditation, the realm of Being which lies beyond the senses. Like all sciences and religions, it professes to be true to the indispensable, the undeniable, the temporally always-the-same, and to embrace an abstract order of all worlds which must hold firm under all circumstances. Its base is mathematics, the science of absolute number and of all orders and relationships--not the material instrument of everyday life, however, but numerical description of everything that is. Its manifestations are high and low, points and lines, surfaces, and stereometric forms. These are interpreted in a limited way by the sense of sight, which makes do for a partial glimpse into universal realities. Its cosmic manifestations are circular and relational, and here the realities are musical--sound produced by motion. The music of the spheres is the phenomenon unheard by base human nature but bringing a universal structure into a One.

That One is a sign of the spiritual and material structure of the All; its aesthetic name is harmony and its goddess is Harmonia. It is the foundation of beauty: indeed, it *is* beauty. The Oneness is expressed in mathematical structures and metaphorically in the harmony of sound in the universe and in both its horizontal and vertical forms on the earth. Arithmetic analyzes numbers *per se* by which harmony is "expressed." Music too involves numbers, but one number in relation to others or all numbers in relations, phenomena and spiritual entities making up compound relations and composed things.

The beauty of this system is that man is at its center. He shares its rationality, the spiritual being and state of the cosmos, and its order. Unfortunately, man, originally created perfect, has lost perfection and needs to redeem himself. The evidence of his lost perfection lies in his sensuality, his irrationality, his corporeality--all of which must be overcome or must disintegrate during his struggle to reclaim what he has lost. His determined appeals to and courtship of rationality and order--physical, mental, psychological, and social--promise to restore him to his original sublime state. On earth this demands a noble goodness, a *kalokagathia* (*kalos* = fine, noble, a state bordering on the aesthetic; *agathos* = good), a personal *arete* (excellence or virtue) through the avoidance of *aischros* (the base or shameful) and the performance of good acts. These acts are political and domestic, and therefore learned through education. Here lies the importance of music in both macrocosm and microcosm. Music is a universal phenomenon expressed in number and leading to right action; it is a primary agent in human life; interpreted in its broadest sense, it makes a bridge between the music of the spheres and the soul-states of men.

The Pythagoreans crossed the bridge, as it were, through the singing and playing of music. Relevant post-Pythagorean comments are legion. Cicero, the Roman orator and politician (106-43B.C.), probably learned of them and their thought through Plato's *Timaeus*. In his *Tusculan Disputations* (4.2.3), Cicero wrote that they conveyed instruction in the form of verse and modified the intensity of their meditations through song and the music of the harp, which calmed their minds. At banquets did they and their guests sing to one another to the music of the aulos, in praise of illustrious men? Cato (the Elder, 234-149 B.C.) thinks so. And possibly to guide singers, string instruments sounded preludes at festivals of the gods and at feasts of the magistrates. Though Ciceronian and Catonian accounts more surely reflect possible aspects of Roman domestic life, what they say corresponds with other efforts to describe a kind of ascetic intellectual life in Greece in the sixth century before Christ. Pythagorean philosophy, its rational explanation of its universe, and its corollaries in the lives of men, has never died. It is a theme on which are played innumerable variations from Plato and Aristotle to today's passionate Idealist.

III

Democritus, the Atomist and Skeptic.   Since it is easy to be skeptical of the Pythagoreans' cosmic and musical theories in spite of the structural beauty they exhibit, it is no surprise that even in their time these ideas should have met with a certain resistance. This came, for one, from Democritus (c.460 B.C.) of Abdera in Thrace.   Democritus was a materialist, empiricist, and determinist, and he accepted Pythagorean doctrine sufficiently among the very first philosophers to liken the cosmological macrocosm to the human microcosm.   Called the "laughing philosopher" and said to be the greatest of the Greek physical philosophers, he adopted and amended the atomistic theory of Leucippus (fifth century B.C.) and thought that pleasure or its absence is a criterion of worth (*Ancilla*, p. 92).

For Democritus, music was the youngest of the arts; it was created not out of necessity, but out of luxury or superfluity (ibid., p. 105). Unlike Philodemus (first century B.C.) later, who thought that music depends on nature, he thought of it not as a product of nature but as a concoction of man; singing, he says (adopting an image frequently used in the future discussion), we learn from the swan and the nightingale. He nevertheless agreed that music is an educational force bringing about a balance between gymnastics and letters (ibid., pp. 106, 108). And in his *Tetralogies*, he made it a separate discipline alongside arithmetic, geometry, and astronomy (ibid., pp. 94-96); in so doing, he anticipated the medieval quadrivium. He was a formalist and skeptic in music and not much of an "ethicist." Later Greek historians thought he had originated aesthetics, and, according to Boethius, he is supposed to have said that the impulses of the soul "are stirred by emotions corresponding to the state of the body."[27] Like many similar remarks, this may have only been a description of psychosomatic states.   In any event, Democritus did not take the extreme position of Diogenes the Cynic (c.413-323 B.C.), who, according to Diogenes Laertius (6.73), thought that music, along with geometry, astronomy, and similar studies, should be neglected as useless and unnecessary. Nor did he take the position Diogenes Laertius (6.104) describes from Euripides' *Antiope* that states and householders are well-ordered (controlled) by the minds of men but not by the twanging strings of the lyre or the trilled notes of the *aulos*. The cynic Diogenes too could be not entirely uncompromising: he wondered that people could tune the strings of the lyre and still leave discord in their dispositions of soul (ibid. 6.27).

Damon and Politics. These dispositions of soul were the ostensible province of Damon of Athens (fl. 460 B.C.), a significant figure in the history of the idea of music who is known for one such idea alone. A character in Plato's early dialogues and a teacher of Socrates as well as of Pericles, the Athenian statesman, he was practically a contemporary of Philolaus and probably younger by half a century than Archytas. According to Pseudo-Plutarch (1136), he invented the Lydian mode. If reports are correct, he stressed an argument, already mentioned by the Pythagoreans, that music can produce ethical effects. In his philosophy, music theory loses its mathematical associations. Primarily interested in social reform, he is said to have written an *Areopagitica*, probably on the subject of politics.[28]

Damon was probably the first practical musician to contribute to any extent to the history of music aesthetics. According to Pseudo-Plato's *Alcibiades I* (118), he taught both music and politics. There are accounts which make him a pupil of Lamprocles, the writer of dithyrambs and especially of an ode to Athens, and of Agathocles, identified as a Sophist in Plato's *Protagoras* (316). In Plato's *Laches* (180), the character Nicias says that Socrates recommended Damon as a teacher of music for his sons because he was accomplished as a musician and also exemplary as a man. Later (ibid. 200), Laches expresses surprise that Nicias, though benefitting from Damon's wisdom, has not yet discovered the meaning of courage. My "friend Damon" is always with the Sophist Prodicus, says Socrates, "who is considered to be the best puller to pieces of words"--that is, a master of nomenclature--because he can analyze words like "courage," with which people "dress" themselves (ibid. 197). The question is to what extent Damon influenced Socrates, who in *Phaedo* (61) equated music with philosophy. "In the course of my life," he said, "I have often had intimations in dreams 'that I should compose music.' The same dream came to me sometimes in one form, and sometimes in another, but always saying the same or nearly the same words: 'Cultivate and make music,' said the dream. And hitherto I had imagined that this was only intended to exhort and encourage me in the study of philosophy, which has been the pursuit of my life, and the noblest and best of music." He conjectures, however, that the dream might have meant music not in the cosmic but in the popular sense of the word, and he therefore composed some verses before he "departed" under the sentence of death.

Did Damon teach Socrates that there were at least two musics, one practical and the other ethical? In the *Republic* (400), Socrates speaks of Damon's knowledge of rhythms which "are expressive of meanness, or insolence, or fury, or other unworthiness, and [of] what are to be reserved for the expression of opposite feelings." But the meaning is vague, because

Socrates additionally mentions martial, dactyllic, and heroic feet and iambic and trochaic rhythms as well as long and short syllables and rhythms of moral quality: all of which, in the absence of analysis, makes for confusion. Is Socrates assuming ignorance, as he often does in order to lead a speaker on?   Indeed, he is not very enlightening, except when (in *Rep.* 401) Glaucon, one of the protagonists, says that "musical training is a more potent instrument than any other, because rhythm and harmony [the fitting together of the individual parts] find their way into the inward places of the soul, . . . imparting grace, and making the soul of him who is rightly educated graceful, or him who is ill-educated ungraceful. . . ." And then Socrates agrees.

We have now entered upon the history of a conjecture first formulated by the Pythagoreans themselves and sometimes asserted even today--that music is or at least may be a moral agent. Laches (188) believes that the Dorian mode is the true beneficial, Hellenic mode, and that the Lydian or the Ionian (whose discovery has been attributed to Damon himself) (Pseudo-Plutarch 1136; *Ancilla*, p. 71) is not socially respectable. (The Dorian was the "middle" mode, the mean. It was flanked on its one side by the Phrygian, Lydian, and Mixolydian, and on the other by the Hypodorian, Hypophrygian, and Hypolydian.) Damon did in part establish the pattern of ancient thought in asking that music be recognized as essential not only to the individual's own liberal education, but also to his behavior as a member of the political state.

For the Greeks, culture, *paideia*, or education was an essential of life, at least for the free man. It was the path to learning, to a love of the permanent and the universal; and it offered resistance to accident and change. The Greeks had a unique sense of state, which persisted from Homer's time to that of Plato and Aristotle and was held as an ideal for centuries. Aristophanes' *The Frogs* of 405 B.C. celebrates that ideal and holds that the poet must teach and advise the leaders of the state. It was expected that the legislator be devoted to the education of youth, whose neglect does harm to the constitution of the state. The good citizen must be trained to fit his own particular station in life under his own kind of government--democratic, for example, or oligarchic.

In education, we know from Plato, Homer was a veritable Bible for the Greeks, who were in effect creating their own culture. The *Iliad* and the *Odyssey* were moral depositories which were frequently allegorized because the Greeks had no holy or priestly books like the *Koran* or the Hebrew Bible, except for what they had received from Egypt; no dogmatic truths were pre-prescribed for them, and they had no scientific or philosophical vocabulary: they themselves were creating such a vocabulary for intellectual exchange. Their thought was a seeking and an inquiry, and they highly valued freedom.   The freedom belonged to the "hero" and aristocrat, however, and not to the slave, whose large numbers made it possible for the overlord to be free of repulsive work. Athens had an educational system, however, and Homer. No wonder Plato closely examined Homer (who in later centuries was supplemented and then replaced by Virgil and the Bible) for his effect on young minds: he was judging the only sacred books which Greece possessed.

The Greek mind as reflected in Greek literature and thought, then, was deep in the communal life of visible aristocrats served by almost invisible slaves. And such a life required stability. For this reason, Damon deplored musical innovation; it is dangerous and must be prohibited, he said, in a state which is a champion of justice. Music must be maintained in its original form to be properly effective. Socrates agrees with Damon that "when the modes of music change, the fundamental laws of the state always change with them" (Plato, *Rep.* 424): the spirit of lawlessness can begin with music, whose license through innovation can pervade every aspect of life. Thus there is no doubt that music is important in the training of character.

It is curious that so little should be known about Damon and that only a few of his remarks are recorded. As late as the first century B.C., Cicero said that Damon "treated music in a way that embraced not merely the particular but [also] the universal" (*Ancilla*, p. 70). But why would the Skeptic Philodemus say that Damon thought music advances all the virtues because "in singing and playing the lyre, a boy will be likely to reveal not only courage and moderation, but also justice" (ibid., p. 71) unless he thought Damon had made an observation considerably beyond the evidence at hand? Athenaeus, a Greek scholar residing in Egypt in the late second and early third centuries, reports (14.628) that in Damon's view his school songs and dances result in the soul's being in a kind of motion, and that noble and beautiful songs produce noble and beautiful souls.

IV

The Hibeh Papyri. In 1905, in graves of mummies near the Egyptian village of Hibeh (called Teuzoi in ancient times), was discovered a group of papyri which contained some words about music. Published, translated into English, and edited by Bernard P. Grenfell and Arthur S. Hunt in 1906, these words have been attributed to various persons. The editors attribute them to Hippias of Elis, a Sophist of the fifth century B.C., thought by antiquity to have been the originator of the pedagogical system called the Liberal Arts. His name has been attached to two (probably spurious) Platonic dialogues in which he is described as more versatile than he should be (Plato's ideal apparently allowed each man to do only one thing well [*Rep.* 397]). A contemporary of Socrates and therefore probably younger than Damon, he is said to have lectured on arithmetic (calculations), geometry, astronomy, politics, and music (rhythmics and harmonics somehow allied with orthography) (*Lesser Hippias* 368). He was contemptuous of the claims especially of people to whom music was foreign-- that is, not a profession--and he was equally contemptuous of theories in support of the idea that different moral effects can be attributed to different harmonies (melodies) or rhythms. He could not accept the idea that music can express the attributes of natural objects like the laurel (sacred to Apollo) and the ivy (sacred to Dionysius). For natural law is one thing, he thought, man-made law another. Enharmonic melody, he asserted, will "no more make its votaries brave than chromatic will make them cowards" (Pt. I, p. 48). He may have been aiming at Damon, or even at Plato (*Rep.* 398-400), or Socrates, and he sounds like Democritus, Philodemus, and, later, Sextus Empiricus.

Up (roughly) to Damon's time, then, there had been a music in classical Greece upon which he and his followers, all conservative in aim and approach, based their opinions of what music is and shall be. His was the usual procedure--to discover artistic principles, as did Aristotle in his *Poetics*, in approved works of art already in existence: what music should be is what it had been. The dramatists were composers themselves. Aristophanes (c.450-385 B.C.) was probably the most musical of them, though Sophocles (c.498-406 B.C.) and Euripides (fifth century B.C.) also created their own dramatic songs. In Aristophanes' *The Acharnians* (971ff) the chorus sings a holiday song celebrating unrestrained drink and love, and in his *The Clouds* there is a powerful address to Zeus (563-74) (which is continued later in 1303ff). In his work, music is everywhere in homes when people are eating, or in schools and musical contests.

The actual turnabout in Greek musical practice--a supposed turning for the worse--was believed to have taken place in the middle of the fifth century B.C., approximately at the time of the death of Pericles. Heretofore, Olympus of Sparta had used the diatonic tetrachord, and Terpander, who established certain changes in tetrachord tuning, had defined the standards. But then a "fall," a decline, took place. Virtuosi appealed to the masses through their showmanship. The guilty parties were Melanippides (fl. 450-440 B.C.), Philoxenus of Cytheria (d. 380 B.C.), Phrynis of Myteline, a player on the cithara (mid fifth century B.C.), and his pupil Timotheus of Miletus (c.446-c.356 B.C.), the last of whom is said to have been extravagant in language and composition and to have introduced the eleven-string cithara. Clearly, he was a virtuoso, and he may have been ahead of his time as Damon, musically speaking, was after his. The music of Terpander was simple; but then came Phrynis. Before Phrynis, the laws (*nomoi*) did not allow changes of mode or rhythm within compositions; the proper scale had "by law" to be retained through each *nomos*. But no more: the *nomoi* are denied and violated. The musical split is made dramatic in a lost fragment of a play by Pherecrates (fl. 435 B.C.) called *Chiron*, in which is described a contest between the old and the new music--that is, between classical and modern, good and bad, simple and complex. In the new type of composition, melody ("changes in modulation"), contrary to past practice, is more important than rhythm; tonality and rhythm are varied; and all kinds of startling and unexpected, contrasting, and chromatic effects take place. Old rules are abandoned for a new personal type of composition.

Complexity and instrumental dexterity become the new rule, and artists are acknowledged as creators, not merely as followers of old and prescribed patterns. Composer and performer are to be different persons, and audiences applaud not the anonymous work but personal artistry and display. The Pythagorean canonists have been replaced. Now there are individual musical forms, the aulos and the lyre make complex music, and in general such freedom prevails that the modes, scales, and genera are mixed (in ways the rhetorician Dionysius of Halicarnasus later termed simply "inadmissible"). It was an early battle of the ancients and the moderns, the ancients claiming all the devotees and patriots of the state.

Another change took place upon which Damon[29] looked with disapproval, but which neither he nor anyone else had the power to reverse: emphasis began to shift in popular practice from vocal to instrumental music. Aulos players tried to upstage the chorus; traditionalists of course thought that instruments should keep to their "lawful" place as servants of the chorus, dramatic action, and poetry. But the divorce between vocal and instrumental music--inevitable, as it seems today--did gradually take place, and eventually the arts once combined in the *choreia* asserted their independence from one another to become instrumental music as such, poetry (eventually to be declaimed, recited, and even read in silence), drama (which, more than poetry, when necessary or desirable retained a subservient music), and the dance (which has always needed music at least for rhythmical accompaniment). The history of music, its idea, and its aesthetics is in part an effort in various ways to put these arts together again. Music was like philosophy: named after all the Muses, it saw its parts, originally a whole of gesture, dancing, poetry, and pure sound, fall away to become individual arts, just as philosophy, once embracing all of knowledge, was to fall into parts as separate sciences. But a rapid progress of such independence among the arts and art-forms, desirable as it seems to us almost twenty-four centuries later, was frustrated even by Plato and Aristotle, who were one or two generations younger than the contemporaries of Melanippides, Phrynis of Myteline, and Timotheus of Mitelus, the radical innovative musician-poets who refused to follow conventional artistic laws.

II
Plato

In the preceding chapter it was necessary to quote from post-Pythagoreans, especially Plato (427-347 B.C.) and Aristotle (384-322 B.C.). This was the case because much of the information about early poets, musicians, and philosophers comes from discussions in Plato's Academy and from Aristotle's historical observations in works like his *Metaphysics*. Plato was an aristocrat, a wealthy man, and probably the possessor of a large philosophical and scientific library. Aristotle was a collector of manuscripts who concentrated on both biological and philosophical works. At the core of Greek philosophy, these thinkers did not work in a vacuum. Firmly grounded in the thought of the past, they became the virtual creators of Western thought. Initially Pythagoreans, they took different philosophical paths. We begin with Plato, who taught Aristotle and who put flesh on the bare bones of Pythagorean theory.

Plato's Academy has sometimes been called the first European university. The primary studies were philosophy and mathematics (which Plato hoped to unify), the physical sciences, arithmetic, geometry, music, and astronomy being the backbone of the curriculum. If Damon was a practical musician, Plato, like most commentators on music both before and since, was not. His idea of music, based on abstract theory, is a major source for the themes of musical thought in the Western world. Its influence, felt well into the nineteenth century and even in some avant garde quarters today, was due in large part to his *Timaeus*, practically the only Platonic work known in the Middle Ages. Uncompromisingly one-sided and based on theoretical absolutes and political conservatism, it had its footing in the conviction that Athens and the political entity called the Greek city-state were showing signs of deterioration because they had abandoned the hard-and-fast organization of a rigidly hierarchical political and social structure. Philosophy in Plato's terms is an investigation of the Ideal. Sad to say, in the case of music, this Ideal was founded on an interpretation of the past and had probably never existed.

I

The idea of harmony symbolized by Harmonia had the same importance for Plato as it did for his philosophical and scientific predecessors. But he went beyond them by concretizing it in startling poetic images or Myths,

31

based on allegories. In the *Republic* (616-17), he describes the vision of Er, a warrior who, slain in battle, returns from the dead to report the vision he has seen in the other world. Among other things, he and his companions saw a

> line of light, straight as a column, extending right through the whole heaven and through the earth, in color resembling the rainbow, only brighter and purer; . . . in the midst of the light, they saw the ends of the chains of heaven let down from above: for this light is the belt of heaven, and holds together the circle of the universe. . . . From these ends is extended the spindle of Necessity, on which all the revolutions turn. The shaft and hook of this spindle are made of steel, and the whorl is partly made of steel and partly of other materials. Now the whorl is in form like the whorl used on earth; . . . there is one large hollow whorl, which is quite scooped out, and into this is fitted another lesser [smaller] one, and another, and another, and four others, making eight in all, like vessels which fit into one another; the whorls (colored in various hues) show their edges on the upper side, and on their lower side all together form one continuous whorl. This is pierced by the spindle, which is driven home through the center of the eighth.

Plato continues: "The first and outer-most whorl has the rim broadest, and the seven inner whorls are narrower" in certain proportions and have colors of different quality and hue. The whorls are the fixed stars, the sun, the moon, Saturn, Mercury, Venus, Mars, and Jupiter.[1] The whole is arranged thus according to size of rim, color, and swiftness of movement:

Whorls	Order of Size	Speed	Colors
8--the moon	4	1	reflects light of sun
7--the sun	5	2	brightest
6--Jupiter	2	2	whiteness second to Venus
5--Mercury	6	2	yellower than 8
4--Mars	3	3	reddish
3--Venus	7	4	whitest light
2--Saturn	8	5	yellower than 8

1--outermost rim of the fixed stars: the broadest; it contains all the rest; in color it is spangled.

"Now, the whole spindle has the same motion; but as the whole revolves in the one [circular] direction, the seven inner circles move slowly in the other. . . . The spindle turns on the knees of Necessity; and on the upper surface of each circle is a Siren, who goes around with them, hymning a single tone or note. The eight together form one harmony"--that is, they sing not one chord, but consonant intervals. The sirens are obviously not those of Homer's *Odyssey*, who are enchanting, seductive, and demonic. These are good and virtuous; they always keep their places among moving heavenly objects and share in the harmony of the cosmos. As they turn around, there is another "band, three in number, at equal intervals sitting upon their throne. These are the Fates, daughters of Necessity" and symbols of the past, the present, and the future.

In Plato's account of world order only sight and hearing make the world palpable to imagination. No other senses are mentioned. According to a recent interpretation, Plato's image, made up of an interpenetration of sight, sound, color, speed, and size, conforms with musical terms: the colors resemble the scale, the speeds (by analogy) resemble a scale, and the song of the Sirens (of eight tones) equals the Dorian octave. Moving in circles to the left, the Sirens sing the Dorian octave, and to the right, a modern major scale. The harmonies of the Sirens even proceed, as do all celestial harmonies, according to equal temperament, which symbolizes justice.[2]

In the dialogue called *Timaeus* (28ff)--the work which was eventually to be reconciled with *Genesis* and thus to be regarded as a most authoritative text indeed for the medieval period--Plato describes the creation of the world. Here he is specific about the mathematico-musical nature of the spheres. There are four elements in the corporeal or physical world: earth, fire, water, air. All are permanent. The world is fair and beautiful because it is like the Creator: each element is a whole and yet part of a whole, and none is subject to decay or destruction. The world was made out of these permanent elements in a spherical globe, in which all extremes in every direction are equidistant from the center; therefore, the globe like all spheres is perfect but, unlike an animal, it has no eyes, ears, nose, mouth, hands, or feet--no senses, in short. It is universal and absolute, not sensual or corporeal. It is a self-sufficient being which revolves on a circle in the same spot and hence represents the most perfect of motions. It is a body entire and perfect. At the center of the universe, which moves in a circle, is the Soul, which is not divisible and pervades the cosmic whole (34).

The creation of the world-soul was accomplished thus: God, or the Demiurge (a sphere with a finite radius), or the Daimon, created the universe out of the indivisible and unchangeable (the Same) and also out of the divisible and material (the Other), and out of them he created a third, or intermediate, kind of Essence. Mingling them together, he made a One, which he again divided into as many parts as were fitting, each part always being a compound of the Same, the other, and the Essence. The division was made according to the proportions of the Pythagorean *tetractys* and the diatonic scale, the entity called the Timaean scale. The Demiurge took one (1) portion from the whole, then a portion double (2) it, and then a third (3) which was half as much as the second and three times the first; then the fourth (4) or double the second, the fifth (9) or three times the third, then the sixth (8) or eight times the first, and finally the seventh (27) or twenty-seven times the first.   Then the three means--arithmetic, geometric, and harmonic--were used up. Thus Archytas and Plato relied on the *tetractys* of the scale-investigations of Pythagoras himself: was musical pattern thought to be an essential of the Real, universal world, or (as is usually thought today) was it merely a fanciful, hypothetical, or symbolical image of it?   The former had to be the truth: the universe as described was (is) real, indeed scientific, as it had been for the Pythagoreans; music also *is* and at the same time symbolizes the genesis and divine pattern of the universe.

The first-mentioned graphic picture of the cosmos and its inherent harmony were less popular (since for centuries the *Republic* was not generally available) than the account of the cosmic creation in the *Timaeus*. Was there a source for the *Timaeus*? On his travels, Plato visited Archytas, studied his physical and physiological doctrines, and then took to Athens Archytas' new doctrine of the spherical shape of the earth.   Archytas may have been a champion (as a lost work of Philolaus may have been the original) of Plato's fairly precise description--however credible or incredible--of the metaphysical construction of the world-soul, of which an integral part was music, necessarily at one with the ideal of harmony in the human body and soul.

Like all theories, this one must be understood in its context; it must be interpreted not in terms of modern "harmony" but of its own: the meaning of the universe lay not in isolated phenomena, but in phenomenal relationships, and musical relationships were primary.   Did Plato believe in the "scientific" harmony of the spheres, was he indulging in a Hesiodic fiction--or was he only indulging in an old man's sober game of play (*Laws* 685)? It must have been the first, or Aristotle would not have taken pains to refute him.

II

In the *Timaeus* (47) Plato also systematizes the senses, the body, and then the soul.   From sight, he thinks, we derive number and philosophy. Indeed, sight was given to man so that he can observe the heavenly spheres in harmonious motion, and the (somewhat lower) sense of hearing was given for a parallel purpose, expressed in speech and music.   Sight was created so that we can observe the paths of intelligence in the heavens, partake of the natural truth of reason, and "imitate the absolutely unerring courses of God and regulate our own vagaries." The same is true of speech and hearing: "adapted to the sound of the voice and to the sense of hearing, [music] is granted to us for the sake of harmony"; the motions of harmony are "akin to the revolutions of our souls," but the intelligent votary of the Muses does not think their aim and end merely to be irrational pleasure. Harmony is meant "to correct any discord which may have arisen in the courses of the soul, and to be our ally in bringing her into harmony and agreement with herself"; and the motions of rhythm have the same purpose.

As man makes music, therefore, he turns towards universal reason and celestial intelligence so as to eradicate discord and to restore the order and harmony of the soul.   Apprehension of the real is through thought, not through the senses.

Thus, discord is evidence of disharmony, of opposites which need solution. Opposites are intrinsic to God's, or the Daimon's, creation of the world. The same reconciliation of opposites, a unity in diversity (or, in reverse, a diversity in unity), is familiar from the Pythagoreans, but was also a doctrine of the metaphysician and philosopher of flux, Heraclitus (fifth and sixth centuries B.C.), known because of his gloomy outlook on life as the "weeping philosopher." The world is less a structure than a process, a becoming; it is that which, being in opposition, "is in concert": from things that differ comes the most beautiful harmony (*Ancilla*, p. 25). Whatever differs within itself is in agreement, is "a One existing in the tension of opposites, a harmony consisting of opposing tension like that [symbolized by] the bow and the lyre" (ibid., p. 28). The bow and the lyre are alike in that their strings must be in a certain tension if they are to be effective: their two ends or extremes are in an unseen strife,[3] but must bring about a hidden harmony, which is stronger, or better, than the visible. It is the only unity worth having--not of likenesses, but of differences or diversities. The unity of the soul is incomparably greater than that of the body; indeed, the soul itself *is* a harmony; harmony is virtue; harmony is the permanent thing for which the body must always strive.

How do the harmonies of body and soul differ? In *Phaedo* (86), Plato, like Heraclitus, likens them to the adjustment of strings of an elemental instrument: when the body is strung together by the elements of hot and cold, and moist and dry, the soul is in proportion; if the strings of the body are somewhat loosened by disease or injury, the soul, "though most divine, like other harmonies of music or of works of art, . . . perishes at once. . . ." What Plato meant was that the physician must produce a proper balance of hot and cold, and moist and dry, if health, which is a state of being in tune, is to be. On the other hand, disease comes from an undue tension or slackness of the physical "strings."   Health is a harmony, an "attunement" or proper balance of opposites. Soul and body themselves are opposites, of course, just as the life of nature is a strife of opposites, one struggling against the other to achieve a harmonious unity. Greek medicine too was based on such opposites, health being an equilibrium.[4]

Properly used, music can influence the soul as gymnastics can affect the body--an opinion probably going back to Solon. The world itself is an animal, and its soul, like our own souls, must have a "first instrument" transmitting its powers to the body (*Tim.* 30, 32, 39). The reasoning soul characterizes men, the unreasoning soul characterizes animals other than men. But what *is* the soul? Here is the puzzle. For the Greeks, the word *psyche* did not mean, as Christians often later supposed, an entity separate from the body, a mere form, as it were. Both Homer and the Hebrews supposed it to be a life-principle that leaves the body at death, goes to the underworld, and exists there as an inanimate and unconscious ghost.

Indeed, the soul or souls are the causes of the stars and the seasons, which are divine beings (*Laws* 899), perfectly good, knowing everything, and having all power (ibid. 900-01). For the gods give evidence of the priority of the soul and of the order of the universe, which gives evidence of the dominance of mind there (ibid. 966-67). The soul, interpenetrating everything, is the cause of eternal reason and is formed within the body of the universe (*Tim.* 37). It is divided into contemplation (observation), judgment, and memory, and must itself be in harmony.

There also was an opinion, closer to that of later Christians, that the soul is an immortal and divine entity imprisoned in the body as a penalty for its ante-earthly and mortal sin, and capable (as in Pythagorean rites) of undergoing purification. Plato as a Pythagorean frequently comes close to stating this second view. For Socrates, soul was a conscious personality, the individual rational ability, both speculative and practical, which leads to scientific knowledge and moral character.[5] It is the principle of life and motion: where these are, there is the soul. For Plato both music and gymnastics benefit the soul; the second prevents the softness towards which music is disposed, and the first reduces the savagery of the athlete (*Rep.* 410). Physical training and habit produce temperance through which the harmony of the soul too is preserved (ibid. 591). To be attuned to harmony or proportion is to possess temperance or self-mastery, which runs through the whole scale and produces harmony among the weaker, the stronger, and the middle classes of men (ibid. 432). In the *Symposium* Plato comes close to explaining why this should be.

Love is the subject of the *Symposium*, and of love there are two types: the higher, that of the soul, and the lower, that of the body--in other words, that which knows moderation and that which leads to excess. Music appeals to the former. Medicine is the knowledge of the loves of the body, which has two kinds of desires, that of the healthy and that of the diseased: the reconciliation of the two is medicine's aim. Music is a reconciliation of opposites too. Eryximachus explains that "harmony is composed of differing notes of higher or lower pitch which disagreed once, but are now reconciled by the art of music; for if the higher and lower notes still disagreed, there would be no harmony. . . . For harmony is a symphony, and symphony is an agreement; . . . you cannot harmonize that which disagrees" (*Symp.* 187). Similarly, rhythm is called "the order of motion" (*Laws* 665), and, again in the *Symposium*, it is said to be made up of long and short elements, "once differing, now in accord," so that "music too is concerned with the principles of love in their application to harmony and rhythm" (*Symp.* 187).

Harmony of body and soul symbolizes the harmony of the world; thus a citizen of an ideal and unified state, like the sage himself, is comparable to the musician whose soul is harmonized through his music (*Rep.* 410, 443). Plato's social standard and aim was self-restraint and obedience to divine law, applied either to the well-organized individual or to the state. For him, harmony invisible, incorporeal, perfect, and divine exists within the lyre, which is constructed out of matter, the earthly, the mortal.

In Plato's philosophy, harmony is expressed through number. The world-soul is a composite of numerical ratios, and lesser souls created in a similar way are parallel cases (*Tim.* 31). Since Plato accepts the Pythagorean theory that everything is number, music or pure tone quite independent of words is endemic to Plato's mathematical description of the ratios of the spheres to one another (*Tim.* 35). For Plato, Reality consists of Forms; it is geometrical, geometry being the science of extension in the directly sensed world. The Real world is imitated by the earthly world, which in Plato's terms is non-real. The Real world is an entity or body of essence called the Forms or Ideas, existent beyond the realm of sense and observation. Number in this system symbolizes order, and sound acts, as does no other sensuous appeal, to connect the sense-world with the rational world of Forms, the outer with the inner.

Most, if not all, of the attempts to reconcile Plato's number system with the basic types or genera of the Greek scales have been arbitrary, willful, and fanciful; usually not related either to sense or musical practice, they have nevertheless included three variants or genera of tetrachords--the diatonic, the chromatic, and the enharmonic, the first being the one commonly in use. There were seven octave-species, two systems of tones covering two octaves of fifteen tones; these were called the "Perfect System" (there were no repetitions, as in modern scales, though like modern scales each system could be "transposed"). As has been indicated, the theory of music was based on the tetrachord (the mystical number 4 of the Pythagoreans), on the unit of four tones which were sometimes said to embrace three "spaces":

Diatonic: Two whole tones (steps) and a half-tone (step) at the end (the entire genus was five whole tones and two half-tones): here was the "standard" of the Dorian mode because a whole step separated the two necessary tetrachords.

Chromatic: a minor third and two half-tones.

Enharmonic: a major third and two microtones (like quarter-tones). The tetrachords could overlap or succeed each other. If they overlapped thus:

```
      f g a  b   or:  b a g f
c d e f                  f e d c
```

the term *synemenon* (conjunct) was used; if they succeeded each other, the term was *diazeugmenon* (disjunct). Nevertheless, the scale or mode was not the basis of composition; the tetrachord was.

The enharmonic genus is the one most difficult for us to grasp and perceive because of the (for us) imbalance of a major third and the generally unusual microtones. Besides the genera, there also were "shades," very refined sub-genera almost too complicated and difficult to be grasped by the unaccustomed modern mind, which is oriented to a coarser and more rigid system of scales in semitones and progressions involving thirds and seconds. Certain successive intervals had of course to be strictly according to scale--the octave, the fifth, and the fourth--because they were basic concords.

Thus for Plato the hearing of music was essentially on the level of the discovery of harmony according to the nature and number of all intervals formed of high and low pitches. (As early as this, one is reminded of the enigmatic remark of Leibniz that music is unconscious counting.) Human affections (emotions) correspond to harmonies, or to numbers, in the systems of sound, and to movements of the body, which, when measured by numbers, are called rhythms and meters. Furthermore, music theory or "harmonics" (better: melodics) is to the ear what astronomy is to the eye: Socrates agrees with the Pythagoreans that these are sister arts (*Rep.* 530).

Language, the greatest accomplishment of man, also is governed by number. In the act of defining, the science of language, which is grammar, is like music with respect to tone or sound. The knowledge of the number and nature of sounds is essential to both the grammarian and the musician. There are the letters of the alphabet, the sounds of each being "one" but yet infinite, whether spoken by one person or many. A good speaker does not know this, but a good (analytical) grammarian does. Sound is one and infinite in both music and grammar, but it is subject to number: there are a higher note (pitch), a lower one, and notes of equal pitch. To know this little, however, does not make the musician either: he must know the numbers, the nature, and the proportions of all intervals and the systems made up of them: and also he must understand affections corresponding to them in motions of the body which can be measured numerically and are called rhythm. (The "musician" is obviously not a "practical" person but a theorist.) Thus each of us must look for number in everything. Out of the infinity of the sounds of the human voice a certain number of vowels was originally identified. Then came other letters not pure in sound; and finally mutes. These were all analyzed (as sounds were analyzed in harmonics) into the numbers of and for them, each and all being given letter-names and combined into a single art of grammar or letters (*Phil.* 17-18). If knowledge is true opinion accompanied by reason, grammar and music each must combine its elements. The grammarian must know the primal elements, the letters; these can only be named; it is their combinations in a proposition which gives knowledge; to know the letters is to know the syllables because the syllable is the sum of its letters. And to learn to read or play the harp or lyre one must of necessity know the separate letters both by eye and ear,[6] or he must know what string answers to a particular note, for the notes are the elements of music as letters are of syllables and other "simples and compounds." Since enumeration of the parts does not produce knowledge, enumeration is not enough (*Thaet.* 202-08). Whereas Plato basically associates music with knowledge and number, therefore, he also lays the ground for a comparison, later given importance by Roman rhetoricians, between music and grammar or language, which is the instrument of knowledge.

If all knowledge comes through numerical order, at least for human beings, then music too is connected with knowledge. Animals have "no perception of order or disorder in their movements--that is, of rhythm and harmony" (*Laws* 653); they do not have rhythmics, harmonics, or grammar. But for human beings, "measure and symmetry are beauty and virtue all the world over" (*Phil.* 64). Formal perfection as found in the harmony of numbers is expressible in proportions governing everything in the universe, and the universe itself appears to be a work of art.

III

Of all the theories about music advanced by the Greeks and tenaciously held by Plato, none was more important and none has had a greater effect on the history of thought about music--or has been more puzzling--than the ethical theory[7] or belief that music in its age-old religious and social functions affects the individual's and community's ethos; and this too is based on the supposition that the universe is a harmony expressible in numbers. In addition, all things human reflect or are a prominent part of this universe and its representative, the state, which ideally too in its unity is a harmony of numbers. The soul harmonized embraces reason, spirit, or passion, and all sensual appetites or desire; all of these affect the total soul and, as well, the total state. Temperance, the ideal of both individual and state (*Rep.* 442-44), is accomplished when the soul is in balance. However, the ethical theory involves not only temperance, but also all psychological states and action itself, which to the Greeks was the chief end of life. Not Pythagorean abstraction but psychological balance was involved. Ethos was closely bound with notions of men's characters and their natures as citizens. Always having the quality of rigidity, the theory nevertheless includes the assumption of possible change, as it did for the Pythagoreans. The four basic virtues were courage, temperance, justice, and wisdom--all of them within a certain person in different ratios at once. Music could shift the balance, and the ratios could be altered almost at will--in the right direction, of course. In this theory, however, love and affection seemed to have no place; morals and moral character were the aims and criteria, as contrasted with mere emotions or the passions. Music was supposed to be the gateway to psychological order and virtue.

It was the musical modes which in some fashion were thought to carry or embody the healthful (or harmful) ethical characteristics and then to influence the listeners. While we ourselves tentatively and synaesthetically compare colors and tones for their effects--and even affects--and sometimes join syllables with colors and musical sounds, we are pretty much unconvinced and sometimes merely amused. But the Greeks dogmatically went

further: each tribe had a different "mode," and its mode reflected its own
nature; each preferred its own mode and (of course) denounced the modes
and qualities of other tribes. The Dorian was austere and encouraged manly
virtues; the Ionian was mellifluous and "relaxed": "soft and drinking."
These were genuine Greek modes. From the east came the Phrygian and the
Lydian modes, the latter also "relaxed," "soft and drinking." The Phrygian
was undeniably passionate. The Dorian was deep and low-pitched, the
Phrygian high-pitched; the former was associated with the cult of Apollo,
and the Phrygian, more foreign and exotic, with the cults of Dionysius,
Cybele, and the dead. Perhaps it is true that the introduction of the Phrygian
mode into Greece inspired the creation of the theory of the ethical effects of
music because it was orgiastic--because, emotionally stimulating, it was
supposed to be healthy, invigorating, but tempering. The Dorian mode, like
the Doric temple, was the standard, the model, the mean between extremes.
Thus, geo-cultural phenomena based on custom and habit could decide what
ethical responses were supposed to be.

In the *Republic* Plato discusses the modes and their characters,[8]
allowing that a song or mode had three parts--words, melody, and rhythm--
and that the words set to music and those not set will be alike because the
laws to which they are subject are the same. The words themselves are in
harmony, and pitch and rhythm will depend on them. Now "we have no
need for lamentations and strains of sorrow," the harmonies expressing
these being Lydian; the Lydian (which uses the aulos, an instrument Plato
rejects) must thus be banished from the state. Nor is there any use for
drunkenness, softness, indolence; hence the low-pitched harmonies of the
Ionian as well as, again, the Lydian must be banished. The only harmony
having military value is the Dorian, which uses the cithara or harp; it
follows the "strain of necessity" and courage; and the Phrygian follows the
strain of freedom and the fortunate as well as temperance. The former is
warlike and sounds "the note or accent which a brave man utters in the hour
of danger and stern resolve," and the latter is used for "times of peace and
freedom of action, when there is no pressure of necessity," for the persuasion of God by prayer, and for the instruction and admonition of man, or
when one is "expressing his willingness to yield to persuasion or entreaty or
admonition" (*Rep.* 398-99). For Plato (or for Laches) (*Laches* 188ff), the
Dorian was the true Hellenic mode.

There were additional modes between the two extremes of the Dorian,
which exemplified the militaristic, repressive, legalistic, and totalitarian
tradition of Sparta, and the Phrygian: the Aeolian, sometimes called the
Hypodorian, was for epics; the Ionian mode, sometimes because of its
closeness to the Phrygian, was called Hypophrygian; others were the
Lydian, the Mixolydian, the Hypolydian.   Each had a character--an
objective character--in connection with words, and an objective ethical or
moral effect, good or bad, good for the state or harmful to it. There is more
than a little here to suggest that the mode and its objective character look to
the unity of the composition.

But reality is not always so simple, for to us the whole series of Greek modes is complex and not entirely clear.[9]   What we know of the actual number of Greek modes, their unequal tones and semitones, and their lack of harmonic structure (in the modern sense) raises more questions than it answers, and in a confrontation of them in the flesh, as it were, we would perhaps think them uncouth and barbaric. The failure would in part be ours because our ears are not attuned to the tiny intervals of the enharmonic genus, for example, just as today many of us find genuine music of the Far East difficult or even incomprehensible, even as incomprehensible as, though probably more defensible than, the productions of John Cage. Contrary to common opinion, music has never been a universal language. It may eventually become so if the world continues to "shrink." But one can guess that only the mysterious ancient Greeks would find their classical and proper music of sound to be "intellectual," sophisticated, ethical in effect, and imitative according to their own lights. The affects, or even merely the broader effects, of their music seem to have been psychological in a kind of objective-mechanical way. The ethical influence of music, when it worked, must have been expected to operate automatically, like a push-button psychology, given the proper predisposition of the listener. This psychology, at least in Plato, was not magical; he had nothing to do with the Pythagorean theory of the magical effect of music as reported later by Iamblichus. Plato not only tacitly rejected a place for magic in musical effectiveness, but he denied that there were legitimate magical effects at all. For him magic was a poison, and in the *Laws* (933) he even thinks that the malicious professional magicians should be put to death.

What is there to this ethical theory of music, relatively specific as its theoretical principles are? Careful analysis probably leaves very little of substance which could be verified today. The musical sounds seem to have combined with poetic statements to be their vehicle and to reinforce their expression. Mode or tone was accompanied by words which pointed to what it meant. Music was intellectual in two senses--it represented the rational order of the cosmos and in its recognizable employment of symbolic movements in pitch and rhythm was directed to mean what the words said. Plato found that it is "one half of the choral art" (*Laws* 673), and that certain modes were therefore allied with certain types and combinations of words based on meaning. Habit must have played a part, however, and helped determine the crystallized meanings of modes and their species. Gesture too must have played a part parallel to words and music, and the combined crafts which were called music appear to have been much more like rhetoric than they are today.

Plato as Socrates is not as frankly sure of himself in applying the ethical doctrine to rhythms. Harmony (or the harmonious effects of linear melody) clearly imparts grace (*Rep.* 401), and the ethical effects can be assigned, because of their nature, to the modes or harmonies themselves. It is assumed that this can be done with rhythms also, but here Socrates cannot be specific. A meter can be reduced to the foot, and it too is subject to the same rules as the mode. What meters are the "expressions of a courageous and harmonious life"? These meters, like the melodies, must be adapted to the words, of course, and should be taught as the harmonies are taught. What these meters are Socrates cannot know, but what he does know is that there are three meters just as there are four notes in a tetrachord: according to Damon, there are a cretic rhythm (of 3:2), a dactylic or heroic (or anapestic) rhythm (of 1:1), and iambic or trochaic rhythm (1:2 or 2:1). But both rhythm and harmony apply to style, good and bad rhythm apply to style, and style is governed by words (ibid. 400).

Could it have been that modal influence was physical as well as psychological? Along with the modes, could there have been rhythms which have not been explicitly described for us? It is possible that there were Greek *rhythmic* modes based on Greek prosody--modes we know nothing of. Since Aristoxenus later seems to describe the affects produced by rhythms with more confidence than those produced by melodies, it is distinctly possible that our information about modal effects and affects is incomplete.

IV

The Greek writer Aristides Quintilianus (second century A.D.) is one source for definitions of the Greek terms *catharsis* (purgation) and *mimesis* (imitation).[10] He indicates that Greek art was an expression of feelings with the expectation that such expression would bring its own relief. On the lower (professional) level, only those participating in dancing and singing feel this relief; on the higher, intellectual level, spectators and listeners feel it too. Plato, who may have adopted the Pythagorean or Empedoclean idea of *catharsis* (*Ancilla*, p. 64), thinks education itself is a kind of purification (*Sophist* 231); this must also belong to the intellectual type of person. But Aristides shows that, historically speaking, "lower" feelings and actions in artful public display were the occasions of catharsis, first in the dance, and later in singing and the theater; and Plato mentions another physical procedure, the use of motion and rocking for their cathartic value in the treatment of children--actions not unlike the orgiastic rites and motions of the Corybantes and the dancing to music by the Bacchic women (*Laws* 790-91).

Now, Aristides (65-67) calls expressive art an *imitation*. As first applied to the triune *choreia*, the term meant expression of feelings through movement, sound, and words; later it was applied to music and even later to poetry and sculpture. It clearly meant the representation of reality through art: imitation follows the virtue of the model, and the proper application of music results in human harmony. Though Plato says little about *catharsis*--he is less "psychological" than Aristotle--he is thorough in treating imitation.

Arguments about Plato's notion of imitation or *mimesis* have been legion. Initially, it seems to be a stylistic classification defining play-acting or something dramatic (like an impersonation) as opposed to descriptive composition. It also means the performance by an actor or reciter. Similarly, it means the action of the student who absorbs lessons and "imitates" what his master tells him.[11] By Plato's time, *mimesis* or imitation had gone through three transformations which ended as an accumulation. First it was like mimicry, a rendering of a characteristic look, action, or sound through human means; then it meant the act of following the actions and apparent thoughts of another person; finally it was a presenting of "images" in the form of pictures, statues, and so forth.[12] For Plato it was an epistemological term: a physical representation based on the knowledge of the Forms (or Ideas) and only the Forms (or Ideas). Unfortunately, the painter and the poet cannot represent such Forms. They can only imitate imitations of them. For Plato, poetry is not functional; it can imitate not Reality but only a human approximation of Reality; it is confused and irrational; the Reality of Forms, on the other hand, is natural, perfect, scientific, good, true, and logical. While the poet is, or should be, a source of information about human life and of moral teaching--a kind of social encyclopedist--he is obviously not a philosopher because his perspectives are local. Is the same true of the musician?

It hardly seems so. For us, the *Laws* is the source for Plato's opinion in his mature years that music has mimetic possibilities (668; cf. *Phaedrus* 248). True, in *Cratylus* (424) he calls the musician and the painter kinds of imitators who are not namers. But there he is speaking of language. And in the *Republic* (397) he mentions the joker who for an effect will imitate anything, including the "various sounds of auloi, pipes, trumpets, and all sorts of instruments." And here he is speaking of performance, as he does in the *Laws*, when he says that choric "movements are imitators of manners occurring in various actions, fortunes, dispositions" (655). It is clear that in making this remark he was thinking of the *nomoi* of music, which somehow had something to do with the Forms, though, like poetry, music can imitate only material things in their appearances and not the Forms themselves (ibid. 596ff).

Presumably, then, whenever it presents harmonic forms, music behaves as an ethical medium. "What is a beautiful melody?" Plato asks, and the answer (*Laws* 654-55) is that "music is concerned with harmony and rhythm. . . . [Y]ou can speak of the melodies or figures of the brave and the coward, praising the one and censuring the other. . . . [L]et us say that the figures and melodies which are expressive of virtue of soul or body, or of images of virtue, are without exception good, and those which are expressive of vice are the reverse of good." The imitation must be clear, and the thing must be imitated according to its quality and quantity. The good is based on the following of certain possibilities of manhood in certain directions. Thus words are important and must be clear because instrumental music in itself, only one component of music, cannot be clear or consistent. There are two really approvable kinds of imitation--the dance of war and the dance of peace (ibid. 814-15). The one of course reflects health, courage, and vigor; the other enthusiasm and excitement.

If Hippias is to be believed (and if he is indeed the Hibeh author quoted above), imitation in ancient times was thought to be of (1) phenomena in the sensible physical world, and of (2) a man's propensities or character.   Thus, for Plato, good imitative and representative musical compositions had to be tested by the character and meaning of the piece and by what it represents. Everyone who wants to be a competent judge must recognize (1) what is imitated, (2) the truth of the imitation, and (3) its adequate and satisfactory execution in words, melodies and rhythms. The goodness of music is determined by its truth (ibid. 669). The poets have brazenly offered truncated types of arts which are entirely unsatisfactory: melody separated from rhythm and the figures of the dance, bare words set to meter, instrumental music and rhythm separated from words--all are ridiculous and absurd because they are mixtures or incomplete mediums which cannot express good imitative meaning (ibid.). Besides, there are at least two kinds of music: the artistic-creative (the "harmonic" in the comprehensive, creative sense) and the educational (*Symp.* 187).   Music is good, therefore, if the imitation is good; the imitation must also be true as well as beautiful or well executed; and the power of imitation is especially great in music because, as an instrument of greater potency than any other art, it extends directly to character and soul (*Rep.* 401-02).

Yet, it must not be forgotten that imitation of the corporeal world and its effects is not true imitation. Poems as simple prose-works stripped of music make poor--that is, superficial--appearances.   The imitator or image-maker knows nothing of true existence; he knows only appearances. Images are used, made, and imitated. The aulos player has knowledge of his instrument, the maker only belief. The imitator has neither. He will not know the goodness or badness of his imitation, and will imitate only what seems good to the ignorant mass of people. Imitation is only a play or sport and is far removed from the truth. Measuring, numbering, and weighing are the real paths to understanding.

V

It follows that young men must be taught only the rhythms and music which are imitations of good characters in men (slaves, criminals, and inferior persons, some of them women, cannot be models of virtue). The educational arm of the state, which ideally is permanent and whose alteration means degeneration, must guarantee so thorough an indoctrination that aristocratic young men will be favorable to the laws and the good characters of men and also harbor an aversion for or at least an indifference to new music in dance or song. The law is this: no one in singing or dancing shall offend against public and consecrated models any more than he would offend against any other law. There are rules for the composing of songs: (1) words of evil omen are to be avoided; (2) prayers are to be offered at sacrifice; (3) good, not evil, must be asked for; (4) there shall be suitable hymns for gods, demigods, and heroes; (5) the good are to be honored after death (*Laws* 799). While Plato criticizes Egyptian mathematics for having only practical ends (ibid. 747), he thinks philosophy alone is able to serve true education; "general education" is of dubious value--hence an apparent restlessness and uncertainty about Plato's grudging allowance that music is educational. He admires the Egyptian mode of fixing forms and patterns and preventing innovation. The Athenian Cleinias shows how the lines are drawn: "a lawgiver may institute melodies which have a natural truth without any fear of failure . . . [but only] in a fixed and legal form" (ibid. 657); this was the custom in Egypt, where forms (*nomoi*) had been fixed for thousands of years (ibid. 656). The legalities extend so far that innovation is both unnecessary and deplorable, and Plato agrees with Damon that "when modes of music change, the fundamental laws of the state always change with them" (*Rep.* 424). And, of course, it is permanent laws that must be taught.

The educational argument covered two stages: the primary and secondary curriculum called *mousikē* and the university curriculum. Mimesis or miming was the foundation of *mousikē*, one of the *technae* of civilization. Learning was based on it. But even in its all-inclusive term as absorbing poetry, which Plato demoted to a place below skilled craft (ibid. 598-99), one finds it difficult to see how a change in music will cause the state to change: just the reverse is true. For Plato, music was of course a technique, a complicated convention designed, as Havelock says, "to set up motions and reflexes which would assist the record and recall of significant speech."[13] Music was in part mnemonic, then, and in a way neither musical nor educational in the modern sense. But it was a preparation for higher thought.

Now, as we have seen, the world of Forms is basic to, or, rather, superior to, all aspects of earthly existence. The world of the senses imitates the ideal world of Forms. The craftsman imitates the ideal world indirectly (as the true philosopher knows it directly). The allegory of the cave (*Rep.*, Bk. 7) shows that what we perceive is only a shadow of Reality, that this level of "unreal" and shadow-like perception is the one on which we live. We deal with and learn imitations. The poet even deals with imitations three times removed: he imitates the unreal world which imitates the Real one (ibid. 597ff). Since for Plato music was hardly anything unless it was allied with poetry--except when he himself treated it as an abstract symbol or allegory of world structure--it too must belong to the imitative world, sometimes three, sometimes four times removed from the Real one. Furthermore, since sights and sounds cannot be judged to be knowledge, the pursuers of them, musical amateurs and similar people, are only imitators and nothing more. They know the fund of tones, colors, forms, and "all artificial products made out of them" (ibid. 476) but cannot be thought to have a knowledge of absolute beauty any more than can the poet, who too is only an imitator (ibid. 601). The perfect world of Forms and the Forms themselves are unchangeable and only reflected in phenomena. And the

Forms cannot be taught; only the forms of the corporeal, sense world can. The arts, unfortunately, are constantly frustrated in reaching the real Forms, but it is their task to try to do so. If they are successful, they can only end in philosophy, the university stage of education.

Plato thought his plan for education was perfect and thoroughly in keeping with the unified and perfect state and the government he envisaged. The Forms defined the state, whose purposes could be best implemented by a system of Guardians (men who, like their pupils, were members of the ruling class). Spirited, gentle, decorous, politically and musically subservient to the state and to tradition--but old (and obviously beyond temptation)--they are preferably sixty-year-old choristers. In their place, they are very good teachers (*Laws* 812).

All Guardians should be philosophers, that class of persons in the state possessing the virtues of wisdom and courage common to all men of character (*Laws* 659). Noble in quality and action, they must play the lyre and cithara (*Rep.* 399), learn only Dorian and Phrygian harmonies (the two heard in serious music), and live according to the rules. (Possession of imagination, initiative, or originality was clearly no requirement.) Nobody was to sing a song not approved by the Guardians, even if his "strain is sweeter than the songs of Thamyris and Orpheus" (*Laws* 829). They were to be censors for the state. They were to discourage any music accompanying an incongruous taste, any obscenities in word or gesture, or any music on instruments which is merely virtuosic and divorced from words. The Guardians, who must indeed be guardians and not boon companions (*Rep.* 421), were to be teachers who, differing from the average person, could distinguish good music from bad--censors who would guide the undependable musical taste of the public. They had to be better acquainted than the public with the nature of music and its effects upon the soul and therefore upon behavior.

Music as an omnibus pursuit (mental training in all subjects of mathematics, poetry, reading and writing, and music itself) should therefore be taught before gymnastic (*Rep.* 403, *Protag.* 326), which is the median activity between music and the dance (*Laws* 813-16); boys should pursue it for three years (14-17) and learn the lyre at the age of thirteen (ibid. 810); and women, like men, should learn gymnastics and the physical arts (ibid. 814). Yet, the ethical difference between men and women must be recognized, the former necessarily being assigned music expressive of courage and the latter that of moderation and temperance. "Now, both sexes have melodies and rhythms which of necessity belong to them"; the necessity is that "the grand, and that which tends to courage, may fairly be called manly; but that which inclines to moderation and temperance, maybe declared both in law and in ordinary speech to be the more womanly quality" (ibid. 802).

Like many educational theorists today, Plato thinks the aim of education is not really to impart knowledge, but to form character and to prepare the young for mature life; philosophy tempered with music is the savior of a man's virtue throughout his lifetime (*Rep.* 549); it is found in education, in a training for the work of the after-life on earth; children's sports as a part of education initially point in the direction which fits men not only for success in life, but also for perfection as citizens (*Laws* 643). Education is "the first and fairest thing that the best of men can ever have . . ." (ibid. 644). First impressions are dominated by pleasure and pain, but through the right training, the goal of life, which is wisdom, will eventually come to us (ibid. 653). Children's unregulated feelings need to be controlled through a developed sense of reason which directs them towards correct habits, which, with understanding, agree with the virtue of the complete human being. For education is in large part a matter of habit. Plato often refers to the fascination of children with song, which under the pretext of play can be a musical source of moral influence: chants have been invented which "really enchant, and are designed to implant . . . [a] harmony" with the laws of the state; these are given to the child because his mind "is incapable of enduring serious training"; they are called plays and songs, and are performed so that "the soul of the child may not be habituated to feel joy and sorrow in a manner at variance with the law, . . . but may rather follow the law and rejoice and sorrow at the same things as the aged . . ." (ibid. 659). Here Plato's idea of play in the young reminds one of, but is in contrast to, Friedrich Schiller's notion that play, obviously adult, is a freedom found in beauty and art, which follow their own rules independent of nature, morals, and duty. (Schiller's theory is, of course, many centuries away from Plato, for whom neither knowledge nor play exists for its own sake.)

Plato of course well knew (or thought he knew) the Athenian public, which he divided into three classes: (1) the greatest number, the uneducated, who cannot sing or dance, or who can only follow the lead of others who imagine they know what is proper in rhythm and harmony ("I know what I like"); (2) next, the working artist and the practical professional man who in body and voice can realize what is beautiful; and (3) finally the society of free men or noble men, thirty to sixty years of age, who need not know how to execute music, which is left to the performer, but must have a complete, a thorough technically-based judgment; the free man, because he has to be a critic, must have feeling and understanding for rhythms and harmonies so that he can follow the melody (*Laws* 670-71). For man alone has a perception of order, of the order of motion called rhythm, and the order of the voice employing high and low pitches called harmony; and these orders together are called choric song (ibid. 665). For rhythms and harmony have to do with the voice, and the whole choral art is the whole of education. The movement of the body, of which gesture is peculiarly a part, shares rhythm with the movement of the voice. Now, the sound of the voice reaching and educating the soul is music, and the two types of physical movement are dance and gymnastic (ibid. 672-73). Choric song has to do with order, which implies measure, the mean, and symmetry, which in the *Philebus* (64-65) are shown along with truth to have the elements of pleasure, wisdom, virtue, and beauty. It is evident that in speaking of music, Plato is speaking of elementary education.

VI

Plato distrusted all working professionalism in music. He was superior to practice. His political aims embraced only the musically educated amateur, but not the professional--who was not "free." Furthermore, he thought of simplicity of melody as the first principle of education (*Rep.* 397ff). And simplicity did not include what we call polyphony: Plato's *Laws* 812 is often cited to show that polyphony existed in ancient times, but the octave separation in singing of man and boy--of mature teacher and immature pupil, the teacher possibly embellishing at the lower octave the melody sung by the pupil--was the exact opposite of polyphony as understood today (though it may have been akin to organum). No, the proper accomplishments occur only if the music is simple and plain: nothing should be in excess; nothing should be touched by professionalism. For Plato, the four notes of the tetrachord were enough for the make-up of all proper harmonies. And rhythms should be simple too: "we ought not to seek out complex systems of meter, or meters of every kind, but rather to discover what rhythms are the expressions of a courageous and harmonious life [the Dorian, the truly manly and Hellenic]; and when we have found them, we shall adapt the foot and the melody to words having a like spirit, not the words to the foot and melody." For "beauty of style and harmony and grace and good rhythm depend on simplicity--I mean the true simplicity of a rightly and nobly-ordered mind and character, not that other simplicity which is only a euphemism for folly" (*Rep.* 399-400). Few working professionals could be so bound and restricted.

If certain modes are to be rejected and others retained, specific instruments too must be judged for their usefulness, this depending upon the extent to which they encourage the use of a multiplicity of notes. Aulos players and aulos makers who encourage complex music should be banished from the state. Only the lyre and the cithara are to be kept in the city in any case, and only the shepherd's pipe in the country. Apollo and his instruments are to be preferred over Marsyas and his (ibid. 399).

For Plato, the mere musician, uneducated and prone to exhibitionism, was a mere tuner of strings and far inferior to a person "who mingles music with gymnastic in the fairest proportions, . . . best attempers them to the soul," and thus may be "rightly called the true musician and harmonist. . . ." The same principles are involved in the dance (ibid. 412). He who sings and also dances gives a pleasurable sense of harmony and rhythm; he additionally "sings what is good and dances what is good" (*Laws* 654). Complexity is a social evil, simple music inspires temperance, simple rhythms can express the courageous and harmonious life, and the true musician is content to mingle music and gymnastic in "the fairest proportions," for both music and gymnastic have in view the improvement of the soul (*Rep.* 412).[14]

Plato is not only a conservative, then, but also a traditionalist and reactionary. Musical degeneracy as he judges it means treachery to the state. There had been good laws for music in the past, when it was divided into prayers for the gods (hymns), lamentations, paeans, dithyrambs, and the song of "laws" (themselves called *citharoedic*). Styles were not confused with one another. Gradually, however, poets introduced lawless innovations, mingled the types, and at the same time affirmed that music has no truth but only offers pleasure to the hearer (*Laws* 700). For there are three kinds of style: the simple, the multiplex, and a combination of the two. And the best is the simple. Harmony (that is, melody) and rhythm should be chosen for their simplicity, and a speaker should keep to the same simple style in a single harmony (melody) and rhythm and avoid great changes in them (*Rep.* 397). In any case, melody and rhythm must depend on the words.

Plato's insistence on simplicity in music may have been both traditional and practical. Both teacher and pupil should use the sounds of the lyre because its notes are pure, and they should play notes in unison. Complex variations in notes are to be avoided. The strings should not sound one note while the poet or composer sounds another. Nor should there be combinations of concords and harmonies made up of lesser and greater intervals, or of notes both fast and slow, or both high and low. Complex variations in rhythm too must be shunned. Such intricacies are not adapted or suited to a three-year education in music, which is the maximum length of time for musical instruction. Of necessity the student must be introduced to music in its simplicity and in its transparency in relation to the words, and this introduction will serve him during his entire life.

Plato's prevailing and broader view is that music or "harmony" was not given to man by the Muses for his irrational pleasure ("which is deemed [by certain Sophists] to be the purpose of it in our day"). Along with rhythm, it was given to help man against "the irregular and graceless ways which prevail among mankind generally" (*Tim.* 47). Primarily music denotes virtue: when Plato heard a man discoursing of nature, he compared "the man and his words, and [noted] the harmony and correspondence of them." Such a person is a true musician, "attuned to a fairer harmony than that of the lyre, or any pleasant instrument of music . . .; for truly he has in his own life a harmony of words and deeds, arranged . . . in the true Hellenic mode" (*Laches* 188). The direct, forthright, honest approach is the musical one, which is lacking in the hypocrite, the coward, and the liar.

VII

Puritan that he apparently was, Plato could not always hold to one single view because his conversationalists would not let him. He had to recognize that music could arouse pleasure for its own sake, an innocent pleasure which in the *Laws* (802) he calls "the characteristic of all music." Also, the end of music is the love of beauty (*Rep.* 403), and the god of love teaches music (*Symp.* 196). Yet in the *Symposium* (176) he relegates it to the status of an entertainment which as a component of a drinking party seems to hinder conversation. But here it is misapplied: true pleasures belong to the beauty of color and form, to sweet smells and sounds, and to an alleviation of pain in both body and mind (*Phil.* 51). Not (as we know) that music is intended to give only pleasure: so much of music as is adapted to the voice and to the sense of hearing "is granted to us for the sake of harmony"--in a sense, to correct discord in our souls (*Tim.* 47). Indeed, it is intolerable to contend, as some people do, that the "excellence of music is to give pleasure to our souls" (*Laws* 655). Music which is judged according to the criterion of pleasure is neither to be sought out nor to be regarded as having real excellence (ibid. 667).

In describing and analyzing the sense of hearing (*Tim.* 67), Plato makes nothing of its possible pleasure. He describes its physical basis, and seems to be echoing Archytas: sound is a blow which passes through the ears and is transmitted through the air, brain, and blood to the soul; the hearing itself is a vibration of this blow beginning in the head and ending in the liver. A swift sound is acute (light = high), a slow one grave (heavy = low); a regular sound is smooth, an irregular one harsh; a great body of sound is loud, a small one soft.

Cleinias, a Cretan, in the *Laws* says he wants excellence in music to be measured by pleasure, but "not . . . that of chance persons" because "the fairest music is that which delights the best and the best educated, and especially that which delights the man who is pre-eminent in virtue and education" (659). Pleasure is an accompanying charm, a sugar-coating of the pill of ethical teaching, almost a constitutional right of the higher or highest classes of human beings, who are so trained as not to be led into false and bad ways by its pleasantness. Grudgingly, Plato admits that there are arts which may delight mankind. Aulos-playing is such an art, as are lyre-playing at festivals, the choral art, dithyrambic poetry, and harp-playing--at least as cultivated by certain people. They never contribute to the higher good of listeners, however (*Gorgias* 501-02). For Socrates, an impure art like music when it is full of guesswork and imitation, an art which Protarcus says must be accepted even by philosophers as having a place in ordinary life as compared with super-human and divine matters, is acceptable only as the lowest form of pleasure (*Phil.* 62, 67).

It is the desire for pleasure devoid of virtue which is the reason for Plato's alarm over the decay of Greek music--especially the music of the Athens of his own day. Thinking, as we have seen, that music had fallen into decline in the middle of the fifth century B.C., he wanted a return of the (supposed) perfection of the archaic art. Poets had corrupted music. Poets and musicians, he thought, both catered to the forms desired by untrained youths in pursuit of indiscriminate pleasure, disregarded the proper relations of melody to rhythm and of music to words, refused to follow the proper models, did not therefore combine those elements of music which correspond with the proper moral virtues, and used the aulos and the cithara without vocal accompaniment so that one did not know what wordless rhythm and tune were to mean or what mode (*nomos* or law) they were to represent (*Laws* 700-01). Used in mystic rites, aulos music should really be excluded from the republic (*Rep.* 399) because it is an art which seeks pleasure alone (*Gorg.* 501); possibly, even uncertainty in the tuning of pitches makes of instrumental music an impure art medium: it is "always trying to guess the pitch of each vibrating note and is therefore mixed up with much that is doubtful and has little which is certain" (*Phil.* 56). For Plato musical license governed by a desire for pleasure symbolized, not a kind of "blowing off of steam," but the license of manners in Athens itself, at one time a city of law and order in which the legislators of music now were no longer in places of power.

In the end, all art, and especially music, renews the soul with grace (*Rep.* 401) or acts as a kind of medicine for it. But men differ, and each man is not always the same. Hearing music, one can be merely passive, or he can be active, or his will power can be overcome and his freedom suspended. One can be attracted to the music because of his own mood; or he can be drawn out of one state of mind into another; or his will power can be suspended entirely so that through inspiration he can be transported out of himself into the spirit of Dionysian ecstasy, like the Corybantic revellers (*Ion* 534) who were possessed by the god. All states of mind can include pleasure, and all music can produce pleasure. It is less accurate than the non-imitative abstract forms, however, and less pure than ship building or house building (architecture) because less accurate in its results (*Phil.* 55-56). Yet, music at its noblest and best is a philosophy, as Socrates said (*Phaedo* 61)--though here he also sounds like a true Pythagorean for whom philosophy is the highest music, entailing number in all things.

VIII

Diogenes Laertius reports (3.88) that Plato recognized three kinds of music: (1) that in which the mouth alone is employed (singing), (2) that in which both mouth and hands are employed (singing by a harper playing his own accompaniment), and (3) that in which hands alone are employed (the harp sounding alone). It is quite clear that Plato preferred the first two for educational reasons. But what about the third? Is it entirely useless? The answer can probably be found in his words about beauty.

In *Lysis* (216), Plato calls beauty a slippery thing, soft and smooth, though Socrates--speaking about friendship--declares it to be at one with the good. In the *Symposium* (206) it is maintained that the beautiful is allied with physical conception and procreation, because both are the result of a desire for immortality, which is good. Here Plato is speaking about generation. Even more beautiful, however, are the creations of the soul which embrace wisdom and virtue. Yet, true beauty is an absolute; to achieve it one must progress from the concrete to the abstract, then to the universal, and then to the universe of truth and beauty (ibid. 209-11). Representative and imitative in nature (*Laws* 668), music nevertheless must in some way approach absolute truth. Its mode of representation as an ally of poetry does not allow it to do so. The sense cannot reach such truth and may even prevent its realization (*Phaedo* 65, 75). Yet in the *Gorgias* (474) Socrates implies that the beautiful belongs to both the useful and the pleasant.

But more important is the beauty of form: in the *Philebus* (51) there is philosophical support for the painting, centuries later, of the Cubists: Socrates describes the beauty of straight lines and circles, and of plane or solid figures formed by turning-lathes, rulers, and measures of angles; this is the form of the eternally and absolutely beautiful. The same is true of sounds which, being smooth and clear, possess a single pure tone: these are not relatively but absolutely beautiful. Measure and symmetry are necessary to such beauty--and are necessary also to virtue; and beauty, symmetry, and truth make up the ideal mixture (ibid. 64-65).

All of this still spells an ambiguity. Plato has not denied beauty to music ("the end of music is the love of beauty" [*Rep.* 403]), especially as it serves the ends of virtue, truth, and wisdom: it can indeed be beautiful if it fulfills a function. Yet certain qualities of sound and tone *are* absolutely beautiful. But sound is not the craft of music. The sounds of instrumental music, for example: Plato does not approve of them. The beauty-in-perfection that Plato seems to find in music is and is not confined to pure sound without regard to its functional use or its share in a piece made up of "crafted" sound, which too is an abstract form. Indeed, there is a beauty in figure, melody, song, and dance, and, in these, man, like no other animal, realizes his sense of order: the order of motion is rhythm, that of the voice is harmony.

Plato the moralist cannot reveal support for "mathematical" music (if one may use the term broadly) or music associated with the (musical) proportions of architecture, which too is at once an art and craft of beauty, a kind of knowledge (*Rep.* 438), and also a thing of grace and harmony requiring a pure taste for its perception (ibid. 401). But as the exponent of the genesis of the world according to musical number, a world to which no one has ever attributed a human language, Plato, like Kepler in the seventeenth century, could easily have seen a parallel between the music of the spheres and the music we today call absolute.

IX

There is a final question: can music be a science? That music is a child of Harmonia is beyond question, and science must at least accept her universal presence. Can it as an art be perfect; can it be the science of perfection? Plato does not really say, and what he does say seems vague and often inconsistent.

In spite of a Pythagorean bias, Plato did not entirely follow Pythagorean principles. For him, terrestrial music is no longer an art or craft of all the Muses but a literary form embracing "melody," harmony and rhythm, among which the dominant element is harmony. It sometimes is and sometimes is not closely related to wisdom (however that may be defined). True, it has allegorical relevance. Though there is still a certain residue of mysticism in its supposed relation to mathematics, it has nothing to do with magic, a reprehensible and quite undependable phenomenon in Plato's eyes. Furthermore, apart from music's own mathematical base--that is, in the form of consonances, dissonances, and scales--it seems to be a mathematical subject only by courtesy. The music of the spheres and its undoubted internal mathematical relationships do not guarantee music itself a place among intellectual studies because such studies focus on the Reality which is eternal and timeless. Its moral effects, and even its immoral effects, do not make it a proper (Platonic) science, which is and should be the study of the "natural harmonies of number" or reflections on "why some numbers are harmonious and others not." These are real problems not even met full face by harmonists, who deal with "the numbers of the harmonies that are heard" (*Rep*. 531). Music and gymnastic are real studies indeed, but they belong to elementary education, and they deal with the realm of things.

For the first subject to have universal application is arithmetic, which has not only a practical but also a higher philosophical use (*Rep*. 523ff). Science is not based on sense or time: things which move in the world of sense are generated forms of time (*Tim*. 38, *Parmen*. 141), and no study of the world of sense can be a science. Higher mathematics and science are not concerned with the visible or tangible, with Heraclitean appearances in flow, but with Forms or the laws of Forms. A kindred study is geometry. It too often treats of what will perish. It should be concerned with the eternal. Astronomy too is practical in part, but it is advisable for us to forget the starry heavens "wrought upon a physical background" and to speculate about the "true motions of absolute swiftness and absolute slowness" relative to one another contained in "the true number and in every figure" apprehended, not by sight, but by reason and intelligence. The eye must ignore the heavens as the ear must ignore harmonics. The object is the perfection of all knowledge; unfortunately, teachers of harmonics compare sounds, they torture the strings of instruments, they examine harmonies as heard--and ignore the natural harmonies of numbers or questions like why some numbers are harmonious and others not. In numbers the scientist can express musical intervals the ear cannot hear (*Rep*. 532). To be a science, music must deal with absolutes; harmonics cannot do this. (There is a parallel here with the love of beautiful things on the one hand and a love of beauty itself on the other [*Symp*. 210] and with evil and good, the latter the standard for the Forms [*Thaet*. 176-77]). The proper medium for science is dialectic (logic), which goes directly to first principles, proceeds by reason alone without the help of the senses, and looks to the discovery of the absolute (*Rep.* 532-33).   Was the possibility of mathematical physics already envisaged by Plato two thousand years before its development in the West, just as he (supposedly) envisaged equal temperament in advance of his day?[15] It almost seems possible.

As for a musical science, however, Plato thought it could not exist. He himself did not recognize a potential *science* of acoustics latent in discussions of sound and tone. The educative force of music: as a social science it could only be a contradiction in terms. But when he denied that harmonics is a science, Aristoxenus of the school of Aristotle frankly but indirectly declared him to be wrong.

III
Aristotle

With Aristotle we enter a new and different philosophical atmosphere--the difference between the Platonic Academy and the Aristotelian Lyceum. In comparing the founders of these two institutions, a Platonist would stress the similarities basic to the two philosophers, the more literary or poetic nature of Plato's writings, and Aristotle's allegedly unfortunate deviation from some of Plato's theories. An Aristotelian would stress the differences between the mathematical Plato and the biological Aristotle, the more empirical nature of Aristotle's thought, Aristotle's greater capacity for classification, for bringing phenomena into rational order out of chaos, and for organizing in treatises the various aspects of thought such as physics, metaphysics, logic, rhetoric, and so forth. Furthermore, the Aristotelian would find a greater honesty (even a greater cheerfulness) and forthrightness in Aristotle, who always allowed himself to be seen, whereas in the Platonic dialogue, made up of question and answer, the characters of the persons speaking are so well highlighted that one can never be sure whom Plato was hiding behind--if he is.

Yet both Plato and Aristotle were scientific in that they aimed at knowledge for its own sake. They shared the belief that their duty was the investigation of the cosmos, a perfect sphere with a finite radius. Neither studied the origins of things, unless the *Timaeus* can be considered a "true" account of genesis; they thought only of that which exists or is.

Though Aristotle allowed for the harmonic structure of the universe, he did not accept the musical (sounding) part of it as asserted by Plato. Nor did he accept the theory of Ideas or Forms or that of number: his attention was turned towards substance, things, and nature (*Metaph*. 992a-b), towards what is observable. For him, Forms could not be numbers, and the number 10 of the Pythagoreans and Plato was especially insufficient (ibid. 1084a).

Not that Aristotle, out of whose Lyceum rose the Peripatetic school of Greek philosophers, was less or more prone than Plato to use the terms 'beauty' or 'art.' For both, 'art' signified a craft with its own rules (witness Aristotle's *Poetics*), a doing something well, a structuring; and 'beauty,' a term used in admiration of the form of the human figure, was a matter of proportion, measure, even of number in the Pythagorean sense--that is, of abstract form.

Unlike modern philosophers, the Greeks were not close definers of terms. They did not differentiate sharply between poetry and prose. Both

55

were "makings," and their creators were "makers." Nor did they distinguish music from artistic language. Though they obviously had in abundance what today is called a creative imagination, they did not have a word for it. The poet was a maker, a fabricator, a craftsman. In the *Poetics* (1460a), Aristotle praises Homer not for having taught poets to speak in their own persons, but rather to frame properly. Poetry was an imitation of men doing something, of men in action (ibid. 1448a).

But between Plato and Aristotle there are profound differences. Plato was an almost completely speculative thinker. At the fore was his idea of the nature and primacy of the state and its legitimate imposition of rules of every kind on the entire populace; he was a moralist, lawgiver, and social reformer. However, with Aristotle, who attempted to define the "arts" according to their human relevancies, there arises the possibility of the discipline of aesthetics. Literary and dramatic criticism are essentially his creations and can be explained as evidences of his agreement with Protagoras' opinion that man is a measure of all things. Aristotle is unwilling to accept the low level on which Plato had placed the arts. For him, experience created art (*Metaph.* 981a), which is near to wisdom--a quality correlated with science and intellect and like them concerned with knowledge and offering proof of certain truths.

Plato would banish poetry, which he thought had capability for harm, from the republic he described and wanted, and he was only a little less kind about drama and painting. Although human nature is a constant for both Plato and Aristotle, for Plato the world of the senses was inferior because it belonged to the material world which human beings must occupy--a world temporary, accidental, and unreal. But for Aristotle it is the world of matter, form, and movement (*On the Heavens* 268a) which the artist, especially the poet and musician, could validly imitate; and for this creator or maker Aristotle shows such respect that he attempts to codify the laws the artist should follow in two (incomplete) works, the *Poetics*, one of the great critical-aesthetic documents of the Western world, and the *Politics*.

In the abstract, both Plato and Aristotle searched for truth, unity, principle, the permanent amid change--all beginning with facts so logically and rationally considered as to conform with the ordered universe and the observable results of necessary law. But Aristotle tried to devise a methodology by mapping out areas of human knowledge and defining a method of scientific inquiry. He in some part codified and indexed Plato for us to use. The intellectual virtues, he thinks, are five: (acquired) science, (innate) intellect, (a certain truth in) the arts, (uncertain truth in) prudence, and wisdom (*Nic. Eth.* 1139b-1141b).

Like Plato, Aristotle thought of music as an art whose laws were partly governed by the requirements of the state. And like Plato he made assumptions about the right of the state to dictate. Yet as scientist he made analyses not only political but also psychological (as he did in connection with the arts and the nature of man from which the arts derive), physiological, and biological. It was characteristic of Greek thought in general to stress the sameness of the physical and metaphysical in man in that the perceptual (the physical) and the conceptual (abstract reality) are held together by an indwelling unity. To a certain extent, the psychological was a middle term entangled in the two on the outside but probably closer to the metaphysical. For Aristotle, however, the psychological was independent. Music as sound is representative not of the music of the spheres (*On the Heavens* 289b-290b) but of psychological states.   Furthermore, while numbers for Plato had been central and intrinsic to the world as a mystical universal whose presence one could only accept and not observe, Aristotle saw them as something useful and external, something appropriate for measurement.

Aristotle explains that one cannot hear cosmic harmony. Is this so because we are like the blacksmith who learns to ignore the sound of his anvil? On the contrary, we really hear no music because there isn't any. The cosmos may indeed embrace a real and symbolical harmony, and heaven may be whole, one, and eternal. It is infinite in time. Its motion is regular and carries no trace of irregularity. Its form is spherical and limited. Its spherical movement is divine and as eternal as it is natural. Sun, moon, earth, and the stars too are spherical; and they move without friction. Therefore, there is not, and there cannot be, any music of the spheres. If such friction existed, the sound it creates would be so great that we could not bear it. Nor do the movements of the spheres produce any other effect in us in place of that of hearing. There is no effect since there is no sound, and the theory is only a poetical fiction (ibid. 284-288a).

Aristotle was also impatient with the Pythagorean and Platonic reverence for numbers, which he found to be neither the essence nor the cause of form and being. Harmony is a ratio of numbers expressing high and low pitches. What is a concord? A commensurate numerical ratio of a high and a low note (*Post. Anal.* 90a). Ratio is the essence; number is the matter (*Metaph.* 1092b). As for the symbolical interpretation of number on the assumption that number can be a cause of things: this, according to Aristotle, is folly. The Pythagoreans, for instance, mistakenly say that the world and everything in it is determined by the number 3 (*On the Heavens* 268a). And how can a number 7 cause such differences as the scale of seven strings, the Pleiades, the seven vowels, the hour of 7 when certain animals lose their teeth(!), and those seven who fought against Thebes? Equally ridiculous is it that there should be significance in the fact that the distance in letters from the *alpha* to *omega* should be equal to the distance from the lowest tone on the aulos to the highest and the "the number of this [last] note is equal to that of the whole choir of heaven." Such analogies can be found everywhere, in both eternal and perishable things.   Ideal numbers are clearly not the cause of musical phenomena (*Metaph.* 1093a-b). Is mathematics synonymous with philosophy? No, because in general philosophy is the study of perceptible things (*Metaph.* 991b-992a) by human beings employing memory, experience, and art (ibid. 980a-981b).

If number cannot cause musical tones, there is something more readily observable that can. Like Archytas before him, Aristotle points out that sound requires the striking together of two objects, a space being between them. "It is generated by an impact," he says. "Hence it is impossible for one body only to create a sound." It is the nature of the material, not its length (as of a string) which is of *qualitative* interest. Not all bodies even upon an impact can produce sound, but for each sounding body there is a characteristic result. (Wood, strings, and metal produce different sounds as qualities.) Sound can be heard both in air and in water, but neither of these is its cause. Two solids are necessary. A mass of air must be set in motion; and speed in motion makes the difference between acute (high) and grave (low) tones. Repeating an early presupposition of Greek thought, Aristotle explains that motion (of which Plato in *Laws* 893-94 had listed ten types) is the most universal characteristic of the world. Now, the "organ of hearing is physically united with air," which itself is soundless; "the air inside the ear has a movement of its own,[1] but the sound we hear is always the sound of something else."

Furthermore, tone is more the expression of the soul than of the outer physical world. Voice produces a sound which has a soul in it: "nothing that is without soul utters voice, it being only by a metaphor that we speak of the voice of the aulos and the lyre. . . . Many animals are voiceless. . . . [But] voice [can be] the sound made by an animal,[2] and that with a special organ. . . . Voice then is the impact of the inbreathed air against the 'windpipe,' and . . . what produces the impact must have soul in it and must be accompanied by an act of imagination, for voice is a sound *with a meaning* . . ." (*On the Soul* 419a-420b). It is even more important that a unity be in operation--a kind of subjective-objectivity--in that the object which can be sensed is at one with the perceiving sense: the activity is one, though there is still a distinction between the two. A man may be hearing but not hearing; sound may not always be sounding. Actual sound and actual hearing are a merging into a one (ibid. 425b-426a).

The unity which occurs in acts of perception can be interpreted as the beginning of artistic unity. Aristotle does not see or even expect unity to the degree Plato and Socrates did, for they had assumed that the more unified the state the better. But Aristotle, though he would agree up to a point, recognizes that life has its pluralities, especially those of state government. The soul is not a harmony but a unity (*On the Soul* 411a-b). A perfectly unified state is on the point of dissolution. It is inferior, just as if a harmony were so unified as to become a single note, or a rhythm were reduced to a single foot (*Pol.* 1263b). In fact, Aristotle even doubts that there is a harmony of the body, or of the soul, or of the two together (*On the Soul* 407b-408a). Where is this highly praised unity? It must be the end and aim of art. In *On the World* (396b), which is probably not by Aristotle at all, it is said that nature in a Heraclitean way may have a liking for contraries, out of which it creates harmonies. Art does this too; in imitation of nature, it creates unities.

Thus in Aristotle, all theories seem to be based on the assumption that they and their consequences can be verified by realities physical and mental, and that physical and psychological theory and observation are the foundation for political theory, which itself is the foundation for ethical and aesthetic theory. It is characteristic of Aristotle, as of Plato when he descends to the lower, corporeal world, that in discussing art he should begin with that arm of the state which is to achieve its aims, namely, that of the *statis sons* (*Pol.* 1339a-b), education which combines with art to fill up the deficiencies of nature (ibid. 1337a-b). For Aristotle, as for Plato, education is for the aristocratic--and Hellenic--few.

Aristotle attempts to describe the kind of Greek people he was writing about and unconsciously sets up a dichotomy for European and Asiatic nations which became a convention. There is the cold Northern climate populated by people "full of spirit, but wanting in intelligence and skill," living in comparative freedom, but, having "no political organization . . . [are] incapable of ruling over others." By contrast, there are the natives of Asia, who are "intelligent and inventive . . . [but] wanting in spirit, and therefore . . . always in a state of subjection and slavery." Between them (and ostensibly in keeping with the principle of moderation and the mean in all things) are the Hellenes, intermediate in character, high-spirited, and intelligent--and thus free, the best governed of all nations, and able to rule the world if they were "formed into one state." Legislators for the Hellenic state should be both intelligent and courageous in their efforts to lead (male) citizens, the proper recipients of education, to virtue (ibid. 1327b).

Aristotle classifies the customary branches of education as reading and writing, gymnastic exercises, and music; he sometimes adds a fourth, drawing. Reading and writing are useful in life, and gymnastics will infuse boys with courage. About the worth of music he has no doubts, but he feels obligated to dispel the doubts of others (ibid. 1339a-b). Although today music is cultivated mostly for the sake of pleasure, Aristotle says, it had originally been included in education because, it was often said (and by Aristotle himself earlier in the *Politics* 1333a-1334b) that nature herself demands that human beings should be able to both work well and to use leisure well: for, he says, "the first principle of all action is leisure" (ibid. 1337b), clearly an end and pleasure in itself.

When human beings are at leisure, however, they should not simply be amusing themselves, for amusement is not the aim of life. Leisure when it gives only pleasure, happiness, and the enjoyment of life is for the worker; then it is a refreshing relaxation having its own purpose. But there are branches of education and learning "which we must study merely with a view to leisure spent in intellectual activity, and these are to be valued for their own sake" (ibid. 1338a). They have no use, but are free and liberal. Therefore music was not admitted into education because of its necessity or utility, though it does give surcease from learning and work (ibid. 1339b), neither of which applies to it as to reading, writing, and gymnastic. It is of use for intellectual enjoyment in leisure, and it was apparently introduced as one of the many ways in which a freeman should pass his time. Boys should be trained in it, therefore, not because of its usefulness or necessity, but because it is liberal or noble (1338a). It is the tool of free gentlemen (as theater is made for the common people).

Thus Aristotle does not demand that music be educationally functional. He thinks one cannot easily determine the nature of music or the reason for our having knowledge of it. One may conjecture that this is because music is not a science (in contrast to arithmetic, geometry, astronomy, and medicine). Furthermore, terms for it are not always single-faceted but rather can have varying differentiae: there is color in bodies and there is color in tunes or melodies, which do not have the same differentiae, as in the realm of sight, piercing ("acute" or "high") colors or compressing ("grave" or "low") ones (*Topics* 107b). This mixture of aesthetic impressions is also marked in a dynamic correspondence of tone and color with feeling just as the most pleasing combinations of colors depend on the same ratios as musical concords (*De sensu et sensibilii* 437a). All of this is contrary to Plato's objection to the use of the word 'color' even metaphorically for a melody (*Laws* 655).

Does music exist for amusement and relaxation, then, because it leads to virtue, or because it contributes to the enjoyment of leisure and mental cultivation? It seems to be reckoned under and to have a share in all three of these. Because it is pleasant, it is included in social gatherings and entertainments. It provides relaxation from past toil. But it also provides the recreation which may have a nobler objective than the mere giving of pleasure to everyone; it can influence character and soul. The songs of Olympus, for example, inspire enthusiasm, and enthusiasm is "an emotion of the ethical part of the soul." And when we hear music which is a pleasure, there is "clearly nothing which we are so much concerned to acquire and to cultivate as the power of forming right judgments, and of taking delight in good dispositions and noble actions. Rhythm [which is a source of motion] and melody supply imitations of anger and gentleness, and also of courage and temperance, and of all the qualities contrary to these, and of the other qualities of character, which hardly fall short of the actual affections, as we know from our experience, for in listening to such strains our souls undergo a change. The habit of feeling pleasure or pain at mere (musical) representations is not far removed from the same feeling about realities. . . . The objects of no other sense, such as taste or touch, have any resemblance to moral qualities. . . ." Thus music has a superiority over the other arts. Figures and colors have little connection with morals. "[I]n mere melodies there is an imitation of character, for the musical modes differ essentially from one another, and those who hear them are differently affected by each. . . . The same principles apply to rhythms; some have a character of rest, others of motion, and of these latter again, some have a more vulgar, others a nobler movement. . . . [M]usic has a power of forming character and should therefore be introduced into the education of the young," because its study is especially adapted to young persons, who reject anything not "sweetened by pleasure--and music has a natural sweetness" (*Pol.* 1340a-b).

As Plato's idea of the beautiful embraces Forms beyond perception, and the eternal, so Aristotle's approach to the aesthetic is based on the acceptance of what Plato would reject--the forms men discover through their senses. For him, the soul is a form of the natural body having in itself a life-potentiality (*On the Soul* 412a), and music exists for the nobler relaxation of this soul. This is because man as virtuous is man in proportion (*Nic. Eth.* 1131a). His sense organs correspond to sensory objects, and his very health is a harmony as characterized by harmonies of elements (*On the Soul* 407b-408a). Physical beauty and physical excellencies are of all types, and the proper affections of each are the influences which tend to "promote or destroy" its very existence (*Physics* 246b).

As an earthly harmony, therefore, music is related to man, for the voice itself "implies a concord, and if the voice and hearing of it are in one sense one and the same, and if the concord always implies a ratio, hearing as well as what is heard is a ratio," a ratio of high and low, an excess of either leading to a destruction of hearing (*On the Soul* 426a-b). In the broader sense, we imitate through the concord, we like to imitate because we like to learn (*Poetics* 1448b), and through music we learn to perceive qualities of affection and of character.

Aristotle seems more generous and tolerant, as well as more practical, when considering the imitation of which Plato had spoken with a kind of derision--that is, the especially low-class imitation by musicians of one another. Aulos and lyre playing, Aristotle says in the *Poetics* (1448a), is imitation, distinguished, as is any imitative piping, from the other arts of imitation (those of color and form, those using the voice, that of the dance, and that of language alone which has no harmony [prose]) in that they combine harmony and rhythm. He admits that, even in aulos and lyre playing, diversities are possible which reflect human character, especially in goodness, badness, and the average which lies between. A more artistic imitation, however, undeniably natural to man, is the presentation in art of the truth of and the faithfulness to character. More than any other sense, hearing (with music) can resemble and imitate moral qualities: required because it mirrors the goodness of the world, music is the supreme art.

But for whom is it the supreme art? Like Plato, Aristotle distinguishes the professional from the amateur, the practical man from the educated freeman. Yet those who do not perform or who have never done so find difficulty in judging the performances of others. For children the rattle of Archytas is a toy, and even "for children of a larger growth" education is a rattle or toy (*Pol.* 1340b). Some people say that music is vulgar (not aristocratic or an art of the privileged). However, those who are proper judges must be or must have been performers; and those whom music affects--namely, freemen--are not vulgarized by it if it trains them in political virtue. They themselves can use certain melodies and rhythms and even play on certain instruments: "for even the instrument makes a difference," Aristotle says, in contrast to Plato. Certain methods of teaching and learning music do indeed degrade music: the learning of music "ought not to impede the business of riper years, or . . . degrade the body or render it unfit for civil or military training, whether for bodily exercises at the time or for later studies." The right degree of training in the arts is achieved just short of the ability demonstrated in professional contests or in attempts to perform the fantastic (that is, virtuosic) marvels of the professionals. The professional performs for the wrong reason, to please the vulgar crowd. Therefore the (aristocratic) young men should study music not to become professionals but only "until they are able to feel delight in noble melodies and rhythms, and not merely in that common part of music in which every slave or child and even some animals find pleasure" (ibid. 1341a).

The educative effect of music is based on: (1) the truth that not only imitation, but also a sense of harmony and rhythm is natural to man (*Poet.* 1448b); (2) the imitation of a model whose virtues and whose proper order it achieves; (3) an imitation couched in music whose harmonious properties call up a human harmony or musical order of a general type; and (4) the fact that this imitation can at will produce a pleasure which for the lower classes alters the strains of working life but which for the upper classes means further high pursuits, including that of knowledge for its own sake. For Plato, as we have seen, preparation for all of this was to be three school years; for Aristotle it is six, with training from age seven to thirteen (*Pol.* 1336a).

If there can be a proper pleasure in the playing of instruments, and if they can imitate in the absence of words, one may suppose that instruments too should be used in education. Their soothing effect, at least for the freeman, is necessarily based on harmony and knowledge. Yet, though the aulos requires great skill, as does the harp, neither should be admitted into education. Only those instruments should be allowed which produce intelligent students of music or of other parts of education (Aristotle did not name them). The aulos is not an instrument expressive of moral character: "it is too exciting" (ibid. 1341a) and should be used not for instruction but for the relief of the passions. Furthermore, the aulos prevents the use of the voice and therefore detracts from educational value. (One cannot play the aulos and talk or chant at the same time!) It is the point made by Alcibiades in Plutarch's biography of him (pp. 5-6), though he may have only been fearful of producing distortions of his own beautiful face in the process. Therefore the ancients often forbade the aulos to young men and freemen. Not that the aulos had not been popular (it had been), but it was ultimately judged to be not really conducive to virtue and therefore was banished, along with the Lydian harp, the many-string lyre, and other instruments which gave a mere pleasure to the hearer and required extraordinary skill. Athena is supposed to have invented the aulos and then to have thrown it away because when played it made the face ugly; but even more important was the belief that it "contributes nothing to the mind," nothing to knowledge and art.

Presumably the music of tragedy, a "not inconsiderable addition," is in its part a very real pleasure of the drama (*Poet.* 1462a) for anyone of any class; and referring to philosophers like Plato (see *Rep.* 398ff), but not naming them, Aristotle speaks of the influence of melody and rhythm as already described by them (and himself). He classified melodies as   (1) ethical,   (2) of action, and   (3) of passion or inspiration, and says that each one has a mode corresponding to it.   In summary, he thinks music should be studied for its many benefits--those of   (1) education (which is treated above),   (2) purgation, and   (3) intellectual enjoyment and relaxation, and recreation after exertion (also treated above).

One might suspect that Aristotle was even more convinced of the ethical nature of music than had been Plato, who believed in the primacy of the eye (*Rep.* 507-08).   Taste, touch, and smell, Aristotle thinks, are not ethical media.   Ethical effects do not follow even from impressions of sight, except for a few pieces of sculpture or painting, and they are only figures (images) of an ethos (*Pol.* 1340a).   The ear is the spiritual sense organ (*De sensu* 437a).   Like Plato, Aristotle records that each (heard) mode has a specific character, and though he admits that all modes may be used, he also points out that they are not all used in the same manner.   Dorian, Phrygian, Lydian, Mixolydian he names for their different effects.   In the *Poetics* (1448a) he called Timotheus and Philoxenus composers who used *nomoi* properly for the reflecting of character in tragedy and comedy.   There are ethical modes which are to be taught and used in education because they are preferred.   But when a person listens to others' performances, other modes of action and passion are acceptable too, according to what is natural to him. Of those ethical modes which endow a man with an ethical stability, Aristotle according to convention prefers the austere Dorian, though he rather vaguely says that others of which musically educated philosophers approved may be used.   He thinks the Socrates of the *Republic* (399) was wrong in retaining only the Phrygian along with the Dorian--"the Phrygian is to the modes what the aulos is to musical instruments" (*Pol.* 1342b)--and Socrates was also wrong in rejecting the aulos merely because it and the Phrygian mode are exciting and emotional.   Bacchic frenzy is better expressed by them, and the dithyramb in any case is Phrygian. The Lydian with its wistfulness (which may be taught to children) and the Ionian (with its enervating effect) both destroy stability (ibid. 1342a; cf. Plato, *Rep.* 399), but they still have their uses. The Dorian, by common consent "the gravest and the manliest" (*Pol.* 1342b), is the mean between the other modes, and in education it conforms to the principle of the mean between extremes. Thus it encourages virtue, a kind of mean (*Nic. Eth.* 1106b, 1107a), just as justice is a species of the proportionate (ibid. 1131a).

But purgation is a function of music too, and this is why the freeman in listening to it may accept different modes of action and passion. In the *Poetics* (1449b), Aristotle speaks of the purgation of pity and fear through the arousal of these emotions. In the *Politics* he explains further: "For feelings such as pity and fear, or, again, enthusiasm, exist very strongly in some souls, and have more or less influence over all. Some persons fall into a religious frenzy, whom we see as a result of sacred melodies---when they have used the melodies that excite the soul to mystic frenzy--restored as though they had found healing and purgation. Those who are influenced by pity or fear, and every emotional nature, must have a like experience, and others in so far as each is susceptible to such emotions, and all are in a manner purged and their souls lightened and delighted" (1342a). Like Plato, Aristotle is less convinced--and his silence on this point is conclusive--that music will heal the body. The purgation is psychological.

Besides these relatively serious kinds of psychological and ethical purgation, possibly allied with medicine, Aristotle recognizes an innocent type, resulting from the use of modes and melodies by theater-performers. These induce pleasure in the uneducated, and are coordinates of moral aims, not necessarily the nuisances seen in them by Plato. Theater-goers may be the vulgar crowd of mechanics, laborers, and so forth, but they need contests and exhibitions for their relaxation. "And the music will correspond with their minds; for as their minds are perverted from the natural state [exemplified by the freeman], so there are perverted melodies and highly strung and unnaturally colored melodies" for them (ibid). Aristotle's acceptance of Athenian social order is no better illustrated than here. Like other philosophers, he doubted that workmen could think or contemplate beauty. He allowed them to sing to lighten the burden of their labors. But he did not grant them minds in the "natural state," which belonged to the rich, privileged, and educated--or at least educable.

Another element of education apparently affected the mind as did music. Plato was near to being the first person of whom we know to compare grammar and music (or harmonics) on the basis of number and knowledge (*Phil.* 17). Aristotle was among the first to write a treatise on rhetoric, which as a subject included metrics, figures of speech, and poetry (elements which would become vital in the understanding of the Roman chant of the Middle Ages).

With regard to rhetoric,[3] Plato and Aristotle adopted different views. Plato believed that it relinquishes truth and honesty. In the *Phaedrus*, he allows it to be called both superficial and untruthful (272-73), and in the *Gorgias* the rhetorician is called ignorant (459) and wanting in an ideal standard (503). In the *Phaedrus* (279), he praises Isocrates (463-338 B.C.), as a young man not satisfied with rhetoric but led to higher things through divine inspiration. Isocrates himself thought his rhetoric was a scheme for education, a union of philosophy and persuasion, a comprehensive science of political subjects and of style in words poetical and varied. In contrast, Aristotle stresses the practicality of rhetoric in that it advances probable and valid arguments based on the ethical character of the speaker and yet subordinates its appeal to the emotional capacities of the audience (*Rhetoric* 1354a-1356a); it is a necessary activity allied with ethics and education.

In the *Laws*, Plato made a technical comparison between the vocal art of persuasion and the vocal art as such. The point of comparison was the preamble or exhortation: "[B]ecause all discourses and vocal exercises have preludes and overtures, which are a sort of artistic beginnings intended to help the strain which is to be performed, lyric measures and music of every other kind have preludes framed with wonderful care."

Aristotle is even more explicit in the *Rhetoric*, where he speaks of the introduction as the "beginning of a speech, corresponding to the prologue in poetry and the prelude to aulos music. . . . The musical prelude resembles the introduction to speeches of display; as aulos-players play first some brilliant passage they know well and then fit it on to the opening notes of the piece itself, so in speeches of display the writer should proceed in the same way" (1414b). Aristotle paints a wonderful picture of the flamboyance of a speech, of its opening flourishes--in words as in music displaying itself, preening itself as it were in preliminary fashion before it begins in earnest--and of the skillful blending of the introduction into the body of the piece itself. Aristotle was quite serious in the *Politics* when he made the observation that "There seems to be in us a sort of affinity to musical modes and rhythms, which makes some philosophers say that the soul is a tuning, others, that it possesses tuning" (1340b). The initial rhetorical flourish is a metaphorical "tuning up."

By calling rhetoric the faculty of following the available means of persuasion (ibid. 1355b), Aristotle clarifies how one aspect of that tuning is achieved. The speaker must have personal power, the ability to stir the emotions of his hearers, and the ability to prove a truth, or an apparent truth, through persuasive arguments which have their counterparts in dialectic (logic). The speaker must remember that he is addressing classes of men, not individuals, on subjects calling for human action. He must put his hearers in the right frame of mind by moving, exciting, and otherwise influencing their emotions--by creating the correlative state of mind in each person.

Then Aristotle listed and described the emotions--the affects--to which the orator (like the poet and bard, or dramatists and actor, or musician) can appeal: anger, calmness, fear and shame, love and hate, pity, and so forth (some of which, no matter how attainable by rhetoric, are not--for example, envy and emulation--within the capacity of music to imitate). Next he describes human beings at various stages of life--old age, youth, maturity--and in various economic and political states and spheres. All of this the orator must bear in mind. Aristotle speaks of style, especially of expression, which should not go beyond the facts or their proper setting in language. Style must conform with the subject even as it enhances it. "It is plain that [oral] delivery has as much to do with oratory as with poetry" (ibid. 1403b). It is plain too that it has much to do with music--or its elements: it is essentially a matter of the correct management of the voice in expressing various emotions--of speaking loudly, softly, or moderately; with pitch high, low, or intermediate; in rhythms adapted to their various subjects. Sad to say, Aristotle thinks, delivery has not been considered an "elevated" subject of inquiry. But it needs to be so treated because it can be taught.

All of this is related to what is moving and expressive, resulting in education whose benefits include utility, moral cultivation, intellectual virtue, purgation, and also amusement. All are under the control of the possible. While it is true that the young should be educated primarily in the Dorian mode, it is not true that the old must employ that mode alone. The old cannot sing in the high-strung modes; nature seems to want them to sing in the more relaxed kind. Thus Socrates (*Rep.* 399ff) was again wrong, as certain rhetoricians insisted, when he rejected the relaxed modes as intoxicating because of their lack of strength. Aristotle maintains that older people should practice the gentler modes and melodies and all others--even the Lydian, which is suited to children and possesses the elements of both order and education. Musical education, which must also include noble music for leisure, should, like all education, be based on three principles: the mean between extremes, which is the Dorian mode; the possible, which is determined by one's period in life; and the becoming or the suitable, which is based upon the purposes of an individual according to his class and therefore according to his life-aims and social station (*Pol.* 1342b). Music gives several benefits: education, release of emotion, and the benefit of culture or cultivation, with which may be linked relaxation and relief from strain (ibid. 1341b). But what must for disciplinary and regulatory reasons be avoided in youth may be embraced in old age. As a liberal education, music does not so much supply knowledge (though it does this too) as form character and serve that character through its changes in the course of life, the highest aim always being contemplation and wisdom.

Thus the Aristotelian theory or idea of music is closely associated with the Platonic, and was in part a political development of it: the superior position of the state and its educational instruments is assumed. Yet Aristotle obviously believes that in the arts, practice precedes theory, whereas Plato's theory (for centuries the more influential) assumes that artistic theory, in the *a priori* fashion, is subordinate to universal principle. While for Plato mathematical science is devoted to universals, numbers are a convenience for Aristotle, and the proper course of human study is theoretical (truth-seeking), practical (useful in society), and productive (a making of good and useful things). Aristotle's view of music is more catholic than Plato's.

Aristotle is more direct than Plato about poetry as an organic form with its own laws rather than as something conforming to a pre-ordained order. Like Plato, he assigns a wide range to music in its ability to order the passions and thus to bring civic and "noble" man under control. Both men think of music as a species of imitation, but in this respect Aristotle holds it in high regard and Plato in low. For Aristotle the imitation of the psychological man in action is enough; for Plato it should have been related to the Forms. Both men believe that music should bring about the psychological state of *catharsis* or purgation. Aristotle believes that music is natural to man, giving him pleasure, and that through the action of *catharsis* it has affinities with medicine and biology. Plato makes less of purgation, though he speaks of both music and dancing as allaying fear (*Laws* 790).

Plato laid down the laws, in part derived from the Pythagoreans. Aristotle defined, refined, and re-interpreted some of them. According to current standards the more scientific of the two and the more directly allied with modern theories of art, Aristotle does not, in contrast to Plato, discredit poetry in either the narrow or the broad sense (as including music), nor does he ban it from the republic, even for the sake of argument, or trumpet the decay of music and the state from the housetops. Though he expresses disbelief in the Platonic Forms and Ideas and in Ideal numbers, he thinks the mathematical sciences are not unrelated to the beautiful (*Metaph*. 6a) and especially to music. While he comes close to contradicting himself about the Forms (in the *Poetics* 1449a), when he says that tragedy at a certain point reached its natural form and there stopped, he does not mean an Ideal form but a man-made form which has been achieved. For Plato what is crucial is a state of being; for Aristotle, motion, not transcendental but physical and mental or conceptual, is primary, and his idea of harmony is confined to physics, mathematics, and the practical and productive sciences as they treat of matter in motion.

For Aristotle, the value of music is human, and a musical mode is almost a symbol of animate and even inanimate things and their ruling principles (*Pol*. 1254a). Indeed, all works of art are like living organisms, and all weave matter and form into an organic whole just as the world itself, like an (organic) animal, is a whole. Here the principle of order is rhythm, the most necessary being the best. And, though he agrees with the proponents of the ethical-moral school of musical thought, Aristotle at the same time implies, as he makes explicit in the *Nicomachean Ethics* (1193b) and the *Poetics* (1147a, 1460a), that art has its own ends and should be judged accordingly.

Though Aristotle questioned the theory that universal harmony and the music of the spheres are one, he believed with Plato that the chief end of man was the exercising of the divine in himself--the divine which is reason. Plato held that pleasure is inimical to man, but Aristotle thought it was a mistake to see pleasure as brutish; instead, he thought it best found in pure thought, in listening to music, and seeing sculpture, sight being superior to touch in purity, and hearing to smell and taste (*Nic. Eth*. 1176a). Pleasure is a fulfillment of desire and a consciousness of the fullness of life (ibid. 1175a). Thus music, that important part of tragedy and of education, itself is a pleasurable therapeutic agent able to restore soul and body as they are afflicted or otherwise deprived.

In his work, however, the poet-musician does not express himself. When the subject of self-expression comes up in the *Ion*, Socrates is skeptical. It is not the person expressing himself but the gods (we think of Homer and Hesiod) and the Muses, whose instrument and mouthpiece he is (*Ion* 533-36); possessed by the divine spirit, the highly emotional poet or musician through a kind of magnetism communicates his state to his audience; he is deeply moved by the god and his message, and his work arouses emotions in the audience similar to his own. But Plato hardly seems serious about this, no matter how frequently he has been taken so to be. Socrates says that the *rhapsodes*, clearly possessed by the god, are also clearly deranged and produce the same nonsensical emotions in their audiences; but Ion suggests that they are only feigning and adjusting their behavior to achieve a certain response--are not, in fact, feeling what they express at all--a matter of dishonest trickery and deception (Hesiod says, "We know how to tell falsehoods that sound like truth") and not of inspiration from the gods (*Ion* 541-42). Thus a work is left as an influence, the subjectivity of the artist is beside the point, and is not even mentioned. To be possessed of the god is not to express one's own feeling. In the world of order which Plato and Aristotle each in his own way admired, the artist can properly reproduce that order or impose it on his chaotic materials. And having imposed that order, he can then see the work and the effect it has on the audience. The *Timaeus*, the *Republic*, the *Laws*, and Aristotle's *Rhetoric*, *Poetics*, and *Politics* are consistent with one another in asking for objective structures designed by the poet and musician to move, please, and educate their audiences.

IV
Post-Aristotelian Theory:
The Peripatetics

After the death of Plato in 347 B.C., not one of his students besides Aristotle made a contribution to the history of the idea of music. The Academy in which Plato lived, taught, and was buried would last as a school until the days of Cicero, though it went through several transformations, the number of which is in dispute. Speusippus,[1] Plato's sister's son, was his follower and heir. Aristotle compares him to the Pythagoreans because he returned to the doctrine of universal number and abandoned Plato's Forms. Two of Aristotle's pupils, however, made contributions to the history of the idea of music; they were Aristoxenus and Theophrastus.

I

Aristoxenus, the Peripatetic, of Tarentum. If Euclid summarized the Pythagorean system of music, Aristoxenus (c.320 B.C.) of Tarentum, who helped keep Pythagoreanism alive by protesting against it, brought music down from the heavens to the earth, as it were, and, at least in the ancient documents which survive, began the history of the technical examination of music as structured rhythmical sound. The Pythagoreans defined music in terms of cosmic phenomena and their corollaries in human life; Aristoxenus examined it chiefly in its relation to human perception. The ancients called him "the musician," and his followers were called harmonists, as compared with Pythagorean canonists, who were rule-followers. Whereas the canonists, who worked with the universal laws of proportion as objectified by the monochord, were supposed to have discovered absolute laws, the harmonists through physical means were still searching for them.

A. Aristoxenus' Harmonics

If Damon is credited with having begun the "ethical" school of music aesthetics, Aristoxenus is credited, perhaps incorrectly (because he may have had predecessors whose works and names are lost), with being at the forefront of the theoretical musical science, of musical theory--that abstraction of the elements and forms of composition according to a system or systems. His subject, previously mentioned by Plato, was the study of the relationships of sound and their tunings--harmonics--and his works were

Harmonic Elements (in three books) and *Rhythmic Elements* (in fragments). A Peripatetic philosopher, he was at first a disciple of the Pythagoreans; he was said to have thought that the human soul is in the same relation to the parts of the body as harmony is to parts of a musical instrument. Along with Plato he may have been one of the first of the musical symbolists because he too followed the numerical-acoustical theory of the Pythagoreans and interpreted it analogically. Abandoning Pythagoreanism, however, he followed Aristotle to become a scientist in the tradition of Lasos of Hermione and Archytas, who also came from Terentum. For the Pythagorean mathematical exactness of the ratios[2] of intervals he substituted the experience of sound and tried to establish the laws of art. His approach was not, like that of the Pythagoreans, *a priori*, mathematical and deductive, but *a posteriori*, empirical, inductive, and psychological; for the reason, or intellect, as the sole judge of the good and bad in music he substituted ear and intellect.[3]

Aristoxenus was not interested in acoustics alone, but in the art of sound--even, perhaps, in an art different from *technē*. Melody is the general science of music (2), and harmonics the science of musical sounds and of knowing how they do or do not commingle. A knowledge of harmonics (one must be warned) can neither make musicians nor enhance moral states. Strictly speaking, harmonics is to melody as rhythmics is to poetry and the dance. It defines the foundations.

His science of harmonics (melodics), though it depends on arithmetic, does its work with properties which cannot be abstracted from physical objects. Aristoxenus' predecessors investigated the acoustical nature of music only to the extent that it could be represented mathematically. But musical form is not that of objects alone; nor is it completely abstract; it is made up of sound, and even though sound depends on string tension (20ff), musical form does not exist *in* material objects. It exists in part within ourselves, whose powers of perception are limited to the "high" and the "low" we are capable of sensing. Instruments and the voice are similarly limited in scope though according to what the ear can discriminate. Through hearing we discriminate the sizes of intervals, and through reasoning we consider the potentialities of the tones (33)--that is, the pitches as they function within a system. Scientific, valid, and conclusive as determined acoustical facts may be, however, the results are analytical; and analysis cannot lead to art itself.

Up to Aristoxenus' time music instruction had been largely based on the rote learning of rules; "canonical" mathematicians and physicists, legitimate in their own way, were concerned with the physical nature and numerical relations of sounds appearing as air vibrations and also with the mathematical relations of high and low pitch, however defined. These scientists had no music as an artful construct. The artists (the "harmonists"), however, were concerned with performance alone; they had no science; this Aristoxenus tried to supply for them. Like Aristotle, he took a balanced humanistic position: for him, to perceive music, which had its own laws, is to hear sounds and then to collect and combine them in memory so as to recognize or receive impressions. According to his (for his time) almost revolutionary theory of perception, the mind is the important agent, but the ear is the judge--especially of the notes of the scale, no matter what their mathematical ratios. In his *Harmonics*, it is as in Aristotle's *Poetics*: the focus is on the minds of men as they contemplate art as it is and as it functions.

He does not think the opinion that harmonics is a non-science should be taken seriously. Harmonics is not to be held in contempt, as it is by some men of intelligence (meaning, probably, Plato) simply because it is only a part of a musician's equipment and on the same level as rhythmics, metrics, and organics (instruments), which he also must know. We miss the truth, Aristoxenus says, unless we take as the ultimate test not what is determined (defined), but what it is that actually determines. Hands, voice, and so forth are only instruments for the process of apprehension (41), and harmonics is not about these but about the laws of the ear; it treats of melody, whether vocal or instrumental, as it appeals to hearing and the intellect. The perceptive ear, whose accuracy of sense impression is fundamental (39), grasps the sizes of the intervals (metaphorical distance described by two notes of different pitches), and the intellect "contemplates the functions of the notes" (33) (which the Pythagoreans had ignored). Thus we can grasp intervals shorter than the whole tone--that is, microtones, though most of them cannot be performed accurately in parallel motion or consecutively.

The hearer's process is to note through the aural sense-perception and intelligence and then to remember all distinctions produced in successive sounds (38-39). What cannot be discriminated by the ear is therefore necessarily excluded from the range of musical sounds (14), but what is discriminated is remembered; the twelfth of a series of fifths will be heard as identical with the beginning note (and will not be detected as the mathematically arrived-at "Pythagorean" comma; though we can *hear* an interval less than a quarter-tone, we cannot estimate its relative magnitude) (15). Neither notations of melody nor the natural laws of harmony based on any instrument is even part of the science of harmonics.

Within a melodic continuity there is a natural law which cannot be shown in the diagrams of the "practical" harmonists (28): the student of harmonics is not like the student of geometry, who, working abstractly, does not need sense perception at all to determine the accuracy of straight lines, circles, and so forth, as do the carpenter and other craftsmen. Nor does the musician work with proportions; he depends on the evidence of a developed ear. He accepts sizes, extensions, and contractions of sound, not numerical ratios: one cannot speak of what one cannot perceive. One is concerned with what is permanent and what changeable, but the ear makes the determination. So, for instance, in observing the types of scales, or successions of two or more intervals, or the genera (diatonic, chromatic, and enharmonic), one sees that the "containing" notes (the octave, the fifth, the fourth) are permanent and give a more secure feeling than dissonances (55), but that the internal variations are changeable. The basic principles of rhythm are similar: the speed or general rate of movement of the rhythm (today, we call it tempo) is felt to change though the basic feet remain the same. The judgment is not mathematical but experiential (phenomenal) (33-34). It is Aristotelian to suppose that art comes to man through experience (*Metaph.* 1.1). But the knowledge is dual: theoretical (truthful) and practical (realized in action) (ibid. 2.1). Aristoxenus therefore takes priority among writers on music--indeed, on its aesthetics--as a speculative philosopher who pursued the technical analysis of pitch and rhythm as they occur in practice.

Where did Aristoxenus find his method of analysis and classification of experience with tone? Probably from Aristotle, who in his *Categories* 5 (2a-4a) lists the divisions for substance as species, genera, differentiae, and accident. In the *Harmonics*, Aristoxenus lists the parts of his science, and later Cleonides (in a supplementary contribution or literally-copied remnant from a manuscript of Aristoxenus) too adopts his Aristotelian order: (1) substance--a note (or "harmonious incidence of the voice upon a single pitch"); (2) an interval of two notes (ratio, it will be recalled, is of the essence; see Aristotle, *Metaph.* 1092b); (3) genus--a division of four notes (the tetrachord); (4) [species] a system [of modes] (of more than one interval); (5) differentiae--modulation (the transposition of a "similar thing to a dissimilar region"); and (6) composition (Strunk, p. 35). All are analytical categories determined by the material substance.

The substance of music is tone, which changes as the voice proceeds. There are two vocal movements (Nicomachus of Gerasa [second century A.D.] said that the Pythagoreans had anticipated Aristoxenus here): the one sound is continuous, as in speaking, the other discrete, or intervallic, as in singing (18). These differences Aristotle called quantity. The discrete quantities are expressed in the singular form: number and (vocal) speech; whereas the continuous quantities are lines, surfaces, solids, time, and space (*Categories* 4b-5a). Because the voice freely produces sounds in motion, the numbers are not fixed. On the basis of what the ear hears, mathematical ratios are adjusted to conform to the aural impression. In this view, proportions are qualities and natural forms, and are perceived so. Unlike the Pythagoreans, Aristoxenus does not deal with ratios or even with sound *production* alone, but only with (metaphorically) linear distances on the line of pitch--and thus with a correspondence between pitch and space.

According to Rudolf Westphal,[4] Aristoxenus was the first of all theorists to use the terms 'high' and 'low' for melody so as to grant it a spatial, three-dimensional property, as compared with the purely physical or acoustical movement[5] of tones, which depend on air set in motion. Thus, in speech the voice travels in space and intermittently stops nowhere special, but in singing the voice rests on one pitch after the other (28)--and the result is song and melody.

Aristoxenus speaks about melody as a kind of chanted speech. The melody of speech (a metaphor for us) depends on the accents of the words causing the voice to rise or fall by a natural law (18-19). Yet the subject of harmonics is all melody, whether vocal or instrumental (34). Sounds of instruments (14, 41-42) are analogous to those of the voice, thought also to be an instrument. And, always interested in the quality of tone, Aristoxenus finds that the tension of a string is the cause of the height or depth of tone (10), though he seems to deny the importance of the rapidity of the string's vibrations (32). Musical melody differs from speech-melody by "employing motion by intervals," and it differs from faulty melody, "which violates the law of harmony, by the different manner in which it collocates the simple intervals."

Hence musical substance is analyzed according to the Aristotelian methods of observation, description, and classification. Number is only an abstraction from objects. In both harmonics and optics, objects are considered not *qua* voice or sight, but *qua* lines and numbers, since a science is more precise if it abstracts. Harmonics abstracts from motion--with time and space, both intrinsic to human thought--and especially from the primary, the simplest, movement (Aristotle, *Metaph.* 1078a).

Aristoxenus seems to rely on Aristotle's attempt to apply at least the number 1 to substance. Substance is matter; it is not a universal because the universal cannot be substance. Nor are unity and being substances. Unity is a predicate, and substance is a cause, a form, something determinate of matter (ibid. 1038b, 1040b-1041b). The crucial number is predicate of unity or 1. This has four meanings: (1) something continuous in general and by nature ("not by contact nor being tied together"); (2) something which is a whole with a certain shape or form; this is a one in a higher degree than something continuous in general, and especially if so by nature and not by force; its movement being continuous in space and time, it is one extended thing; (3) something the thought of which is indivisible in number; (4) or indivisible in kind: "that which is intelligibility and in knowledge is indivisible," that which causes substance to be one in "the primary sense" (ibid. 1052a). The 1 in color is white, from which all other colors derive; it is the 1, a particular one, of white. So in music: the 1 is the quarter-tone. Among articulate sounds the 1 is the vowel, and among rectilinear figures the 1 is the triangle (ibid. 1053b-1054a). For Aristoxenus too the quarter-tone unit is crucial--the least of the (successive) musical substances for perception, though the voice cannot sing it (14).

There are three genera in music, and of them, Aristoxenus thinks, the diatonic "must be granted [to be] the first and oldest, inasmuch as mankind lights upon it before the others"; and then come the chromatic and enharmonic, in that order (19), and their "shades" follow.[6] Distinguishing the genera is the first job of the study of harmonics.

The second is to deal with intervals. Here Aristoxenus does not hesitate to contradict Plato and the Pythagoreans. He declares that the interval between the fourth and fifth steps is a whole tone which can be divided exactly in two to produce two equal semitones. This, he thinks, is because he is dividing tonal space and not relying on arithmetic. The Pythagoreans thought the tone (9:8) could be only unequally divided, one of the two "halves" necessarily falling short of the other. For the Pythagoreans a tetrachord was made up of two whole steps (tones) and a *leimma*. But Aristoxenus disagrees. He thinks it made up of two whole steps and a half. But the division of the whole tone has a history of its own, encouraged in part by Plato's acceptance of the *leimma* in the *Timaeus* (36).

Aristoxenus found the semitone intense in quality, and, quite apart from any mathematical description of it, he thought it compared favorably with the weaker and softer larger intervals. Indeed, according to where it is placed, it is the "soul of music" since its location determines the character of the tetrachord. Thus, for Aristoxenus it has not only a purely sensuous position with respect to intervals, but also a psychological one as well.

The third task of harmonics has to do with notes, their number, and the means of recognizing them, a further question being "whether they are certain points of pitch, as is vulgarly supposed, or whether they are musical functions"--and also with what a musical function is.

The fourth deals with scales (systems), their number and nature, and "the manner of their construction from intervals and notes" (36): how the melodious is distinguished from the non-melodious, or what musical melody is.

Fifth come modes, or scales, in which the systems are placed "for the purpose of melody" (37): the Phrygian system is a tone above the Dorian, the Lydian a tone above the Phrygian, and so forth. Thus the ethos of the modes depended on their pitch.[7]

Sixth are modulations, their nature and number, and how they arise (this is recorded by Cleonides).

Finally, with the seventh, comes the actual composition of melody comprising the choice among the many melodic forms of every character (38).

Beyond the perceived work lies judgment, and at its core must lie harmony, recognized through the correct observation of phenomena, description of what is prior and what derivative, and conclusions legitimately derived from the premises. Hearing and reason, reason and hearing: separate but cooperative--every proposition must be true and evident and must be accepted by sense-perception as primary truth. But what must be demonstrated cannot itself be a primary principle (44), for there "is a certain [prior and permanent] marvellous order which belongs to the nature of harmony in general" (42) but not to instruments except as they follow the demands of sense-perception.

As regards the ethical theory, Aristoxenus seems to reflect the skepticism of the Sophists and of Euripides and Aristophanes, the latter especially in *The Clouds* and *The Frogs*, when he qualifies it with the clause "in so far as the musical art can improve moral character" (31). He does not directly deny that music can improve moral character or that it may carry within itself such a character. In fact, he specifically believes that it has characteristics like strength of character and licentiousness. But he speaks so only when discussing rhythm. Even then he does not insist that "virtuous" rhythms can improve a person. He was not questioning the objectivity of the moral or ethical properties of rhythm and music; nor was he denying the uniformity of their appeal for and effect upon persons of like education and social origin. But he clearly had not observed the moral improvements the proponents of the ethical theory expected. And in his remark about the limited moral effect of music, one detects an admission that the modes did not after all produce the effects that Plato and Aristotle had ideally and dogmatically ascribed to them.

Following Aristotle's notion of continuity as comparable to a (geometrical) line with its infinite number of points, each having a space-line position, Aristoxenus finds that "we must follow the guidance of natural laws in the search for continuity" (53); each sound is what it does as a part of the whole and any sound introduced without a legitimate function has no place in the music. *Harmonia* governs the law of melody. Even the elements of melody are abstracted, however; the material of musical sensation is not found in nature, but is determined through selection; from the infinitude of terrestrial sounds are selected tones to be made into sound-relational systems. And then the ear, without which the science of music cannot proceed, plays its part, while the intellect or understanding judges the organic system of tones related according to functions the ear perceives. Whereas the Pythagoreans described the system of music as it supposedly is--that is, as the science of mathematics assures us it is-- Aristoxenus always had in mind the function of each element within an artfully created organic structure. Thus his analogy of music with the new geometry--the science of functional relations--of his day, not with mathematics in general or with arithmetic.[8]

Like Plato and Aristotle, Aristoxenus was not very sympathetic with "the style of composition now in vogue." He sounds like Plato modified: "The ground of this fashion lies in the perpetual striving after sweetness . . . time and attention [being] mostly devoted to chromatic music . . . [and] the ethical character of the music suffers a corresponding deflection" (23). The implication is that beyond local fashions lie positive laws and, for Aristoxenus, especially the law of function, which makes of a harmony a systematic or organic whole.

B. The Cleonidean Supplement

A certain Cleonides of the second century A.D. was a thorough-going Aristoxenian whose *Eisagoge*, or *Harmonic Introduction*, now thought to be a popularizing of Aristoxenus and a completion of lost sections of his work, was for a long time attributed to Euclid. Translated into Latin by Georgias Valla, it was published in 1497 and would serve as one source for the Renaissance musician's understanding of ancient Greek music (which, of course, he never heard). Primarily descriptive of harmonics as a practical science, it carries definitions of the note, the interval, the genres (diatonic, chromatic, and enharmonic) and their "shades," the system, the tone, the modulation, and the melodic composition--all of course prefigured in Aristoxenus.

The most valuable and most frequently cited of Cleonides' statements supports the theory that the ethical effect of melodic composition was based on pitch. He names three types:

1. Music with a "diastaltic [exalted] ethos" reflecting grandeur, virility, and heroism.
2. Music with a "systaltic [narrow, contracted] ethos" lacking in manliness and encouraging effeminacy, dejection, and amorous and plaintive feelings.
3. An intermediate music of "hesychastic [tranquil] ethos" characterized by internal stability, calmness, and peaceful disposition of mind.

In theory the first belonged to tragedy, the second to laments and expressions of pity, and the third to hymns, paeans, eulogies, and so forth (Strunk, p. 45). This classification was adopted literally by Aristides Quintilianus, who may have been Cleonides' contemporary.

If Cleonides is a reliable authority, modulation (Aristoxenus' sixth task for harmonics) meant to the Greeks the transfer or change from (1) one genus to another: diatonic to enharmonic, for example; (2) a conjunct to a disjunct system, or vice versa; (3) any one of the thirteen tones (modes) to another: Dorian to Phrygian; and (4) in melody, one ethos to another: diastaltic to systaltic, for example (Strunk, p. 45). Cleonides thus looked back to Aristoxenus and "completed" him, and, as will be clear later, he looked ahead to Ptolemy or may have even been paraphrasing him.

C. Aristoxenus' Rhythmics

Man's mind cannot, of course, grasp time in its completeness or, indeed, any series of events in their completeness. Infinity is a pure concept eternally unrealizable or even unimaginable by man. One can speak about it only metaphorically, in terms of space and movement. In imagination, time can be cut off; or extended; or proceed faster or slower. A temporal movement can be treated as complete. Thus, time is constantly being manipulated, and never more so than in music, whose essence is time expressed in rhythm carried by and in sound. A pattern (say, a rhythm) constantly repeated, or what seems to be an interminable series of likenesses "taking" time (which it cannot do), causes impatience: time may seem out of control and may become oppressive; passed in certain ways, it can give men pain, encourage violence in them, or even in extreme cases cause them to lose consciousness. But a rhythmical pattern which does not cross the threshold of tolerance pleases as though time were now in the artist's control.

Aristoxenus' work on rhythmics, or the division of time, has been restored from many manuscripts. Almost as important in the history of rhythmics as his *Harmonics* in the history of melody, it describes the classical quantitative system. Here, as in the *Harmonics*, vocal music is the foundation and sung poetry the starting point. Both works are related, apparently, to the formal theories of Democritus and the Sophists, from whom Aristoxenus probably took over his theory of perception.[9] His successors, and even Cicero,[10] who thought him not sufficiently moral, included him in the company of Archimedes, Aristophanes, Pythagoras, Plato, and Democritus because he had a passion for knowledge.

A true Aristotelian, Aristoxenus thought that movement alone was essential because movement measures time. While the arts of repose and space--architecture, painting, and sculpture--carry symmetry as form, those of motion--music, poetry, and the dance--require proportional rhythm,[11] and for the Greeks, as for the Jews and Arabs, rhythm more than melody had to do with ethical effects.

Rhythm, we are told, is number and regulated movement, and these refer usually to syllables or musical tones. Time or duration divided quantitatively, movement, and measurement are the essentials. Music must always be sung to verses composed of long and short syllables, the short syllable being twice as fast as the long (and the long therefore twice as long as the short--a rule accepted later by the grammarians of Latin in imperial times). But the rule was not rigid, and may not have been so for Aristoxenus.

There was a difference of degree: "the ancients did not, as far as we are aware, extend a syllable so as to embrace a whole musical phrase, but only as far as was necessary to make the time-divisions recognizable."[12] The purpose was audience comprehension, not only its musical enjoyment--clarity of understanding, not aural pleasure.

Verses were composed of a certain number of feet formed by different combinations of short and long syllables; the rhythm of the melody was regulated by these feet, and thus was divided into two parts to correspond with the short and long syllables. The equal or long was called "down," the short or unequal "up," and when time was beaten to the verses, the hand came down on the long and went up on the short. Now, at the beginning of each lyrical poem a canon or rule of the rhythm was indicated (much like a time-signature in modern music), the numbers 1 (for short) and 2 (for long) only being used, though of course in various combinations according to the verse-foot.

There were two "natures," according to Aristoxenus: the *rhythmizomenon* was the one and rhythm the other. The one was like an object undergoing a plan, the other was the plan.[13] The *rhythmizomenon*--the raw material or substance, called music, poetry, and the dance--was subjected to rhythm. Melody, made up of a succession of intervals, was given form by rhythm. Governed by rhythm, everyday speech, ordinarily made up of syllables of no definite accentual or unaccentual order, becomes poetry, just as one's steps are unorganized until rhythm gives them order and transforms them into dance; intervals, speech, and steps are *rhythmizomena* to which rhythm can be applied. The material or substance is not rhythm, but is that to which rhythm is applied. It is the thing divided in time.

In *rhythmopoeia* (the art of poetic rhythm), rhythm is applied to the *rhythmizomenon*. The rhythm of a long section like a phrase (in modern terms) Aristoxenus calls "continuous rhythmopoeia," and each rhythmical form, like each melody, is expected to produce a particular emotional effect on the mind. The spondee as an individual measure was suited to the solemn hymns of the gods, and the anapest to energetic and vigorous marches. Each unit (as compared with the long phrase or continuous *rhythmopoeia*) was made up of regular longs (*theses*) and unaccented shorts (*bases*, later *arses*); the "beat" of the foot came with the *thesis* and its elevation with the *thesis* (*arsis*). In general, the "foot" beginning with the elevation of the foot seems to have been more common than that beginning with its down-beat.

The foundation of Aristoxenus' entire rhythmic system was "primary time," the smallest unit of time used in a single composition (*Harmonics*, p. 31).[14]   (It was a concept later stressed by Aristides Quintilianus and especially by St. Augustine.) This primary indivisible time depended for its length upon the mood or speed of the piece; it was the shortest quantity and could not be divided. From primary time was built the foot, and from the foot were derived compound feet. In the *Harmonics*, as I have shown, Aristoxenus indicates that the actual magnitude of the individual foot is decided by tempo.

Now, phrases could be enrhythmical when the lines are so arranged that they are clear and convincing (prosaic, "flat") whether or not they are inspiring or expressive. Arrhythm is brought about in the phrasing of a composition in such a way that the rhythm is incomprehensible. But eurhythm (being rhythmoid), or "beautiful rhythm," is always the aim-- something adequately and skillfully performed. The three species of foot are the iambic (3:4, uneven proportion), the dactylic (1:1, even proportion), and the paeanic (a ratio of 3 to 2: a quintuple). The last (far more common to the Greeks than to us) was a long *thesis* (two simple feet), a short foot, and a long *arsis* (two simple feet): thus, where a simple foot is ♩ the (modernized) paeanic species looks thus: 5/4 ♩ ♩ ♩ . It was used for hymns and invocations to the gods. Rhythm was more varied than ours because the rhythms and micro-rhythms of verse were more closely (even more religiously) followed; we use a more strict and limited measure, and "harmony" supplies us with variety. Variety in ancient times had to be rhythmical, and it was achieved partly through "irrationality," the rational being the ratio of a foot, but the irrational being a middle value between the two (short and long) values (thus it was something like a dotted quarter or eighth or like a *Luftpause*). Aristoxenus warns against the use of five rational component syllables--that is, the use of five primary times--in the paeanic species (*Oxyrhynochus Papyri*, Pt. I, p. 18). Why? Because to the

Greeks a succession of short notes was mean and vulgar, though Aristoxenus thought the rule could be broken if the result were effective[15]--another example of Aristoxenus' empirical approach to music.

Now, the attention span of the human mind has its limits: hence, prose is divided into sentences and smaller units and poetry into verses. The reasons are psychological.   Thinking of rhythm or harmonics, Aristoxenus resembles Aristotle who in the *Poetics* (1450b-1451a) says that a tragedy must have a definite (not too small and not too large) magnitude-- that is, one which can be held in memory.   An artistic principle is involved as well as an affective one.

For Aristoxenus the phrase is an enlarged form of the foot.   The smallest foot to be used for divisions is the iamb (three "times") and the longest is conjectural, possibly sixteen.[16] But the total rhythmical composition has its ethical effect (Aristides Quintilianus here possibly supplying what of Aristoxenus is lost):   quintuple rhythm is inspiring or "enthusiastic" and in tragedy expresses intensity of emotion.   The iambus and the trochee are suitable for the dance.   Compound or complex feet, irregular forms, produce disturbance.   Too violent changes are dreadful and destructive; spondees produce moderation and strength of character, trochees and paeans warmth.   Short equal notes are mean and ignoble, long and short notes mixed without rhythmical proportion are licentious; rhythmless music is only distracting, not uplifting to the mind[17]--and so forth.

The total, the divisions of larger forms into smaller--that is, the arranging of periods of the whole in recognizable and comprehensible magnitudes--is governed by the superior principle of symmetry, as is the totality of any architectural piece.   Each part has its place; each part is integral to the recognizable form and can be literally tagged, named, and placed; and each part must be heard, because in Aristoxenus' time music was heard, not read, and the ear had to be satisfied, not "internally" through imagination, but "externally" through stimuli from the outside.

His contribution to music aesthetics was to turn attention to hearing as basic to judgment.   This is his most frequently-mentioned accomplishment. But, like Plato in the *Theaetetus* (163, 166), he remarks that memory is needed in perception: *Harmonia* and motion must rely on the mother of all the Muses.

Much of what Aristoxenus says has been variously interpreted. Technical matters are puzzling, and it is unfortunate that no work by him on "organics" survives.   But his *Harmonics* and what has been reconstructed of his *Rhythmics* were to stand as sources of comment and as models for centuries to come.   His separation of *a priori* theory from aural experience was to be a permanent point of controversy for more than two thousand years, appearing, to cite two examples, once in Ptolemy, the Alexandrian astronomer of the second century A.D., again in the sixteenth-century controversy between Zarlino on the one hand and Vincenzo Galilei on the other.

Disagreement seems indeed to have characterized the study of music, therefore, from the time of Aristoxenus. Besides the war between the ancients and the moderns, there was a constant war between the Pythagoreans and the Aristoxenians, and it was almost as though a writer on music had to be one or the other. The conviction that the mathematical Pythagoreans were right was widespread and extended to the predominant belief that the theorist, or Pythagorean, was the true musician, while the non-mathematical Aristoxenian, the performer, was only a practical man and no true judge of musical value. The former was indeed thought to be on firm ground, and the latter dependent only on the ear, an inconstant, irrational, and unreliable instrument. Here was the reason, then, that Aristoxenus spoke of the "ancients" whose highest accomplishments occurred during the Periclean age, at least a century before him.

II

Theophrastus, the Peripatetic. Aristoxenus wanted to be Aristotle's successor in the Lyceum. Much to his chagrin, however, the mantle fell on the shoulders of another disciple, the scientist Theophrastus (d. c.287 B.C.), today best known for his *Ethical Characters*, an analytical, satirical, and objective literary treatment of typological ethical qualities in human beings.

Theophrastus did pioneer work in the physiology and psychology of sense perception: the relative capacities of physically large and small sense organs, he thought, seem to exhibit no correspondence between acuity and size. In the course of sense-perception, an element within us simply meets a similar element outside us. The medium of hearing is air, as it is that of smell. But each sense has its own function and characteristically modifies its medium, so that we do not hear odors or smell sounds. Now, in music the air is controlled by the voice, and the "springs" of music (pain, pleasure, and inspiration) can change the nature of the voice so that it no longer has its usual form but becomes musical.[18] Of all the senses, hearing the most deeply agitates our emotions, and through sympathetic hearing "two musical tones that harmonize can be quantitatively equal [outside us] while still revealing a difference in quality [within us]." Therefore music as a "movement of the soul" can purge us of the evils coming from passion. Nevertheless, pain and pleasure in sensation are extremely close, and both of them or either, and also inspiration, can elevate the voice to a plane of beauty.[19]

Recalling Aristotle (*Poetics* 1449b), Theophrastus declares for a *catharsis* contributing to psychological health through expulsion (but not psychological change through the artistic presentation of ethical affect). Like Aristotle, he thinks the voice is a reflection of the individual soul, but he does not agree with Aristotle's classification of melodies into the ethical, the active, and the enthusiastic.

Theophrastus diverges from the Pythagoreans when he doubts that design and purpose play a role in the universe. Nevertheless, his *Metaphysics* is based on the Greek desire to embrace the unchanging, or the objects of reason, as distinguished from those of nature.[20]   Rational and natural science are related in that universal reason is prior and presupposed by objects of sense.   The first cannot be mathematics (as the Pythagoreans and Plato insisted) because numbers are the creation of the human mind (as Aristotle thought); nor can mathematics give life or movement.   Reason must therefore cause motion, though it cannot move by itself; it must itself be an object of desire, a single cause indivisible and non-quantitative. (It is Aristotle's Unmoved Mover, which is given activity, as compared with Plato's soul as self-mover.)

Though the universe is not a simple entity without parts, we are satisfied to find it to be a harmonious whole attaining all possible perfection.   Opposites, like matter-form and good-evil, depend for judgment on sense-perception, which grasps the different kinds of being reason must explain: knowledge presupposes differences among universals, classifies individuals under different universals, and treats of members of the same universal. The purpose of knowledge is to discover identity in multiplicity; its aim is sometimes a universal and at others a particular.   It alters its method to suit the class of object--intelligible (intellectible) or natural, for example, and also mathematical.

Consequently, there is a difference between heavenly and animal movements, matter and form, and the characteristics and essences of the sciences and the arts.   Indeed, "order and definiteness are most appropriate for things of highest worth . . . , for grammar and music and the mathematical sciences; . . . and again [also for] the arts, which imitate nature, both the instruments and everything else depend on ruling principles."[21]   Music is therefore a science like mathematics because it has order and definiteness; it is like the science of grammar (or rhetoric as Plato saw and Aristotle thought of it), but also like the arts (crafts) because its instruments are the means to an end and depend on ruling principles.   Theophrastus does not burden these sciences and arts with cosmic significances or relationships; each art has its own order and definiteness, its own harmony and consonances.   Like both Aristoxenus and Aristotle, he sets aside the Platonic-Pythagorean-mystical notion of objective cosmic harmony and holds to a concept of harmony as a feature assumed by human beings to be present in and appropriate to each art.   Each art may be a symbol of the goddess Harmonia because, speaking metaphorically, each has its own harmonics.

If music is not mathematical, then what is it?   Theophrastus wrote an *On Music* which has been lost, though a fragment of it is published with Porphyry's *Commentary on Ptolemy's Harmonics*.[22]   Here, as often is the case also in Aristotle, the focal point is motion: the movement of the melody is expressed as the voice acts on the soul in the way the singer wants it to; the motion enters the soul, calms it, or purges it of its passions. Without movement there is no music.   The effect is definite, but it is not mathematical or quantitative.   Physical vibration is not an aspect of number; it is movement: thus Theophrastus contradicts both Archytas and Heraclides Ponticus as well as Plato.   Nor does he accept the idea, also related to number, of Plato and Aristotle that high tones have a higher transmission of velocity than low ones.

Indeed, quantity, in tone as in color, is different from the essential in nature, which is quality: high and low tones do have number, but, more important, they depend on qualitative peculiarities. Theophrastus sees that tones, acoustically considered, follow special quantitative laws, but (in a not too clear discussion) he shows that high and low tones differ, like spatial quantities in other sense-modes, according to power of voice in singing, to the narrowness and width of *auloi*, and to different thicknesses of strings-- that is, according to quality. Here, as in consonances, a balance of forces seems to be decisive and the fundamental differences in nature are deter- minative (and "spatial"): high notes sound forward and upward, low ones go the same in all directions, but consonances of both high and low notes travel with the same speed. For intervals are not the cause of tonal dif- ferences, and there Theophrastus resorts to the Aristotelian theory of privation or awareness of negation[23] to support knowledge of an actuality. Tonal differences have a qualitative basis, though in consonances these differences are in balance.

But all movements are prior to either quantity or quality, and for Theophrastus (as for Censorinus later) many expressions of music in the voice stem from movements of the soul. All is natural and physical, and so is the sympathy between movements. The drive for melodic motion thus begins in the soul, is expressed in the voice, and is instinctively sent in a certain direction. The effects are even physical: it must be this view which encouraged Theophrastus to affirm that music can give health to the body--or which prompted legend-makers to create stories in his name illustrating the therapeutic effects of music.

Unlike Plato and Aristotle, however, Theophrastus does not link the modes with mankind's ethical nature. He does not think music can arouse ethical affects. Indeed, for him it is linked with the passions and with them alone. "Music moves souls," he says, "and provides them with rhythm."[24] It begins with emotion and ends there. As Plutarch reports, he declared that love "contains all the causes of music--grief, pleasure, and enthusiasm," and that "it should . . . incline us more than any other passion to poetry and songs" (*Moralia* 8.67).

Theophrastus has a fairly large place as a source of scientific observa- tions in the *Natural History* of Pliny the Elder (23-79 A.D.), and he has been called the first philosopher to teach the power of music to heal illnesses. Athenaeus (624) reports that in his *On Inspiration* Theophrastus said that persons having sciatica will avoid its attacks if the ancient aulos is played in the Phrygian mode over the part--an effect resembling reported accomplishments of Pythagoras. And Aulus Gellius (second century A.D.) similarly says (4.13) that Theophrastus claimed that playing strains on the aulos in the Phrygian mode would relieve severe gouty pains in the hips. These reports, whether apocryphal or authentic, persist in later writings about music.

The sense for musical harmonic expression no longer seems, as in Homer, Hesiod, and Plato, to be a special gift of the gods, but rather appears to be something integral to the human soul itself.   This view of Theophrastus--that is, that harmony is buried deeply in the soul and acts as its movement--made a deep impression on Aristoxenus.[25]   It was Theophrastus' Aristotelian position that we act in ways which are natural, that man is more a political being than an animal, that he is endowed with speech (as animals are not) and has a moral sense unique to himself. Theophrastus' model stressed the uniqueness of man in the natural world, and he himself created or at least followed a naturalistic aesthetic beginning from the notion that man's indigenous characteristics and capacities are the source of his arts because his movements--and in music those of voice--are ordered and reflected back to his soul.

In three specific respects Theophrastus was the undoubted pupil of Aristotle: in his emphasis on movement and the corresponding evidences of it in body and soul, including the catharsis of bad emotions; in his discovery of one of the sources of music in enthusiasm (religious ecstasy), which Aristotle had called the ethical part of the soul (*Pol.* 1340a, 1342a); and in his concentration on the psychological and perceptual. If one adds to these his (probably spurious) acceptance of the idea that music can heal the physical man, it may indeed be said that, despite the relative incompleteness of his work as now known, Theophrastus may be called the author of the first naturalistic music aesthetics in the Western world.

V
The Hellenistic Dispersal
of Greek Musical Theory:
Epicureans and Stoics

The period extending from the birth of Socrates to the death of Aristotle marked the golden years of Athens and also the beginning of its rapid political and economic decline. It was almost identical with the age of Pericles, the great orator, statesman, and leader of the democratic party (which Plato did not admire). He took over the city in 460 B.C. and almost immediately began to prepare for inevitable conflict with Sparta. His military preoccupations did not prevent his making Athens a center of art and literature, however--as it already was of philosophy. With the architect Ictinus, who designed the Parthenon, and the sculptor Phidias, he made it into one of the most beautiful cities of the world. Anaxagoras and Socrates were his teachers.

Pericles died in 429 B.C., and Socrates thirty years later. Approximately ten years before the death of Plato in 347, Philip II of Macedonia (383-336 B.C.) successfully overcame the combined armies of Athens and Thebes. For centuries thereafter, Greece was subject to foreign governments; it was merely a section of empire and no longer a combination of independent city-states which had been the origin of the political and social thought of Plato and Aristotle. At first the city-states were united under the rulers of Macedonia. Philip's successor--his son, Alexander III, the Great (356-323 B.C.), a man in some quarters more famous than his teacher Aristotle--placed Athens in a subordinate political position. Ironically, the city at this point began to be influential in science and philosophy which, throughout the world and especially in the East, took on a Greek cast. Hellenism became a dominant component of culture wherever it fused with oriental thought and life. This was particularly true in Alexander's own city, where philosophy and criticism were already in full flower. Greek science, Greek (transportable) art, Greek religion, and political thought travelled throughout Europe and Asia or, as has been observed, from the Aegean to the Indus and from the Caspian Sea to Ethiopia.

In general, the so-called Hellenistic period in world culture extends from the domination of Greece by Alexander to that by Rome (from c.30 B.C.). During this long period, philosophy--and the aesthetics or idea of music--underwent a change in character and divided itself into four schools of thought. Originally there had been three Socratic schools as well as the

Athenian Academy led by Plato and the Athenian Lyceum led by Aristotle.

CLASSICAL GREECE	HELLENISTIC GREECE & ROME
SOCRATIC:	*End of 4th century B.C. to middle of 1st century B.C.:*
1. Megarian: led by Euclides of Megara (c.450-374 B.C.), disciple of Socrates: taught that the good is the one and the only true being: chiefly known for attacks on others.	EPICUREAN: led by Epicurus (324-270 B.C.): taught that the human soul is material and shares the fate of the body; assumes that life is materialistic, mechanical, sensual; believed that the soul is the "harmony" of the body.
2. Cynic: led by Antisthenes (c.444-after 371 B.C.), pupil of Socrates, present at his death: taught the importance of virtue and education.	STOIC: led by Zeno (4th-3rd century B.C.): the aim of life is moral, is virtue.
3. Cyrenaic: led by Aristippus of Cyrene (c.435-c.356 B.C.), pupil of Socrates: taught that the chief end of life is pleasure, intense and immediate pleasures being preferred.	*c. middle of 1st century B.C., to middle of 3rd century A.D.:*
	SKEPTIC: Pyrrho (c.365-c.275 B.C.): a school of miscellaneous people who thought all judgments questionable, all problems insoluble, and all other schools too dogmatic.
PLATO	
ARISTOTLE and the Lyceum: became the Peripatetic School led by Theophrastus.	ECLECTIC: combined hedonism, moralism, and Platonic idealism in rejection of both skepticism and moralism.

The last four schools flourished in Athens and also in Rome, which gradually assumed a central position in the known world of the time. While the Peripatetics transferred from Athens to Alexandria, the Epicureans (represented by Lucretius [95-52 B.C.]), the Stoics (represented by Seneca [4 B.C.-65 A.D.] and Cicero [106-43 B.C.]), and the Skeptics of all shades all taught in Rome.

Though Athens fell and Rome began its long period of hegemony over the world of antiquity, the Mediterranean continued to be the seat of civilization. Greece was in effect extended westward to southern Italy and eastward to Asia Minor (the Anatolian seaboard). Alexander had gone east into Persia and the plains of India. Greek influence was neither political nor economic, but intellectual; it was localized and supreme in the so-called Hellenistic civilization of Alexandria, Pergamum, Dura, and other eastern cities. Alexander and his armies never crossed the Alps, the Carpathians, or the Cévennes in southern France.

Now Italy became the Mediterranean power. It was able to subjugate Gaul. Germany remained unconquered except for its eastern part, which is now Hungary, Poland, and Czechoslovakia. Italy controlled all of the mediterranean littoral, including Africa and Syria. Southern Britain was a Roman province, and remained so for three and one-half centuries. But the Greeks continued to be highly productive under the Latins. Their travellers' accounts (some true and some apocryphal), ethnographic works, and topographical investigations increased the number of Greek writings still extant today.

The Greeks introduced the Romans to art and thought. When the Roman general Sulla conquered Athens and Greece late in the first century B.C., he confiscated the treasures of Delphi and Olympia as well as Aristotle's library at Piraeus. Thus began a tremendous activity of collecting Greek monuments and manuscripts, with the result that great library-museums gradually included the works of the Greek poets, dramatists, philosophers, and historians. Some of the treasures were moved, and some simply stayed where they were, to remain the possessions of Roman emperors like Hadrian. Under the first Caesars, Hellenistic culture, now an aspect of Roman civilization, was represented in the libraries of Alexandria, Antioch, Athens, Pergamum, and Rhodes. The most famous, often thought to be the greatest of all, the Museum and Library at Alexandria, was partly organized by a Peripatetic scholar from Athens. The Greek Academy and Lyceum of Plato and Aristotle, respectively, had been private collections and institutions. But the Museum (Home of the Muses) in Alexandria was a historical and scientific collection, a state institution lavishly supported by the reigning Ptolemies.

For centuries it was accepted as fact that the Romans had little to do with music and wasted little thought on it. However, especially after the publication of Wille's *Musica Romana* (1967), one can no longer agree with the traditional assessment. Using Greek and Roman literary materials and archaeological, epigraphic, and numismatic remains, he arrives at a highly convincing conclusion: that music was an integral part of the daily life of the people, of public and military activities, of the theater and the circus (the Roman substitutes for Greek tragic and comic spectacles), and also of the artistic side of private life in the home. Of vulgarity there was plenty indeed (as there had been in Greek times and as there always will be at any time). The aulos had become a large, impressive tuba-like instrument, and lyres were huge, chiefly for the immense power of tone needed in huge theaters and circuses. Instruments were played in unusual combinations, and huge masses of musicians often performed at the same time. The water organ, the syrinx, and the *scabellus* (clapper) were for all practical purposes new instruments, and they took front place in the theater, the arena, and the meeting-houses, where they initially served secular ends and eventually even influenced religion.   The *tibia* (pipe) underwent development, and even the syrinx was used for artistic ends.

According to traditional and proverbial judgment, no singing or dancing was to take place in the Forum, but in every other realm of life music had its place.   Musicians in a sense had a social position, though frequently they were slaves (who sometimes were freed).   Social classes from the lowest to the highest employed music in their religious ceremonies and in public festivals.   Furthermore, out of Roman life came, in some part, even some aspects of the music of the infant Roman Church in the West. Not everyone approved of musical activity, of course, and the Roman historian Ammianus Marcellinus (second half of the fourth century A.D.), looking back, deplored the use of the lyre and in fact of all music in domestic life: music, he thought, was a poor substitute for philosophy (14.6.18).   Philosophy was still a gentleman's occupation, though the practical Romans adopted a substitute--namely, rhetoric--for it.   Indeed, the emphasis on rhetoric provides the best illustration of the contrast between the Greek interest in ideas for their own sake and the Latin preoccupation with the influence of ideas in politics and law.

Like everything else Roman, music was "practical."   Yet there was, comparatively speaking, no dearth of reflection about it, its place in the world, or its part in other activities.   In several respects, Roman music was a pioneering music.   Its basic, indeed primitive and naive, aspect in general remained unaltered.   True, song was both magical and artistic, but as it lost its original simplicity it gave way to complicated melodies and rhythms. The sensuous possibilities of music were exploited from the very first, and musical enthusiasts granted great respect and encouragement to virtuosi of all kinds.   Nevertheless, the daily manifestations of urban life remained constant: the simple cries of beggars and street-peddlers took on musical form and were musically interpreted.   Indeed, Rome supplied part of the first chapter of the history of folksong in the Latin West.   Military signals were combined with music for purposes similar to those of the work-song. And as the empire grew, Rome, more than ancient Greece, was the recipient of the most diverse kinds of music from abroad.   In turn, the Romans disseminated music and the idea of music throughout the world.   Horace and Nero, different as they were in person, mind, and temperament, were active musicians.

Roman music and Roman interest in music can therefore no longer be considered an appendage to Greek history, a decadence, a deterioration, and a flattening out.   The picture of the Roman as uneducated, lacking in taste and feeling, and musically barbaric is patently false.[1]   But he was not "original," and the quotations used by Romans from Greek writers reveal that they relied unquestioningly on Greek thought for authoritative musical opinion.

I

The Epicureans. Little, if anything, is known of Epicurus and his ideas about music. He wrote an *On Music* which has disappeared, and his actual ideas were probably appropriated by Philodemus. He interpreted existence materialistically, thought that action should be judged hedonistically, and held that knowledge is a matter of the senses. For him, beauty and pleasure were almost one; beauty would not be beauty if it were not pleasurable. He even allied the good with pleasure, so that anything not pleasurable should be rejected. Like his followers, he had to allow for the existence of determinism (as in the fall of a statue), but he also admitted to the presence of indeterminism. It is hard to see how Epicurus could have admired music as anything more than a superficial pleasure, but even this is only a supposition.[2] His whole school derided the Platonic vision of Er and the music of the spheres. His objective was repose and almost a state of non-being or at least non-response. Pleasure was really a negative thing, the absence of (and therefore the freedom from) pain and disquiet (see Lucretius, *De Rerum Natura*, 2.16, 964f).

Epicurean philosophy was founded in Epicurus' Garden and followed two paths: (1) the cynical or utilitarian, which did not favor aesthetics at all; and (2) the Democritean, which was naturalistic, empirical, and violently opposed to idealism and mysticism. Both Lucretius and Philodemus of Gadara (c.110-c.50 B.C.) followed the latter path. And both have a philosophical consistency which the Stoics as a whole lack.

Lucretius (Titus Lucretius Carus). Lucretius' *De Rerum Natura* (*On the Nature of Things*), despite Cicero's neglect of it, was a veritable bible for Epicureans. This is understandable because the poem is a complete philosophy in verse. It begins with an invocation to Venus, clearly a symbol, and a prayer to her in supplication for peace. Her good offices, Lucretius maintains, have heretofore been frustrated by the gods and religion. For the world is not divine. It is a vast organic whole including earth, sky, and all creation, life in its origin, and man in his advance from savagery to a higher type of civilization. Fire, despite Heraclitus, is not a constituent of things. Nor are earth and air. The only immortal substances in it are atoms, as Leucippus and Democritus insisted, and empty space. The atoms are limited in their number but not in their variety, which is not governed by necessity but comes about by way of their ceaseless and restless motion in infinite time and space. The human soul and body are both "atomic" and exist or cease to exist together. Atomic behavior, because it is free and spontaneous, is able to control man's fate.

During his evolutionary advance, man in his first purely animal existence was subject to natural forces. He began to control fire, to cook, to make clothes and shelter, and to transform his animal cries into speech. The tribal and social existence which gradually followed was accompanied by agriculture, the domestication of animals, the use of metals, and the accumulation of wealth. Social evolution resulted in the forming of governments. The arts gradually arose during this evolution. The entire process was governed by nature, which established the natural rights of everyone. Thus justice, which is superior to natural rights, was and is not a permanent ideal object but something fluid which alters with time and place. It is an idea subject to change.

As man appropriately searches for true happiness, he is not led by the gods or religion, which have "brought forth criminal and injurious deeds" and destroyed happiness by denying that death is a pleasant sleep: Agamemnon's sacrifice of his daughter Iphigenia is an example of how perfidious the gods can be. They have attempted to smother that joy in life which comes from man's submission to the Mother of the gods--that is, to the earth, which is the source of truth. Through perception, man discovers the laws of nature--and he avoids the untruths which are the teachings of old superstitions. Through philosophy and virtue men achieve happiness and joy in life. Such joy is based on a universal human pleasure which is an absence of pain and the presence of love. Though the universe has no designated purpose, human beings do. They accept truth, reject the false, and aim to achieve happiness and dignity in life. But these are not the end of life. The good and simple life, and not immortality, is the legitimate human goal; it results in peace, a contented mind, and a heart purified and free from corrupting passions, especially those of ambition and avarice.

Far from being indifferent to art, and especially to music as was Democritus who thought it the result of superfluity in the lives of men, Lucretius shares with Epicurus a lukewarmness about the arts; but this lukewarmness may only seem so because both explain that art, its forms, and its uses derive from man's model--nature, an earthly nature to be seen and heard--and from neither the mystical nature of the Pythagoreans nor the terrestrial imitation of Platonic Forms. It is the nature symbolized by the bird songs which men imitated before they could sing polished songs for the ear. The whistling of the wind through the reeds taught them to blow their breath into hollow hemlock-stalks or the pipes of Pan. Nature thus even supplied them with models for making instruments: men may have been inspired by the sound of Zephyr in the reeds to cut holes in the first reed-pipe just as perhaps, in their early wandering through nature, they lived in divinely inspired leisure and discovered the air of the aulos (*De Rerum Natura* 5.1384-87). Primitive men themselves were the real Muses when they set music in motion: they lay in the grass, perhaps alongside a brook in the shadow of a tree, and were so refreshed that they felt a spontaneous drive to make wreaths for themselves and to dance, which at first they did noisily and in unrhythmical measure (ibid. 5.1380-1402). With the sweet sounds of nature to guide them, they created music by themselves.

Was there any assurance whatsoever that, however men may have been inspired to create music (and other arts), the flush of success would continue? Not necessarily. And yet there was progress. Take watchmen and sentries: they learn the rhythm of a song as a matter of tradition, but they probably find less bliss in it than did the children of nature of long ago. There follows the generalization that pleasure resides in what is present and new, and may better replace the greatest pleasure in something old (ibid. 5.1409-17). As the source of one of life's refinements, therefore, music comes from nature, from the earth, the mother of man. From the very beginning, like painting, poetry, and sculpture, it represents a spiritual advance or progress and an achievement in the development of mankind from animal existence to that of cultivation (ibid. 5.1448-53). Through his own inventiveness and reason, man created the arts and caused them to evolve: at first nothing but a game and a relaxation, they eventually arrived at a "topmost pinnacle" of perfection (ibid. 5.1148-56).

Here his assumptions are completely naturalistic. The universe he envisages is cold and indifferent; it includes innumerable worlds. Furthermore, the principle of harmony is not a characteristic of the soul (ibid. 3.131-36), though it is of use to musicians (who assume its validity). There are different kinds of atoms of infinite number: smooth and round, and pointed, for instance, so that the rasping of a saw cannot be made up of atoms as smooth as those of the melodies of a skilled musician (ibid. 2.410-13). The atoms set in motion by the blare of the trumpet are different from those of the swan's mournful cry--and so forth. Roughness of voice comes from roughness of the atom particles, and smoothness from their smoothness (ibid. 4.540-49). Harmony is not a universal principle but the result of atomic behavior.

Now, one thing cannot be denied: the evidence of the senses, which reason is helpless to modify or explain. For Lucretius, the soul is not immortal, knowledge is psychological, and perception, upon which knowledge is based, is an activity of the five senses (ibid. 3.624ff, 4.973-83). First there are physical changes; all sounds and voices are heard when they make their way to the ears and strike the organ of hearing with their corporeal substance (ibid. 4.524ff). Voice and sound are physical and material. The elements of sound make their way from a narrow passage of the voice to the outside. Both voice and words are made by parts of the body, while the consumption of physical energy continues through speech and voice, the harshness or gentleness of the latter depending on the roughness or smoothness of the atomic particles (ibid. 4.526-46).

Then, sound must travel. The further away the voice is from the hearer, the more confused the diction and the meaning; the closer the voice, the clearer the diction and meaning. Entering into more detail than can be reported here, Lucretius continues to describe the origin of sound in its material physicality. The voice is expressed from the body by way of the mouth, articulated by the tongue, and formed by the lips; and the same physical powers are in evidence as the voice is broadcast afar. Coming from one physical source, the sound can be divided and spread out among people in a large audience, where it divides like a stream and exerts its force on separate individuals.

Part of the utterance escapes into the air, and some parts beat on solid rock and, driven back, give off a sound and "sometimes mock us with the echo of a word" (ibid. 4.550ff). Later, Lucretius describes the echo, which Aristotle had mentioned in *On the Soul* (419b), and in his account of it he includes miraculous stories accepted by the naive and ignorant from legends about satyrs, nymphs, fauns, the great god Pan, and the music of all of them (*De Rerum Natura* 4.573-90). The marvel of sound, he insists, is that it can pierce through walls and doors and go through the "winding pores [passages]" of things which eyes can never penetrate--except, of course, that eyes can see through the "straight pores" of glass. Since one sound rises from another, a single voice can go in all directions to form a choir of many voices joined together. Through a splitting apart, the heard parts can fill large distant places. In penetrating to spaces behind the door, however, the voice is blunted, sounds are confused to the ears, and the words sound only like noise (ibid. 4.596-614). But the voice can penetrate the soul, which is something mental or physical. And it works even in sleep. Then it is at times "pushed deep down within the frame," and the chant of the lyre is heard nevertheless. Interpreted sometimes as a psychology of musical perception, this passage is, rather, a psychology of the dream and no more than an expression of a suspicion of the truth that passionate devotees of music who constantly hear music in waking will hear it echoing too in dreams (ibid. 4.971-83).

Lucretius is completely consistent in his treatment of music: originally an imitation by man of the material aspects of nature, it has been man's pleasure and stay, a component of his deep psychic and spiritual being. Like Epicurus, Lucretius thinks pleasure is the end of art. But, also like his model, he expects the pleasure to be more than a mere dwelling on the sensuous. Indeed, it goes beyond the sensuous, to be a balance of pleasures and pains beneficial, as are all pleasures, to body and psyche, but "cool"-- that is, not a source of ecstasy or transport but of repose.

Philodemus.   It was one of Lucretius' fellow Epicureans and Democriteans, a teacher in Rome, a utilitarian, and, like Sextus Empiricus later, a kind of rebel in music aesthetics, who through his prose writings and his erotic poetry most clearly presents us with the Epicurean philosophy of music. While Lucretius finds a prominent place for music in the evolution and development of man, his capacities, and his arts, Philodemus analyzes it for itself alone.

For Philodemus (first century B.C.),[3] Epicureanism meant not only a peaceful but also a gay and sensuous life. He contradicts the idea of the Stoic Diogenes the Babylonian (second century B.C.) that music, like anger, pleasure, and sadness, resides within us.[4] It is a common experience, Philodemus says, that all Greeks and barbarians (foreigners) cultivate music in all phases of life, and that the same melody produces different effects in different people in different times and places. Both Pindar and Philoxenus, for example, used the Phrygian mode with different effects. It may be true that every child, even before it attains reason, surrenders to the powers of music (65), but, taking a formalist position, Philodemus does not think music is an imitative art at all.

Nor does he agree with Diogenes that, though music does not mirror character in an imitative way, it reveals magnificence or baseness, heroism or cowardice, politeness or arrogance in human character. Indeed, music does not reveal these any more than does cooking, or culinary art (an opinion Aristotle would have thought absurd [*Pol.* 1339a]); it is less an art than an experience (as Plato said in *Gorgias* [510] of cooking alone; and one may add that as cookery, it is like rhetoric as Plato describes it, rhetoric and cookery both meaning flattery [*Gorgias* 462-63]). In fact, music is an irrational pursuit: poems allied with it are useful because of their thoughts, not because of their melodies and rhythms.

Music was of course not invented by a god (95); it is a creation of man, and there is no analogy between it and atmospheric phenomena (that is, the cosmos and planets). Nor is it related to mathematics, as Plato had thought (30). Like Protagoras (c.481-411 B.C.) and Democritus, Philodemus sees man as the measure of all things: he is also the measure and control of music, which behaves unexceptionably like any other human product. It is limited in its effects, good or bad. Heraclides Ponticus is wrong to think that melodies can be suitable or unsuitable for manly and weak characters or consistent with the characters of the men performing them. Yet Philodemus thinks that music is not far from philosophy (which he seems also to hold suspect) because it brings value into human life; taking an interest in it, we will (at least) be properly attuned to many or all the virtues (92). But it has no influence on the soul or on character. As for the study of harmonics, Philodemus does not mention this pursuit at all.

For him, music, rhythm, and melody are of a purely outward formal nature and entirely independent (65). In religious song, too, music seems of little significance alongside the poetry. Furthermore, it is wrong to think with Diogenes the Babylonian that music is inseparable from true devotion (38) (or the divine, or the gods, whether all together or individually). Nor will Philodemus have anything to do with the idea that music is significant in love-life or at drinking parties (84). In these connections, poetry, not music, is the inciting factor. For, as Democritus said, music is a luxury and a relatively young art (108). One must admit that Plato and Aristotle are right in thinking that it lightens the ennui of work (82); it can therefore be a refreshment and an amusement; but it cannot be of significance in the education of youth or in the moral improvement of adults. It is indeed pleasant, but it has no ethical or moral effects--and it surely has no connection with justice (90), the aim and purpose of the state. All in all, Philodemus may serve as an antidote to previous musical speculation. Fortunately, he does not go so far as the fourth century B.C. historian Ephorus, who thought that music is a path to deception and sorcery (Polybius 40.20.5).

The rationale for his position is based on the Epicureans' special theory of perception.[5] For them, all senses are alike, especially in their manner of operation. Sound itself has no special individual properties. All sensation is irrational and devoid of cognitive meaning. Therefore, music must be purely formal because it has no cognitive effect. And, if no cognitive effect, then there is no ethical effect, since passions and morals can be influenced only through cognitive effects. Furthermore, music does not include reason, on which social and moral judgments rest; it gives a direct pleasure and stimulation to the ear and nothing else. Epicurus himself denied that there is any value in the labor of learning to play instruments or in discussions of technical points in music, and his disciples agreed.

Philodemus thought music not even general in its effect: it influences only individuals who are predisposed to it, especially women and ef-feminate men. Sensuous impressions may be the same in all men, but the resulting images are different. True, it influences people differently, but this is because tastes and temperaments differ. Reactions to music actually depend on a memory of ideas and the incidents related to them; and the most important of them come from the words. Associations explain the ecstasy of religious music and also the "connections of ideas" caused by noisy instruments played during ceremonies. Music has no moral functions and no metaphysical significances.

In thinking that music is a luxury, an entertainment, a form devoid of content, Philodemus was in rebellion against a formidable group of "ethical" thinkers--Stoics like Diogenes the Babylonian, the Pythagoreans, Plato and the Academicians, Aristotle and the Peripatetics, Theophrastus, and Aristoxenus.   He shared with Aristoxenus, however, an empirical approach.   He was not exactly a cynic, and he attempted to justify the existence of music through his own experience, which declared that music had the high station it had been awarded. Music is a Democritean luxury. To the Sophists and the Epicureans it was largely a means to enjoyment and amusement: morally considered, it can lead to laziness, drunkenness, wastefulness, and extravagance. Cynics like Philodemus simply reject it as only a combination of sounds and rhythms. To say that it has an ethical effect is merely to indulge in empty talk. For Philodemus it is formalistic, not ethical.   It is purely aesthetic.   Diogenes of Babylon is wrong, Philodemus says, to think music influences affective life. Perhaps it can if it is assisted by the rational word. But by itself it is incapable of imitative or ethical effect.   It actually deflects its alleged result.   Reports of its wonderful effects are nonsense: ecstasy, for example, results from illusions caused by noise and not from sound itself. True, it can lighten work-loads, but only because it is a servant of sensuous pleasure like eating and drinking. It is not and cannot be a useful avenue to the enrichment of a noble life.

II

The Stoics. The Stoics who wrote about music were chiefly three: Diogenes the Babylonian, who, as we have seen, was Philodemus' object of disagreement; the Roman Cicero, who is often more an Eclectic than a Stoic; and Seneca, also of course a Roman, who wrote about musical practices and habits but had very little to say about theory.

The Stoic School of philosophy, with its Portico outside Athens, was founded by Zeno of Citium (c.336-c.264 B.C.) and flourished in the early Roman period. Its crowning glory, achieved when the Roman empire was in decay, was embodied in two men, Epictetus (60-100 A.D.) and Marcus Aurelius (121-80 A.D.), both of whom wrote in Greek. Stoic philosophy had three emphases: logic (which included a theory of knowledge), physics, and ethics. Physics was thoroughly materialistic and included theology and psychology. Real substance was found in bodies served by the sense-organs and other physical substances in space which make their impress on the soul. For the Stoics, the *pneuma* (like Aristotle's *æther*) or living substance of the universe surrounds the body and makes up the living organic universe. Denying that the human will is free and believing that it is subject to the will of nature, the Stoics took as their motto "Virtue for virtue's sake." They rejected Plato's theory of Ideas or Forms and the doctrine of innate knowledge. Yet they thought that the universe is harmonious, good, and one; Being and reason belong to this unity. They stressed man's duties as a rational and wise being. They disliked mere flattery of the ear. In the name of freedom they rejected the passions, encouraged apathy or freedom from all passions and affections, but did accept nature and fate as the two forces which determine all human thought and action. Stoic philosophy aimed to bring back to life what was left of Greek religion.

They were, however, not so much philosophers as literary men and moralists. Devoted to logic and semantics, they became the first consistent allegorizers. They allegorized Homer and started the flood of comparative and symbolical thought which was to be all-pervading in the Middle Ages. For them, right action in private and especially in public life was a *sine qua non*; reason in the individual, the universality of nature, the virtue of an ordered life, action according to standards of decorum, and tranquillity and detachment of mind were their guiding principles. For them, reason was expected to govern art and poetry as well as life: anything irrational was to be rejected as inferior. Their principle and rule was not pleasure, not the titillation of the senses, but rational judgment; pleasure was either irrational (based on movements of the soul founded on incorrect judgment) or rational (based on a certain elevation of the soul which may sometimes be derived from poetry). Like Plato and Aristotle, the Stoics were teachers, and for centuries most manuals of learning and most encyclopedic works were modelled on their writings.

Like Plato, the Stoics taught that the harmony of music is modelled on universal harmony. But they were Aristotelians in thinking that one should live according to nature and that the musical modes and rhythms to which one is exposed should correspond with human gifts and values. They admired beauty and art and tended to accept them as emanations of soul or spirit in the restricted human sense in which they used these terms.

Cicero (Marcus Tullius Cicero). An orator, politician, and moralist, Cicero played a major role in Roman public life and nevertheless found time to write philosophical works. Most important for the present study are his *De finibus bonarum et malorum* (*About the Ends of Goods and Evils*) and *Tusculanae disputationes* (*Tusculan Disputations*), both dialogues devoted to the ethical opinions of the Epicureans, the Stoics, and members of the New Academy, along with *De natura deorum* (*On the Nature of Gods*). He wrote three essays on oratorical subjects: the longest, *De oratore* (*On the Making of an Orator*), the second, *Orator* (*The Orator*), and the shortest, *De partitione oratoria* (*The Division or Partition of Oratory*). Himself supposedly a Stoic who belonged to the New (Platonic) Academy, he was an admirer of Plato and an enemy of Epicurus and his followers, whom he judged to be anti-traditional and superficial in thought. He was admired by Lucretius, and despite all evidence about Cicero's attitude toward Epicureans in general, St. Jerome later said that he had edited *De Rerum Natura* in 54 B.C. Cicero attempted to romanize Greek philosophy, and therefore the *Timaeus* and part of the *Republic* again take their place upon our stage. Through its translation into Latin, Cicero in effect returned the *Timaeus* to the public attention which, for good or ill, it was to enjoy for a millenium or more. In this respect, Cicero is not an original thinker, but originality itself carried no premium in ancient times. The mark of authority was preferred to that of conjecture or experiment, and the task was to select the authority who guaranteed legitimacy.

Diogenes the Babylonian and Cicero were probably not exactly contemporaries, nor did they come from the same geographical area. Their philosophical Stoicism may be thought to be approximately the same, however, in its general outlines, for Stoicism was an omnibus type of thought which underwent only gradual change. In general, then, they were concerned with ethics and religion, morals, and individual salvation, with truth-seeking not for its own sake but for its application in everyday life. That which had been the highest realities for Plato and Aristotle, and especially the doctrine of Forms, would be set aside in favor of an emphasis on moral action and the life-states of human beings. Further, most Stoics and their basic philosophical system found symbolical support in the power of the physical world, the sun, the universal substance (or fire), and the Heraclitean flux, which all together encompassed everything.

Hercules and Ulysses were favorite heroes who illustrated actions of moral import. The Stoics believed in the god Zeus, and one of their number, Cleanthes, wrote an extensive invocation to him. They did not apparently have faith in the living and life-furthering gods shared by the Greeks--a faith probably shared even by Plato. In *On the Nature of Gods*, Cicero like Euhemerus explains that men like Hercules were given immortal status (of the god-warrior or the god-king, for example) to serve as cosmic symbols of the harmonic union or of the strife of universal elementary forces in nature and as allegorical figures for moral or philosophical ideas or concepts (2.23-27). It was thought that these gods and man could communicate, however mysteriously, through divination, omens and portents, and oracles. Unlike Plato and Aristotle, who theorized about politics but had contempt for concrete political action (since they rated all theory above practice), the Stoics took it as their duty to serve the state through politics. And as teachers they appealed to all members and strata of society, not merely to nobles and so-called freemen. Virtue (the perfection of anything, adding to the health of the state) was their watchword, and right reason the proper approach to it. Macrocosm and microcosm, they thought, are material in substance, and motion and tension are primary principles; and since matter and force are one, pleasure in the world is an accompaniment to right action. As for right reason, its virtue is formalized in grammar, rhetoric, and dialectic.

As a member of the New Academy, Cicero admired Plato. His philosophical apparatus includes the Vision of Er from the *Republic*, which he recapitulated for his own purposes in Book 6, Section 8, of his late work, the *Commonwealth* (or *Republic*)--a section called by him *Somnium Scipio* (*The Dream of Scipio*). Like the *Timaeus* and the revelation of Er, it belongs to vision literature. Here Cicero re-describes the music of the spheres. From the Milky Way the soul of Scipio Africanus addresses his grandson. There are nine spheres. The intervals between them are unequal but exactly arranged in fixed proportions which produce various harmonies (intervals) through an agreeable blending of high and low tones. The first, the uppermost, the sphere of heaven, which carries the stars, revolves the most rapidly and produces a high shrill tone, whereas the lowest revolving sphere, that of the moon, produces the lowest. The earthly sphere, the ninth, at the center of the universe is stationary and makes no sound. The other spheres, two of which (Mercury and Venus) move with the same velocity, produce seven different sounds--the number which is the key to almost everything, including music and harmony. (Later, Boethius [*On Music* 1.27] called the scale here described "Ciceronian," but gave Venus and Mercury different tones.) By imitating this harmony on string instruments, Cicero adds, "learned men have gained for themselves a return to this region" (*Comm.* 6.18-19). We cannot hear the ever-present harmony of the heavens, however, because our ears are dead to their constant sound, as though we were living near the cataracts of the Nile. In this apparent re-phrasing of the Vision of Er, Cicero mentions two harmonies: that of the spheres and that of instruments. The Pythagoreans, of course, expanded the number of harmonies to include human physical and psychological relationships. Plato had made this third type a matter of education and citizenship in the city-state. Cicero either subdivides this third or makes it a fourth: that is, political.

Elsewhere, Cicero maintains that there exists a harmonic movement which is cooperative and inward; it is made certain because astronomy has treated it and because heavenly music is a model for earthly music, both being the rational design of an intelligent being (*On the Nature of Gods* 2.46.119). Thus he arrives at a *musica humana* to support the reasoning that everyone should play a part in making the state harmonious. (For Plato's republic he obviously substitutes the ideal state exemplified by Rome.) The universe is large, man is small, the possibilities of the good life for the average man are limited, and the chances that there is a paradise are nil. But there is an amazing process in the interrelations of the universe and politics, and there can indeed be a paradise on earth for man in politics, which, according to the image of the universe Cicero has relied on, makes man acceptable to the state itself and to the higher state of the cosmos. While everything may be transitory, the statesman has a permanent aim in view throughout life: he is both philosopher and politician; through politics he is good for his fellow men and for the state.[6]

The image of the music of the spheres makes graphic the ontology of both universal harmony and political structures. Cicero sees an all-embracing harmony in the structure of the cosmos in its ebb and flow (ibid. 2.7.19). For Zeno, the father of Stoicism, Balbus says, the world is possessed of mind and reason, is animate and rational, and gives birth to animate and rational creatures. The universe is a living intelligence. How can one doubt this, Zeno asks, using old but telling comparisons, if one would ascribe competence in music to olive trees should flutes playing music grow on them? Or think a plane tree was something of a musician if it bore lyres which played in harmony (ibid. 2.8.22)? These are imaginary possibilities declaring the real harmonic rationality of the world, which, animate and wise, produces offspring rational and wise. If any man is not moved by the harmony of creation, he has never considered such matters (ibid. 2.46.119). But he should do so because even the very structure of the human body says he must.

In his *Tusculan Disputations* Cicero admits that in Greece everyone learned music, instrumental and vocal, and that everyone not acquainted with it was deemed uneducated (1.2.4-5). But he is skeptical of the results, or at least he thinks the results are not well defined. The virtuous man knows that harmony of action is far superior to the harmony of sounds; there are parallels here, however, in that just as the musical ear detects faults of tone in harp or *tibia*, so one can observe moral faults in men; probably echoing Aristotle, Cicero believes that "something in our life [can be] out of tune" (*On Moral Duties* 1.40.145). Positively stated, the aesthetic quality of harmony encourages virtue in action.

Nevertheless, music alone cannot be a comprehensive avenue to virtue through education for action. On this point, Cicero abandons Plato. This is not to say that as a citizen of Rome, the city and hub of empire, Cicero does not adopt the politically and conservatively motivated attitude of Plato that music, like everything else, has a duty to the state. As one of the pleasant matters for study, music does indeed have an importance in communal life (*The Division of Oratory* 23.80). But Plato's (and Damon's) opinion that people in the state change because of the songs of musicians is false. It is the morals of the nobles or aristocrats that will influence people (*On the Laws* 2.15.39, 3.14.32). Though ancient song and the music of harp and aulos were governed by moderation and though Romans have turned from "stern" tones to modern ones, the consequences (despite Plato in his *Republic* 424) are nil (*On the Laws* 2.15.39). Not the arts but philosophy is concerned with men and manners and the nature of good and evil. Here Cicero's adherence to Stoicism is manifest, and he takes the historical position that the social position of music, its definition, and society itself have all changed since ancient Greek times.

Whatever may have been the place of musical intervals in Scipio's dream, music itself is not a universal phenomenon. It is not universal harmony itself. It is "natural," to be sure, and begins in sense perception. For all of the arts are products of nature and can lead to the discovery of the highest truths. Each sense has its own powers. Percepts (like white, for example) are based on them, and their powers are developed through practice and artistic training. Thus, people trained in music through hearing notice what most people do not perceive (*Academica* 2.7.19-20).

Now Cicero is almost Lucretian: training develops sensitivity. It is more than significant, for example, that the ear is always open: a sound heard in sleep awakens us, even if the ear has wax and its passages are affected. Normally, of course, it is important that the ear's outside parts project from the head--a projection allowing for the easy passage of words and sounds. The orifices, hard, gristly, and sinuous, are like the tortoise-shell or horn of the lyre and its crooks and turns, and make possible the relaying and amplification of sound (*On the Nature of Gods* 2.57.144).

By virtue of its senses, which are the gifts of nature, mankind is superior to animals; for only the ears of men are refined enough to perceive the pitch and timbre of the human voice and human instruments (ibid. 2.58.146). Consider the physical origins of the voice: the Stoics metaphorically compared the tongue to the plectrum, the teeth to the strings of the lyre, the nostrils to the hollow arms of the lyre vibrating as the music comes from the strings (ibid. 2.59.149). And the hands too are wonders of nature, because in functioning they enable one to paint, mold, engrave, and make sounds on the cithara and the tibia (ibid. 2.60.150). All of which demonstrates that not the gods, but nature holds the universe together in accord, harmony, and sympathy and is the source of our faculty of speech, our knowledge of numbers, and the art of music (ibid. 3.11.27). Emphasizing the natural and physical origins of harmony in the universe and on this basis contrasting men and animals, Cicero seems to be only superficially Platonic and more Epicurean than he supposes.

He is equally ambiguous about Aristoxenus, whom he judges to be both profound and trivial. Aristoxenus in his early Pythagorean period was both musician and philosopher because he maintained that the soul is a special tuning-up of the natural body analogous to harmony in vocal and instrumental music--an assertion said to be supported by Plato (probably *Phaedo* 86) but denied by Xenocrates, for whom, as for Pythagoras, soul had no form or substance but was pure number (*Tusc. Disp.* 1.10.20). Cicero, who mentions these comments and additional ones from Aristotle and others in order to question contradictory ideas about the soul, remarks that the soul, if it is really the harmony of the post-Pythagorean Aristoxenus, will disappear (ibid. 1.11.24) as does the harmony of music: both are temporal and temporary. And thus Cicero maintains that the post-Pythagorean and post-Platonic Aristoxenus should be philosophically ignored, for he is a man so pleased with his own "tunes" that he tries to bring them into philosophy, where they do not belong. Aristoxenus is not scientific in the Platonic sense: we all can recognize how melodies are produced "arising out of differences in pitch" and how further melodies arise; these are only sensuous matters, however, and Cicero asks how a physical body in its positions and attitudes can produce melody unless there is a soul (which Aristoxenus ignores in his preoccupation with music theory). This is the one question unanswered by Aristoxenus, who should have left philosophy to his teacher Aristotle and himself gone on with his singing lessons: let each man, Cicero thinks with apparent disdain (as did Plato and as did Aristophanes in the *Wasps* [1431]), remain at his own trade (*Tusc. Disp.* 1.18.41-42).

Yet he also thinks that Aristoxenus must be included in a list of great men who have given delight to our ears through the discovery of combinations of sound of diverse qualities. Music belongs to the finer arts even though it is not necessary to life (ibid. 1.25.62). Cicero questions Epicurus' opinion that, pleasure being the absence of pain, positive good consists of the pleasures of taste like that of listening to music (ibid. 3.18.41). There must be a higher pleasure. Will Epicurus listen to the music of the water-organ rather than to the music of Plato (ibid. 3.18.43)? True pleasure is indeed found in the metaphorical music of the intellect and not merely in that of sounds in their interrelations. (The music of Plato of course can be a metaphor for music defined in the comprehensive fashion of the Greeks as leading to the good life.) To live the good life is to live in consistency, dignity, wisdom, and courage, and, Epicurus to the contrary, the happy life is no different from these (ibid. 5.5.13). Such a life may even be passed in obscurity in spite of the rejection of others, but it must be one in which a person holds to his own principles in order to maintain his self-respect. The tibia-player or harpist must be true to his art; he should follow his own taste, not that of the multitude, just as the wise man must look for what is most true without regard for the pleasures of the populace (ibid. 5.36.104; cf. *Brutus* 50.187, 51.190-92). Truth to nature and fact is not truth to art, however.

This truth is the truth of craft. In his *Academica*, a dialogue on epistemology in which he defends Skepticism, Cicero admits that one cannot fail to notice the power of the musical sense; sounds (like light, smells, and tastes) lead to truth, but are not themselves truth. Indeed, the musician, like all craftsmen who work with the senses, partakes of a certain science, an organized body of the knowledge of making and doing, whether only in theory--the mental envisaging of form and facts--or in practical application; he is a craftsman like the harpist who knows how to round off rhythms and complete verses (*Academica* 2.7.22).

But his craft, like geometry and literature, eludes the powers of the dialectician (logician), who sometimes claims that he can judge of the truth or falsehood of music (ibid. 2.28.91). Here Cicero as it were anticipates Sextus Empiricus, the Skeptic of the second and third centuries A.D., who thought that music is a technique with its own brand of truth.   It has something irrational in it, and the ear decides about its completeness (*Brutus* 8.34).   Philosophy, not dialectic, is its superior; and in the process of construction, like the other art-crafts, it calls for cold-bloodedness and clear-mindedness. Delusions and dreams give the musician no confidence if he is to sing (that is, to invent songs and orations) either with or without the accompaniment of the lyre. In art, one must rely on skill and knowledge, not on dreams (*On Divination* 2.59.122). There is a natural divination based not on reason or deduction, but on mental excitement inspired by outside influences such as music, like "certain vocal tones . . . [or] Phrygian songs" (ibid. 1.50.114; see also 1.18.34).   Music is indeed a skill capable of possessing the mind. Yet it is not an essential of life: deaf persons who formerly were charmed by it should remember that many wise men lived quite happily before it was invented and that a greater pleasure can be had from reading than from hearing verse (*Tusc. Disp.* 5.40.116). In this latter instance, the mind is approached directly through words and not through a sensuous medium which attracts for its own sake.

Now, though music is naturally non-rational, it shares with oratory a substratum of all the human senses, a readiness for perception in all listeners. Certain types of recognition are sub-rational. Ordinary people as well as the educated are moved by numbers (measures) in the sounds produced by the voice. This comes clear when, not really understanding the scientific relevances, they raise objections to an actor whose sounds are too long or short or to musicians who do not play the same rhythm or are out of tune (*On the Making of an Orator* 3.50.195). Furthermore, the learned are not much better judges of the numbers or harmony than the uneducated. Derived from nature, art moves and delights because all minds are naturally affected by numbers and the harmony of sounds: these excite us, stimulate or soothe us, and make us calm, cheerful, or sorrowful. All members of the public are therefore equally severe with poets and orators who deny the natural gratification demanded by the ears (ibid. 3.51.197).

And oratory, like music, is a medium, but more complex. It cannot be intellectually or mentally direct because the voice is the indirect instrument by which the orator carries on his work. Manner includes delivery and use of language, and delivery is the language of the body--that is, movement or gesture, which includes facial expression. Now, voice, whose variations depend on feeling, has three registers--high, medium, and low--through which are produced a "rich and pleasing variety in song," because even in speech there is a sort of singing--not, however, the kind which appears in the epilogue of a play and is almost like a song, but what Demosthenes and Aeschines mean when they accuse each other of using vocal modulations

(*The Orator* 17.57). Employing numbers in language and modulation in notes to produce pleasure, musician-poets of former ages varied verse and song so as to avoid satiety in the listener. They agreed that in oratory the music of the voice and the harmonious structure of words should be poetical to a greater extent than prose, a freer art than poetry, will allow (*On the Making of an Orator* 3.44.174). The harmony of numbers must be free of sameness. And since numbers are inherent to the human voice, nature has modulated the human voice for the ear. As the Greeks maintained, proportion is the rule, and nature, which combines utility with dignity and beauty, is the model to be imitated in the creation of harmonious numbers in speech. For nature is at one with the order of the firmament, of earth, sun, moon, and the five planets, whose beauty is so powerful that the slightest modification in it will destroy it and whose artful beautiful appearance, which includes the figures of men and animals, has the perfection of a work of art and not the effect of an accident (ibid. 3.45.178). The artful forms of nature and men are oratory's models.

Not unlike Plato, who in *Philebus* 17-18 describes an undifferentiated ("one and perfect") sound which needs division, Cicero sees that originally the elements of the arts were uncoordinated, uncorrelated, unorganized, unformed. Consider the rhythms, the sounds, and the measures of music. They originally lacked order, organization, symmetry, and proportion, which are important even though, along with philology and poetry, music is one of the more trivial arts (as compared with the law) (*On the Making of an Orator* 1.49.212) and even though Plato is said to have been pre-eminent in it, as he was in geometry. Yet music does not belong to moral philosophy (ibid. 1.50.217). The orator depends on it nevertheless; all his performances are accompanied by it; and as he gets older, the tibia player accompanying him must slow down his rhythms and lighten the music (ibid. 1.60.254). The orator must also of course have (the music-like) characteristics of gesture, intonation, and eloquence (ibid. 1.59.251). His aim is organized language. Is there any music sweeter than a well-balanced speech (ibid. 2.8.34)?

Like Plato and Aristotle, Cicero is concerned about the technical matter of the prelude to or opening of a speech: it should be so clearly connected with what follows that the oration does not seem to be its appendage. A musical prelude sometimes produces such an effect when it makes more of an impression than does what it introduces. Indeed, the prelude must be an integral part of the entire structure, and not something (as often in music) not really asking to be listened to (ibid. 2.80.325).

Proper tone of voice (not soft or effeminate or unmusical or "rustic"), delicate and precise enunciation, precise language, and charm of utterance are of equal importance (ibid. 13.11.42) in the whole, which must be artistic and suitable in style; speech must be clear in both matter and language-- explicit, and full, and endowed with melody and cadence (ibid. 3.14.53). The thought, however, is the thing, and both philosophy and music, the latter being useless without the former (ibid. 3.21.79), are the concern of the orator, who is a total man of broad culture.

Rhythm, cadence, sentences coming to rhythmic conclusions, and the well-ordered structure of the whole: these are the elements of good (prose) oratory and of music. Rhythm is not a continuous undifferentiated flow, but a dividing up--a beat marking equal and frequently varying intervals of time. It organizes what could have been an interrupted sound. The turning point of a rhythm in speech marks a "period" in Greek (ibid. 3.48.186). But in the oration, the rhythm of speaking and writing is not strictly regulated, as it is by metricians or musicians (ibid. 3.49.190). Because rhythm and words excite, calm, and lead to mirth and sorrow, they are naturally suited for poetry and song (ibid. 3.50.195-97). But rhythm is primary; it is antecedent to melody, which it forms and shapes.

Because nature has given every motion a look, a tone of voice, and a bearing of its own, a person's frame, expression of face, and sound of voice "are like the strings of a harp," which "sound according [to how] they are struck by each successive emotion," "the tones of the voice [being] keyed up like the strings of an instrument . . ." (ibid. 3.57.216). Consequently, the skillful orator arouses emotions because it is the expression that counts: the human soul is powerfully moved by a sonorous voice or a song (*On Divination* 1.36.80). "Sympathetic vibrations" are involved, as when the Stoics assert that one can pluck certain strings on the lyre and hear sounds from the other strings (ibid. 2.14.33). All of this is of course related to universal nature and the harmonies of the heavenly bodies (*On the Nature of Gods* 3.11.27). An aspect of expression, music is almost its embodiment.

Can it be that Cicero prepared us for Descartes? It is possible. For Cicero, as for Descartes in his *Passions de l'Âme* of 1650, every emotion has its characteristic look, tone, and gesture, and man's entire body, his features, and his voice--all sound like the strings of the lyre. The tones of his voice (an instrument) are like the strings of a musical instrument, tuned so as to respond to each touch--sharp, flat, forte, piano, and so forth. Thus tones are smooth or rough, of lesser or greater volume, long or staccato, pizzicato or legato; and in other ways with varying gradations they produce the expression of the affect. All are regulated by art, all metaphorically are the colors of the actor as there are colors for the painter (*On the Making of an Orator* 3.57.216). They are an integral part of the whole which embodies expressive ends.

Cicero says nothing about self-expression. Nor does he refer to that peculiarly modern theory, that the artist's own feeling is transferred to his audience. True art is a matter of calculation and planning (of craft, of *technē*); what you do is decided by the effect you want to produce, not by how you feel. An oration has the (indissoluble) parts of invention, style, arrangement, memory, and delivery (ibid. 1.42.187): here is an analysis which became a prescription later to play a profound part in writing about music in the baroque period.

To the objective, ethical-modal, even impersonal music theory of the Greeks Cicero added an affective psychology of tonal (and gestural) expressive effect based on sympathy. The realistic possibilities seem to defy analysis. The Greek theory that the proper modes objectively considered can (possibly) willfully produce certain effects in hearers and the oratorical-rhetorical theory of Cicero (and of others who would follow him) who held that certain gestures, tones of voice, and total bodily attitudes can produce certain effects, are equally objective. Both theories anticipate the "classical," still "objective" doctrine the Germans later were to call *Affektenlehre*.

Along with Quintilian, who followed him by more than a century, Cicero created the rhetorical-oratorical tradition. For him, the philosopher who had been at the pinnacle of the Greek world is the inferior of the orator, who (ideally) combines rhetorical skill with a mastery of that whole range of human knowledge which philosophers have claimed as their own. Oratory is both a science and style. The art of persuasion is a discipline in itself (cf. Plato, *Lesser Hippias* 368), and musical elements are its hidden resources. Philosophy and science are both subject to style, and, recognizing this, the Romans have raised the orator to his deserved position of eminence (*On the Making of an Orator* 1.12-14). For the Greeks, music was ethical and political; for the Romans it is an expressive and necessary adjunct to oratory, the political art *par excellence*.

As incidental historian of the philosophy and culture of his day Cicero is just as convinced as Horace of the decline of music in Roman times. Public pleasure, he thinks, should be tempered by song, harp, and tibia at public events like games or the race-course and wrestling-matches (*On the Laws* 2.9.22). Romans prefer the Colosseum and the trumpets of soldiers playing there; the Greek system of music with its complexities and subtleties would be wasted on them. For the urbanized Romans, the pipes of the rural Greeks are entirely out of place. For them, all is for show, and the "austere sweetness" of the music at one time found in the Roman theater is wanting. In its present state, music is the source only of a childish pleasure and lacks the power of bringing lasting happiness: "For as art started from nature, it would certainly be deemed to have failed if it had not a natural power of affecting us and giving us pleasure; but nothing is so akin to our minds as rhythms and words--these rouse us up to excitement, and smooth and calm us down, and often lead us to mirth and to sorrow" (*On the Making of an Orator* 3.51.197-98).

Actually, for the Romans music is an idiom in itself as it was not in ancient Greece (*About the Ends of Goods and Evils* 3.1.4), when it served to embody and transmit content, often rational. For the songs the Sirens sang were enticing, not because of their vocal sweetness or their novelty and diversity, but because of the supposed knowledge they imparted. Homer knew that his story would not sound plausible if mere melody alone were to captivate Odysseus; enchantment had to be due to the knowledge offered him (ibid. 5.18.49). Similarly, Aristoxenus found pleasure in his knowledge of music, but fortunately only in its speculative theory and not in its sound; for the mind delights, not in the advantage offered by knowledge, but in knowledge for its own sake (ibid. 5.19.50). The mind's content, not the enticements of the senses--that is, speculative theory, not its practical application--and also the intellectualism of Plato establish true knowledge of harmony in *esse* and in action.

With the Stoics and the Epicureans, regardless of their moral-religious orientation, the idea of music became naturalistic. Although Harmonia remained to govern it, the specific number-theory of the Pythagoreans seemed to be completely forgotten and was tacitly treated as irrelevant, though it would be revived later by Neoplatonic mathematicians. While numbers remained elements in oratory and poetry, the Vision of Er in the *Republic* and the Timaean image of the genesis of the cosmos took on moral-political tones. The strict Greek ethical theory sometimes received polite comment, but the psychological effects of music, its special cooperative role in rhetoric, its role as amusement, whether superficial and sensuous or more deeply spiritual, its influence as relief from the burdens of life--in short, music as a phenomenon of nature interpreted in the broadest sense--these continued to make their mark.

VI

The Hellenistic Dispersal: Various Theorists

The aesthetics and idea of music, at first the province of such philosophers as Plato, Aristotle, or Theophrastus, were to be widely disseminated throughout the Hellenistic period in the Western world. Such thinking about music was thus to reach far beyond the purview of such later thinkers as Lucretius or Cicero, and it became in part a scholarly pursuit and a secondary or supporting member of the theoretical structures based on rhetoric, oratory, or architecture. It was of necessity at least in part subordinate to religion because of the frequent use of music in religious practices, though of course religion was itself changing, with the abandonment of the gods of the Greeks and Romans and their laws that, based on nature, had previously determined how men should behave. Of necessity, then, the idea of music had to adapt itself to the teachings of the Hebrews and Christians, for whom the world and its doings and human life itself were given the purpose of obeying, honoring, serving, and worshipping God. The more external and objective religion of the Greeks became exchanged for religious experience that was internal as well as intensely communal.

Remaining in the secondary place which early philosophers, theorists, and moralizers had most frequently given it--the opinions of the majority of the population, including especially workers and slaves, continued to be ignored--music was for centuries denied autonomy, which it achieved in fact only in the nineteenth and twentieth centuries (and then not always without qualification). Music served definite purposes and was "practical." It was discussed by scholars in their sometimes encyclopedic and often systematic works; usually it was included as a matter of course, but, since the tendency was merely to repeat the opinions of predecessors, little that was new in thought was added to the idea. Originality, as we have seen, was no authorial aim, and notions of the relation of music to the cosmos, mathematics, poetry, speech-crafts, dance, and so forth, as embodied in theoretical writing and in legends of all types, became standard fare for learned writers, who handed them down, as tradition, from age to age.

Music, singing, instruments, musical effects, and musical "personalities" were subject-elements in literary works of the highest type and renown, even more so than they had been in Homer, who of course because he had lived in an earlier age could not take advantage of the benefits of classical philosophy. For though Rome found itself unable to contribute very much with regard to theory, music in some part entered prominently into its works of literary art. Here it is necessary to call attention to three of the very greatest of Roman writers, Virgil (70-19 B.C.), Horace (65-8 B.C.), and Ovid (43 B.C.-c.17 A.D.). All were admirers of Lucretius and imitated him, and all made important use of musical legend and of an unstated theory of musical effects or affects. Like the gods depicted in their work, the music to which they refer is romanticized. Some references appear to have been used for purposes purely literary, elegant, and ornamental; almost all were conventional; some are obviously symbolical.

Virgil, the Latin Homer, may be described as the more operatic. His *Aeneid* flourishes with scenes of war and military success, of popular celebration and feasting, of national aspiration and success. One meets with Orpheus and his Thracian harp--Orpheus, who with Amphion and Arion, symbolizes the power of music--and with the Thracian priest who "makes eloquent" the seven "divided notes" (of the musical scale). So too the reader is introduced to Iopus "of the flowing hair" who was taught by Atlas and who sings to his golden lyre of the sun, the moon, and the origins of human beings, cattle, rain, and fire. Since Virgil at the outset sets out to *sing* of "arms and the man," he embeds many musical references in his treatment of war--the "bray" of the clarion, war-trumpets, war-songs, and so forth. Achilles-as-cithara-player is a prototype of the music-playing Greek, as compared with Aeneas, a man as unmusical in reputation as the nation he founded. In Plato the Phrygian mode is sometimes acceptable, but for Virgil the Phrygians are womanish and for warlike inspiration cultivate the pipe with its "two-fold note"--that is, the aulos or the tibia. He also pictures more domestic occasions: Triton blows on his shell, vows are chanted to Juno, boys and unwed girls sing litanies, and marriage-songs occur when they should.

In Virgil's *Eclogues* and *Georgics*, songs and singing are everywhere. Orpheus of course mourns for Eurydice, while Linus, Pan (the god of shepherds' music), and Corydon as well as shepherds sing songs consistent with the unreal, irresponsible, indefinite, bucolic state in which they live. All is artless, erotic, and "natural." The *Georgics* are formal and artificial within the terms of artlessness. The singers pursue bucolic themes and in their ideal pastoral state never hear the "hoarse brazen note" recognized by warriors. True, some vacant minds are charmed by song, and "wives" can soothe their labors with it. In these "country poems" all references to music seem formal, metaphorical, literary, and artificial in the best sense of the word. The writing is as it should be about country lives and loves, country allegory and pastoral refinements, and there is an evident desire to supply entertainment through moralistic but primarily idealized, romanticized, and picturesque accounts of life.

Virgil's friend Horace is to the lyric ode--celebratory, politely erotic, ironic, moralistic, satirical, and autobiographical--as Virgil is to the epic. Virgil imitated Homer, but Horace wrote in complicated verse forms inherited from the Greek poets. Of all Roman poetry, his was the most frequently set to music, and this was so through the Middle Ages and Renaissance. Further, his *Art of Poetry*, always much respected, was a basic text for European neoclassicism.

The Latin ode has been thought of as a speech or text performed with an admirable sweetness, a sweetness and euphony endemic to the Latin language itself, even, as had been the practice in Greek, when presenting catalogues of the names of gods and goddesses, nations, ships, men of distinction, and objects of nature. It had a beauty held in place by rhythm. Not only the poet but the orator too was expected to modify his tones of voice and to maintain its timbre according to the instrument which accompanied him, which designated his proper pitch-ranges, and which held him to the dictates of pitch and rhythm appropriate to his voice and oratorical intentions. Horace himself, an admirer of the Greek poet Archilochus, regarded the lyric as a musical phenomenon designed according to accepted good taste in timbre and rhythm. In one of Horace's odes, Alcaeus, a favorite model, plays the cithara, and in all of his odes Apollo, the god of poetry and music, is everywhere. In Ode 6 (Book 4, ll. 26-41), Horace calls upon Apollo to keep the "lesbian measure," to place the poet's own finger upon the string of the cithara, and to sing of various gods and goddesses. In the final lines of Ode 11 of the same book, Horace apostrophizes strains which will suit the winning and attractive voice, and he praises the charm of music itself. For him Sappho is *the* musical poet, and he also especially admires Anacreon.

Frequently it is asked whether Horace himself played an instrument to his own singing. Surely the poet's position was in fact little different from that of the orator--also a type of performer, as Quintilian said, who must rely on poets just as the poet must rely on musicians (*Ins. Orat.* 1.10.28-30). Quintilian was thinking of style as well as matter, and with regard to style Horace was nothing if not elegant. To display his meters he must have sung, or chanted, to the accompaniment of the cithara, which he frequently mentions (for example, in Ode 1.31.18ff). Cicero probably had the less skillful poet in mind when he said that in poetry certain meters require musical accompaniment because without it the words seem to lack rhythm (*The Orator* 55.83). However, Cicero may have anticipated Horace's Jubilee Hymn (*Carmen Sæculare*), written for singing by boys and girls at the festival of Octavian, at that time Caesar Augustus, in 17 B.C. At its presentation, Horace himself may indeed have played the cithara. Perhaps modelled on the choral odes of Greek drama, this work is in marked contrast in nature and intention to the antiphonal singing of the future Christian Church, on which of course it exerted no influence.

Ovid presents a distinct contrast to Horace and Virgil; he is satirical, naturalistic, erotic, and sometimes bitter. When compared to Virgil, he seems more musical not only in his lyrical verse but also in his use of imagery. He selects the respected civilizing instruments: the art of the lyre taught by Chiron to Achilles is a symbol of the taming of a wild spirit; the lyre itself is a symbol of Ovid's own poetry--and of the cosmic constellation--and the harp, created by Mercury, with its seven strings represents the Pleiades. References to the lyres of Apollo, almost universally the god of music, and Orpheus are frequent: the lyre responds to harmony and represents the poet's verse. But darker meanings also emerge. Orpheus may sing to his lyre, but in the *Metamorphoses* crazed women are shown to be moved by the sound of flutes or *auloi*, by discordant horns and drums, and by the howlings of the Bacchanals. Instruments are profound forces: the rattlings of the *sistra* are a symbol of the Egyptian goddess Isis; and brazen cymbals accompany bacchanalia and the cult-rites of the earth-goddess Cybele. There are realistic effects also. Do you want to discourage a lover? Scoff at his singing or playing. On the other hand, workers, rowers of ships, ditch-diggers, servant girls, shepherds, and so forth are all refreshed and consoled by music. Even the Eumenides are conquered by song, and who can deny that everywhere possible there is concord through harmony?

I

Varro (Marcus Terentius Varro). The richness of the musical imagery of Virgil, Horace, and Ovid often found its counterpart in the work of scholars who more prosaically repeated the "truths" and legends and applied them to more practical pursuits. Such a scholar was Varro (116-27 B.C.), a friend of Cicero and almost an exact contemporary of Virgil. Though a politician, he wrote extensively about literature, history, and antiquities and on broad subjects like law, philology, and philosophy. No ancient writer exceeded him in quantity; he himself calculated his works as numbering 490. He classified past accounts of music, and included it among the nine Liberal Arts, which also comprised grammar, logic, rhetoric, arithmetic, geometry, astronomy, medicine, and architecture. These nine, of course, were later reduced to seven. In the history of musical thought he is best known for his lost book on music, Book 7 of his *Disciplines (Disciplinarum Libri IX)*. That we know anything of the contents of this book is due to one of the miracles of German scholarship. Ernst Holzer in his *Varronia*,[1] on the basis of statements by later writers, attempted a reconstruction of Varro's work from such sources as Pliny, Quintilian, Gellius, Censorinus, St. Augustine, Macrobius, Martianus Capella, Boethius, and Isidore of Seville, all of whom had the advantage of relying on Varro for a bridge between themselves and the Greek past.

Apparently Varro began with the general theme of the importance of art[2]--its cosmic significance as the Pythagoreans saw it in the music of the spheres, the rational, the numerical relations of tones, the relation of tones to meter or verse, the overarching control of "music" over physical and mental events, and its embodiment of rhythm in all physical structures, as demonstrated by the Pythagoreans, Aristoxenus, and Cicero. Probably adopting Lucretian, or even Ciceronian, explanations, he discussed instruments, the legends surrounding them, the use of music in the announcing of laws, and its function as cures for medical, psychological, mental, social, and ethical ills. Nor did he forget the wonderful effects achieved by Orpheus or the powerfully magical effects on elephants, lions, and dolphins.

Very different for his time is Varro's incomplete *Menippean Satires*, an imitation of the satires of Menippus, a Cynic who, in the third century B.C., wrote about men's, and especially philosophers', foibles. Varro's work contains an important section on music titled *Onos lyres* (*The Ass and His Lyre*) in which he contrasts the opponents of music with its adherents. He does not preach, except indirectly through satirical description. His purpose is to assert the positive value to the listener of musical activity and to offer an apology for it.

Varro attacks the philistine foes of music, and begins with an idea traceable back to the Sumerians and repeated by the Aesopian Phaedrus, that the donkey who hears a lyre wiggles his ears. Often pictured in plastic art,[3] the donkey is unsuited to harp-playing because he is deaf to universal harmony. (He is so described in Latin, German, French, English, and Italian sayings and proverbs. Sometimes he is replaced by an ape.[4]) What and how much does a donkey have to do with music? Exactly as much as a philistine. Varro thus concentrates on the rejection of music by limited and narrow-minded Romans who have no understanding of music as a universal subject.

He first stresses the parentage of music in Pacuvius, a Roman playwright and poet (c.220-132 B.C.), his uncle Ennius, a Roman poet (c.239-169 B.C.), and the Muses. Tradition has little to say in objection to music, he thinks, though one cannot really dispute the judgment of people's tastes. It is reasonable to think that Hercules did not achieve his advertised results by way of the psaltery, yet the power of music has been demonstrated over and over. There is one single strong argument against it, of course--the discredited position of the professional musician and his pampered mode of life. His voice-production (*phonaskia*) resembles that of the crowing cock that wakes us up in the morning. In the area of practical training, which Romans respect, he is deficient.

The real defense of music lies in its conformity with the principles of general education. These principles, given a poor reputation by arrogant and superficial musicians, are based on the conviction that the music of the spheres in their harmony moves the entire world. This aspect correlates with the natural disposition born in human beings (workers singing in the vineyard, or women singing to lighten their work), with the natural reactions of animals, with the traditional "miracle" of the Cybele, and with the success of the Gauls, celebrated in a Greek epigram, who tamed a lion by playing on the tympanum. Music has an ethical effect, even in the theater, but modes, meters, and styles must be under such control as to conform to the individual and the occasion. (Achilles and an effeminate man require different meters.) Thus, the name of an artist like Amphion not only guarantees the musical quality of the tragedy, but also shows how necessary is long study.

Indeed, the classical Greek view of the significance of music for statesmen seems to Varro an argument for music on all levels, and for him it follows that a person not devoted to the Muses is unsuited for official life. In all of this, Varro makes clear the towering position of Aristoxenus.[5] His final justification for music, however, is Damonian--that is, that it benefits the state--and how, one may ask, could the philistine-donkey have overlooked that?

Varro's scholarly attempt to preserve the historical beliefs about music is in sharp contrast with the close examination of the art from mechanical, acoustical, or aesthetic points of view which we find in Pseudo-Aristotle, of its application to architecture by Vitruvius, and its continuing place in the art of rhetoric and in the education of a speaker as described by Dionysius of Halicarnassus and Quintilian.

II

Pseudo-Aristotle. It is known that Aristotle wrote a work titled *Problems*, which he and others refer to as his own. A *Problems* consisting of thirty-eight books does exist, but it is not genuine, though it does seem to be derived from Aristotle's works. In all probability it was gradually assembled by members of the Peripatetic school, who had (possibly beforehand) written tracts called *On Things Heard* (concerning the qualitative, not the "mathematical," elements in the production of sound), *On Tones*, *Physionomics*, and *Physical Problems*. All were concerned with empirical observations on the nature of sound and its production and were in fact anticipated by the Pythagoreans who, one remembers, knew about the vibrations of strings and the pitches they produce; by Euclid in the *Canon*; and by Aristotle in the *Politics* and even perhaps in *On the Generation of Animals*.

Possibly completed in Alexandria and usually dated in the first or second century B.C., the *Problems*, Hellenistic rather than Hellenic, is a work that reflects Aristotle's theory of music but supplemented with Pythagorean and Platonic elements. Yet mostly it adheres to the naturalistic tradition of Aristoxenus and Theophrastus and ignores the music of the spheres. Book 11, on voice, concerns sixty-two problems, mainly technical, about the qualitative, the physiological, and acoustical differences in the human voice, though here, as in all books of the *Problems*, the questions posed are not so much answered as followed by further questions. Chapter 32, on ears (thirteen problems) also contains questions and their "solutions" impinging on physical phenomena. Subjects related to the nature of Greek scales, Greek singing, and certain aesthetic-critical matters are contained in Book 19 (fifty problems). Despite the unknown date and authorship of the *Problems*, however, it has not infrequently been treated as Aristotle's own. Its philosophical support is clearly based on Aristotle's division of ultimate "causes" of phenomena into four: (1) the material, (2) the form or archetype, (3) the source of change or coming to rest, and (4) the end (aim) of the thing (*Physics* 194b).

A. Physical Observations

Having recorded observations about almost every aspect of the physical man and considered even the universe as a physical entity peopled by moving bodies according to certain mathematical relationships, the Pseudo-Aristotelians turned to the human voice, and interpreted it as the medium of music and all human expression because of its centrality to the physical human being and the human psyche. As the voice expels air, it makes sound, and sound reflects human nature in general and the individual and his characteristic in particular. Something (like a blow) causes air to be set in motion, and the air then causes sound to move and become a motive power. (It itself moves, and incites or stimulates certain psychic actions in listeners.) The results are qualitatively various--for example, low, high, shrill--and they gradually spend themselves (*Problems* 899a). The quantity of air can be explained in terms of the number of persons singing, for a group of singers will produce a sound which will travel further than that made by an individual alone. Is this the result of multiplication or addition (917b)? But the quality comes first and depends on men's physical types and on the conditions of audibility.

Why do "hot-natured" men have big voices (899a)? Why do nervous people have deep voices, and fearful people shrill ones? The answer has to do with heat and air in motion (903a). Why are voices deeper in winter (905b)? Why does weeping sound shrill, but laughter relaxed; why do children and younger animals sound more shrill than the adults of their species? Breath in motion, violent (and swift) or slow, small or great in quantity, tense or relaxed according to the air-propelling medium--these apply in different degrees in the vocal activities of human beings of different types, sexes, and ages (900a-b) just as they apply to the singing of easy and difficult intervals (917b). These subjects are aspects of the acoustics of the human voice itself.

There is also the acoustics of place and situations. Sounds are more audible at night, and voices sound more shrill from a distance (899a; see also 903a). Furthermore, deep voices are more audible nearby and less so from a distance (901a). And sounds are more readily heard from outside if one is within a house than from inside if one is outside it (903b). These observations of course concern resonance. Physical mediums make the difference: night air, voices in their own physical natures, and wood or stone used for architectural structures; empty earthenware, water, bronze, vessels buried in the earth (899b). We are reminded of certain observations of the Roman architect Vitruvius. Texture, for example, decides that sight (which "can only take one direction"--in a straight line) cannot "pass through hard objects" though the voice can (904b, 905a).

The question of resonance brings up echoing sound, an Aristotelian and Lucretian subject. A voice or air having a certain form carried along often "loses its form by dissolution," but an echo, "which is caused by . . . air striking on something hard," does not dissolve and can be heard distinctly. The echo persists because refraction, not dissolution, has taken place (901b; see also 904b). It is clear that echo is the refraction of voice in contrary motion (904a). But there comes an unanswered acoustical question: Is the voice higher when it echoes back because it is smaller or because it has become weaker (918a; see also 899a)? The mystery remains only partly answered and explained.

One would expect the Pseudo-Aristotelians to apply number to sound, but they seldom do so. They are impressed with the number 7, not because it is symbolical--symbols seem not to interest them at all--but because the number of tones in the ancient Greek scale was 7 (918a). Number and ratio are mentioned (920a, 901b). When are sounds in harmony the most pleasing to the ear? The answer, consistent with Pythagorean principles, is: when they are in simple numerical (that is, consonantal) relation, the simpler the more consonant. And that is all.

More than any preceding observers and analysts of music, however, the Pseudo-Aristotelians mention its psychological pleasures, which will be listed in the following section.

B. The Analysis of Pleasures

1. *Pleasures in rhythms and melodies.* In *Problems* 920b, it is asked why rhythms, melodies, and concords in general cause pleasure. The answer is that (a) we delight in natural movement, as children do, (b) though we delight in types of melodies for their moral character, we find pleasure in rhythm because "it contains a familiar and ordered number and moves in a regular manner," and (c) through sense-perception we delight in concord because "it is the mingling of contraries which stand in proportion to one another." Here one finds the Aristotelian doctrines of (a) the naturalness of all ordered movement (including that of eating and drinking), (b) musical motion, (c) the (Damonian, Platonic, and Aristotelian) idea of the moral influence of music, and (d) the notion of the resolution of contraries, a Pythagorean or Heraclitean principle.

2. *Pleasure in recognition or discovery,* along with the element of familiarity (as in Aristotle's *Poetics* 1448b and 1452a). In *Problems* 918a and 197a, it is asked why we find greater pleasure in hearing men sing music we already know than in hearing them sing what we do not know. First, we find pleasure in recognition and also in noting the singer's achievement of his aim and end; second, we acquire knowledge from what we do not know (a discovery which is pleasant), and we also use and recognize what we know. The familiar is always more pleasant than the unfamiliar. This may be because the listener is in sympathy with someone who sings what he himself knows: "For [one] sings with him; and everyone enjoys singing what he is under no compulsion to sing." (The idea is that

the knowledgeable aristocrat is content not to take part in the professionalism of the singer but nevertheless admires what he himself cannot, for whatever reason, do.)

3. At the same time there is a pleasure rooted in the recognition of a certain objective beauty based on desire. But it is a desire unrelated to sex or drink (896b); it is a beauty-in-itself. (Here one may see an anticipation of St. Thomas Aquinas and Immanuel Kant.)

4. *Pleasure in the expression of feeling. Problems* 918a: Recitation with musical accompaniment produces a tragic effect when it turns into singing, probably because the resulting contrast achieves an expression of an extreme feeling of calamity or grief. Uniformity is less mournful. (Pseudo-Aristotle contrasts singing *per se* with singing with accompaniment: Note-by-note accompaniment of a recitation seems not powerful emotionally, but the accompaniment of actual singing by aulos or lyre seems to give stress to the singer's achievement and to increase his emotional impact.)

There is another possibility (922a). Singing and aulos playing mingle with each other because both are accomplished through the use of breath, and therefore, combined, they give a greater pleasure than, say, the lyre, which is not an instrument of breath and hence is inferior as an accompanying instrument. Here is suggested the primacy in artistic effect of the breath of man mystically sharing in a universal breath. There is also a hint that breath is the agent of man's soul and thus a forceful medium for art. There is a further, lesser observation: the aulos is like the voice and serves to conceal the singer's mistakes; an accompanying lyre cannot do this because it only reveals and emphasizes such mistakes.

5. *Pleasure in combinations of voices.* A single note (homophony) sung or played by like voices or instrument is pleasant; however, a concord (antiphony--of the octave made by the voices of young boys and men) is attractive "because it is a mingling of contraries which stand in proportion to one another," and proportion is naturally pleasant (921a). Rephrased: why is antiphony in the accompaniment (two notes, one of which [the octave] reproduces the singer's) more pleasant than symphony in the accompaniment (note-for-note duplication by the instrument of the singer's part)? Possibly because the singer's note and the octave of the accompaniment make an obvious consonance (918b). In short, they are analogous concordant notes, not the same one (918b).

Thus, concord itself is more pleasing than a single note, and the concord of the octave is the most pleasing. Fifths and fourths do not have the accord of the octave and do not therefore sound antiphonally (and so cannot be used consecutively). *Hence, the octave is the only concord used in singing* (918b-919a). Now, singing in the concord of the octave is called *magadizing* (921a), a term derived from the harp-like instrument called the *magadis.* Just as syllables in verses are in the proportions of equal-to-equal or of two-to-one, or any other kind of proportion, so the sounds of the concord are in proportion as they move to one another. Magadizing is made up of contrary notes in accord with the octave. The fifth and fourth, however, are not made up of two notes equal in force, and these give a different impression or sense-perception. Even when the singer and string accompanist do not make the same sound (or note), they will (must?) finish on the same note to give pleasure at the end, just as they earlier gave pain with their differences. It is another case of unity in diversity.

There is, further, pleasure in the beauty of the lower note when there are two. Why, it is asked, does the lower of two strings sounding together always give the tune? Possibly because the low note is large and strong and "contains" the upper one (as the greater contains the lesser) (918a)--that is, the lower note is a fundamental in sound, and the reverse is not true. There is the effect of unison with the high note, a unison high does not give with the low one (918b). When there is accompaniment, it should be above, not below, the singing voice. The melody itself is naturally soft and tranquil, but suffers from the addition of rhythm to become harsh and full of movement. The high note (of the accompaniment) is full of movement, and the melody (in the lower position) is soft, as befits the more melodious of the elements (922b).

Yet, why is it that singers of low notes seem more out of tune than (or not so much in tune as) singers of high notes? Probably the period of time taken by the low notes is longer than that of a high one and is therefore more perceptible: taking a longer time, it creates a greater impression than a high note, which, being swifter, is less noticed (919a).

6. In *Problems* 918a, it is assumed that the human voice produces more pleasure than do instruments because the human voice is better able to imitate or follow the principle of *mimesis*. Why, it is asked, is the aulos or lyre less pleasant than a wordless song? "Or is it true that even in the case of an instrument we get less pleasure if it is not expressive of meaning?" (Aristotle himself at the beginning of the *Poetics* says that most aulos and lyre playing is a mode of imitation.) The answer is that, while the human voice is more pleasant, instruments "strike the note better [that is, are more accurate] than the human mouth" and are therefore more pleasant to hear than meaningless (i.e., wordless) warblings of the voice. At the same time, the voice is the basic instrument. (The *mimesis* is of course in the words of the voice; if there are no words coming from the voice, there is a greater pleasure in the wordless instrument because of the precision with which it sounds tones.)

C. Music and Mimesis

The Pseudo-Aristotelians hold to the ancient idea that music can inspire ethical affects and reveal ethical character. *Problems* 919b and 920b show concern with how and why music, even when voiceless (created by instruments alone) expresses character (as tastes, colors, and odors do not). It does so because what is heard has movement. It is not the movement which results in action--even color has this--but the movement of sound as such. In melody and rhythm a movement of high and low notes resembles moral character, a resemblance which does not happen, however, in the mere "commingling" of high and low notes. Nor does "symphony" (an "ordering") as such possess moral character. Movements are necessary, are connected with *actions* indicating moral value. (It will be recalled that, according to the *Poetics*, "Tragedy is . . . an imitation of action and of life" [1450a].) Also in *Problems* 920a, it is asked why a singer's passing from a high note to a low one is more satisfactory than the reverse. The question is answered equivocally but may seem to us to suggest a knowledge of medieval plainchant, or melody-writing, possibly (if the *Problems* is misdated) now in its infancy: to go from a low note to a high one is to begin at the end; the highest note is the beginning, the leader, in the tetrachord (and one should not begin with the lower end-note). Yet the low note has a greater nobility and euphony than the high one.

Nevertheless, there is a further question (in 920b): Why, if height in a voice is consonant with smallness and lowness with largeness (a low note being slow and the high note fast [in vibration]), does it require more effort to sing a high note than a low one: setting something small in motion is easier than setting something large, and this ought to be true also of the passage of air. The answer is not that the possession of a naturally high voice and the singing of high tones are the same thing or that high voices are a sign of weakness because they are able to set only a little more than a small amount of air in motion which quickly disappears. Instead, "height of note in singing is a sign of strength": carried along violently, it is carried swiftly. Singing high notes requires effort; singing low notes is easier. High notes are therefore a sign of a strong and healthy character.

There is also the more "objective" *mimesis* of modes: neither the Hypodorian nor the Hypophrygian mode, for example, is suitable for a chorus in tragedy. Yet they are used on the stage because they are imitative (920a). But of what? Of action; and therefore they are not fitting for choruses which do not take an active part in the proceedings. The Hypophrygian is the mode of marches and arming, and the Hypodorian is magnificent and steadfast (and therefore also more suitable for lyre accompaniment). Since the weak are more passive than the strong, the Mixolydian mode suits choruses (922b) for its mournful expression (*Pol.* 1340b); so too does the Phrygian mode, which is exciting and orgiastic. The actors on the stage who imitate the great heroes or leaders use the Hypophrygian and Hypodorian modes, and to the chorus, which represents mere men--beings more human in stature--is suited the more woeful and quiet kind of music.

These positive kinds of *mimesis* are dramatic. In everyday life, the *mimesis* of moods may achieve contrary results. People in opposite states of mind or mood ask to have the pipe or aulos played for them. But the results may be that personal grief can be mitigated while the same means can increase personal enjoyment (917b). Thus the idea that music can in everyday life affect people in specific or prescribed ways, as it can in dramatic presentations, is placed in jeopardy.

The solo singer too is mentioned. He is the virtuoso, who had been for Plato the bad singer because he obscured the message of the music by indulging in complexity instead of simplicity. The Pseudo-Aristotelians, however, accept both the solo singer and the virtuoso, and probably reflect the secular in music to the exclusion of the religious which was asserting itself.

The crux of their argument seems to be the *nomoi*, the melodic formulae memorized and repeatedly used prior to the widespread adoption of notational systems. Now used by both voice and instrument and in singing sometimes combined with improvisations, the *nomoi* were the basis for the defense of the virtuosi, those skillful men who employed them and were "able to imitate different characters and sustain their parts" in the long, elaborate songs they were accustomed to sing. The words were constantly different, and so was the music. And it was essential that the music be more imitative than the words. Choruses sang in a single mode "in the old days" because singing in more than one mode was too difficult for them. But the virtuosi could effect changes: being professional, they preserved the character of music. On the stage the actor is the virtuoso who imitates; the chorus is less imitative and sings simpler songs (918b).

The type of suggestive question-and-answer discussion pursued in the Pseudo-Aristotelian *Problems* is hardly unique in ancient writing about music, but is spare and incomplete when compared with Plato's dialogues and later (lesser) similar works. Lacking is the political context of the state or governing body. Concentration is almost entirely on music itself and especially, of course, on vocal music examined for its aesthetic characteristics of tone and psychological effect. Further, unprecedented emphasis is placed on the sheer pleasure music arouses; post-Grecian and probably Latin uses of music in dramatic presentations by singer-actor, chorus, and singer-virtuoso also receive attention. In all of these respects it may be supplementary to Aristotle's *Politics* and parts of his *Poetics*. What it attempts will seldom if ever be matched in the future, even in Neoplatonists like Aristides Quintilianus. Noteworthy is its failure to say anything about voice production. But this is a characteristic of succeeding books about music, which ask for sweetness in singing, following, one may say, certain Latin models. This pseudonymous work seems to have been attributed to Aristotle early in the fourteenth century by Engelbert of Admont.

III

Vitruvius (Marcus Vitruvio Pollio). If Varro was the first great Roman scholar whom we know seriously to have placed music in an encyclopedic context of subjects, Vitruvius (first century B.C.), younger than he by probably a good part of a century, was the first theorist of architecture to apply it to his art. An engineer as well as an architect, he wrote an *On Architecture* which was eventually treated as a classical depository of principles in all building construction. It is a kind of recipe book which had numerous followers in all fields and in all the arts in the centuries to come. One of the first whole-hearted admirers and direct disciples of Aristoxenus, Vitruvius devoted the fifth chapter of his book to musical harmony, though he admitted that the subject was so obscure and difficult, especially for persons who, like himself, were unacquainted with Greek, that anyone explaining it must sometimes use Greek words because Latin does not have the proper equivalent expressions.   He therefore translated ("as well as I can") from the *Harmonics* of Aristoxenus (*On Architecture* 5.4.1).

The broadcasting ("throwing") of the voice always had to be of primary concern for him because (fortunately) there were no electronic methods for amplification. Two requirements had to be paramount: (1) the voice must be used for something worth saying, and (2) it should have a quantity or power and a quality of attractiveness which couched thought in sounds or in tones easily "thrown," readily projected and heard, pleasantly modulated, and expressively controlled.

To be readily heard was of course the prime criterion for speech. And therefore the acoustical characteristics of buildings had to be taken into account.   Amphitheaters like the one at Epidaurus with unbelievably transparent acoustics were probably less rare then than now, but very likely many were less than perfect. In nature herself there were special geographical places uniquely useful for the transmission of clear vocal expression. Barring the unnecessary repetitions belonging to it, the echo seemed to serve as a natural example of what the well-produced voice could accomplish under the best circumstances, and it pointed up that acoustical rules could be discovered (as they or their applications still are). For acoustics is the science of sound, its production and dissemination, and Vitruvius in following musical principles began to apply acoustical principles to architectural structures.

He refers to Aristoxenus' divisions of expressive sounds between speech (constant changes in pitch levels by conjunction) and singing (changes from one definite pitch to another by disjunction, the note or notes between the sounded ones not being heard) (5.4.2). There are three kinds of modulation: harmonic (the enharmonic, in which quarter-tones are used), *chroma* (the chromatic in which smaller than quarter-tones are used), and the *diatonon* (diatonic, in which a wider, or "easier," kind of interval is used). The first is artificially constructed and produces a singing which is solemn and impressive in effect; the second produces a greater impression of sweetness; the third is closer to nature. Thus nature divides the limits of the voice by the quantity of the intervals and by the qualities of the different modes. All is based on fixed and varied tones, and all instrument-makers follow those fixed proportions of nature (5.4.3-4). How do these principles apply to architecture?

For Vitruvius it was basic that architects must have an understanding of the laws of tone and rhythm in their mathematical relationships (1.1.8-9,

15-16) and that they must go beyond their field to know geometry, music, and other studies if they are to become proper mathematicians (1.1.17). The principles which are fundamental in architecture--*taxis*, proportion, *diathesis* (arrangement), symmetry, and economy (1.2.1-9), and, in terms of beauty, the principles of strength, utility, and the grace of symmetrical relationships (1.3.2)--all point to the musically effective factors in the composition of the architectural work. The three columns--the Doric, the Ionian, and the Corinthian--seem analogous to the three musical genera, which Vitruvius describes anthropomorphically as imitations of the typical physiological proportions of the masculine, the feminine, and the maidenly (4.1.6-10). The five types of temples (3.3.1ff) and their proportions have their correlates in the theory of music, since from the very beginning harmonic relations are necessary for the combining of basic architectural materials (2.1.7). Even the structure of a theater follows musical principles. Its curved level gangways should be proportional to the height of the theater; taller, they will send the voice, which moves in a circular fashion, upwards and will not allow word-endings to be clearly heard. Some of the voice, like a floating air (melody), must range in utmost clearness and describe innumerable modulating circles so as to move horizontally and vertically (5.3.5-8). For resonance Vitruvius would construct thirteen cavitied vases among the seats of the theater at twelve equal distances to supply twelve notes, so that when the voice from the stage strikes them, the sound will be clear and concordant with the vases it sets in motion (5.5.1-6). He would also use harmonic proportions according to the Greek *canon musicus* for the construction of war machines (10.12.2) and water-organs (10.8.1-6).

A word about the vases: bronze vases must be made in mathematical relationships according to the size of the theater. Touched, they should sound in relations of a fourth, a fifth, and so on, up to the second octave. And the whole theater would be constructed so as to correspond to musical ratios; voices and vases will then make for clarity of sound and at the same time create concords of sound in harmony. The arrangements will have to change according to changes in theater size. Even the material of the construction is important, wood or solids calling for different treatment and offering different degrees of resonance (5.6.1-4).[6] Wooden theaters which contain resonant boards do not need the vases. Singers to the lyre, especially when they perform in a higher key, turn towards folding doors on the stage, which reinforce the sound of the voice. When the material is masonry, stone, or marble, however, the principle of the sounding vases needs to be applied (5.5.7-8).

Nor is the influence of climate unimportant. Climate determines architecture in a musical way. Initially, it determines the physical characteristics of the people, and thus people in the North lack moisture and have deep voices. For Vitruvius, the world seems to be triangular, laid out like the shape of the *sambuca* of the Greeks. Southern people have higher voices than northerners because the strings of the instrument produce higher

tones in the South than in the North. Thus the whole world-system is
adjusted to the harmony of the sun's temperature, with people in the North,
South, and middle regions having different voices (just as their other
characteristics are different); therefore their buildings must also be different
(6.1.4-12). (This curious theory of how climate and geographical position
determine what people shall be interestingly has its counterparts in the
thought of the eighteenth-century German theorist Wilhelm Heinse and the
nineteenth-century French writers Mme. de Staël and Hippolyte Taine.)

Vitruvius refers to differences in architectural structures which may
be visually observed by everyone. He explains permanent architectural
principles as they are forever based on relations inherent to music. For him
architecture is metaphorically a frozen music, and the point of contact is the
mathematically ordered nature of the universe by which everything is
ultimately shaped. The musical order puts its stamp concretely on objects
of the world, even on the instruments created by men. The entire Vitruvian
account is a description of such an instrument, the Roman theater. The
emphasis on sound is an emphasis on the players' voices and their
audibility. Actor and voice take precedence, and visual effects like scenery
are secondary. Harmonious sound, acoustical and musical theory realized in
practice, and the aural perception of the audience are basic, and the rest can
then follow in theatrical production. Vitruvius' work was aimed at carrying
universal rules over to the practical and necessary art of theater-building, a
transference which for painting was not to take place until the Renaissance.
The aim was an organic unity constructed on musical principles, principles
basic to the clarity of sound and the intelligibility of what the sound
conveyed.

An admirer of ancient architects, Vitruvius himself eventually came to
represent the principles of "ancient" architecture; he was the model of
architectural theorists for subsequent centuries, with a significant burst of
renewed interest during the Renaissance. Bramante (1444-1514), Alberti
(1404-44; see his *De re aedificaturia*, 1485), Andrea Palladio (1508-80),
Michelangelo, and Vignola (1507-73; see his *Regole de' antique ordini*,
1562) all studied him and frequently adopted his principles, which deeply
influenced European architecture up to the nineteenth century's Greek
Revival architecture. Apparently less a force in his own times than later, he
and his work were the inspiration for buildings constructed during the
Middle Ages and the Renaissance according to his "musical" principles.

IV

Dionysius of Halicarnassus. In Cicero and Vitruvius there is a clear
effort to apply Greek thought to the Roman condition. In Dionysius of
Halicarnassus (d. 7 B.C.) there is an apparent attempt to Hellenize Roman
history and at the same time to console the Greeks for being under the
political control of Rome; his aim, it is said, somewhat impugns the
accuracy of his (almost complete) *Roman Antiquities* of twenty books. In

his *On Literary Composition*, however, he writes as a rhetorician and thus typifies the literary critic of antiquity. To begin, he criticizes certain Greek orators, judging theories of rhetoric like those of Lysias, Isocrates, Plato, and others adversely.

Supposedly the first writer to insist that the style is the man, Dionysius was probably also the first after Cicero specifically to give high importance to the musical element of speech in oratory. He directly calls public oratory a musical science which differs from vocal and instrumental music in degree but not in kind. Like Aristotle, he refers to the natural pleasure of melody and rhythm easily observed in the well-attended popular theater when the reaction of the masses is engaged.

The essentials of oratory are melody, rhythm, variety, and appropriateness--all aiming at delight and pleasure. Unbelievably anticipating Jean-Jacques Rousseau, Dionysius declares that rhythm and harmony (melody) are essentially one: and he seems to remember Aristoxenus and to anticipate St. Augustine in thinking that a linear rhythm is harmonious since it is perceived in time and stored in memory. Rejecting a mystical understanding of such aspects of music, his meaning is that the ratios of musical intervals and of rhythmic feet (which the early Greeks had already thought were the same 1:1, 2:1, 3:2, and 3:4), or the "melody" of spoken language, are likewise measured by pitches, and that, though vocal and instrumental music employ a greater number of intervals, Greek speech itself may have had a quasi-musical character. The interval of the fifth is crucial in spoken language (as in music). The voice as it rises does not exceed three tones and a semitone (the tetrachord), and when it falls, the resulting interval is no more than a fifth. The entire word is not on one pitch, of course, but, by syllable, partly high, partly on low, and partly on both. Here music has a greater variety. Both vocal and instrumental music use intervals exceeding or less than the fifth, potentially including the octave, the fourth, third, second, semitone, and even the quarter-tone. Euripides in the *Orestes* asks Electra to produce such (musical) variety in melodious speech (11; p. 127).

Dionysius accepts the Aristoxenian differentiation between speech and singing, however. A speaking voice is melodious, but it is not a melody; symmetry is the quantitative aspect of words in rhythmical form, but it is not rhythm (11; p. 131). The design of melodies, whether enharmonic, chromatic, or diatonic, and of strophe and antistrophe in the ode, must remain the same: the rhythms must not be modified; they must be invariable (19; pp. 193ff). Thus, he lays ground for the dissemination of neoclassical principles of versification in succeeding ages. Prose is not so limited, however: full of variety, it has its own charm and beauty (19; p. 197). Each category--oratory, poetry, and music--thus has its own melody and rhythm, and here Dionysius attempts to be less metaphorical than literal.

But music seeks its independence from and its own power over the words it accompanies--an independence from oratory and poetry in which it may be rooted. Dionysius approvingly says that it wants words to be subordinate to "tune," not the "tune" to the words (11; p. 127)--an observation clearly carrying aesthetic consequences, recalling the euphony emphasized by Lasos of Hermoine. Rhythm, which the Greeks stressed above melody, is a parallel case: ordinary prose speech keeps the qualities of noun and verb constant, but longs and shorts are determined by meter. Yet musical melody and rhythm may change the longs and shorts so much that one quantity can enter into its opposite (11; p. 129). Intrinsic to Dionysius' thought is a schematic scale with poetic and musical rhythms at its opposite ends, so that poetry and oratory are at one pole and vocal and instrumental music at the other. The end-positions indicate independent existences and constitute an opposition forgotten or ignored until Salinas in the sixteenth century and Mersenne in the seventeenth mentioned them, after which they were ignored again.

V

Seneca. About Seneca there is little to say. Named Lucius Annaeus Seneca, he was born in Spain and, after studying in Rome, became a lawyer, statesman, and philosopher. Like Cicero more than a century earlier, he thought of himself as a Stoic but was in fact an Eclectic; he took a high moral tone in advising and judging his contemporaries. Less theoretical than Cicero, he deplored the large sizes of orchestras and choruses, which in his day often had more participants than listeners. He showed that in his time emphasis was on rhythm, and he has even been interpreted as implying that a rudimentary kind of counterpoint was current. Stressing the tyranny of military instruments and especially of the brasses, he rebuked musicians for striving for harmony of sounds instead of harmony of soul. In this he resembles Plato and Cicero. In general, he felt that the arts were superfluous if one follows nature. And yet one wonders why he thought that anyone lacking a knowledge of music can know other things to no purpose (*Lett*. 83.3). On a personal basis he reveals a healthy skepticism, however: how, he asks, when he himself is in adversity, can other modes than doleful ones keep him from feeling doleful (*Lett*. 88.8)? Can certain tonalities or modes change one's mood? He supposed not. Yet he includes music among the five Liberal Arts of grammar, arithmetic, geometry, astronomy, and music (*Lett*. 88.3-14, 2.349ff). Delete grammar and the result is the scientific quadrivium of the later-defined Seven Liberal Arts.

VI

Quintilian (Marcus Fabius Quintilianus). During the centuries of the heyday of the Roman Empire, even when remnants of Greek civilization were defended, imitated, and cherished, as was very frequently the case, there was a tendency to associate music with grammar rather than with mathematics, though number was often declared to be common to all three. Cicero and Varro thought the association of music with grammar the natural one. Seneca and Quintilian (first century A.D.) took a similar position.

Quintilian was born in Spain. Whether he was in fact a Stoic or not, he disliked the lax moral tone of his time. His *Institutio Oratoria* (in twelve books) is a practical account of the proper education of a Roman citizen and of the methods of teaching actually used in Roman schools. He expected the orator to be good and useful--a man following the Divine, the architect of the universe who had given speech only to men of all living things (2.16.12). He thinks too that the music of his own time did not realize its proper function, but that it "has been emasculated by the lascivious melodies of our effeminate state and has to no small extent weakened such manly vigor as we still possess. . . . I refer to [and desire to see taught] the music of old which was employed to sing the praises of brave men and was sung by the brave themselves. I will have none of your psalteries . . . that are unfit even for the use of a modest girl. Give me the knowledge of the principles of music, which will have the power to excite or assuage the emotions of mankind" (1.10.31-32). The Greeks, especially Lycurgus of Sparta, had the right system: "nature . . . seems to have given music to men to lighten the strain of labor," while music itself has the functions of bringing voices together in sweet unison and of giving solace to solitary workers (1.10.16-17). When Orpheus, a figure who joined musician, poet, and philosopher in one person, was able to draw beasts, rocks, and trees after him, music was united with things divine. Music is therefore a necessity even for the orator. The true musician is both prophet and sage (1.10.9-11), and, as Cicero maintained (*Making of an Orator* 1.6.21), the orator's province is everything in the life of man.

The rhetorical aim must be an artistic structure which gives force and direction to thoughts, penetrates the emotions, stirs the soul. This cannot be accomplished by merely anything that happens to stumble into the portals of the ear. Men are attracted by harmonious sounds. Were this not so, musical instruments by themselves would not excite the different emotions they do. Different melodies like war-songs and songs of entreaty excite or calm the soul. Trumpet sounds are different as they call men to arms or to retreat. Of these things the Pythagoreans had been aware. Rhythm and melody in themselves have a secret power--an important consideration in eloquence. Disarrange a vigorous, charming, or eloquent sentence, and all of its force, attraction, and grace immediately disappear. This is why all great orators from Demosthenes to Cicero have called for artistic rhetorical structures (*Instit. Or.* 9.4.9-18).

For his basic text, Quintilian supplies the classic account of the Latin *numerus* contrasting rhythm and meter, prose and poetry. The best judge, he says, is the ear. The ear is superior in evaluating rhythm, the foundation of artistic structures in which both trained and untrained people find pleasure (9.4.116). Musical rhythms determine the values of metrical feet for dancing as well as for melodies (9.4.139). All of the three rhythmical arts (oratory, music, dance) are combined in the orator who concentrates on voice, delivery, and gesture (10.7.9, 26). Voice appeals to the ear, gesture to the eye, and the two senses together to the soul through emotion. Of these, voice is the more important because gesture must be adapted to it. The voice may in quantity be loud and strong, or weak with variations of strong and weak; in quality it may be clear or husky, full or thin, smooth or harsh, wide or narrow in compass, rigid or flexible, sharp or flat, and great or small in lung power. Methods of producing the voice may be sharp, grave, circumflex, intense or relaxed, high or low, slow or fast in time--with all the immediate possible variations. Training improves, neglect impairs these qualities (11.3.13-21). The orator supplies the ear with all types of delivery because the voice is "like the strings of a musical instrument," slack and deep, or tight and shrill and thin (11.3.42). The first element of good delivery is evenness. Also important are variety of tone, the adaptation of tone to the various subjects, and the avoidance of monotony (11.3.43-46).

The harmony of gesture, expression of face, and speech (11.3.67) must change with the audience, however, and even with the speakers themselves and their judges (11.3.150). Since different tones and modulations are based on different aims, the species of rhetorical style are as countless as are the many gradations of tone in music (11.3.166-69). The orator's task is indeed great: his art is like the harp and will be perfect when all strings are "taut and in tune" (2.8.15).

Quintilian frequently stresses the musical accents of his own art. They are second only to grammatical aspects (1.4.1ff). Music is a practical skill as demonstrated by Pythagoras' heptachord or lyre--that is, by its notes, which correspond to the sounds played by the (spherical) heavenly bodies in their music (1.10.12). It is the most ancient of all liberal studies; its theory explains Plato's *Timaeus*, and even Socrates in his advanced years received instruction in lyre-playing (1.10.13). The greatest of military generals (Alexander?) played the harp and the aulos, and the armies of Sparta were inspired in war by music. "Today," unfortunately, soldiers use the tuba or trumpet (1.10.14). For Plato, the study of music was a necessity for the ideal statesman (*pace* Lycurgus), and even the Stoics thought that a wise man might well pay attention to such studies (1.10.15). Quintilian recognizes that he is really speaking about music and literature as one, and that formerly music and grammar were united with music, in each case taking the subordinate part. Archytas was patently wrong in supposing that letters are subordinate to music; the reverse is true (1.10.17).

Thus, the orator's training is not complete in the absence of rhythm and meter, an intricate study in which the ear cannot always appreciate the correct sounds of the different letters any more than it can those of the different notes for musical strings (1.4.4, 7): it cannot always distinguish Latin tenor, tone, and accent (1.5.22) and follow their laws (1.5.30). During poetic declamation, a boy's voice must be so raised and lowered--that is, so modulated--and its speed and energy so varied that he can demonstrate an understanding of what he reads. And his reading must combine dignity with charm. The result must be manly, and neither a sing-song (to which

Cicero too objected) nor an effeminate kind of modulation. Music is one of the subjects which thus, along with literature, must be studied as part of the training of the ideal orator.

Expression occurs through voice and body, then. The orator must vary his delivery of tones and rhythms according to the emotions he wants to express: sublime thoughts call for elevation, pleasing thoughts call for sweetness, ordinary thoughts require gentle utterance. All call for raising, lowering, and inflecting the voice for the purpose of stirring emotions in the hearers. Certain stories about musical effects are obviously fictitious. Though instruments alone can arouse emotions which speech cannot (1.10.25), they make the right point (1.10.26-33): the orator must pay attention to his voice, a musical concern. The orator must be able not only to invent, but also to dispose (arrange), elocute, remember, and pronounce (or act): structure and euphonious sound are his constant preoccupation.

He must also know what to avoid: affected speech, for example; the sounds of shrill women, of old men speaking tremulously, of drunkards or slaves; and also expressions of love, avarice, or fear (presumably, displays of weakness). He must not use the actor's gestures, but through art must produce the highest expression by concealing it (1.11.1-19, 4.2.39-40). He is more like the performing musician. Like the harpist, he must do several things at once, but the citharoedus has the more complicated job (1.12.3). His focal point is sound, the result of the conflict of two bodies (3.6.6) and the cause of a bewitchment of the hearer with sounds having the charm of music (9.2.5).

Oratory is a union of elements, then, and in it music plays a major role something like that of instrumental music and its effects. Dance is a medium of expression, and it is a part of oratory as an art of gesture: it has an appeal of its own, and it reveals the temper of the speaker's mind in a way comparable in everyday life to the meaning communicated by a glance or a manner of walking. (Such physical manifestations are found too in animals though they cannot speak to show anger, joy, or desire to please. Even pictures, silently and without motion, penetrate to our innermost feelings, and sometimes seem more eloquent than words themselves.) Alone, movement and gesture produce grace (11.3.68), but the focal point is always musical rhythm which draws together music, metrical feet in poetry, and movement in the human body in order to make them one art. The time-arts together make the total impression.

It may seem unusual that in ancient times the art which itself never appears to have been granted any rightful autonomy (that is, when it was "alone" as instrumental music, it was often called decadent or degenerate) should more than any of the other arts act as a model for and be an integral and integrating element of arts like grammar or literature, architecture, and speech and oratory. Music of any kind is ignored in the suggestive dictum of Simonides: *Ut pictura poesis*. This saying refers, however, to content and to the process of poetical imitation, which are not themselves aesthetic principles. For music was not a matter of content but of style. Unwittingly, the aesthetic nature of music was nevertheless recognized in other structures in sound. On the other hand, music could be thought to be flowing architecture, or architecture could be thought to be a rigidified music; music was the principle of structure in buildings as in language. It was a synaesthetic prototype. If its structural aspect as found in oratory or speech was especially attractive and beautiful, this is because structure itself was the universal, the Real, the model of human existence in everything, not only in the arts but also in conduct: the basic musical structure of the universe is both aesthetic and ethical.

But this is merely analysis. In the end, for Quintilian, oratory itself is the most attractive and noble of all the arts. It is a complete whole, whereas music falls into two parts: (1) its own practice, and (2) its "theory," the latter productive of the "rhetoric" which the former can only accompany. Quintilian cannot be denigrating philosophy, but he is virtually replacing it with rhetoric and its musical characteristics. To his mind these have a nobility of their own beyond that of the other crafts and techniques.

The theory of rhetoric emphasizes content and additionally the beauty of form, the latter for the sake of attractiveness, pleasure, the expression of pathos and ethical impressions and affects, and resulting actions. In ancient times, as we have learned, a slave with a musical pipe called the *tonarium* stood near the speaker, gave him his proper pitch, and helped him to adjust his pitch if his tones were too high or too low. The speaker was like a singer; he appealed to his audience out of a natural capacity based on a universal sense of hearing in both the simplest man and the most sophisticated. Ideally, his appearance, voice, modulated language as required for understanding, and gesture were a totality. The practical Romans in public speech and in dramatic and oratorical delivery approximated something like the broadly ethical effects the Greeks expected of music. Cicero and Quintilian, the classical teachers of rhetoric in Roman times, came near to describing the ancient *triune choreia* but as realized by a single speaker, who, using all the thought and technical musical effects at his disposal, proved himself the vessel of wisdom for his hearers.

It is clear that in the days of the Roman empire there were no works on music comparable to the writings of Aristoxenus. The collection of questions and observations of Pseudo-Aristotle (probably more Alexandrian than Roman) was not a work conforming to a single plan. Acoustical in approach, it yet made one of the earliest attempts to describe the source of musical pleasure. What the Romans left behind were incidental remarks and observations about music which were part of other writings. Like Greek literature and critical commentary, however, the extant Latin theory is probably only fragmentary and our understanding of it is hence probably very incomplete.

Furthermore, though Cicero in his incomplete *Commonwealth* discourses on the Vision of Er through Scipio's Dream, one finds it hard to be convinced that the doctrine of the music of the spheres and the theory that music is an integral part of the world of Being were generally accepted. One detects not scientific dogma, but literary interest. In the end, for all the people here discussed--all living within the century-and-one-half before Christ except for Quintilian--music is not a reflection of universal processes but rather a creation of naturalistic man. The more attractive, literary, and legendary accounts of its effects and its alliance with cults and mysteries are traditional, and Ovid, Virgil, and Varro, who could make them seem matters of history, establish this clearly. Lucretius, for whom divinity was suspect, described it in terrestrial-evolutionary terms. Even the doctrine of number, transcendental and mystical in import in earlier times, loses its cosmic significance and serves only as explanation of craft-like and technical principles in poetry and song, to say nothing of grammar. It also comes as no surprise that there should be skepticism at the hands of Philodemus and the Stoics about the effects attributed to music by the Greeks.

Despite the frequent recognition of the usefulness of music in social occasions involving eating, drinking, and fun, therefore, the Roman attitude towards music as handed down to us is sober, non-symbolical, moralistic when moralism applies: music is chiefly an accompaniment of and surely not a substitute for what is a matter of intellect, of the higher things in life. The idea that music can be devotional, as Diogenes the Babylonian maintained, is exceptional and probably derived from Plato. Duty, morality, and political responsibility seem closer to the facts.

During the Renaissance, and at one point (by Nicolo Vicentino in 1555) quite directly, it was said that rhetoric is the true original of music. By this time it was assumed that music should do what rhetoric had done so well--but for a different purpose.

VII
Hebraism and Hellenism

The Peripatetic philosophers, who remained genuinely Greek in character, had effected a move from Athens to Alexandria where they had access to the magnificent Museum and its manuscripts of Greek, Egyptian, Babylonian, Hebrew, and Indian works. Because of the character of this city, they probably also were affected by a new element which would influence music aesthetics both directly and indirectly for centuries into the future. This element was Hebraic.

Alexander's city, which in approximately 300 B.C. had seen the writing of Euclid's *Elements* and possibly also his *Canon*, now had become cosmopolitan. Though the Jewish seat of power still lay in Jerusalem, Jewish people had begun to move to Alexandria as soon as it was established. There they joined a Greek population with which they strove for a civic power that was continually denied to them, while Greek political activity, still under Roman domination, increased. Here and elsewhere many Jews took up the Greek language and thus were Hellenized; significantly, the learned among them helped to prepare a Greek translation of the Hebrew Old Testament, the famous Septuagint which, begun sometime in the latter part of the third century B.C., was completed in c.130 B.C. Among religious writings by the Jews in Greek was also the important anonymous work called the *Wisdom of Solomon*. Written with the intention of promoting the mystical union of Jehovah with man and revealing Stoic and Epicurean influences as well as connections with Egyptian rites, it is now included among the apocryphal books. Here Wisdom is personified as a divine agent in the government of the world, and she is further linked to the destiny of the Jewish people. This book has also been compared to early Christian writings, especially those of St. Paul, and we are reminded that, most important, out of adherents to the Jewish religion there rose a sect of people who would eventually be called Christians.

The new religion would put its mark on the idea of music. It would complete a new trend initiated by the outstanding member of the Jewish school in Alexandria, the scholar and philosopher Philo of Alexandria. Like many new trends of significance, Philo's approach to music was relatively unperceived, especially among thinkers of the West. Thus while the Pseudo-Aristotelians, legend-purveyors like Pseudo-Plutarch, theorists like Cleonides (who, it will be recalled, "supplemented" the work of Aristoxenus), and scientists and mathematicians like Nicomachus of Gerasa,

Theon of Smyrna, and Ptolemy added new insights to the Greek theory that music is a universal phenomenon, all behaved as though Philo had not been, because they pursued music not as an art but in the Greek manner as a mathematical science of universal import. The below-ground stream of Philonic theory, however, eventually became the full coursing river of Roman and Christian music philosophy.

I

Philo of Alexandria (Philo Judaeus). As a representative of Hellenistic Jewish philosophy, Philo of Alexandria (c.20 B.C.-c.50 A.D.) has been called the Jewish Plato, partly because he tried to harmonize the thought of Plato, Aristotle, and other Greeks with the Pentateuch and partly because his philosophy was closely related to a rising Neoplatonism. He thought that God had created the Ideas which are imminent to his mind, because without beautiful prototypes nothing beautiful could be created (*On the Creation* 4). Philo himself was an intense and passionate servant of religion, and, like the Greek Stoics, he thought that allegory was a way of wrenching essence out of experience, of mediating between religious faith and learning--and between revealed religion and scientific knowledge. He thought that all wisdom was embedded in the Scriptures and that the discovery of the full range of this wisdom must depend on transcending literal interpretations of the Old Testament. The object, then, was to discover those meanings which were hidden behind the literal meaning of the words. A text, he insisted, required allegorical interpretation. Thus Philo's attention as focused on the works of the psalmists became crucial for his interpretation of the meaning of music. While the date of the Psalms is now in dispute, with some modern scholars suggesting a date in the tenth century B.C. (nineteenth-century scholarship had dated them in the fifth century B.C.), these ancient writings from Jerusalem became, in the work of this Alexandrian writer, highly important texts and sources of musical knowledge. Hebraism and Hellenism were thus joined, and they remained joined in the thought of Clement of Alexandria (c.150-220 A.D.) and other Fathers of the early Church.

Philo believes with Aristotle that all art is imitation (*On Drunkenness* 22.90.390) and that musical imitation should calm the passions and through catharsis return the soul to order (*The Sacrifice of Cain and Abel* 37-38, 168). Because it is a sensuous art, however, music as such is of no concern; in fact, its sensuous tendency is its chief hindrance to true knowledge (*The Migration of Abraham* 10.437; 4.137; 52.444; 4.16). Since it can be the mother of the madness in any soul which associates with it, the wise man must treat it with caution: his first duty is to achieve liberation from all desire and all emotion (*Allegorical Interpretation* 140-41, 115). Philo thus replaces the Greek aristocrat free from hand labor with the neoplatonic religious man free in mind because he is insulated against earthly wants and feelings. It follows as a corollary that music has the task of eliminating, if it can, repugnant currents from our spiritual lives. As Clement of Alexandria (*Miscellanies* 1.29) was to suggest later, we must not overlook the mistress (the soul and religion) and be seduced by the love-potion of the servant.

But music is a servant also to philosophy. In this respect it is an encyclopedic number-science. Like the Pythagoreans, Plato, and the Stoics, Philo sees an intimate connection between heaven and earth (*On the Creation* 168, 4), and also vaguely adopts what he knows of the musical system of the Greeks (*Preliminary Studies* 75-77, 530). Returning to the number symbolism of the Pythagoreans, which he "biblicized," he holds that anything not worthy of being comprehended by number is not sacred but profane (*On the Posterity of Cain* 28, 243). He himself preferred the numbers 4, 6, 7, and 10, among others (*Who is the Heir, passim*). The concept of number is of universal significance for him, as it was for the Greeks.

Before a writer and imposter who called himself Dionysius the Areopagite (now called the Pseudo-Areopagite), writing c.500, adjusted Christian imagery to the idea of the music of the spheres, Philo had already transformed Plato's Daimon into the Judaeo-Christian God, a change for which the Scriptures provided the clue. When we hear the harmony of the spheres, Philo thinks, we are like Moses on the fortieth day of his fast; we then resemble the divine (*On Dreams* 1.36, 626; 5.314-15). Heavenly harmony is the very archetype of all musical instruments; through its structure, songs devoted to the honor of the highest God are accompanied musically (ibid. 37, 626). The seven-string lyre, the guide of all musical instruments, is the earthly copy of heavenly harmonies. Since everything in the universe is ordered numerically, the harmony of the soul is analogous to that of the universe--and also to a well-tuned lyre which produces the best consonance of all (*The Unchangeableness of God* 24-25, 276)--as well as to the (earthly) fourth, fifth, octave, and double octave (*Preliminary Studies* 76, 530). The number 7 especially has descended from heaven to earth; it is the source of the harmonic relations of the arts (*The Unchangeableness of God* 12-14, 274). Number 4 is related not only to the other numbers, but also to the elements and the seasons. In all of this, Philo is like his Greek allegorist predecessors, the Stoics--or like Democritus, who tried to find hidden meanings behind literal ones ("Man is a universe in little"; *Ancilla*, p. 99), or Empedocles, or Zeno, who sought natural principles and moral ideas in symbolized form in all legends and in the poetry of Homer and Hesiod.

For Philo, human beings fall into three classes: (1) those who are caught up in a life of the senses, (2) those who explore the outer world, and (3) those whose world is the super-sensuous and divine. The arts of human beings must and can never be an end in themselves. They are rather the initial steps toward philosophy and must never be followed entirely; indeed, anyone who pursues them is exposed to the danger of being enchained by their enchantments and of being deflected from higher purposes. In the relationship between the earthly and the divine, the number-symbolism of the harmony of the spheres is the important mediating factor. We do not hear the harmony--not because our senses are not attuned to it, as the Pythagoreans thought, and not because our mortal state means a loss of universal harmony, but because if we heard it, we would be at one with God. And to achieve such an almost impossible oneness, we must adopt the attitude of contemplation, an attitude and state both Pythagorean and Neoplatonic.

Alongside contemplation is ecstasy. Philo finds it in the Platonic *Symposium* (209-11). For him it is even more significant than it was for Plato because it delineates the sole avenue to a participation in the super-sensuous. As we are penetrated by the divine light, we are transported out of ourselves and even out of our consciousness (*Who is the Heir* 15, 475); and thus every wise person can be a prophet who, like a musical instrument, serves the spirit of God. For classical Greek thinkers, ecstasy was an exceptional event; for Philo it is the enduring spiritual state of a good man.

In stressing ecstasy he anticipates the mystic states of Neoplatonists like Plotinus, Porphyry, and Proclus and of the Christian saints. It is a means of sharing in the super-sensuous world which supplants the sensuous sphere that one is able to forsake for the divine light (ibid. 16-17, 484-85). The nine heavens and the nine Muses themselves as they sang offered harmony to man for his imitation, and the resulting ecstasy is ultimately only a recognition of the presence of harmony, mortal, universal, and divine.

Philo writes his own hymn to harmony (*The Sacrifice of Abel and Cain* 6.37-38, 168). The tension and relaxation of the well-tunedness of the soul (of which Aristotle spoke) can be regarded metaphorically as indeed belonging to an instrument, but a moral one. The scale itself is made up not of high and low, but of moral opposites which the soul keeps in an equal tension in a "concord of virtues and things naturally beautiful" (*On the Unchangeableness of God* 6.24). Such a soul is a perfect instrument fashioned by nature, and the pattern is made by our own hands. The perfectly adjusted soul will produce the most beautiful symphony (concord) in the world, by way not of cadences and melodies in sound, but of consistency in action in life. It is in the state of contemplation and internal harmony that we celebrate the All-Highest with songs of praise and with hymns--not with loud voices, however, but with those attuned to our invisible and pure spirit (*Noah's Work as a Planter* 30.126, 348). As the Church Fathers were to say, *Non voce sed cor canere* ("sing not with your voice but with your heart"). The model of all Christian hymns was to be the song of Jesus and his disciples at the Last Supper: as the Authorized Version reads, "And when they had sung an hymn, they went out into the mount of Olives" (*Matthew* 26.30).

Thus according to Philo music is in a subordinate place because it is in the service of God and secondary to him. It is in the position of every-thing else in the universe. It is not an autonomous art, but a mediating one; it should not be musically (that is, sensuously) beautiful but religiously serviceable. Plotinus later tried to find beauty-as-such in art-as-such. But Philo, who knew the works of Homer, Euripides, Plato, Parmenides, Empedocles, Zeno, and Cleanthes, was less attracted by beauty in the abstract and in its apparent mirroring of number and universal order than by a reflective, mystical, and religious type of humanism.

Philo shared his Eastern influence on young Christianity with other Neoplatonists like Plutarch and Nicomachus of Gerasa in the first century A.D., Plotinus, Porphyry, and Iamblichus in the third century A.D., and Proclus, Macrobius, and Martianus Capella in the fifth century.   In Neoplatonism, Neopythagoreanism, and the Judaic-Alexandrian philosophy and number-symbolism, the Church Fathers frequently recognized their own spiritual bent. Like Philo, they thought that music achieves and maintains its importance only as a servant of religion. They too frequently interpreted it allegorically and symbolically. Philo, with the Stoics and Neoplatonists, began what the Church Fathers continued, and, though a Neoplatonist like Plotinus recognized in music a beauty for its own sake, the Church Fathers held to Philo's view that music best serves men when it facilitates an understanding of the Scriptures and turns men's minds toward the Eternal.

Only after almost two centuries did the influence of Philo of Alexandria exert its full effect, an influence as *sub rosa* as it was germinal. By the year 220 A.D., when Clement of Alexandria died, the Greek idea of music had been once and for all surveyed by Aristides Quintilianus, a Neoplatonic Greek living in Smyrna, and Christianity itself had been established, not necessarily as a startlingly new and "foreign" religion, but as an offshoot of a Judaic group whose members refused to worship the Roman emperor. From Plutarch to Boethius (d. 524 A.D.), sometimes called the first great medieval thinker, musical speculation followed two paths: (1) that of the Hellenists, Neoplatonists, and Neopythagoreans, who added their own symbolical and mystical adjustments to the ancient Greek idea of music; and   (2) that of the Neoplatonist-Hebraic Philo whose religious philosophy was in part adopted by the Fathers of the rising Christian Church.   Beginning in Asia Minor and also especially in Alexandria, this Church carried a basically new musical idea to the West, eventually to make it Roman and European.

II

Plutarch and Pseudo-Plutarch. I have several times referred to the pseudonymous work attributed to the Greek biographer and Platonic moralist Plutarch (48-120 A.D.). The foremost man of letters of his day, Plutarch himself was a conservative whose primary interest was the moral speculation and general thought of the past. He was educated in Athens and taught at Rome. His remarks about music are published in his *Moralia*. He found pleasure not, apparently, in music itself but in musical theory, which "makes the lover forget his passion" (*A Pleasant Life Impossible* 109). Cicero-like and equally self-righteously perhaps, he chides the Epicureans for rejecting the pleasures of the contemplative and intellectual life and for avoiding discussions of choruses and the production of plays--and for ignoring questions about "double [*auloi*] and rhythms and harmonies" and about why the chromatic genus relaxes the hearer whereas the harmonic makes him tense (ibid. 1096). Not music itself, but theory and analysis are intellectual and passion-dispelling, and are better than passion itself.

In his *Table Talk* (or *Symposiacs*), he approves of singing accompanied with wine, especially that of the *scholia*, usually performed impromptu to the lyre's accompaniment, whether by one person or many. Singing is characteristic of men who drink in moderation (3.1.645), he says, especially on occasions like victory celebrations (1.10.628). At a drinking party, he thinks, music is more appropriate than philosophy (1.1.613). It may have the virtues of a mean between extremes. Like Theophrastus, he thinks that music is attached to the passions alone, primarily those of sorrow, joy, and religious ecstasy (1.5.623).

Thus Plutarch subscribes to the intellectual's view: Callistratus says that music can cause lascivious dancing and encourage effeminacy; it can be more intoxicating than wine; it is not really a more proper preoccupation for men than for irrational animals. We must secure ourselves against it, he says, against the misleading pleasures of songs, cadences, and tunes, which are more corrupting than the finest cooking or perfume because they affect our intellectual and judgmental faculties. In these words, Lamprias supplements Callistratus' words: when we are intoxicated by the Muses, we should fly to the helicon of the ancients, to Euripides, Pindar, and Menander (7.5.706)--that is, to literary ideas and not to music.

Plutarch exhibits all the contradictions and inconsistencies which seem to be the delight of the dialogue or symposium writer. He allows the ardent lover of music to be the best qualified judge of that art (*Table Talk* 4.4.668). But while he himself is possibly a lover and expert of music, he may also be neither. His conservative and authority-ridden mind allows him to say that harmonious instruments like the lyre, the harp, pipes, and *auloi* make no sense except as they accompany songs and strains of grief and joy, and only then as they accord with human experiences to reproduce the judgments, feelings, and morals of the people who use them: as Zeno has said, gut and sinew, word and bone send forth the harmony and music which partake of reason, rhythm, and order (*On Moral Virtue* 443). No wonder he did not completely agree that planets make up a cosmic instrument, of which the earth is the lowest of the strings on the universal harp. Yet he thought that the distances between the speeds of the stars were in proportions parallel with those of musical instruments (*On the Generation of the Soul in the* Timaeus 1027-29).

Like Cicero, Plutarch writes his own version of the *Timaeus* 35-36. He addresses his extensive remarks to his two sons, but rather than applying Platonic principles to politics, as Cicero did, he explains these principles in mathematical terms. Pointing to Plato's description of the soul, he emphasizes the World-Soul and rejects all astronomical interpretations because he thinks Plato meant ratios and numbers to represent the harmony and concord of the Soul (1029-30). He recalls the Sirens of Plato's *Republic* (617), each of them singing a single tone which blends with the others to make a single concord; free from strain as they chant, they "entwine" things divine into a harmony of eight notes "over the sacred circuit of the dance." Neoplatonically, Plutarch thinks the Soul, both contemplative and practical, guides heavenly bodies, reorganizes the chaotic and stupid soul according to concords and numbers, and gives to all things, even those lacking sense, potentialities, including those sometimes found in medicine. The product of all fixed ratios is the soul's harmony and concord with itself (1030). Plutarch makes the familiar comparison between speech and musical sound, contrasts the thought-properties of the former with the proportional characteristics of the latter, and brings together the ideas that the affective part of the soul is indeterminate and unstable and that limits are put on it by motion, visible and variable (1026). He makes a digest of Greek musical-mathematical theory based on Plato (1027-30), contrasting the simultaneous and separate striking of intervallic tones, and finds that the tones of music in their mathematical arrangements regulate the soul. Thus, he demonstrates that he is a Neoplatonic contemporary of Nicomachus of Gerasa and Theon of Smyrna.

The name of Plutarch has also been applied by commentators to an equally learned but pseudonymous writer of uncertain date who was likewise a Neoplatonist. The title of his book reads: *On Music: Concerning the Archaic and Classical periods of Greek music. Excerpts from the works of Plato, Aristotle, Heraclides Ponticus, Aristoxenus, and others, brought together into two discourses ostensibly carried on by the musician Lysis and the philosopher Soterichus in the home of Plutarch's teacher Onesicrates of Chaeronia on the second day of the Saturnalia.* Lysis and Soterichus represent the Peripatetics and the Platonists, respectively, and are parallel with the Epicureans and the Stoic-Platonists in Cicero. However, Pseudo-Plutarch is more squarely in the Neoplatonic camp than Cicero. This work is less a dialogue than two reports inviting comment.

Soterichus points out that Lysis, the performing musician, who dwells on "not only . . . music, but . . . the whole round of the liberal arts" (1135), depends on written accounts, whereas he himself follows other sources such as hymns and statues. And Pseudo-Plutarch himself asks the question, why is there not more agreement about music among the Platonists and the best of the Peripatetics (1131)? Lysis tells his side of the story, which is sometimes legendary and sometimes "real."

In ancient times, music was a study of grammarians and students of harmonics. Under the banner of letters and rhetoric, or culture, it benefited family, city, nation, and race more than did military exploits. The host, Onesicrates, says that human voice was its focal point. "Beaten air perceptible to hearing" is what the grammarians called vocal sound, and it had two parts: the one was grammar and letters, used for preserving vocal utterances in memory; the other was music, or "an act of piety and a principal concern of man as he sings hymns to the gods, who granted articulated speech to him alone . . ." (1131).

Relying on Heraclides, Lysis recounts the history of the origins of music in Amphion (son of Zeus and Antiope, who invented music in his cithara-accompanied poetry), in Linus of Euboea (who composed dirges), in Anthes of Anthedon in Boeotia (who wrote hymns), in Pierus of Pieria (who wrote poems on the Muses), in Philammon (who set up choruses at Delphi), in Thamyris of Thrace (the very challenger of the Muses themselves), in Demodocus in Homer (*Od.* 8.266-366, 499-520), and in Phemis of Ithaca in the *Odyssey* (1.325-27). All of these, commonplace in history or legend, represent vocal music (1132). And all, whether poet or musician, adhered strictly to the rules. Sacadas of Argos, mentioned by Pindar, was a composer of music, a writer of elegaic verse set to music, and an aulete. He offers an example of modulation from one mode or system of music to another: he wrote a chorus called *trimeles* (three-aired) because each of three strophes was in a different system of "tuning"--that is, first in Dorian, then in Phrygian, and finally in Lydian. Unfortunately, however, it became fashionable not to follow the *nomoi* exactly, and in the time of Phrynis simplicity was abandoned, as was the *nome*, harmonic or rhythmic, in any piece (1132-33).

Lysis also makes much of instrumental music, undervalued by Plato but granted the power of imitating and representing character by Aristotle. Greece must have had important music for instruments alone, for Olympus (a descendant of the elder Olympus, the disciple of Marsyas) composed a *nome* for *auloi* in honor of Apollo. It was called "many-headed" (by Athena because according to Pindar [*Odes* 12] it imitated the lament of the Gorgons). And this Olympus had many successors (1133).

Then there are the musical genera--diatonic, chromatic, and enharmonic, the last of which comes first from the hands of the elder Olympus (1134-35). Rhythms too occurred in genera and species. There was the lofty and noble manner of rhythm, sometimes abandoned for purposes of novelty, popularity, or the "mercenary" so that restriction to a few notes of simplicity and grandeur in music had become obsolete (1135).

Thus Lysis. For Soterichus, however, music is not earth-bound. The inventor of music was not a man, but the god Apollo, who created both the cithara and the aulos. Thus music, "in every way a noble pursuit," is an invention of the gods (1135-36). But, alas, modern corruption has entered in: the ancient respect for dignity is gone and "effeminate twittering" in the theater replaces the "music of former days, strong, inspired, and dear to the gods. . . ." Such effeminate music had been deplored by Plato along with the Lydian mode (*Rep.* 398ff), "high-pitched and appropriate to lamentation." The Mixolydian suits passion while the Dorian has grandeur and dignity, and the two were blended in tragedy. Thus Plato rejected the plaintive Lydian as well as the enervated Mixolydian, and championed the noble gravity of the Dorian (1136). These modes--three among many of which the ancients knew--were preferable to those which carried "variation and many notes. . . ." The use of certain notes, indeed, caused singers to be ashamed because of the moral character they expressed in certain contexts. Thus tragic poets did not use the chromatic genus, though a far older music, that of the cithara, used it from the very beginning. Its use was clearly a matter not of ignorance, but of choice (1137).

Choices were everywhere in evidence in ancient times. Thus the great ancients on principle avoided "the chromatic genus, modulation, multiplicity of notes" and "rhythms, scales, styles of poetical or musical composition and rendition" that were current in their time. Choice, not ignorance, was the determining factor. Even rhythm: it was more complex in the past than now, and was cherished, while the interplay of the accompaniment was more varied because the ancients liked the beat (whereas the moderns like the tune). They preferred music not over-modulated on principle. Thus Plato rejected forms of music because they were inimical to the state, not because he did not know of them.

Soterichus goes to even greater lengths to prove Plato's undoubted familiarity with universal harmonies. The *Timaeus* (35-36) is examined for that purpose: mathematics and music are distinguished; so are the arithmetical, harmonic, and geometrical means; the harmony of the four elements of the soul and the concord produced by two dissimilars of the soul by means of musical ratio; the duple ratio (6, 8, 9, 12) of the octave. All of these prove Plato's study and knowledge of mathematics and its relation to music (1138-39).

Nor is Aristotle ignorant of the mathematics of music as a divine and august creation. For him, the body itself is made up of concordant dissimilarities, like those of music. The octave or harmony itself has four terms, the constituents and terms being even, odd, and even-odd. Harmony is concordant with itself as a whole and with its parts (1139-40). All is consistent with the senses themselves: sight and hearing are celestial, divine, and in a harmony revealed in sound and light (*On the Soul* 425b-426b). The other senses, inferior to sight and hearing "being divine" but not separated from them because they are in the train of the first two, also conform in harmony (*Pseudo-Plut.* 1140). And this very harmony is the basis of Greek education.

Soterichus describes a complete catalogue of evidences that the Greeks had employed music for educational reasons. Music would have molded and modulated the minds of the young and made them graceful in bearing in all occasions, in serious activities, and in war with its perils. The Lacedemonians used the aulos in war, the Cretans the lyre, and others the trumpet. Music was used for wrestling matches and pentathletic contests. Before theaters were set up, temples were the home of music. But now, the educational purpose of music has been abandoned, and only the music of the theater remains (as the Pseudo-Aristotelians too seem to complain).

The catalogue continues in answer to a question: Did the Greeks, then, never engage in innovation in music? The answer is, of course, yes, but not at the expense of nobility and decorum. Terpander invented several modes and verse feet and the *scholion* sung at banquets. Archilochus invented a rhythmical system, declamation with instrumental accompaniment, various verse feet, and accompaniments "of higher pitch than the song" (an elementary or archaic organum?). Others invented additional modes and rhythms, expanded music beyond its original confines, and, when auletes were no longer paid by the poets they accompanied, they themselves established a more complex music. The last, however, made up of added strings, many key-shifts, new and strange modes, small intervals, and rapid notes, became undisciplined and the butt of comic jokes (1141).

Pseudo-Plutarch himself was clearly on Soterichus' side on this subject. Order, sobriety, virtue--these are the rewards. Thus Aristoxenus, writing on Telesias of Thebes, illustrates that music can rectify or pervert the taste and perceptions of the mind (1142). Musical education encourages the adoption of the noble and the generous in youths, the rejection of their contraries, and the pursuit of decorum, temperance, and regularity. There is only one conclusion: whoever expects to have a just taste and discernment in music in order to use it for rational and laudable purposes must follow the ancient model, and he must perfect his knowledge of music with the help of all other branches of science, especially philosophy (1142). It appears that Pseudo-Plutarch would institute a Platonic renaissance.

In one sense he was almost an original: generally non-innovative in an age of theoretically prescribed social, political, and moral law and order, he seemed to initiate the idea that law is not the final word in the creation or judgment of art. His historical sense allowed him to see that new laws constantly struggle to supplement or transcend old ones. True, he called for the fashionable return to old ways, and he was not the first nor the last to call for simplicity. But laws are not created in advance, and he expanded the doctrine of Aristoxenus that the musician should decide what genera are required by the character and sentiment of certain verses and what styles of composition and execution contribute to the same end (1142). He found the usual method of instruction (of the "freeman") too restricted: music should cover the curriculum since, as part of the world and therefore having its share in the encyclopedia of knowledge--and as a symbol of world harmony--it is a universal element with mysterious, magical, and religious powers.

III

Nicomachus of Gerasa. Pseudo-Plutarch concluded with a grand reference to the music of the spheres. Nicomachus of Gerasa, in Arabia Petraea (fl. 100 A.D.), the Neopythagorean and Neoplatonic philosopher and mathematician, in his *Introduction to Harmonics* stresses number-theory and also conjectures about the music of the stars. His little treatise was written at the request of a noble lady and is admittedly brief and incomplete. Somewhat younger than Quintilian and professing to follow

Pythagoras, Nicomachus, like many philosophers and men of letters, again took up the threads of thought of the great age of Greek philosophy; he was an eclectic in whom are intermingled Pythagorean, Platonic, Aristotelian, and Stoic elements.   His primary sources were Apollonius of Tyana, a Greek Neopythagorean traveller and, by reputation, a magician; and Aristoxenus--the former for biography and the latter, through certain lost or extant works, for mathematical philosophy, music, and medicine.   He also drew on the *Timaeus*.   Thus the *Arithmetic* and *Harmony* form a consistent whole.

Nicomachus follows the Platonic idea of the Forms, which are eternal and not subject to change: they are real as things themselves, caught in a changing Heraclitean flux, are not. Number is the clue to the mystery, and thus he attempts (*Arith*. 1.2, 2.24) to explain the mathematical principles in the different passages about the world-soul in the *Timaeus* (35ff) and the marriage number in the *Republic* (546-47).   Things are twofold: those which in themselves constitute a coherent and indivisible whole, and those which can be reduced to individual parts. Consequently, the sciences are twofold: (1) arithmetic and music are concerned with multiplicity or multitudes, that is, separables, arithmetic with multiplicity itself (it is the foundation of all other sciences), and music with the mutual relation of one element and another; and (2) geometry and astronomy are concerned with inseparable unities (that is, multitudes), the former with the unmoving and the latter with the moving unities *(Arith*. 1.3).   Here in Nicomachus is in fact the quadrivium, named later by Boethius, which out of its germ in Archytas and in Plato's *Republic* (523-34) developed into a staple of scientific theory.

To put the classification differently: quantity is (or multitudes are) of two kinds: (1) that having no relation to anything else, absolute and discrete quantity: arithmetic; and   (2) that relative to something else; relative quantity, mutual relations, ratio, proportion: music. Size (or magnitude) is of two kinds: (1) a state of rest and stability, continuous, unchanging: geometry; and (2) a state of motion, revolving, changing: astronomy.

For Nicomachus, the harmony of numbers is evidence of good order, fellowship, and cooperation. Indeed, numbers are the source of energy: they are dynamic, convey qualities, and sometimes take on human characteristics (*Arith*. 1.14-16).   They are symbols reflecting the universe of things. For Nicomachus the use by the Greeks of the seven Ionian vowels for the seven planets and the sounds they supposedly produce illustrates that number pre-exists in the mind of God; it is number immaterial and conceptual and the true essence of everything created--that is, of time, motion, the heavens, the stars, and the entire revolution of celestial being (*ibid*. 1.6).   For Nicomachus the vowels are divine numbers through which the immaterial nature of God is revealed.

Unity, that Greek passion which comes to a head in the thought of Speusippus, is the basis of theory, and Harmonia remains its symbol. Harmonic ratios are arithmetic ones (1.5.1), though the three-dimensional proportion of the cube is the proportion properly called harmony (2.29.1) and the formula for this perfect proportion is 6, 8, 9, 12 (2.29.1-3) (called *harmonia perfecta* by the Middle Ages). Scientific number, which is superior to everything, pre-existed in the mind of God; it governs everything in the universe, because that which is harmoniously constituted is also in accord with itself (1.6.1-2). The stars, therefore, exist in a perfectly harmonious state, as do string and blown instruments (1.5.2), though everything harmoniously knit together is made up of opposites of real things--of those things which not only are real, but also are different and in some relation to one another (1.6.2, 2.19.1). Sounds, the elements of melody (2.1.1), too are governed by harmonic proportions. Nicomachus believes he is following Pythagoras (though it may be Aristoxenus) in dividing sounds into the ruleless, non-measurable ones of speech and the intervallic, measurable ones of singing (*Harm.* 1.2). It is the latter which exist in proportions or ratios.

Unlike Euclid, Nicomachus is not devoted to pure number to the exclusion of its possible symbolical meaning. Pure mathematics, like pure music, cannot satisfy his mind. Numbers 1 to 10, he thinks, are divine and represent gods and goddesses. The number 5 and others are symbolical of even other realities.

He treats number 1 extensively and almost lyrically: it is the *monad*; it begins all numbers and all things; it is the divine itself, and it is reason; it is the form of all forms, harmony, goodness, excellence, and the basis of natural things; it is represented by Apollo, the sun, and Atlas. Number 2 is inequality or difference, opposition, change, contrast--though also equality. From it derive multiplicity and division, and consonance in music, where it is called harmony. Three is the first perfect number, the first which is beginning, middle, and end--all three, but also the sum of the first two numbers. It means perfection in all areas, especially in ethics, where it is the source of all goodness. It is the special governor of music. Number 4 is the potential of 10 (4 + 3 + 2 + 1), the quadrivial number, the number of elements, heavenly powers, seasons, virtues, and the species of being. In music the four (tones) embrace the three perfect consonances. The four numbers are the harmony of the soul.

Five has no connection with music, but 6 symbolizes the harmony of the soul (Nicomachus followed Aristoxenus in thinking of the octave as made up of six whole steps, in contrast to the Pythagorean division). It is the source of the three perfect consonances, and it has its effect in the harmony of the types (or species). Seven is the root of the phenomenon of sound in the entire cosmos, the harmony of the seven planets, the seven-string lyre, an important element in the creation of the world--and all Becoming and Growth. Eight is 4 doubled and the representative of all harmony. If there is an eighth sphere (8 tones) inclusive of 7 (intervals), it is the basis of all heavenly harmony and of musical proportions. Number 9 is less rich. In musical terms it is only the largest, the sum of the number-ratios of all three consonances. But 10 is the God of Gods.

Taking the mathematical stance, Nicomachus follows Pythagoras and his handling of the tetrachord; from the mythological standpoint, he believes that Mercury invented the lyre; and with reference to the symbolical-allegorical, he declares that Saturn, in motion the planet farthest from us, produces the gravest (lowest) sound, the moon producing the most acute (highest). In descending order, Saturn through Jupiter, Mars, Sol (the sun), Venus, Mercury, and Luna (the moon) give their names to musical sounds, and, making up two planetary scales, they take their places in the zodiac (*Harm.* 2.3). We cannot hear these intervals, of course, but reason locates them with clarity.

Nicomachus became the mathematician most frequently quoted because his arithmological observations were renewals of thought supporting current "science" and tradition. He had returned to universal arithmetical "music" in which--and especially so in the "harmonic" branch of number as defined by Archytas--there explicitly lay the idea of ratio: it was through the ratio-as-form in Aristotle that Nicomachus demonstrated the nature of the consonance. Basically and physically, the consonance is a two-in-one, a separate two which together sound like one. The very blending is a unity. Nicomachus' design is to classify Being (*Arith.* 2.26.1), and it must include the opposite of unity, which is the non-blending of dissonances. Thus the octave or number 8 as a supreme blend could be a symbol of the universe (*Harm.* 1.16), the basis of heavenly harmony and of musical proportion (probably as declared by Philolaus [*Ancilla*, p. 74]) and the essence of a truly mystical Neoplatonic mathematics.

But Nicomachus' ratio, like that of his predecessors in mathematics, was musically static. Music moves, and the relationships within it are constantly changing. While custom and habit, supported by Pythagorean mathematics, have decreed that a few of its relationships are unalterable, they too pile up in metaphysical and metaphorical space to undergo continual transformation, both among themselves and accompanied by imperfect ratios. Like his predecessors, Nicomachus identified the constant, permanent, universal ratios as perfect. The perfection he recognized, however, was only something guaranteed by reason and not by a universal ear. It was the perfection of rationally ordered universal harmony.

In his translation into Latin of Nicomachus' *Arithmetic*, Boethius later ignored its mystical and numerological aspects and favored the philosophy of number and ratio as applied to sound alone. (Of rhythm, as of the actual music current in his day, Nicomachus said nothing.) Thus, Boethius tacitly ignored Nicomachus' role as Neoplatonic allegorist *par excellence*; at the same time, Nicomachus' *Arithmetic* continued to be a popular basic text throughout medieval and renaissance Europe.

IV

Theon of Smyrna. Theon of Smyrna was probably a contemporary of Nicomachus. Neither refers to the other, but both find a magical and mystical character in the universality of the mathematico-music (or musico-mathematics) they describe. Theon relies more closely on Plato (*Timaeus* 35-36), though both employ Pythagorean calculation. Theon mentions Archytas, Aristotle, Adrastus (Aristotle's pupil in mathematics and harmony), Philolaus, Plato, Eudoxus (Plato's pupil), and also others, all in large part Pythagoreans. Both Nicomachus and Theon stand in contrast to Euclid, who separated number and especially geometrical science from mystical speculation and almost completely from philosophy. For them, number, metaphysical and mystical thought, and cosmology were practically one subject. Mathematical and spiritual insight of life are combined within the spiritual Oneness of the universe. Theon's major work here is *Mathematical Principles Useful for the Study of Plato*. It too is a textbook.

Theon, like Nicomachus, starts from Unity: God, the soul, the beautiful, the good, all essences like beauty and justice, and equality are one. One as a number is unmixed, cannot go beyond itself--that is, cannot be changed through self-multiplication. It is the beginning of everything, the permanent, identity, reason, the Idea, substance, like and unlike; if it is not reality, it is the possibility of everything. For the other numbers and especially the *tetractys*, Theon takes positions similar to those of Nicomachus.

But more frequently than Nicomachus he quotes Plato, especially the spurious *Epinomis*. To know Plato, he thinks, one must first thoroughly understand geometry, music, and astronomy (p. 1). Palamedes in Plato (*Rep.* 522) believes that Agamemnon's lack of power to rule is probably due to his not knowing number. Like Plato, Theon censures the musician who deals with sound-relations instead of real number as studied by the arithmetician; the practical musician is unable to study real numbers in the scientific Platonic sense, and it is such study which leads to an understanding of the beautiful and the good. For Plato, arithmetic, a gift of God to man, is the path to virtue. And all the arts are useless if number is denied them. Thus music, the result of motion in sound, is measured by numbers, can be the source of good, but is never the cause of evil. An astronomer is like the practical musician; he scrutinizes the planets but does not employ abstract numbers, which are unconnected with matter and reveal the nature of things (p. 5). Such numbers--4, for example--govern the universe:

magnitudes: point, line, surface (the triangle), solid (pyramid)
simple bodies: fire, air, water, earth
figures of simple bodies: pyramid, octahedron, icosahedron, cube
living things: seed, growth in length, in breadth, in thickness
societies: man, village, city, nation
faculties: reason, knowledge, opinion, sensation
parts of the living creature: body and the three parts of the soul
seasons of the year: spring, summer, autumn, winter
ages: infancy, youth, manhood, old age

Numbers are harmony, and for Plato the greatest and noblest harmony is wisdom (*Laws* 689). Thus, only the philosopher is the true musician, for right reason is accompanied by decency in song, cadence in rhythm, and accord in harmony (*Math. Pr.*, p. 7), and his science--philosophy--is the initiation into holy things, into authentic mysteries (ibid., p. 8; cf. Plato, *Phaedo* 69).

Music therefore brings number, spirit, and matter all together. Though arithmetic comes first among the sciences--it is basic, the foundation of number and reason--musical mathematics comes second and enables one to understand celestial music (1.2) or the music of the spheres, which is the fifth step after arithmetic, music, astronomy, and stereometry. Music divides itself into the instrumental, the mathematical, and the spherical types (3.44). Arithmetic allows us to find the consonancy (symphony), the greatest power, the "truth to reason, fidelity in life, and harmony in nature," a harmony "diffused through the world." Consonance is an intelligible harmony, one more easily perceived than a perceptible one. For this understanding of consonancy Theon goes to the Pythagoreans (2.1), who define music as the "perfect union of contrary things, unity within multiplicity, even accord within discord." It is God's great work abstractly and mystically to "reconcile inimical things through the [harmonic] laws of medicine and music" (p. 7).

With Theon, even more than with Nicomachus, we feel ourselves in the heady realm of faith in universal mysteries leading directly back to Platonic realms of Being populated by Ideas among which are abstract numbers far removed from and superior to facts and truths identified by empirical science. It is a Platonic science denied to all practical, sensuously-bound arts and investigatively-arrived-at knowledge. It has sub-species, as it were, but they exist all together, as an imagined One, as a coherence that is accepted as though reason and pure intellection could identify it and its elements, which exist all in a blend. It is a faith in an unperceivable ontological state of things, of number in the abstract, the divine, forms in the abstract, goodness, truth, and beauty, cosmic elements (though not their "realizations"), souls, justice, equality, and, above all, relationships which make up an abstract music (which can only be "visualized" and felt as a presence and not observed). It is, of course, a Neoplatonic world that will also be found in the non-mathematical world of Plotinus, in which the human soul moves actively in a mystical relation to God and Spirit. Before Plotinus, however, in the early days of the Christian Church and the late days of Greek and Latin thought lived the greatest mathematician of them all.

V

Klaudios Ptolemy (Claudius Ptolemaeus). While Nicomachus was writing in Arabia Petraea, another Neopythagorean and Neoplatonist, Ptolemy (also second century A.D.), one of the world's universal geniuses, was probably working in Alexandria. Like all scientists of his time, he thought nature simple and unified; in such terms he designed a scheme of planetary motion made up of a dynamic agglomeration of cycles, epicycles, and other expedients to explain the observed motions of the planets. Though, according to hindsight, he may frequently have been wrong, yet he explored this subject in greater depth than had any of his predecessors; he did equally well by the science of harmonics. A systematizer, he thought that the Pythagoreans had not given sufficient attention to the ear and had expressed differences in sound by ratios which often did not conform with the physical evidence. And he believed that the Aristoxenians had ascribed chief weight to hearing-sensations and then had applied numbers, the symbols of relationships, not to differences in sound, but to intervals (of distance). Ptolemy himself tried to adjust the two faulty approaches by using the *helicon* (the harmonic monochord-like canon of his own invention) which could adjust ratios properly (1.2). And, like Nicomachus, he preferred the proportions 6, 8, 9, and 12 for the major intervals.

The first two books of his *Harmonics* are technical, and the third is in great part humanistic and psychological in the Aristotelian sense; it also contains elaborate comparisons of the music of the spheres with existence, the sciences, art, and beauty. The whole (with a second book on ratios and their measurements) adds up to a doctrine of harmony, its nature, its connection with the universe and music, and its influence on the moral man and the "affections" of the mind--in short, with every subject governed by number, proportion, or correspondence. Like Aristides Quintilianus, Ptolemy sees every aspect of life, including virtue, as a universal idea, but, more than Aristides, he "proves" his points mathematically.

Most important is the strictly harmonics section of this work by this astronomer, mathematician, and geographer of Alexandria, designer of the Ptolemaic system of astronomy and geography based on the notion that the sun, the planets, and the stars revolve around the earth--a system initially proposed by Aristarchus of Samos (third century B.C.) but rejected by his followers in astronomy. Ultimately this system would be refuted by the Polish astronomer Copernicus (1473-1543). However, Ptolemy's harmonics segment became a standard mathematical work on music and in part replaced the *Harmonics* of Aristoxenus, which for five hundred years had been used extensively by practicing musicians and teachers (who, however, were less interested in its mathematical aspect). Ptolemy himself, like Nicomachus, Aristides Quintilianus, and almost everyone else before the ninth century, in general ignored the techniques of contemporary music, though his discussion of instruments and the singing of tetrachords (1.16, 2.1-2, 16) seems to describe the music of the Roman empire of the second century A.D.[1]

His center of attention is entirely abstract, geometry, astronomy, and music in its elemental organization being related to musical instruments. His aim is to be logical, not to direct attention to practice. He presents the Greek Perfect System of modes, which included all smaller systems, and he rationalizes keys in a scheme perhaps not of his own invention. He thinks modes are limited to an octave (or seven spaces) of intervals and thus contradicts Aristoxenus' opinion that an octave is made up of six whole tones. Aristoxenes had allowed for thirteen modes, Alypius (c.360 A.D., in *An Introduction to Music*) and Aristides Quintilianus for fifteen,[2] but he thinks there can be only seven just as there are only seven harmonic proportions and only seven planets. His perfect, rational system, parallel to his astronomical system, was still another example of the attempt to realize the ideal of Harmonia;[3] his reform was aimed at providing a new and legitimate set of scales, each one made of a succession of specific intervals without regard to pitch. His theory of modes again shows that ancient speculation about a no longer existent classical Greek music lacked general agreement. Reason alone, as always, was helpless in reconstructing the actual past musical practice.

For Ptolemy, actually more Platonic than Aristoxenian, reason is simple and uniform, enclosed and organized within itself, always the same within the same relationships. But sense impression is caused by multiple-formed, inconstant, and changing matter. Perceived by hearing, an interval is either too small or too large until reason assigns it a proper mathematical ratio. The same law applies to sight, which needs help from reason for proof (of lines, circles, and so forth) and which with hearing is in the forefront of any pursuit of understanding. For the astronomer the several movements of the heavenly bodies agree with their observed limits. But seeing is not enough, and the theorist shows that in nature, whose works are created according to reason and on purpose, nothing is produced without plan, at least in the most beautiful of arrangements which appeal to sight and hearing. And it is through sight and hearing that science reveals the most beautiful world which exists (1.1).

Though sounds and hearing both have limits (1.4), together they complete one another to declare that the art of harmony is a wonderful and sublime reality. The explanation goes thus: the principles of everything existing are matter, motion, and form. Matter is an object (material) from which arise motions as cause, and through cause arises form as an end in itself. In this dynamic process, harmonic power is neither an object (it is something acting, not something taking impressions from outside) nor an aim (because it is self-contained and in itself achieves something like harmonic or rhythmic correctness and legality: like order and beauty, it is governed by laws). As a cause it gives to the formless object a determinate and genuine form (just as, for Aristoxenus, rhythm is applied to the *rhythmizomenon*). Not itself an object, harmonic power is a source of ordered and natural form.

Causes are related to (1) nature and pure being, (2) reason and excellent being, and (3) the Divine and eternally excellent being. Harmonic power is not a cause related to nature (it does not give existence to formless being), nor is it related to the Divine (because it is not a cause of eternal existence); but it is related to reason, the middle of the designated causes, which brings about the good on either of its sides. The cause related to reason falls into three parts: (1) understanding, related to the more Divine form; (2) art (craft) related to reason in the proper meaning of the word; and (3) custom and habit, related to nature. Reason is the creator of order and balance (art), and the laws of harmony which it comprehends are equally valid in the realms of hearing, sight, and judgment. Harmonic power puts an order into the sense of hearing which results in what we call harmoniously beautiful sounds in the true sense, and this occurs partly through the theoretical discovery with the help of the understanding of well-measured relations, partly through the practical production of these relations with the help of art, and partly through the consistent utilization of those practical knowledges which support custom. Reason in general, therefore, (1) finds beauty through theoretical speculation, (2) realizes the perceived through its means of expression (through the activity of hands, for example), and (3) through custom forms the formless material (object) into an identity with itself. Mathematics is concerned not only with the mathematical investigation of the beautiful, but also with the production and the practical application of such matters as fall within its realm of judgment. Sight and hearing are the avenues of such judgment. Both senses use the indispensable media of arithmetic and geometry to designate the quality and the quantity of the chief structure (not only music, but the visual arts too are now unconscious counting). Because they are of related stock, they are sister-daughters; sisters themselves, their foster-mothers are arithmetic and geometry (3.3).

Sight and hearing both present sense impressions to reason for the judgment of the presence of harmony. Low and high pitches are discovered in air moved by the hitting of something, whereupon they are sensed and perceived by the ear--and then reason makes a judgment (1.2). But sense perception causes difficulties. It is constantly subject to matter, which is many faceted and always in a state of flux. Because of this instability and inconstancy, perception, whether of all persons or even of the same person in varying states or relationships, never leads to the same observation. Yet hearing and seeing are ancillary to knowledge and the rational part of the soul. Truth is the aim: larger intervals, for example, are more easily judged correctly than small ones. Reason as leader must always supply the needed corrective.

Ptolemy thus recognizes a human variable beyond sense perception, the variable among individuals as such. The educated gentleman, aristocrat, and scholar has an easier task than the creator even though he makes the final reason-based judgment. For in general, Ptolemy says, it is easier to judge something than to make it, to judge a wrestling match than to be a wrestler, to judge dancing, aulos playing, or singing than to perform (1.1), and thus to judge music than to compose it.

The instrument for analyzing a musical object for the judgment of the presence of harmony is the harmonic canon, that is, not the monochord, but Ptolemy's own *helicon*. Sense perception receives the rough impression, which reason takes over to make into a specific, accurate understanding (1.1). Hearing judges the matter, reason judges the form and cause. The sense or ear receives and takes in the ratios of different genera, and then transfers them to the harmonic canon so that reason with the assistance of numbers can judge whether or not they are true to nature. Again, we are not far from the internal counting which Leibniz attributes to musical perception. Ptolemy supplies an example out of Aristoxenus: our perception can hear and even go so far as to identify a fifth but will clearly and unambiguously know it as such only when the canon calls it a ratio of 3:2 (1.10). "Counting," then, one kind of counting, is interval recognition by the ear supplemented by reason.

High and low are the qualities of pitch. What are the sources of quality? The answer can come from Plato and Aristotle with possible supplementary information from Vitruvius. Being acoustical considerations, they are (1) the force of the blow, (2) the physical nature of the object struck and the origin of the blow, and (3) the distance of the struck object from the beginning point of the motion. Obviously, a change can be effected if only one of these elements is altered, all others remaining the same. The material of the object (to recall Aristotle and Vitruvius) can be porous or dense, thin or thick, smooth or rough, and it may differ in form: mouth and tongue, clapper, an uproar, voice, noise, and so forth; and terminology can take account of all of these (for example, a tone can be thick or thin). Copper gives forth a sharper tone than does wood, and catgut a sharper one than string.

Tension too is a contributing factor: the more tense a string, the more forceful, uniform, and sharp it will be. For sound is a continuing tense state of air which starts from the inner place where the blow occurs and enters into an outer place of air. Some sounds are sliding, others demarcated. The former--in an image later adopted by Boethius and Guido of Arezzo--are like the colors of a rainbow. The lower range of a long sliding tone sounds like the bawl of a cow, the upper like the howling of a wolf. But demarcated sounds are like rungs of a footbridge or a ladder, and are each confined to one degree of tension (1.4). Tones are higher as the tension is greater, lower as it is reduced. According to their own material, strings, *auloi*, and (human) windpipes have different tensions (1.3). It is the tensions which produce tones, for a tone is a sound of a single invariable tension. (Therefore a single tone is irrational because it is only one, and cannot be compared with itself.) And when two strings of unequal tension are in a relation, they please the ear, or do not please it; they are *emmelic* (consonant) or *ekmelic* (dissonant) respectively (1.7). Symphonies are the most beautiful of the intervals the voice impresses on the ear; diaphonic relations cannot be judged so.

Ptolemy turns to *musica humana*: what is the connection between music and psychic movement (3.4ff)? Different tone-types (*genera*) have their individual colorations (1.12, 16; 3.5). Each *melic* type has its own aesthetic significance; it calms or represses the soul, or makes it furious or enthusiastic (2.6-7). He also describes how he thinks the Greeks recognized modulations from one genus or psychic state to another (3.7) and accepts their notion (expressed by Aristoxenus and others) that ethical effect is based not on the mode but on pitch: the "same melody has an activating effect in higher keys [modes] and a depressing one in lower keys [modes] because a high key [mode] stretches the soul, while a low one slackens it" (2.7). For Ptolemy, as for most of his predecessors such as Aristotle, the Dorian was on a middle pitch and took a middle place in the producing of affects; for him, however, all modes at the middle pitch are like well-ordered and stable states of the soul, higher modes are like exciting and stimulating states, and the lower ones like relaxed and feeble moods.

Musica humana reflects the world-soul. It is a bringing of the human soul into conformity with harmonic tone-relations. There are four divisions: (1) three psychic activities (thinking, perceiving, living) based on a parallel with the octave, fifth, and fourth, and (2) virtues (based on reason, feeling, desiring) parallel with them, also based on the octave, fifth, and fourth. (The highest virtue is the consonance of the psychic aspects among themselves, and the total philosophical harmony of all the virtues is the equivalent of the harmony of the entire musical system as well as the harmony of the spheres. In contrast, disharmony represents evil [3.6]). Then, (3) theory and practice involving the three *genera*: the diatonic theoretically is related to the theological and political life and, practically speaking, is a matter of straining or exertion; the chromatic is theoretically mathematical as a matter of economy; the enharmonic is theoretically material and is a matter of the ethical or falling off (*see* Appendix A); (4) the modulations from one of the *genera* to another representing modifications or variations in psychic states: the higher (the pitch of) the genus the more tense, the lower (the pitch) the more relaxed; and there is a middle position between these. The relationship between music and the mind allows for changes from joy to sadness, from peacefulness to rapture, and so forth (3.4-7).

There follow ontological explanations and illustrations of *musica mundana*. The background includes the Pythagoreans, the *Timaeus*, and other sources. The logic is deductive, the presentation deceptively inductive. All is extended analogy and imagination run riot. First, there are parallel relations between intervallic and circular motions in tandem with tones and the universe. True, Ptolemy thinks that tones in succession seen as pitches have a straight motion, not, according to function, a circular one. Yet though on an instrument they represent a straight line, their relative characteristic meanings are represented in a circle or in rotation (3.8). Thus the zodiac must be compared with the Perfect System of the double octave. Therefore, also, consonances and dissonances are analogous to the divisions or signs of the zodiac and their relations to one another. The basic division of twelve corresponds with the whole tones of the double octave. But there are also differences in the motions of heavenly bodies: the longitudinal movement of the stars from east to west (and the reverse) corresponds to the movement of tone scales from low to high (and the reverse). Thus the low tone corresponds to a lower space or place and the high tone to the opposite, while in the writing of notes the lower ones begin and also conclude. The relationship between the lowest movement of the stars and the distances near and far on the earth corresponds with the harmonic genus: if the distance from the earth is small or great, the related *genera* will be enharmonic or diatonic. The diverging breadth of motion of the stars during different seasons corresponds to the change of mode; the modes higher than the Doric are like summer, the Doric has the middle value, and those lower ones are like winter. Ptolemy finally compares the tetrachord of the Perfect System with the relation of the constellations of the stars to the sun (3.8-13). The moving parts of the universe, the stars in their paths, make musical harmony intelligible to the ear. Can the multiplicity of parallel lines and movements, we may ask, prefigure the wonders of counterpoint? But of course Ptolemy could have imagined only multiple melodies, but no counterpoint made up of passages both linear and vertical.

At the top of the deductive pyramid is number, as the Pythagoreans taught and as their successors were never weary of repeating. Ptolemy completes his system with a numerical-relational treatment of a comparison of the "permanent" tones of the Perfect System with the first spheres of the cosmos. He organizes the entire zodiac into 360°, then numerically realizes the relationships of the individual movements, and finally compares the planets with the system of tones: the differences between the stars of the day and those of night, the difference between masculine and feminine principles, and the differences within the system of the music of the spheres. The beneficial and non-beneficial stars in the interval of the fourth are Saturn (negative), Jupiter (positive), Mars (negative), and Venus (positive)--a division, to be sure, quite obscure since Mars in any case should have been a symbol for the Dorian-like masculine virtues. Ptolemy extends the comparison: the sun and Jupiter are day, manly, warm, dry, and active; the moon and Venus are night, feminine, moist, and soft; Saturn is day, but moist, and Mars night, but dry; Mercury is both day and night.

The German scholar G. Junge impatiently calls Ptolemy's classifications and codifications of ideas about music (especially the more abstruse astrological categories such as that of the music of the spheres) a *Spielerei*, an idle amusement, a pleasant pastime.[4] Archytas and Plato, as we know, had wanted to tie divine numbers to earthly music; both were like Ptolemy, who was also in the geocentric tradition of world harmony, though, unlike them, he also was an astronomer, a proper empirical scientist. Denied access to the kind of instruments which would be later developed for observation of the heavens, he still pursued the musical astrology which assumed that the music of the planets was based on circular orbits having no deviations of distance or speed. Incorrect in this, he was also hardly alone in being wrong. He did observe the angles of the descending rays of the planets and made valuable and accurate observations about the moon. He had as his musical-theoretical followers in the Renaissance (at first indirectly through Boethius) such men as the Spaniard Bartholomew Ramis de Pareia (1482) and the Italians Ludovico Fogliano (1529) and Zarlino (1558). But it was only with Johannes Kepler in the seventeenth century that musical world-theory was properly based on the planets not in their circular motions but in their elliptical orbits, all following variable distances and speeds as they circle the sun.

VIII
Aristides Quintilianus

Sir John Hawkins (1719-89), a biographer of Dr. Samuel Johnson and competitor as music historian of Sir Charles Burney (1726-1814), was enthusiastic about Ptolemy and his works, but was far less charitable towards Aristides Quintilianus (first and second centuries A.D.). Hawkins thought that Aristides preceded Ptolemy (in fact they seem to have been unaware of each other) and found the former extremely abstruse and overly fond of describing analogies.[1] In fact, Aristides was no fonder of them than was Ptolemy; he merely set out to describe more aspects of nature and life. Ptolemy was the more abstractly scientific, while Aristides was the more humanistic.

The most systematic of the Neoplatonists, Aristides wrote the single almost complete and authentic musical textbook of ancient times, a veritable compendium of theory from Archytas and the Pythagoreans onward. He concentrated on the structure of universal and earthly music and avoided what must have seemed irrelevant to a scientific work, in particular the scores of interesting but unreliable legends which in past ages had clustered around the subject of music. He was an eclectic who followed in great part the school of Damon and remained true from first to last to the "divinely wise" Plato of the *Republic* and the inevitable *Timaeus*, works which supported his own Neopythagorean and Neoplatonic tendencies. He may have been encouraged by Pseudo-Plutarch to recapitulate in systematic order what the Greeks had taught, just as he may have been influenced by the philosophies of Porphyry and Iamblichus. He also showed familiarity with Aristoxenus. His is an expanded summary of the traditional music aesthetics, both speculative and practical, of ancient times.

His *On Music* is divided into three books arranged inductively. The first treats harmonics, rhythmics, and metrics in the Aristoxenian fashion. The second, following the school of Damon, has to do with theories of education and expression, the latter endemic to the soul and to song; and there is an important appendix on instrumental music. The third, which is Pythagorean and Platonic, deals with the ontology of nature, the cosmos, and world harmony. Though the thought is organized inductively, I shall present his discussion deductively in the belief that this way of proceeding will best do justice to his work. Aristides Quintilianus is no doubt abstruse, as Hawkins maintained, but despite his repetition of much of what we have already heard, his text has the fascination of fiction, which, like much

151

ancient music speculation, it of course is. He weaves a texture of relationships from God to inanimate objects, and, like Ptolemy, he never questions
the validity of his theories.

I

Book III (The Cosmos and Its Elements). For Aristides, as for the
Pythagoreans, music was a symbol of world organization or universal order:
in the structure of the universe, there is a clearly recognized preview and
model of the structure of sounding motion, of music and its three basic
consonances found in the intervals of the fourth, the fifth, and the octave.
These consonances are eternally fixed intervals determined by number-ideas
which can be arithmetically and geometrically demonstrated in the tone-
relations of the canon or monochord (113-15).[2] But, the perfection of music
can be regained in a purely mental fashion through numbers rather than
through sensuous hearing--regained because it pre-exists in the universe
(116). The greatest and strongest agreement of nature or Being with music
is intellectual because numbers, whether of nature or Being, are metaphysically significant. The number 1, the ancient said, is the principle and the
source and creative origin of the harmony of the All (Plato, *Sym.* 187; *Parm.*
137, 159). The number 2 is related to matter, the first manifestation of
contraries. Three is the universe completed and perfected by the reconciliation of opposites. Four is physical or solid; 5 is sensation or sense; 6 is the
completion of perfection of the body made up of the first uneven and the
first even numbers geometrically considered (thus, in Plato, *Rep.* 546; in the
old sexual metaphysics, uneven is male, even is female). Seven is un-
blemished purity or chastity (of all the first ten numbers, it is not geometrically created, nor does it beget any other number); 8 is material body (the
first material number 4 multiplied by 2; it is reproduced in the cube); 9 is
"musical" (made up of the three consonance-relations: $2 + 3 + 4 = 9$); and
the harmony of the course of the spheres of the All agrees with this number:
there are seven planets + two spheres (that of the fixed stars or zodiac and
that of the earth); 10 is the "first consonant" ($1 + 2 + 3 + 4 = 10$); it is also
the first of two numbers whose internal number has two internally equal
intervals--that is, 2 and 8 ($2 + 2 = 4, 4 + 4 = 8$). (Also, 2, 4, and 8 sometimes are called the primary harmony.) Twelve is termed the most musical
of the numbers because it has relationships of consonances to 9 (4:3), to 8
(3:2), to 6 (2:1), to 4 (3:1), and to 3 (4:1). Twelve embraces tones sufficient
for human nature to reach the upper register of the voice (122-24). Like
Nicomachus and Theon of Smyrna, Aristides has adopted a mysticism of
number based on Plato and the Pythagoreans.

Now, according to divine teaching, earthly things have an imitative
relation to higher divine ones. In the latter, the active power of the world
soul is pure; in the former, because of the confusion and impotence of
matter, it is stained and hemmed in. The sun's rays, for example, are the
least (but not completely) cloudy and the most pure as they occur in the

atmosphere, but dark, dim, and hazy in the depths of the ocean. The sun is not different, but our sense of sight is restricted and limited by the surroundings; physical nature keeps us from seeing the sun as it is. Thus rays from heaven are not consistently the same everywhere, but only as the material or substance in question allows them to appear. Divine perfection is radiant like the sun, and through moral effort human beings can win and earn back a portion of the divine perfection they have lost.

As the sculptor in stone effortlessly works out the form he has in mind from incongruous materials, so the power of the universe hews out things which are favorable, more harmonious, and better, in contrast with the things below which are duller, weaker, and more blind. Yet there is a sympathy between earthly and heavenly things: seasons, wind-directions, waves of heat, the growing and fading of plants, and so forth, as well as the stages in the development of human life are all influenced by the divine. Earthly music, which is a sounding tone-resonance, is not so pure as the heavenly, which rests on clear mathematical calculation (124-26), but is material and "confused."

Thus Aristides Quintilianus, as one might expect, glorifies number and proportion, the Greek basis of beauty, as the medium of imitation. He allies the natural beautiful proportions of the human body with form and color in painting, finds them in the beating of the pulse as measured by the physician in the human body where they correspond with the three musical intervals, and sees them as intrinsic to life, action, custom, morals, and politics in everyday human existence. In all of these, there is a median size, area, or concept, like the number 3, which symbolizes perfection or completion because it includes two opposites and a middle. Elements tending towards disharmony are brought into harmony. This relationship resembles the soul, for the soul has a volitional part which lies between rational thought and sensuous, instinctive life and is in a fitting conformity with both of them. And the political state: where is this median element in it? Plebeians are the military middle or median between the Senate and the great mass of people. There are other parallels, and anyone who, recognizing the dependence of these matters on median numbers, yet denies this dependency on music is completely uneducated and by nature artistically untalented (127-28).

Of all the arts, music is the most like the universe: it could not do its own powerful work if it lacked a strong ontological relation with superterrestrial phenomena or if, through a unification of opposites, it did not resemble the very creation of the world. It is like both natural physical creation and the harmony of the entire universe. The other arts are material coming to terms with nature through form. Of course, sounding movement too, in its restricted, purely natural and material sense, is simple and unformed and lacks corporeal differentiation in terms of Form (of Ideal Beauty). Its material, on the one hand, is not substance but continuity of movement (rhythms) and, on the other, a breaking up of movement into intervals (ratios). Universal providence divides what is all-too-cohesive into material forms and then, according to measured relations (ratios), reunites what has been separated. Music, unlike the other arts, behaves similarly. It rejects, on the one hand, sounds flowing into one another in an undifferentiated manner and, on the other, sounds which, too greatly separated by incalculable distances, lie outside experience: it shapes melodic song out of well-adjusted and moderate (median) intervals. Tones share "high" and "low" with the universe, some tones (like those of the three concords) remaining fixed and others unfixed (129-30). Some things in the universe, like the earth and its occupants, are fixed in space; tones correspond to them. Tones of the higher degree turn towards the infinite, but are confined by art; they are directed by the power of the world-creator in so far as it is external and irrational, and by material nature on the other to the extent that it is controlled by reason. Dynamism and rationality are united in the tonal art.

The first system of consonances and their cosmic correspondences appears in threes (133-34), for which see the chart on the following page.

Aristides Quintilianus' imaginative exposition of the metaphysical significance of numbers affecting the entire system is exceedingly detailed. It is sufficient to say that the fourth has a material four-foldness, the elements of earth, fire, water, and air; the fifth looks towards the bodies of the ether,[3] and the octave to the movement of the planets (145). Poets speak of the dance of the stars, but wise men speak of the melodic movement of the planets, who in their spheres produce sounds not perceivable by the human ear. Here, as heretofore, metaphysical symbolism has a strong anthropological and astronomical flavor, and the mysticism of number accompanies a mysticism of sex. The stars give order to tones, which are partly masculine, partly feminine, and partly mixed, in a fashion fixed, as the ancients thought, in an individual way according to the stars' potential and active energy.

Aristides treats the sexual in a state of excitement realistically: the masculine is dry, hard, and inflexible, and in spirit energetic and industrious; the feminine is moist, soft, pliable, permeable, inactive, quiet, indolent, and work-shy. These qualities are of course frequently mixed. Thus the sphere of the moon is moist, permeable, and the chief cause of physical becoming because its femininity produces a feminine tone, though it spills somewhat over into the masculine. It is chiefly feminine in that it receives the discharges of the other stars, but masculine in that its body-begetting and body-nourishing energy in turn descends to earth. Thus, the priests of the Mysteries called the moon male-female. Mercury on account of its size is in an equality with the sun because it is dry, but it is a little moist when it is far from the sun; since it prefers to appear during the day, it too has a male-female sound. Venus in her sphere is the goddess conforming to the bright, clear, lovely, and acceptable; she is soft-moist and the creator of joy; because she is happiest when she appears at night, her tone is extremely feminine. The sun, dry, glowing with fire, and hot, applies itself to

The Three-fold System of Natures or Essences

The Cosmos	spirit (non-physical) (the perfect octave, including all tones)	the middle nature (the 5-tone interval of the 5th)	bodies (the physical) (the 4-tone interval of the 4th)
Things	divine and eternal	mortal existence	inanimate existence
Physical dimensions	the line (the physical dimension associated with 1)	the surface (plane) (associated with 2)	extensions (the cube) (the corporeal, the 3)
Melodic species	the enharmonic (single and undifferentiated)	chromatic (surface color)	diatonic (associated with depth)
Interval size	uses the smallest (micro) intervals	uses half-tones	(uses mostly whole tones) (two whole tones, one half tone)
	(1/4 + 1/4 + large third) uses finest, narrowest intervals	more artificial, artful intervals	natural intervals
Numerical parts	1 (+)	3 (+)	2 = 6
Being and nature	the soul (undivided, simple)	inter-soul (body, physical matter: female creator of life for the body)	observable body
	the universe (creative power)		natural matter

lively and resolute action: its tone is masculine. Mars is at once warm and hot and also pleased by moist and nocturnal places. As a mixture, it inclines more to the masculine. The sphere of Jupiter almost rivals Venus in its acceptability; it modifies war like heats and meliorates the coldness of Saturn; a good mixture of both masculine and feminine, it is fruitful like Venus and encourages earthly-ephemeral states of mind; it is vigorous, encourages the marriages of bodies and the producing of children, and therefore may suitably allow the more feminine tone to sound. Saturn is arid, rough, hard, and in tone masculine (147-48). All of this is based on Galen's doctrine of the four temperaments or humors: hot, cold, dry, moist, in different mixtures.

The relevance of number to the elements, movements, and seasonal change is thus readily outlined. From Plato's *Timaeus* (53-56), Aristides Quintilianus in part derives ideas which too may be expressed in diagrams:

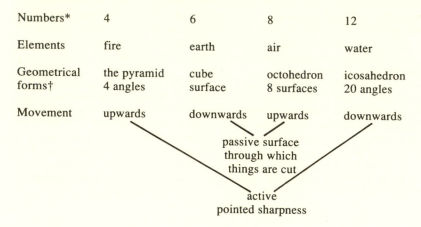

Numbers*	4	6	8	12
Elements	fire	earth	air	water
Geometrical forms†	the pyramid 4 angles	cube surface	octohedron 8 surfaces	icosahedron 20 angles
Movement	upwards	downwards	upwards	downwards

passive surface
through which
things are cut

active
pointed sharpness

The Seasons	summer	autumn	spring	winter
	warmth	saplessness dryness	youthfulness tenderness	moisture dampness

* The proportions of the Doric (standard) octave which Nicomachus calls the first (superior) *tetractys*, the source of consonance (*Harm.* 2.7). The 6-8-9-12 *tetractys*, based on the double octave, precedes 1-2-3-4 not in time but in quality alone as superior in rank. Nicomachus (*Ar.* 2.29.3) and Boethius later (*Ar.* 2.54) see the 6-8-9-12 *tetractys* as realized physically: the cube is harmonic or geometrical harmony (Nic., *Ar.* 2.26.2; Boeth., *Ar.* 2.54).

† Supposedly from Pythagoras, who described five solid figures, the fifth, the dodecahedron representing the sphere of the universe (Freeman, *Pre-Socratic*, p. 86n). These five "solids" have also been called Plato's discovery (*Timaeus* 55-56).

Furthermore, according to Pythagoras,

4:3	spring is to autumn as a relation of the fourth	the
3:2	spring is to winter as a relation of the fifth	three
2:1	spring is to summer as a relation of the octave	consonances

(144-45)

The ultimate proof of musical proportions is to be found in the development of living creatures and in the beauty of human beings. Aristides applies numerical calculations to seven-month, eight-month, and nine-month children. Consonance-intervals, he thinks, are shared in beautiful bodies, dissonance-intervals in unbeautiful ones. Here we return to the sexual question: beauty of the body is not recognized in shameful effeminacy, but in the manly soul which human beings are impelled to attain and which they judge in establishing friendship. It is the teaching of the divine Plato that the aim of music belongs to the love of the beautiful (144; Plato, *Rep.* 403). Harmonic and rhythmic (beautiful) proportions in the structure of the body are both arithmetical and geometrical (150-53).

But the soul was created before the body: out of the indivisible (the Same) and the divisible (the Other), God created Essence. (The *Timaeus* is of course copied here.) These elements were then mixed and divided into parts according to the proportions of the Pythagorean *tetractys* and the diatonic scale. Thus was created the unequally divided system of the seven planets in their spheres (cf. *Timaeus* 35-37). Later God created four types of animals--the heavenly gods (fixed stars and planets), birds, sea animals, and land animals. But he created human beings with seven qualities because there are seven numbers:

1. rational insight
2. courage
3. temperance
4. justice

5. success and well-being
6. beauty
7. health

He divided human beings into two general types: (1) the higher, rational, and theoretical who partake of reason and the divine and are called cultivated, moral men; and (2) the irrational, pathetic, practical (passionate Dionysian, Bacchic, enthusiastic) men called rough and brutish. As music works on the practical part of the soul, the latter type undergoes a kind of catharsis, is purified of sickness and madness. The intent is that the former type of man (in Plato the guardian and educated man) is to be attracted by the ethical-pedagogic type of music which touches the logical part of the soul.

If there are two general types of men, there are also two human futures, the one governing the realm of the divine and unalterable, the inescapable, the universally determined and necessary, the immaterial, non-physical, logical, *noetic*, and eternal; the other governing the earthly, the changeable, indefinite, equivocal, the material, the alogical, and the aesthetic. Each type of man is symbolized by melodic change and development just as the universe over long periods of time observes changes among generations of men, revolutions in the state, and increases and diminishings (evolution?) in plants and animals.

Though Aristides Quintilianus here seems to echo Lucretius, his world-ontology is a free footnote to Plato; nevertheless, his exposition makes music a more primary subject than it was in the *Timaeus*: melodic song is a copy of the beautifully arranged order of the spiritual (or psychic) world; the soul presents such a copy in speech and orders the movements of the physical world through the singing of tone-syllables (Schäfke, p. 146). Furthermore, consonance, sense, and the elements are connected:

	1	2	3	4	5
Senses	feeling	taste	smell	hearing	sight
Elements, from lowest to highest	earth	water	air	fire	ether

In his Timaean genesis of the world, Plato mentions only the senses of sight and hearing (though he accounts for the others later [65ff]). But here, alongside or parallel to the elements in their order in space, Aristides names all of the senses, and places at a metaphorical top the two most sensitive because they lead to knowledge and wisdom. He names hearing and sight in ascending order. It is an order followed almost universally in Western thought (notably by St. Thomas Aquinas) because sight gives knowledge.

Usually Aristides categorizes in threes, and the median is the "concordant" element. As we see above, he also uses divisions of five when necessary. But he additionally employs four when he must--for instance, he lists (Schäfke, pp. 137-38) psychic relations in terms of the four virtues, which are cumulative:

the wisdom of the statesman	the courage of the soldier	temperance (self-mastery)	justice[4] (the result of the three others)

II

Book II (Human Beings).   The ancients, including the Neoplatonists, did not live in our unfriendly and indifferent universe, for they always assumed that there was a sympathetic relation, however severe and austere, between the cosmos and men. Sometimes this relation was embodied in "white" magic. The order of the universe always descended to human social and political levels, and a similar order (conforming to social and political laws, however arrived at) was integral to human beings, their bodies, and their minds or psyches. Contemplation of this relationship in itself seems to have been a matter of emotional exaltation. Cosmic speculation could call up an intense wonder, just as the application of "universal" principles to men and their arts could excite linguistic eloquence. The pivotal turning point was the human soul.

Because of its origin in the universe of things, this soul is both rational and irrational; it either realizes what accords with reason or is zealous about physical matters. Its zealous, irrational part too is dual: there is the soft, relaxed, degrading, depressing slackness of the affective sort, called sensuously inordinate desire; and there is a disproportionate, extraordinary, soaring, pushing forward which is called the powerful will. As a result of the dual nature of the soul, there are two different kinds of instruction: the one maintains the rational realm of the soul in its natural freedom; through thought it makes things intelligible and also preserves their unalloyed purity. The other kind of instruction cultivates habits and remedies and controls what is lacking in reason--that which moves like a wild animal, that which is untidy, unseemly, and undisciplined.   In the first instance the guide is philosophy; in the second it is music, which through harmonies forms ethical ideas in men from early childhood and through musical rhythm trains the body (61). Aristides thus describes the two elementary social controls of music and gymnastics as they are found in Plato.

Of moral education for the soul there are two types. The first, which is curative and changes what is bad into something good, functions in two ways: (1) it attempts through reduction not suddenly, but gradually and persuasively, to mitigate a passion or to free an individual from it; and (2) it also may attempt to substitute one state of mind for a completely different one.   The second type of ethical education struggles to attain the good and to increase virtue by destroying passion (80; Schäfke, p. 113), while in the first that which already exists is preserved and carried up to a higher plane, increasing virtue by degrees. The art of moral education on the basis of (Platonic) ideas is also twofold: we make use of physical things, of objects in their materiality, and aim for a beneficial spiritual state of mind. But if we are unclear or confused, we can trace out the necessary (physical) signs through artifice (80)--that is, through symbols.

Now, in play all children are inclined to sing and make happy movements which enchant people who find pleasure in music. There are gifted and ungifted children, however. The former accept instruction immediately; the latter must wait to receive its benefits. For music, when it is compared with painting, sculpture, poetry, dance, and dramatic art, is a powerful imitative art, and of all the arts it obviously is

the most convincing and influential.   And, clearly, Aristides defines
music comprehensively as producing imitations of what in truth is
carried out in actions themselves.   Even melodies and rhythms without
words are imitations.   The determination of the will initiates, rational
deliberation in thought follows, and then comes the execution; music
imitates the ethical ideals and emotional impulses of the soul, the verbal
expressions of the thinking intelligence in harmonies and sound-
formations, and deeds of violence in rhythms and physical movements
(62-64).

For these reasons all children or youthful people should be given
an education based on imitations and likenesses. Habit and practice will
then turn them in directions consonant with adult life, and they will be
prepared to adopt proper states of mind and to act correctly in their
maturity.   Indeed, no human activity for either immature or adult
persons is complete without music. Religious songs and divine services
are beautified by it.   Special celebrations and festivals, wars, battles,
processions, sailing and rowing, difficult mechanical activities, each for
different reasons is accompanied by it (65)--all of which proves that its
primary aim is not pleasure, but the control of souls through virtue.

Music is a medicine and remedy for the passions. People sing and
make music to achieve three results: joy and good humor through
pleasure and delight, sadness through melancholy and grief, and the
divine through religious transport and enthusiasm.   These may be
combined in external events as fate dictates or in the ways which cause
young people in their immaturity or elderly people with their
weaknesses in different degrees to be delighted by certain states of mind
or soul. The resulting catharsis can occur on two types of occasions:
(1) when a person is only moderately burdened by one of the passions--
that is, by pleasure, melancholy, or religious transport--and (2) when, if
he has fallen into an immoderate state of mind, he can be influenced and
instructed as a spectator (music is then therapeutic). The three moods
can be recognized in divisions of the soul: in the realm of sensuous
desires, where pleasure predominates; in the realm of melancholy and
madness, which is the daughter of feeling; and in the realm of thought
and enthusiasm. For each of these passions, music offers an appropriate
medical treatment leading the disturbed person unconsciously but
necessarily into the right mental state (66).   But the limitations of
therapeutics depend on the physical characteristics of the individual, and
everyone undergoes catharsis according to his age and sex (67).

In what he says about the place of music in the state, Aristides
Quintilianus seems to rely on Plato's Laws. Besides the types of people
susceptible to education through music, there are two (more alarming)
types: those who understand neither melody nor poetry, and those who
do not open themselves properly to music and poetry and therefore do
not undergo a completely satisfactory character development--that is,
those who are inclined towards things not worth striving for (67-68).

Pursuing its ethical-educational aim, music brings the power of melody and the word to bear; it is a moral influence through law; and when it aims at pleasing by way of amusement, it goes through many modulations and new transformations in sound so as to effect a close sympathy and identification of the hearer with the thing performed. Because music is a powerful medium for education, human beings who are not able to follow this discipline or be improved by it often degrade it by calling it base and common or wild and crude in feeling. Taking the ethnological approach, Aristides Quintilianus says that faults in taste and a failure to accept music as an educational force are found (in the Roman world) among certain "barbarians" (foreigners) from the west coast of Asia, along the north coast of Libya, in the north of Greece, and among northern people, including the Germans, the Celts, and so forth.[5] The people who gave a place of honor to the theory as well as the practice of music were the Greeks, blessed in virtue as well as in all knowledge, possessed of a surpassing humanity, and emulated by the Romans.

The purpose of the state is, of course, its own maintenance and continuation, and if music can delight and transform whole cities, states, and people, why should it not also be able to transform the individual? It is a matter of knowledge that the melodies and rhythms people enjoy in private as well as in public life indicate and identify the manners and morals that please them (73). Bad things will bring the good to naught, but good things--for example, good words, and natural dispositions and habits--like beautiful song and the most noble actions, preserve it (74, 79-80). Music was not unuseful when in ancient times it improved the relations of people and their neighbors and moderated the antagonisms of cities and nations among themselves because social betterment through music is comparable to medicine, the science which concerns our entire lives (74-75). It if is to behave properly, the presuppositions of music as a medium are these: (1) the idea is appropriately represented--that is, imitated--in (2) the linguistic expression necessary for a real impression and for the persuasion of fellow-creatures through (3) harmony (melody), which employs height and depth according to measured intervals, and (4) rhythm (76).

How does music cure spiritual passions? Here Aristides is like Plotinus: the soul is independent of and indifferent to objects; it wants to be associated with what is better and greater; as a companion of reason, it is divorced from desire.

But as soon as it begins to turn towards earthly matters and feels impelled towards an earthly or material precondition, it must select one part of a duality, masculine or feminine, a duality present not only in living beings but also in inanimate creation. Originally simple and lacking in distinct form, the soul takes on human shape, constructs itself in space, as it were, hides the beauty of its original nature, and assumes the stamp of a human form or frame, in part according to will and in part according to necessity. It struggles not only to enter a body but also to have a certain character of its own: it may prefer the masculine, or the feminine, or sometimes a form made up of the two mixed (the androgynous), or sometimes even a special, peculiar, truly paradoxical and absurd blend. Thus some men can look like women, and vice versa, and we suspect and deduce that their moral characters correspond to their appearance (76-77; Plato, *Sym.* 189).

The two sexes thus differ as indicated in the chart which follows:

Masculine	Feminine
rough, harsh, austere things causing thought, decisive action well made and formed, eurhythmic	the smooth, the agreeable, the sweetly enticing
	pleasure-enticing, mental ability gradually revealed, the slack, disintegrated, arrhythmical
	refined, colored, gay, ornamented
erect, hard, serious, grave, brave, soldierly	affected, vulgar
noble, dignified, proud, sublime, good	
	cowardly, common, bad, inferior
everything purposeful, vigorous, violent, spontaneous, energetic, active, eventful	
depending on pure thought: logical, reflective, pensive	pathetic-feelingful, passionate (joy and sorrow, but especially female complainings), tearful, sad, passive, impulsive, desirable, sensuous, vicious, enchanting or intoxicating, hindering thought

And all of the characteristics listed above are evident in the idea or representation. Furthermore, one person admires white, another blue, one sweet pleasure, another the bitter--differences which extend to impressions, images, affections, and so forth. And music is able to appeal to and change men as it conforms with the many possible transmutations, sexual and temperamental, which human beings can display.

Since the human soul is moved by song, Aristides accepts that words are the necessities of education. While analysis suggests an origin in Plato and Aristotle (even Cicero, or certain Neoplatonic writers), Aristides' illustrations come from Homer (80), whom he treats allegorically elsewhere (105):   necessary to education, by way of grammar and linguistics, are apposition, epithets, and adjectives, substitutions, inversions, transfers in meaning, metaphors, comparisons (similes), allusions, paraphrases, symbolical expressions, allegories, and other devices (80).

If these rhetorical devices assure affective melody, however, such melody can also be produced on instruments alone. True, he admits that only the complete tonal structure, which includes melody, rhythm, and word, possesses curative, morally uplifting and educative power, just as the doctor of medicine uses not just one substance from the earth to heal physical infirmities but a mixture (30-31). And he also admits that the perfect (complete) affectiveness of music includes Ideas and their representation (102). Yet he holds that the soul also is naturally moved by instrumental music. There are two explanations. (1) The soul is a harmony, and indeed a harmony on the basis of numbers (as Philolaus and the Pythagoreans said). (2) The earlier original formation of the soul when it entered into its union with the body was in accord with the material and the natural shape of instruments; as soon as it adopted certain Ideas (representations) conforming with its inclination towards the corporeal world, the soul gradually forgot the beautiful superior things of its God and became entangled in mere representations (103).

The further away the soul was from the upper regions and the closer it came to this world, the more it sank, laden with increasing error, into the nightlike darkness of corporeality: first, because of its descent from its original sublime rank, it lost its ability to encompass the universe in a pure, intellectual Idea, and then, because it forgot super-earthly beautiful things, an astonishing confusion took place, and it was attracted downwards to the physically more powerful region attached to matter.   But salvation and purification are possible. Aristides in Plotinian terms describes the fantastic progress of the soul "upward": as it goes through ether, it overtakes everything radiant and at the same time becomes part of the material being which it holds together naturally with skin-surfaces, fibers, lines, and air for breathing, all the roots of the human body (104), which the ancients also called a harmony (105).

Is it any wonder, then, that the soul should be stimulated, not only by the voice in linguistic expression, but also by instruments in which strings or columns of air are resonantly set in motion, instruments to which the soul is related *in essence* because of the nature of bodies? When a breath of air sounds in melodic-rhythmical form and our own breathing of air sympathizes with it, or when a string is struck in harmonic fashion, why should not the soul in matching fashion with its own fibers or nerves harmonize and sound in sympathy? Something similar happens on the cithara when one of two strings an octave apart is "stopped" and the other is struck: the first vibrates in sympathy. Music is the sacred art in that it causes reactions and effects through the medium of inanimate objects. How much greater is the necessity, then, that it should work through an instrument set in motion by an emotional being and arouse the same kind of excitement as his (107)?

Consequently string instruments conform to the ethereal, the dry, the simple realm of the world-structure as the permanent part of spiritual nature. Wind instruments are analogous to windy, moist, and more changeable things. They make hearing womanish and soft, tend to undisciplined modulation, and owe their construction to dampness. String instruments are better because they resemble the better things; the latter are inferior. Thus Apollo invented the lyre, a superior instrument for educated people, and Marsyas the aulos, an inferior instrument for artisans and others who are uneducated (107-08).

Even instrumental music has an ethical purpose, then, though song is still the basic form. As examples of the non-ethical there were the Sirens, those animal-like and mortal women who sang melodic songs which had to be avoided because they led to vice and corruption. The Sirens wanted to entice and conquer men, and to avoid temptation Odysseus passed them with averted eyes turned forward. For (as Aristotle indicated) theory and practice agree that truly useful, valuable encouragement of the arts is twofold: it serves (1) the outstanding, capable, and educated, and (2) for their innocent recreation, the great mass of people and the even lower classes who are quite insignificant. Thus the Greeks attributed the educational music of the cithara, as masculinely formed, to Apollo; however, they assigned the music necessarily aimed at pleasure because it concerns the masses to a woman among the gods, Polyhymnia (108-09). They allied the educational and beneficial music of the lyre with Hermes (idolized by Ficino in the Renaissance), who is supposed to have given it to Amphion. To Eros they attached what is suitable for the amusement often beneficial to the feminine and instinctive part of the soul. But they ascribed to the aulos the type of music which flatters the mass of people devoted to pleasure, and the corresponding part of the soul to Euterpe, who, as her name indicates, recommends that the pleasant and desirable be sought at the same time as beauty.

Not only our souls, but the entire universe is arranged in opposites resembling pleasure-pain, vice-virtue, aristocrats-masses. The creatures who live under the moon in realms replete with currents of air and damp formations receive their power from ethereal life and are soothed and made happy by both kinds of earthly instruments--the blown and the strung. Wind instruments stain the soul and send it earthward; the cithara and the lyre are purer and more holy and are appropriate for hymns of praise. And wise and holy creatures imitate the ethereal sphere and freely renounce the confused, restless, ugly, agitated world of earth; they devote themselves to the divinely beautiful, to perpetual simplicity, and to mutual concord on the basis of moral judgment (110). It is this last assertion which, ascetic in suggestion, has earned Aristides

Quintilianus the merit of having points of contact with the Mysteries, and with Plotinus and Iamblichus--to say nothing of the Christian Church.

III

Book I (Theory and Practice of Craft). Aristides Quintilianus divides earthly music into the theoretical and the practical (6-9), a distinction which had been made by Aristotle. As the chart which follows sets forth in detail, it is possible to call these the natural (theoretical 1), contemplative (theoretical 2), and the artificial (practical). To melody (harmonics) and rhythm, Aristides adds a third aspect, meter, which is an integral part of both. This division was probably derived both from Cicero and Quintilian and from the practical, "harmonist" school of Aristoxenus.

	THEORETICAL		PRACTICAL (Damon)
1.	physical (as in physics) (Pythagoras) a. number-theory (arithmetic) b. physical things (acoustics)	1.	applied a. melopoeia b. rhythmopoeia c. poetry } educative
2.	technical (art: technē) (Aristoxenus) a. harmonics b. rhythmics c. metrics	2.	executional (expressive) a. instrumental b. vocal c. mimical, dramatic, declamatory

For the musician there are, of course, practical consequences of the ethical theory. Like many of his forerunners, Aristides finds that the ethos of tones (modes) is different as they are higher and lower, and that at its very beginning the art of composition depends on the musician's choice of a register of the voice, a decision based on the different parts of the scale (and the different branches of lyric poetry). For other effects, there are three kinds of melodic structure, the *nomic* (or Apollonian), the *dithyrambic* (or Dionysian), and the *tragic*. The first is depressive, contracts the soul, and awakens sad feelings; the second expands and raises our spirits; the third is in the middle and puts our souls into a state of peace. (Aristides does not mention, but hints at, Aristotle's theory of catharsis in tragedy.) These, as we have seen, are conventional divisions found in Cleonides and others who described ancient theory and aesthetic realities. Even when he is concerned with Aristoxenian technical matters--and the theory of rhythmics is almost literally Aristoxenus'--Aristides cannot set aside the moral-educational idea which for him must come first. Melopoeia has three general kinds of influence or affect which Cleonides has listed and Aristides rearranges and interprets anew:

> *systaltic* (in songs of love, gallantry, and lament): it is soft and tender in passion, and plaintive; it affects and penetrates the heart.

> *hesychastic* (the intermediate): it produces a state of tranquillity and moderation.

> *diastaltic* (with tragic and heroic subjects): it exhilarates, kindles joy, inspires courage and magnanimity, and expresses sublime sentiments.

Allied with these three, as well as with mode, is modulation (which, according to Cleonides, moves from genus to genus, system to system, tone [mode] to tone [mode], and from ethos to ethos). Aristides Quintilianus illustrates modulation primarily as a going from one rhythm to another, however, just as St. Augustine later used it primarily for changes in time or duration. Aristides takes this view because he accepts the "masculine" position as he again turns to sexual description to bolster what was the ancient understanding--that rhythm is the superior of melody and gives it life or soul.

In harmonics Aristides is what one would expect, a man eminently conventional. He divides the whole tone in the Pythagorean manner: having the proportion of 9:8, it cannot be equally divided and therefore can become only two unequal "half-tones" and the tetrachord only two whole tones and an imperfect half-tone. Like Plato, he sees this necessary decision as the failure of sense to reach the heights of reason and intelligence (30).

For certain Greeks, he says, rhythm is masculine and melody feminine. Without rhythm, melody lacks energy and form. Rhythm takes unshaped material and informs it with spirit; it also shapes the matter of tonality; it brings the unformed mass into ordered movement. It is active rather than passive. As the masculine element, it organizes and gives active form to the feminine element of the melody (43). Rhythm is a system of times, many units of time being put together "according to a certain proportion of each other" (31). Meters are in the words, rhythm is the motion of bodies. A measure beginning with an unaccented syllable is calm and gentle, one with an accented syllable is troubled and agitated. Time composed only of 2's (entire feet) is noble in effect; less so are measures from which a foot is missing at the end, its absence being supplied by a short rest. Time of equal proportions is graceful. Everything here is Aristoxenus *redivivus*.

As must be clear, one staple of Greek thought--indeed, one of its passions--was the principle of the *natural*. Just as eighteenth-century harmonic practice commonly accepted the major as the natural key, so Aristides Quintilianus sees the diatonic species as the most natural because of its singability for the educated and uneducated alike. The chromatic, he thinks, is more artistic (artful) because it is played by or sung exclusively for the educated and cultivated; and the enharmonic is even finer and more precise (because of its micro-intervals). Used in the music of the most accomplished professionals, it is impossible and impracticable for the great mass of people (19).

Thus Aristides tries to demonstrate that rhythm (according to Plato [in *Protag.* 326], necessary for the life of man) and also meter not only conform to nature but even have their source in it. Certain species of rhythm are like the gaits and movements of human beings (and, according to Plato in *Laws* 802, different in men and women). An action or a walk resembling the spondee shows measure and fortitude. When it is like trochees, it indicates fire and velocity. With the pyrrhic measure it reflects something low. And a movement based on all of these implies dissoluteness and disorderliness. Movements and rhythms therefore can and must express ethical characteristics.

Again there is a three-fold division: the term 'rhythm' is used in relation to static or motionless bodies (when, for example, we speak of a rhythmic statue), to bodies in motion (thus we say that someone walks rhythmically), and to the realm of sound (31). Rhythm is a scale of "times" brought together in a certain order, and its effect we call *arsis* and *thesis*, strong and weak (49), noise and stillness (31). In speech it is determined by syllables, in melody by the ratios of *arsis* and *thesis*, in (physical) movements by human figures and their limitations. There are five parts to rhythm: (1) primary times, (2) kinds of feet, (3) rhythmical tempo, (4) modulations, (5) *rhythmopoeia*. There are three kinds of rhythmical feet based on *arsis* and *thesis*: a 1:1 ratio, a 1:2 ratio, a 2:3 ratio, and sometimes a 3:4 ratio (all of which are the ratios of consonances; he disallows the 1:3 ratio). The foot, which has two parts, itself is that part of the whole rhythm which allows us to understand the whole (32-34). Is meter to rhythm as a part to the whole, or is it like matter, related to form? Is the essence of rhythm found in *arsis* and *thesis* and the essence of meter in syllables and their unlikeness? The answers are that rhythm is made up of like or equal syllables and antithetical feet, but meter is *not* made up of like syllables and rarely of antithetical feet. Rhythm depends on an (unstructured) rise and fall; it has its own regularities, and especially the repeated sameness of the ratio of *arsis* to *thesis* which informs syllables of speech and produces a variety of meters according to a variety of syllabic structures and a variety of strong syllables against weak (49-50). But meter is a regularity, not of speech, but of (poetic) song; it is a measuring off of rhythms, a measuring so as to bring out the character of the rhythmic foot, and it has one element which is meaningless for speech: the rest, which is an empty time, a moment lacking sound, used for the filling out of the meter (40-41). Aristides thus defines rhythm and meter much in the traditional way of his namesake Quintilian or as St. Augustine was later to do. But he has nothing to say about the rest as having a vitality of its own.

Aristides was one of the first Greek writers about music repeatedly in classifications to name a third element, a middle one, though it cannot be

said that he *created* the rule of 3. Sounds had been frequently classified as
high, low, and median, and an oration analyzed into *inventio, dispositio*, and
elocutio. While he may have had in mind the three consonances *in extenso*,
as it were, or even the perfect number 3, his predecessors were concerned
mainly with opposites, with a duality and its "reconciliation"--a practice
going back to Aristoxenus and his school, and even earlier, where emphasis
was on harmony and rhythm, or to Aristotle, who distinguished theory from
practice. For Aristides, for example, there are three types of rhythm (just as
there are three types of affective melody): the erotic, the comic, and the
encomiastic. There are also the *eurhythmic*, the *arrhythmic*, and the
rhythm-like. In musical structure there are melody, rhythm, and meter. He
names the original three modes: Dorian, Phrygian, and Lydian (25). The
chromatic genus lies between the diatonic and the enharmonic as does a
color between black and white. Of course, there are dualities too: the mind
is rational and irrational, soul is contrasted with body, the infinite with the
material, the higher (educated, rational, theoretic) man with the lower
(irrational, practical) one, inferior instruments (wind) with superior
instruments (string).

But the triple organization is more marked: the soul is between
reason (divine thought) and the earthly body. The willful state of mind
stands between rational thought and sensuous existence, musical sound is
neither continuous nor completely disjointed, but intervallic in melody.
Divine and eternal things, physical dimensions, musical species, being and
nature--all can be analyzed into threes. Musical tones and effects can be
masculine, feminine, or mixed; in ethical education through music there are
(1) the will to effect change, then (2) a rational thinking about method, and,
finally, (3) execution. Ethical ideas are imitated through ideas and
concepts and expression through words and harmonies, while the imitation
of greater vigor is achieved through rhythms and physical movements. The
reasons for singing and playing are three: pleasure and delight, the
assuagement of sorrow, and religious transport. There are three kinds of
voice-use: in speech, in song, in poetry-reading; and there are melody
(tones), rhythm (motion), and performance; perfect melody has motion of
tone (in the sounding body), time, and (most of all) rhythm. More importantly, there are three divisions under which music can be discussed; and,
employing these divisions, Aristides recapitulates ancient music theory: the
theoretical-Pythagorean-Platonic, the Damonian, and the Aristoxenian.
These are the three divisions which were implicit even in Pythagorean
musical thought but not clearly explicit until Aristides Quintilianus himself
made them so. Three or four centuries later Boethius, who does not
mention him, would give these divisions names which have remained with
them even up to the present day.

Unfortunately, the work of Aristides Quintilianus was lost to the
centuries between his own time and Franchinus Gafurius, who commis-
sioned a Latin translation (completed in 1494) of it for his private use. This
translation was not generally available until the middle of the seventeenth

century, however, when it was published in Marcus Meibom's *Antiquae musicae auctores septem, graece et latine* (Amsterdam, 1652). The loss of Aristides' work for more than a millenium was, needless to say, a matter of considerable gravity for the history of the idea of music.

IX
The Fruits of Hellenism:
Plotinus and Neoplatonism

To the creators of the most significant body of philosophical doctrine relating to music in ancient Greece--that is, to Pythagoras and Plato--we need to add the name of Plotinus--a philosopher who actually lived during the early Christian era and who extended this ancient heritage of thought in some very significant directions. For Pythagoras and Plato, philosophy had been the pursuit of wisdom, formal and abstract, but for Plotinus the Neoplatonist it would be the pursuit of a state of being. Emotion and intuition take their place beside reason and even supersede it.

In Plotinus, three systems of thought affect music aesthetics: the Judaic-Platonic-Pythagorean exemplified by Philo, the Neopythagorean, and the Neoplatonic, these last two more or less amalgamated. All three had their base in Alexandria, the rallying point, as we have seen, of most elements of ancient Greek and oriental thinking. Among thinkers in Alexandria, music was no more an art than painting or architecture, but it continued to hold the high intellectual place given it by the Pythagoreans, whose concern was to establish it as a science. It was an important part of encyclopedic knowledge. In addition, all Neoplatonic and Neopythagorean tendencies possessed a theologizing character which points the way to knowledge and happiness attained not through rational thought but through immediate and divine revelation and a mystical identity of the soul with the Godhead. Abandoned was a systematic exploration of what is best for the state and its citizens, and substituted was an obsessive concern for the individual soul, its moral character, and its religious and ecstatic experiences. The contrast between God and the world, the mystical interpretation of transmitted religious and philosophical writings, the numerous inner and outer means of purification for the soul so that the individual may share in the highest wisdom, which is the spiritual, and in a divinity long lost-- these, *in esse* embracing all the realities of existence, were the chief preoccupations of the Neoplatonists. The paths to the realization of mystical aims are incantation, prayer, and sometimes even magic, with the goal being to effect a spiritual catharsis through religious ecstasy. Music is still not thought to be an art in the modern sense, but rather it is seen as a scientific study and at the same time a medium for the soul's betterment. Accompanying incantations, prayer, and magical ceremonies, it is often thought to be a mystical agent between the soul and the illimitable divine.

For the Neopythagoreans, Pythagoras was less a scientific thinker than a moral-religious reformer, miracle-worker, and prophet. In his long life he exemplified as did no one else the ideal of man in a mysterious union with the divine. His relation to music, intimate and intellectual but at certain times resulting in action, was accepted by all who recognized that in his philosophy arithmetic principles supported geometric (spatial) and harmonic (sonic) theory. The true founders of the mathematical treatment of music, the old Pythagoreans, based intervals, modes, and systems on numbers and adopted the doctrine of the harmony of the spheres along with the assumption that there is an intimate sympathetic relationship between cosmos, the human body, and the human soul. This relationship is expressed in numbers defining the stars as they necessarily move in their orbits, the musical ratios and proportions which govern the motions of the human soul and the acts of the individual, and the ethical, psychological and physical effects music can produce. Concrete examples of such effects are embodied in stories and legends which few persons dared to doubt.

Now, music is often related either positively or negatively not only to mystical-religious but also to ascetic ends, though asceticism hardly represented a stance that had been encouraged in ancient Greece. Numbers become symbols not for scientific realities beyond sense, but for ideas and concepts in a blend with feelings. An almost uninhibited subjectivism in symbolical interpretation held sway. As an abstraction, world harmony was still thought to be realized in numbers. At the same time, it symbolized the great human virtues of purity, health, the good, and divinity (*Diog. Laert.* 8.33). And the microcosmic human soul was also a moving number carrying within itself all human relations (ibid. 8.24-30). If piety and holiness are higher than wisdom (and so the Neopythagoreans thought), they too must carry the hallmark of cosmic and psychic movement. For the old Pythagoreans, the soul "descended" from the Illimitable; for the new ones it had left the spirit to enter the material. In both cases, it had become unclean and through retribution and penance wanted to return to its source. These and similar doctrines of the Neoplatonic and Neopythagorean schools of thought, anchored in the ancient past as they were, now spilled over into Christianity.

In the ancient past, redemption was achievable partly through the rites of magic. Greek and Jewish adherents of the new Christian sect approached it through baptism and the Eucharist, rituals which had been adopted as purgatives, not for the sake of God, but for the people. In Neoplatonism, however, devotees wishing to achieve purification and atonement followed the way of the middle daemons, the keepers of this world (so says Nicomachus, who compares these middle daemons to Judaic angels), and along this path they proceed on to the Divine itself. Neoplatonists searched for the Divine but blended their understanding of that search with a "good" demonology of the gods, to which they added the principles of natural law. Out of this matrix, superstition and magic would appear to have triumphed for several centuries, indistinguishable from religion. Thus, Neoplatonism also adopted theurgy. Gods were "forced" to do, or in negligence would fail to do, what men demanded.   The aim and purpose was a spiritual self-purification as compared with the Greek social-political purification resulting in a personal or behavioral inner balance within a social context. An individual's own discipline and employment of divine signs in nature led to the salvation of his soul.

We may suppose that we are again touching upon the ancient theory of ethos since the Pythagoreans saw that the soul, threatened from the outside by defiling evils, must be freed and put in a condition which alone corresponds to the admission of divine, healing truths.   But the new Pythagoreanism stressed a more negative theological-musical morality under the control of asceticism and self-denial. The soul must strive toward what is beyond the world, and for this it must achieve moral states of being which existed before the world began and which still exist outside it. Even art must obey this law.   Though all artistic images are sensuous, the soul striving upward, though it uses them, must not dwell on them.   Such images are valuable only as they encourage and advance the flight from the sensuous to the supersensuous world. The phenomenal world is denied and hence is a negation, something to be overcome.   Thus music, which in ancient Greece seemed to take on a certain freedom despite the frowns of aristocratic philosophers, was again treated as a servant; it was constrained by ascetic doctrine which forbade the real and genuine artistic enjoyment of musical forms.   In this, the Neoplatonists encouraged and supported the views of the Christian Church, though as we shall see they both provided stages through which music would move on the way toward its independence in recent history.

I

Plotinus.   Often identified as the last philosopher of antiquity, Plotinus (204-69 A.D.), the chief figure of the Neoplatonic school, was a native of Alexandria and taught at Rome. Often a major influence in later philosophizing even when his thought was rejected, he believed that the individual soul can be directly attracted to what is vital in the soul of the world, the spheres, and the stars (*Enneads* 4.3)--that is, to the heavenly bodies which perform a choral dance (4.8). By the self he never meant body-and-soul, as the Christian theologians did, but always only soul. He was thought to support astrology, medicine, music, and (though he had qualms about these) initiations and talismans. Though he was an admirer of Aristotle's *Metaphysics*, he was hardly representative of Aristotelian thought. Indeed, his lack of agreement with Aristotelianism may perhaps be compared to what Plato's would have been since he turned attention away from the (exclusive) social group toward the individual soul in the Organic Whole of the universe and, on account of his divorcement of music from the state and politics, encouraged its assuming a share in personal religion. He did not always emphasize harmony (or sometimes symmetry in the visual arts) so much as mystical experience. He gave a high place to music in his system of moral values and provided a crucial impetus for it (and its idea) in its long journey from its subordinate position in a mixture with poetry, dance, myth, and so forth, to its ultimate position in modern times as an independent activity parallel with painting, sculpture, architecture, and poetry--independent as an art, independent of politics, morals, religion, and subject-matter, for none of which it has necessary responsibilities. Ultimately, therefore, Philodemus on music seems in part to have been vindicated, though he would have shuddered at the thought that music is a symbol of the Object which is a One or Universal-All.

Plotinus, who was concerned not with dogma but with authentic and mythological problems and spiritual states, posited the existence of a quality-less metaphysical Being who is the One and All, a One supra-Intellectual and undifferentiated, absolute and "negative." For Plato there were two worlds, the Real or the eternal one of Ideas or Forms, and the unreal, subordinate one of the material, sensible realm. But for Plotinus everything is the unimaginable One, without thought, act, will, or consciousness. That One is immanent, and from it descend: (1) the *Nous*, being both intelligence and the intelligible; then (2) the Idea, being both archetypes and forces; the (3) Nature; and finally (4) Matter, which is division and plurality. All of these are linked by harmony, and all move by the force of divine emanation.

Thus, the One sends forth emanations of all forms of life and all forms and phases of existence; and all forms of life must return to it. The One is Divine and also Mind, Intellect, and Universal (or All-) Soul. Man shares in the universal life through the emanation of the universal Life Principle, or All-Soul, which has three phases: (1) the Intellective-Intuitive Soul, (2) the Reasoning Soul, and (3) the Unreasoning Soul. The first realizes itself through man's eternal contemplation of the Divine. The second constitutes the normal nature of man and includes will, intellect, imagination, and memory. The third, the "unreasoning Soul," is the principle of animal life and includes sensible imagination, sensible memory, the fleshly appetites, sensation, and the vegetative, nutritive, and generative appetites.[1]

Briefly put, the stages in men's lives are these: first, the civic or lowest whose virtues are attractive but do nothing for the soul; second, that of the purifying virtues which lead men away from sensuality and evil and back to the *Nous* (Mind and Reason); the third, contemplation, which leads one back to God. When it reaches God, the soul is perfectly passive and reposeful. A state of *ataraxia* prevails. For Plotinus, therefore, the perfect subjective state is purposeless, motionless, negative, and inactive.

For Plotinus, the beauty of a work of art is in the idea, and the chief object of longing is the One. Spirit and matter interpenetrate, and through Matter runs the way back to the Spirit. The Idea descends through multiplicity; thus Nature is beautiful only in exceptional cases. A work of art is the Idea appearing in matter. It rescues man from multiplicity and can act as a religion through which the spiritual is rendered visible to men's ideas. All art is an immense symbolism. And the very idea of music is an Idea.

The work of art is not mechanical. Nor is the creative in Nature mechanical, for both are a matter of the *Logos* which impresses itself upon materials. As a substrate of forms, Nature is soul. Yet the arts return to "the Reason-Principle [Ideas] from which Nature herself derives" and have the power of improving on her (5.8.1). Art does not improve on the One: it cannot because its realm is the inferior one of matter. But through a wholeness, art does create beauty, and like the *Nous* it fights for a victory of form over the formless (1.6.3). In imitating not the visible but the principle upon which nature herself is founded, the artist's mind shares in the nature of the *Nous* (5.8.1).

Plotinus may be writing a gloss on the *Symposium*: in music, whose melody and rhythm belong to the beautiful, harmonies unheard create the sounds we hear "and wake the soul to the consciousness of beauty . . . : for the measures of our sensible music are not arbitrary, but are determined by the Principle whose labor is to dominate Matter and bring pattern into being" (1.6.3). Not having mentioned song, Plotinus is already speaking, at least in part, about an abstract instrumental music, for he compares it favorably with the imitative arts of painting, sculpture, dancing, and pantomime, which he thinks are earth-bound because they copy physical forms and movements and do not refer, except indirectly, to the "higher sphere," that of the "Power There which observes and mediates the symmetry reigning among all beings in the Intellectual Cosmos" (5.8.i, 5.9.11). Even Plotinus, who encourages the subjective, the intuitive, and the contemplative in art and thought, stresses the general and typical: when the sculptor works, he says, he does not have an image of a specific piece of work, but of a beautiful general image--of god or man, a Grace or a Muse--that the art of sculpting in which he has been trained allows him (5.8.1, 5.9.12). Nevertheless, sculpture belongs only among the arts "born here below." Nor does architecture fare very much better: it takes a lower position in comparison with music because it copies the physical forms of number and ratio whereas music draws on patterns and forms in the Intelligence and through a dynamic process assumes a humanistic-mystical role by which one attains a spiritual catharsis. Harmonies unheard are the originals of sounds we hear (1.6.3). Beauty is a musical proportion, and beauty-as-such, or spiritual harmony, is what attaches itself to outer things. Art of this kind reveals the structural principles of nature.

The thought of music is melody and harmony, then, and it must therefore "be the earthly representative of the music [which] there is in the rhythm of the ideal Realm." Here Aristotelian form and content seem to combine with Platonic Idea and its imitation: the sensuously beautiful is not inimical to the spiritual. Not until Schelling (1775-1854) will we again meet with such a thoroughgoing Idealism. The crafts like building and carpentry, Plotinus says, sounding like Hugh of St.-Victor, give us matter in wrought forms: they take their "principles from the realm and from the thinking There"; but they are not wholly in the intellectual realm, except as they are contained in the Idea of man, for, unlike music, they are in touch only with the order of sense. Music, on the other hand, does not begin from an unmusical source but from music (5.8.1), originating "not with the forms of matter," but "with the observation of the symmetry of living things" (5.9.11).

According to his student Porphyry (c.232-c.304), who revised his works, wrote his biography, and served as observer of his four beatific visions, Plotinus had a thorough theoretical knowledge of music and other subjects, but had no practical capacities for any of them. What did this matter? For him, they were components of the spiritual world, and his temperament did not allow him to treat them in any other way. One *can* copy the Ideal directly, he thought (as Plato did not). The musician can copy the Ideal: he is inspired by the world of Ideas as represented by the Muse; he is inspired by the Realm of the Ideal. But he of course of necessity deals with the world of sense.

At the same time, he must be "exceedingly quick to beauty, drawn in a very rapture to it . . . : as the timid are sensitive to noise so he to tones and the beauty they convey; all that offends against unison or harmony in melodies or rhythms repels him; he longs for measure and shapely pattern." Drawn by tone, rhythm, and designs in things of sense, "he must learn to distinguish the material forms from the Authentic-Existent which is the source of all these correspondences and of the entire reasoned scheme in the work of art: he must be led to Beauty that manifests itself through these forms; he must be shown that what ravished him was no other than the harmony of the Intellectual World and the Beauty in that sphere, not some one shape of beauty but the All-Beauty, the Absolute Beauty; and the truths of philosophy must be implanted in him, to lead him to faith in that which, unknowing it, he possesses within himself" (3.6.4; cf. Plato, *Symp*. 210). To know beauty is to exist on the highest degree or rank of life; then the soul is freed from and purified of earthly dross, and is transformed. Beauty is beyond mathematicizing. Plotinus is as far removed from the thinking of Nicomachus and Theon as one can be: music is not arithmetical specula- tion. It is the reconciliation of opposites, of high and low; it is the principle of the harmony governing the world (3.2.16). In it, the *Logos* brings opposites into a unity, for the *Logos* is the Reason-principle of the universe.

The individual soul actively strives for beauty as an ultimate reality, and its assistant may be music, which has the power of ("white") magic. What draws the soul to beauty is love, which is given in nature. The soul is in the power of the "tune of incantation, a significant cry, the mien of the operator." That soul is reasonless; it is "not the will or wisdom that is beguiled by music, a form of sorcery"--that is, the hearer proceeds not rationally, wilfully, or wisely, and the soul is hardly aware of the beguile- ment. We can capture even planetary influences through "prayers, either simple or sung with art," and Proclus, Plotinus' follower two centuries later, resembling in practice certain Renaissance figures like Ficino, sang Orphic hymns and saw magic in them. Music is like a prayer which is answered not by will, but by "some influence [which] falls from the being addressed by the petitioner." Such influence is possible because "that part and other part are wrought to one tone like a musical string which, plucked at one end, vibrates at the other also. Often, too, the sounding of one string awakens what might pass for a perception in another, the result of their being in harmony and tuned to one musical scale; now if the vibration in a lyre affects another by virtue of the sympathy existing between them, then certainly in the All--even though it is constituted in contraries--there must be one melodic system; for it contains its unisons as well, and its entire content, even to those contraries is a kinship" (4.4.40-41). Sympathy is an ultimate rule.

In another context Plotinus seems to be thinking of the lyre, the seven-string instrument of Pythagoras embracing the world and functioning as a symbol also for Philo when he describes the relation between the Ideal and matter according to movement and form. It is a passage admirably suited to serve as the Neoplatonic source of the idea that the aeolian harp is the soul of the poet through whom the Ideal speaks. (Here one may think of the English poet Shelley.) The affective phase of the soul or mind, Plotinus indicates, is not corporeal but ideal in form. The Ideal itself is tranquil, is in perfect repose, is impossible of being disturbed or affected. But matter is set in motion by the mere presence of the ideal form. The Ideal originates motion, but is not moved by the motion it induces. Its own act is different from what it has caused. Thus ideal form is itself an activity, but it operates only by being present--as if Melody (the Ideal) itself plucked strings and set them in motion. The affective phase of the soul remains unmoved though it originates movement--exactly as Melody dictates the music. The Ideal cause is like the musician, who moves the string of his instrument though the melodic principle remains unaffected. Only the strings move. And the musician himself (by this Plotinus also signifies the poet himself) could not pluck the strings unless the unmoved, tranquil, and undisturbed principle of Melody were there to dictate to him (3.6.4). The sympathetic influences in all of this take place in either natural or artistic ways.

In this respect, music and rhetoric are alike in that they both lead sometimes towards the good and sometimes towards the bad because both have an inner magic (4.4.31); and music has a clearly evident affect besides. It is in the nature of the soul to be charmed by song (4.4.43). Therefore music is like a prayer, for prayer, whether simple or complicated, when it is in an alliance with music (4.4.38) is magical.

The point is that music (through the movement of vibration and "tuning") in its identification with the reasonless soul and the intellectual principle produces ethical results. Through the beautiful, man's soul can be purged and his soul led by degrees to the Divine. This cleansing was of course a catharsis directed towards spiritual salvation, and it differed from the earlier Greek understanding of catharsis by admittedly being a subjective, mystical experience. Rhythm in music (one thinks again of Schelling) is an earthly manifestation of the rhythm of the Realm of the Ideal and is thus the most able of the arts to raise man to the universal Godhead. The aim is the suspension of normal awareness in the state of mystical ecstasy or transport, which Plotinus frequently delineated according to his own experiences. The highest aim of philosophy is to see the Divine (the Intellectual Realm). This is accomplished by a suspension of reason and self-consciousness and the acceptance of ecstasy in experience (4.8.1), which is an enlightenment taking the place of reason (6.9.4). It cannot be doubted that the mind is separated in itself from all other matters and principles (4.8.1, 5.5.7). Ecstasy is mind, is spirit. It is a penetration and an elevation of the individual soul into the innermost sanctuary where the Good radiates Beauty and where both are identical with the Ideas of the Intellectual Cosmos (1.6.9) and the transcendence of Being (6.9.11).

Thus, Neoplatonic doctrine did not remain conformed with scientific thinking but went beyond it to embrace immediate and direct divine revelation. The immediate perception of the divine as the highest aim of philosophy was to be reached only with the suspension of rational thinking. Through music, love, and philosophy the soul can return to God, perceive the Divine, and undergo an illumination which raises it to a state even beyond reason. It cannot be described (6.9.4) because the soul, separated from everything external, is drawn into itself (5.5.7). Magic is the state, deriving in part from prayer, which divorces one from a sympathy with things (4.4.26). Unlike some of his followers, however, Plotinus does not hold to superstitious and fantastic ideas uncritically and without reservation, for he tries to provide for them a philosophical basis in the great coherence and contest of nature, of the "heavenly [symbolical] script of the stars" (2.3.7).

Plotinus was no Christian himself, and, though his disciple Porphyry wrote fifteen books against the Christians (but not against Christ), his own thought, like Plato's was a source and support for Christian dogma. He exerted a profound influence, for example, on St. Augustine. For Plotinus, philosophy and theology assume an identity which was not to be pried apart for a thousand years. Much as he sees music as an integral part of the universe, he nevertheless takes the position which the Church Fathers and the Scholastics probably derived from him, that beauty addresses itself primarily to sight (1.6.1, 2.9.16) but that it does so also to hearing in certain combinations of words and whenever melodies and cadences are beautiful (1.6.1). He represents a "softening" of Platonism because he takes up and alters the doctrine of Forms and ignores the austere, unbending, and elitist part of Plato's philosophy of music--that it is an educative force for the right people of the state, which determines what that force should be. "Toughness," like science, is so alien to Plotinus that he excludes politics from his system. His focal point is humanity--indeed, the religion of humanity--and its goodness, not its behavior as citizens of the state. And in the realm of thought about the One and the Transcendent, it was easy to transfer the One to God, to interpret beauty as God's, to find that it can be internal to man, and to harbor the conviction that music is an identity with the Unreasoning and pure Soul and a medium for the glorification of God.

II

Porphyry (Porphyrius). Porphyry, a Greek from Syria, said that he had experienced only a single beatific vision (Plotinus had seen four such visions) and that it had occurred at the age of sixty-eight. A confirmed mystic, he had an intense concern for music, which is mentioned throughout his works, especially in his *Commentary on Ptolemy's Harmonics*, a work dedicated to a certain Eudoxus (not, of course, the so-named pupil of Plato). Porphyry relied not only on Ptolemy but also on the Pythagoreans, Eratosthenes (third century B.C.), Plato (he quotes *Timaeus* 35-36), Archytas, and Euclid.[2] He quotes Aristoxenus by name and also Dicaearchus, a Greek peripatetic philosopher of the fourth century B.C. He does not discuss music from the ideal standpoint of Plotinus, whose student he was, but returns to number theory. For him, the Pleiades are the lyre of the Muses (and for this he was remembered during the French Renaissance); furthermore, he puts the Muses in the place of Plato's planetary Sirens. He adds nothing to Plotinus' idea of the beautiful. By nature he was a scholar and teacher rather than an artist.

He was the first Greek thinker actually to label philosophy the servant of theology. As a pagan Neoplatonist and not a Christian, he nevertheless served as a mediator between Plotinus and St. Augustine. But he was also a grammarian and rhetorician, a student of Homer and an explicator of Plato and Aristotle, whose *Logic* he is said to have understood better than anyone else in his time. He was versed in non-philosophical fields like natural science and medicine. Yet he unaccountably took a monistic position in philosophy: all scientific knowledge, he thought, is meaningful only when it agrees with essential knowledge, and this essential knowledge is theological. He replaced mathematics and numbers with the divinity. Believing that thinking by way of reason is superseded by an immediate direct revelation of the Divine leading to mystic understanding and bliss, he turned to professional philosophy based upon an increase of knowledge. For him, belief and knowledge were one and inseparable; they were a theology without a Church. How, then, can an art like music fit into universal or transcendental knowledge or Being?

He returns to some of the preoccupations of the Pythagoreans. For example, he revives the psychological doctrine of the musical harmony of the soul. Based on the diatonic species, this harmony is also a copy of a higher divine proportion. But he is more "practical" than Plotinus. How is music to be used? What is the relation of soul to body, sensuism to morality? His morality basically is a pure asceticism, while sensuism is inimical to the love of God (*De Abst.* 1.36, 45). To reach the supernal one must free oneself from sensual passions and deny oneself sensuous enjoyment, no matter how harmless. Indeed, the germ of asceticism in action was one of Porphyry's contributions to Christian behavior, in which religion and asceticism became joined.

Porphyry is the first philosopher totally to reject the sensuous charm of music (even Plato had allowed it an educational place in the state, and Philo did not reject it entirely).   Yet he recognizes only the religious vocation of art, and condemns the seductive lure of the sense of hearing, whose influence, not denied even to the animal world, human beings under certain circumstances must avoid (ibid. 1.31).   Theatrical performances and dances as well as the music allied with them (all of which are placed on a level with horse-racing) come entirely from evil and draw men away from their high spiritual aim (ibid. 1.33).   Sexual intercourse makes its participants impure (ibid. 4.20).   Like the Church Fathers he adamantly declares war on worldly profane music, but he is also a pagan in that he identifies the Society of Apollo with the Muses and the harmony of the world.

How does music serve God?   Not sensuously, but through spirit, and the accepted cliché appears once more: sing not with the voice, but with the heart.   We may approach God not with audible prayers, but in "pure silence and pure thought."   Porphyry contradicted certain popular beliefs, one of which, exorcism, was gaining in popularity, as were superstition in general and divination in particular.   He himself referred to the enthusiasm effected by music, an enthusiasm which played a great role among the Corybantes and Cybele, the Great Mother, who were imbued with the god.   But he referred to it to reject it: does it have something in common with that immediate highest vision of God raised above all reason?   No, he said, and he threw it out along with all forms of ecstasy.   All should be intellect and intellectual application.   Nor does he acknowledge prophecies.   Yet he encourages solar piety, and there are some popular beliefs from which he was not aloof: the highest original Being is far above the sensuous; and the middle beings, the daemons, the good as well as the bad, are accessible in their different degrees through action and the proper serving of God.   The good ones are individual parts of the world, and Porphyry entrusted the realm of music to one of them.   But he ascribed to the bad ones that which above all seems pernicious in folk religion, and this category included for him that which is incantational.   For magical means affect not the primal Being, God, but only the gods of the second and third rank.

Thus Porphyry forsakes the Ideal heights of the Plotinian view of music and indeed retains hardly anything of it.   What he does in not recognizing Christ and in believing in daemons, or "middle" beings, is to play into the hands of Christian writers.   Eusebius, bishop of Caesarea (c.314), a younger contemporary, in his *Ecclesiastical History* (6.19.8-9, NPN2 1.266) took him severely to task, and St. Augustine quotes him in order to refute him (*City* 10.26-30).   Porphyry denies the Plotinian assertion that music mediates sense and spirit, and, as we have seen, derides all secular music.   But his student Iamblichus, called the "Divine" by his own cultish followers and already frequently quoted in these pages, takes a different stand.

III

Iamblichus (Iamblichus of Chalcis).   Porphyry was a Greek Neoplatonist, but Iamblichus, like Nicomachus, was a Syrian of the same school.   All accepted Plato's doctrine of ultimate principles.   Iamblichus was a fabulist, "historian" of the universal marvels, and a "magician."   He blended Plato with magic, a superstition Plato deplored.

Dying approximately in the year 333 A.D., he had been a citizen of Smyrna, not Alexandria.   He studied with Porphyry in Rome and was preoccupied with the Mysteries of Egypt and with the doctrines of the Pythagoreans and the Chaldean-Babylonians which derived from Egypt.   He called himself a Pythagorean, but *theurgia* was more important to him than theory or theology.   Only five books of his comprehensive work on the *Egyptian Mysteries* remain, though there is some question about his authorship of this work.   Here is treated the physical and ethical significance of numbers in music, geometry, and the spheres (astronomy)--a mystical mathematical and symbolic theory much like those of the Pythagoreans and Nicomachus.   There is little, if any, resemblance to Plotinus.   The metaphysical-symbolical aspect of numbers, the musical elements as expressed in numbers (which he probably derived from Nicomachus), and the theological (as beyond the philosophical)--these elements come to the fore, as do the Pythagoreans themselves.   The ancients (like Aristoxenus early in his life) had been receptive to such Pythagorean teachings, and Iamblichus loved the wonders and the anecdotes about them (which ultimately were spread abroad throughout the Middle Ages).   He attributed the invention of music to the Babylonians, from whom Pythagoras took it for naturalization in Greece.   Iamblichus' mysticism is poetical, musical, religious, and he incorporated it into ritual.   For him, universal sympathy combines everything into a system of correspondences (*Mysteries* 5.24).

Yet he never thought of music as a pure science.   Like Aristoxenus and Aristides Quintilianus, he sharply separates its theoretical from its practical realizations, and (following Democritus, perhaps) he even calls it a younger art which, having arisen only in a period of prosperity, contributes chiefly to pleasure.   He held to the ascetic, moral, and cathartic doctrines of his predecessors.   Plotinus and even Porphyry were ambiguous about the place of music in moral purgation and ecstasy, but Iamblichus, whose book is entitled *The Mysteries*, is as clear on this point as one perhaps can be when treating the mysteries.

There are three levels of being: God (or the gods), daemons, and man.   The daemons (previously encountered in the work of Porphyry and not to be confused with devils) exist in a hierarchy.   The question is how human beings are to relate to them.   Iamblichus believes with Plotinus that God cannot be influenced by prayer and actions of a physical type (*Mysteries* 1.15).   Yet he is overwhelmed by the effect of magic in primitive art.   The use of symbolic indications (he agrees with the Stoics and Plato) will apparently solve the contradiction: he also thinks that if magical practices do not affect the gods, they do open the human soul to divine influences (ibid. 3.6).   There is here a sharp contrast to the views of Porphyry. The result can be ecstasy when the soul separates from the body, but he prefers to call it enthusiasm, which he defines as the entrance of the God to his worshippers. Ecstasy is produced by the influence of (good) daemons; it can degrade and impair our spiritual states. But enthusiasm (called by Aristotle the emotion of the ethical part of the soul) is entirely the work of the gods; it raises our souls in all circumstances to what is better. Enthusiasm comes not from man's soul, but from God, who uses human beings like instruments (ibid. 3.7).

Though instrument, spirit, and song can be a mystical One, music of the physical type is motive in nature, it excites the affections, and its instruments can heal the passions of the soul when it is in disorder, change the body's "temperaments and dispositions," and through certain ordered tones arouse or soothe "Bacchic" fury. Furthermore, when it is unstable and variable and can by way of its differences "accord with the several dispositions of the soul," it induces to ecstasies. Physical and human, it produces the human work of art; possessing nothing divine, it is foreign to enthusiasm. Harmony and rhythm are its portion, but in itself it is only human and ecstatic.

The soul, however, before it entered the body, heard the divine harmony, a harmony which it retained through the inspiration of the gods after it entered the body. This kind of music is not an "ablation, purgation, or medicine." It is an enthusiasm, a realization of a harmonious state which it wants to retain. If the instrument, music, and song can be an enthusiastic One, then the sounds and harmonies which they create are "appropriately consecrated to the gods" (ibid. 3.9). When the sensuous element is mixed with divine harmony to tarnish it, prophecies become false, and then true enthusiasm is so disfigured as to revert back to ecstasy, a corybantic ecstasy which is inimical to it. Ecstasy is human, but enthusiasm is divine and can be aroused only by divine harmony (ibid. 3.7).

God alone is its source, but it can also be aroused by the harmony and rhythm, the musical element of the soul. Before its birth, the soul heard divine harmony (as the Pythagoreans had insisted), and on earth it is capable of giving itself over to the harmony which has traces of divine origin. In enthusiasm, the soul "remembers" supernatural music. But physical music cannot call up enthusiasm itself. Instead, divine enthusiasm brings musical expression along with itself--but not always, since singing and playing music form only one of the concomitants of the enthusiastic state, which differs with the individuality of each enraptured person (ibid. 3.5). In theurgic ritual, however, the chanting of magic sounds and names brings about a mystic union.

For music is one of the magical arts. Thanks to it, we can "relate" to divine beings and even influence them: each divine being has its own sacred song. Every god in his place in the universe is in a certain strong relationship to different harmonic sounds (ibid. 3.5). Should I employ music corresponding to those sounds, the god immediately makes his appearance in order to sympathize with me, and then I am completely possessed and fulfilled with a higher nature. The music is in the god and "descends" with the god to me. Iamblichus adopts Plotinian negativism: it is not that the soul is transported so much as that it experiences a flight from the sense-world. The godhead, never divested of the supernal harmony entrusted to it, reacts (as it were) to its earthly imitation and realizes itself in a corresponding degree in a union with the individual soul on its way to enthusiastic transport.

Iamblichus takes a position far from Plotinus, Porphyry, and most ancient aestheticians of music: (1) he makes no references to the concrete ethical theory: "catharsis" is a matter of religious and spiritual salvation; (2) his religious theory is "tarnished" by the use of magic and prophecy; (3) he seldom refers to psychological states: the real effects of music depend on spiritual events brought about by the intervention of supernatural beings; (4) like Plotinus and Porphyry, he recognizes and desires a flight from the senses; (5) he says nothing of Plotinus' idea that beauty can be a stage on the way to the highest moral purity; (6) yet he agrees with the idea, approved by the Neoplatonists, that knowledge is achieved not through rational thought, but through immediate divine revelation. Iamblichus qualifies even this last theory by juxtaposing enthusiasm and ecstasy and by granting a place to ("white") daemons in the arousal of these emotions.

IV

Proclus (Proclus Diadochus). Proclus (c.410-85), the Greek Neoplatonic philosopher whose thought is an extension of Plotinus' and yet independent in some respects, lived approximately two hundred years after Porphyry and is thought to represent the final phase of ancient thought. He was born in Constantinople, taught in Athens, and adored Plato's works. His life extended beyond that of St. Augustine, the greatest of the early Church Fathers. More faithful to the philosophy of Plotinus than Plotinus' pupil Porphyry, he is thought to be the last great teacher of the Neoplatonic school. Like Porphyry, who was a contemporary of the earliest Church Fathers, he defended paganism and vigorously opposed Christianity, which was in the ascendancy in the Roman Empire and was replacing philosophy in men's minds with its theology. He especially spoke out against the Christian idea of the creation of the world. Like Porphyry, too, he was a scholar and commentator on the philosophies of the past, especially Plato's. He wrote a commentary on the *Timaeus* in which he stressed the macrocosm-microcosm analogy, an aspect that he interpreted as supporting idealism. He thought that he himself was a link in the "golden chain" of true philosophy which connected men with heaven in the fashion of the golden chain mentioned by Homer. He studied and sang Orphic hymns and, like Iamblichus, followed both Orphic and "Chaldean" methods of purification through occult art.[3] And on occasion he wrote his own hymns. In certain works that in the fifteenth century were translated into Latin by Marsilio Ficino, he described astrological music, using mostly sun-images, which he may have found in Porphyry. He wrote chiefly commentaries.

Nichomachus, whom Proclus admired, wrote a *Theologumena arithmetica* (later probably compiled by Iamblichus), but Proclus wrote not only an *Institutio Theologica* but also a work in six "books" on the theology of Plato. He expressed his ideas about music in his commentaries, however: in the one on the *Timaeus* (already mentioned), one on Euclid, and three on Platonic dialogues (*Alcibiades I*, the *Republic*, and the *Parmenides*).[4]

In his commentary on *Alcibiades I*, Proclus says some instruments are repressive and other "motive," some adapted to rest and others to motion. He thinks the repressive ones the more useful for education: they give order to manners, repress turbulency, and quiet and temper agitation. Motive instruments serve to produce enthusiastic energy. Therefore the pipe (aulos) was useful in the ancient mysteries and mystical sacrifices: then rational power was excited "to a divine nature." In the education of youth, the irrational aspect should be subdued and the rational excited. As the irrational element is disciplined, reason-"initiators" (motive instruments) "energize enthusiastically."

Unlike Iamblichus, he tacitly rejects magic, but also like him he accepts the idea of enthusiasm. He shares the Neoplatonic predilection for music, but nevertheless believes he contains the soul of Nicomachus, whose organization of four sciences he accepts. He therefore too counts music among the mathematical sciences; he sees it as a younger art deriving from (the mother) arithmetic, as astronomy is a younger art to geometry (*On Euclid* 35.28ff, 36.24ff, 59.20). He attributes great significance to mathematical symbolism (*On Tim.* 216a, *On Euclid* 22.2ff) and treats the harmony of the spheres in the Pythagorean manner (*On Tim.* 238b). Like Plato, he thinks the mathematical sciences are indispensable preliminaries to philosophy. But they are not self-contained as to aim: they are only copies of true Being (*On Tim.* 193c). In this respect he opposes Plotinus.

In his own mythology, as in Porphyry's, there is evidence of a subtle substitution of the Muses (from whom, according to one account, music got its name) for the Sirens, by whom it was represented on Plato's cosmic spindle. The Sirens are accompanied by the Fates in the vision of Er (*Rep.* 617). Proclus insists that the Muses provide the Cosmos with the form of Harmony while the Fates provide it with the form of order (*On Rep.* 2.241). Though the Muses are not attached to the spheres (ibid. 2.237.17), they are close to Apollo, the origin of the universal music (his right hand) and universal harmony (his left hand). As sources of intelligible harmony, they control the Sirens, the sources of the corporeal harmony of the spheres (ibid. 2.239-40). Intelligible harmony and corporeal harmony are supplemented by a third harmony, which the Sirens grant man as a gift to serve as their "ultimate image" (*On Alc. I* 205). Here Proclus comes close to defining the "musics" of Boethius.

Proclus separates the arts into two classes: those which can express

Ideas--that is, all of those later called the quadrivium (*On Parmen.* 5.58)--
and those denied this capacity (those useful for daily needs). He finds that
there are three groups of musical devotees--the musical persons themselves,
the admirers, and the philosopher (*Comm. on Euclid* 27.7)--in an ascent
from sensuously perceptible harmonies to the super-sensuous just as the
enthusiast is carried from visible beauty to the invisible (ibid. 21.10ff). This
activity is an augury of the intelligible divine of the future (ibid. 21.14ff).
To turn to this divine music is truly to be a friend of the beautiful, and to
experience one revelation of divine harmony is to see the entire organization
of the world and the foundation of the lordship of the Creator of the
universe. Like Plotinus, Proclus refers to the well-tuned (Pythagorean) lyre
of the cosmos on which the *Nous* (reason), the soul, and the body represent
the "highest," the "middle," and the "lowest" steps of the scale (*On the Rep.*
2.4.15, 2.49.25).

In symbolical and metaphysical fashion and possibly following
Iamblichus, he also allies the three perfect consonances with the three levels
of the beings who have souls. The octave, the most satisfactory in itself,
includes all other consonances and symbolizes godlike souls. The fifth,
below the octave but above the fourth, is reserved for daemons. And the
fourth, on the lowest level but necessary in common with the others if
harmony in its totality is to come to be, is the representative of partial souls,
to which the human soul belongs. Such comments come partly from the
Pythagoreans, of course, and probably from Porphyry, but the position is
modified by Proclus' dependence on the ethical theory of Plato (*On Euclid*
24.4ff).

This last subject causes him to remark on practical matters. He tries
to modify and moderate Plato's harsh rejection of poetry, though he
ultimately agrees with Plato after all that it is good or bad only with respect
to the aim it serves (*On the Rep.* 360ff, 392ff). The highest aim (as the
Neoplatonists show) and value of poetry and music, therefore, will involve
the recognition of the highest things (ibid. 361)--a principle which can be
interpreted to lead either to the ascetic ideal or to the purification and the
sanctification of human beings. Tragedy, comedy, and theatrical music do
not reach that aim (ibid. 1.50.2ff). Worldly dramatic and religious music
are real opposites because religion, superior to philosophy, has values and
meanings which music must attain either by releasing human emotions and
passions or, through genuine art works, in a restrained fashion expressing
religious and moral perceptions, conceptions, and experiences. Only sacred
songs allow us to become at one with the gods, to have a mystical relationship with them (similarly, Plato thought the hymns to the gods to be
acceptable). Other music cannot lead directly to God. Only philosophers
have that true enthusiasm which fills the soul with that symmetry whose
representatives are rhythms and meters (*On Tim.* 331.68, *On the Rep.*
399-400). Music may produce its harmful effects in the theater, therefore,
but its undoubted purpose is theurgic, magical, and mystical.

The Greek aesthetics of music, then--the Greek Idea of music--includes the abstract (faith in mathematics), the fantastic (the ranking of the gods and music among magical arts), the symbolical (the parallels between every aspect of music with the cosmos and of musical consonance with the states of souls), the educational, the classificatory (the inclusion of music among the sciences), and the religious (sacred music as the highest form of art leading to the divine). In all of these areas Proclus and the Neoplatonists who preceded him found models in the Pythagoreans, Plato, and Aristotle.

Not that Proclus' work summarizes the older doctrines. Plotinus, Porphyry, Iamblichus, and Proclus all together modified the doctrines or truth of tradition into what may seem to be an eccentric, peculiar, or special arrangement of ideas--ideas which again demonstrate that the past is not repeated but modified--ideas which, despite the sometimes violent anti-Christian feeling accompanying them, were taken up by the Fathers and scholars of the Christian Church, willing at least in this instance and able to take encouragement from their enemies. But the Neoplatonists in one sense come at the end of an era. Their support of magic and theology means a gradual abandonment of the sciences, of Plato and Aristotle. Their support of the Forms, however imagined, remained, and their rejection by the Christian Church seems in some part a symbol of the closing of the schools of Athens by the Emperor Justinian approximately forty-four years after Proclus' death.

In another sense, however, they are ostensibly at a crossroads: relying and building on old Greek music theory, they turn in another direction. But the new direction is interrupted by the work of the medieval Latin Church and then is returned to life, but in a much modified form, in the Renaissance.

X
The Decline of Hellenism

The late classical milieu, as described in the previous chapters, may be summarized as follows: by the end of the second century A.D., the idea of music as described by the Pythagoreans (or by an imagined Pythagoras), Plato, Aristotle, and Aristoxenus had become common property. Whereas its more numerical-technical aspects as described by Euclid were developed arithmetically and numerologically by Nicomachus with astrological additions by Ptolemy, its moral and therapeutic aspects had for long become an accepted part of theory devoted to other concerns--the moral and political purposes of Plato, the rhetorical-oratorical aims of Cicero, Dionysius of Halicarnassus, and Quintilian, and the more historical ones of Varro and Pseudo-Plutarch. There had been the protesting voice of Philodemus, who is sometimes called the formalist among the early theorists, but it sounded alone and, after the catastrophic eruption in 79 A.D. of Mount Vesuvius, was heard no more. Aristotelian and Pseudo-Aristotelian acoustics seemed to be forgotten. But there was the difficult and perhaps even magnificent attempt of Aristides Quintilianus to combine all musico-theoretical threads into one mystical body of Neoplatonist correspondences. Also, the Greco-Jewish thought of Philo of Alexandria was blended with Neo-platonism to set a new pattern for the aesthetics of music, a blend which more and more persisted, so that, by the time the Roman empire finally disintegrated and the period known as the Middle Ages began, the classical idea of music had undergone significant adjustments and changes. The political fundamentals and realities were altered, the classical gods, goddesses, and Muses were replaced by a Christian God in turn kindly and vengeful, and the secular political group of men represented by the state was replaced in large part by the congregation of religious worshippers led by the clergy. Antecedent to the Middle Ages were the Church Fathers, who, forming a group by themselves, based their thought not only on the Hebrew Bible but also on Plato's *Timaeus*, Philo, Varro, Cicero, and Plotinus. Roughly concurrent with the Church Fathers was a group of writers and thinkers--the subject of this chapter--who may be called retrogressives.

I shall discuss first the skeptic Sextus Empiricus and then two Varro-like writers who, by repeating old notions and varying them slightly, passed them on for the use not of musicians but of scholars. Finally, I consider two explicators of Plato and the Platonic Cicero. Thus, philosophical Neoplatonism achieves a kind of consistency of its own in music theory, makes its own impression on the growing Christian Church and the patristic writers, and, serving as a record from the past, assists in the development of a new theory of music which, almost independently it seems, was growing out of the musical practice of the Church and its ceremonies.

I

Sextus Empiricus, the Skeptic. The two most illustrious skeptics of the ancient world lived approximately three centuries apart. The first was Aenesidemus (first century B.C.) and the second was Sextus Empiricus (second and third centuries A.D.). The former is of no interest here, but the latter, practical, positivistic, and methodical, is. Sextus Empiricus also lived approximately three centuries after Philodemus, whom as a formalist he resembled, though the latter was an Epicurean and Sextus a Pyrrhonic Skeptic.

As such, and like Epicurus, Sextus looked for tranquillity, impassivity, and moderation in all things. Though a physician, he was yet suspicious of all learned studies and wrote against the professors (in the original sense) of them all: of grammar, rhetoric, geometry, arithmetic, astrology (or astronomy), and music. Unwittingly he named six of the seven Liberal Arts (that is, except for dialectic, or logic). And, keeping close to the realities of concrete existence, he gave the word 'music' several layers of meaning: it is a science of melodies, notes, and rhythm-making, as Aristoxenus in his *Harmonics* showed it to be; it also means instrumental skill like that of aulos and harp-players. These are the proper senses of the the term. But there is a third: its use for correctness of performance, which we call musical even though the work of art is a piece of painting: the term then stands for the correctness an artist has achieved ([*Against the Professors*] *Against the Musicians* 6.1-3). But Sextus himself wanted to take up only the first sense because, of all the kinds of music, this is the most perfect. It is of course acceptable because it is scientific.

He questions that music is conducive to goodness or has any special psychological effects, or that its sound causes rejoicing, or that, heard in hymns, feasts, and sacrifices to the gods, it "incites the mind to emulate the good and console those in grief" (ibid. 6.18). Animals are not affected by it; nor can a certain kind of melody produce stately and refined motions in the soul, or another kind produce base and ignoble motions. Nor should musicians use the term 'character' for melodies because they supposedly form character. Music is not a superior craft even though it affects the educated; it affects the uneducated as well (ibid. 6.31-32). This is because it actually resists virtue, works against those striving for it, and can easily lead young people into incontinence and debauchery (ibid. 6.34).

Not for Sextus is the idea that the world is constructed harmoniously; even if true, he says, "a thing of this [harmonious] kind can be of no help towards felicity, just as harmony in instruments is of no help" (ibid. 6.37). He would accept the idea that musical "tunes" by nature are "some of this kind and others of that kind"--that is, they differ among themselves. They are really not one thing or another in fact and reality: it is only our own thinking which makes them so (ibid. 6.20). In Sextus' philosophy, subjectivity has now replaced the objectivity of the qualities of modes, rhythms, and melodies. Indeed, musical knowledge is not even a source of general pleasure, and thus the non-musical do not miss the art when it is absent. We do actually enjoy delightful melodies (that is, one supposes, those melodies we presume to be delightful). And the really expert musician who better than the layman understands what is performed really gets no greater feeling of pleasure from his music than the professional cook or wine-taster from the results of his work.

But then all studies except one are suspect. Learning about literature is impossible because there is no art of grammar, because poetry is useless, and because learning about literature by way of grammar has no value. Only philosophy has value; even the grammarian is interested only in words and not in what lies behind them. Furthermore, literature (grammar) is not necessarily useful to the state ([*Against the Professors*] *Against the Grammarians* 1.293-94). On the last two counts, Sextus is of course correct, and on the first, on grammar, he anticipates St. Augustine.

Music is even less valuable than grammar: it is not even useful to life. It simply distracts. It does not exert a moderating influence on the mind, but deflects it from its proper occupations. In this it is like sleep or wine, turning attention away from the rigors of war, from the toils of labor, and from the passions it cannot rectify. Though Plato argued that music contributes to happiness, Epicurus, who is declared to be correct, denied his contention and called music unprofitable (*Against the Musicians* 6.27).

As a representative skeptic, Sextus Empiricus even denies music's very existence. If there were no sounds, he says, there would be no music. Musicians base their theory of music on notes; but, as a matter of fact, notes do not exist. According to the Cyrenaics (Aristippus, c.435-356 B.C., was their leader), only sensations or feelings exist, and all sentient creatures strive for pleasure and avoid pain; sound is not a feeling and does not exist as a producer of feeling; if pleasure is the chief end of life, the immediate pleasures are the best; the individual himself is the reality because Platonic universals have no being. And if sound, which is an individual thing, is not a feeling, neither is it a sensation; it is something which evokes sensation; therefore sounds in themselves do not exist. Does not Plato agree? For him only Ideas exist, just as for Democritus only atoms exist.

Sextus Empiricus is suspicious of a phenomenological philosophy of depth. We know only phenomena, not the inner nature of things. Thus phenomena are neither true nor false; they just are. Not able to know things as in themselves they are, we can only know their appearances. We cannot accept or reject things themselves because all we know is our sensations. To suspend judgment is to recognize our own failure to understand things.

Nor is a thing a soul, for the soul does not exist either. It is not an object. Since it is only an experience, music too is not an object, and it is not objectively able to effect, soothe, or refine emotions. Its supposed effect depends on the individual and that individual's psychological responses. Thus, there can be no science of music, only a psychology of it. Similar arguments apply to rhythm--and even to time (ibid. 6.41-45, *Outlines of Pyrrhonism* 3.136ff). Sextus Empiricus is the model of a naturalistic phenomenalistic skeptic. Anti-Platonic, psychological, and "realistic," he rejects universals and objectivities and accepts as primary only subjectivity and experience.

This is not to say that he did not grant to the musician, if not some of the virtues, at least some of the processes of the learned. He agreed with Speusippus that some things are perceived by the senses and some by the mind, the latter being objects of educated thought and partakers of reasoned truth. For Sextus the fingers of a wind or string player perform actions which have their origins not in themselves but in mental activity and therefore in cognitive experience as described by Speusippus. Similarly, a musician who can accurately divide that which is harmonious from that which is not harmonious produces impressions which are derived not from nature but from thought. Educated impression benefits in a natural way from the accomplishments of learning, which are based on reason and grant a faultless knowledge of the object.

Sextus Empiricus is thinking of technical knowledge as art and science. A musician's ear, he says, recognizes the accuracy or inaccuracy in the tuning of an instrument. Furthermore, he thinks, when a player seems to perform spontaneously, he does so on a foundation of practice and "reasoning" (*Against the Logicians* 1.145-46). Art is a specific body of knowledge or skill which can be learned and put into practice. It is knowledge organized by the mind.

Skeptical, therefore, of the much lauded beneficial effects of music, Sextus still accepts the Speusippian psychology which allowed the musician an objective knowledge of the object, no matter how questionable the value of the object itself. But it is not a therapeutic; rather, it is a craft, a technique, of forms about which one can acquire a body of knowledge. Impersonal in every respect, it is merely formal. Clearly, Sextus' entire philosophy is purely intellectual, an avenue to intellectual delight for its own sake, and not an empirical treatment of human experience and its objects.

What influence could the writings of Sextus Empiricus have exerted? It is hard to say. A follower of the teachings of Pyrrho (c.365-c.275 B.C.), the skeptical philosopher, he was unknown to the Middle Ages. It was as though the lava of Vesuvius which covered the works of Philodemus had covered his works too. Only in 1562 were his writings translated into Latin by Antonius Gogavinus and did the publisher Étienne issue them as a whole. And during the English Renaissance Sir Walter Raleigh (c.1552-1618) wrote *The Skeptic*, which seems to have been a summary translation of a fragment of Sextus Empiricus.

II

Not Skeptics, however, but a large group of commentators on Plato and Aristotle dating from the first century B.C.--Philo, Cicero, the Peripatetics (Pseudo-Aristotelians), Neoplatonists, and Neopythagoreans were their models--make up the bulk of writers who in the most eclectic of writings passed on old ideas in pleasant and palatable form. Men like these, popularizers in any age, write a "gentle" literature for the aristocrat with pretensions to learning. Like Varro, they were quotable authorities for centuries to come, and they preceded the encyclopedic scholar whose work in the Middle Ages became the repository of almost everything known or at least accepted. Their names are Aulus Gellius and Athenaeus.

Aulus Gellius. Aulus Gellius (second century A.D.), like many of the lesser figures treated in this volume, is almost a blank from the biographical standpoint. A lawyer and part-time resident of Athens, he wrote a *Noctes Atticae* (*Attic Nights*), a compilation--really his own commonplace book--in which was recorded, in heterogeneous fashion, and in twenty (not quite complete) "books," everything that interested him in books or in what he had heard in conversations. Almost every branch of knowledge, including grammar, geometry, philosophy, and history, was covered by scholarly quotation. He cannot be accused of originality. He repeated "facts" and opinions by now familiar to us.

He likes to take the position of the receiver--indeed, the connoisseur--of art; the philosophical "Greeks" would have accused him of triviality: "Musical" as the orator's technique may be, the audience is his final test. There are listeners, he says, who hear words of "warning, . . . persuasion, or . . . rebuke." or a discussion of a philosophical theme, and then praise the speaker inordinately without thought or restraint; or they shout compliments to him. Aulus Gellius is disillusioned: they pretend to be charmed by the rhythm of his words and the musical notes accompanying him, but reveal that they have not heard the speaker at all and that both they and he have been wasting their time. They act as though they had been at an aulos player's recital (5.1.1-4). The implication is clear: they must have empty minds. Gellius does not dispute the legitimacy of the musician's performance at an oration. Located in the audience, he often at intervals sounded a "deeper note" on a short pipe to restrain the calm the "exuberant energy of the orator's delivery." Yet the practice was not uniform, and Cicero (*The Making of an Orator* 3.60.225) reports that Gracchus the orator used a skillful musician for both purposes--to calm and to arouse him (*Attic Nights* 1.11.10). More questionable are specific psychological effects.

Gellius finds contradictions among reports about the effects of instruments. The Pseudo-Aristotle of the *Problems*, for example, says pipers were used in armies to spur on the cowards (ibid. 1.11.18). On the other hand, Thucidydes describes the Lacedaemonians in battle as making use not of horns and trumpets but of the aulos--not to stimulate the warriors as horns and trumpets do, but to calm the men and to cause them to advance in better order, for the effect of the aulos player's notes is to "restrain impetuosity." Feelings were kept under control, and "fierce impetuosity" was checked by the "quiet, pleasant, and even solemn" prelude in conformity with the discipline of military music. The Lacedaemonians (Spartans) advanced slowly to the music of aulos players, who helped them march to the attack in ranks unbroken rhythmically. Similarly, the lyre regulated the steps of the Cretans in battle. And, if female aulos players were indeed the delight of wanton banqueters (ibid. 1.11.1-9), the sensual Greeks had a different reason for their reaction, which could not have been tranquilizing. Nor could facial expression have been the cause. Do we not know that the beautiful Alcibiades broke his pipes in two and threw them away (as did Athena) because playing them makes the face ugly (ibid. 15.17.1-3)?

Gellius does not forget medical effects. To Theophrastus' idea that gouty pains in one's hips can be relieved by soothing measures played on the aulos, he adds that Democritus (in *On Deadly Infections*) said that snake bites too are cured by skillfully played and melodious aulos music. Indeed, music is the medicine for many ills of the flesh (*Attic Nights* 4.13.1-4). Physicians say that music sets in motion the veins (the arteries) of men according to the number 7 (of the seven-string lyre) because of the harmony produced by the striking of four different strings. And Gellius then illustrates the mystical value of the number 7 (ibid. 3.1.0.13, 15-17). Music must share in this universal value, the recognition of which he traces back to Varro and his *Hebdomades* (*On Portraits*): the number 7 has various powers. It is the Greater and the Lesser Bear in the heavens, and the seven "wandering" planets in seven circles in the heavens perpendicular to its axis. The Zodiac is influenced by the seven, as are the nesting of kingfishers, the course of the moon, the birth of human beings (seven-month children are especially weak), the height of the human body (no one is taller than seven feet), the teeth, and the wonders of the world (which are seven). "These remarks by Varro," Gellius adds, ". . . show painstaking investigation" (*Attic Nights* 3.10.15-17).

Gellius' *Attic Nights*, then, is a record of serious amusements, scholarly gossip on a broad scale, a compendium of anecdotes which adds little or nothing to musical theory or speculation. It is a kind of historical journalism which does not even have the virtue of the imagination found in Athenaeus and Censorinus, though they too are not primarily original thinkers but interested recorders of ancient quotable opinion.

Athenaeus. Of all the documents examined thus far, the most charming in a casual and sometimes clumsy way is the *Deipnosophists* (*Banquet of Learned Men*) of Athenaeus (fl. c.200), a grammarian of Egypt, already cited because he treats music historically and because his material is said to come from (the lost) *Concerning Music* of Heraclides Ponticus.

Dilettantish in tone, the work is in fifteen books, most of them complete. Following Plato and Pseudo-Plutarch, it, like Gellius' *Attic Nights*, is filled with information on every conceivable subject, contains references to something like eight hundred writers and to something like 2500 writings, most of them lost--quite an accomplishment for a series of drinking parties. A genuine antiquarian, Athenaeus must have benefited from the treasures of the great library at Alexandria.   There are vivid references (1.15-16) to dancing to aulos accompaniment as described in the *Anabasis* of Xenophon (c.434-c.355 B.C.), Greek historian and disciple of Socrates, and to Sophocles' dancing, naked and oil-anointed, to the accompaniment of his lyre (1.20). Furthermore, the *Deipnosophists* is an example of "banquet" or symposium writing of which Plato furnished the classical model.

Like Plato and Pseudo-Plutarch, Athenaeus speaks of the latter-day decay or perversion of music (1.18): "today" choruses instead of performing in the traditional fashion must follow innovative aulos players (14.617). He contrasts the orderly beauty in the music of old, when "auloi were peculiarly adapted to every mode, and every player had auloi suited to every mode used in the public contests," with that of "today," when "people take up music in a haphazard and irrational manner." He quotes Aristoxenus on the modern corruption of music, especially in the theater (14.631-32), as well as the unknown author of the *Helots*, who deplores the change in song as represented by Gnesippus, the inventor of serenades for adulterers when they want to lure their loves by playing the *iambyka* and the triangle (14.638).

In Athenaeus' list of classical instruments is named the water-organ or water-clock and its pleasures.   It is a wind instrument governed by water. He also mentions the triangle and the *nabla*, a Phoenician instrument that was struck.   Instruments of the past, in this symposiac environment, seem called upon to justify the use of those of the present. And so in a welter of descriptions of ancient musical life reconstructed from ancient works there stand out remembered luxuries accompanied by music.   Named are the triangle, the tambourine, the *sambuca*, the single pipe (invented, it is said, by the Egyptians, especially by Osiris), the cithara and triple-cithara, the transverse flute called the *photinx*, and the half-bored or half-holed *auloi*, called by Anacreon tender and by others boys' or children's pipes. Many of these were used at banquets (4.174-82). Nor is the *magadis* forgotten, a string instrument which (likened to the harp) is played in octaves following the ancient practice of combining men's and boys' voices--that is, of *magadizing*.   The list continues with the *phoinix* (invented by the Phoenicians), the *pektis* (something like but different from the *magadis*), the *clepsiamb* (for accompanying the reciting "in distorted fashion [of] metrical verses"), the *scindapsus*, the *iambyka* (for the chanting of iambic verses), and others like the *barbitos* (similar to the lyre) and *barmos* (undefined). And in ancient times there were others for solo playing (14.636ff). Whatever the instruments of the Greek past, they seemed not different except by name from those of the late Roman period.

Now, the Lacedaemonians, the Thebans, and the Athenians, to say nothing of the Pythagoreans, all learned to sing to the harp or cithara; and in his essay on the Greek poet Stesichorus (c.640-c.550 B.C.) Chamaeleon says that the poems of Homer, Hesiod, Archilochus, Mimnerus (late seventh century B.C.), and Phoclides (sixth century B.C.) were chanted musically. The verses of Archilochus were the object too of rhapsodizing from a raised chair in theaters by Simonides of Zacynthus--this according to Clearchus in his *Riddles* (14.620).

The aulos played alone was of course generally disliked. Its tone was harsh, and Horace in his Ninth Epode (1.5) speaks of the barbaric quality of an instrument often felt to have been similar to it.[1] "'Tis the song," says a speaker (as Athenaeus reports) "that is queen, established by the Pierian Muse, but the [aulos] must be second in the dance, for he is e'en a servant...." But "the music of [*auloi*] with lyre is a joint partner in stageplays; for when one adapts his mood skilfully to that of his associates, then, and then only, do we get the greatest delight": this was called concerted music, "a kind of contest in harmony, aulos-music, and dance-rhythm exactly corresponding, with no singer adding words to the performance" (14.617-18). The ubiquitous aulos, a stimulating instrument though not an especially pleasant one, like other instruments could in combinations create moods, and instruments and dance without words could produce concerted effects. Other kinds of music produce different results even in social gatherings at which everyone sings in chorus, either simultaneously or separately in groups; usually the skilled singers sing last because they "believed that the beautiful song was the one which seemed to contain advice and counsel useful for the conduct of life" (15.694).

All those present at Athenaeus' dinner table praise music as an amusement. But Masurius has taken up the playing of instruments because he thinks it is deep and intricate and because it always supplies something new. Those learned and educated call it a treasure since it "trains character [and] tames the hot-tempered and those whose opinions clash." The Pythagorean Cleinis always played the lyre when he was exasperated to the point of anger. Again Theophrastus is quoted about the aulos played in the Phrygian mode over a sciatic part of the body. But the company present doubts the existence of that mode; Heraclides Ponticus indicated that there are only three modes because there are only three kinds of Greeks. They are the Dorian, the Aeolian, and the Ionian, of which the last is hard, neither bright nor cheerful, but austere; it has a not ignoble seriousness, and is a mode well adapted to tragedy. Ephorus (the historian of the fourth century B.C.) thinks that music was introduced for purposes of deceit and quackery because, as Polybius the historian of Megalopolis (c.205-125 B.C.) says, the Lacedaemonians had good reason for substituting the aulos and marching rhythm for the trumpet in battle, just as the earliest Arcadians had good reason to carry "the art of music into their entire social organization" and to make its pursuit mandatory and habitual for boys and young men who were otherwise not austere in their habits of life (14.623-26).

Thus Athenaeus, whose reports of musical discussions sometimes suggest rhapsody, repeats many of the old stories, takes the old conservative positions with regard to music, and sufficiently stresses the pleasure it supplies to serve as an antidote to skeptical writers. But, then, the term 'conservative' is a modern one and hardly applies to thought in an environment dominated by the belief in the existence of certainties long established and asking only to be uncovered. The mood of Athenaeus is that of fun in discussion.   His is occasional thought about basic, inherited, and even old-fashioned and out-of-date subjects seen through a romantic glass.

III

Censorinus, Chalcidius, and Macrobius. Sextus Empiricus was an iconoclast. Gellius and Athenaeus were antiquarians in the realm of ideas. Censorinus, Chalcidius, and Macrobius in effect were inheritors of the notion of Porphyry that philosophy is the servant of theology. Their method is expository and ontological: world, mankind, and musical art form a kind of interlocking but yet descending series of realities, of correspondences, in which world harmony surrounds human harmony, both being made up of "musical" intervals based on musico-mathematical relationships.   The traditions making up this theology are of course Pythagorean, Platonic, and Neoplatonic.   These traditions are supported by transitional figures who of necessity were aware of a rising Roman Church and yet were determined to hold to a classical past.

1. Censorinus, a Roman grammarian, along with Varro, Gellius, and Athenaeus, is another of the scholars and men of letters who took over ideas from the past to reconstruct them for their own popularizing purposes. His work, *De die Natali* (*Concerning the Day of Birth*) (238 A.D.), is one of the many surveys which appeared in late Latin and early medieval times. It is a short book, even a fragment. Censorinus was among the first (the others being St. Augustine, Favorinus, Macrobius, Martianus Capella, Boethius, Cassiodorus, and Isidore of Seville) to transfer the collective elements of Greek musical and intellectual tradition to the Middle Ages. His sources, like theirs, were Varro, Cicero, Pliny, Quintilian, and certain Greek theorists who remained practically unknown until his work was first published in 1628 by Erycius Puteanus of Louvain.

2. In approximately 340 A.D., there appeared a *Commentary on the Timaeus* 35-36. About its author, Chalcidius, almost nothing is known except that he was a grammarian and probably a Christian. He is one of the first people, including Cicero, to find it necessary to comment on the musical section of the *Timaeus*, of which, along with Macrobius, he fairly created a revival. Though Cicero in his *Dream of Scipio* in connection with music mentioned only the harmony of the spheres and its political emanations, Chalcidius is more elaborate.

3. Macrobius (Ambrosius Aurelius Theodosius), like his predecessors in this chapter, was a type of writer more and more common as time went

on--the scholar, translator, and commentator writing for readers of Latin who could not read Greek. Living in the fourth and fifth centuries A.D., he was a Neoplatonist and a virtual contemporary of St. Augustine. His best-known work is a commentary on Cicero and his *Dream of Scipio*, a work for which he unconscionably copied from Porphyry and Plotinus.[2] He also wrote an incomplete *Saturnalia* (*Conviviorum saturnaliorum libri septem*), a picture by way of dialogue of a company of learned men discussing mythological, historical, and grammatical subjects. He is intellectual brother to Chalcidius. Neither probably had read Plato or Aristotle, but both tried to preserve the Liberal Arts and philosophy. Macrobius' exegeses of Virgil (*Saturnalia* 1, 3-6), whom he trusted as an infallibly wise man, became staples of literary, rhetorical, and encyclopedic study in the Middle Ages. For him, Plato and Cicero could hardly do wrong, and Virgil seemed to him to be universal in his learning.

Censorinus, Chalcidius,[3] and Macrobius all accepted the idea of the cosmos and its eternal harmony. Censorinus dramatized the mystical relationship between cosmos and universe which was an assumption in the thought of all the Neoplatonists--a relationship which obtained also between heaven and the stars, between the earth and its inhabitants, and between the physical and mental well-being of these creatures. What he described was a kind of Neoplatonic magic.

On this subject, Macrobius (*Commentary*, Book II) repeats Cicero's description of the spheres and their music, to which he later applies Neoplatonic modifications. He agrees with Cicero that we cannot hear this music because our ears, having a narrow range of hearing, are like those of someone standing near the Great Cataract of the Nile: we must harden ourselves to its deafening roar--or, if someone deserving to "participate in the heavenly secrets were filled with the vastness of the sound," other mortals less deserving "would [nevertheless] not catch the sound of celestial harmony" (2.4.14).

At the top of this celestial harmony, Macrobius says, is the celestial sphere, which, containing all others, moves from west to east. The lowest of the spheres is the earth, which does not move. Neither of these spheres makes sound. But the seven "errant spheres" do: these, above the earthly sphere but within the celestial sphere, revolve from east to west and make seven tones. From the highest to the lowest, they are Saturn, Jupiter, Mars, Venus, and Mercury, which follow as satellites the earth and the moon (2.4.8ff). Chalcidius too announces the doctrine of the music of the spheres (*Commentary on the Timaeus* 73), often mentions the seven planets and their spheres whose organization in circles he attributes to Eratosthenes (third century B.C.), and recalls that Plato described the Sirens as having their positions on individual spheres (ibid. 95). The harmony of the spheres, according to Censorinus, is a ladder of nine rungs making up eight pitches which include six tones (the Aristoxenian octave). Between Saturn, he thinks, and the heaven of fixed stars there is only a half-tone (not one-and-one-half tones as in the comparable ladder of Pliny [*Natural*

History 2.22.84]); from this half-tone the otherwise unfamiliar series of three half-tones results. The interval between heaven and the sun contains a fourth, that between heaven and earth an octave of six whole tones. Thus, Dorylaos could call the world an instrument of God, but others, because of the seven planets, called it a seven-string object (13.5).

The universe is obviously a harmony of the whole and is a soul which Chalcidius, echoing Aristoxenus as theorist and also Plato's *Timaeus* 36, thinks is musical and based on the six intervals of harmony with three tonal spaces and harmonic divisions (40). How does the soul which is the universe descend to earthly beings? Censorinus' answer, reminding one of both Plato and Aristides Quintilianus, is that the harmony of the whole affects births, and he refers to a (supposed) teaching of Pythagoras about the growth of the embryo in the mother's body after its conception: the embryo in the womb is composed of milk for the first six days, of blood for the next eight--thus it is in a relationship of four--then its growth of flesh is nine (thus in a relation of 5 [the fifth] to the first period of time); and then in twelve days the body is formed--an octave in relation to the first period of time (11.3). In speculation, then, music is proved to be the principle governing the day of birth, achieved through musical modulation. Numbers are decisive: making changes in those to be newly born, they express the relations of musical concords (9.3).[4]

Censorinus too describes the descent of the soul into the body as a kind of musical modulation (10.3). The original "modulation" is lost to the soul when it enters the body. It is the soul's primary movement or journey from the intelligible to the corruptible-corporeal. In this change the soul has forgotten its original state. The proof? Most human souls are inharmonious. But when they earn a re-entry into the intelligible and incorruptible, the soul remembers. Divinely intelligible music will cure and save us because only it can carry our troubled souls into pristine harmony; vulgar music, of course, cannot achieve this effect. The process of ascent and descent may be Pythagorean, but here Plotinus is surely Censorinus' dominant influence. Macrobius, less a Neoplatonist than Censorinus, however, and probably relying on Plato's *Republic*, asserts that the human soul is itself divided into reason, emotion, and appetite, and is derived from musical concords (1.6.42). For Macrobius it is not certain that the soul loses all harmony when it enters the body. Cosmic modulation has allowed to man his own high faculties for understanding the harmony which the universal soul demands.

None of these three men is a music theorist--that is, a describer of the laws of tone according to current or past practice. One might almost say that Aristoxenus was the sole ancient theorist until certain men of the Middle Ages outlined the practices of musical composers. His successors were often moved to correct his "mistakes"--concerning the division of the tone into two semitones (half-steps), for example, or his division of the octave. Censorinus claims to present facts to musicians (10.1), whose melodic structures are more important than the structures of the geometer

(10.2), but he is no theorist. Chalcidius gives more detailed information about intervals, the three tonal spaces (of the tetrachord) and the three-fold harmonic distribution (the species diatonic, chromatic, and enharmonic) (40), and the mathematical relationships of the elements of the perfect or permanent intervals (45). Censorinus thinks of tracing the discovery of the numerical nature of tones to Pythagoras and the monochord, but has doubts about this and instead follows the tradition of tracing proportions of tone back through Nicomachus to Aristoxenes.[5] For Chalcidius, all of this theory belongs among the sciences, of which geometry is the basis of education, harmony and music being, as it were, its substructure (32).

The primary interest of Censorinus, Chalcidius, and Macrobius is less in musical structure, however, than in universal relationships. Clearly Aristotelian, Macrobius explains that universal sounds and their earthly "imitation" can be transmitted only by ether or air. In ether, they are the purest, the clearest, and the most highly placed of such creations. In second place is air, less pure and slightly heavy. Then comes the third part, still clear but graspable by the sense of touch, and corporeal: it forms "bodies of water." Finally comes the "impenetrable solid" which is the dregs of the purified elements: these dregs more and more settle down and take the last (lowest) place in the universe which, far from the sun, is called *terra* (1.22.5-6) and remains in one place never to move. Rhythms as well as sounds are transmitted, as Censorinus thinks; they correspond with pitch intervals, though of course the cosmic pitches and rhythms are themselves beyond sound and are inaudible to the sense of hearing (13.1). Close and mutually active relationships between earth and cosmos are indubitable: for both Censorinus (12.2) and Macrobius (2.3.4) the heavens sing.

From the Pythagoreans on, the cosmic-terrestrial connection has been expressed in a symbolism of numbers, and Macrobius fairly dances with this subject. He agrees with Cicero (*Commonw.* [*The Republic*] 6.18.18) that the number 7 is almost the key to the universe (Macrobius 1.6.45, 2.4.9) and that its properties and almost magical influences are seemingly endless (1.6.45-83). Eight produces a solid body (the cube). It is "full" and allied with the harmony of the spheres, of which eight are revolving (1.5.15); it is the number the Pythagoreans called Justice (1.5.17-18). And he carefully relates that in Plato a Siren sits on each of the eight spheres (2.3.1); and that Hesiod in the *Theogony* shows that the eighth Muse, Urania, the star-bearer, is above the seven spheres and is correctly called the sky, while the ninth sphere and Muse (*Theog.* 1.78-79), as the greatest, is a result of all sounds occurring in universal harmony: "Calliope . . . is preeminent among all," Calliope meaning "best voice" (Macrobius 2.3.2). Apollo is called god of the sun and "leader of the Muses" as if he were the chief of the other spheres. Similarly, the Etruscans "recognize that the Muses are the song of the universe: their name for them is Camenae, a form of Canenae, derived from the verb *canere* (to sing)" (2.3.4). Thus there can be universal singing--or at least human consequences for such melodic activity.

Macrobius mentions that priests use music for sacrificial ceremonies accompanied by lyre, cithara, pipes, or other instruments. In hymns set to cosmic music, the strophe represents the forward motion of the celestial sphere and the antistrophe the reverse motion of the planetary spheres, both motions producing the first hymn in honor of the supreme God (2.3.5); and the most varied of people have allowed music in funeral processions because it was thought that the souls after death return to the source of sweet music, which is the sky (2.3.6). No wonder that Orpheus and Amphion could influence dumb creatures, rocks, and people barbarous, irrational, and stolid.

Censorinus too would see music as divine in origin in that it exerts power on the mind in scenic presentations (12.1), in sacred affairs in which the *tibia* is played, in triumphal music, in the legendary music of Apollo and the Muses, and in religious rites accompanied by *tibia* players whose social position is in high respect (12.2). Pythagoras taught a musical hygiene of the soul, Aesclepiades cured men of their illnesses, and the Greek surgeon Herophilus (c.300 B.C.) had knowledge of its physical benefits (12.3). Commenting on the ability of music to relax and stimulate, Macrobius holds, Lucretius-like, that the nightingale and the swan and other similar birds practice music, "creatures of land, sea, and air willingly fall into nets under the spell of music," and shepherds' pipes call flocks from their pastures (2.3.10). But the best effect of music is moral, as Chalcidius maintains. Divine music is forever joined to reason (267), and the first harmony of all is moral; its realm is a mutual harmoniousness which completes and supports the most rational part of the soul and restores the original natural soul as constructed by the Creator.

The Pythagorean-Platonic system as summarized by Aristides Quintilianus and Chalcidius and their followers encouraged the acceptance of a Grand Assumption seldom disputed. It was an assumption which spelled the Basic Perfection of the All. It was comfortable; it encouraged "harmonic" political actions, suggested ways of improving psychological and medical states, and justified well-organized social organizations. It was an Idea, however unrealistic and unrealizable.

It was the ground-base of a religion called Neoplatonism, among whose adherents Macrobius included Cicero. Early in the Christian era it was one among the many religions and cults competing for favor with Christianity. But since the Greeks had not accepted a holy book, Pythagoreanism and Neoplatonism could not be recognized as state religions. Yet, the *Timaeus* could serve as a Greek Genesis, as indeed it was so interpreted by certain of the Christian Fathers. Macrobius' work is a homily on Genesis. The Daemon, however, is less personal than the Jewish God. The Greek Genesis has the merit of teaching a broad doctrine of harmony which is all-inclusive, and it was probably more easily useful in human life and less demanding than the more austere moral instruction of the biblical *Genesis*. It presents a "scientific"-symbolical and vivid picture of the cosmos which is attractive and allows man to be an integral and fundamental part of the universe. Harmony, not sin, is its core. Therefore it conforms to an underlying aesthetic principle of universal order which it is pleasant to contemplate, an order in which man shares.

Macrobius rightly prefers the legendary, upon which this Greek religion is based, to the immediately at hand and observable. Primary when he writes about music is the universal and not the local, the state of the soul and not the nature of practical earthly music. Since his thought became part of the broad tradition of universal theory easily absorbed into Christian thought and modified by it, it may indeed be true that he is a *sub-rosa* influence on the description of the spheres in the *Divine Comedy* (*Paradiso*, Canto 10), though there the mystic power is not sound but light.

As St. Augustine, his near contemporary and great Father of the Christian Church, wrote a veritable rhapsody on number, so Macrobius furnished his readers a metaphorical ode to Harmonia, Pythagoreanism, and Platonism. Harmonia had kept her place in music theory from legendary times, when she symbolized the ideal and organic organization and operation of the universe, to the fifth century A.D. Music and she were one.

The late antique scholars we have surveyed here ignore Christianity. Contemporary with the Church Fathers, their aim was not proselytizing but transmitting "scientific" information from sources they knew (or merely named), not to plan or further a new course but to revitalize an old one. Not Athens but Rome was in the center of their consciousness. It is highly possible that they were distant disciples of Julian, called the Apostate (331-63), who was vocal about his desire to disestablish the Christian Church which Constantine I had made a state religion in 313 and to re-establish the Greek pantheon of gods and religion while he himself was emperor (361-63). To Hellenize Rome seemed to be the ideal. The ancient gods like Orpheus and Apollo were again religious symbols, now Neoplatonic in their appeal. But they were already being reduced in scholarly attention, and their godhead, along with the vague religion they vaguely symbolized, was being denied.

PART II

THE CHURCH FATHERS
AND THE MIDDLE AGES

XI
The Fathers of the Church

The music aesthetics of the Greeks was more frequently than not based on a speculative philosophy which in modern times has often been considered to be fanciful, extravagant, unscientific, and even imaginary--a play of mind having no anchor in reality. But for the Greeks of the classical period it was thought to be scientific because they were absolutely certain of the objective unity and solidarity of the universe and of the close identity of music with it. The view was to continue in literal and metaphorical use for centuries to come. Its support was number theory with an attendant symbolism which also haunted men's minds for centuries; number had seemed to be the one element, abstractly conceived or not, which is the common ground for all existing things, animate and inanimate. Even in the twentieth century nothing less than a renewed Pythagoreanism of number is sometimes found in musical thought, especially among the avant-garde.

Not unrelated to cosmological phenomena, number theory, and symbolism was the more mundane belief that musical modes and scales as heard can produce affects, quite precise ones indeed, and influence morals and action, both private and public. Hardly any age has been without its opinions about the possible emotional, purgative, psychological, and even medical benefits of music, but none has been more dogmatic about such matters than certain ancient Greek thinkers. Basic to this music speculation was a belief in universal law which applies to all phenomena everywhere and, of course, to music as a craft. The constant, though unexpressed, question was: how well or ill are the laws of craft followed and for what legitimate ends? These laws tacitly are acknowledged everywhere in ancient documents about music, even where they are refuted. As we have seen, Aristides Quintilianus in the Hellenic age brought them together in the most succinct shape that they were to have.

During the Middle Ages these elements of theory would remain as pagan remnants. Certain naturalistic and acoustical observations disappeared from view, not to be taken up again until the sixteenth century. The scientific or speculative, the ethical, and the theoretical aspects remained, but the scientific or speculative predominated not because it applied to the physical world alone, but also because it was modified to embrace the growing theological and spiritual worlds as defined by Hellenism and Christianity. Music was social but, insofar as we have record of it, primarily religious. Its aims were devotional, moral, and practical. Its practical role in the Christian community is particularly deserving of attention here.

During the Patristic period and the Middle Ages--or, more exactly, during approximately the first 1400 years of Christianity itself--the boundaries of city-states and nations were to be superseded by a declared unbounded and universal worship of God. The Greeks had used their kind of music to prepare young men for citizenship in the state and therefore to assist in the preservation of the state itself. But now the hierarchies of government were replaced by a hierarchy of Being descending from God to man through his representatives in the Church, a new political organization over which for practical purposes the layman had little control. The eschatologically oriented Fathers of the Church saw music as a way to prepare men and women for a future life, for a spiritual life here and now as well as after death, a new life which was to be accomplished through good deeds and contemplation, through the worship of God and the pursuit of holiness. The aim of the Greeks was aristocratic, that of the Church Fathers, apart from the governance of the Church, largely democratic in that it embraced all classes of men. For the Greeks, only noble families, and then chiefly the men, were the concern of musical writings. But the Fathers of the Church aimed at the people of God, who might come from any social class. Congregational singing and communal activity through song at first belonged to the people themselves, who of course were not without supervision. The community might include monks or lay people led by clergymen, and in the case of secular churches those clergy devoted to and trained in music (for example, the canons or singing men of a cathedral) would eventually be more and more responsible for the singing of psalmody, sequences, hymns, antiphons, and responsories. In monasteries, the purpose of the music was meditational, and singing indeed remains an important communal activity in monasteries to the present day. In the early Church, whenever professional musicians (in the secular sense) asserted themselves, especially in technical displays, they were typically disciplined and advised to direct their skills toward the universal effort of providing wholesome and plain music for those in the Christian community so that they can share in a worship service which transmits divine grace to them. Music was the servant of devotion and theology, and the latter formed the body of principle and doctrine which was permanent. The Nature and possible First Cause of the Greeks gave way to a God present in men's hearts and worshipped in the liturgy with music.

We may speculate on the basis of the present study whether both the Greeks and the early Christian writers lacked a sense of the historical process. Surely it is true that Plato and many others for one reason or another deplored the decay of music, which also implied a decay of scientific and political standards. Never was there a desire, recommendation, or prediction that it be improved in terms of progress. Always reference was made to an earlier situation, in the one case of a long-gone healthy, socially viable music, in the other of an art of a lost paradise. The Fathers had little feeling for historical change except toward a "closed" state in eternity, which of course cannot undergo alteration or improvement. The aim and purpose of the history of music was not to be found within itself, and hence it could contain no goal toward which it might aspire within itself. Robert Nisbet, on the other hand, insists that Plato and Aristotle and, even more so, St. Augustine follow a theory of unilinear progress in history.[1] But evidence for such a conclusion is lacking in what they say about music. From the ninth century we inherit documents based on contemporary practice as well as on the assumption that what is past is not only best but also an exemplification of what is permanent and inviolable. Yet as we examine church music and the idea of music as it developed in the Patristic and medieval periods, it is clear that the musical tradition did advance in the direction of greater realization of purpose and more mature artfulness and that it did experience change.

However, even lacking a belief in the possible advancement or progress of music as such, the spirit of endless crusade for the propagation of the Christian faith and the battle against rival religious practices and heresies were everywhere in evidence in the early Church. It must not be forgotten that the early intolerance against the Christians shown in religious trials and persecutions was based not upon their beliefs but upon their unwillingness to participate in official cults and ceremonies, especially those which directed veneration to the emperor. They called themselves *ecclesia* (group, an assembly of people), a word which had been used in the Septuagint for God's chosen people. The state was not predominant in their view, not absolute in its demands, and hence not of necessity to be obeyed in all respects. They themselves were the new Israel, and their beliefs were uniquely their own. Of course, they at first represented only one of several current religious cults, and on the whole their world view was one which the pagan leaders of the state did not ask them to renounce or reject. But the matters of faith, the beliefs of the early Christians, must not be denied by participation in pagan rites or other overt acts demanded by political rulers. Even when Constantine the Great in the Edict of Milan in 313 A.D. gave Christianity the official blessing of the Roman state, it was not yet tolerated in all countries because it contradicted local secular or religious practices.

To achieve spiritual health and to repress sensuality: these were chief among the Christian aims. And nothing could contribute to sensuality as much as that most bodily of arts, the dance and its concomitant rhythms. Thus, though King David took the place of Greek demigods like Orpheus in the early Church, clerical writers seldom mentioned his dancing before the Lord (*2 Sam.*1.14). In fact, the dance was eventually banished entirely from the liturgy.[2] Nevertheless, Theodoret of Cyrrhus (c.393-c.466), a Greek Christian theologian of Antioch, does mention that in his day hymns were sometimes accompanied with hand-clappings and dance movements (*PG* 83.426). Later, during the Middle Ages, the depiction of angel musicians was frequent in the visual arts, and there was of course the popular image of the dancing of the angels. Nevertheless, creatures here below, especially members of the clergy, were discouraged and even forbidden from imitating such heavenly dancing, though secular men and women could and did use dance rhythms, which we cannot document with any precision because of the lack of notation or other evidence. Even though certain of the Fathers like St. Jerome would banish instruments from the church services because they were associated too closely with dance rhythms, the rhythms themselves must have persisted in folk music.

There was also strong resistance to poetic rhythms as established and codified in Greek and Latin verse. At the time of the early Church, the old refinements and complexities of rhythm were very frequently being ignored and hence were being forgotten. Feeling for a subtle quantitative time measurement in poetry was lost, though regular accent and stress were not ready to take its place. There was at first considerable opposition to rhythmical hymns and a preference for a chant modelled on psalmody; meter, or approximations of it, was thought to be pagan and anti-ascetic. Psalms and antiphons[3] to be repeated at certain hours of the day every day were regarded as of benefit to people at all times and of greater effectiveness if sung rather than recited. The lack of a definite meter seems to have been preferred, while the words, set to simple, unadorned, "sweet," but not excessively enticing melodies, were expected to be clearly understood, devout, and exalted in mood--but not beautiful or excessively pleasant.

There were among the Fathers those who believed that silent contemplation was the proper approach to God's worship, and thus to allow singing was only to grant a concession to the weakness in those human beings who found silent contemplation difficult or impossible. The Fathers found their precedent in *James* 5.13: "Is any of you sad? Let him pray. Is he cheerful in mind? Let him sing [psalms]." Silent singing, the singing of the heart, as St. Paul advises (*Eph.* 5.18-19), occurs when one is filled with the spirit; then one should speak "in psalms, and hymns, and spiritual canticles, singing and making melody in your hearts to the Lord."

The ban against the liturgical use of instruments in the services of the Church was the result of regarding them as relics of paganism and hence as inimical to the worship of Christians. Nevertheless, the Bible had reported that men had used instruments when they sang the psalms. Yet, instruments were used in Roman and Hellenic rites also, and thus only purely vocal music must be appropriate for services in the worship of God--a practice which has been retained until the twentieth century in the Eastern Orthodox Church. This is not to say that instruments were never used in the early Church. For example, the use of harplike instruments was sometimes approved because King David was said to have played them. Still, though the Bible also mentions use of the trumpet, cymbals, and other instruments, these nevertheless were widely prohibited since they were also symbols of Greek and Roman paganism.

The asceticism of the early Church--not something new, but an inheritance from Neoplatonism--called for two rejections: (1) that of worldly secular music in general, especially that of the skilled virtuoso, and (2) that of the "empty" music of instruments. Especially disliked was music which might be valued for its own aesthetic significance--that is, as something artistically or sensuously beautiful. Pagan civilization was to be subdued, and a new religion and a new ideal vaguely related to Neoplatonic philosophy--and more precisely related to the Hebrew religion out of which it sprang--was to triumph in its place.

Thus there was much feeling against poetry and complex music in the early Church--feeling which seems in some sense to echo Plato's attacks on poetry and complex music. However, the Church Fathers also expressed very serious reservations about sculpture and painting, and their attitude was based on their rejection of the profane and worldly which they saw to be in competition with the sacred and the opportunity of the sinner for salvation. The pagan culture of Greece and Rome embraced a false religion which needed to be replaced by the true one. It was even declared, as an extreme but not uncommon point of view, that no Christian was to pursue any studies which reflected profane or secular learning. Yet certain Fathers like Jerome and Augustine allowed the classics to enter the curriculum for whatever positive values they had to offer, although the choice of works to be read and of the values to be absorbed by the students was selective. Origen, Clement of Alexandria, and Basil gave approval to poetry while categorically rejecting drama, acting, and the theater, which seem to have been particularly disliked by the early Church (see especially Tertullian's *De Spectaculis*). Frequently, but not always, they condemned the visual arts as idolatrous, and only accepted them when they supplied images for religious use; such images, including the works of art found in the catacombs at Rome, set the stage for innumerable battles, dogmatic, theological, and sometimes even aesthetic, aimed at restricting their subject matter or style or even aimed at destroying examples found unacceptable. It was not nature but Christ and Christian stories and legends which were to be imitated in the arts.

One important idea was taken over from the Greeks--an idea which also derived from the Orient. This idea held that the universe is one undivided whole, a structure created in its completeness by God. There is a potential inner harmony between the cosmos and man, a spiritual harmony which moral discipline and an appropriately directed ascetic way of life will assist men to achieve. The ancient unity of the heavens and earth--of their spheres--was accepted as universal law, and men extended such thinking in their understanding of the Church, which served as a point of juncture with the Eternal. And thus man's institutions, like the state, his nobilities and monarchies, and even his wars, might be reflections of the divine Order. After the time of Constantine, Church and state indeed were to be united, and the Church was to be the dominant partner. Soul and body were one in the universal Being, and both were under the governance of the Church.

As we know, Greece was the mother of symbolism and Plato its midwife. In the *Laws* (898) the sun has a soul and is like the soul of man; furthermore, it is the child of the good (*Rep.* 508). Time is an image of eternity. Sometimes it is not connected with eternity (*Parm.* 141), yet it is (symbolically) so connected that it moves forward (ibid. 151-52). The very doctrine of Forms is a vast symbolism of temporal and physical objects and beings. Following Plato's example, symbolical practices and symbolical systems of the Patristic period and the Middle Ages were attempts to bridge the gap between spirit and matter through the discovery of supposed similarities between them. When music stands for the universe and its structure, it is a symbol, at least for those who do not think it has a positive identity with the essence of the cosmos. When its elements--modes, tones, instruments--are parallel with cosmic or religious elements, it serves as both symbol and allegory.

It is almost impossible to speak of medieval art and not consider symbolism and allegory--those popular devices for teaching spiritual or intangible and transcendental truths. They were not, however, a medieval invention. Allegorizing began with Greek commentaries on Homer as early as the sixth century B.C. and was continued by the Stoics. Jewish rabbis had used allegory to expand the meanings of the Scriptures, and Philo of Alexandria, combining both the Greek and the Jewish traditions, tried to reconcile the Old Testament and Platonism. Origen and certain of the other Fathers continued this effort, which became a standard form of biblical explanation and exposition. Through its use, Virgil was made suitable for and acceptable to Christians, and Origen declared that only through allegorizing could the more profound meanings of biblical stories be discovered. He defined three kinds of meaning--literal, moral, and spiritual (mystical)--representing the letter of a text and its significances. Allegorical significances thus would abound in medieval Latin literature. Ovid told mythological stories with moral meanings; so later, in Italian, would Dante. Similarly, in Patristic literature, to mention one example, a close connection was assumed between virginity, sightlessness (and virginity and deafness), and celestial music, as if to have closed senses is to have an open mind to God. Indeed, the Virgin, like the virgin and prophetess Miriam in *Exodus* 15.20, was thought to be in perfect harmony with God because she saw and heard heavenly rather than earthly things and because she sang music beyond the capacities of ordinary mortals (*Rev.* 14.1-5; St. Ambrose, *Concerning Virgins* 1.3.12, NPN2 10.365; 2.2.17, NPN2 10.376). In popular books of "universal" knowledge, the literal level was frequently the level of the least significance. Old Testament events were seen as typological prefigurings of events in the New Testament; hence, for example, the sacrifice of Isaac prefigures the sacrifice on the cross, which sets men free from the death demanded by a just God. Everything in nature also had an allegorical meaning relating to some part of Christian doctrine, as the famous Bestiaries would illustrate in the early medieval period. Allegorical figures like Greed, Lust, Goods, Knowledge, Courtesy, Humility, Rumor, Mischief, and others would eventually populate miracle and morality plays, political pamphlets, and the ubiquitous homily or sermon.

Both Philo and Plotinus provided encouragement to the Fathers in their use of symbolism. The One of the orthodox Trinitarian Christians was a child of Hellenistic Neoplatonism, which dovetailed with or melted into Christian philosophy as the Church left its plebeian origins behind and rose to realms of respectability and power. As reason was the basic principle of Greek philosophy, so the first principle of Neoplatonic One, as we have seen, was the super-rational, that which embodies faith and lies beyond both reason and physical reality. This principle was also one that supported Christian mysticism and encouraged a devaluing and even contempt for empirical, scientific knowledge.   Despite the hostility of such non-Christians as Porphyry and Proclus, Christianity assimilated and in a sense conquered both Neoplatonism and the Judaic-Alexandrian philosophy represented by Philo.

In some ways it may be said that the Christian Church was born in Alexandria, the world capital of Neoplatonism and Neopythagoreanism, though its first adherents--the first to call themselves "Christians"--were, to be sure, Hellenists of Antioch (*Acts* 11.26). The early Fathers, with whom this part of our present survey begins, were part of a culture which valued music only in a certain way, and their attitude toward music is hardly surprising when compared to that of their pagan contemporaries and predecessors. Somewhat regretfully, they sometimes turned away from music as an art. It was for them either sacred or profane, even the former being, as we have seen, not necessarily approved if it did not conform to certain standards. Like Plato's probable influence on music, theirs was eminently, though certainly not entirely, repressive. Their cultural influence at first would seem to have been negative because they actively discouraged whatever they saw as worldly. The important thing, therefore, is that they saw the Church, its services, and its music as a kind of corrective to the popular profane stage--that is, the Church functions as a theater in which its drama and music establish in worshippers the means and desire to follow the holy way of life.

Just as the early Greeks admitted that their musical inspiration came from Egypt and Asia Minor, so now the Alexandrian Christians among the Greeks based their music primarily on the Eastern models of Hebrew psalms and canticles and pagan litanies. In the very oldest liturgy with music of which we have documentation, a psalm was followed by the reading of a biblical text, after which there was sung a *troparion* or interpolation by the choir. This type of liturgy was a Syrian development. Early Christians also adopted unison singing according to Eastern practice. The more usual church service of the early Christians was modelled upon the Jewish synagogue service.   A homily was embedded in scriptural readings, sung prayers, and chanted psalms and songs of praise. First there was a Eucharist (a giving of thanks) for the Christian faithful, along with readings from the Old Testament, responsorial singing of the psalms, readings from the new Testament, and prayers for the faithful. In all of these parts of the service (except for the homily), singing, in imitation of Jewish models, was direct, responsorial, or antiphonal.[4]

Early Christian church music was chant, designed to accompany the

Greek or Latin prose of the worship service. Probably of almost a spontaneous growth once it was separated from Jewish and Syrian forms of service, it rapidly took on the marks of an oral tradition. In the absence of written notation, it had to remain simply monophonic, and it was normally sung without instrumental accompaniment. The text of the psalm was cantillated, clear verbal statement being its purpose. Other segments of the service were subjected to a similar purpose. Constantly under pressure to remain simple, direct, and relatively unornamented, chant was encouraged to allow tone as an independent movement only in the rarest of circumstances.

When we examine the entire early period of Christianity, we see that liturgical chant developed not only in the East but also in Italy, Gaul, and Spain. Based on the ritual of the churches of Jerusalem, Antioch, and other locations in the East, the oldest preserved chant has been said to be the *Ambrosian* (from Milan), and it also includes borrowings from the old Roman chant. Leaving aside the scholarly arguments concerning these kinds of chant (including, in the case of Ambrosian chant, the lateness of the manuscripts), we may nevertheless confirm the very great importance of the forms which developed in Italy during the period leading up to Gregory the Great, who was pope in 590-604 and who lent his name to the chant afterwards known as "Gregorian."

The chant, then, was the backbone of the church services, including the Eucharist, which was (and is) called the Mass in the West after its closing words *Ite, missa est.* By the fourth century this service had taken on two forms in the East: the liturgy of St. Basil for the New Year and other special feasts, and that of St. John Chrysostom for ceremonies sung on ordinary Sundays and holidays. In the West, however, there was at first no uniformity either in the Mass or in the Office (or prayer services) dispersed throughout the day and night at monastic churches. The liturgy took on various forms according to locality (Ambrosian, Gallican, Mozarabic, and so forth). With the imposition of the Roman rite throughout the West, the modern shape of the liturgy emerged, though again with local and regional differences, as in the case of the very elaborate Salisbury (or Sarum) rite which developed in England in the Middle Ages. Following practices already traditional, antiphons, hymns, responsories, and so forth were produced in great profusion not only for the Mass but also for the various Offices, ceremonies, and festivals. Such creativity was indeed not discontinued after the Roman practice was propagated throughout his realm by the Emperor Charlemagne in the early ninth century. Like the Latin language, the Roman rite was expected to draw the peoples, lands, and nations into a unity, even though their own special language, folk music, and even everyday religious practices and social customs differed. Indeed, the Gregorian chant was yet another *nomos* which, like its forerunners in Greek practice, had to be consistently applied because it was deemed both valid and legal.

As suggested above, during the infancy of the Christian Church not all teachings to which people were exposed were religious and mystical. In their schools,[5] the Fathers and subsequent Christian teachers were to adopt the old, but still not sharply defined, secular doctrine of the Liberal Arts--a fortunate development for the West. Quintilian, reminiscent of Aristotle's theoretical, practical, and productive sciences, had divided the arts into three kinds: one of things contemplated by the mind (theoretical), a second of things in action (practical), and a third of things produced and accomplished or made (productive) (2.18.1-2); astronomy illustrated the first, the art of dance the second, and painting the third. Here there was an apparent preview of the classification of the arts by Hugh of St.-Victor (1096-1141) into the theoretical, the practical, and the mechanical (with the addition of the logical or dialectical).

Cicero's division had been dual: (1) those arts based on the senses which supply the material for knowledge and science of the highest truth. The senses, where observation begins, must be trained artistically: and who can deny their powers? Musicians hear, grasp, and judge more at one time than does the untrained listener. But there are percepts, like the identifying of white or melodiousness, which are qualities grasped by the mind, and not by the senses. Since man is rational, his mind receives notions of things from such percepts, and in the absence of such notions, understanding, investigation, and discussion are impossible; for memory is the foundation of all philosophy, of the conduct of life, and of all the sciences. Besides the arts, there are (2) the sciences, which also fall into two classes: (a) the envisaging of facts mentally and (b) the doing of or making of something. According to the first, the geometer envisages things non-existent or indistinguishable from fictitious things whereas, according to the second, the harp-player, as an example, rounds off his rhythms and completes his verses (*Academica* 2.7).

Though the term 'Liberal Arts' included the trivium of arts (grammar, logic, rhetoric) and the quadrivium of sciences (geometry, astronomy, arithmetic, and music), each art was never thought to be its own end and aim; it was a "lower wisdom" which, rightly used, could "ascend" to something higher--that is, to the divine. Knowledge of a liberal art is good, but it is no more than the beginning for the soul's rise to its ultimate attainment of God, and the soul's secret wisdom is only a step towards the unattainable. (The practical arts themselves are mechanical.) Like the Neoplatonists, the Church Fathers through their doctrine of art strove to achieve not the political ends favored by Plato or Aristotle, but those of a purely spiritual and human ideal, their own requirement being that this ideal should be reached according to the tenets of Christianity. Man, unsupported by grace, was thought to be innately corrupt on account of his heredity (his descent from Adam and Eve), while the source of everything good, true, or beautiful was God himself--the source of grace and the Creator of the universe. Thus the good, the true, and the beautiful were after all the Christian's path back to the perfection which had existed in Adam before the Fall--a perfection to be achieved only through harmony with God.

In the end, then, the Fathers, whose chief duty was to proclaim a revealed religion embodying redemption, salvation, and love, gave attention to music for primarily practical reasons. Pagan or non-Christian music of the theater, the circus, the dance, and so forth was inferior and harmful because its aim was sensual. The music of the Church was a *musica practica*. From its very beginnings, however, there were evidences, typical of art when it is under dogmatic restraints, that the practical and prescribed were eventually to be superseded; as the services became more elaborate or as the liturgy adjusted to changing calendars, the musician, then both composer and performer, was more and more frequently required to supply memorable melodies for the various liturgical items, and inevitably these sometimes became more elaborate and "sensual" than was deemed appropriate. In addition, the Fathers gave attention to the tradition of *musica speculativa*, of music treated as a "mirror" of the universe from Pythagoras onward and studied by theologian and philosopher alike--hence the distinction between *cantus*, the performing musician, and the *musicus*, the musician-as-philosopher.

As there was diversity of liturgical practice in the centuries before Charlemagne, so diversities of opinion regarding music were also not lacking. Like Philodemus and Sextus Empiricus, for example, Theodoret of Cyrrhus makes the familiar comparison of music with cookery, but only when it is improperly used. (He also leaves us an account of multi-linguistic antiphonal singing.) That worldly music encourages diabolical illusions became an obsession of the Fathers. In contrast, they set the religious aims of music in sharp relief.

No science, said the Venerable (or Pseudo-) Bede (in *Musica quadrata sue mensurata*, a late seventh- or early eighth-century work), has dared to cross the threshold of the Church except music, which, according to experience, is of all sciences the most noteworthy, the noblest, and the most alluring.[6] Music is therefore in the closest relation to the holy Scriptures and is as essential to it as is a servant in family life: so wrote Abbot Rupert (c.650-after 715) (*De Sancto spiritu*).[7] For Theodoret, it is an art of imitation; it is a copy of God's created nature, the prototypical original (*De providentia* 3, *PG* 83.588-90). Furthermore, it has a task: to affect the hearing, to modify the mental frame of mind according to need, and to change dejection into joy and instability into energy and bravery (*De prov.* 5, *PG* 83.623-24). In short, Theodoret tacitly revised Greek principles of musical effect to satisfy Christian demands. Art is innate to man, as Aristotle taught, and the pleasantness of music is only God's concession to the weak in spirit so that the psalms and other religious songs can be clearly enunciated. According to this view, God, in order to save the weak from error, has decided, so to speak, to put up with sacrifice and with musical instruments so that he can mercifully overlook the weaknesses of men and strengthen their deficiency of understanding (Theodoret, *Comm. on Isaiah* 1.11, *PG* 81.226).

God himself takes no pleasure in singing or the playing of instruments, but in order to clasp humankind closer to himself he has allowed such things, such lesser defects, so that he can prevent the larger ones (Theodoret, *Comm. on Ps. 150* 4, *PG* 80.1994).   Similarly God does not need our praise; instead, he wants a basis and reason for the evident blessings he has conferred upon us.   The Greeks employed music in the education of boys and young men for its moral influence.   But in the Middle Ages music would officially be neither a matter of secular instruction nor an object of pure observation; whenever it did not serve religious purposes, the Fathers had treated it as an exercise-ground for horrendous descriptions of every kind of spiritual danger.

The psalms as chanted or sung according to rules that tended to ignore theory utilized a responsorial manner of performance.   Psalmody of this kind was undoubtedly representative of the earliest music of the Church.   In responsorial singing, the cantor sang a portion of the psalm, and the choir answered with another portion.   Whereas the Jewish cantor sang a florid and ornamented melody, however, the members of a Christian congregation or monastery were expected to chant the psalms simply and straightforwardly, though in time Christian singing too seems to have become more complicated and colorful, specifically in responsorial practice.   In *The Contemplative Life* attributed to Philo and dating from 83-90 A.D., there is a useful description of the singing of an ascetic brotherhood among the Egyptian Jews called the *Therapeutae* ("worshippers" or "physicians").   Two choirs were formed, one of men and one of women (who of course sat in separate sections of the synagogue).   Suddenly both choirs rose up and each selected a leader who possessed personal dignity and skill in music.   Then they sang hymns to God which were composed in different meters and melodies.   Sometimes they sang together, sometimes they answered one another.   Then they became a single choir, "as did the Jews when they went through the Red Sea," and the deeper voices of the men and the higher voices of the women together created a "sweet and true" musical symphony (in octaves).   Eusebius (c.260-340) in his *Ecclesiastical History* (2.17) also mentions the Therapeutae, which he believed represented an early Christian community, and Tertullian (c.160-c.230), a Carthaginian, a Father of the Church, and a Latin ecclesiastical writer, describes a similar responsorial psalmody sung in Latin in Carthage (*On Prayer* 27, ANF 3.690).

Initially psalmody apparently did not involve conscious differentiations of mode, but always moved within one and the same tetrachord.   It was enough if its effects were immediate, real, and personal and if it seriously expressed the suffering and longing of the individual worshipper.   Later, with Ambrose in the fourth century, modes seem to have been distinguished, and by a process of accumulation the construction of a theory of music appropriate to this practice followed, an abstraction from many sources, mostly anonymous.

When finally an effort was made to formulate a theory of music, the Fathers had to forge some new directions because under the Romans, who were not inclined toward fine distinctions in sound, the genera of the Greeks had been gradually lost except for the diatonic species, which absorbed all others in the music of the Latin Church. Similarly for rhythm: while a long syllable the length of two shorts in both Greek and Latin was generally sung to a long note and a short one to a short, quantity was, as we have seen, being displaced, eventually to be replaced by quality (accent and stress). In hymns, the early Church used simple iambs and trochees. The rhythmic complexities found in the poetry and drama of the Greeks faded away to re-appear later in the complicated rhythmic structures of the *Ars Nova* and the polyphony of the Netherlands School.

In the earliest plainchant and psalmody, then, there must have been a lack of the kind of meter which came to dominate the later hymns and sequences. Nor were definite rhythmical divisions or planned musical accentuations a part of it. Prose rhythms were basic, but such chant was probably not even as rhythmically sophisticated as the early baroque recitative form cultivated by the Florentine Camerata in supposed imitation of Greek declamation. The musical settings of the psalms involved a one-to-one syllabic relationship. Thus the florid singing of the psalms in the Jewish synagogue was rejected, and simplicity in performance practice was the approved way of singing psalmody and other chants.

I

Clement of Alexandria (Clemens Alexandrinus, or Titus Flavius Clemens). The earliest of the Church Fathers to stress music was St. Clement of Alexandria (c.150-c.220). Probably born in Athens, he was a theologian and scholar who thought philosophy, defined as *gnosis* or knowledge, was a gift of God. A convert to the Christian faith, he was knowledgeable in Greek literature and philosophy, which he regarded as necessary to an understanding of the scriptures. Deeply influenced by Philo and a teacher (later head) of the Catechetical School in Alexandria, he taught Origen (c.185-254), who also among the Fathers would be a prominent writer and teacher as well as a contributor to the allegorical interpretation of the Old Testament. Clement, who wrote in Greek, was a model rhetorician and orator, a veritable inheritor of the Ciceronian tradition.

Blending Platonism, Neoplatonism, and Stoicism, Clement was a Hellenist with respect to world harmony. Before the triad of heaven-purgatory-hell entered Christian mythology, or at least prior to its adoption by the Councils of Florence and Trent in the fifteenth and sixteenth centuries, world-theory was still vaguely Pythagorean and Platonic. Thus Clement believed that God created the world as harmony and constructed the blend of elements as if he had combined Dorian and Lydian harmonies. We must therefore, he thinks, be wary of testing divine harmony with that which belongs to earth. This is the basis for the difference between sacred and profane music and between pagan harmony and the Christian. Clement's universal symbol is of course Christ. Like Philo, he thinks Plato borrowed his wisdom from Moses and the Prophets; he further thinks that Plato heralded the coming of Christ, the only tamer of that "most intractable of animals" called man--flighty, crafty, passionate, pleasure-loving, and rapacious man. Christ superseded the minstrels: his pure song is the harmonic principle of the universe. All creation is a melodious, organized order; the elements of the universe, commonly in discord, are now, under Christ, attuned and in concert so that the whole universe is in harmony. It is an order which prevents the ocean from encroaching on the land and which causes the atmosphere to mitigate violence, just as the Dorian mode blends with the Lydian. It is the harmony of the Whole, not that of the music of Orpheus or even of music's inventor Jubal, but of God's counsel which inspired David, and therefore of the God whom David sought (*Exhortation to the Heathen* [sometimes called *Exhortation to the Greeks*] 1, ANF 2.171-72).

Despite his mastery of the Greek language and his insistence on the importance of certain Greek ideas, Clement paradoxically has little direct praise for Greek thought. The Greeks were pilferers, he says, of all kinds of writings, even from the Egyptians. He mentions the more picturesque aspects of the writings of the mysterious occultist Hermes Trismegistus. He describes a procession of Egyptian priests at whose head walked the Singer carrying two books of music and hymns by Hermes, and he makes note of as astrologer who could at all times chant from four books of Hermes about the stars. There are forty-two books by Hermes, Clement says, thirty-six of them carrying the whole philosophy of the Egyptians and six on medicine (*Stromata* [*Miscellanies*] 6.4, ANF 2.488). (Was this the same Hermes Trismegistus who was so highly regarded in the Renaissance?)

The Greeks, pilferers or not, must ultimately be rejected and confuted. Christ the leader has revealed absolute truth, and his devotees sing a new song--not the ridiculous songs of Amphion, a minstrel who allured fishes, or Arion, who was said to have surrounded Thebes with walls, or Orpheus, or Eunomous, the last of whom was solemnly thought by the Greeks with the aid of a grasshopper to have played a funeral ode to the dead serpent at Pytho at Delphi. All of these legends are without value, says Clement in his *Exhortation to the Heathen*, though the grasshoppers, one of whom supposedly took the place of a string on Eunomous' cithara, were really singing the new song of God. Clement asks that the truth of God be brought to the dwellers in the temples of initiations and mysteries and that the new Levitical song be sung in the immortal measure of "the new harmony which bears God's name." The minstrels, he thinks, were deceivers; under the name of music they misled men into doing deeds of violence and into idolatry, subjected them to "the yoke of the extremest bondage," and caused them to be denied the freedom of the citizens of heaven. And then he makes his own joyful shout: in God is his "harp, and pipe, and temple" (ANF 2.171-72).

Clement's distinction between the new song and the old[8] became a veritable cliché among the Church Fathers. It stems from St. Paul's comparison of the New Man (Christ) with the Old (the pagan). The new melodies spell love and charity and the old ones the evilness of the flesh. It is the theme of St. Augustine's sermon *De cantico novo* (*The New Song*). Reference to a new song had appeared in Psalm 32.3 and in *Isaiah* 42.10, and St. Paul had established the comparison in his epistles to the *Ephesians* (5.19) and the *Colossians* (3.16). The suggested parallel is between the Old Testament which is to be rejected except as it anticipates the New Testament. (The Old, according to St. Augustine [*Contra Faustus* 4.2, *PL* 42.218], was the "pre-missive" figure of the New.) There are the old and the new laws, the old prefiguring the new, and the new prefiguring a future glory. The new law is what men ought to follow in practice, a moral law accompanying the renewed soul on its journey to eternal bliss. There are echoes of St. John the Evangelist: the instrument of God is the Word, the *Logos*, the New Song, "the manifestation of the Word that was in the beginning and before the beginning"; it is the path by which God and the Good are revealed to man. God is in his new home, and Christ is the new song; the song of Salvation is replacing the mistaken, corrupt songs of the ancient minstrels (*Exhortation* 1, ANF 2.172-73). King David was a harpist, and yet Christ, the Word of God, scorns instruments which, like the lyre and the cithara, are lifeless, and prefers the instrument of many tones he himself has made--that is, man. David "exhorted [men] to the truth and disuaded [them] from idols" just as he healed the possessed Saul through his harp-playing (*1 Sam.* [*1 Kings*] 16.23). The new song--manifested in the Word and Christ--is God's instrument, and so too is man.

Clement himself seems to be singing a rhetorical prose-poem in celebration of the new allegorical music. He ecstatically substitutes Christian truths for Greek philosophical thought, especially for Greek legends, and even for Greek instruments. And yet he makes compromises: skeptical of the use of the lyre and the cithara, he still tolerates them--but only because David used them (*Paedagogus* [*The Instructor*] 2.4, ANF 2.249). He rejects the aulos and the syrinx for the Christian church service. Though the syrinx was the instrument of the shepherds at Bethlehem and the aulos belongs to the superstitious and the idolatrous, both should be rejected because they appeal to wild animals and irrational men. Pagan instruments like the psaltery, cymbals, trumpets, and the *auloi* are antithetical to the single Christian instrument of the Word, through which we venerate God.

The inadmissible standard of earthly harmony is exemplified by the use of instruments at feasts, where it furthers licentiousness (*Instructor* 2.4, ANF 2.248). "Grave and modest strains" are acceptable, but liquid harmonies marked by modulations and encouraging "effeminacy and scurrility" are to be avoided; so are enharmonic harmonies, which should be "abandoned to immodest revels, and to florid and meretricious music" (*Instructor* 2.4, ANF 2.248-49). Over-colorful melodies are to be "left to shameless carousals, and to the honeyed and garish music of the courtesan"

(*Christ the Educator* 2.4, FC 23.133). Music can indeed be used "for the sake of the embellishment and composure of manners," for example, when people "pledge each other" to the accompaniment of music at banquets, when their desires are soothed by song, or when God is glorified for his gifts to man. But other music is "superfluous" and must be rejected (*Stromata* 6.11, ANF 2.500-01). Clement almost thunders in saying that truth and wisdom should "abandon Hellicon and Cithaeron and take up their abode where is the true law." The Church itself is not the theater or the circus, and the Word of God is the true athlete "crowned in the theater of the whole universe" (*Exhortation* 1, ANF 2.171).

In a rare reference to music theory, Clement quotes Aristoxenus on the harmonic species. But he prefers the symbolical to the technical way: the lyre figuratively stands for the Lord, and also for the people who are redeemed. Music itself is like "the ecclesiastical symphony at once of the law and the prophets, along with the Gospel . . ." even though it has the secular aim of embellishing and composing manners (ANF 2.500). He pursues in detail the Stoic's Christianized allegory of man as God's instrument: the tongue is the psaltery of the Lord, the lyre is the mouth struck by the Spirit as if it were a plectrum, the body is an organ and its nerves are strings from which it receives harmonious tension; and when the Spirit strikes, it gives forth human voices. The tongue is "the cymbal of the mouth, which resounds with the pulsation of the lips": "man is truly a pacific instrument," whereas other (artificial) instruments incite to war, inflame lusts, kindle loves, or arouse wrath, impropriety, effeminacy, and licentiousness (*Instructor* 2.4, ANF 2.248). At least one instrument as such has its own symbolical function: the ten-string psaltery indicates "the Word Jesus, who is manifested by the element of the [Pythagorean] decad" (*Instructor* 2.5, ANF 2.249). Clement is thus suggesting that man is ultimately capable of sharing in universal harmony through the application of the principles and rituals of religion--through the proper "song" of love and charity. The allegorical song which is the right measure for all things bridges the gap between the sacred and the profane, the heavenly and the earthly. The new song is the celestial song not of instruments but of words, of the "mild and loving yoke of piety" (*Exhortation* 1, ANF 2.172). In making these distinctions, Clement separates the instrument man from the instrument voice and from other instruments made by human hands. Later in the Middle Ages these distinctions will be used for purposes of classification.

Clement's pupil Origen, also influenced by Philo Judaeus, describes the use of singing in Christian worship. The Greeks use Greek, he says, and the Romans Latin, "and everyone prays and sings praises to God as best he can in his mother tongue" (*Against Celsus*, ANF 4.653). Like Clement, he does not apologize for his knowledge of matters Greek, which he thought essential to a Christian education. He too attempts to reconcile the Greek and Christian views of life, though Porphyry said that he profaned Hellenism by such an effort. Again like Clement, he treats instruments as symbols: the *tuba* or trumpet symbolizes the efficacy of the Word of God (*Homily on Jeremiah* 15-16, *PG* 13.319), the *tympanum* or drum the destruction of lust, and cymbals the eager soul enamored of Christ (*On Ps. 150* 3-5, *PG* 12.1683). Origen carried allegory and symbolism to such an extreme that he wrote a three-fold commentary on every book of the Old and New Testaments.

II

St. Hippolitus. Hippolitus (d. c.236) was an ecclesiastical writer in the early third century who was banished from Rome, where Greek was still viable as a literary language, during the persecution of Emperor Maximin. According to a legend, he was martyred, but this story seems to have been a later invention. His early years and the nature of his education are not known, though he was credited with being a disciple of St. Irenaeus. In his commentaries on the *Psalms* he makes an important distinction between *psalm* and *song*, a distinction which also was the concern of others (for example, Eusebius, St. Hilary, and St. Gregory of Nyssa). Indeed, the distinction was to become a cliché in early Christian thought.

According to Hippolitus, psalm (*psalmus*) or canticle (*canticum*) may be arranged in four categories: psalm, song, the psalm of song (*psalmus cantici*), and the song of psalmody (*canticum psalmi*). The psalms are "played to an instrument without the accompaniment of voice and [composed] for the musical melody of the instrument"; songs "are rendered by the voice in concert with the music"; psalms of song are those in which the voice takes the lead while a sound appropriate to it is "rendered harmoniously by the instruments"; and songs of psalmody are those in which the instrument takes the lead, while the voice is secondary "and accompanies the music of the strings."

Hippolitus interprets further: metaphorically speaking, when an instrument is struck--that is, when a body is "struck" with good deeds and succeeds in action--there is a psalm. Here speculation is secondary. Speculation is primary only in the song, which, not being practical, treats of the mysteries of truth, assents to them, and induces in us "the noblest thoughts of God and his oracles," so that we are enlightened by knowledge, and "wisdom shines brightly in our souls." A song of psalmody is one in which good action leads while wisdom follows, and we are judged by God to know the truth of things heretofore withheld from us. The psalm of song occurs when with the light of wisdom we consider some abstruse questions relating to morals and then become prudent in action because we know what, when, and how that action is to be taken. The psalm is without "degree" (accentless), the song has "degrees" (accents), a sign that "the saints will be engaged in nothing but in speculation alone" (*Argument on the Psalms* 2.7, ANF 5.199-201).

In effect, Hippolitus attempts to distinguish very carefully the nature of the psalm as contrasted to the hymn. Perhaps reflecting the evidence of biblical practice rather than contemporary conventions, he indicates that the psalm was accompanied in imitation of King David by a musical instrument. As performed, it was less a song than a group of chanted words often repeated in responsorial fashion. Here the sensuous side of music was at a minimum, and the psalm in essence was more like a prayer than a song. Its verse was "biblical"--that is, free of regular meter. Dynamics were limited if not absent; tempo was what was proper, neither too fast nor too slow; rhythm was determined by the text; the musical limits were set by the tetrachord. All limits were prescribed: nothing could occur which emphasized the music, and everything stressed the religious or devotional and pedagogical text.

On the other hand, the hymn, a liturgical strophic poem, at this time was less traditional and less restricted than the psalm already. The hymn had no refrain, all stanzas were sung to the same melody, and its *melos* was plainsong, though this form did not even then rule out tunefulness. Its purpose was to praise God in song; its performers were a congregation of people--a community. The hymn was capable of being a contemplative form which might express the feelings of the individual Christian, whether such feelings were of grief and remorse or of joy in God's love and hope for mercy and salvation. Sometimes based on the *Psalms*, the hymn was a medium for creativity among poets and musicians, who were given a certain range of freedom in reflecting in verse and music the subjective states of the singers--that is, of feelings and thought which are ideally more significant than the musical setting itself.

The Church of course had already created its own mythology[9] which gave King David first place among musicians. For Hippolitus, he was the first and only person to think of psalms as prayer (supplication to God for anything needed), vow (engagement of soul), hymn (song of blessing to God for benefits enjoyed), and praise (of the wonders of God). David himself had been concerned with such categories as soon as he had taught his fingers to tune the psaltery, which probably had been used only for idle amusement before he reduced its use to rhythm, order, and art; in addition he married song to melody when he sang to humble shepherds of God and also later when he attempted something higher and more in the public interest. He also appointed four leaders of choirs (because "there are . . . in all things visible four primal elements"), and these four men led the choirs of men selected from the remaining tribe of the Levites (*Arguments on the Psalms* 8-9, ANF 5.201-02, *PG* 10.719). Curiously, the number 4, a perfect number in pagan science where it was first applied to the four elements, is here transferred to a religious use in worship.

Whatever his ideas about the psalms and the singing of them, Hippolitus is best remembered today for his partial outline of the early Christian Mass. In approximately 200 A.D. he compiled an *Apostolic Tradition*. Not surprisingly, the early Church's liturgical ceremonies were both formalized and formulaic. The formulas made improvisation by clergy or congregation unnecessary and constituted the organized procedures for the ordination of bishops, the baptism and confirmation of Church members, and other activities which were thought to be the responsibility of the Church itself. Psalms were the musical staples for ceremonies, short or long, and they served also for oral readings, for prayer silent and oral, and for singing at various points in a service. In a sense they modernized their supposed creator, King David, and became an integral part of a Church whose international inclusiveness he could not have imagined.

There were, and still are, two large sections of the Mass deriving partly from Greek but mostly from Jewish practices. When Hippolitus wrote the *Apostolic Tradition*, the Roman liturgy was in Greek. He said little or nothing about the first division, called the Service of the Word, which included a lection (the reading of a lesson), a psalm, a second lection, and a sermon. Hippolitus described the second section, which is called the Eucharist (communion) and is referred to as the Canon. It has three parts: (1) the offering of gifts (as found also in short services like the evening "agape" or "love feast"), (2) the saying of a prayer over the gifts, the consecration of the symbolical bread and wine, and the saying, as a conclusion, of the doxology, and (3) the breaking of the bread and its distribution with wine among members of the congregation. This ceremony as outlined persisted for many years and in time met with competing forms. The greatest change, however, took place when Latin replaced Greek as the ceremonial language.[10]

III

Eusebius Pamphili of Caesarea. For the Fathers, Christianity was an eschatological religion based in the expectation of the *parousia* or return of Christ in glory (to be announced by the sounding of trumpets), though as the apostolic period receded the hope of eternal life increasingly was applied to the individual believer's personal aspirations. Nevertheless, Eusebius (c.260-340) saw the pattern of history as important for Christianity, which had historical roots in Judaism and looked forward to triumph at the end of history. Like Clement, he saw Platonism in the heathen world, like Jewish history described in the Old Testament, as a preparation for the acts of salvation performed by Christ at the center of the historical process. During his lifetime, Christianity would be joined with the Roman state under Constantine the Great in 312-13, and thus a new complication appeared in the understanding of the historical position of the religion. Called the "father of ecclesiastical history," Eusebius in his *Historia Ecclesiastica* surveyed Church history up to his own time, and his *Chronicon* provided a summary or universal history up to 325 A.D. For him, Moses was the predecessor in time of the great thinkers of Greece and Rome, the Bible was the first historical narrative, and the fall of man was the dividing line between Paradise and man's expulsion from it. Eusebius was among the first of the churchmen--he preceded St. Basil as bishop of Caesarea, the city founded by Herod the Great (c.73-74 B.C.)--to condemn the use in the Church of all instruments, and especially the cithara (which Clement had accepted).

But like Hippolitus, he allowed vocal music, which, as in Jewish worship, was an essential aspect of the religious ritual. He divided the sacred from the profane, the Jewish-Christian from the pagan, and thus established conventions which he regarded as proper. And, though he wrote in Greek, like others he was already thinking of Christians as Romans. "We praise God on the living psaltery," he cries, for the harmony of the whole Christian people is more pleasing to God than any instrument. "Our cithara," he says, "is the whole body, by whose movement and action the soul sings a fitting hymn to God, and our ten-stringed psaltery is the veneration of the Holy Ghost by the five senses of the body and the five virtues of the spirit [wisdom, temperance, courage, justice, holiness]" (*Comm. on the Psalms, PG* 23.1171). "We sing the psalms in melodious tones," he writes (*PG* 23.1174), and he assures us that the singing of both psalms and hymns was extensive and well defined in his time (*PG* 23.647, 658).

Eusebius is an additional contributor to the "law of allegory," as Abert calls it. Like Philo and other Church Fathers, he thinks of the human body as a musical instrument. But man's soul is the voice which should sing. According to this view, enunciated also by Hippolitus, the psalm is an allegorical harmonic impulse of the soul toward good action, even if no meditation accompanies it. The song is a seizing of truth without action because the soul is contemplatively occupied with God and his Word. But a psalm-song comes to be when the understanding is influenced by action, and the song-psalm occurs when the action is directed by understanding as to how and when it is to be practiced (*Comm. on Ps.* 19.7, *PG* 23.74). Pure unaccompanied song is the symbol of pure seeing (intuition) by the soul not shackled by the instrument of the body; but if that instrument is added, the accompanied song is the copy of the active life effected by the soul and body in unison (*Comm. on Ps. init.*, *PG* 23.71, 74).

Already during the lifetime of Eusebius, the Church in the West seems to have abandoned Greek, with the exception of the *Kyrie* of the Mass. Such was not the case in the East, and the use of different languages was influential in dividing the Christian Church into two principal branches. While in neither East nor West was there uniformity of liturgy as yet, the West chose Latin as its ecclesiastical language even in regions where the local liturgy differed very considerably from the usage at Rome--that is, from the Roman rite which would eventually be adopted throughout the West. Latin, in addition to its liturgical function, came to function as the universal language of Western Europe, where it brought together the most diverse nationalities and occupations. The Romans had used Latin for the law, both domestic and in the courts, and for both everyday and commercial correspondence. The Church Fathers were especially devoted to its literary expression, drew upon it without reservation, and praised or blamed the language according to demand. From Latin texts they drew quotations and moral (or immoral) lessons, and, above all, they received from such texts precious advice about rhetoric and therefore about speaking publicly and sermonizing. The use of Latin in the liturgy in the Western Church also would have very great significance for the development of its liturgical music. Yet it is not possible to ignore such Eastern Fathers as St. Basil and certain others whose influence on the development of the idea of music was strong.

IV

St. Basil the Great (Basilius). The Church Fathers all agreed that the singing of the psalms should not be ornate and that the instruments which they distrusted (and often failed to tolerate) were only symbolical in meaning. Such views are found in the writings of St. Athanasius of Alexandria (c.298-373) and also those of St. Basil, who was successor to Eusebius as bishop of Caesaria. Athanasius repeats the ancient doctrines in somewhat altered form: beginning with the harmonically tuned aulos which produces a unified perfect consonance, he assumes that in the soul there are different motions which sympathetically determine the movements of the parts of the body and that therefore, according to reason, a human being resides always in a spiritual state corresponding with musical consonances (*Epistola ad Marcellinum, PG* 27.11ff). Like Eusebius, he compares the ten-string psaltery to the body with its five senses and five mental powers (*Expos. in Ps.* 143.9, *PG* 27.543), while the *tympanon* or drum is a symbol of the mortification of the flesh (*De titulis in psalmorum 150 7, PG* 27.1342) as it had been for Origen. The Neoplatonic symbolism of instruments, here as in Clement of Alexandria and Origen, is applied in Christian terms to the body, whose members are like strings correctly bound together, and to the mind, whose thoughts are like cymbals: both body and mind through song and marked by the Spirit receive movement and life (*Ep. ad Mar.* 29, *PG* 27.39, 42).

Like Athanasius, Basil was acquainted with the Greek and Latin classics. He was the first founder of the Basilian Order of monks on the desert of Pontus, and was in a sense the administrative genius behind Greek monasticism. In his *Ad adolescentes* he called for the study of the Greek poets, orators, historians, and philosophers, but these he wished to have bowdlerized for Christian consumption. He rejected Greek philosophy and aspects of Hellenism which he thought were inimical to Christian teaching. Ancient doctrine could be educational, but not a depository of truth. He thus thought that the good Christian could be a *rhetor* and a teacher of rhetoric. He was a great preacher and theologian who held moral instruction to be superior to literary education. He shaped the liturgy of the Eastern Church, as has been indicated above. He loved music, knew a great deal about it, and made it the focal point in a series of homilies on the *Psalms*. Like Clement, he believed that psalmody has a practical reason for being.

The book of *Psalms*, he felt, reveals what is profitable in the prophets, the historians, and the law. It is useful because in each psalm one can find a remedy for his own condition (*Homily 10*, "A Psalm on the Lot of the Just Man" [*On Ps.* 1], FC 46.151). But words alone do not suffice. The Holy Spirit blends the delight of melody with the doctrines taught, so that "by the pleasantness and softness of the sound heard we might receive without perceiving it the benefit of the words" just as physicians prescribe medicine supplemented by honey. The result is educative: because the Holy Spirit sees that men are attracted to virtue less through example than through affection, it borrows pleasure from melody, adds it to the heavenly mysteries, and causes a "pleasantness and softness" to the ear in order to place, as if surrepticiously, the treasure of good words, of good things, into man's mind. Basil is describing a sugar-coating of the pill that heals: the harmonious sounds of the psalms were so devised that men young, old, and imperfect can learn as they sing (FC 46.152). Pleasure makes the difference: it binds socially, spiritually, and communally, and then leads to virtue.

Psalms when sung can also effect changes in mood. In the home and marketplace, they have been known to bring calm to persons in wrathful moods. They can tranquilize souls, arbitrate peace, restrain disordered and turbulent souls, soften the soul's passions and moderate its unruliness, form friendships, unite the divided, and mediate between enemies. If Basil's objective is not secular-political like Plato's and Aristotle's but societal-communal, it is nevertheless consistent with the idea that music can be therapeutic and useful to the social order. He sees choral singing as a bond, as it were, which creates unity; it joins people into a harmonious union of a single choir and "produces the greatest of blessings, charity" (ibid. 46.152). Even better: psalmody drives away demons, summons the help of angels, supplies arms against nightly terrors, gives respite from toil, safety to children, adornment to men, solace to the old, and a fitting ornament to women; it "peoples the solitudes," "rids the marketplace of excesses," is "the elementary exposition of beginners" and "the improvement of those advancing, the solid support of the perfect, the voice of the Church." It "brightens feast days" and "creates a sorrow which is in accordance with God," can call forth "a tear even from a heart of stone," and is "the work of angels" (ibid. 46.153). It is of the most importance, however, that we learn something (spiritually) useful while we sing, and, whereas what we learn by force does not always last, what we learn with pleasure does.

But what do we learn from the psalms? The "grandeur of courage," "the exactness of justice," "the nobility of self-control," "the perfection of prudence," "a manner of penance," the "measure of patience." The psalms, Basil thinks, constitute a perfect theology predicting "the coming of Christ in the flesh," acting as a threat to (final and fatal) judgment, and arousing a "hope of resurrection," a "fear of punishment, promises of glory, [and] an unveiling of mysteries" (ibid.). Like Hippolitus, then, Basil finds a connection between the psalms and active states of mind.

Basil is more psychological than Clement, and is probably the first of the Church Fathers in the East to discover a relation between the song (hymn) and not only contemplation but also everything connected with what is highest and noblest--even theology itself. Like other Church Fathers, he took biblical tradition as the arbiter of morality and adopted what he found there as the basis for the well-ordered life. Seeing how difficult it is for human beings to pursue virtue and to avoid a life of sensuous enjoyment, God "sweetened" dogmatic rules with the charm and enchantments of music, which includes both vocal and instrumental manifestations. The prophet adopted "the so-called harp" to show, "as it seems to me," that the gift from the Spirit resounds from above. In the cithara and the lyre, the bronze from beneath responds with the sound as it is plucked, but the source of its harmonic rhythms in the harp is above, so that "we may be careful to seek the things above and not be borne down by the sweetness of the melody to the passions of the flesh" (ibid. 46.153). The words of the prophet shine through the structure of this instrument "because those who are orderly and harmonious in soul possess an easy path to the things above" (ibid. 46.154). Thus Basil too suggests a symbolical significance for musical instruments, and he sounds like Clement: in *Homily 15* (FC 46.229) he discusses the harp (for praising God), the psaltery (a symbol of the divine and the soul), and the cithara (a symbol of the body and human existence on earth) and finds that anyone knowing how to bring to full consonance the laws of God will sing of God with the ten-string psaltery because 10 is the number of God's commandments (as 10 was the perfect number of the Pythagoreans). Music both vocal and instrumental assists in the propagation of the faith.

In his fourth homily on the *Hexameron*, called *The Gathering of the Waters*, Basil mentions the secular theater. The Church Fathers, as we have seen in Clement, endlessly compare the theater of this world with the Church, or make reference to the theater of the soul and of God. The world's theater embraces "the manifold spectacles of conjurors" and "soft and dissolute melodies" which cause great impurity of soul; a theater of impure sights, it is a "public school for licentiousness" whose elaborate melodies of the *auloi* and lewd songs move people "to unseemly behavior." The great contrast is the "vast and varied workshop of the divine creation" (*Homily 4*, FC 46.55), the vast theater and school of the psalms for the propagation of the Orthodox faith, whose music is a practical means for effecting and producing spiritual change in human beings.

Basil will have nothing to do with the untruth of the "fabulous invention" and "artificial nonsense" of the music of the spheres (*Homily 3*, "The Firmament" 3.3, FC 46.39-40). Nor will he accept criticism for his approval of psalm-singing: it is agreeable to the Church that people who worship at night should sing psalms in their distress and affliction; they may even sing antiphonally with one another and thus produce a heedful temper and a heart free from distraction. When they "allow one person to intone the melody and the rest chant the prelude of the strain . . . in response," they "offer up the psalm of confession to the Lord," and then each person forms his own expression of repentance (*Lett. to the clergy of Neo-caesarea*, FC 28.83-84).

In provincial life the psalms were in the foreground; they were the most important of vocal forms, and to "psalmodize" became a symbol for the carrying out of the practical life of a Christian. Though St. Augustine objected to this view, later theorists who accepted it maintained that to sing means to announce God's Word by way of mouth and that to psalmodize means to fulfill divine missions through good works. Augustine likened correctly schooled choir singing to a well-ordered state (*City of God* 17.14), while his disciple Prosper of Aquitaine (fl. 440) said that with words man makes a union of singers whose voices when they do not harmonize cannot arouse pleasure, though when they harmonize and sing a true song they produce a pleasure based on a general similarity between the conduct of life and each individual confession. Himself a lover of music, Basil saw in it an almost total symbol for the struggle for and the attainment of a Christian life.

V

St. Hilary of Poitiers (Hilarius).   The rapidity with which the Christian Church spread in the West is nowhere more discernible than in the career and work of St. Hilary of Poitiers (c.310-67). In c.353, when the Church had already been very well established in Gaul for a considerable length of time, he became bishop of Poitiers, only to be exiled c.356-60 because of his opposition to Arianism, which he opposed as an orthodox Trinitarian who remained loyal to the definition of the Trinity set forth in the Nicene Creed. In contrast to the orthodox position which held with Athanasius that the Father and Son are co-eternal and of the same substance, Arianism proposed that God is real, unknowable, and separate from all creation and that Christ is not God by nature--but because of his position as an instrument of righteousness he was granted a special dignity by the Father. Hilary's theological views were set forth in numerous theological treatises in Latin, and in these he proves himself to be devoted to the methodology of allegory. In going beyond number, imaginative images, emblems, and allegories, and in speaking enthusiastically about the *jubilus*, however, he showed himself to be thoroughly enthusiastic about the possibility of reaching out to the reality which is beyond the reach of senses--that is, about mystical experience.

Hilary contributed to the history of the symbolism of instruments: for him, as for Hippolitus and Eusebius, the resonance of the cithara was due to the arched form of its body, resembling the human chest, and that of the psaltery to its level surface, its rectilinear construction being comparable to the body of Christ (*Prologue to the Book of Psalms* 7, PL 9.257). In the great bulk of his works (like that of other Fathers, ecclesiastical, exegetical, dogmatic, hortatory, and controversial) music is of course a minor subject.

He was nevertheless the first champion in the West of hymn singing, which gradually adopted a broader range of subjects than merely those drawn from the Bible. As noted above, the form of the hymn also became linked to the new form of verse adopted for Latin by the time of Charlemagne. Hilary encouraged the dissemination and use of the early hymn.

During his exile in Phrygia, he learned to know Syrian hymnody, which appears to have been metrical; this kind of hymnody was widely disseminated in the eastern Mediterranean region and had been translated already into Greek. He is said to have been responsible for translating these hymns into Latin, while he himself also wrote original hymns. Such hymns were designated for use in the congregational and communal singing of the faithful, but, possibly because of their musical difficulty for people living in a region far removed from the East, he was disappointed in their reception and in their failure to be effective in the propagation of Trinitarianism. Rightly or wrongly, St. Ambrose is credited with later successfully winning acceptance for the metrical hymn in the West, but Hilary's own composi-tions in this genre won him Isidore of Seville's praise as the first Latin poet of hymns, which have been called characteristic of the medieval achieve-ment in the Latin lyric.[11] The hymn form was traced back to the Last Supper, which, held in the evening, was a common meal (a communion) in which such song was mingled with prayers. The starting point of the allegory of singing allied with contemplation and good works, then, was found in the Orient, from which both Hilary and Ambrose imported it. Hilary indicates that psalm-singing is not so much a duty as an activity of the voice (*Tract. to Ps.* 146.1, *PL* 9.869). In psalmody one must think of work pleasing to God, and God is pleased only by harmonious and appropri-ate alternation or modulation of the movement (gesture) of the body. In psalms which may only be described by the term 'psalm' one finds either the teaching or the avowal of good works well pleasing to God; should the word 'song' (hymn) be in the superscription, however, a spiritual recogni-tion of the heavenly secrets which men can reach through the knowledge of wisdom is present. One speaks of the psalm-song if the teaching of knowledge is bound with the practice of good works, but of a song-psalm (hymn) if the practice of good works is attached to knowledge (*Prol. to Ps.* 19-20, *PL* 9.244-45). Here he sharpens the distinctions made by St. Hippolitus, and also, like Hippolitus, he adds an analysis of the practical modes of psalm production: the psalm is pure instrumental music without song; the song is pure vocal music; the psalm-song is choral singing which follows an instrumental piece or introduction; the song-psalm occurs when an instrumental section follows a choral piece (*Prol. to Ps.* 19-20, *PL* 9.244-45).

Hilary recognized a third kind of song--the jubilation, interpreted as the song style of the shepherds to whom on lonesome fields certain questions were revealed (*On Ps.* 65.3, *PL* 9.425). The practice was Byzantine and highly ornate; the congregation responded to the cantor with a melismatic *alleluia* ("praise the Lord") of varied duration, sometimes as long as fifteen minutes! The jubilation (*jubilus, jubilatio*) was named for the triumph and exultation expressed in the last syllable of the *alleluia*. It was an expression of joy of indefinite extension. A melismatic decoration, it was one of the first musical forms adopted by Christianity that stood in direct opposition to the requirement, established by the early Church for the singing of the psalms, of melodic simplicity in order to insure the dominance in the chant of the text. Its indulgence in tone, as it were, was in contrast to the accepted ascetic ideal. Was it therefore a denial of the power of the Word, of the *Logos*? Its speech-text very nearly disappeared beneath the repeated and lengthened syllables. But St. Augustine, more attracted to music than many of the other Fathers, praised the *jubilus*; so too did St. Jerome, who said that he continued to find it in many places in Bethlehem in the fourth century. The song was based on an intention either contemplative or devotional; but the *jubilus* was a free-flowing ecstatic melisma, a fervent and unbounded praise of the Lord for which language with its restraints is inadequate.

The hymn, a comparatively plain form compared to the *jubilus* in any case, did eventually overcome the objections of strict clergy and others who would object to its music, and it became an integral part of the services of the Church. Its entry into the services was probably due to the attractiveness of melodic-rhythmic singing--an attractiveness that guaranteed the popularity of the form so that it could not easily be rejected. It would appear that congregations and monastic communities liked precisely those purely musical aspects of the hymn and of melodic singing (not impossibly, in some instances, with some instrumental accompaniment upon occasion) which the more conservative clergy would have suppressed if it had been possible. The positive attitude of Hilary and Ambrose toward such hymns also very likely made a considerable difference in the survival of the form, while others, as we have seen, helped to conserve the *jubilus* which would round out the *alleluia* to add its own attractiveness to the church services-- an attractiveness that was aesthetic rather than rational or text-oriented.

VI

John Chrysostom. As a student of rhetoric, John (345-407), a Greek Father of the Church who became bishop of Constantinople, was particularly expert in sermonizing; after his death, his remembered oratorical skill earned him the title of *Chrysostomos* (the golden-mouthed). He was also a poet. His oratorical skill was often turned to oppose the theater, primarily for its evident corruption: actors use foul words and gestures, they cater to licentiousness by the way they adorn their hair or walk or dress or use their voices or move their limbs and eyes, and they also employ *auloi* and pipes for improper plots and actions (*Homilies on Matthew* 7.37, *PG* 57.78-79). More interested in the practical than in theory and dogma, he was, however, a contentious individual: he was twice deposed and sent into exile because of his asceticism which he wanted to impose on others and because of his lack of tact. Since he thought that antiphonal singing had utility through its practical spiritual and moral effect, he encouraged its use in the Church.

Like St. Basil, he thinks God has deliberately put the psalms into musical form to insure the blending of melody with prophecy so that even rather indolent persons will want to sing hymns to God. Psalm singing is popular in the East, he says, and the very efficacy of music lies in its ability to make spiritual reading easy for the indolent since its charm leads men gladly to sing hymns (*Exposition of Ps. 41*, *PG* 55.156). Nothing "uplifts the mind" to give it wings and to free it from the earth, nothing gives it a "love of wisdom" and philosophical thought, nothing causes it "to scorn all things" related to earthly life so much as "modulated melody and the divine chant composed of number [meter, rhythm]" (*Exposition of Ps. 41*, Strunk, p. 67). Infants are put to sleep with music, and travellers refresh themselves with it. Like scores of the writers he had read--Quintilian (1.10.16), probably Ovid (*Tristia* 4.15-16), and Athanasius come to mind--he agreed that peasants, sailors, and women sing as they work in order to make their work easier. Even St. Paul had sung when he was in prison (Strunk, pp. 68-69).

Since this pleasure is innate, God "established" the psalms to counter the bad effects of lascivious songs and all things harmful and vicious. The psalms contain so much of value, utility, and sanctity that they lead one to philosophy: the words purify the mind and allow the grace of the spirit to be invoked (Strunk, p. 68). Chrysostom is definitely echoing St. Paul, who had told the Ephesians (5.19) that they should speak to themselves "in psalms, and hymns, and spiritual canticles, singing and making melody in [their] hearts to the Lord"; or the Colossians (3.16) that they should let the Word of Christ dwell in them "in all wisdom" and should teach and admonish "one another in psalms, hymns, and spiritual canticles, singing in grace in [their] hearts to God." For demons,[12] Chrysostom maintains, congregate where there are licentious chants, but the grace of the spirit gathers where there are spiritual ones. At feasts, Satan seeks to ensnare souls; it is therefore best that psalms and hymns sacred to God be sung on such occasions. Psalmody banishes evil and depraved advice and wipes away mental stains. On the other hand, the comedians, the dancers, and the harlots--and thus jealousy, adultery, debauchery, and countless evils--call up demons and even Satan himself. But those who invoke David with his lyre address Christ. To call up demons and Satan is to make homes into theaters; to call upon Christ is to make them into churches.

Sing the words, John says, even though you do not understand them: they will make your tongue holy. Sing even if your voice is made weak by age or youth, or is harsh, or if you do not know musical proportion. What God wants is a "sober mind, an awakened intelligence, a contrite heart, sound reason, and clear conscience." Instruments are not needed for these ends. You yourself may "become a cithara, mortifying the members of the flesh and making a full harmony of mind and body" (Strunk, pp. 69-70). Thus he would expel (artificial) instruments from the Church. "I should like to allege," he wrote, "that people in older times were so excited by tympanums [drums] and psalteries because of the dullness of their senses and because they had, to begin with, even then extracted themselves from the false images" (*Ps.* 149, *PG* 55.494). Instruments are acceptable only as symbolical images: the cithara is a symphony of virtues (*Ps.* 97.2, *PG* 55.779), and trumpets are in a symbolic relation to the twelve Apostles (*Ps.* 4.4.5, *PG* 55.45-46). When a spiritual melody is created, flesh no longer lusts in contradiction of the spirit. A slowly perfected art is not a necessity, but a lofty purpose is. Place and season are irrelevant because all places and seasons are good; and singing without voice is acceptable too because if the mind resounds inwardly, we sing to God.

The Church Fathers only vaguely followed the ethical theory of the Greeks, and then, as we have seen in Basil, the ethico-musical doctrine of the ancients is in the process of being replaced by a personal spirituality and moralism regulated by Christian theology and by the Church's developing legal system. Believers must first be in sympathy with God and reconciled to him through the forgiveness of their sins, as the Creed dictates. The emphasis, as noted above, is no longer on life, manners, and citizenship, but on an indifference to them in favor of a self-denying and, in the extreme, ascetic ideal. The catharsis of pity and fear is thus fully completed in the experience of living as a human being and Christian on this earth and does not require the artifice of music and drama to accomplish this aim. The Fathers therefore tacitly ignore this kind of purgation. For them, the aesthetic effect of music--an effect which might include catharsis--is of no moment, and indeed, as we have seen, music's value lies strictly in its usefulness in modifying religious or spiritual states. For the earlier Greeks, music was to act on the wills of men. The Fathers normally limit the effects of music to negatives like the prevention of evil and immorality or to a certain sweetness which disguises the true disciplinary feature of the psalms; the positives are general (spiritual) moral improvement and a sense of exaltation and ecstasy in the presence of God.

For Chrysostom, song must lift men into the realm of the Spirit. David sang his songs not to tickle the ears, but to refresh and benefit the soul. All worldly song pleases the ear, but its sensuous part is far from profitable; heavenly music, on the other hand, leads the soul to discipline and order (*Ps.* 100.1 [spurious?], *PG* 55.630). The ear should be firmly directed only toward its proper aim--namely, to a grasp of the divine Word and the full-toned spiritual connection whose governance over a soul is so powerful that he who is swept away by the melody can with pleasure enjoy neither meat nor drink nor sleep. Thus bad spirits fear the music of the Church, because by hearing it and being influenced by it we will be lost to them (*Ps.* 145.5, *PG* 55.474). Indeed, not only among the heathen, but even among the community of Christians there are many who secretly find pleasure in "diabolic singing" and are occasionally backsliders in this direction (*Ps.* 7, *PG* 55.80ff). The singing of psalms for the dead does surely have an especially ethical effect, however: its purpose is not to lament for the dead but to express gratitude for death itself (*De lazar. concio.* 5.2, *PG* 48.1019-20), since death is in fact a stage that must be passed on the soul's journey to Eternity.

Chrysostom too believes that the psalm leads to action and the hymn to contemplation. Hymn singing, for example, is a matter not of words alone but also of a state of mind which brought the words together (*Sermo cum presbyter fuit ordinatus* 2, *PG* 48.695-96)--an inner state of mind in which subjectivity leads to worship. Hymnody especially, in contrast to all spheres of psalmody, belongs to the domain of higher powers (*Colossians 3*, NPN1 13.301-02). Chrysostom objects to the systaltic *tropos* as defined by Cleonides, the ethos described as lacking in manliness and encouraging amorous dejection and plaintive feelings. The well-ordered melody, he thinks, and the rhythmically divine song of all things refresh men the most, give wings to the human soul, save it from all earthly dross and all the chains of the body, and make man a philosopher and a despiser of all earthly and profane artifices. Properly used, music is a kind of ecstasy transporting the soul to God.

VII

St. Ambrose (Ambrosius). St. Ambrose (340-97) was bishop of Milan, a city which was a favorite residence in his day of the Roman emperors. It was during his lifetime that the Church became divided between East and West, an event that occurred after 395 and the death of Emperor Theodosius I (the Great), the last sole ruler of the Roman Empire and the target of Ambrose's violent censure. Thereafter, the Western Church, like the Western arm of the empire, had less and less to do with Eastern traditions, including the use of the Greek language. Greek philosophy, literature, and science had more and more to be translated into Latin, and by the year 600 Greek works were generally to be known only through Latin translations, many of them poor précis or misinterpretations, with texts even attributed to the wrong authors.

The independence of the Western Church meant that some progress would be made in the codification of liturgical and musical practices, including progress toward the making of a canon of church modes--an achievement for which Ambrose had received credit for initiating--though this process was not completed until the time of Pope Gregory the Great. At one time it was erroneously supposed that Ambrose adopted the seven modes and reduced them to four, to be increased in Gregory's time to eight. Ambrose's sources were probably Eastern and Roman, and the eagerness of scholars encouraged them to "discover" facts and to advance interpretations that are now seen as unconvincing. Ambrose did not, for example, compose a *Te Deum* often attributed to him.

Ambrose's promotion of congregational singing has already been mentioned above. The traditional view, which may well be correct, is that his contribution also involved the successful introduction of the antiphonal singing of hymns in the West. In any case, he thought that psalms should be sung by the whole congregation and that its members might adopt the music of the liturgy as true folk songs. His love of music and its theory seems indeed to have led him to encourage the hymn form, which, as we have seen, appears to have been introduced to the West from the eastern Mediterranean. St. Augustine reliably attributed the authorship of several Latin hymns to him. The notation of these hymns, however, comes from a much later period.

When we examine one of Ambrose's hymns (for example, *Aeterne rerum conditor*), his contribution of meter as an ordering principle (something absent, of course, from psalmody) becomes clear. Here, then, we can observe the replacing of the old quantitative verse of earlier Latin poetry by accentual verse, the old measures (the hexameter, the elegiac, and the sapphic) being ostensibly retained but becoming transformed into trochaic (♩ ♪) and iambic (♪ ♩). Often a hymn was made up of stanzas of iambic dimeters, such as two measures of four iambic feet, a unit mentioned for the song by Quintilian (9.4.45-51). For Ambrose, the hymn was a song in praise of the Lord in which all three elements (pitch, words, and meter) enter into an inseparable unity.[13]

Not among the earliest parts of the liturgy, the hymn would henceforth appear in many different guises, including a rich extension of medieval traditions reaching into Protestantism. The same melody could be used for various texts on account of the adoption of metrical and stanzaic forms that now were developed, and a single text may have been sung to different melodies--or to variants of the same melody, as we may expect would have been the case in different regions in the West. Its form was to be a permanent fixture in the Church's worship because it had a devotional aim, while also it was potentially useful as a polemical vehicle for anti-heretical statement in times when orthodoxy seemed to be threatened. Its popularity also arose from its use of popular words and music and from its use of a rhythm based, as we have seen, on quality (accent).[14] In the history of music, Ambrose has been regarded as one of the seminal figures; whether or not this is an accurate assessment of his actual contribution, the Church in Milan in his day clearly played a crucial role in musical and liturgical developments.

Like Clement of Alexandria and Gregory of Nyssa (but unlike Basil), Ambrose stressed the old but useful theory of the harmony of the spheres, which gradually among these thinkers shades into the idea of a universal harmony created by God. For world (cosmic) music is the prime model of the earthly, he says, and King David set up the art of the *Psalms* in imitation of the musical conversation carried on by the world bodies among themselves, a conversation audible in the farthest reaches of the universe (*Explanation of the Twelve Psalms of David, PL* 14.965ff). His own hymns are an embodiment of world harmony echoing throughout the Church. At the margin of this earthly world, the music of the spheres can still be heard: this is not at all unnatural since the echo in forests and on walls of rock sounds delightful, and even birds find a joy in charming song (*Ps.1* 2.1, *PL* 14.922). The Prophet heard cosmic music in the rush of wings, and for Plato it sounded in the musical movement of the stars (*De Abraham* 2.8.54, *PL* 14.480). Ambrose even finds musical therapy in birds' songs (*Hexaemeron* 5.24.85, FC 42.222).

He goes beyond his predecessors in his mystical-symbolic speculations about aspects of the Bible. Like other Fathers, he thought that biblical figures were superior to Greek and Roman models because they alone reflected the truth. He deplored the debasement of music in the theater, and, like Eusebius of Dorylaeum (d. c.452), bishop of Constantinople and Dorylaeum, St. Hippolitus at Rome, and St. Hilary at Arles (from 429 to 449), he applied symbolization and allegory to most spiritual and temporal matters. For him the number 7 was not to be treated as it was by the Pythagoreans and other philosophers, but in the form and organization of divine grace (*Lett.* 50, FC 26.265). For example, the cithara is our flesh when it dies to sin in order to live to God: when the tortoise lives in sensuous enjoyment, it is in mud; when it is dead, its shell is used for song and holy teachings because it sounds the changing seven notes in rhythmic measure (*The Prayer of Job and David* 4.10.36, FC 65.419). These seven tones are an image of the seven-fold gifts of the Holy Ghost (*Jacob and the Happy Life* 2.9.39, FC 65.170-71). David with the rod of the Holy Ghost caused the psalm to sound for virtuous people like the instrument of heavenly sweetness on the earth. When, using strings as dead relics, David directed his praise to heaven in the sounds of different voices, he also pointed out that we must first destroy sin before good works can be discerned in the body (*Ps. 1* 11, *PL* 14.926). According to these symbols, the strings and the body of the tortoise are dead relics which resemble sin destroyed, but now the body of the cithara is alive and reveals its good works at the same time that the deadness or death of sin is realized. Instruments are lifeless (destroyed by death), but out of them comes life. Ambrose's defense of instruments is always symbolic: the Apostle Paul was like a psaltery that spontaneously produces the song of sweet grace in perfect harmony in which the Holy Ghost like a plectrum brings into sound the inner string of prayer and the outer of psalmodizing (*Ps.* 48.7, *PL* 14.1158). Confession takes place on the cithara, which is struck upon by the plectrum of the Holy Ghost: the cithara is the flesh which in baptism receives the seven-fold mercies of the Holy Spirit according to the number of the strings ("seven changing notes in rhythmic measures") (*Job* 4.10.36, FC 65.419). The number 7 will not be denied: even the seven old Greek modes are in symbolic relation to the seven mercies and grace of God (*Jacob and the Happy Life* 2.9.39, FC 65.170; *Prayer of Job and David* 4.10.36, FC 65.419).

In Ambrose, the old magical-sympathetic view of music is now fully transformed into the communal-sympathetic. There is a sympathy in reverse, as it were, when God is pleased not only by being praised in the hymn but also by being appeased by it (*Ps. 1* 5.1, *PL* 14.925). Better yet, psalm-singing is a bond of unity between social levels of people and between private and public life. It brings the congregation into a unity. In fact, the practical use of the singing of the congregation is the achievement of communal attention and order. The Holy Ghost can find no error in congregational singing--in contrast to that of the virtuosi (*Ps. 1 9*, *PL* 14.924-25). An example of the pneumatic (spiritual) character of such congregational singing comes clear in the song of gratitude after the return of the prodigal son who was spiritually and physically weak (*Ps. 118* 7.26, *PL* 15.1224, 1232). Thus, psalm-singing is suitable for every stage of life. It is sympathetic-cohesive, and therefore Ambrose did not feel bound to the demand in *I Corinthians* (14.34) that women should not sing: every class is threatened by the danger of profane music; at the same time, Ambrose valued the opulent voices of young and married women as they melodically sounded out the praise of God (*Ps. 1* 9.3f, *PL* 14.924), though he was enough of a conventional churchman to think they should otherwise remain silent in the church (*Ps. 36* 4-5, *PL* 14.968)! For Ambrose thought that the secondary aim of the psalm-singing of people in competition with one another is both a musical delight and religious training (*Ps 1* 10.1, *PL* 14.926). But at his most serious he compares people united in psalm-singing to the harmony achieved by the unequal (in length) strings of a cithara (*Ps 1* 9.5, *PL* 14.925). Indeed, the entire world is made up of the contrast of elements as is the harmony of deep and high tones (*De Noah et arca* 1.23, *PL* 14.400), and the liturgical chant is itself a realization of cosmic harmony and peace with God (*Hex.* 3.5.23, FC 42.84).

Like Hilary of Poitiers, Ambrose encouraged the use of music to teach and to combat heresy. But foremost among his accomplishments were his use of antiphonal practices in communal singing as an integral part of the liturgy at Milan and also, if we can believe the traditional views, his successful introduction of the hymn. Through participation in the singing of psalms, hymns, and other liturgical music, the minds of all classes and groups of people could direct their songs to God in honor and praise of him. Through such song, in all humility they might express their joy, lighten any heaviness of heart, and reach an improved spiritual condition.

VIII

St. Jerome (Eusebius Hieronymus). St. Jerome (c.340-420), a Doctor of the Church, is best known for his translation into Latin of the Bible, subsequently known as the Vulgate (the version that was translated into English in the Douay-Rheims Bible and which for convenience I cite in this book). An extreme ascetic, he was a superb scholar, a poet, and a humanist in the sense that he took seriously questions of a linguistic nature. His respect for classical texts was based on his belief they could serve the Christian and his Church. His literary legacy includes numerous commentaries, works of biblical exegesis, writings on archaeology, and, especially, *De viris illustribus*, an ecclesiastical history. He translated into Latin and revised the chronology of Eusebius Pamphili. He admired Aristoxenus as "the musician," just as he himself would be later greatly admired by Erasmus.

Though at one time he condemned all musical instruments (*Lett.* 107, NPN2 6.190), he also commented in a positive way, as had others such as Clement, on an important verse in the epistle of St. Paul to the Ephesians (5.19): "Speaking to yourselves in psalms, and hymns, and spiritual canticles, singing and making melody in your hearts to the Lord." Keeping from drunkenness, Jerome says, and therefore being filled with the Spirit, one can accept all things spiritually--through psalms, hymns, and songs. Hymns declare "the power and majesty of the Lord and continually praise his works and favors"--especially the psalms to which the word *alleluia* is added (Strunk, p. 72). As a controversialist, Jerome was tireless in contrasting sacred music, especially the psalms, with the profane. Poetry could be the food of devils (*Ep.* 21.13, *PL* 26.880), but David was the Christian Pindar and Horace (Pref. to Book 15 of his translation of Eusebius' *Chronicron*, *PL* 27.56). The Sirens' song symbolized all that was bad-- sensuality, false doctrine, and temptation. But good music can banish bad spirits (Pref., *Comm. on Eph.* 3.5.19, *PL* 26.528). Concerning ancient learning, Jerome took the "charitable way: in general, if used it should be rejected in favor of the Bible and the Scriptures, but should serve Christianity," and it can do so in no better way than through providing the methodology which might be used for the allegorical interpretation of the Scriptures, which it is the duty of the Christian to pursue in order to purify secular learning of all errors.

He too holds the psalms in high reverence. The psalms achieve ethical effects by which through the instrumentality of the body we recognize what is and what is not to be done. But one can speak of higher things--of the harmony of the world and of the harmony and concord of all creatures--and then one sings a truly religious song (*Comm. on Eph.* 3.5.19, *PL* 26.528). Body and soul are in opposition because the psalm is directed toward the body (action) and the song to the soul (contemplation). Again we hear that we should praise the Lord more with the heart than with the voice, and Jerome adds: not as tragedians do, "smearing the throat with a sweet drug, so that theatrical melodies and songs are heard in the church, but in fear, in work, and in a knowledge of the Scriptures." If a man performs good works, "he is a sweet singer before God." He advises the servant of Christ to "sing . . . not through his voice, but through the words which he pronounces, in order that the evil spirit which was upon Saul may depart from those . . . similarly troubled" (Strunk, p. 72). Jerome's envisaged ethical effects are those appropriate to the devout Christian whose concern is not narcissistically with himself but with his relation to God.

More than the other Fathers mentioned here, Jerome was protective of the moral and spiritual lives of women. Whereas the Fathers usually seemed to be addressing congregations of the faithful and, separately, male students in church and cathedral schools, Jerome specifically addresses the guardians or parents of young girls. While all the Fathers made a dogma of virginity and censured sexual intercourse outside marriage, they valued the souls of men and women alike, as the ancient Greeks had not; and Jerome, veritably obsessed with virginity and the salvation of women's souls, made a special issue of the matter and studied the Bible with groups of patrician women. His description of the educational methods to which a virgin should be subjected is, in modern terms, disturbing, to say the least.

He advises a Roman woman to teach her daughter the psalms and to avoid worldly songs (*Lett.* 107.12, NPN2 6.194); he would deny women a knowledge of the world's songs entirely (*Lett.* 107.4, NPN2 6.190-91); and he thinks the young virgin should avoid female companions who can "warble songs with liquid notes"--instead, she should rise at night to recite prayers and psalms, while in the morning she should sing permissible hymns (*Lett.* 107.9, NPN2 6.193). He gives similar advice to a Roman father: his daughter should be rewarded for singing the psalms (*Lett.* 128.1). There follow warnings: at banquets the efforts of singers can be so seductive as to allure the young girl to pleasure--a point proven by heathen legends of the songs of the Sirens and Orpheus' music on the lyre (*Lett.* 117.6). The good virgin should be deaf to the sound of the organ and quite ignorant of the uses of the pipe, the lyre, and the cithara (*Lett.* 107.8).

Outside and beyond the physical world is a music beyond imagining, that of choirs of angels: these are the model to keep in mind. The theater and the devil's songs sung in it must be avoided, and a widow should be very careful not even to be seen with a "devilish singer of poisoned sweetness" (*Lett.* 79.8, NPN2 6.167). Psalm-singing in the open air is a good adjunct to the sweet songs of birds (*Lett.* 43.3, NPN2 6.58). And women, who should obey their husbands, especially should delight themselves with songs and canticles--but only in private (*Against the Pelagians* 1.25, NPN2 6.461-62). Jerome seems to admire a restricted kind of Roman *Hausmusik*, which Tertullian too had recommended in an example of a married couple who chant to the Lord as they compete with each other singing "echo" (antiphonal) psalms and hymns (*To His Wife*, ANF 4.48). One's private life too--and probably even more than one's public--must be devoted to God and be subject to the teachings of the Church. For secularism is to be scorned: the clergy hence should not sing the *Ecologues* of Virgil (*Lett.* 21.13, ACW 33.118-19), and women should be protected from Greek and Roman writers, including Plautus, Terence, Cicero, Virgil, Horace, and others (though Jerome himself admired and read such authors for an understanding of Christian dogma).

The composer-performer receives advice from Jerome too: if a writer is so clever that nobody can understand him, he is only singing for himself--and for the Muses (*Lett.* 50.2, NPN2 6.80-81). For, essentially, face and voice are not one and inseparable: the outer and inner are inter-dependent (*Against the Pelagians* 1.23, NPN2 6.460-61). Yet even a singer of a bad performance will merit God's approval if he is able to do good works. The servant of Christ sings not that his voice but that his words will please. The choir leaders themselves should not cultivate the theatrical kind of singing which they exhibit: it impairs the religious character of what is uttered (Pref. *Comm. on the Eph.* 3.5.19, *PL* 26.528).

Despite his emphasis on the message of sacred song--what you sing with your mouth, you should believe in your heart, and what you believe in your heart you should prove through your work--and despite his condemnation of all instruments, he favors the *jubilus*, that musical decoration and expression rather than verbal statement coming at the end of the *alleluia*. He himself is said to have encouraged the addition of the *alleluia*[15] to the service of the Mass: he calls it "that which neither in words nor in syllables nor letters nor speech it is possible to express or comprehend how much man ought to praise God" (*On Psalm 49, PL* 26.970). He demonstrates too a sense of symbolism, and he makes it concrete when he speaks of the "tropology of numbers" (*Comm. on Amos* 3, *PL* 25.1073).

The Fathers of the Church, then, were in specific ways unfriendly to music as such, often in spite of themselves. They could not publicly tolerate secular music. According to Athanasius, sailors', millers', and wanderers' songs (the conventional examples in ancient times of music having good effects) are indecent in that they follow the traditions of song and dance in city folk festivals. Thus for centuries actors, players of native music, and minstrels were anathema. For Jerome, there was a better--indeed a more exclusive--path to refreshment of spirit, to the lifting of sadness, to the feeling of good fortune--through the praise and glorifying of and giving thanks to God. The words of the Bible, and especially the *Psalms* supposedly composed by Kind David, the hymns and canticles, the very Mass itself--all were the important core of what the Christian should attend to, and music was only a servant to the activities of men who hoped to please God. The *jubilus* was exceptional: it could express praise, love, honor, and worship through contentless sound itself. In their passion for the eternal truth, the Fathers insisted that music is subordinate to words. But as they favored the *jubilus*, they unwittingly took account of ecstasy, which they often called enthusiasm; and, even more important for the future, they unconsciously paved the way for sound in motion or rhythm as an autonomous art. But even the *jubilus* was not always admired, and later in life even Augustine, who once had praised it, seemed to reject it with all of music and its corrupting effects.

These men were thinkers and theologians, if not philosophers. Indeed, philosophy itself was not yet considered to be legitimately theological. They were no more professional musicians than were their predecessors who wrote about music. They were compelled to recognize music--while they virtually ignored the other arts--because it was useful and necessary in the Church. Nevertheless, these were men of imagination, of vision, and, above all, of conviction and passion. None of them forsook the requirements of the worship services, including the Mass, and of Christian education in the narrow sense. As a rule, they were not speculative thinkers; they were men of action, even administrators. Few of them had original minds or were capable of creating abstractions such as we find, for example, in Plato.

The late Latin and pre-medieval use of music for arousing devotion in clergy and congregation, who would be inspired with a worship of and appropriate admiration for God as the Creator and sustainer of all, was of course not new. The pagan world had found music efficacious for magical-religious activities, rites, and ecstatic experiences. The Phrygian musician Olympus, for example, had used the aulos or was accompanied by it when he sang, and his melodies inspired enthusiasm (Aristotle, *Pol.* 1340a); and in the cults of Cybele and Dionysius, in the Orphic rites, and in the religious rites of Thrace and Phrygia singing and instrumental music had effected a transport which can be called transcendental--a union of soul and universal spirit. Plato and Aristotle mentioned the Corybantes, who were not in their right minds but out of them, and music and dance were thought so to affect people who were in the proper state of enthusiasm that, at one with the god, they were transported outside their corporeal selves. Similarly, in the Middle Ages music could be said to have the power to make a person at one with the Christian God. This was effected primarily in a mystical experience which is as convincing and all-embracing as it is ineffable. In its ability to move and transport, music was the most important contributor of all the arts to the Christian life.

XII
St. Augustine

St. Augustine (354-430), the most influential of the Church Fathers, did not become a Christian until he was thirty. The story of his conversion, in his *Confessions*, is justly famous as the record of the life of one who suffered a spiritual crisis, accepted Christianity at the hands of St. Ambrose (then bishop of Milan), became bishop of Hippo (now Bone, Algeria) in 396, and emerged as a theologian of the very greatest significance. He had been eight or nine when the Emperor Julian attempted to restore pagan religious practices, and he was thirty-eight when the Emperor Theodosius acted in favor of Christianity by forbidding worship according to pagan rites. Augustine--a scion of a wealthy Carthaginian family, lover of women in his early years and a natural father, a sensualist on his own admission-- was to become, following his conversion, a force behind the cultivation of pagan learning among Christians, though he never consciously tried to reconcile Hebrew and Greek traditions.

In another famous work, his *City of God*, and in his other writings he explicitly or implicitly compared the world and temporal existence with heaven and eternity in terms of the Earthly City and the City of God, both concepts that were foreshadowed by the thinking of the Neoplatonists. The one is a passing thing and yet dependent, the other permanent and independent; the one is a state of becoming in which one may find oneself caught up to one's great loss, the other is pure Being, which is ultimately freedom and salvation. More than any of his predecessors, he was a powerful personality and also someone who was intensely autobiographical and subjective in his thought. He may be said to be a thinker convinced of the universality of his own thought, yet he is the most philosophical of the Fathers. His *Confessions*, the prototype of the intellectual and spiritual biography in the Western world, stood in contrast to the usual hagiographical biography that had been the rule. The *Confessions* serves as an account of his journey from aesthete and hedonist--a lover of music for its own sake--to passionate Christian who would need to understand all things, including music, in terms of the framework provided by the idea of the two cities, the Earthly City and the Heavenly City. His comments on music are more penetrating than anything in the writings of the other Fathers. He is to music what St. Basil and St. Ambrose are to the aesthetics of light, a topic which of course has a history of its own.

Augustine knew the works of Plato, Plotinus, Porphyry, Proclus,

Varro, Cicero (whose *Hortensius* is said to have helped him to a love of wisdom), and the old and contemporary grammarians his *De musica* (*On Music*) was designed in part to replace. In contrast to the Neoplatonists, he insisted that the created world is good, yet he agreed with them that evil is only an aberration of good. Though he was not well versed in mathematics or science, his knowledge was in large part rhetorical. He admired classical literature for humane and aesthetic reasons and thought that it has practical benefits (*City of God* 18). For a thousand years his words stood as an acceptable outline for certain philosophical problems and their solutions. In his writings, the Platonic Idea undergoes a transformation which was to remain a constant in the Western world: the Idea is a content of divine origin, a locus for a creative world-soul, and the mode of Being of the personal God. For him, philosophy had three divisions, based, he said, on Plato: physics, ethics, and logic. Moral philosophy or ethics is related to action, natural philosophy or physics is related to contemplation and affords an approach to universal truth, and reason or logic distinguishes between truth and error. Augustine's first two categories of action and contemplation (ibid. 8.4) are precisely those by which the Church Fathers characterized the psalm and the hymn respectively.

He is to the Middle Ages as Plato and Aristotle were to the ancient world. He marks a change in thought, and his *Confessions* gives us its clue. The ancient stance had been objective, as we have seen. Faith had meant knowledge of cosmic, elemental, earthly, and human things, all mutually influential, and of the proper moral states and actions which they required. Though symbolism of the imperceivable, eternal, and permanent as well as a certain mysticism were not lacking, the idea of transcendence in experience was not as yet developed. But, extending the thinking of the earlier Fathers and the Scriptures, an internalization arrives with Augustine. As established in *Romans* 8, God, the world, faith, human behavior and judgment have a share in the human mind and soul. The moral, the good is within one. Inner life is a given, and this precept is consistent with personal as well as communal religious experience and the existence of a God who is personal as well as revealed in the Christian community and its traditions. For Augustine, then, the inner life is to be an awareness of God's own presence through faith as a personal act of will. In the battle of life--a concept adopted from St. Paul--one's allies are faith, reason, and the deity himself. Knowledge is thus not identical with virtue, as had been the case for Socrates; instead, goodness is an entirely separate condition, and God is immaterial Spirit and Absolute Beauty experienced through revelation.

In origin, he thought, wisdom is truth both moral and rational. To find it, the soul must turn to God, for illumination comes from God himself. Therefore the importance of the symbolism of light becomes clear, for intelligence needs the light, the sun, the truth of light, the light of God, the divine light which reveals truth eternal and immutable. The angels achieve it through active intellect alone because knowledge is revealed directly and cannot derive from sensation. It penetrates the soul, acts on the body, not the body on the soul; the soul can affect the body so as to cause something luminous in the eyes and a clear and mobile air in the ears. The soul affects all the senses but is not affected by them (*On Music* 6.5.10). Here we have a direct inheritance from Plotinus, as we also have from Pythagoras according to tradition, when Augustine says that philosophy is the love of wisdom, a love which is the desire for the good, depends on knowledge, and is eternal. All faith is therefore not in worldly objects but in God. Augustine elaborates his metaphysics in his *City of God*, a counterforce to Plato's *Republic* and a major source of the later doctrine of luminosity as it will appear in the Middle Ages.

Despite his well-known love of music, his (incomplete) *On Music* disappoints at first because its primary subject is rhythm governed by time and number. An early work, it reflects Augustine's interest in rhetoric, a staple of all Christian education which he studied at Carthage and which he was induced to teach at Milan. He was to include both rhetoric and music among the Liberal Arts, which Varro said were nine in all but which he reduced to seven by deleting medicine and architecture and substituting philosophy for astronomy (*Divine Providence* 1.35-42, FC 1.313-19; *Retractions* 1.5, FC 60.22).

On Music is a part of a cycle of dialogues on the Liberal Arts, each of which Augustine thought had its own theory because no single theory can be all-inclusive. Never written was a final book which was to follow, focusing on harmonics (that is, melody). This section was expected to make advances in musico-rhetorical theory, in contrast to the productions of the grammarians, all conservative traditionalists (*On Music* 2.1.1). Books 1 to 5 of *On Music* are devoted to rhythm, metrics, verse, and associated subjects; Book 6 is a treatise on pure numbers as they are constitutive of the soul, the universe, and time. Augustine's basic aesthetic principle is Platonic: beauty is unified simplicity. "[God] has ordered all things in measure, and number, and weight," he quotes from the *Book of Wisdom* (11.21), and God therefore maintains all things in mode, form, and order. Beauty belongs to the higher order of God.

It is music, not Latin grammar of the conventional sort, which is his subject. Words the same in sound but different in meaning, and words different in sound because their accents are differently placed--both are rhythmically ordered and can be rhythmically imitated even by drum or string. These sounds and their rhythms do not concern the grammarians, who are mere namers and analyzers and do not deal with sounds based on pure number. The proper discipline for the examination of sounds in rhythm is not grammar but metrics in music, which (poetically speaking) reflects the omnipotence of the Muses in song (*On Music* 1.1).

But what is music? Augustine seems to have learned from Varro that it is the science of modulating, of measuring well (*musica est bene modulandi scientia*). This is not the modulation of nineteenth-century music, that of transfer from key to key, but one of the kinds of modulation listed by Cleonides which involves changes in sound: it is sound in motion.

It is the regular (or regulated) rhythmical measure of classical Latin, for one thing--a measurement of time. It may have to do with the singing or playing of a melody, but at present Augustine is interested only in temporal order, because order is the rule of all things. Like Aristotle (*Physics* 218b-222a), he believes time to be the measure of motion. Like Plotinus (and Henri Bergson [1859-1941]), he thinks it has two forms: (1) the objective (external) which is bound to the object and takes place in space; and (2) the subjective (interior), which takes place in time. The soul, originally motionless, is set in motion by a spiritual force going from object to object. For Augustine, the principle of life is rhythm manifested in the motion of the soul, which in turn is the principle of time. Here motion (rhythm) and time are pure ontological matters.

Mensurating or measuring well is an aesthetic matter whose harmoniousness can be either an in-itself or a relation to an occasion or to a psychological situation. Movements exist not to accomplish something else, but to be themselves, to exist only for their own sakes and to give us enjoyment. They are not ethical-aesthetic, though the ambiguity of meaning of the Latin word *bene* (good, well) suggests that they are. True, Augustine once said that music and dancing could be reprehensible, and in later life he surely thought them so to be. Such moral judgments would have entered into his unwritten "On Harmonics" which would treat melody; there word-meanings would apply and ethical significances would be expected. Here, however, he shows that in music there is mensuration as in oratory there is diction.

Essentially mathematical, mensuration is a skill in moving well, especially in music and the dance. Mensuration of plastic works in wood, silver, or another kind of non-motive material[1] is one thing, but mensurated movement is another; it occurs when a dancer moves gracefully and harmoniously for the sake of the movement itself. This movement (and that of music) is a superior thing because it is desired for its own sake, is free, and does not subserve something else (*On Music* 1.1). Later Augustine talks about the sweet quality of meter, its delight to the ear, and its charm (ibid. 3.7.16). The idea of the superiority of the thing desired for itself points forward to Kantian doctrine.

The idea is not so very different, either, from Quintilian's (9.4.50) view that modulation belongs to everything in poetry, music, and dance which involves motion. To keep movement going harmoniously is to measure "times" well--and intervals of time well. Yet harmonious mensuration is sometimes out of place or even reprehensible--for example, in graceful dancing or sweet singing which are gay in a serious context (*On Music* 1.3). Mensurable rhythm operates in the realm of time (*Free Will* 2.42, FC 59.151-52), and in a letter to St. Jerome, Augustine writes that a composer who is also a good musician is, like God, an artisan: a man composing a song knows what metrical lengths to give to tones so that melody can flow beautifully in a succession of slow and fast times. God allows no periods of time to proceed more rapidly or more slowly than the recognized and well-defined law of rhythm he has created, in a wonderfully rhythmical song of succeeding events (*Lett.* 166.13, FC 30.19). We recognize what we cannot quite understand, however: the even regularity of the natural movement of a meter soothes our perceptions before we give consideration to the mathematical relations of the sounds (*On Music* 3.8.19).

But music is a *science* of measuring well. Nightingales measure well but are not trained to do so. Furthermore, beasts like to hear singing, and birds like to hear their own voices. Certain men who know nothing about music can hear it with pleasure and so relax from mental work. (They take in measuring well, but should not be "taken in" by it when it is improper.) Now, instrument-players have a certain art (the nightingale merely functions out of its nature), which they can achieve only through imitation. But their art is not a science, which is located in reason alone, even though the player tries to join reason with imitation. Science is mental, but the player imitates only by means of the body. Yet the sense of hearing is connected with both body and mind, while memory, necessary to both science and imitation, is related to the mind alone. The sense organs are only a *means* for the grasping of universal forms, among which is number. No more than the rest of us could Augustine by physical means perceive numbers in their separations and combinations. But he could posit the very duration of the "numbers" of the body (as in the perception of sky and land): 7 plus 3 are and always have been 10 and at no time have they not been nor will they not be 10. However perception fails us, the incorruptible truth of number is the possession of anyone who reasons (*Free Will* 2.21, FC 59.130-31). Science is mental, is closed to irrational living things, is not in sense or memory, for it exists in intellect solely. The mobility of the instrumentalist is not related to science but to practice (*On Music* 1.4.9), which too is based on sense and memory, elements that Plato, Aristotle, and Aristoxenus likewise mentioned. Both science and music-as-science are thus in the intellect. But the mass of people judge ignorantly, and, like actors and some musicians who want to please, think more of the praise than of the song. No man on the stage loves his art for itself. He loves it for the advantages it grants him (ibid. 1.4-6). In St. Augustine music earns respect but actors and acting none at all. Like Boethius later, he explains that the actor's art cannot be a science, but that music intellectually judged as number can.

There follows a discussion of "times." Because music is a knowledge of lengths, all measure and limit is its province: here humanity chooses what is necessary and sets aside infinity and immeasurability, which are beyond its grasp. Movements made according to proportional relationships are more desirable than those that are not. The first are rational, symmetrical, the other non-rational, non-symmetrical. In movement there are numbers which reveal sure and fixed laws. Take the progression from 1 to 10. Everything to be a whole must have a beginning, a middle, and an end, and all of these are present in the number 3, the first uneven (and divine) number. Even numbers do not have this unity: they are divisible. One is the unity from which other numbers come; 2 is the number through which they come.   No other two numbers make a perfection (3) with their following number arrived at through addition. The first whole even number is 4 (1 + 3 or 2 + 2). The greater the harmony the more compressed it is, the tighter is the unity of a one among many.   The unity is called proportion, and the first four numbers are the greatest and most honorable of all numbers because they add up to 10 (the Pythagorean decad), after which (at 11) there is a return to 1.   All measured movements in song and dance are related to 4 and are ornamental and delightful to the extent that they keep to the proper compressed ratios in time. What in time is beyond the capacities of our senses is set aside (ibid. 1.22-26).   A numerical system well accepted in Augustine's time, it of course stems from Nicomachus or Theon of Smyrna and Pythagorean and Platonic arithmetical systems.

It is well known that architecture and music were Augustine's two loves.   Both are governed by the conjunction of number and reason--or even by their identity.   Reason, which has fashioned grammar, dialectic, and rhetoric, notes a difference between sound and what it symbolizes.   Sound, which pertains to the ears, is   (1) "the utterance of an animate being,"   (2) "what breath produces in musical instruments," and   (3) what is "given forth by percussion": specifically, the sounds of tragic and comic actors--or of everyone giving vocal renditions, or tibias and similar instruments, and of instruments like the cithara, the lyre, and cymbals, which are struck. Reason sees little value in these sounds unless there is a fourth step of ascent into words fixed according to measure and according to high and low modulations of pitch so that there result accents and feet, syllabic longs and shorts, units in segments or members of verse, and rhythm.   And all of these are number, which clearly shows that reason begets poets who then "produce the finished product."   Reason declares that numbers are divine and eternal, and it reluctantly endures the clouding of the "splendor and serenity" of numbers "by the material stuff of vocal utterances."   Numerical proportions are immortal.   But sound, which is sensible, "flows away into the past and is imprinted on the memory"--and therefore the sense-effect accompanying the intellect in poetry was called music (*Div. Prov.*; *Problem of Evil* [*De ordine*] 2.14.39-41, FC 1.316-18).

In the first five books of *On Music*, Augustine plunges into poetics, especially the treatment of feet, rhythm, meter, verse. He attempts to create a new system based on musical rhythmics and metrics. There is the usual comparison: rhythm is the conjunction of feet with no determinate end, whereas meter is a conjunction of feet having a determinate end (*On Music* 3.6.14).   All meter is rhythmical, but all rhythm is not metrical (ibid. 3.1.2, 5.1.1) or at least is a combining of several "unstructured" meters.   Rhythm is based on a relation of syllables in time on the (qualitative) duration of syllables.   Rhythm flows, meter is bound.   There are at least two rhythmic principles: (1) rhythmic feet must be equal with respect to number of primary times (as Aristides defined them)--that is, they must have at least two and not more than four (syllables), and   (2) the ratio of *arsis* to *thesis* within the foot must always be the same (ibid. 5.2-4).

Augustine does not discourage the mispronunciation of "lengths" in words as grammar requires. The reason is aesthetic, and thus music insists on pronunciations according to *its* requirements, according to laws of short (1 time) syllables and long (2 times) syllables. The elementary syllabic feet are those of two syllables--four possible feet:

$$\cup\cup, \cup -, - \cup, - -$$

and multiplications of them; three syllables:

$$- \cup\cup, - \cup -, \cup\cup -, - - -$$

four syllables:

$$\cup\cup\cup\cup, - \cup\cup\cup, \cup-\cup\cup, \cup\cup - \cup$$

and so forth. Rhythm is infinite, is made up of numbers of longs and shorts in succession in time, but not of feet which are in harmony with one another. Meter is finite and measured according to a strictly limited flow of lengths of long and short: it is a measuring off of rhythms. Thus all verse is meter, but not all meter is verse. Meter is the joining together of feet, of which there cannot be fewer than two.

In outline, Augustine's theory of poetics and musical metrics is a comprehensive analysis of the subtleties of Latin verse into 568 meters, as it were to illustrate a musical, non-grammarians' method of delivery. More than usually important in his schemes is the pause, rest, or silence, which for him holds an important place in versification (ibid. 3.7.13-16). For Aristides Quintilianus, it will be recalled, the pause is merely an empty time lacking in sound; like a pause in oratory and other types of speech, it is used to fill out a meter. But for Augustine a pause has a psychological meaning in that it is expected. It corresponds, he thinks, to the basic law of identity. Empirically speaking, in the established meter there is an expectation of a time-lag (delay) in the sense of hearing at the conclusion of a meter; it is satisfied by the two possibilities of lengthening or interrupting the completion of the temporal interval (ibid. 3.7.16). The ear declares what the length of this interval should be (ibid. 3.8.17), which is no less than one "time" and no more than four "times" (ibid. 3.8.18). All meters must end with a complete foot or with part of a foot completed by a rest. Within the verse and foot the ratio of times must be kept constant. The same holds for silence or the rest. It must be exact according to meter, and especially at the end of a meter (of at least 2 feet) or phrase, where it may replace the second half of a final beat (ibid. 4.1.1ff). Elsewhere, Augustine examines Pythagorean number theory psychologically: time is measured not in terms of speech and movement, but of formed, shaped, and ordered tone in memory (*Conf.* 11.28). For him the subjectivity of the listening individual corresponds with the objective musical phenomenon, and sound and rest correspond with the expectations of the ear.

Not the judgment or the authority of the grammarian but of the ear is the test of rational numeration of sounds, whether in meter or verse (*On Music* 2.2.2). Ratio is the key, and like Aristides and Greek and Latin poetic theorists, Augustine, having asserted the primacy of the Pythagorean tetrad and decad, now asserts the decisive nature for rhythmic feet of the four ratios 1:1, 1:2, 2:3, 3:4, or the proportions of the first four classical consonances as the Pythagoreans defined them. (Aristoxenus disallows 3:4, Aristides allows it, but neither they nor Augustine will allow the 1:3 ratio.) Modulation or measured motion occurs according to these modules or measures of musical units. In the realm of rhythm, therefore, Augustine preferred musical to rhetorical or grammatically approved rhythms-- Dionysius of Halicarnassus set them side by side as equals--though for literary scholars he probably introduced an unnecessarily ambiguous element into rhythmic and poetic theory.

Augustine's analysis of sound in motion and time gives him a scientific justification for the art he loved. In this sense he is Platonic, for though Plato denied that music was a science at all, he had to admit that the musician, who was no philosopher of number, could nevertheless perceive number in rhythm. Augustine is in Plato's camp at the beginning of the sixth book of *On Music* when he (unnecessarily) disparages what he has said so far about rhythm and reaches for higher things. He has dwelt childishly, he says, on the number-traces belonging to number-intervals; the more mature and intelligent pursuit of the beauty of tones is concerned with purely intellectual-mathematical relations--Platonism restored. Augustine's musical hierarchy is still cosmic and Catholic at its pinnacle. It is the same perceptibility of number, of Intelligibility in itself, the same idea of truth, the same mystical philosophy which, we are told, influenced Gothic architecture.[2]

Book 6 of *On Music* is a veritable hymn to number[3] and universal rhythm, of the passing of corporeal to incorporeal things (6.2.2), number and proportion being the explanation for Augustine of the superiority of music over the other arts. As he combines sense and memory, his theory is Aristoxenian; but it also is Neoplatonic in a re-affirmation of the soul, God, and order and in a turning from the physical, sensuous imitation to what is beyond, to a non-physical, supersensuous original of music. He contrasts the knowing of number with the sensing of harmonious sound, even though number governs the sound and even though we find ourselves approving or disapproving of it (ibid. 6.3.4). Sound, like the true, is made by the body and enters the soul, where is lodged the form of the insubstantial dream. Bodies are the better as they are more harmonious by reason of numbers since beauty itself is number; as the soul turns away from carnality, it is reformed in wisdom by divine numbers (ibid. 6.7.19). Numbers are not only Euclidean--that is, "real" and "universal"--but also Nicomachean--that is, symbolical, mystical, and metaphysical--and they were to remain so throughout the Middle Ages. They are more: they are there, but not sensible. They come in three kinds--those in memory, those in sensing, and those in sound (ibid. 6.6.16), and certain among them are pre-eminent by reason of beauty and ratio. Numbers are the basis not only of the ear and bodily motions but also of light and color (ibid. 6.13.38). They are eternal. Sounds pass away, but the numbers which are music remain in intellect and memory alike (*Div. Prov.* 2.14-15; *Free Will* 2.16, FC 59.127-29). And in systematizing rhythms or numbers, Augustine makes the not so incidental remark that one should not worry about names (like those of the gram- marian) because the thing is in its meaning, and names are only "imposed by convention, not by nature" (*On Music* 6.9.24). Numbers of music are identical with the effects (or affects) produced, and the harmony of tones (which depends on numbers) reminds one of the ideal unity of God's state (*City of God* 17.14).

St. Augustine's system of number, based on reason and interpreted by the human mind, falls into several parts (which have been variously evaluated). There are five elements; four involve physical number, and the fifth embraces mental-spiritual number:

1. Rhythms or numbers exist in sound: the tones themselves are in a well-ordered relationship. This rhythm is corporeal: it is a sonant rhythm. (Augustine in no sense revives the study of acoustics, which is nevertheless suggested here.)

2. Numbers exist in the rhythms or numbers of the ear of the hearer: the well-constructed relationship is already within the comprehension of the hearer. For example, one can hear music without "hearing" it--that is, our tonal consciousness is able to grasp the tonal phenomenon: music exists in sound, but in the ear it is directed towards a number-experience of perceived sound (*On Music* 6.2.3). Here sound-number is encountered, it is occursive.

3. Rhythms and numbers exist in the act of presentation: the well- ordered relationship of tones is in the presenter. Sounding rhythms exist in the creative act of the producer. They are what we hear and that to which we react. They move. There are inner melodies which take the same time as those outer, played ones; they are inseparably connected with memory. There are also inwardly sounding forms which, variously modified, are governed by will and are not unconditionally governed by memory (6.3.4). Here rhythm is outgoing; it is progressive.

4. Rhythms and numbers exist in memory: the well-ordered arrange- ment is in the memory of the receiver. Number-allied tones are conditioned by time and are subject to memory (just as the Muses are daughters of memory [*Div. Prov.* 2.14.41, FC 1.318]). Rhythms in memory come later than rhythms heard and presented (*On Music* 6.3.4). Here rhythm is capable of being recorded.

Augustine sees the senses as an integral part of memory. With each goes the image for which it has its own special capacity. All images are stored in memory, which in some way secretes them inside itself; and each can be brought back into imagined sensation outside memory. The things we see, hear, touch, and smell are not brought back, but only the images of them. In darkness I can recall images of light and color. Sounds too can be recalled, and they do not change or confuse color-images. I can sing internally through memory without moving any of my physical singing parts. Nor will images of sight intrude. Thus, though I am not tasting or touching anything, memory will return to me scents which I can distinguish--tastes, smooth and rough things--all this while I am not hearing, tasting, or touching anything (*Conf.* 10.8.14). Clearly, memory records according to its capacities and our demands.

5. Rhythms and numbers exist in judgment by way of imagination or phantasy; they are ordered, intellectual numbers given through reason, which applies the right measure to the tones and arranges them to correspond with an intellectual prototype that the mind (of both artist and perceiver) intrinsically possesses. These numbers are eternal; they stimulate judgment; one assents or dissents in terms of rhythmic numbers; one feels pleasure or pain; the material sound has aroused natural musical judgment. As the sound is presented and perceived, tonal memory completes the process. This rhythm-number is judicial.

Though in connection with the second, third, and fourth elements Augustine touches on the psychology of musical creation, perception, and memory, his chief interest is in the fifth, the critical, the judgmental, the process of measuring a remembered sonant rhythm against the eternal. For certain rhythms are immortal. True, some rhythms depend on time and on differences of degree in individuals (ibid. 6.7.18-19), but these are constituents of human nature, which itself is not universal. Certain judged rhythms can be ascribed to the rhythmicizing of every continuous physical activity (like work, for instance) (ibid. 6.8.20), but even they can be judged only through memory, which grasps and holds the object of judgment. Memory is the recalling of thoughts, physical movements, and musical formations which have been realized earlier. Numbers remain in the memory quite independently of what is thought of at any single moment; memory perceives (1) the fresh signs of music carried out fleetingly (active or reacting numbers), and (2) the remnants of old remembered music (memorial numbers); and the judging person, following acts of memory, then passes the sentence (ibid. 6.8.21-22). Augustine also finds number in dance, the other art of pure motion, just as there are numbers belonging to Harmonia and numbers of celestial harmony.

Now, the judge clearly undergoes pleasure, which naturally arouses judgment; but pleasure cannot be an ultimate, because alongside the pleasure deriving from feeling there is still a higher realm of evaluation deriving from understanding (ibid. 6.9.23). In false and corrupt art only the physical--the sensuous--pertains, but in art which approaches the imagination, the memory of physical number and the representational image of eternal number aroused through reason must be present and in harmony. Beauty and true delight lie in the harmony of the physical and the intellectual. The aim of true music is to raise the common up to eternal harmony. It purifies as it stimulates the soul of the hearer, awakens in that soul a like harmony, and leads it to the love of God.

Later, he adds a sixth, perceptive (sensing) rhythm (or numbers), to his list of psychological elements in the judgment of music. By perceptive rhythm he means judgment through feeling. Moved by the things to which the body is passive, judgment through feeling precedes those judgmental or judicial rhythms which operate through understanding. Both sonant and perceptive rhythms turn the mind away from eternal things (ibid. 6.13.39), and these, especially rhythms related to dance or physical movement, are physical and in sharp contrast with rhythms present in the soul (ibid. 6.9.24). In adding perceptive rhythmical judgment through feeling, Augustine does not merely recognize new physical aspects of a rhythmical system of number. Rather, he indicates that human feeling is not divorced from the human soul (interpreted either in the Greek fashion or in the Christian). One can only think that Augustine is writing his own partial *Timaeus*. Reason is the focal point: a knowledge of music leads to reason, which first sought for the nature of correct form and found it in free, beautiful motion.   In physical motions reason distinguishes different time-intervals and different slow or fast intervals in space. Then the soul further divides time-lengths into different rhythms according to intervals conforming to the demands of the mind and establishes types and orders leading up to different varieties of verses. Finally, it learns which psychic activity to measure, operate, and sense, and then separates these activities according to body and soul (ibid. 6.10.25).

Reason is eternal, but sensuous pleasure (the reaction to [occursive] rhythms met from the outside) deflects the soul from a contemplation of the eternal. Progressive rhythms operating in physical bodies too turn the mind from eternal things, divert the soul, and make it "restless" (ibid. 6.13.39). Phantasies or imagined rhythms, recorded rhythms which can divert the mind from eternal things, also can direct the soul, as do perceptive rhythms and the knowledge of rhythmic things. But a person who is occupied with non-physical rhythms implanted in man by the Creator as an eternal standard need not turn away from the practical use of music in physical movement (nor, indeed, from cithara playing) (ibid. 6.15.49). For such a person already has an insight into the fundamental basis of the complete harmony and order of the world, a cosmic, intelligible beauty of pure forms, recognized by Augustine as the action of numbers as they present themselves in musical perception, just as the numbers of the artisan and his work are present to be met by the perceiver. In him resides proportion, which is equality in perfect form. And then in a letter (*Lett*. 166.13, FC 12.18-19), Augustine justifies his view of eternal music which is intrinsic to the human soul: God, he asserts, is the rhythmic mover of the world and the creator of many arts. In him resides proportion, which is equality in perfect form (*On Music* 6.11.29). Altering one of the ancient opinions about the origin of music, Augustine adds that God (not the pagan gods) gave music to man as a gift of mystical insight.

In the singing of the hymn *Deus creator omnium*, Augustine finds that hearing occurs through reacting (emotional, affective, occursive) numbers; reacting occurs through memorial (recordable) numbers, is identified through progressive (advancing) numbers, delighted through perceptive (sensuous) numbers, and judged by reason through judicial numbers. The final judgment is whether our delight is right or not, whether the whole is fit or absurd (ibid. 6.9.24).

The focal point once more is reason, which carries Neoplatonic overtones: reason perceives the numbers which, eternal and divine, govern and make perfect everything in rhythms (mensuration) and song, and, having examined them, finds they are eternal and divine. Led by faith, reason looks at heaven and earth and is pleased only by their beauty, by their beauty only in their figures, by their figures only in their dimensions, and by their dimensions only by numbers--which it brings together in the discipline of geometry. Examining the movement of the heavens, the seasons, the regular and harmonious courses of the stars, and distances, reason has found that dimensions and numbers can be apprehended through reflection and study, but that all things perceived by the senses alone are only shadows and images (*Div. Prov.* 2.14-15). (Augustine is recasting Plato's Allegory of the Cave and his idea of science.) Reason distinguishes its servant senses from an interior sense which governs them all (*Free Will* 2.3-4). Therefore number science is of the highest significance for educated people. Perceived by no sense of the body, the reason or the nature of numbers is the same as wisdom and motion, and is also a general metaphysical aspect--if not a determinant--of Being (*Div. Prov.* 2.11.30-34, FC 1.308-13). Number represents the visible principle of beautiful form, but the significance of number is more recognizable in moving things--and thus in tones--where there is a progress in numbers stepwise on the path of wisdom to truth (*Lett.* 101, FC 18.146). Moving things embody time. Yet music, the supreme art of time, is timeless. As a phenomenon, it is in time and depends on our own grasp of present, past, and future. But we make it--the child of Jupiter and Memory--beyond concrete time when we recall it (*Div. Prov.* 2.41, FC 1.317-18). There is a going from "what is" to a "what is not," and the three cooperative elements are time, motion, and memory. It is a process of going from the outer world into the inner.

"What is Time?" is the question of Book 2. If nobody asks the question, one knows the answer; if the question is asked, time cannot be explained. Past time is gone, future time is not yet. The present is always the present, but only because it passes into past time. Is time a tending not to be? Time is short, but some intervals are shorter than others. Past times are in memory only as images, and future times are foretold by the present. Time is measured as it passes. By it we measure the motion of bodies. We measure times in our minds. Time must exhibit unity and order. Sensible things exist only for the moment and are perceived in part by the senses, are contemplated by the intellect, and are given a history through memory.

In the *Confessions* (11.28.38), Augustine describes the temporal experience of music. When he wants to perform a psalm which he knows, he must first turn his expectations to the whole. But after he has begun, everything he has allowed to flow into his mind from the past in anticipation stores itself in his memory, and the life of the singing activity splits itself between memory of that which was expected and the anticipation of what is to come: only his attention helps him to carry what he sings over into the future so that it will become the past. To the extent that this experience unrolls, as it were, expectation is decreased and memory enlarged, until finally the entire expectation is exhausted and the entire action has entered into memory. As the song runs its course, every one of its parts, every syllable, shares in the change. What resembles the whole process is the life of man. The song is a psychological experience; it is a symbol of the journey of man through life. If it is a symbol, however, the skeptic finds difficulty in believing it to be outside time.

It is clear, then, that St. Augustine's *On Music* is much more than the rather mechanical treatise on rhythms and meters it has often been thought to be. And its sixth book is more than a merely rhapsodical mystical poem recited, in the probable fashion of the Pythagoreans and certain Neoplatonists, to celebrate everything in the universe as number. True, there is the idea that God as number created everything in the universe according to number in its eternal being and that through music reason can ascend from the corporeal to the incorporeal. Plato's *daimon* has been replaced by the Christian God, and the musical gift, instead of deriving from ancient anthropomorphic gods unique in their powers and their weaknesses, derives from the One God, the rhythmic mover of the world, at once superior to man and at the same time part of him. Furthermore, Augustine's psychological system of aesthetic epistemology is probably the first of its kind in the history of art criticism, as it certainly is the first in the history of music aesthetics.

Despite his peculiar procedure of describing his system and then later adding to it the element of feeling, either as a corrective or as a recognition of his own impatience with what remained an unfinished work, Augustine nevertheless provides a possible and legitimate account of aesthetic judgment. Taken from one side, the work of art is a physical object, created and made by someone, encountered by someone (perhaps even by the artist himself), introduced into that someone's memory as a total work, then perceived and felt by that person, and finally judged by him according to standards inherent to his very being. Taken from the other side, a person in the presence of a physical work (deriving from a presenter) encounters it, stores it for treatment in memory while he perceives and feels it, and then judges it according to standards ("numbers") within himself or within his conscious mind. The prevalent modern view is that the standards are derived from an amalgamation of experiences; Augustine's view is that standards are God-derived and intrinsic to human existence. But the system is there and comes about by way of Augustine's own analyzed experiences and his Christian feeling. It is more subjective than any preceding aesthetic theory, and for this reason was ignored by aesthetician-listeners who either saw art works as objects of craft or could not understand the transcendental position maintained. Augustine's psychological theory was not an especially admired aspect of his work, though repetitions of his definition of music were legion. Despite its having been revived by Robert Grosseteste, Augustine's psychological approach had to wait until the twentieth century fully to be appreciated.

One cannot, then, ignore the essential subjectivity of Augustine's thought in this early work, which, written at the age of thirty-three (*Retractions* 1.6, FC 60.21-22), foreshadows the revelations of his later works, the *Confessions* and *The City of God*. A love for music--as a sign of order itself symbolizing love--shines through his "cries," and their cause is not always words-and-music, but music by itself. "How abundantly did I weep to hear those hymns and canticles of thine," he writes about his baptism in his thirty-third year and the overwhelming effect the music of the hymn had on him; "how abundantly did I weep . . . being touched to the very quick by the voices . . . [and] thy truth [was] pleasingly instilled into my heart, which caused the affections of my devotion to overflow, and my tears to run over . . ." (*Conf.* 9.6). And then there is the *jubilus* (so admired as we have seen, by Hilary), the exuberant *alleluia*, which after all is more music, more a feeling of joy, than words. Distinguishing between the divine and traditional forms of song, the former being indefinite and infinite, the second clear-cut in meaning and precise in outline, Augustine finds in the *jubilus* such excessive joy as cannot be translated into words (*Ps.* 100 [99].4; NPN1 8.488).[4] "And to whom does that jubilation ascend if not to God, the Ineffable?" (*II Disc. of Ps.* 32, ACW 30.112). It is an ecstatic joy, as much Neoplatonic as Christian. In commenting on Psalm 100[99], he writes that "He who rejoices pronounces no words; his joyful song is without words"; the heart melts in joy and strives to express its feelings "even when it does not understand their meaning."

In youth, he tells us, he had been misled by the cult music of Cybele [Bere-cynthia] (*City* 2.4), but later he was devoted to the Hebrew psalms and the singing of them. Those who follow Old Testament and New Testament figures, he thinks, will use music as an accompaniment to all stages of life; they sing in hope, they sing out of love and longing, sometimes in sorrow, sometimes in joy (*Ps.* 123[122].2, NPN1 8.596). Yet, certain musical incantations appear more to gods of the second and third rank[5] (*City* 10.9), he says, and here he may be recalling the question of whether or not Christianity was connected with the Mysteries of older times--or he may simply be recalling what he had read in Iamblichus and especially in Porphyry, just as he was anticipating some of the more "transcendental" ideas of Marsilio Ficino. But for human beings, he thinks the voice-heart cliché describes a higher level of music based not on the state of a voice but on the text and the singers' mental attitudes (*II Disc. on Ps.* 18.1, ACW 29.182).

Consistency, one may exclaim, thy name was not Augustine. As he gets older, his opinions become rigid, and he stresses words more than music. He reverts to the dichotomy of Clement: the promises in the Old Testament, he thinks, are temporal and earthly, and anyone who loves the earthly sings the old song, but he who loves eternal things sings the new--that is, of Christ (*Ps.* 143[142].1, NPN1 8.651, *PL* 37.1845-46).

It will be recalled that hymns and responsorial songs of the Eastern Church were of a type adopted and spread throughout the West, and that St. Ambrose was given credit for encouraging such music. The instrument of Augustine's conversion to Christianity, Ambrose induced him to adopt the general Christian position that heathen music was the work of demons or devils from which the young should be protected. In his later writings Augustine encouraged a turning away from the profane in art, learning, and life. Ecclesiastical music nourished spiritual development, he said, and licentious secular music was not alone in standing in the way of apprehension of divine law: all worldly power did that. Voices and hearts, mouths and customs, should sing to God in agreement (*Sermons* 34.3.6, *PL* 38.211). At the feast of St. Cyprian he praises Bishop Aurelius for banning the cithara and instruments of the theater (*II Disc. On Ps.* 32.5, ACW 30.105-07). For him heresy is like the inharmonious singing of false voices (*Ps.* 149.4, NPN1 8.678). Neither praise which is not the praise of God nor the praise of God which is not sung deserves the name of *hymn*, which, in contrast with all other merely pneumatic (spiritual) singing, expressly requires hearable singing--not necessarily instruments. Hymns are praises of God accompanied by singing (*Ps.* 71[70].1, NPN1 8.315). Like other Church Fathers, Augustine sees Sunday as a commemoration of the Resurrection and a day on which singing was not to be restrained (*Lett.* 36.12, FC 12.150). And, like Plato, he asks for simplicity, here, of course, in the psalms. He contrasts the lascivious songs of worldly people with the holy songs of the Church and enjoins people that biblical singing serves as a banishment of songs like those of Babylon (*Ps.* 65[64].3, NPN1 8.268-69). He always seems torn between a judgment of earthly music and the higher judgment of universal music, the two antithetical judgments by the senses and by a superior reason or spirit.

Nor are his attitudes always unambiguous. He classifies instruments but is really interested only in their symbolical significance. Possibly relying on Varro or Aristotle, he lists voice types (human and animal), wind sounds, and stringed instruments (*Ps.* 150.5-6, NPN1 8.682-83). The voices of human beings are represented by tragedians, comedians, and choruses (in general, by all who sing); wind sounds come from *auloi* and similar instruments; and struck sounds come from instruments like the cithara, the lyre, cymbals, and such instruments (*Div. Prov.* 2.14.39, FC 1.317). All instruments are combined under the word 'organ' (*Ps.* 150.5-6, NPN1 8.682-83; also *Ps.* 57[56].14, NPN1 8.228-29). These are only matters of definition, but yet all instruments praise God--voice in the choir, breath in the trumpet, and striking in the harp, representing mind, spirit, and body.

He is like the other Church Fathers, too, in symbolizing instruments through analysis. Because of its ten strings, the psaltery is closer to heaven than the cithara (*II Disc. on Ps.* 32.5, ACW 30.108). The wood of the cithara, like the physical aspects of all instruments, is indispensable when the strings create tone, just as in prophetic history much is narrated which lacks special meaning: much is mere narrative alone (*City* 16.2). The cithara, like narrative, has no significance until it is employed. Instruments and human organs have certain parallels, too: the lungs are like the bellows (of an organ); the tongue, as the Stoics insisted, is like the plectrum, the teeth like the strings, and the entire harmony like the physical organism (*Sermons* 243.4, *PL* 38.1145). The human body itself is an instrument of God. The timbrel and psaltery have mystical meanings because on one there is stretched leather, gut is on the other, and on both the flesh is crucified. Ideally, the whole world should be the chorus of Christ (*Ps.* 149.4, NPN1 8.678), though the earth is round like a timbrel (*City* 7.24). People whose different lives are in agreement or harmony are like consonances made up of diversities (*Ps.* 150.5-6, NPN1 8.682) and are not unlike choirs of saints. The unified and well-ordered state is like a schooled and well-directed choral song made up of different voices (*City* 17.14). The Christian instrument is a symbol of those on which God is praised (*Ps.* 150.6, NPN1 8.683). All motions of the soul are figuratively musical (*Ps.* 95.1-3, NPN1 8.467-68). Yet the love of music and of God are essentially different (*Conf.* 10.6).

On a lesser plane, number is allegorical, too, though Augustine warns against an overemphasis on allegory (*Ps.* 67[66].1, *PL* 36.813-14). The course of the day and year are accomplished by the musically crucial number of 4: morning, noon, evening, night; spring, summer, fall, winter. The psaltery with its ten chords (strings) is like the Ten Commandments and can be ascribed to both the Creator and his creatures. Indeed, the number 10 symbolizes the knowledge of the Creator and the creation. The number 3 is the Trinity of Father, Son, and Spirit, and 7 (the musical scale) symbolizes a creature in terms of his life and body (three commandments to love God with our whole hearts, souls, and minds, and four discernible elements-- earth, water, fire, and air--making up the body (*On Chris. Doc.* 2.16.25, NPN1 2.543). The commandment of God rests upon two rules, the love of God and the love of man, three strings (of the ten-string psaltery) being related to the love of God and seven being related to the love of neighbor, all ten being a symbol of the Ten Commandments (*Ps.* 33[32].2, NPN1 8.71).

In *On the Trinity* there is an elaborate section which is a veritable cadenza on the numbers of perfection and completion. We ourselves contain the consonance of "single to double" (the octave) planted in us by God and recognized even by the ignorant when it is sung by themselves or by others. Treble and bass are in harmony, and anyone whose "note" is not harmonious gives offense through the ear. The ratio of the single to the double derives from 3, which is $1 + 2$, and all three ($1 + 2 + 3$) make 6, the senary, the perfect number because it is complete: 6 itself is 1, in its third part 2, and in its half 3. Six is the number in which God completed his work of creation, and on the sixth day man was made by him. The Scriptures in many other ways celebrate the number 6 just as the cosmic year furnishes many examples of it. It is "commended" in the building up of the body of Christ and of the temple at Jerusalem, and the ratio of single to double is evident even in the three days of the Resurrection (*On the Trinity* 4.2-6, NPN1 3.71-75).

St. Augustine could never forget his sensual youth--and, in reaction, wanted to prohibit all tendencies to sensuality in others. From first hand he knew that pagan happiness depends on rich living and eating, on daytime and nocturnal drinking, and on band-playing and theatrical entertainments available both day and night (*City* 2.20). He discredits the conventional and traditional call upon the gods to favor solemn festivities or scenic performances, and thinks the theatrical canticle is an especially irresistible but demoralizing stimulant (*City* 2.25). He would eliminate the daily performances of sung-and-danced adulterous scenes of Mercury and Venus, though he finds the cult of the great mother Cybele to be even more repulsive (*City* 7.26). Frivolous songs are initially sweet but eventually debilitating and misleading (*Sermons* 9.4.5, *PL* 38.79). Christians must separate themselves from pagans and their corrupting dances and songs (*Sermons* 198.1, *PL* 38.1101-02). Augustine thus learned to loath the theater music he had loved in his youth. But he never fails to approve of the practical (moral) music of everyday emotional life and the theoretical "music" which was a help in the understanding of the Holy Scriptures. He (*Retractions* 1.3.2, FC 60.14) deplores his early exaggeration of the value of the Liberal Arts. Nevertheless, we may almost say that his motto could have been "Music for moral and spiritual strength."

This hardly means, however, that Augustine adopts the old *ethos* theory of musical effects. He is never as specific as the ancients, nor does he follow the example of Ambrose here. In his later greatly reformed state of mind which led to his writing retractions of his early work, he emphasizes that musical harmony is indeed a simile for the music of the soul (*Retractions* 1.10, FC 60.46). He had been far more specific in his book on the Trinity (4.2.4, FC 45.133-34): through the death of Christ, man is redeemed in body and soul--a fact which involves the numbers 1 and 2. Harmony is the word properly expressing reconciliation through Christ. Now, the octave (1:2) has a value deeply implanted in our nature by God so that even people uneducated in music and mathematics respond to it. The consonance of the octave conveys even to human ears the mystery of the meaning of redemption. For Augustine, the musical consonances to which he had referred in his discourse on rhythm are reflections of theological truth. But he limits the effects of music in general to emotional ones allied with religious transport and mystical experience rather than with love or hate (which the Greeks too avoided) or with a social affect like military courage. The different affections of our spirit (*spiritus*) have in their diversity their own moods in voice and song "by whose secret association they are aroused" (*Conf.* 10.33); and here he returns to the doctrine of the sympathetic exchange between spiritual (soul) movement and musical movement.

But Augustine is not consistent in his views. In the *City of God*, he deplores the sensuous and "carnal" effect that music had once had on him. Music had been a real temptation, and because this art is still so, it is best that it should be banished from his ears and from the whole Church-- including even the sweet music accompanying the psalms of David, which should be closer to spoken speech than to song. Thus he agrees with Athanasius that the chanting of psalms should avoid the full resources of melody in favor of a plain style of singing (*Conf.* 10.33). Music is stripped to the bare essentials, and his final judgment is that words are of first importance. Yet he fluctuates in his characteristically agonized way between the dangers of pleasure and approved wholesomeness, and he favors singing in the church so that delights of the ears can raise weaker minds toward devotion--an opinion not unique, as we have seen, among the Church Fathers. Yet at times, his fear of music is almost pathological, and he does not allow himself even what other Fathers granted the ignorant members of their congregations: he thinks he sins when he is more moved by voices than by words, and would therefore prefer not to hear music at all. For us, of course, his very indecision and fluctuations are signs of the constant and obsessive temptations the early Christian thought he had to overcome.

He seems ultimately in his agonizing to take up the position that works are superior to faith. One should praise God, he says, not only with one's voice, but also with one's actions and works. One should sing psalms not with voices alone, but with works: only then will one psalmodize not only on the cithara, but also on the psaltery (*Ps.* 98[97].5, NPN1 8.481).

We may regret the transformation of the enthusiast of music who wrote an *On Music* into the bishop who felt the need to castigate every trace of pleasure, even in the art of numbers; for in later days Augustine seems to have forgotten the numbers except allegorically. Even the passions are necessarily suppressed rather than, as in ancient days, purged; the ethical-moral situation is everything and individual emotions nothing--except for a possible ecstasy which could conform to the ascetic ideal. Human emotion was to be transcended and artistic pleasure tolerated only to the extent that it served religion. One approaches Augustine's later works with the conviction that in them something has been lost in the philosophy of music, no matter how great were his accomplishments in theology and philosophical thought. And, indeed, though he was a powerful influence on the thought and dogma of the Western Church, his effect on later music theory was much less than we would expect. Yet, his definition of music as a science was often repeated, and his words on rhythm and the rest are joined with those of other grammarian-rhetoricians to define the basic rhythms of twelfth-century polyphony. Reason and number easily became the dominant aesthetic principles of the Middle Ages--as was the case with luminosity. And Augustine's own analysis of musical perception was to be repeated quite literally by Robert Grosseteste.

XIII
The Latin Textbook Pioneers

In contrast to the ambivalent attitude of the Church Fathers to the Greeks, their successors such as Boethius, Cassiodorus, and Isidore of Seville in a less carping and more "scientific" frame of mind accepted the speculative-scientific aspects of the Greek idea of music. These textbook theorists held the speculations of the ancients in high regard, whereas the majority of the Fathers had viewed their religious and philosophical opinions with a certain contempt at the same time that they were deeply indebted to them in other ways. The theorists, on the other hand, accepted the musical theories of the ancients and gave them the weight of their own authority.

It will be recalled that such Fathers as St. Ambrose, St. Jerome, St. John Chrysostom, and St. Augustine all had reservations about the philosophical ideas flowing from antiquity. Boethius was their junior by approximately a century and a half, yet, Christian that he probably was, he wrote almost as though the Fathers had not existed. Using and giving prominence to ancient ideas and documents, he attempted to bring light into what has been (to some extent inaccurately) called the Dark Ages, a period which is normally dated from the generation following the death of Augustine and lasting to the age of Charlemagne.

The summaries of theory and aesthetics of the then ancient world by Aristides Quintilianus and Ptolemy during the first and second centuries A.D.--summaries designed for the intellectually moribund Roman world--combined and preserved Pythagorean, Damonian, Platonic, Aristotelian, and Aristoxenian elements, as we have seen. Between these first and second century thinkers and Boethius (c.480-c.524 A.D.), who interpreted the same music, the same theory, and the same aesthetic views by combining the same elements (in different proportions), there was a gap of nearly four hundred years (roughly a time equivalent to that which separates the age of Elizabeth I of England from the present). In the fifth century, then, there was a revival of the old theories somewhat in their original form. Neoplatonism, which had interpreted them in its own way, was not extinct, but the writers treated in this chapter in general ignore this philosophical school, particularly because it embraced magic and difficult symbolism, though along with Pythagoreanism it had been the best known of the pagan philosophies at the end of the Roman empire. Yet the Church Fathers had served as a bridge between the older period of pagan philosophy and science which came to the end of its creativity in the first and second centuries and the period of textbook writers who would look forward to the theorists and aestheticians of the Middle Ages. This was especially the case because of the widespread destruction of the libraries of antiquity through natural disasters, decay, and human destruction.

As inheritors of ancient learning, the monastic and lay scholars of the so-called Dark Ages gave their attention to theoretical, technical, and other principles, but they also studied poetry, grammar, oratory, and music. While at times it seems that the language arts were more important to them than the supposed scientific certainties, it was certainties that they wanted to understand and transmit. Many of their assertions about music have two aspects: an occasional reiteration of the tenets of speculative philosophy based on the principles of a music they had never heard and could never hear, and an emphasis on the religious and the divine. Through them, Christianity achieved a very broad influence in subsequent thought across Western Europe. But, unlike the Church Fathers, they continued to think of the arts, including music, as something objective and impersonal. Yet, as inheritors of the Christianity propagated in the writings of the Fathers, they also often wanted to superimpose religious doctrines and attitudes and moral prohibitions on their inherited ground bass, as it were. Aside from Boethius, the result was an aesthetics of allegory which penetrated not only musical philosophy but also mathematics and philosophy themselves. A further result was a degree of repetition which is wearisome to the modern mind. Not until the Greco-Arabic revival in the twelfth century did the ideas of Greek and Latin authors again take their place alongside independent observations about music as a structure. In the meantime, the realms of knowledge, as well as moral and spiritual matters, were classified and codified in terms of the Seven Liberal Arts--the types of knowledge assigned by the Greeks to the freeman--which were not subjective constructions of the human mind, it was said, but discoveries of the objective and basic structure of the world--that is, a structure ultimately created and existing in the spirit and mind of God.

I

Martianus Capella. In the early fifth century A.D., there appeared an important work by a Latin writer, Martianus Capella, who was a key figure in the intellectual history of the West. A North African and probably like St. Augustine a Carthaginian, he produced a popular handbook entitled *De nuptiis Philologiae et Mercurii et septem artibus liberalibus* (*The Marriage of Philology and Mercury and the Seven Liberal Arts*), formerly sometimes called the *Satyricon*. This work was to be considered authoritative in the Middle Ages. For its setting it was inspired by Varro's *Menippean Satires* and Apuleius' *Golden Ass* (second century A.D.).[1]

A kind of romantic allegory, the *Marriage of Philology and Mercury* contains two books of allegory and seven of textbook exposition. Book 4,

reminding us of Aristoxenus' analysis of harmonics, carries unacknowledged Aristotelian listings from the *Categories* (5.1-9): substance, genus,
species, differences, accident, oppositions, propositions, and syllogisms.
The last book, the ninth, is an almost literal transcription of Aristides'
Harmonics and *Rhythmics*.   For Martianus Capella, almost certainly a
lawyer and not a professional musician at all, music is perfect when it
appears in the ("wedding") form of chanted poetry (song) joined to mime of
the triune *choreia*, in which poetry, music, and dance are in simultaneous
performance. Music is a total synthesis, a harmony, and the synthesis is a
musical form. Its understanding calls for both the exercise of a craft and the
scientific investigation of a composition. It is a rational search for harmony,
for a universal and divine marriage of all elements.   Varro was one of
Martianus' sources, but Varro did not establish the system of the Seven
Liberal Arts.   This was Martianus' accomplishment, partly since he
discarded architecture and medicine from Varro's list of the arts and
adopted as crucial the number 7, already selected by St. Augustine
(*Retractions* 1.6), Cicero, and others. Like such ancient philosophers as the
Pythagoreans and Plato, who discussed every known branch of knowledge
as a part of philosophy--therefore as wisdom ("the noblest kind of
music")--Martianus gives the term 'philosopher' even to grammarians,
poets, and geometricians.

Scholar and admirer of Virgil and Horace that he was, Martianus
undoubtedly knew that Seneca (*Epistle* 88, 2.349ff) had identified the
system of the *artes liberales* and the *studia liberalia*, which were free--and
classical--and which were not designed to prepare one for the making of
money.   Excluded were painting, sculpture, and other manual and
"mechanical" arts. Martianus' own list finally held, though he did not name
the two major divisions that would be (1) the *trivium* (grammar, dialectic or
logic, rhetoric) and (2) the *quadrivium* (geometry, arithmetic, astronomy,
music, all of which lead to a knowledge of quantity). Occasionally he uses
the language of Neoplatonism and Neopythagoreanism, while also one
senses that the *Timaeus* is in the background.   An agglomeration of
elements, the work of Martianus Capella was in fact a recapitulation of the
essentials of the Roman curriculum and was perhaps most widely used as a
textbook in the schools of the Middle Ages. In the Renaissance as well it
served as a basic work in the revival of learning of ancient arts--an unusual
accomplishment for a compiler of other men's ideas.[2]

The Marriage of Philology and Mercury is a book of travels through
the spheres and may have served as a model for the allegories of Alan of
Lille and Adelard of Bath in the twelfth century as well as for other
heavenly journeys of the Middle Ages, including the visionary journey of
Dante in his *Divine Comedy*. The use of allegory by Martianus is further
said to have been an influence on medieval art, which made visible the
allegorical depiction of the Liberal Arts and also a great many other
allegorical sciences.

There is, first, a song of invocation to Hymen, son of Bacchus and

Venus, god of marriage, and singer at weddings. Mercury (eloquence), excited by a story about marriage among the gods, meets with disappointment because he cannot marry Psyche, who has been snatched away by Cupid (1.7). With Virtue, he goes to ask advice of Apollo, whom he finds dwelling with Fortune on Parnassus, where trees make music. A melody is caused by the wind blowing through the trees, which make contact with one another: under the resulting tension, the tall trees make a sharp (high) sound, while the trees which droop near the ground make a "heaviness of [low] sound." The trees of middle size in their contacts sing together in the fixed or permanent harmonies of the duple (octave), the fourth, the fifth, and even the second. Sometimes semitones came between, but in any case the trees produced a harmony which was "the whole music and song of the gods" (1.11). Thus Apollo's grove is the symbol of song.

Mercury explains that Apollo brings everything into tune musically, and this is so in his grove of trees as well as in the heavenly spheres (1.12). An exceptionally sweet sound and pleasant harmony also characterize the motion of the spheres because separate Muses appear on individual planets--eight Muses from Urania through the fixed heavens to Clio and the moon (1.27-28):

> Urania -- high pitch
> Polyhymnia -- sphere of Saturn
> Euterpe-- sphere of Jove
> Erato -- sphere of Mars
> Melpomene -- the middle region (the sun)
> Terpsichore -- golden Venus
> Calliope -- Mercury's sphere
> Clio -- the moon

The parallels established here may usefully be compared to Dante's in the *Convivio* 2.14.

Apollo recommends that Mercury should marry Philology (learning) (1.23), and Juno demands that Jupiter expedite the wedding since his love for her had existed for a long time. During this period of time he had learned to play the tibia and psaltery and had taken into his house the several disciplines--that is, the Seven Liberal Arts (1.36). Preparing for a parliament of the gods, Jupiter and Juno both are elegantly and symbolically robed; he carries a nine-string lyre in his left hand and she a timbrel "which reverberated with fearsome thundering" (1.66-67). Later Philology attempts to determine the numerical symbolic permanent relations and finds that they are 3 and 4, the 3 representing perfection, the beginning-middle-end, and 4 a definition of solids, its own triplication being the first to yield a cube of all numbers. The three harmonies of music (1:2, 2:3, 3:4) are perfect and embrace all concord as well as masculinity. In addition, to multiply 4 by 2 and 3 by 3 is to arrive at 8:9, the whole tone (2.104-05).

Before the door of the marriage bedroom all the assembled musics make a well-voiced harmony. Tibia, lyre, and water-organ blend in song, and then are silent so that the Muses can sing *a capella*. Each Muse in turn sings according to the art which she governs and thus produces a better music than that of instruments (2.117-25). Calliope sings of Philology's ability to chant the prophecies of the Muses, to play the lyre of Pindar, and to command "the strings and the sacred plectrum . . . to pour forth the Thracian song" (2.119). Polyhymnia tells Philology that she knows sounds according to the rules of rhythm and can judge melodies, tones, and tunes (2.120). Melpomene reminds her of her ability to sing tragic songs in tragedy and comedy (2.121).

After each Muse has spoken, the Graces to a booming of tabors and the ringing of cymbals will lead the wedding dance, and, as a palanquin is brought in to carry the bride to the courts of heaven, they sing ritual songs to the mysteries (2.133-34). The Arts and the Disciplines, all women, by way of Philology's mouth then spew forth books about the arts and sciences, some containing musical notation, others mathematical symbols, "harmonies of music," rhythm-notations, and pieces for singing (2.138). Leaving in the palanquin, Philology is accompanied by the singing of the Muses (2.145). She will follow the road to heaven, which is that of the spaces fixed by the knowledge of the sounding spheres (2.169). These spaces are a whole tone to the moon, and then are arranged as follows:

	a half-tone to Mercury	
	a half-tone to Venus	
	a tone + a half-tone to the Sun	
from low to high	a tone to Mars	6-1/2 whole tones
	a tone to Jupiter	
	a half-tone to Saturn	
	a tone + a half-tone to the fixed stars	

That which they had traversed (six and one-half tones, inconsistent with the six-tone octave of Aristoxenus) gave forth the "concord of the whole octave in full and perfect harmony" (2.199). And when Polyhymnia meets Mercury for the marriage, the voices of the Muses are heard in "sweet strains of varied songs" (2.209). They, among other beings from the earth (now gods) who had become celestial beings by virtue of their accomplishments, are all met by Linus, Homer, Virgil, Orpheus, Aristoxenus, Plato, Heraclitus, and Pythagoras (2.212-13).

The wedding takes place in Jupiter's castle. The Muses sing with a sweet sound accompanied by tibias, trumpets, and the water-organ. The music blends perfectly because it follows the sacred numbers; Mathematics himself embraces the perfect harmony of the spheres and also the perfect harmony of the chorus of the Muses (4.227-28). Of individual numbers, he selects three especially--these are the three consonants (7.733)--and also 6, which numbers the whole tones of universal harmony (7.736) (as declared by Aristoxenus). He thus, following Nicomachus, plays with the numbers 6, 8, 9, 12 (for the 1, 2, 3, 4 of the *tetractys*) (7.737).

Memory and Philology symbolize the union of eloquence and learning, the former (the trivium) being the preoccupation of the Romans and the latter (the quadrivium) that of the Greeks. Arithmetic and geometry are universally applicable, and metrics can belong to either grammar (or rhetoric) on the one hand or the mathematics of harmony on the other. Minerva declares that harmony or Harmonia belongs to music (3.326; Stahl, p. 25). Harmonia is the daughter of Venus, the celestial twin of arithmetic, and as she comes into the hall of the gods, a concord sounds from the shield she is carrying. Ages ago she assigned notes to the moving planets, "assigned numerical relations to the perceptible motions and the impulses of perfect will, introducing restraint and harmony into all things" (9.922; Stahl, p. 204). Martianus describes the stereotypical examples of the origins of music, its powers, its therapeutic effects as produced by incantations and instrumental music, and also its appeal to animals. Much of this comes from Varro. Then he outlines musical characteristics: good proportion in rhythm and melody; movement, modulation, the three consonances (*symphonia*) in every octave species (*tropi*), the three divisions of three which are subject matter (*harmonica*, *rhythmica*, *metrica*), practical composition (*melopoeia*, choice of pitch, relations of pitches), and practice (instrumental music, vocal music, recitation). Like Aristoxenus and Aristides Quintilianus, Martianus thinks voice production is continuous, discrete, or intermediate (in conversation, in song, or in poetic recitation). Also, *melopoeia* may be divided into three distinct styles: the tragic, the dithyrambic, and the nomic, though the erotic, the epithelamic, the comic, and the encomiological are also possible (9.965). Thus Martianus Capella seems to follow Aristides Quintilianus in most things. As he describes *tonoi*, concords (*symphonoi*), and dissonances (*diaphonoi*), and the modification of tones according to ethos, intervals, octave species, and tetrachords, he is only repeating what an encyclopedist would say whether he knew his subject or not. He mentions pentachords, but his source is unknown (9.961-63; Stahl, p. 217). He returns to Aristides or possibly Cleonides when he comments on changes of system (*modulatio*); and to Aristides or St. Augustine when in defining rhythm he thinks of a "time" as an indivisible unit (like the geometric point and the arithmetic *monad*); and again to Aristides when he calls rhythmic types *enrhythmic* (definite proportions), *arrhythmic* (no rule, no definite ratio), and *rhythmoid* (rhythmic in some places, not so in others).[3]

Martianus Capella, as an encyclopedic and textbook thinker, adopted a tone which is eminently affirmative, and thus was widely adopted by students of philosophy and the arts since he was thought to represent opinions universally and scientifically accepted or commonly held. The practical or worldly arts were not treated (as for Augustine, medicine and law are banished from his list of accepted studies); instead, his interest was in teaching what was accepted as eternal. Empirical observation is lacking in his work. The Middle Ages, like the Renaissance and also like neoclassicism in the eighteenth century, likewise believed that "what oft was thought" was likely to be the most true, especially if it was "ne'r so well expressed," and that the "Rules of old [were] discover'd, not devis'd."[4] Beauty was under the same restriction. It was a universal, discovered and not created by man, and was itself a test of the resemblance of objects of the material world to the beauty of the divine.

II

Boethius (Anicius Torquatus Severinus Boekius). *The Marriage of Philology and Mercury* of Martianus Capella, written when Christianity had thoroughly triumphed over paganism, was constantly cited in the time of Charlemagne when British and Irish scholars visited and migrated to the region now known as France, while this region became the center for renewed interest in learning and church music and liturgy. Martianus' chief competitors were to be the works, largely translations from the Greek, of Boethius (c.480-524), whose classic *Consolation of Philosophy*, a work of intense personal and noble thought written when its author was a political prisoner preparing for his execution, is still widely read and studied today.

Centuries of logical and metaphysical discussion and analysis were to be based on Boethius' Aristotle-defined classifications. Sometimes regarded as the last Roman and by others as the first Scholastic, Boethius, like Martianus Capella whom he may have used as one of his secondary sources, was primarily a transmitter of ancient writing and thinking. His work and translations in mathematics (Euclid, Nicomachus, Ptolemy) and logic (Aristotle) were the basis of scientific discussion in the Latin West. Like most learned Romans, he was acquainted with Cicero as rhetorician. But he also knew Greek, a rare accomplishment for a Roman in his day, and his aim was to translate all of Plato and Aristotle into Latin--a task that, for whatever reason, he failed to complete, though he did write a commentary on the latter's *Categories*. His failure may possibly explain the long delay in the revival of an interest in Aristotle and in Platonic works thought to be lost. Boethius, however, did complete a translation of the *Isagogue* (*Introduction*) of Porphyry, testimony to the continuing interest in the Neoplatonic thinkers. On the whole, his own work is a conglomeration of Platonism, Pythagoreanism, Stoicism, Aristotelianism, and Augustinianism.[5]

Boethius' treatment of theoretical music is of immense importance. As a music theorist and in the methodology adopted in his *Consolation of Philosophy* his purpose was an attempt to bring Pythagoras, Plato, and Aristotle into harmony--an aim also evident in his other works, for example in his commentary on Aristotle's *On Interpretation*. But his sources were almost universal, additionally including such writings as those of Archytas, Philolaus, Euclid, Iamblichus, Nicomachus, Albinus,[6] Aristoxenus, and

Ptolemy. On some he relied, and others he tried to correct. His aim was purely scientific. Attempting to revive the ancients, he ignored contemporary Christian thought and practice, however, and a section of the *Consolation* (3.9) has been called a summary of the *Timaeus*.

Among his earliest works was his *Principles of Music* (*De institutione musica*), in five books, written at the age of twenty. Its subject was (as he thought) a permanent part of the *quadrivium* ("four roads"),[7] studies of permanent entities in ontological independence of the material or physical world. A remarkable performance for one so young, the book had centuries-long use in the schools. Boethius' book on music, which is speculative and technical, is in marked contrast to the early work of Augustine, which treated rhetoric, rhythm, meter, and the psychology of musical or artistic judgment. Augustine was always the innovative thinker, but Boethius was a scholar and an expositor, following Ptolemy closely, of the Pythagorean theory of music as a mathematical science of sound (and therefore of truth) and of ethical affects according to the theories of Damon, Plato, and Aristotle. Out of these--and additionally, probably, out of Euclid's *Section of the Canon*--he attempted to create a system.

Repeating his predecessors, he surveys: the "history" mentioned by Plato and further developed in Pseudo-Plutarch (whom he does not mention) of the rise of Greek music governed by *nomoi* and rules and of its eventual decline; various statements about the education of boys; doctrines like the preferability of "masculine" to "feminine" music; judgments of the perfidy of Timotheus of Milet for having added a string to those already in use on the cithara and for having created so complex a music that he was ostracized from the state of Lacedaemon; and the accounts of the effects Pythagoras produced on the love-sick youth through music and inducements to sleep effected by the Pythagoreans in troubled people through song. The last, Boethius thinks, demonstrates the complete joining of soul and body in a musical harmony perfectly aligning the movements of the soul with the beats of the heart in motion. Citing Democritus' advice to Hippocrates, he is describing sympathetic transfer on the assumption that spiritual or psychic states are composed of the same proportions as those of harmonic modulations.

Like certain ancients previously discussed in this study, he believes that music is a therapeutic agent. He repeats statements about the effects of sad music on mourning people, about the influence of trumpets on warriors, about changes effected by soft melodies in excited minds or in minds tending too greatly toward lust or voluptuousness. The song, the *cantilena*, itself stimulates impulses in the body which excite imitations of similar movements in the mind and soul (*Of Music* 1.1.1). And all of these effects set music off from the other mathematical arts. Music is of course a gift of nature, and here Boethius adopts Platonic-Aristotelian "objective" psychology. Proportions in sound are the proportions to be observed in human beings and the universe. If music is thus inseparable from the existence of man and is also a gift to be cherished and cultivated, where are the roots of this intimacy and how are they to be discovered? But such questions are not answered except in terms of universal truth or of cosmic interdependencies.

As a scientist and mathematician, Boethius (*Arith.* 1.1) thinks the roots of musical effect can be discovered through inquiry and knowledge--a knowledge, according to Nicomachus, of essences. True, one must know comprehensively about melodies, their rules, their relationships, and their function in a composition. But first Boethius begins to categorize and classify music in all of its aspects, essential and accidental. He seems to re-create Aristides' system, which he may have known, and also more certainly the system of Ptolemy as he enunciates his famous classification, afterwards repeated, criticized, and modified over many centuries, of a triad of (1) *musica mundana*, (2) *musica humana*, and (3) *musica instrumentalis constituta*.

His general approach is simultaneously intellectual and theoretical (and, by implication, aesthetic), metaphysical and cosmic, and eminently humanistic in what may be called the Aristotelian fashion. He thinks that music is interwoven with human nature, which, for example, limits the boundlessness of sound by restricting the ability of men to produce high and low pitches vocally and to extend their musical phrases beyond our breathing abilities (*Of Music* 1.13). Limited as our physical capacities are, however, we share in reason and understanding.

Now, understanding initially created sight (cf. *Timaeus* 45) and then voice and hearing. As the gateway to the soul, however, music is the clearest path for the mind and the sciences. The mathematician can tell the observer how triangles or squares differ when he perceives them, but the hearer can so perceive sounds that he can not only judge and tell the differences between tones, but also experience delight from the well-ordered melodies (pitches) and be offended by disorganized and incoherent ones. Since hearing was granted to us for the sake of harmony (*Timaeus* 47), music is allied not only with speculation and understanding but also with the heart. Thus it is a characteristic of human nature to be calmed by soft melodies and to be excited by the opposite kinds, and this is true for people of all ages and of all professions. There is no period in life in which delight in good melody can even be avoided. As Plato said (*Timaeus* 37), the entire world-soul is musical harmony. We are pleased by what is in agreement with ourselves, by what is allied with or adapted to us, and by what is beautifully and tastefully related to tone. Similarity is agreeable, dissimilarity unpleasant. A person prefers what is suited to him. Thus some melodies (modes) are called by the names of the peoples who invented them.[8] Lydian and Phrygian melodies were pleasing to their originators because they conformed to Lydian and Phrygian morals and manners. Extreme opposites like the delicate and the rough do not combine, though love and joy do. Plato's idea (*Rep.* 424) that one must beware of changes in a true music because a change in music brings about a change in the state--this notion is correct, but without such influence the populace neverthess changes (as Cicero suggested)--and sometimes for the worse. No other way exists of instructing and guiding the heart than the ear, and when rhythms and melodies descend from ear to the heart, they instruct, guide, and mold the mind to be exactly as they are themselves. And all of this is based on a musical structure which is universal and tripartite:

I.   World (cosmic music): *musica mundana.*
       (The harmony of the universe: how can it be that the machine of heaven moves so quickly and silently if it is not in harmony? Though its sound does not reach our ears, so quick a movement of such large bodies will not produce no tone, especially since the orbits are united with a great harmony; but nothing so joined by law, nothing so blended, can be perceived. Some orbits are higher, some lower, but they go with uniform speed so that the rational order is permeated with different dissimilarities. Nor can such celestial rotation diverge from a rational order.)

1.   Celestial bodies
       a. position
       b. motion
       c. nature
2.   The elements
       a. weight
       b. number
       c. measure
3.   Times (periods)
       a. years (4 seasons)
       b. months (the moon's cycles)
       c. days (alternation of light and darkness)
       The four elements produce a single body and mechanism through harmony.
       Diversity plus variety of seasons and fruits: the year becomes a unity of differences held together by harmony.

II.   Human (human music): *musica humana.*
       (The harmony of soul and body: nothing can be so excessive that one part can destroy some other part. The beauty of the world is perceived through the senses, but we find our own basic harmony by looking into ourselves: human music is understood by anyone who descends into the depths of himself.)

1.   Body
       a. partly vegetative (in all living things)
       b. partly human (the sensitive nature)
       c. partly mental (the rational nature)
2.   Soul
       a. partly in powers like anger and reason
       b. partly in virtues like justice and fortitude
3.   The connection between body and soul: natural friendship (the chain which ties soul to body)

III.   Instrumental: *musica instrumentalis constituta.*
       (The mathematical relation of tones: an imitation of world music.)

1.   Striking (strings and timbrels [lyre, cithara], cymbals, tympanum: symphonies)
2.   Blowing (pipes [aulos, tibia], organ)
3.   Voice[9] (songs and chants)

Everything, clearly, is harmony, but harmony of the eternally constant, not of the corporeal flux. Cosmic harmony is related to man as an entity-- that is, to man as a musical harmony and to the harmony man himself makes through the objects he constructs. All musics are unities, and each imitates the unity "above" it. The interpenetrating harmonies are so sympathetic and reciprocal that mundane and instrumental music can awaken virtue in the human soul and give health to the human body. Boethius' three kinds of music, the music of Plato's *Timaeus*, and the Pythagorean music of the spheres all describe a science of harmony which is more than a mere science. It is like the imagined universe of the present day scientist who declares that he deals with the most perfect and most beautiful world there is. Harmony, reason, and beauty are almost interchangeable.

The structures of music which produce such results are tonal relations, ratio, proportion (as described by the Pythagoreans, Augustine, Ptolemy, Nicomachus). The initial relations are acoustical. Sounds are continuous or separated by a silence between them. Continuous sounds are blended, joined together, by a common boundary like a rainbow of qualities just as colors can be so close together that their very boundaries are indefinite. Similarly, a string gradually tightened will give forth one long tone from low to high, and one gradually loosened will produce a tone extending from high to low (*Of Music* 5.5). A striking or a blowing produces a movement of air without which there can be no tone. Quick movements of air produce high tones, slow movements low ones. A string in tension produces high tones, one more relaxed lower ones. The vibrations combine to produce the individual tone just as a spinning top colored alternately red and white will appear red when it is in motion (ibid. 1.3). But a sound results from a binding together of certain parts in a proportion which can be expressed in number (ibid. 4.1), and a consonance is a combination of tones differing from one another but brought into a unity (ibid. 1.3). Dissonances have complicated mathematical grounds. Consonances are a blending; dissonances are not.

For the judgment of relations, however, one cannot rely entirely on one's sense of hearing, though the ear to a certain extent clings to ratios still existing in memory, as St. Augustine had demonstrated. The final accounting is made through the power of understanding; it is a judgment based on certain rules and is not subject to error. Though both eye and ear apprehend proportion (ibid. 1.32), the senses cannot make this judgment independently because they deal with illusion and confusion. Furthermore, all men do not have the same powers of perception; nor does one individual have identical powers for all kinds of perception. While the Pythagoreans rejected the evidence of physical hearing and depended only on numerical calculations, Boethius takes a modified Aristoxenian position which he derives from Ptolemy: the ear hears consonances and dissonances and realizes which tone is higher and which lower, but exactly how far apart they are it cannot say because its judgment is insufficiently precise. Sense because of its inherent limitations is misled equally by the smallest and the largest of phenomena. Furthermore, sense is like the listening servant, while intellect is like the judge. And however well the senses grasp all parts and aspects of life, they cannot grasp the truth (even that of proportions), which is revealed only through calculation and reason (ibid. 1.9).

Another example: we may see that a circle described by the hand is correct; but the written circle is matter, and it is matter with which sense has to do; all circles declared by sense to be correct are correct only insofar as they conform to an ideal type; reason knows that the man-made circle or circles can only be approximate and that eye and feeling can only judge approximations. Reason, however, judges the correctness of the approximations as they conform to the ideal circle. Thus number, not sense, is the basis of beauty--a view which suggests that Boethius had read both his Ptolemy and his Augustine.

Yet Boethius took a step in the direction of the subjective judgment of music. The objective harmonic thing, the consonance, suits both body and soul and is recognized by the subject in the pleasure he feels. The pleasure principle had already been found in Censorinus (10.6), and Augustine saw feeling as a step on the way to artistic judgment. If Aristotle thought that to know is a pleasure, Boethius finds it a pleasure to know or recognize harmonic structures. Both Plato and Aristotle allied heard music with pleasure, but with different degrees of approval. Boethius finds pleasure in hearing the consonance, displeasure in hearing the dissonance. The pleasure, we may be sure, is that of the man of high quality of mind, learning, and social status.

When he describes the purely intellectual approach to music, he often names Pythagoras and his supposed designation of philosophy as the science of wisdom, of scientific principle. His assumption, like that of all thinkers from Plato to Descartes, is simplistic, non-naturalistic, and made up of sharp distinctions and contrasts. He ignores or is blind to objects as they exist in material life, as they are in everyday existence, but instead looks for forms, dimensions, qualities, figures, and other concepts in themselves clear, unchangeable, and, though manifest in physical changes and metamorphoses, rigid and pure in outline (2.2). Thus the foundation of reason must be mathematical, no matter how synaesthetic the character of the observed object or the sensed reality: line, surface, and the cube in its geometrical harmony (*Arith.* 2, 49, *PL* 63.1158) are optical impressions taken in by the eye in a way not mathematically different from the sound-impressions (*Of Music* 2.32). It is the mathematical which makes him prefer the Pythagorean theory that the whole tone cannot be divided into two equal "semitones" to the Aristoxenian theory that it can. His decision is based on reason: 9:8 cannot be divided equally, and any such effort results in two unequal semitones and a comma (ibid. 3.10). He finds equally unacceptable Aristoxenus' division of the octave into six tones (ibid. 3.3). Since reason is superior to sense, the senses gather in the confused impressions for reason to join into one clear, harmonious knowledge.

Much of what follows is repetition from other authorities. There (from

Iamblichus and Nicomachus) is the legend of Pythagoras and the hammers (ibid. 1.10). He adopts the Nicomachean numbers 6, 8, 9, and 12 for relations of tone. He follows a mysterious Albinus in pointing to a median position of the voice in the reading of heroic poetry. With Aristotle he recognizes that the human voice has two limitations, one caused by the nature of human breath and the other by the "spread" of pitches the voice can reproduce (ibid. 1.13).[10] He compares sound waves with the waves caused by a stone thrown into water (ibid. 1.14). He ascribes, as though scientifically, characteristics to the musical species: the diatonic is hard and natural, the chromatic softer in its deviation from the natural, and the enharmonic beautiful and tasteful (ibid. 1.21). Nor can he forbear mentioning (ibid. 1.28) the astronomical symbolism of Ptolemy and possibly of Cicero (*De republica* 6.17) also, though he makes little of either. But he ignores the number symbolism of Nicomachus.

Boethius was among the first thinkers to attempt a definition of the word 'musician,' which Plato, for one, did not hold in high regard. For the Middle Ages, *ars* or 'art,' like *technē* for the Greeks, was a kind of knowledge and craft. There was a knowledge for its own sake (*artifex theorice*) and technical knowledge existing for the creation of forms (*artifex practica*). Music was art (artifice, practice) and science. Both Boethius (*De inst. musica* 1.1.34) and Cassiodorus make this distinction. Now, as we know, no written music of hellenic antiquity was known to the Middle Ages or even to Roman writers. But the musical theory memorialized in written documents was known, and these variously supported the two kinds of knowledge labeled here as *artifix theorice* and *artifix practica*. Boethius had the basic distinction in mind when he asked: "The musician--what is he?" And his procedure is what one would expect of a man who himself was thought in that era to be a true musician though he neither composed nor performed. It is more important and more noble, he thinks, to know what every practical artist or craftsman does than to make things oneself. Hence, though Ptolemy thought it more difficult to create than to judge, for Boethius the purely physical accomplishment of a work of art carries with it the mark of the servile slave. Conversely, learning serves as a mistress. Yet if the hand cannot do what the science says, then all is wasted effort. Boethius is rephrasing Plato, for whom the thinking freeman and philosopher are greatly superior to the artisan, which is what the practicing musician is in social station. Science is more laudable than mere craft, and the scientific knowledge of music is higher than practical performance just as the soul is superior to the body. Scientific investigation does not require practical accomplishment, but its results are a guide to hand-workers. The cithara player gets his name from the cithara, and the flute player his from the flute. But a true musician is in the service not of practical performance but of a science which he has mastered.

Three types of people occupy themselves with music: (1) instrumentalists, (2) poets, or composers of songs, and (3) judges of instrumental performance and the composition of songs. The first are the farthest away from musical science; they only serve others and, having no learning, also have no share in intellectual investigation. The second succeed because they have a natural instinct for making a song, though they are not scientific investigators and have no connection with the highest in music. The third have true knowledge and true judgment because they can perceive and measure the rhythm, the melody, and the entire composition. Strictly speaking, the third are the only musicians of the three; they have the ability, in conformity with scientific knowledge and rule, to judge mode, rhythm, and species of sound (acute and grave) in their blending as well as composed songs--in short, everything (ibid. 1.1.34). For Boethius, the true musician is the philosopher-critic as compared with the mere performer who can follow the rule without knowing the scientific reasons supporting it. He is certainly the *musicus* as contrasted in the Middle Ages with the *cantor*. In modern times his place seems taken by the mathematical physicist, who is usually compared with the technologist and engineer.

Thus for Boethius music is a matter of pure scientific speculation. His aesthetics is mathematical and structural. The recognition of harmony is an intellectual achievement. Therefore the universal importance of number is for him affirmed. The entire Middle Ages would hold to the inherited opinion that there is a close relationship between number (or arithmetic) and music. The former was thought to be a study of relationships *per se* in the scientific sense; the latter offered the sensuous enjoyment granted by those relationships in sonorous movement. Both furnished a pleasure of reason and sense. Aesthetics was mathematics realized in physical form. For Boethius the odd indivisible numbers are the foundation for identity, indivisibility, simplicity, equality, immutability, massiveness, virility--all masculine--while duality and even divisible numbers represent multiplicity, divisibility, infinite variety, fluidity, nimbleness--all feminine. In this way quantity becomes quality, and the opposing characteristics of stability-movement, equality-inequality, unity-multiplicity, masculine-feminine, and odd-even can be integrated and harmonized in simple proportions (ibid. 2.23ff).

In the Middle Ages Boethius' *Arithmetica* and *Principles of Music* were to be the principal sources for the aesthetics of proportion. They are the chief basis of the medieval conception of the ordered universe and of an aesthetic psychology founded on pure numbers, and their influence lasted into the twelfth and thirteenth centuries and beyond. Boethius' theory of proportion can be traced back to the ancient philosophers just as the many physiological details can be traced to Theophrastus. The general principle remains--that of unity in diversity (*Of Music* 2.5, 8, 12) and the Augustinian ideal of equality. The learned of the Middle Ages as well as the ancients upon whom they depended never questioned the doctrine of proportion, local or universal--the doctrine that everything is "musically" beautiful and that even a certain symmetry of the parts of the human body achieves beauty, as Aristotle had claimed in his *Topics* (3.1), a work translated by Boethius.

Furthermore, the world is made in the image of God, and man is the image of the world. Macrocosm determines microcosm. In the *Consolation of Philosophy*, Boethius speaks of the divine beauty "which bears in mind the idea of the beautiful universe, and creates the image of this idea in matter" (3.8). This statement explains and justifies Boethius' care in stressing the philosophical and judging side of the musician at the expense of the natural predispositions of the musical composer. For Plato too, a true musician had been one whose words and deeds harmonize (*Laches* 188) and in whom beauty of soul harmonizes with beauty of form (*Rep.* 402)--ample justification according to Boethius' thinking that such a harmony need only be intellectualized.

Though *De institutione musica* was an early work while the *Consolation*, written years later in prison, was his last, the two, musically speaking, seem of a piece. The *Consolation* is an extended dialogue and song--like Martianus Capella's *Marriage of Philology and Mercury*, in both poetry and prose. The character of Philosophy is the Muse, whose poems are verses or songs doing the work of music, the servant of rhetoric and the singer of "sometime lighter and sometime sadder notes" (2, Prose 1). Helped by strings, music brings about miraculous soul-states which had been noted in *De institutione musica*. Instrumental music is of two kinds, corrupt and virtuous, the latter fostering wisdom through melody (*harmonia*), rhythm, and poetic text. Skillfully abridging the first part of the *Timaeus* (in 3.9 and 1.5.1-24), Boethius considers *musical mundana* and speaks of a love, illustrated by that of Orpheus for his Euridice (3.12), which rules the movements of the souls of the consonant members of the world-soul (1.5.42-49), which praises God forever (3, Prose 9), and which exists in the music of the seasons, the elements, and the stars, all in coordination describing beautiful motions. To understand the world is figuratively to understand music, and since God governs everywhere and since concord proves that God orders all things (4.6), God himself must exist (3, Prose 12). The universe is a very music of laws (1.6, Prose 6, 3.2), and man in his music must order his own moral and intellectual activity--his reason (1, Prose 1)--as do world and instrumental music. Though the ideal of human music is less explicit than implicit in what Boethius says, it works along with rhetoric--that is, in pleasing sound with weighty sentences (3, Prose 1). Yet he everywhere accepts the idea of the motion and unifying of the soul, and suggests that the soul is in a musical as well as in a moral condition. The aim of man must therefore be ethical-musical. Virtue is musical, vice is not (1, Prose 3).

Did Boethius add divine music to his famous triad? He does not mention it, though it seems implicit to *musica mundana*. Later writers like pseudo-Dionysius, John Scot Erigena, and ninth-century and subsequent writers associated with the Church who were also music theorists clearly found divine music to be intrinsic to "universal" world music--a favor to the world from God who uses the angels as his medium, an emblem of God penetrating directly into the place of worship, God's own expression, and a model to be emulated by man himself when, through his own music, he worships and praises the Lord.

If Boethius was influenced by traditions coming to him for systematization, he in turn made the system so clear and vivid that his influence was felt for centuries to come.   There were two principal reasons for his continued popularity as a music theorist: those who followed him in the West would cease to read and understand Greek, for which in any case texts in the original language became extremely rare; and he was thought to have covered in compendious fashion all the Greeks had known about music. He became the chief source in the West for advanced musical instruction concerning not only that theoretical part of ancient musical science which he could safely summarize, but also music aesthetics. Later called *Doctor Magnificus*, he gave no hint that he knew the church modes, which would be defined later. In England alone everyone before the beginning of the fourteenth century seems to have copied him, and when students were first admitted for music degrees at Oxford in c.1499 and already at Cambridge in 1463, musical instruction was based on his work. In the University of Cambridge, the student was required to give a lecture on Boethius,[11] while study of his *De institutione musica* was compulsory up to the sixteenth century for all graduates and until well into the nineteenth century for candidates for the music degree. His division of harmony and music into cosmic, human, and instrumental figured in classifications until the end of the seventeenth century, by which time it had ceased to have meaning except as a literary metaphor.

Perhaps Boethius retained his influence because his ways of thinking were in fact more Greek than Latin or Roman. For music, and in all that he did, he is the theorist reviving or explicating Hellenic thought. However, with the increased activity in the writing of music textbooks and their necessary concentration on current practice, the Greek ideal was eventually doomed to be replaced in spite of how frequently it continued to be celebrated. Practical knowledge was eventually substituted for speculation. Boethius' failure to take note of Christianity and its musical practices will, however, not surprise us when we understand that such neglect was also to be found elsewhere, and the real reason was perhaps not actually a question of allegiance to the Christian religion but rather that there was still only one true source for scientific learning, Greek thought. Boethius, like Jerome, John Chrysostom, and Augustine, served as a conduit to communicate the permanencies of mathematical, abstract, and scientific thought which had been discovered in the past. Paganism and pagan philosophy died slowly, and the latter indeed may be said to have cast its shadow down to the present day. Education continued in the Middle Ages to be based ultimately on Greek thought, Roman literature, and even on the legends of pagan gods like Orpheus, who was sometimes allied with the concept of immortality. Ideas and ideals derived from Neoplatonism and of Stocism, joined with an emergent Christianity and supported by rhetorical instruction (though not joined by ideas derived from Epicureanism or Skepticism), were in varying degrees taught in the schools, and all signalled an attempt to make present what was held to be permanent from the past.

Cassiodorus, in the name of King Theodoric, gave Boethius the ultimate compliment for a scholar of his day and age: "You have thoroughly imbued yourself with Greek philosophy. You have translated Pythagoras the musician, Ptolemy the astronomer, Nicomachus the arithmetician, Euclid the geometer, Plato the theologian [which he was thought to be by Proclus and other Neoplatonists], Aristotle the logician, and have given back the mechanician Archimedes to his own Sicilian countrymen (who now speak Latin). You know the whole science of mathematics, and the marvels wrought thereby."[12]

III

Cassiodorus (Favius Magnus Aurelian Cassiodorus). In contrast to Boethius who, as we have seen, wrote about music out of a scientific motivation, his pupil Cassiodorus (c.485-c.580) worked in the service of theology and wrote to educate not in science but in what was functional. The one wrote with the learned adult in mind, the other very much for the less advanced student. Both were attached to the administrative arm of the court of Theodoric the Great (b. c.454), Ostrogoth ruler of Italy in 493-526 at Ravenna and passionate devotee of Roman culture and political administration. Boethius was consul in 510, and his execution, without trial, occurred in 524, while Cassiodorus, apparently one of Theodoric's favorites, was already an official sometime after 503, a *quaestor* or royal minister, remaining in this and other similar political positions until he retired from such work in c.537 in order to found possibly one of the first monasteries to be devoted to learning and scholarship. In the East, the Emperor Justinian in 529 had not only closed Plato's Academy but had published his own edicts against all philosophers. The destruction of the great libraries of antiquity, as we have seen, signaled the decline of culture in general. Cassiodorus set out to establish a counter-trend by founding a large monastery at Vivarum in southern Italy, his aim being to perpetuate learned traditions within Christianity--an aim which he had found impossible to accomplish at the Christian institute for advanced studies in Rome. He also encouraged the setting up of libraries of classical texts and the founding of scriptoria for the copying of the works most in demand. He furnished the model for numerous religious establishments throughout Europe for centuries to come.

Throughout his career he praised the Liberal Arts constantly, encouraged the spread of classical learning among the Christians, and, like Augustine, gave a place in Christian education to the pagan classics as a prelude to the study of theology, Church history, and the Scriptures. It is sometimes said that he derived an interest in these studies from Ammonius of Alexandria (third century A.D.), but his teacher Boethius too was at hand. He collected manuscripts and wrote books, including a (lost) history of the Gothic kings, among others. In *De artibus et disciplinis liberalium litterarum* (*PL* 70.1167), he defined ancient philosophy as (1) knowledge of what exists, (2) knowledge of divine and human things, (3) preparation for death, (4) the assimilation of man to God, (5) the art of the arts and the science of the sciences, and (6) the love of wisdom.

Like St. Augustine and other Church Fathers earlier, Cassiodorus thought the Liberal Arts to be permanent aids to the study of theology and that all literary culture and profane science is contained in and derived from the Scriptures. Though pagan learning should not be ignored, the Bible supplies the roots of the tree of truth. He agreed with Clement of Alexandria that the Muses derived their name from *maso*, to seek, and that thus were explained the power of their song and the harmony of their voices. His *Institutiones divinarum et humanorum lectionum* (*An Introduction to Divine and Human Readings*), a treatise written after 551 for the instruction of the monks at his monastery, is divided into two books: the first concerns the nine codices of the New Testament and their commentators and includes advice to monks about how they should carry on their occupations and duties; the second is a brief account of the Seven Liberal Arts, which he held to be indisputably constant and eternal, the required studies of every worthy man of the cloister. In the chapter on music, Cassiodorus recommends Gaudentius (?second century A.D.), Varro, Nicomachus, Boethius, Censorinus, Augustine, and other sources. Not produced with an audience of experts in mind, the book does not include Boethian abstractions and in fact has little originality--a school book, a textbook about sung poetry that indeed was more widely disseminated than Boethius' more scientific work on music. Cassiodorus was interested in music less as a cosmic factor than as an art or craft addressing the senses and extending religious experience.

Much earlier than the time when he wrote the *Institutiones*, Cassiodorus as a government official, sometime between the autumn of 506 and 511, had written a letter for King Theodoric to Boethius, asking him to recommend a harper for Clovis, the Frankish king. He added learned comments to his request, and in a discussion of the antique modes and their characteristic differences he noted their psychological effects. The Dorian mode produces modesty and purity, the Phrygian fierce combat, and the Aeolian tranquility and slumber; the Ionian sharpens the intellect and kindles a desire for celestial things, and the Lydian soothes the soul oppressed by care. The ancient Dorian seems to have lost in manliness, which is sexual, and to have taken on a purity which is spiritual. Indeed, Cassiodorus transfers the context of the modes from the pagan to the Christian. Like Boethius, he includes the human voice among instruments of music, to which he also adds oratory and poetry. He is certain that music has great power and recalls the story of Odysseus and the Sirens as an illustration. He playfully calls for that *citharoedus* to go forth like Orpheus to charm the beast-like hearts of the "barbarians," and, not missing a pun, he says the lyre is called "chorda" because it easily moves the hearts (*corda*) of men--that is, through what we call sympathetic vibration or resonance. The lyre is the loom of the Muses and comes from Mercury, who invented it according to the idea of it he received from the harmony of the spheres. Astronomers placed the lyre among the constellations to show that music is heavenly. For there still is an "astral music . . . [which], apprehended by reason alone, is said to form one of the delights of heaven." In this letter,[13] Cassiodorus the Christian cannot abandon the pagan stories, and, as was not uncommon, he almost seems to find it hard to allow Orpheus the god with his lyre to give place to Christ the Son of God.[14] But Orpheus is a symbol for the music which enters our ears and changes our spirits and is the queen of the senses. Music is in effect psychological and even, it would seem, a hedonistic pleasure, yet paradoxically it is moral and celestial.

While Cassiodorus was, as we have seen, no originator, he nevertheless set out to relay the proper information, and, like Boethius himself, he knew the proper authorities and the appropriate legends. (Actually, his celebration of certain aspects of pagan learning helped to preserve a place for it in Christian education subsequently.) Unlike his teacher Boethius, however, he cannot be classed as a philosopher, but merely as a kind of collector, an antiquarian who made compilations for the admiration and use of the students and monks who were the chosen audience for his work.

In the Introduction to the *Institutiones*, Cassiodorus notes that mathematics is a theoretical study. Though he writes as a religious man rather than as a scientist about music, he nevertheless like Augustine defines music as a science treating measure in relation to sound (3.6, 21).[15] It "deals, among other things, with the relationship between a simple number and its double" in multiples of 2 and 4 (2.4.1). This is because, according to the book of *Wisdom* attributed to Solomon (11.21), God ordered all things in number, measure, and weight. Thus it must be that music is spread throughout our entire lives if we obey God's commandments and with pure hearts observe his rules. Because of God's commandments, we have music in us; when we sin, it is absent (2.5.2). To follow God's commandments is to be in harmony, just as sounds are differences but in concord. Even the beating of our pulse is "joined by musical rhythms to the power of harmony" (2.5.2). Like Augustine, Cassiodorus thinks that music is the science of proper modulation, but he adds that when we follow the good, moral way of life we are always "musical." Music is manifest in sky and earth: Pythagoras witnessed to the fact that the world "is founded in the instrumentality of music and can be governed by it" (2.5.3). Music, of course, permeates religion: let us note the ten-string instruments symbolically representing the decalogue, the reverberations of harp and timbrel, the melody of the organ, the sound of the cymbal; and even the psalter was named after a musical instrument (the psaltery) because it contains "pleasant and agreeable modulation of the heavenly virtues" (2.5.2).

Ignoring Boethius' triple classification of music, Cassiodorus names other triple divisions: harmonics (the melodic structure of high and low pitches), rhythm (number-formed melodic movements corresponding to a text), and metrics (the quantitative measures of poetic verses). Rhythmic power is musical: it examines the meeting of words with melody to determine whether the sounds fit together well or badly. Metrics is literary, for it investigates the measures of poetic verses like the heroic, the iambic, the elegiac, and so forth (5.5-6).

There are three types of musical instruments: percussion (percussible: bronze and silver bells, and all struck objects), string (tensible: plucked instruments including the cithara), and wind (inflatable: blown instruments like trumpets, pipes, pandora, and so forth, producing a "vocal" sound when filled with air). All instruments have the same duties--to produce consonances, which are the proper mixing of a bass with a treble, or a treble with a bass, to produce euphony (or *symphonia*) (5.7). Cassiodorus, like Gaudentius (*Isagoge*) and others, follows convention and identifies six consonances, the octave (1:2), the fifth (2:3), the fourth (4:3), the octave plus a fourth (24:8, really a compound musical fourth), the compound musical fifth (3:0), and the double octave (4:1). Like Aristides, he names fifteen "tones" (pitch keys) (5.7-8). Like other similar inherited arrangements, Cassiodorus' entire musical plan was accepted so rigidly during the Middle Ages that the intervals of the third and the sixth were not thought respectable until quite late.

Since for Cassiodorus music is the branch of learning soothing our ears with sweet harmony and leading our understanding to heavenly things, he feels compelled to refer to the miracles supposedly performed chiefly for cathartic or therapeutic reasons, miracles publicized by the Greeks and by Neoplatonists such as Iamblichus, but of course modernized and Christianized. Like certain Church Fathers, therefore, he rejects Orpheus and his lyre and, naturally, the songs of the Sirens as merely pleasant fables; like almost everyone else in his day, he substitutes for them David's deliverance of Saul from the unclean spirit by means of a redeeming melody--something doctors had been unable to do with herbs. The physician Aesclepiades (fl. 100 B.C.), for example, restored a madman to sanity through music. This was possible because everything and all is governed by celestial harmony (2.5.9), as had been made clear by Alypius (300 A.D., in his lost *Introduction to Music*), Euclid, Ptolemy, Albinus, Gaudentius, Apuleius of Madaura, Cicero, St. Augustine, and Censorinus (5.9-10). Sweet melodies, and all beautiful forms, delightful tastes, pleasant fragrances, and sensations of touch--all pleasures of the senses--are in a resonance with eternal beauty, infinite sweetness, and divine tenderness. Following Cicero on art and science (*De natura deorum* 2.22), Cassiodorus thinks that art, which aims at action, is a skill and works with unforeseeable contingencies, whereas science, or speculative knowledge, deals with immutable laws. Art is a creation and a making, it is so governed by rule as to control us, and it looks to action just as knowledge looks to understanding. Art works with the probable and the conjectural; science treats of the demonstrable, of true argument dealing with unchanging principles (5.17). Thus Cassiodorus, in contrast to Boethius, overtly combines pagan learning with the Christian faith. More than Boethius and much like the Church Fathers, he promotes the idea that all earthly knowledge is of use for the understanding of divine revelation. This was an expression of faith which could and did justify science in later centuries. With Boethius, Cassiodorus began a tradition which was reflected in the High Middle Ages in the works of Domingo Gundisalvo, Hugh of St.-Victor, Vincent of Beauvais, and others. Different in many aspects, their works on music are all philosophically introductory and are concerned more with observation and speculation than with performance.

Like other religious men of his day who were largely under the influence of the writings of the Church Fathers, Cassiodorus wrote extensively about the psalms, producing an *Expositio in psalterium*. Like St. Augustine, his model, he was erudite and resourceful in devising symbolic interpretations of biblical and secular phenomena. For him the union of four hundred Israelitish psalm-singers accompanied by an orchestral sound produced by every kind of instrument is like the unity of the Christian faith, which is a harmonizing of many different tongues and voices (*Ps.* 2, Pref., *PL* 70.35). He compares the *organum musicum* of the psaltery and the cithara (*pandurium*, cithara) symbolically (*Ps.* 4, Pref., *PL* 70.47; *Ps.* 146, *PL* 70.1034). Song has three symbolical divisions: *cantare* or song, *exsultare* or a votive offering, and *psallere* or good works (*Ps.* 20.14, *PL* 70.151; *Ps.* 46.6, *PL* 70.334; *Ps.* 56.11, *PL* 70.405). And the entire enumeration of instruments in the *Psalms*, which must work on the heart and not on the senses, is to be understood as symbolical in the spiritual sense since, as a symbolical elucidation, music is a discipline concerning itself with congruences arising out of inequalities; it can easily be used for spiritual purposes; the demand for psalmodizing and for the jubilized playing on instruments (like the *tibia*) is therefore an allegory or parable for the ordering and agreement of spiritual deeds (*Ps.* 97, Concl., *PL* 70.691). The playing of tubas, horns (*corneis*), citharas, and cymbals, and choral singing too, have only one aim, religious praise of the Savior. Such a concordance of sacred harmony opens up not the fleshly ear but spiritual contemplation (*Ps.* 150.5, *PL* 70.1054). Yet the *tuba* represents earthly power, the psaltery God, and the cithara--with the remaining instruments-- earthly love (*Ps.* 150.3, *PL* 70.1052). Like Augustine, Cassiodorus sees wordless song aroused by worldly joy as a jubilation. He admits that there are hymns of happiness which, contrary to the view otherwise followed by certain Church Fathers, were not concerned with the text, but were made up of a whole and carried out in unarticulated expressions of sound (*Ps.* 46.1, 5, *PL* 70.302). But secular situations are different, and thoughtful spectators at pantomimes must recognize the wide difference between the psalmody of the Church which will bring salvation and theatrical presentations which serve only to corrupt (*Ps.* 39.6, *PL* 70.288-89). He describes antiphonal singing, the rotation in song between choir and congregation (*Ps.* 104, *PL* 70.742), and later adds that the music of the *Psalms* pleases not only human ears but also the spirit of angels (*Ps.* 145, Pref., *PL* 70.1029).

It is clear, then, that in every respect even prior to the Middle Ages, the political value of musical influence had been thoroughly replaced in Western Europe with the religious value of serving God (*Ps.* 20, Concl., *PL* 70.151; *Institutiones* 2.5.11); music was considered subject not to the state but to divine Christian law. It exemplified the relation of the sensuous to the supersensuous or supernal as Christianity interpreted them (*Ps.* 80.3ff, *PL* 70.587; *Ps.* 97, Concl., *PL* 70.692). Though in his letter to Boethius he had mixed the pagan and the Christian, in his commentaries on the Psalms Cassiodorus is thoroughly Christian, and the pagan is recognized as the fabulous (*Ps.* 80.3, *PL* 70.587). Even the old ethical theory of music seems completely replaced by the opinion that for all the faithful, music should act chiefly as an appeal to the goodness of God, whom it serves. Theology thus came to dominate in Cassiodorus' thought and became his principal concern in his own writing, and it remained the major concern of most of those who would follow him in writing about music in the Middle Ages.

IV

Isidore of Seville (Isidorus Hispalensis). Cassiodorus is a symbol of the de-secularization of thought which, in process since the time of Philo of Alexandria, was to be complete by the beginning of the seventh century when the distinguished St. Isidore of Seville (c.560-636), one of the prime influences on the Mozarabic rite and its chants, was named as one of the bishops destined to dominate Spain between the conversion of the Visigoths and the Islamic invasion of that country in 711 A.D. What was left after the de-secularization process was complete was a kind of debris of earlier scientific thought, though Isidore's own contribution was much more accurate and respectable than often has been believed.

In Isidore's time, Spain was a richly civilized and thoroughly Roman-ized country with large numbers of its men having previously won distinc-tion in the empire. Persons of intellectual stature had come from this region in the first and second centuries (e.g., the two Senecas, Lucan, Quintilian, Martial), and indeed Spain remained the equal of Rome intellectually, ancient culture being more steadfastly retained there than at the old center of the empire. This was in part true because the barbarian invasions had in large part spared the Spanish. Only the Visigoths had become a permanent factor in the development of that country, but their arrival was only in 419--well after 326, when they had first entered the Roman empire, themselves to be influenced by Roman culture.

Isidore, archbishop of Seville, belonged to the Visigothic aristocracy. In spite of his lack of knowledge of Greek, he has been called the most learned scientific writer in Europe during his lifetime, and the comprehen-siveness of his work remains impressive even to the modern reader who takes the effort to look at his *Etymologies*, compiled during the years 622-33. This work is the product of the first genuinely Christian encyclopedist, though it is important to see that the book is in fact more of a dictionary than an encyclopedia since its stated purpose is to be comprehensive only in defining the origins of things especially as information may be derived from the writings of the ancients.   Yet in effect the book was regarded subsequently as a kind of universal history of the Seven Liberal Arts and also as a binding authority to which reference might be made.   Its audience was intended to be broader than Cassiodorus', since he directed his work toward young men of his own ruling class as well as presumably toward the usual clerical and monastic readers and students.   Like Cassiodorus, whom he literally copied, Isidore tried to realize certain ideas of Augustine, but unlike Augustine he forbade the reading of pagan writings except by special permission.   He accepts the euhemeristic principle that the ancient gods are derived from especially noble human beings.   As a historian, he allots six periods to the world as defined by the Bible--a division of history that regarded the seventh age as the present one, which would reach its culmination at the Last Day of divine judgment at the Second Coming--but he includes fabulous characters as parallel in time with biblical persons.   In his *Etymologies*, he attempts to provide instruction according to educational goals reached through the learning of the past--but not through that of his own day, of which he says nothing in this work. Indeed, contemporary thought is outside the scope of the *Etymologies*, as we have seen.

Nevertheless, he is concerned about the quality of singing and technique, and even regrets that music cannot be preserved in notation[16] so that it might be more easily and perfectly retained than in memory alone.   In his suggestion that some kind of notation might serve as a superior substitute for memory, he seems to oppose Plato, who of course thought that writing is injurious to memory (see *Phaedrus* 275).   But Isidore's interest here (as often elsewhere) is practical, for he desires to have a text sung repeatedly in the same way.

Though he was particularly concerned about the definitions and origins of technical terms, his *Etymologies* do not indicate any knowledge on his part of a technical nature.   Arithmology was his love, and in other writings, specifically his *Moralia*, he displays his interest in allegorizing the Scriptures.   His aim in the *Etymologies* in large part is summarized in his words about the orator, whom he calls "a good man skilled in speaking."   By a good man he means someone with a natural capacity for learning from instruction and with knowledge and certain accomplishments (*artibus*) or practical abilities, which are the result of labor.   And he thinks these elements are to be sought in every artist (*Etymol.* 2.3).[17]

Isidore provides a summary of what he has learned of the Seven Liberal Arts.   They consist, to begin with, of discipline, which is knowledge or science, and art, which is something requiring fancy and imagination. Discipline or science calls for studying and discussion, and the relevant subjects are: grammar, or proficiency in speaking; rhetoric, or eloquence; dialectic, or logic, each contributing to the separation of truth from error;

arithmetic, or the relationships and divisions of numbers; music, or songs and chants; geometry, or the measurements and dimensions of the earth; and, finally, astronomy, the study of the laws of the stars (1-3). In these categories, Isidore tends to ignore the former place of music among the mathematical sciences, and gives it a place in terms of its contents, songs and chants. Furthermore, he is uncertain of his position when he compares a discipline and the arts, and seems throughout to depend on Cassiodorus.

Indeed, to read Isidore about music is to read Cassiodorus on new manuscript pages and under a new name. Less concerned about numbers in his comments on music than Cassiodorus, he describes music essentially as consisting of poetic texts and chants and songs (3.15.1-2), though to be sure he does include it among the mathematical sciences and as an art. Music is a modulation consisting of time and song, the latter being the practical knowledge of melody (3.15.1). It is "a science that treats of numbers that are found in sounds" (3, Pref.). Its name derives from the Muses and probably from the idea of inquiring or learning because the Muses inquired into the power of songs and the modulation of the voice, the sound of which makes an impression on sense, "passes along into past time [as Augustine indicated] and . . . is impressed on the memory." The Muses (who divided learning among themselves) were supposed to be daughters of Jupiter and Memory: "unless sounds are held in the memory by man, they perish because they cannot be written" (3.15)--that is, music is not literature and does not have its content or notation. The "history" of music begins with Jubal, who discovered music before the Flood (*Genesis* 4.21) ("he was the father of all such as handle the harp and organ"). Like the Church Fathers, Isidore was clearly attempting to take musical priorities away from the ancients, to whom he usually seems hostile, and to give them to biblical figures.[18] He made Jubal the predecessor of Pythagoras.[19] But he gives credit to Linus the Theban, Zethus, and Amphion: following the time of these originators it was considered as disgraceful for one not to know music as not to know letters, because sacred rites, ceremonies of all kinds, hymns to the gods, glad and sorrowful occasions, banquets, and funerals--all were the occasion for music (3.16).

Though he does say that music is a mathematical science, therefore, he is only repeating what he has read. He relies on an accretion of statements about music rather than on any numerical concept of it. He recites the usual remarks about the harmony of sounds (concords), of man (health and virtue), and the universe;[20] about the harmonic guidance of heaven, the sensuous arousal through music of different feelings and emotions, the effects of music on men in battle, in boats, in the fields, in states of weariness, sadness, and pain. He somewhat changes Cassiodorus' classifications of instruments (voice, which is struck by breath; blown, *tuba*; and struck, cithara) and hints at the symbolism of three--that is, of mind, spirit, and body--but he returns to the divisions of harmonics, rhythm, and meter. He stresses motion and modulation, concordance (symphony), *tonus* (mode), and the pitch of voices. Of some interest is his list of *organica*, instruments which are filled with a current of breath and animated to sound like the voice: these are trumpets, reeds, Pan's pipes, organs,[21] and *pandoura* (a stringed instrument), and others.

In one respect, Isidore mentions an aesthetic quality which, not stressed by the Church Fathers, was to become a hallmark for good singing in the age of Charlemagne and after. This is the quality of sweetness, which the Romans frequently had mentioned. He describes melody synaesthetically as sweetness of *mel* (honey) and sweet voices as "fine, full, loud, and high." It is true that Isidore describes other kinds of voices: thin, for instance-- those of children, women, and the sick which lack breath. And there are penetrating, fat, sharp, hard, harsh, blind ("choked off as soon as produced"), and pretty voices. But the perfect voice is "high, sweet, and pure": high to be "adequate to the sublime," pure to please the ear, and sweet to soothe the minds and souls of the listeners.[22] Perfection is of course a higher criterion than sweetness, and for perfection all of these qualities are needed (3.20). Isidore was quoted throughout the Middle Ages about his preference for the high voice. It is in contrast to the low voice which Pseudo-Aristotle (918a) thought to be large, strong, and a "container" of an upper one. Can the difference be that the high voice was preferred because of the "celestial" or "ethereal" character of the high voices of the boys trained in monastery or cathedral schools and choirs; and that the low voice was preferred by the ancients for its greatly admired masculine quality when it was contrasted with boys' voices which, after all, would "break" and slide downwards, as is proper in a maturing male?

The really important thing about Isidore's use of numbers in his study of music, however, is that numbers themselves would never be treated in such a cavalier way in the Middle Ages. Proportion exists in the universe, which is made up of revolving circles; similarly, in the macrocosm--"not to speak of the voice"--proportion has so much power that man does not exist without it (23.2). Without music, not even a science can be perfect: without music there is nothing because the very structure of the world is said to be based on a certain harmony of sounds (of the music of the spheres) (17.1). And thus Isidore repeats "knowledge" about music without at any point extending it. Like all "science," music is based on authority, not on research and investigation. In its most practical manifestations, it is a craft; the craftsman (*artifex*), as several of these encyclopedists think, is a person who makes an object (*ars*) just as the goldsmith makes things out of gold (9.1.2). One may observe that Isidore's *Etymologies* shares with Boethius and Cassiodorus a curious neglect of contemporary music, meaning chant or church music, especially that species called Gregorian chant following the time of Gregory the Great. However, such a charge is unfair, since elsewhere in his writings Isidore does deal very specifically with the music of the Church of his time. His *De ecclesiasticis officiis* not only treats the music of the Offices but also throws very specific light on the Mozarabic liturgy which was in use in Spain during his lifetime.

A certain professionalism had already entered church singing.

According to the evidence of the Canons of Laodicea which have been linked with a Council of Laodicea in the mid-fourth century, the first step had already been taken to recognize church singers as professionals. The cantor, originally a member of the laity, was given status as the guardian of the music which the Church prescribed. In the centuries which followed, the cantor was unlikely to be a composer in his own right, and indeed it is important to see that the music on the whole carried a degree of anonymity with regard to authorship. For practical purposes (and on Isidore's own evidence), music could not yet be transmitted by written manuscripts with notation, and in fact it was only much later that the neumes which would be developed to assist the singers would be placed on staves and provided with a system what would make them fully readable. Thus the antiphonal and responsorial practice described by Isidore in his *De ecclesiasticis officiis* (1.3-7, 9, 13-15, 2.12, *PL* 83.743ff) involves a purely (or, almost purely) oral tradition.

Plainchant is usually regarded as based on rhythm as opposed to meter, following the unmeasured rhythms of prose of the Bible. However, the meter of the hymns, as opposed to psalms, suggests that the entire chant practice was more complex than has been previously believed by many earlier scholars. The most recent research suggests a tradition which in its richness was idiosyncratic, likely to be different according to the region and even the local church practice. Nevertheless, it is possible yet to say that in comparison with oriental song it was relatively "pure" and objective, and this is apparently the case also when Roman and Mozarabic chant is compared with the more florid developments in liturgy before the time of Charlemagne in the region now known as France. Especially in the Roman chant, then, the sensuous aspect of music was kept to a minimum. Hugo Leichtentritt has suggested that nothing in European literature, philosophy, painting, or sculpture can compare with Gregorian chant, except perhaps Romanesque architecture of 900-1200.[23] While what Cassiodorus has to say about singing does not constitute even a recognition of this developing practice of chant or its importance in cultural, albeit religious, life, Isidore shows that he is actively interested in the developments in his region of Spain, though one would not be able to guess this merely from the *Etymologies*.

XIV

The Carolingian and Post-Carolingian Age

During the period of a little more than a century and a half between the death of Isidore of Seville and the crowning of Charlemagne as Emperor in 800 A.D. there seems to have been no outstanding contributor to the idea of music. Charlemagne--"the father of the whole world," according to Aurelian of Réôme--in his establishment of the Holy Roman Empire acted as a cohesive force for diverse people and, most significantly for the subject under study, was a strong stimulus toward intellectual activity. Following the often troubled times of the disintegration of the old Roman empire, Charlemagne's regime and its influence were positive forces for culture in the West. The Franks, who were his special responsibility, assimilated ideas of classical antiquity and used Latin as their sole means of communication wherever they were dominant. Earlier the region of Gaul had even developed its own unique liturgy, but in the Carolingian period its people allowed themselves to be Romanized. Since under Charlemagne's influence they retained the Roman ideas of state, Church, and culture, they in effect fostered a kind of "universal" political, religious, and cultural state of mind. For them, the *orbis* (world), the *urbs* (city), and Rome were the same, so that, with the encouragement of the Emperor, the Roman *imperium* could be transported anywhere. The Franks studied the classics, and they also entered the fold of the Roman Church and adopted the Roman rite for worship (see Appendix B). There resulted two opposing tendencies, one classical and the other anti-classical. The latter resembled oriental art because it employed adornment, extravagance, and richness in order to realize abstract forms and mysterious and abstract symbols. The classical, as one might expect, predominated in literature, philosophy, mathematics, and theoretical and aesthetic speculation--and in the liturgy and its music.

In Spain at this time, however, the intellectual and cultural patterns would differ considerably from those of the Frankish region, especially on account of the Arabic presence which influenced them deeply. The Arabs, though an Islamic people, were avid students of Greek writings, including the philosophical texts. While the Arabs attempted to encourage (and sometimes to coerce) European thought into submission to Allah and the *Koran*, Charlemagne nevertheless maintained connections with them and sympathized with their scientific, naturalistic, and trans-national aims. Thus both the comparative docility of the Franks and the assertive ambition of the Arabs contributed to Charlemagne's renewal of intellectual and cultural pursuits, which in his mind were right and proper for the Holy Roman

Empire, the symbol--and more than symbol--of internationalism.

Church and state had, to be sure, been in a more or less close alliance since the time of Constantine the Great. Charlemagne, who had become king of the Franks in 768, was made emperor thirty-two years later at Rome, the seat of the empire. Eventually his court migrated northward to Aachen. Church and state were now to be even more closely joined. His government embraced northwest continental Europe (though not Scandinavia), much of Italy, and a small portion of Spain, and the universalism Charlemagne attempted to foster also laid the ground for an intellectual revival or renaissance. In order to encourage cultural activity, he attempted to educate the clergy--many clergymen and even bishops were ignorant of Latin except by rote and preached in the local vernacular--as well as to establish a uniform liturgy based on the ritual of Rome throughout his provinces. Not only the clergy were given education, but also, in so democratic a manner as the world had perhaps never seen, many serfs and freemen were required to study grammar, music, and architecture.

The head of the palace school at Aachen was Alcuin (c.735-804), an Englishman from Northumbria who had been trained under Archbishop Egbert at the cathedral school of York, an institution which was deeply indebted to the scholarly ideals and the work of the Venerable Bede.[1] An encyclopedic and scientific scholar, Alcuin established the study of the Seven Liberal Arts on a model which encouraged their acceptance as a guiding curriculum throughout the Middle Ages. He called them the Seven Pillars of the House of Wisdom--or seven steps to theology (*On Grammar* 9.1, *PL* 101.853-54). Sharing with others the many manuscripts of the magnificent library at York, he was only one of the learned men who in the eighth and ninth centuries linked Britain with the continent prior to the period of the ravages of the Vikings in Northumbria. It was, of course, natural for Charlemagne to go abroad for his learned men when such scholars as Alcuin could be brought to his territory for the purpose of enriching the previously weak intellectual climate among the Franks. England, Christianized for the second time following the Anglo-Saxon invasions in the mid fifth century, had found itself relatively protected and had developed a strong monastic and intellectual tradition. Charlemagne of course also attracted to his court the learned from the various centers of learning on the continent.

Curiously, though Charlemagne's own literacy may be seriously questioned, the intellectual accomplishments of his reign were sufficiently significant that a case may be made for recognizing him as the first modern man. Under him, interest in the Latin classics was renewed, and grammar (that is, meters, figures of speech, poetry) was encouraged as a study. Alcuin, for example, wrote not only theoretical works but also a grammar (applied to the study of literature) and a rhetoric as well. Musical settings are reported to have been made for the odes of Horace, for portions of Boethius' *Consolation of Philosophy*, and for parts of Virgil's *Aeneid*. We hear of instrumental accompaniment to vocal music as a widespread practice. The social context seems to have been favorable for both religious and secular expression. It thus may be claimed that Charlemagne's was the first consistent and consequential cultural era to follow that of ancient Rome itself. He championed official Christianity, which was a state religion and imposed in a manner consistent with the usage at Rome insofar as possible, and encouraged the establishment of new schools in cloister, cathedral, and church. The court and monasteries were places of intense musical activity. Charlemagne was himself deeply interested in church music and its reform, rejecting the music not only of the Gallican rite but also of all other rites (e.g., Ambrosian, Mozarabic, or Byzantine) in favor of the Roman rite and its chants. Gregorian chant and its practice were to be followed strictly.

In Charlemagne's court, Alcuin restored the Muses to their old status as guardians of art and knowledge. In antiquity the Muses belonged not only to poetry but also to higher forms of intellectual life. To live with the Muses was to live humanistically (Cicero, *Tusc. Dis.* 5.23.66), recalling the identification of the library in Alexandria as the Home of the Muses (Museum) as well as also the epic invocations to "our Muses" ("the most holy virgins") in Virgil. Now, through the climate created by Alcuin and his contemporaries, secular poetry, especially that of eulogy or of friendship, entered the court. The genre of *versus*--that is, rhymed, rhythmic poetry, usually in strophes--appeared in this era, as according to report did a long series of Latin songs, many of them now lost, in classical verse, about historical events, love, politics, and human mutability. The Carolingian renaissance also extended to segments of society outside the monastery and court and school, and there it took forms about which we would like to know more. Unfortunately, these were the least permanent aspects of Carolingian culture.

Secular and monastic learning and traditions nevertheless proved incompatible, it would seem. For example, monks were not disposed to accept secular poetry. In Alcuin's pupil, Rabanus Maurus, monastic attitudes toward secular and religious poetry became clear: churchmen in general disliked the former; poets who need to be inspired, they thought, should go to Sinai, Mount Carmel, Horeb, or Zion for inspiration. To such sources indeed the writers of poetry and music for the Church went, for in Frankish territories in the period following the time of Charlemagne and extending to 1150 A.D. was a flourishing of such writing, particularly in the sequence and in the tropes which were added to such liturgical items as the Introit, *Kyrie, Sanctus, Agnus Dei,* and so forth. The sequence in particular is interesting here, since increasingly this form took on the meters determined by stress and accent, as in secular verse of the Middle Ages. This was also a great period of hymn writing, and this form too reflected the new metrical patterns of medieval practice rather than classical practice which had been based on quantity and length of syllables, The immense quantity of this production may be suggested by the modern collection *Analecta Hymnica*, which presents fifty-five volumes of texts alone!

Simplicity remained the main characteristic of chant for the

Carolingian period, however, or in any case it was the approved ideal toward which church music was to strive. In chant, voice alone on the one hand and voices in unison on the other--individual and community--could pray to, appeal to, and praise God. In psalmody its rhythm remained controlled by the sacred texts, and its melodies were unharmonized (in the modern sense). Simple in principle and yet fixed by an idea of Gregorian tradition and of a superior Roman practice the music was ostensibly undefined; it could therefore symbolize the timeless. Like all prescribed art forms, it was imagined to be always the same (so long as practice imitated the way that music was believed to be done at Rome). When it replaced the Gallican chant in Frankish areas, it was thought to be the highest kind of music to which man can aspire. It also represented an important stage for the development, codification, and systematization of music in the Western world. Sweetness (*suavitas*) and tranquillity were its characteristics. But it was sweet (beautiful) without being more than minimally sensuous; in every respect austere and spiritual because it supposedly denied the physical, it was divorced from "real" life in that it avoided the weaknesses and corruptibilities of actual life--and also, supposedly, the sensuous delights of hearing. In a way, its appeal could be universal because it was the least common denominator of what song can be.

Music speculation too was in the nature of being non-local in time and space. In the ninth century, music aesthetics (or the idea of music) and music theory were an undifferentiated pair disposed gradually to establish separate realms of existence. Earlier writers like Boethius had theorized about ancient speculations and had ignored actual contemporary practice. Along with Cassiodorus, and like Martianus Capella and Censorinus, Boethius supplied a universal theory to pass as basic truth everywhere. The universal was always to be a corrective for the merely local in time and place. Nowhere had the split seemed more obvious than in Isidore of Seville, who, as we have seen, failed to treat contemporary church music in his *Etymologies*, while elsewhere he treats such music as it appeared in the Spanish churches and ignores theory and questions of aesthetics. Musical change, however, was frustrated by the earlier writers of the Christian era, who still laid down the laws. Boethius was known as the profane and speculative scientist-philosopher, but Cassiodorus, because he was a man of the Church, was more powerful than all other teachers of music. For the Church, music was primarily a practical science subserving moral and devotional purposes.

Nevertheless, during and immediately following the Carolingian age, the arts in their physical and technical aspects began to be treated as separate from the universal harmony which had been their burden for centuries and to be regarded as the primarily human creations described by the Epicureans and other naturalists. For Alcuin, who in certain respects followed Augustine, beauty was earthly, divine, and classical in that it realized the ideal of measure, equilibrium, and harmony; but he called it a "divided" sound (as had Virgil in the *Aeneid*), a varied sound, and "good modulation"; it was the discipline of number realized in sound (G 1.26).

As a social phenomenon, according to Zoltai,[2] music was also sometimes found in a context of secular actors, mimics, and dancers who, allowed into one's house, ended by attracting a crowd of followers of impure soul. Such behavior naturally triggered priestly displeasure, and indeed the practical aims of the Church had often to be expressed negatively, as they were by the Synod of Tours of 813, when the clergy was warned against the spell of music. When the Synod of Aachen met in 816, it proclaimed:

> Singers should make the greatest effort not to sully with faults the gift given them by God, but to further adorn it with modesty, purity and sobriety, and with all the other adornments of saintly virtues. Their melody should raise the minds of the assembled people to mindfulness and love of heavenly things, not only by the loftiness of the words which they sing, but also by the sweetness of the sounds. The singer, in accordance with the tradition of the Holy Fathers, should be distinguished and illustrious in voice as well as in art, in order that the soothing sweetness of his melodies may arouse the minds of his listeners.[3]

The music discussed is, of course, chant or plainsong.

Hence by Carolingian times the groundwork had been laid for another incipient quarrel--the quarrel between the ancients and the moderns, which came to the surface in the thirteenth and fourteenth centuries with such writers as Jacob of Liège. Ancient theory repeatedly rejected modern practice and tried to make it conform to old fashions of which no examples were known and to which contemporary practices in church, monastery, or palace of the aristocracy were in any case indifferent. But, as long as Charlemagne's realm remained intact, the fruits of his organization were apparent in all educational institutions. The curriculum was in a sense both "pagan" and Christian. Alcuin, to whom the Carolingian *Musica* was formerly attributed, did not, however, live to see the end of either the educational reforms or the political unit Charlemagne had established. During his lifetime, Alcuin had carried on the work of Isidore of Seville and the Venerable Bede, who had brought cloister and cathedral schools to a high state of development. The accomplishments of Alcuin and his contemporaries created a climate in which the Carolingian *Musica* could be written. Next to Alcuin, the most dominant of these educators was Rabanus Maurus.

I

Musica. This treatise, formerly attributed to Alcuin, was perhaps the first writing in the Occident to describe the division of the ecclesiastical modes into authentic and plagal (G 1.26). (We may treat this work as

Carolingian in spite of the the the lack of early manuscripts.) Said to have used the Byzantine system of melodic formulas (the *Octoechos*) rather than scales, the author of this treatise continued the Greek patterns in the tradition of the ancient *nomoi*. To the original *tetractys* for each authentic mode he added a second or *plagal* mode, the Greek terms for the four tones of *protus, deuterus, tritus,* and *tetrachius (tetrardus)* being retained. The modes were numbered but not named. For convenience, the following listing of the medieval modes, as eventually named and systematized by Guido of Arezzo in the first half of the eleventh century, is provided here:

AUTHENTIC 1 (Dorian)
3 (Phrygian)
5 (Lydian)
7 (Mixolydian)

1. { 1. Authentic (Dorian)
{ 2. Plagal (Hypodorian)

2. { 1. Authentic (Phrygian)
{ 2. Plagal (Hypophrygian)

OR

3. { 1. Authentic (Lydian)
{ 2. Plagal (Hypolydian)

PLAGAL 2 (Hypodorian)
4 (Hypophrygian)
6 (Hypolydian)
8 (Hypomixolydian)

4. { 1. Authentic (Mixolydian)
{ 2. Plagal (Hypomixolydian)

The author of the Carolingian *Musica* meant that each pair of authentic and plagal modes had the same *finalis*, or final note. Here he relies on the modal division of 4 (the *tetractys*): 4 x 2 (eight tones), as in Pythagorean and Platonic speculation. But his own text (G 1.26-27), as Rudolf Schäfke indicates,[4] is more than a classification or laying down of rule. He uses the *tetractys* as a kind of musical sociology: the authentic means the superior and greater value, and the plagal the lesser, these in analogy with the feudal stratification of society and of the political order. The authentic is the leader, the master, the ruler; the plagal is indirect or secondary, the master's subject. In these terms, the organization is hierarchical. It finds its full exposition in the *Musica disciplina* (8) of Aurelian of Réôme.

It must be noted that an eighth mode has been added to the seven Greek modes. The addition is suggested by Ptolemy and made concrete by Boethius (*Of Music* 4.16ff). The eighth mode was necessary, it was thought, so that the music of the spheres could be brought to fullness: the fixed stars needed a mode, and Urania (as Martianus Capella had made clear) would be without sound if no mode were ascribed to her--clearly, an irrational state of affairs. It was both logical and convenient, then, for the early writers of the Church, should they indeed concern themselves with pagan lore, to find a parallel between the ancient modes and the modern, the Hypomixolydian then being regarded as parallel with the Fourth Plagal.

Like many of those who followed him, the author of the *Musica* formerly attributed to Alcuin compared music with speech: the smallest part of both is sound indicated by a note or letter, and in its unity (in which it is arithmetical) both music and speech are the result of multiplication (G 1.26). Thus he (presumably) anticipated or set the stage for the rest of the Carolingian age, which was primarily technical, not aesthetic, in its interests. It was an age of copying, or working encyclopedically. There seems to have been little or no interest in the *value* of literature as such, but much in technical analysis, allegorizing, and symbolizing. In music aesthetics it tended toward the scientific abstraction exemplified by the modal system as described in the Carolingian *Musica*. This work relied on St. Augustine, Boethius (especially his Nicomachus-derived *Arithmetica*), Cassiodorus (especially his commentaries on the psalms), and Isidore of Seville (his *Etymologies*).

II

Rabanus Maurus (Hrabanus or Rhabanus Magnentius Maurus). Not all of the Carolingian writers who expressed opinions about music followed the pattern of the *Musica* formerly attributed to Alcuin. Technical, analytical, or aesthetic matters were morally neutral, but they existed in a moral and spiritual context of the Church's teachings. Their *pied-à-terre*, as it were, was the Divine Whole of Harmony which contrasted sharply with the physical, cosmic whole of the Greeks. Writers like Rabanus Maurus (c.776-856), a polymath and encyclopedist, wrote about music and other subjects according to the expectations of the Church. With him, allegorizing and symbolizing experienced renewal. A Frankish theologian, scholar, and teacher, he had been educated in the great monastic schools of Fulda and Tours; in the latter he was taught by Alcuin, whose every word he claimed to have written down. He became head of the school of Fulda and its abbot, and in 847 he was named archbishop of Mainz. He helped to spread Roman learning throughout Germany. In addition, he was given credit for the authorship of hymns, one of which was reputed to be *Veni Creator Spiritus*, and was the undoubted author of various commentaries as well as theological and pedagogical works, all of which, written especially for the school of Fulda, were in large part in answer to questions posed by the brothers of the monastery. He compiled an *Excerptio*, popular throughout the Middle Ages, of the grammar of the Latin of Priscian. As might be expected, he followed Augustine, Cassiodorus, Isidore, and Bede. As a religious man, he stressed not so much cosmic matters as the usefulness of a knowledge of biblical interpretation.

For Rabanus, the arts are the work of both eternal wisdom and human invention. They were a construction not of the human mind, but of the mind of God, who gives them an objective and divine structure. Like Bede, he thinks music, of all studies, is capable of crossing the threshold of the Church (*De cleric.* 3.24, *PL* 107.393-94). For him, all of the Liberal Arts, like the planets, meteors, wind, thunder, water, and so forth, are ultimately based on the divine, objective structure of the Spirit of God. Music is a factor in universal perfection (*De universo* 18.4, *PL* 111.495-96), and its perfection lies in its sweetness and clarity. This is so because music and the universe interpenetrate, and the divine structure of this interpenetration--that is of harmony--is of primary ontological importance, since arithmetic, geometry, and astronomy--the lesser branches of the quadrivium--can do nothing except discover its laws (*De cleric.* 16, *PL* 107.393). Music *is*; these subjects only explain.

Echoing Isidore literally, Rabanus thinks no branch of knowledge can be complete without music, because nothing can exist without it: the whole world is held together by harmonic laws, and heaven itself moves within them (*De Univ.* 18.4, *PL* 111.495). He draws upon Philo for symbolic and allegorical commentary. In the Old Testament, for example, David was a union of singer and instrumentalist who vouched for the song of the human voice, for the sound of the instrument, and for both in combination. The voice is produced by forced breath, and the perfect voice (as Isidore said) is high, sweet, and pure--high to express the sublime, sweet to delight the mind, and pure to please the ear. Lacking any one of these qualities, the voice is imperfect (*De Univ.* 18.4, *PL* 111.496). Like Isidore and St. Ambrose, Rabanus clearly equates voice with Spirit (*spiritus*), the breath of which was used by the Father when he impregnated the Virgin Mary. Through vocal and instrumental treatment like David's, lovely and pleasant music characterizes the Catholic Church which some day under God's leadership will blend into a harmony of faith through different languages and in many kinds of songs (*Comm. in Paralipomenon* [*Chronicles*], *PL* 109.309-11). Song is a sign of spiritual knowledge, and the perfection of wisdom is the study of the Scriptures. To sing to the psaltery means to achieve a good work. As the song is contemplative, the singing to a psaltery is part of active life. Concerning the psaltery, Rabanus ascribes an especially prominent significance to the number of its strings (*Comm. in Eccles.* 8.18, *PL* 109.1041). The cithara, on the other hand, symbolizes the Church whose twenty-four dogmas correspond to the cithara's twenty-four strings.

Arithmology, treated in his *De numero*, was one of Rabanus' specialties. The senarius (a verse of six feet), he thought, is perfect not because God created the world in six days, but rather God created the world in six days because the number 6 is perfect. God therefore seems of necessity to be co-eternal with number. Numbers are undisputed realities, everywhere more real than "appearances." Even the number of the elect, following the Bible, is described (symbolically) as 144,000.

Music, then, is a comprehensive symbol in which voice, instrument, and song combine to create a harmonic whole. Our own lips are beautifully sounding cymbals, and both lips and cymbals can be counted among musical instruments because they can produce sweet harmony (*De univ.* 18.4, *PL* 111.495, 500). The lyre represents the exultation of the saints, and thus music plays a part not only in the physical world but also in the moral one (*De cleric.* 2.47ff, *PL* 107.562ff). As Cassiodorus had believed, a virtuous man possesses music whereas an evil one does not. Even higher than the physical and moral worlds, however, is that realm of significant meanings which are beyond description (*De univ.* 18.4, *PL* 111.495-96). Jubilation is a cry whose power of expression is conditioned by passion and enthusiasm; it means a joy beyond the ability of human speech to utter. In music there are even more significant meanings than those suggested by the great men of the past. These are meanings which extend far beyond the power of words, the nature of things, and all mystical significances. We have gone entirely beyond the expressible.

III

John Scot Erigena (Johannes Scotus Erigena). After Rabanus, musical theory became more specific, and the three types of music identified by Boethius were combined into two further types, *musica naturalis* and *musica instrumentalis*. For several centuries prior to the career of John Scot Erigena (c.810-c.877), medieval musical scholarship had existed in part to preserve in encyclopedic form those portions of classical scholarship which were considered valuable and which were still available. With John, Irish in origin but apparently ultimately appointed the head of the court school of Charles the Bald (823-77), Charlemagne's grandson, a change in attitude becomes noticeable. In Ireland, classical poets were still read, and Greek had not been forgotten, as was the case in other academic circles in the West. But Erigena was interested in something more ambitious than learning about language and poetry, and thus he attempted in his *De divisione naturae* (*Of the Division of Nature*) to achieve a complete philosophy. Also of tremendous importance were his translations of *The Divine Names* and *The Celestial Hierarchies* of Dionysius the Areopagite (fifth century), more accurately identified as Pseudo-Dionysius. Thus Erigena added a very significant Neoplatonist supplement available in Latin to the musical thought received from Plotinus, Martianus Capella (upon whose work he wrote a commentary, *Annotationes in Marcianum*), Boethius, Augustine, and others.

For John, the sources of truth are two: reason and revelation, and if they are in conflict, reason must be chosen. Yet true religion and true philosophy are one and interchangeable: in his work on the *Division of Nature*, John held (with Plato) that universals are anterior to particulars. He divides nature into four classes: (1) what creates and is not created (God), (2) what creates and is created (ideas which subsist in God), (3) what is created but does not create (things in space and time), and (4) what neither creates nor is created (God as End and Purpose of all things).[5]

To know a thing, he thinks, is to know not an individual, but the idea: this is the assumption of his *De divisione naturae*, a work of metaphysical inquiry in which Plotinian "emanations" (*PL* 122.139) are a constantly recurring theme. Geometrical figures exist only in the notions of geometry, and, similarly, man himself is an intellectual idea existing in the mind of God, where there is a Oneness above unity (as Porphyry also had said). To know is to grasp an essence leading to God, but neither God nor essence can be known by finite minds. Experience does not supply notions of the mind, nor do sensations "check" them. Yet things exist more truly in the ideas or notions of men than they do in themselves. The divine *Logos* is the true light shining in the darkness and enlightening all men who come into the world. God, who is the essence of all things, possesses a knowledge which is causal; man's knowledge is merely an effect. The Liberal Arts, created not by man but by God and based on the structure of the universe itself, are such an effect leading back to their origin. How does this apply to the art of music? Erigena says that there are a *musica naturalis* and a *musica instrumentalis*. The former is not made by man, the latter is. The former is created by God, the second by man.

How does John the Scot arrive at such a distinction? The answer is not far to seek. For Plotinus, it will be recalled, the artist is not the mere imitator Plato (*Rep.* 602) made him out to be, for he is the producer of an object which reflects divine beauty; the musician is especially able to carry out this task because he is sensitive to tones and the beauty they convey. The arts are more than a *mimesis*. Nature herself is the imitation. The arts imitate things seen, but return to the principles of form from which nature herself emanates. They go beyond imitation because they possess a beauty which is intrinsic to the world and themselves and is only an addition to any sensible object which lacks it. Having in his possession the truths of philosophy, the musician rises from music to the condition of the lover and then to the summit, the realm of intellect (*Enneads.* 1.3.1-3). The highest place achieved by the musician is the philosophical, where divine beauty can be perceived. His medium is less the sensuous than the spiritual; physical desires are absent from his state and condition, and in earthly terms his proper pursuit is not secular but religious.

John the Scot's source may also have been Proclus, who accepted Plotinus' three degrees of *mousikos, erotikos,* and *philosophos*. Commenting on the first book of Euclid's *Elements*, Proclus describes the artist's progress from visible to invisible beauty. The musician, the lover, and the philosopher are located beyond the sensuous world because their achievement touches upon the primary life of the soul. The musician travels from harmonies perceptible to those imperceptible, and imperceptible harmonies contain the ultimate principles of Being.

Both Plotinus and Proclus describe a path from the visible to the invisible: following it, the truly philosophical and religious musician is indifferent to the senses and in union with the ultimate ideal, or beauty. But the true source of John the Scot's distinction between natural and instrumental music is the *Celestial Hierarchies* of Pseudo-Dionysius, for whom reality was a great Chain of Being, the material world was an image of divine harmony and beauty, and the two orders of reality were the divine, or celestial, and the ecclesiastical: hierarchy being a cosmic property, the musician receives from heaven (the divine or celestial) the hymns sung there and transmits them to the (ecclesiastical) Church (*Cel. Hier.* 1, *PL*

122.1039); psalms, canticles, and hymns are all reflections of spiritual chants brought to earth in a form of sacred music audible to human ears but nevertheless embodying the divine (*Cel. Hier.* 2.3, *PL* 122.1082).

Pseudo-Dionysius, as noted above a ?fifth-century imposter (pretending to be an Athenian of the first century A.D. who was converted by St. Paul [see *Acts* 17.34]), was nevertheless tremendously influential with regard to the iconography and mythology accepted by the medieval Church. A writer who Christianized Neoplatonic and Neopythagorean ideas from Plotinus and Proclus,[6] he was accepted as very nearly scriptural by most of the subsequent doctors and other significant thinkers of the Church, including Thomas Aquinas. His work, probably a deliberate expansion of *I Corinthians* 15.38-53, became accepted as a part of orthodox theology especially in his handling of the music of the spheres, for which he substituted the image of a heavenly organization that must have been as believable as it was logical. The nine Muses were replaced by nine orders of angels, who in nature were spiritual and divine and lived above and beyond the spheres of the universe. In Plato's *Republic* were described eight discs and in addition a surrounding globe, and, as we know, for the Greeks 9 was a sacred number. Hence where there had been a previous structure based on 9 there were now in Pseudo-Dionysius nine choirs. The position of Plato's Sirens was thus taken by angelic sirens who, through their incredibly beautiful singing, would set in motion a celestial dance.

The angels are grouped into three triads, each group attached to a person of the blessed Trinity. (In Dante's *Convivio* 2.6, they will further be correlated with the spheres of the cosmos.) The universe, static and immutable, is divided hierarchically, according to Proclus' hierarchy of divine orders,[7] thus:

> The Seraphim turn the Primum Mobile
> The Cherubim turn the sphere of the Fixed Stars
> The Thrones turn the sphere of Saturn
>
> The Dominions turn the sphere of Jupiter
> The Virtues turn the sphere of Mars
> The Powers turn the sphere of the sun
>
> The Principalities turn the sphere of Venus
> The Archangels turn the sphere of Mercury
> The Lower Angels turn the sphere of the moon

The harmony of the spheres was now no longer a mechanically produced sound but the harmony of the angels. With this in mind, clergy and monks often organized three choirs in monastery, cloister schools, and churches, and the choir of boys in the loft would face the west (the altar was in the east end normally) because the high voices at twilight resembled angels' voices and would thus serve with their unusually sweet voices to present a strong challenge to the powers of darkness. Thus was attempted an earthly realization of the Pseudo-Dionysian mystical image of the heavenly choirs.[8]

And the picture thus presented of God and man in their mutual relations is dramatic and compelling. God's love is universal and infinite; it includes all of nature and every conceivable piece of matter; everything emanates from him and everything is drawn back to him just as one piece of matter is drawn to every other. Thus perceptible beings and images, material and immaterial, in their differences and multiplicity harmonize with God and bring higher beings down to their own level (*Cel. Hier.* 1, *PL* 122.1038-39). The individual soul must turn towards the living reality of the surrounding outer world, which is a complex combination of multiple-faceted symbols, a spring-board by which it can lift itself to a perception of absolute beauty. The beauty of art helps human beings return to the intrinsically beautiful Oneness of God, from whom all good and beautiful things of the world derive (*Div. Names* 4.4, pp. 95-98). Such doctrines permeated Catholic thinking for centuries and made their imprint on art and aesthetic theory--and in a sense they represent the highest form of knowledge (intellectual understanding).

The individual approaches the wonders of God through contemplation (intuition); in beauty he finds perfect Being, and in art-forms he finds symbols of reality. Like Augustine (*Divine Providence* 1.7, FC 1.255-56), Pseudo-Dionysius includes under beauty the bad, the ugly, and the repulsive (Augustine names locusts, lice, insects, and fleas [*The Way of Life of the Manichaeans* 1.17.62-63, FC 56.107-08]). The bad is only the absence of the good. Demons too reveal their relative perfection, God having made them as part of Being; their relative imperfection is a deficiency which is not total: total deficiency is not an unformed thing; it is non-existence itself. Therefore, doomed souls, non-rational animals, all creatures even if they are misshapen, and all of nature are beautiful on the borders of their own perfection. For everything is beautiful which comes from God, the universal cause, and all in their own perfectibility and beauty return to him.

It seems odd to say that the Pseudo-Dionysian description of the soul's search for perfection leads both to religious salvation and to science. Yet for both aims these ideas dominated medieval thought up to the fourteenth century in Italy and well into the fifteenth in the rest of Europe.

John Scot Erigena, then, accepted the theories of Pseudo-Dionysius in addition to those of Plotinus and Proclus. Literature and architecture are human arts, he says, but the laws of music exist in the universe itself and in everything in it, since everything is measure and number (*De divisione naturae* 3, *PL* 122.651). The world can be a painting, a speech, or a poem; it can be more: a symphony (a concord). Oneness is like voices in a concert, as Seneca had said (*Epistle* 84). Music has two facets--sensuous sensation and correct proportion, each of which is enjoyed within the other. But the pleasure of music is entirely formal because the pleasure of harmony is produced not by sounds but by proportions which can be perceived through sounds only in our inner sensibility. The entire passage needs to be read: "I am convinced that nothing pleases the soul and nothing produces beauty but the rational intervals of different sounds, which, grouped together, produce the sweetness of musical melody. It is not the various sounds which produce the sweetness of the harmony, but the relationships of the sounds and their proportions, which are perceived and judged by the inner sense of the soul" (*Div. nat.* 5, *PL* 122.956; trans. Tatar. 2.133). Harmony is not only an organized movement of universe and music--is not only a set of parallels--but also an inner state of the elements of being existing simultaneously in the cosmos, in social and political life, and in musical works.

On the higher level is the intelligible, the invisible, which illuminates the soul; this John calls the natural level. It shines in the sun and heavenly bodies. The lowest level is artificial, a symbol of artificially created human things. The Liberal Arts are natural, are made to help us know the order of the natural world or universe; through the methodology which they provide, we may thus arrive at intelligible truths on the highest level of the being of nature, a knowledge which leads us towards a knowledge of everything-- that is, of God (*Div. nat.* 3, *PL* 122.639-40). Music is like geometry in that it distinguishes in the light of reason the harmony of all things mobile and immobile in their natural proportions (*Div. nat.* 4, *PL* 122.774). The study of music is the study of discord and concord in nature; music, like geometry, is intrinsic to the study of philosophy; the study of nature is the study of philosophy itself. These precepts express the kernel of thought which later encouraged the scientist, first of the Renaissance, but especially of the seventeenth century, to carry on his work.

John attempts to be practical-theoretical as well as mystical. He briefly describes *tonoi* or modes. In looking for a unity in the composition or in the use of modes, he says that the end of every movement is in its beginning (*Div. nat.* 5, *PL* 122.866). Astronomy describes the movements of the heavenly bodies in their constant returnings: music begins with a tone and ends with it; it sets consonances in motion and eventually returns to the tone again; thus the very power and potency of music is derived from its beginning (*Div. nat.* 5, *PL* 122.869). In short, the unity of music is brought about by the tying together, by a kind of coalescing, of beginning and end.

He also describes organum (*Div. nat.* 5, *PL* 122.965), which conjec- turally he feels may have derived its name from the organ, and thus provides documentation for the beginning development of a practice that will lead to counterpoint or polyphony. The sweetness and sonorous beauty of symphony (concordance) is also present, he thinks, where it compares with the inexpressible beauty of the universe (*Div. nat.* 3, *PL* 122.638). He describes it as singing of verses of different kinds and ranges, separated by wide intervals or sounding in well-measured ratios, but alternately dividing and coming together in conformity with one of the modes and producing a natural and agreeable symphony. He seems to be giving a broader meaning to the word 'symphony' than was usual, and he obviously accepts what seems to us a simple counterpoint (note-against-note) which may have become common practice. John was probably the first philosopher to speak of such practice with praise, and only in the *Musica Enchiriadis* (usually dated some years later) was it clearly under discussion.

The beauty and sweetness of organum, he thinks, represents aesthetic beauty. He contrasts practical beauty with practical interests. A vase may serve as an example. Regarded as beautiful, it pleases the corrupt man, who wants to possess it at the same time that he feels aesthetic pleasure, yet it also pleases the virtuous man, who is not motivated by a drive or by egotistical passion, but who sees it as a reflection of Infinite Beauty (*Div. nat.* 4, *PL* 122.838). The sweetness of polyphony therefore reflects universal or Infinite Beauty, and it appeals for different reasons to sinful and virtuous men alike. In essence, however, it attracts the virtuous. John has described the contrast between autonomous and dependent beauty as St. Thomas Aquinas and Immanuel Kant were to describe it much later.

His approach rests on an insistent desire to know and grasp the universe of music whose structure is objective and formal; all men in their subjectivity struggle to know the essence of the universe of which music is an organic part. And in his effort to define a total picture and comprehend a universal totality, Erigena proves his right to the label of 'scholastic philosopher.'[9]

IV

Music Instruction Books of the Ninth and Tenth Centuries. Ostensibly following the example of Aristotle's *Poetics* and *Rhetoric*, which, however, were then no longer known in their entirety, a new kind of instructional manual appeared for technical specialists in singing. These were "how-to" reference books reminiscent of the design of Dionysius of Halicarnassus' *On Literary Composition*, Cicero and Quintilian on oratory, or Vitruvius on architecture, all of whom had divided their work according to subject matter, form, and technique. The most exact model, however, was grammar, the art of speaking correctly, which had been treated by Donatus (c.350 A.D.), Diomedes (late fourth century A.D.), and Priscian (c.500 A.D.), who had laid down rules and definitions and in addition had listed and described parts of speech, syllables, letters, and verse-feet. The approach was businesslike, mechanical, and in general not particularly conducive to aesthetic analysis or conjecture. Books on music theory, treatises or tracts written in the early Middle Ages, will often belong to the same type and have similar purposes. And the questions which they try to answer are: What is the aim of music? What are its ontological sources? What are its structural and compositional characteristics? And what are its effects?

From the ninth to the fourteenth century documents concerning music fall into two types. The first concerns itself with chant and organum and their connections with grammar and rhetoric; the second, appearing in the thirteenth and fourteenth centuries, concerns itself with polyphony and the problems it raises regarding time-values or duration.[10] The interests which had appeared in the Carolingian period thus fully emerged in this new and more technically oriented kind of writing, which was designed to serve an educational function, in this case for the edification of future singing masters or singing men who would be employed in the Church. Sometimes addressed to a ruling abbot or nobleman, each work was indirectly aimed at pupils in monastic, cathedral, or convent schools, which during the ninth to eleventh centuries were located at such centers as Fleury, Corbie, and Ferrières in the West, and Fulda, Reichenau, Trier, and St. Gall in the East. Sometimes too these works were addressed to more mature students of the Liberal Arts.

Dealing with chant, though with side-glances at organum, the instruction book was at first devoted to aspects of the liturgy and accompanying monodic singing--the antiphon, responsory, psalmody, sequences, tropes, and parts of the Office as well as the Ordinary and Propers of the Mass. These works sometimes introduced, in various stages of development, a tonary, a compilation or catalogue listing the ecclesiastical modes of antiphons, responsories, and other vocal items used in the Church, including the elaborate wordless *jubilus*. Outstanding among these anonymous tracts was the *Commentario brevis de tonis et psalmis modulandis* (G 1.213-29), in which is found the tetrachordal NOEANE system of notation. Basic in these works were melodies and their pitches explained in terms of a larger system of tones and rhythms--explanations which sometimes included aesthetic observations. Written in a time of considerable flux with regard to practice, these treatises were attempts to codify the liturgical and musical practice supposedly established in its perfection by Gregory the Great by the beginning of the seventh century.[11]

They were part of a process of slow induction whose aim was the improvement of vocal music in the Church and its uniform use throughout Western Christendom. The book of this type was not an instructor in harmony but in *harmonics*, as the Greeks had used that term. It said nothing about the techniques of voice production, a science no doubt governed by the taste of the cantor or master. The first body of such writing in the Western world based upon a music by which it could be tested and which it could test, the medieval instruction book, coming first at a time when music surpassed the other arts in clerical approval, reveals a quiet rejection or avoidance of the quadrivial approach to music in favor of one ostensibly modelled on, at least related to, grammar (in elementary education) and rhetoric (in secondary education), which had served as the usual staples of education among the Greeks, the Hellenistic thinkers, and the Romans.

Who was it that attempted in short works to codify early medieval church music? Remembered, in contrast to those whose works are no doubt lost, are the following:

1. Aurelian of Réôme (Aurelianus Reomensis), a French monk and scholar of the middle of the ninth century, seems almost the prototype of the music theorist of the following five hundred years in that his observations on music are surrounded by literary traditions. He easily proves, however, to be a transitional figure. Largely and unadmittedly based on Boethius, Bede, Cassiodorus, and Isidore, his *Discipline of Music* (*Musica disciplina*) is addressed to Abbot Bernard of St. Jean de Réôme, whom he calls an "archsinger" of the entire holy Church. His subject, nevertheless, is current church music, especially antiphonal chanting, and its proper treatment.

2. Rémi of Auxerre (Remigius Autissiodorensis (d. 908), a pupil of John Scot Erigena, wrote innumerable commentaries, including one on the *Timaeus*, and a treatise on liturgical ceremonies. He thought the Liberal Arts had been devised by the Egyptians and transmitted to Greece. Whereas John had regarded them to be perfect and ideal emanations from the mind of God, Rémi seems to ask for a concrete art which derives from the soul of the artist who observes the world about him. Into the arcana of God-created, pre-established harmony, he thinks, man has no insight. Thus he looks forward to Nicholas of Cusa. A dialectician in various French schools of his day, he wrote a commentary on Martianus Capella which includes a treatment of the musical section (Book 9) of the *Marriage of Philology and Mercury and the Seven Liberal Arts*. He probably wrote not for musicians but for pursuers of the Liberal Arts. Most interesting in his work is his theory of rhythm.

3. Regino of Prüm, a German monk, was abbot of Prüm (892-99) and thereafter of St. Martin's at Trier until his death in 915. Best known as chronicler (his *Chronicron* is a history of the world from the beginning of the Christian era to 906), he also wrote a treatise on church jurisprudence and an *Epistola de harmonica institutione* (c.901) addressed to his superior, Archbishop Radbod of Trier. His purpose was to correct the intonations of improperly sung responsories, antiphons, and other forms. He also prepared one of the first *tonaria*[12] to appear in the West. In his *Epistola,* he mentions Pythagoras and Philolaus and relies on (and sometimes literally quotes) Martianus Capella, Virgil, Horace, Cicero, Cassiodorus, Macrobius, Chalcidius, Aurelian, and Rémi. In his work Boethian abstractions and the Cassiodorian devotion to sung poetry are replaced by a devotion to sound (intonation) itself.

4. Hucbald (c.840-930), a monk of St. Armand (near Tournai in Belgium), a fellow student and colleague of Rémi and a composer and theorist, is credited with several writings, including an *Alia musica* (tenth century), a composite work applying unfortunately incorrect attributions of Greek modal names to the authentic and plagal church modes classified in the *Musica* formerly attributed to Alcuin. Also claimed for him were the *Musica enchiriadis*[13] and the *Scolica enchiriadis* (see Sec. 5, below), which were not his work at all. However, he did write *On Harmonic Instruction* (*De harmonica institutione*), a theoretical and practical manual about chant with some attention also to organum. This work probably recorded an early

step in the direction of polyphony. His model has sometimes been thought to have been Boethius, from whom he takes certain Greek concepts of music, but his subject is mainly plainsong and clear directions for singing it--a subject which is foreign to Boethius' purposes. Hucbald also had read Martianus Capella and Chalcidius and must have had a share in Rémi's immense learning based on Italian authors, and like Notker Balbulus (c.840-912), the Old High German theorist and composer, he was a poet.

5. An unknown author is represented by a group of manuscripts entitled the *Musica enchiriadis* (*Music Handbook*) and the *Scolica enchiriadis*, a question-and-answer catechism of principles. Both stem from the ninth or early tenth century. Like the work of Aurelian of Réôme, they recognize the rationality of the Pythagorean-mathematical systems but turn toward musical theory based on plainsong practice.

6. A widely-distributed *Dialogus de musica*, or *Enchiridion musices*, of the tenth century was formerly attributed to Odo of Cluny (d. 942), who probably had been a pupil of Rémi of Auxerre and a canon, choir singer, hymn writer, and, later, abbot. Nor was this work produced by another Odo, an Abbot Odo of Arezzo in Italy who was the author of a treatise on music and a tonary. The attribution to "Odo" was continued by the eighteenth-century editor Gerbert. The *Dialogus*, which is in the form of a catechism, contains a very early use of letter-names for scale-pitches of two octaves, including the letter G as the lowest.

All of these writings on music were presumably produced by men associated with the Church. It is certain that none was from Rome, and indeed all appear to have been Northerners. This is hardly surprising, for political power too had retained its northern shift after Charlemagne. Otto I (the Great) (912-73) and his predecessors, Conrad and Henry I (the Fowler), who was Otto's father, were kings of Germany and Holy Roman Emperors; all saw their domains as surrogate Roman Empires whose Church and its art glorified the Almighty. For them and for the theorists who wrote in their day, the Emperor's power was a Christian power, and the Emperor, like Constantine or even the biblical King David, was a guide to Christendom, the world which belonged to God and in which music, through the liturgy of the Church, played a major role.

V

Natural and Instrumental Music. For the structure of the world, God's creation, in essence determined what music is to be. As we know, the ancient harmony of the spheres was supplemented and supplanted by the Pseudo-Dionysian idea of the harmony of (the Christian) God's creation. Aurelian (pp. 9-10), following Boethius, names the three musics (1) of the universe, (2) of humanity (the microcosmic world which is an adaptation of incorporeal reason to the body, of the rational to the irrational, of the sun-derived soul to the moon-derived body, parallel with that of the universe), and (3) of instruments (voice and man-made instruments creating sounds in their proper proportions). But this reference only introduces a more genuine harmony--the divine music of God's universe.

Both Aurelian and Regino are eloquent in celebration of universal harmony. Aurelian indulges in a characteristic medieval enthusiasm, introduced by Cassiodorus, for the natural wonders of the world. Pure air, flowers, the calmness of the seas all occur as the sun rises higher, and all illustrate universally interrelated and integrated harmony, a harmony found also in man's throat, which is a pipe for singing, and in his chest, which is a kind of harp adorned with strings--that is, having fibers in his lungs--with pulses that beat, and with fluctuating "ascents and descents." Music reflects the wisdom of God, whom all creation would extol (pp. 7, 56): thus the ancients like Solomon had choirs because it is a disgrace not to know music. Proportion is the essential principle: the harmonies of spheres, the seasons, and the strings of the cithara whose harmonic limits are restricted by its lowest and highest strings--all are proportional. What is disproportionate? All Christian men agree with the heathen that disproportion is evident when an inadequate heat from the sun causes water to harden into stones (ice) and when clouds driven by the wind thunder upon the earth (p. 10). Disproportion is discomfort, ugliness, a denial of harmonic beauty.

For Regino (G 1.230ff), universal harmony remains embodied in motion and sound, the two elements which since time immemorial have been part of sublunary music. Because he relies on Boethius, Cicero, and Martianus, he repeats traditional observations: there is music, as the Pythagoreans had said (G 1.239), in the motions of the heavens; some of these are faster, some slower than others. The faster ones produce higher sounds and the slower ones lower sounds because they move according to certain ratios. Now, the consonance on which all measurement of music is based cannot derive from sound itself. Why? Regino cites astrologers and musicians who say that all musical consonances fall between the highest sphere and the circles of the planets, the earth being the lowest point from which consonances can arise. Martianus Capella likened this system to the musical tree of Apollo, where harmony is the united grouping of different voices. Very nearly agreeing with John Scot Erigena that music is a formal art yet a natural one, he finds its characteristics in the relationships of tone, not in the tones themselves. The ratios are there in either natural or artificial music.

For Regino, too, music is either natural or artificial. The first is produced not by a musical instrument or by human activity or touch, but by divine inspiration as exemplified by nature in the motions of the heavens, of the spheres, of the human voice (G 1.233). Natural sounds result from movement, either the rapid ones of the stars in outer space or of the air in the hollows of the throat. The elements of musical organization too are natural: from God come the four source-tones (modes) of natural music (*musica naturalis*) and from them derive the other (plagal) four--in all, eight natural tones. Natural music offers a beautiful variety of harmonic delight in a mixture of high and low like a sprinkling of flowers, and it gives loud and fitting sweetness to melody (G 1.232). To grasp natural music, the music of God in its true power, however, one must study artificial music. Natural music is superior to artificial, but it is beyond our grasp because invisible things can be proved only through visible (or symbolic) ones (G 1.236). It can nevertheless be recognized on earth in a song in praise of God, praise which must be founded on the eight tones (modes) of five whole-steps and two half-steps--or in an *alleluia*, which is above and beyond the artificiality of earthly things. For Pseudo-Dionysius, John Scot Erigena, and Regino of Prüm, the sensible in which man participates and which he must manipulate leads directly to the knowledge of the harmony of the natural world of God, to *musica celestis* (G 1.233-34).

It was an ancient truism that the human voice is superior to instruments; thus for Regino it is a superior avenue to God, who created it. Song is natural music made up of natural sounds; artificial sounds are those made by instruments fabricated or invented by men (G 1.236). Artistic (artificial) music is invented through art (craft); its instruments are of three types: tensible, inflatable, and percussive (named by Cassiodorus). There is also another kind of music, that which is made by irrational creatures. Both the vocal-natural and the instrumental-manual (or artificial) artistically follow the laws of divinely established objective harmony. For music blindly made by natural objects like stars, wind, birds, and so forth is not artistic, nor can it reveal the nature of God. But human intelligence even with its artifices can bridge the gap between nature and God. It is intelligence that counts. The natural laws are objective, unchangeable, and divine; those of artificial music are subjective, variable, and human; and the human mind brings the two together in Christian song, which is a kind of natural music, a religious song which is grounded in the nature of divinity itself.

VI

Numbers and Numerology. One of the invariables of the cosmos was thought (as we have seen) to be sound in movement governed by number. It had been so from Pythagoras through St. Augustine to Boethius. Number has a hidden power, and arithmology was its evident science. Following Cassiodorus, Isidore, and the *Musica* attributed to Alcuin, Aurelian in a mixture of pagan and biblical reference repeats numerological legends. The eight modes seem to imitate celestial motions (p. 21). The zodiac (also called *aplanes*), a high circle in the sky, is a standard-bearer; it does not wander, but moves in straight lines to the right, from east to west. Its whole course is finished in twenty-four hours--that is, in twice twelve. Under this circle there are planets (wanderers) moving to the left, toward the east. But the planets complete their courses in different time-periods: Saturn in thirty years, Jupiter in twelve, Mars in two, the sun in one, Mercury in 329 days, and Venus in 348 days. These motions are eight (seven of the planets and one of the zodiac), and they make the sweetest harmony of song, consonance or the harmony of heaven, which the Lord declared to Job (p. 22).

Regino also gives his own version, coming from Pythagorean astrology by way of Martianus Capella, of the spheres of the nine Muses as they represent the nine heavenly orbits (those of the seven planets, the heavens, and the earth). Urania represents the spheres of heaven, Polyhymnia that of Saturn, Euterpe that of Jupiter, and so forth (G 1.245). Between the outer spheres and the circles of the planets are found all of the musical consonances (G 1.234). And from the universe of things symbolized by the planets and the Muses comes earthly music.

Indeed, number is the basis even of the aesthetic effect of music. Regino uses the almost ubiquitous word "sweet" (*suavitas*) for melodies (G 1.233), and though the sensuous impression here seems to be of prime importance, his remark is consistent with Erigenian thought in that the aesthetics of sensation corresponds with that of numbers of an ideal order. The author of the *Scolica enchiriadis*, quoting from St. Augustine (*Divine Providence* 2.14-15, FC 1.316-18), is also impelled to attribute aesthetic effect to number. For him, too, sweetness of melody is produced by fixed relations, and number is indeed the source of everything pleasant in rhythm whether of movements or of melodies. This is so because sounds (as St. Augustine had said) disappear quickly while numbers remain--both outside the mind and in it. Without numbers nothing can be understood. Knowing the numbers 3 and 4, we can know what triangles and quadrangles are. And the "equal sounding" of the octave, fourth, and fifth (in symphonies of the "sweet agreement of different sounds joined together") gives evidence that arithmetic is absolutely necessary to an understanding of music. It is the "proportioned dimensions of sounds" which serve as the musician's proper pursuit. Such a pursuit results in symphony and harmony and is governed by the same principle that regulates the concord of voices and the nature of mortal beings themselves (*Musica enchiriadis*, p. 31). The delight, the symphony, and the harmony are only evidences of the presence of numbers as treated by mathematics. The numbers lose their importance (are not so easily noticed) only through the physical materiality of tones and movements, but they remain present behind the proper arrangement of musical sounds.

Aurelian (pp. 8-9) shares with the entire ancient and medieval arithmological world an enchantment with the number 4. There were the Pythagorean four blacksmiths, four hammers providing the four intervals of the octave, fourth, fifth, and second, the four primary intervals of the tetrachord, four authentic and four plagal modes (4 x 2). If Aurelian is otherwise skeptical of the number theory, one can only guess so from his assertion that "they say" that this order is a harmony (as Nicomachus taught) of numbers stable and abstract in arithmetic, stable and pertaining to forms in geometry, mobile and always pertaining to forms in astronomy, and equally abstract in music, yet mobile and in proportion (p. 23). Philosophy has three parts: physics, ethics, and logic, called, in Latin, natural, moral, and rational. All are arts of number, of which the whole theory of music consists (p. 22).

While certain principles of Pythagoreanism--number and proportion--could have been given for music and letters in Platonic terms (*Sophist* 253), medieval theorists, concerned primarily with describing preferred musical practice, were nevertheless less concerned with mathematical theory--so that the *Dialogus* formerly attributed to Odo failed to mention it at all, while later writers accept it without stressing it. Quadrivial music, however, when it was mentioned, easily took on mystical accretions.

VII

Liturgical Chant and the Art of Singing Well. A piece of sculpture, or a cathedral, or a painting is usually more easily and quickly grasped--even if more superficially--than a piece of music. Each is more easily recorded in the mind because the sense of sight is more facile, moves and comprehends more rapidly, and achieves its sensuous imprint more incisively than the sense of hearing. Memory, in complicated ways necessary to all the arts, is especially complex in its function with respect to grasping music at all. The present-day listener, even if his experience with medieval music has been extensive (perhaps being grounded in actual liturgical experience as a singer), must have a special kind of aural memory, both analytical and composite, to hold in mind what the music is, and he almost needs to see in visual terms the abstract forms of sound with which he is confronted. Performing or listening to medieval music, he must be able to ignore or "forget" music that has intervened. Plainchant, performed in the way it was presented a thousand years ago, is also quite foreign to modern experience. Ninth- and tenth-century texts already describe many of the basic elements of this art form. Nevertheless, in these early chants the very pitches themselves are in question; even more, the performance practice utilized tuning systems and rhythms and even pronunciation of the Latin that set early chant off from what passes as Gregorian chant today in the churches. In addition to tonal memory, the person who sings or hears chant which attempts to approximate the practice of this early period must have a feeling for the historical changes which have taken place and a respect for the ways in which music was performed in the past insofar as it can be reconstructed.

In the view of the writers on music under discussion here, this music is a sublunar type whose origins extend back indefinitely, and often its origins are confused with its supposed first practitioners. According to Aurelian, music took its name from the Muses, those daughters of Jupiter who served the art of memory, an art necessary to man if he is to keep musical motion in mind.

For the ancient legendary men of music like Apollo, Orpheus, and Amphion or any other minor Greek god who supposedly began practical music in performance, medieval writers substituted Jubal, who (according to *Genesis* 4.21) invented the harp and the organ. Through calligraphic error

Jubal was mistakenly replaced often with Tubal or Tubalcain, who produced weapons (*Gen.* 10.2, 4.22). Like the Church Fathers earlier, Aurelian added the psalmist, King David, to his list.

In a more immediate sense, of course, Pythagoras remains the discoverer of music and its founder as an abstract science. He had overheard the blacksmiths' hammers which supposedly established the permanent, perfect intervals; and though the legend was confirmed by Nicomachus, who was regarded as an authority, Aurelian calls on both Euclid and Ptolemy for scientific support. He also continues the tradition of giving the weights of 6, 8, 9, and 12 to the hammers for further use in the defining of permanent, universal intervals (pp. 7-8) and proportions, which are the basis of the placing of music among the mathematical sciences of the quadrivium.

But now the Pythagorean explanation of music as number, no matter how frequently it is apostrophized, can legitimately be replaced by the Augustinian notion that music is the art of singing well through the correct controlling (regulating) of modulation and mensuration ("controlling variations of sound") (Aurelian, p. 7; "Odo," in Strunk, p. 111). Furthermore, it is related specifically to rhetoric, as Augustine in his own *On Music* in part had assumed, and is a possible parallel to rhetoric itself, called by Quintilian (2.17.37) the art, or the science, of speaking well. The arts of production--the trivium--take over, and in music theory, for practical purposes, Latin rather than Greek supplies the basic sources.

VIII

The Intervals. Singing well is like speaking well, and both are based on relations. The single tone is only a cipher for acoustical-grammatical study, but it is a first step in the art of music. As sounds symbolized by letters must be combined to form syllables, words, and sentences, so a single tone must be combined with another tone in a metaphorical space to create an interval, the first step in the realization of music. The number of intervals in nature is infinite, but it is the recognition by man of tones according to numbers, a selection conforming with his inner nature, which establishes terrestrial music.

The result is that the interval is the very backbone of musical form. The ancients stress it, and so do medieval theorists. Both give first place to perfect consonances, and both extend them from one octave to two (the Perfect System). About the perfect intervals there is agreement, but not about the others.

Hucbald describes nine intervals: the "minor" second (semitone), the second (the whole tone), the minor third, the major third, the perfect fourth, the tritone (augmented fourth), the perfect fifth, the minor sixth, and the major sixth. These are the only rational intervals, he thinks, larger ones being both irrational and impracticable for the voice (even the major sixth is hard to perform) (p. 16). Not all are consonances, of course. Musical consonances are musical wholes such as are produced when men and boys sing at the same time. This is the simultaneous singing and thus blending of two sounds in a concordant effect. Of the nine intervals, only two are consonances, the perfect fourth and the perfect fifth, whereas the octave is probably not a consonance because it is not made up of different tones but rather of the same tone sung by men and boys (p. 19). This last opinion is in sharp contrast to other views, theories, and purposes that identify the octave as complete, perfect, and symbolic of the entire world.

This, according to the *Musica enchiriadis*, is because the largest symphony is an octave, which contains a consonance more perfect than the other consonances. Singing in octaves proceeds as though there were an infinity of sounds, each reborn at the octave, which is "the first, the primal, consonance." The octave is a fresh start, the whole series being in the seven of the different strings. The symphony of the diapason "preserves the consonance" (p. 17). The octave, then, assumes a transcendental importance in medieval music theory, and one would suppose that the double octave (double diapason), which Hucbald (p. 34), following Boethius and Martianus Capella, pursues with some ardor, would be of double importance. But it turns out not to be, although it is used to enclose an order of tetrachords in composition.

Hucbald tells us that almost all intervals used in medieval music were small and that the effect was one of rising and falling in a restricted musical space. Compositions were kept to a narrow range. Even unusual extensions of range were confined to the smaller intervals, as in the *Dialogus* where the intervals for both chant and organum are limited to six (Strunk, p. 109): the semitone, the whole tone, the tone and a semitone (minor third), two tones (major third), the fourth, and the fifth. There are no other "regular conjunctions of sounds" (and thus sixths or the seventh are not included). There are three consonants, of course: the fourth, the fifth, and the octave or diapason (meaning "of All") (Strunk, pp. 108-09), the staples and elements of musical motion and form.

These elements must be kept under control, however, and thus certain quantities serviceable for the making of melodies must be subject to rule. Whatever is sung must keep a proper course, and anything non-rational must be excluded. According to Hucbald, as words are communicated through speaking, "so sounds enter[ing] the mind by means of . . . phthongi" or sound "elements" are suitable for song and for "maintaining a steady pitch." They are exemplified by the vowel sounds the voice produces or by sounds "in unison with a stretched string" (pp. 20-21). They are organized in ladder form, from lowest to highest, and *vice versa*, each being a proper distance from the others (but none identical with another). And they are arranged according to the system of intervals already described. There appears to be one exception: the semitones are themselves not always equal (a problem which Aristoxenus and Plato already had mentioned). They may be either more or less than one-half of a tone, as can be illustrated on the six-string cithara and the water organ (p. 22).

Since it is the relationships of tones which are important, the tones themselves ideally must be precisely determined. As far back as the time of the Greeks, there was an instrument which scientifically had set the pitches of the tones in their permanent relations. This was the monochord (or sometimes the Ptolemaic helicon). It was tuned according to the rational mathematical system of intervals, and it was thought to be the physical representative of universal harmony and thus infallible as an instrument and guide. The series of seven tones which it establishes (the octave, the eighth, was often thought identical with the first) is sometimes symbolically likened to the Virgilian Orpheus and his seven-string lyre (*Aeneid* 6.646), as in the *Musica enchiriadis* (p. 17) and as had been the case in the *Etymologies* of Isidore of Seville.

The monochord was the favorite device for tuning up to and following Ugolino of Orvietto (fourteenth and fifteenth centuries). It systematized pitches and provided a standard against which purely vocal music could be checked.   According to the *Scolica enchiriadis*, mistakes in pitch are defined as flatness and sharpness, as unpleasant qualities, and as a destruction of the true character of the tone or of the whole piece (this cannot occur in musical instruments because each tone keeps its pitch once it is tuned) (G 1.173-74). Following the ancient and medieval convention, the author of the *Dialogus* formerly attributed to "Odo" goes a step further by claiming the string of the monochord to be of more use than the voice in the learning of singing, because the string is divided (that is, tuned) by the art (craft) of learned men--that is, not by the mere practical performer--so that, "If it is diligently observed or considered, it cannot mislead"--and "it never deceives" (G 1.2525-53, Strunk, p. 105). The monochord indeed was a guide not only for the cantor and singers, but also for the non-practicing judge (or critic) who used it in passing his opinion about the music as constituted and performed.

The monochord was also the path to judging the correct qualities of intervals. Quality is a concept superior to quantity. Yet they are both coordinates. Basic number and measure seem foreign to quality: rather, they are another example of the reality behind the sensuous effects of objects; they are reason supporting sense. Intervals can be "expressed" quantitatively, but their "givenness" to sense, their actuality, is qualitative. Quantities appear mentally or "spiritually" real as givens of the order of things of the unsensed world. The numbers 1, 2, 3, 4, and so forth are used in physics and acoustics--and also in music theory as it is practiced. This application of number to music is a serious concern of the binding kind. In the Middle Ages, people were widely held to have an inner calculator which instinctively makes music and responds to it. But the most important aspect of music is its embracing of quantity.

IX

The Modes and Tetrachords. It was agreed that there are eight modes (or "tones"), four authentic (greater) and four plagal (lesser), made up of tetrachords. Every Gregorian melody was assigned to one of these modes. Named in the Carolingian *Musica* formerly attributed to Alcuin and probably derived from the Byzantine *octoechos*, they are given in more detail by Aurelian (pp. 20-24), who initiated the practice of supplying examples from the chanting in the Roman Church of psalm-verse and antiphonal singing. He (p. 24) reported that Charlemagne (Alcuin?) felt the need for enlarging the number of the original four church modes to eight. They were enough: "Pass not beyond the ancient bounds that your fathers have set for you," cried Aurelian (p. 24), following *Proverbs* 22.28. Only in the tenth century, in the anonymous *Alia musica* (G 1.125-52), were modes (or tones) interpreted as octave scales. In Aurelian as in the Carolingian *Musica* and possibly in an intervening tonary now lost, the term 'mode' (manner or way: an abstract organization of pitches) may have meant a melodic formula (like a *nomos*), varieties of formula, or an organization of tones in terms of successive pitches appropriate to the rhythmical scheme of the words they accompanied. (The rhythmic system could be prosaic or "loose," or it could be metrical, arbitrary, or rigid.) The melodic mode was the first step toward a guarantee that the composition would have a unity.

The modal system was far more complicated than our major-minor system. The plan[14] looks like this:

The Ambitus (octave range)

protus (1) {	first authentic	[D] E F G (a) b c d
	first plagal	A B D [D] E [F] G a
deuterus (2) {	second authentic	[E] F G a b (c) d e
	second plagal	B C D [E] F G (a) b
tritus (3) {	third authentic	[F] G a b (c) d e f
	third plagal	C D E [F] G (a) b c
tetrardus (4) {	fourth authentic	[G] a b c (d) e f g
	fourth plagal	D E F [G] a b (c) d

The bracketed letters represent the finals (or last notes) of each mode which, as it is sung, declare the mode. The letters in parentheses represent the notes in each mode on which words are chanted or recited by the tenor (*tuba*). The tone for changing in each mode is the reciting note or tenor (*tenere* = to hold). They all are "dominants," but not in the modern sense. Each pair of modes, one authentic and one plagal, ends on the same final. Thus for the Dorian or first authentic and first plagal:

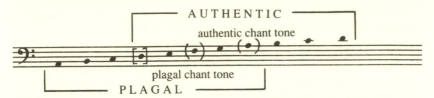

Of the first qualitative importance in these modes is the position of the semitone. According to the *Scolica*, each mode gets its quality from the position of the semitone, the species of tetrachord (four strings) and pentachord (five strings) used, and the internal relations of chants. Aristoxenus' dictum has become a commonplace: the semitone is the heart and soul of the melody (G 1.210-11). Thus in the first authentic it appears between steps 2 and 3, in the second authentic between 1 and 2, in the third authentic between 4 and 5, and in the fourth between 3 and 4.

FORMULAE AS TETRACHORDS

T S T	S T T	T T T	T T S

Dorian
(Gk. Phrygian)

Phrygian
(Gk. Dorian)

Lydian

Mixolydian
(Gk. Lydian)

T = whole tone
S = semitone

FORMULAE AS PENTACHORDS

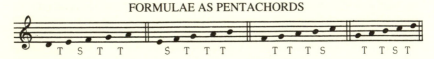

T S T T	S T T T	T T T S	T T S T

It must be remembered that the above are melodic formulae, not scales. They are abstract octave species. The scales and their steps (and also the resulting 'harmony,' in the modern sense of the term) have no place here. Also, it must be remembered that these intervals are created by successive, not simultaneous pitches. Usually the fifth above the final in the authentic (though the sixth in the Phrygian), it was a third below that of the final in the plagal (thus the first plagal chanting tone is f).

How do authentic and plagal modes proceed? The *Dialogus* formerly attributed to "Odo" answers quite simply that the high (*acute*) melodies are sung in authentic modes and the low (*grave*) ones in the plagal modes.

Each mode, it will be seen, includes a pentachord (inexplicably mentioned, as one recalls, by Martianus Capella) (in the first authentic: d e f g a) and a tetrachord (a b c d). Of these, the tetrachord, the more important, was organized into a system. In the system recommended by the *Musica enchiriadis* (and by Hucbald) there is a series of four groups of four descending tetrachords, each of which has a semitone at its center (tone, semitone, tone) (p. 3). They are called, from low to high: *graves, finales, superiores,* and *excellentes* (deep, finals, high, highest). In the *Scolica* (G 1.177-78) they are synaesthetically likened to red, green, yellow, and black. They form a double octave and are measured on the monochord. I present a diagram which includes a different version of the system by Hermanus Contractus (eleventh century):[15]

Hermanus Contractus:

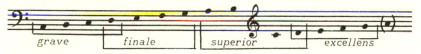

Musica enchiriadis:

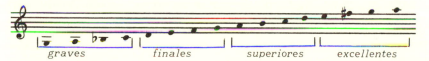

So as to retain the order of tone, semitone, tone, it will be noted tht Hermannus overlaps tetrachords, as the *Musica enchiriadis*, which employs accidentals, does not.

It was through the recognition of the mode[16] that one could establish the unity of the piece. From where could this recognition come? A few theorists said that the beginning establishes the mode. This was supposedly the view of the author of the *Musica* attributed to Alcuin. But Aurelian insists (p. 28) that the specific mode must not be anticipated except where "the ends of the verses are inserted" and where not the melody but the sense of the text must be kept. This is especially true in offertories, responsories, and invitatories, where the last note must suffice. In introits, antiphons, and communions, however, it should be found at the beginning. Regino agrees almost verbatim (G 1.231). The *Dialogus* formerly attributed to "Odo" indicates that the last note determines the mode, and that the beginnings and endings of phrases (*distinctiones*) must conform with it (Strunk, p. 113).

The *Musica enchiriadis* (p. 10) simply maintains that authentic modes begin on their note in the tetrachord called *superiores* and end on the *finales*, whereas the plagal modes begin and end on the *finales* and seldom reach the *superiores*.

Such, in brief outline, is the apparent system of modes with their basic tetrachords. They were designs made after the fact, like most rules in art. They were different from the modes described by Boethius, transpositional (after Cleonides), apparently "Greek" even in his day, and academic. Probably derived from a lost book of Nicomachus, they have an interest purely abstract. Described by Calvin Bower,[17] they have only a tentative, if any, relation to the medieval modes. But the medieval modes were the basis of actual music--the basis as they were employed of the music which the Church Fathers at different times described and judged, sometimes in aesthetic terms, sometimes only in literary or theological-symbolical ones.[18] The modes are the working tools of compositional forms. Underlying musical formulae, for one example, they support the aesthetic, literary, rhetorical, and religious modes of order and thought endemic to the music of the medieval Church.

It is important to see that what is under discussion is not anything approaching a modern view of the unified work of art, but rather a combining, a meshing, in the instance of psalmody a series of concatenations of psalm sung by a soloist or responsorial singer or by a soloist and choir antiphonally. The example of the psalm is particularly useful, since the psalms served, as it were, as the backbone of the Mass and especially the Office, and the binding involved in the singing of the psalms was the antiphon, which might as in the case of the introit serve as introduction, linkage, and conclusion, resolving differences by the maintaining of the tetrachord. The recognition of the mode or tetrachord, then, was a plea for consistency, psalm and antiphon maintaining the same tetrachordal form. Thus the dogmatic assertion of the *Dialogus* formerly attributed to "Odo" indicates a practice still followed--that the end of the antiphon must correspond with the beginning of the psalm.

To be sure, more was expected of the cantor or chanting monk than recognizing the mode. He was pulled in two directions: toward liturgical and biblical texts, and toward music in itself. The first had a rational basis in the words, in the verbal organization with its various levels of punctuation; the second had a musical basis embodied in melismas which in both pitch and rhythm push for independence. The latter denies the sober text, moves toward rhapsodic and ecstatic musical expression in ornamental and elaborate passages which, it was thought, can express the praise of God, a plea for his mercy, the glories of his creation, and his promise of the soul's salvation. It ignores all linguistic punctuation, and its apparent irrationality made it the frequent object of censure; it obscured word-messages, it was senseless, meaningless, merely ornamental--indeed licentious--merely a medium for the singer's display of his technical virtuosity and therefore of himself. The possibilities of such display are perhaps most pronounced in the *alleluia*, as we have seen for earlier periods; the melodies of this item continued to be composed and re-composed throughout the Middle Ages.

X

The Treatment of the Text: Music and Grammar. But the cantor was constantly being pulled back from the purely musical and turned toward the grammatical-rhetorical. His model had to be reading aloud, which after all seems to have provided one of the models for plainchant. Thus, probably, the reciting tone developed, and in any case music and language of necessity remained in a close parallel relation. Not literary-critical works like those of Aristotle, Horace, or Longinus but rather the rhetorical treatises of Priscian and the anonymous *Rhetorica ad Herennium* were the models for analysis of the internal order of sacred musical compositions.

Priscian had perhaps already been made use of much earlier by Isidore of Seville. In connection with the first authentic mode, Aurelian (pp. 46-47) employed familiar technical terms from grammar like *acutus*, *accentus*, *circumflexus*, and so forth. Possibly to indicate an embryonic form of notation, Rémi begins at the beginning; the note is the material beginning of music and functions like the point, the unity in arithmetic, and the letter. Though Rémi seems terminologically careless in equating the colon (a pause in the middle of a melody and its words) and the comma (the end of a song where the last note is the same as the first), he nevertheless uses these terms in a comparison of the voice in continuous conversation with its use in song (G 1.68).

Musical linguistics thus became a system in its own right. Inner connections bound the whole musical piece together, and inner punctuation conformed to the requirements of verbal meaning. Verbal text and music were a technical unity. The text, of course, was beyond criticism. The traditional psalms, the Office appointed for the day, the Mass itself, all were already "set" and had a certain permanency. The words were the already accepted ones, and the complete music was therefore music inextricably tied to the sacred *Logos*. The author of the *Musica* drew a parallel: letters randomly placed, so that "neither words nor syllables are joined properly together," are like the non-concordant joining of voices in music, and letters joined properly are like the concordance of disparate voices (p. 11). Thus the tetrachords themselves are technical units variously modified to fit the words as if they were parts of speech, or they are modulated according to their functions in the discourse.

The author of the *Dialogus* formerly attributed to "Odo," like most of these early theorists, thinks that the root of song is language. As in spoken languages, he says, two or more letters stand for a syllable or a single letter for a single syllable. So in music sometimes a single tone is sensed as an independent element of the melody, and sometimes a number of tones which are connected make up one consonance, a phenomenon well designated as a musical syllable (a neume). Here theory is derived from practice (and probably from Plato and Chalcidius): the parallel between music and grammar clearly means that the musical syllables are the ultimate characteristic members of an artistic melody-song securely held together in a unity of expressive meaning. If a complex of many syllables in language can produce a unified section of utterance that has independent meaning, then in music one or more "syllables" can produce larger melodic segments of different tonal sizes which, because we sense them as melodic and rhythmic entities--unified (indeed, often beginning and ending on the same tone), euphonious, and symmetrical--we can call *distinctiones*, that is, punctuations or, as Guido was to say, "a suitable place to breathe" (*Micrologus* 15), thus a pause. For the author of the *Dialogus* attributed to "Odo," this was a way of harmonizing beginnings and ends of phrases with the final tone (G 1.280).[19]

These segments--we would call them phrases and even motifs--become higher unities or segments of the song, whose limits are set by the linguistic expressions, and these expressions the voice of the singer follows exactly. The sense of the text comes to the fore whether a segment is made up of one or of several such phrases. The segments are not completely independent clauses (or phrases), but members of a statement which, like other sub-divisions, are held together in larger segments of the primary forms of sacred song, versicles, antiphons, responsories, and so forth. Even in larger forms, the "phrases," like the first representatives of an undivided section of meaning within a system, are recognizable as such (G 1.276). While the *Dialogus* keeps the dominance of the text in view, it allows for a purely musical organization. We follow all rules, the author says, only to the degree that we are not led to neglect the demands of beautiful sound, the highest law of the art of music (G 1.278).

Thus the musical line could be: (1) syllabic--one note for one syllable (though only occasionally a few more), (2) neumatic--several notes to one syllable: that is, elementary ornamentation, or (3) melismatic--a melisma, or long vocalise sung on a single syllable with added ornamentation (e.g., the *Alleluia* and the *jubilus*, especially mentioned by Augustine and others, and sung by the cantor). Furthermore, movement is usually step-by-step, though skips of a third are also common.

Punctuation is indicated through sound or pitch. Small units of sound (*syllaba*, later *neuma*) correspond to the verbal dipthong and are organized into smaller phrases (*comma, colon*) or larger ones (*periodus*) to make a complete sentence (*distinctio*). The punctuations, poetic caesuras, and longer subdivisions are indicated by departures from the reciting tone. Colons and commas, distinctions, and periods--all are separations of lengths depending on the text.

The linkage of rhetorical units to musical phrases is seen in the tones for readings, prayers, and psalmody, of which the latter may be used as an example to show how text and melodic formulas are joined. (The antiphon, a brief, freely composed melody in a compatible mode, preceding each verse of the psalm and following the last verse, is not germane to this discussion and therefore will not be treated here.) Each verse of the psalm proper is made up of two half verses. The first half is set to a beginning formula (*intonation*) leading to a reciting tone (*tenor*) which is reiterated for much of the text. Immediately before the point of punctuation there is a formula (called mediation or *mediant*) which in its descent or ascent, signals the half-close. A long and complicated half verse will also be subdivided by a flex, another small formula for the relief of the monotony of the long text, after which comes the return to the reciting tone. Following the half-close, the reciting tone or *tenor* is once again pursued until near the end of the verses, when the *termination* is invoked.

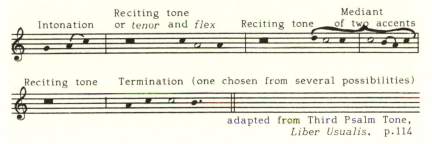

adapted from Third Psalm Tone,
Liber Usualis, p.114

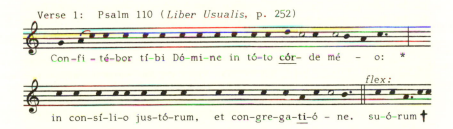

Clearly, plainchant composing was not self-consciously "creative." Types of melody, including musical formulae, were adapted to the texts of different types, to be contracted or expanded as the text or custom required. Designed initially to be memorized, types of melody could follow one another whenever necessity, mode, or formula decided. Amalarius of Metz, a pupil of Alcuin and a well-known writer on the liturgy, comments in his *De ecclesiasticus officiis* on the differences in the responsorial singing of the Franks and the Romans when they sang the sequences, the *Alleluia*, and the *jubilus*--geographical differences due to the historical break perceived between the Gallican and the newly imposed Roman liturgy. The selection of melodic types was thus a regional matter. But did the selection of melodic types also depend on the ethical effects expected? In ninth- and tenth-century music theory there is little mention of such effects or affects. If we are to believe the theorists, expression existed to gain the attention and favor of God, who was to be praised and implored for forgiveness of one's sins as well as for other favors, and not to alter the psychological state of the singer, soloist, chorus, or congregation. In the course of the liturgy, the Mass was felt to have an objective effect--to make the transcendent actually present among the worshippers--and to make past events such as the Passion and Resurrection present among the congregation. But the liturgy was never regarded as merely something which would make an audience feel better or achieve a modification of mood.

Following ancient social psychology and ethnography, Regino tries nevertheless to distinguish different modes according to the character of the people from whom they derive (G 1.235). Though Aurelian (p. 6) mentions the physician Asclepiades and health, the physical benefits of music have almost no place in this realm of thought, health--physical and mental--being instead the province of God and the Church (though not of its music). Hence, while ethical considerations are not entirely absent, insistence on a close and "programmed" attachment of mode to affect is lacking. Thus the *Musica enchiriadis*: the moods (peace, joy, sadness) of the text may be expressed well in different modes (pp. 31-32). And Rémi: melodies qualitatively have different pitches and therefore different expressive values, though the same melody can be played on the high, the medium, or the low strings of the cithara. Describing the psychological effects of melodies, he classifies them as *hypotoid* (tragic, the sounds being low), *netoid* (high and sharp), and *mesoid* (medium) (G 1.79). Again we meet with the ancient opinion that effect and affect are based on level of pitch. He makes it clear that in the time of Martianus Capella, the diatonic was preferred (G 1.75 and n. b), but when he says that modes came from Greek sources, he means the Byzantium of his own day.[20] Greek modal-affective rigidity had disappeared from medieval chant practice based on prose (however poetic) as well as on meter explored in hymns but not on the hexameter.

XI

The Rise of Organum. The apparent simplicity of these rules (and their exceptions are many) is complicated by the rise of organum or the writing of music of more than one voice, a practice which of necessity antedated the discussion of it in the *Musica* and *Scolica enchiriadis*. Its locale was the monastery church or cathedral, where it was likely to have involved considerable improvisation by the singers. The author of the *Musica* says that each step in a tetrachord has its own "status, different from the others" and that modes or tropes rise from the aesthetic principle of harmony in diversity (p. 20). Now there is a new kind of diversity in singing, hardly mentioned by Aurelian and Rémi, though Regino of Prüm

(G 1.237) defines consonance and dissonance so as to suggest contrapuntal or parallel movements of voice. Hucbald, who (along with the author of the *Musica enchiriadis*) speaks of "symphonic" singing, defines a new practice, that of diaphony--unison or uniform singing--"because [in the words of the *Musica*] it does not unvaryingly agree with the melody, but in [its] different harmony, it is more concordant" (p. 20). Diaphony is a departure from the preferred monodic regularity; it is organum or symphony, the singing of two voices together, not merely in octaves as men and boys do, but in parallel intervals of the fourth or the fifth--or sometimes with parallel doublings of these voices an octave below or above, so that the "symphonies" move within the greater perfect octave. Hucbald describes two types of organum, which may be called (1) the simple, or the parallel concordance in the fifth or the fourth of two voices, a *vox principalis* and a *vox organalis*, and (2) the composite or parallel concordance in parallel fifths and fourths of two voices doubled by one or two more voices. But there occurs something of a problem in the successive appearance of vertical intervals. Now there appear dissonances in addition to consonances as *symphonia*, dissonances in simultaneous (as well as successive) form, a structure resulting from the musical, not poetic impulse. An important correction must be made if consonances are to remain perfect. The offending dissonance is the tritone (*diabolis in musica*).

It was a rule that the tritone was to be avoided. The classical examples of this interval are from B-flat to e or from f to b. It is a diminished fifth, being a semitone less than the three and one-half tones which comprise the perfect fifth; or, by another way of reckoning, it is an augmented fourth, being a perfect fourth with a semitone added. The tritone, therefore, is an interval of three tones. Avoiding the tritone is possible if, for example, a pitch (usually of the f to b interval) is flatted a semitone or if the parallel motion of organum is interrupted by non-parallel movement. To the medieval mind, the tritone was a rational problem to be solved by rational solutions.

The demand that the tritone be avoided in successive simultaneous fourths has been said to contain the kernel from which came chromaticism and contrary motion in voice-leading: in the *Musica* it is shown that oblique motion can through the use of unisons, seconds, and thirds avoid the tritone (pp. 26-27).

Vox principalis

Vox organalis

Te hu - mi-les fa-mu- li mo - du-lis ve-ne-ran-di pi - is.

It is hard to see that the rule against the tritone can have been anything more than an intellectual matter. It surely cannot at first have been an aesthetic one. Organum itself was not in actuality as yet the new polyphony. It was a duplication of voices and supposedly not an addition of new melodic lines. It simply added ornamental enhancement to a more bare melody. It was based on rules as rigid as those for chant. But it was a first crack in a break away from rigid voice leading made necessary by abstract principles supposedly coordinates of universal truth.

It served as the ornamentation of ecclesiastical sounds, according to the *Musica* (p. 31). Regino defines it by contrasting *concentus*, or "the uniform fusion of the same melodies," with *accentus*, or "the best possible combination of different tones" (like the ancient practice of "magadizing," the fusion of men's and boys' voices in singing in octaves). More poetically, he again follows Martianus Capella in placing the echo of the high original melody (the *cantus firmus*) of the god Apollo's sacred groves at the tops of the trees while the lower branches echo the lower octave and the middle branches echo the divided middle tone of the fourth or the fifth (G 1.234). Using the Pythagorean division of the monochord, the medieval touchstone, Regino was allegorically describing organum.

Regino emphasizes the original melody but indicates the parallel importance of the accompanying voices. The leader takes first place even in the later polyphony of the thirteenth and fourteenth centuries which grew out of organum. The original melody dominates, and the accompanying voices play secondary roles, even though their contribution to the texture of the piece becomes more and more complicated. The *vox principalis* carries a clear statement of the thought or sentiment to be expressed, and the accompanying *vox organalis* becomes more and more complex and even, in new practice, undergoes improvisation. There could even be voice crossings, the *organalis* sometimes being as much as a fifth above the *principalis* when the latter was in a low register.

One must not interpret either plainchant or organum romantically. They are governed by the aesthetics of number, not of ethical states, moods, active or passive impulses. They *in general* do not foster word-painting of height or depth, though Schäfke suggests[21] that the text of the Mass can call up painterly results through certain mystical analogies: "qui venit" of the *Benedictus* may be sung by quickly moving voices; "cum Sancto Spiritu" of the *Gloria* can signify the three voices of the Trinity; "invisibilium" in the *Credo* may be represented by having a four-voice texture (the numerous *solidus*) reduced in number to express the defect of evident corporeality. Types of chant--formulaic devices remembered--could be and were applied to a variety of texts. Music, formulaic or free, had an aim: to allow the text to perform its function, and thus along with the words realize its own spiritual purpose. Its abstractness did indeed make it "timeless."

XII

Rhythm and the Unified Arts. The difficult problems of the nature and quality of tones, their relationships to one another, their larger organization into musical wholes, and the rational or aesthetic criteria which govern these matters at various points--these are problems intrinsic to an art which has liturgical and ecclesiastical purposes, and they belong to music *per se*. But music also has another characteristic or element which it shares metaphorically with certain other arts but in a real sense with prose and verse. I mean rhythm. In the early Middle Ages it was seen as the terrestrial concomitant of universal movement, not only as a mystical binding for everything, but also as a musical phenomenon equal with harmonics and metrics (in the Cassiodorian system). Rhythmics and metrics govern prose and verse, respectively. For metrics Aurelian turns to Nicomachus: "it takes its origin from [human] music, should . . . be separated from it [that is, is not a part of it], since it is applied to song not so much through reasoning and through the rationality of this art as through natural impulse." Metrics is a system of verses of various characteristics: the heroic, the elegiac, the sapphic, and so forth (p. 12). Rhythmics (as found in most Ambrosian hymns) is a "moulded [or sung, *modulata*] composition of words" analyzed by the number of syllables and seems similar to metrics but "is judged by the discrimination of the ears" (p. 11). Metrics (quantitative measurement by feet) is for verse or poetry, and rhythmics (without quantity but measurement by the number of syllables) is for chanted prose (or even for elevated and eloquent sermonizing oratory). Meter is instinctive, whereas rhythmics is rational, intellective, and based on words proper to music. Is the sound, in other words, appropriate to the words? Aurelian is defending plainchant through a classical distinction between rhythmics and metrics, prose and verse.

The theory of Rémi of Auxerre is more general than Aurelian's and yet more specific. He begins with the usual Cassiodorian triple division of harmony, rhythm, and meter. But for him harmony has nothing to do with the meanings of words or even with rhythm--that is, with longs and shorts or accents (as in ancient verse-practice). Truth and harmony are as one, and harmony would be impossible except for the law of numbers. Rhythm too is a special kind of number, but in this instance Rémi recalls Aristides Quintilianus and Augustine. Its kernel is duration as that of metrics is the import of words (G 1.67-68). Here number includes a special unity of sound-accents, of sounds and silences, of longs and shorts--all of which obey the law of modulation. What are the characteristics of rhythm? First, rhythm does not necessarily imply or stress the significant word; second, the rhythm of language occurs in verbal succession and (at this point Cicero and Quintilian are followed) does not imply ideal or fixed limits. Such limits are defined by meter (G 1.67, 80). Rhythm is a general matter which does not involve melody: it is a movement of number without melody--that is, without the regular and measurable return of certain elements following one another in time. Rhythm or meter has not as yet achieved an independent notation as, to a limited extent, pitch has. Rhythm is literary, not musical. Thus it has no dominant musical features.

In fact, Rémi views rhythm synaesthetically in the fashion of the ancients: it appears in three manners--in sight, hearing, and feeling. The eye sees rhythm in gestures and in movements of the dance, the ear hears it in the sounds of instruments and the human voice, and feeling detects it in physiological phenomena.   Leaving biological and tactile rhythms to biology and medicine, Rémi comes to certain practical conclusions: the musician is interested primarily in plastic or sonorous rhythm.   In form, dance is in perfect unity with mimetic poetry.   The order of succession of syllables depends on verbal music, and the modulation is marked through melodic accent--that is to say, through *arsis* and *thesis*--in pure musical order.

But rhythmical structure, even that of the Gregorian chant, seems not to be totally dependent on the rhythm of the text if we observe carefully the musical phenomena involved.   Melodies can have a significance outside the text and therefore strive toward independence.   They follow the text, which possibly (and in chant such as in normal psalmody) serves as a model. Movements and physical attitudes are a plastic music (G 1.80-81).   Thus three types of rhythm declare themselves: (1) the unmeasured: that of biological order, supple, indefinite, and varied, which governs oratorical movement;   (2) that which is consonant with the musical value of sound; and   (3) that of the sound-value of the word.   Of these three rhythms--of the three numbers without "melody"--Cassiodorus preferred the third, but Rémi seems to be defending the first two.   And in granting to sound or music a rhythm of its own he recalls Dionysius of Halicarnassus.

He also calls to mind the ancient triune *choreia* and suggests that there is a hierarchy of the arts.   In general, music is highest because it embodies number *and* harmony "without which nothing can exist." Harmony is the status quo of the universe, and by its presence literature through eloquence and the poetic arts can transmit wisdom, the very foundation of society.   Thus, the Greek ideal is frequently re-discovered and re-asserted: the perfect work of art combines dance, poetry, and music in the harmony of movement combining choreographic arrangements with vocal and instrumental sounds.   Like Rémi, others, including Roger Bacon (c.1214-94), were frequently tempted to take this position, patently encouraged by ancient aesthetic thought.

XIII

Some Characteristics of Musical Form and Its Judgment.   There was also a recognition of inherent qualities in musical forms.   Aurelian's entire Chapter 19 (pp. 45ff) is devoted to rules for discovering the qualities of verses in all modes--that is, their density, sparseness, height, and depth. Furthermore, in discussing the first authentic mode, he stresses verse and its proper declamation as well as the proper "projection" of the parts of the Mass, especially of sections in which antiphons and poetic verses are joined (pp. 25-29).   It is clear that "differentiae" are necessary because the antiphonic beginnings following the psalm-verses are so varied as to call for different endings in the psalm-verses themselves.   Naming more than a hundred examples, he points out when, within the modes, certain syllables are to be "raised," to be "pressed down," or to be pronounced emphatically (p. 26). Sense and meaning of text, custom, local practice (in Gaul or Rome), occasion or context (when necessity or even euphony asks for changes in syllables or words) create a need for all the varieties of the modes, which govern "every sweetness of music, and bearing flowering shrubs as it were, . . . decorate the field of the whole antiphoner . . ." (p. 45). (Examining similar examples of antiphons in the *Tonary* of Regino, the nineteenth-century historian François Gevaert attempted to reduce this qualitative variety to forty-seven formulaic themes.[22]

The aspects of plainchant which Aurelian emphasizes are formal elements. The total piece is the text, and music is its aesthetic support. Sweetness and pleasing effect are expected, but the pleasures are in the details, not in the textual whole, which has its own purpose. The ubiquitous semitone, for example, has a formal aesthetic effect governed by its nature as proportion. In the *Scolica enchiriadis* we read that semitones when they are alterations in the right places put their individual stamp on the context and add to the pleasant sound; in the wrong places, however, they are dissonant with their surroundings (G 1.195). The author of the *Dialogus*, formerly thought to be "Odo," approves of the altered semitone in the right place: too many whole tones produce boredom, and all-too-wide steps produce dissonances. When semitones follow one another immediately, however, the spicing of the song is like the excessive use of salt at table, with a resulting taste of bitterness (G 1.2167ff). In the *Dialogus*, music had a kind of independence as an aesthetic structure. Music is thus clearly distinguished from theology.

Like semitones, the device of repetition, appearing in both chant and organum, was aesthetically acceptable. An essential characteristic of musical form, it is also an essential in the creating of significances in music. But the *Dialogus* warns that its excessive use achieves only monotony (G 1.277). On the other hand, dissimilarity among parts of a composition can be too great. Symmetry (about which one may again invoke the ancient name of Harmonia) is the governing principle, is the rule, guaranteeing full aesthetic effect. When symmetry fails, the singer as well as the auditor will find the result unpleasant, but when it is present, the singer finds that difficulties evaporate and the hearer's pleasure is increased. Pleasantness and euphony at all costs: this is the motto of the author of the *Dialogus* here cited.

The rules properly followed will produce a euphony which does not contradict the total aim of music (G 1.278) but which is unfortunately not sufficiently satisfying in the contemporary worldly or profane music. Like the Church Fathers, the author of the *Dialogus* thinks that the secular music of his time is wicked, licentious, and overly elegant and that its many voices are frequently inauthentically voluptuous and effeminate (G 1.272). Ignorance of the true principles of music is the real cause of the problem, for such ignorance allows a good man to be transformed into a charlatan--or into a popular singer (G 1.275). This author makes one of the few remarks on record in his century about secular music. Only with Johannes of Grocheo in the fourteenth century, however, does secular music become a matter of disinterested commentary.

This is not to say that, in contrast to secular music, the rule of the Church can be so rigidly prescribed as to guarantee inevitable propriety and perfection. Setting down the rules for melody, the *Dialogus* notes that it is difficult to find them violated in the melodies that are written down, those improvised patently being a different matter. He admits that there is a general mandate for any art and that things "singular do not obey the rules of art" (Strunk, p. 115). Aristoxenus thought that to know the rules is not necessarily to be the musician (composer). According to the author of the *Dialogus*, general rule is one thing: it is valid and objective, and probably traditional. Though the singular individual rule may be at fault, school rules nevertheless do not create the perfect piece of music. Written down, music is rule-bound, but when it is sung in the absence of the written text, the ear is free to judge. The ultimate artistic judgment lies with the musician himself acting in the spirit of contemporary practice (G 1.277).

Who, besides ecclesiastical and moral critics, is to make the artistic judgment? The singer is no authority; he is the guided, not the guider. The *Dialogus* speaks of "presumptuous and corrupt singers," and we must remember the state of music notation and even the extent of musical literacy among this class of musicians--and also how physically cumbersome their music books were. A musician, says Aurelian, echoing Boethius, "is one who has the faculty of judging without error with regard to reasoning, purposeful reflection, and musical convention, regarding quantities and rhythms, the kind and relationships of melodies, and the songs of the poets" (p. 12). The musician (*musicus*) who follows music and mathematics is to the cantor as the grammarian is to the "mere reader," as intellect is to physical skill. Like Boethius, he thinks that "physical skill obeys like a servant" and that "reason rules like a mistress." Any art and any discipline in the nature of things is more honorable than a craft performed by hand or through work. It is greater "to know what someone does than to do what someone knows" (p. 19). A musician who acts by the rule of intellectual contemplation is to the singer as teacher to pupil: "the former creates poems, the latter analyzes them." The "singer stands before the musician like a prisoner before the judge." Noble singers still exist, but (of course) there are no musicians like the old ones (p. 20).

Boethius had defined the musician as an intellect, as a knower, as a Platonic intellectual aristocrat, who does not work at singing. Theorists, while they felt compelled to follow Boethius, also felt it necessary to describe a man who later would be called the *musicus perfectus*. Regino, for example, transforms Boethius' almost pure critic into a man who practices music but who can also discuss music and explain its significance in terms of theoretical and scientific principles. The complete musician is a three-in-one (singer, musician, mathematician): he has been taught mathematical rules, can account for the laws of his art, can debate about them and it, and can know the rationale of musical creation and performance. Art and science are more venerable than handicraft. The hallmark of their greater importance lies in that the musician knows what he is doing rather than in his merely doing what he has learned from another person (G 1.246). The musician is not merely the medium through whom the knowledgeable free man is offered something for his judgment. His knowledge is his characteristic.

XIV

The Divine Aim of Music, Its Difficulty, and Orpheus as Anti-Hero. Ultimately--and it is a point to which we must return again and again--the purpose of music is affirmed as the praise and glorification of God. Always and everywhere this aim was proclaimed: to sing the praise of God, the eternal *alleluia*, is music's primary function. The source of music in celestial patterns and its translation into human praise commingles in actual musical activity among men. For Aurelian, the monk writing a practical work, there are concrete indications that music is in fact divinely inspired. "The whole physical world and sky," he says, "carries sound; music moves the affections of men; it stimulates emotions of different mood; it restores the strength of combatants in war, influences beasts like serpents, birds, and dolphins, and, like the angels, renders praise to God" (p. 56). Such praise is prefigured in monastic experience: a monk heard the song of angels, remembered it, and gave it to the Fathers of the Church; a monk in Auxerre heard the *Alleluia* sung by angels and gave it to the clergy; and St. Gregory (*Dialogues* 4.27, FC 39.222-23) reports that a boy, after learning heavenly words and being made to speak in tongues, could predict and reveal how many were about to die and who they were. Similarly, St. Paul (2 *Cor.* 12.4) heard words not to be repeated, and St. John was told not to write about the voice of seven thunders (*Rev.* 10.4) (p. 57). Elisha "filled his mind with sweetness through a melody" so that the Holy Spirit came to him and taught him things he did not know before; hence Elisha too shared in divine wisdom through music. Aurelian finds emblems of the art of music (the harps of God) in the *Apocalypse* (*Rev.* 14.2, 15.2), and he asserts that singing pleases God because through it we imitate the choir of angels who sing his praises without end (p. 6).

Aurelian also describes, though ambiguously for modern minds, a practical formulaic device said by some scholars to stem from Byzantine formulaic intonations called the *enechemata*. Supposedly employed in celebration of and in gratitude for God's goodness and mercy, it was a kind of antiphon which did not follow any of the rules for melodic structures. Charlemagne, Aurelian's "father of the whole world," is supposed to have defined four new modes called ANANNO, NOEANE, NONANNEANE, and NOANE; the Greeks, not to be outdone by men of the West, added four more. The eight modes thus were represented by eight nonsense-syllabic formulas, or short melodies (as in the *Commentario brevis* [G 1.214-16], where it is said that the syllables are used for studying melody in each of the modes). Regino (G 1.247) allows them no meaning but says they were taken over from the Greeks for a display of the "wonderful variety" of the words. He seems also to be referring to Aurelian's remark (p. 25)--one of the few personal anecdotes in all the theoretical works in music written in medieval times--that "a certain Greek" said they were untranslatable and in Greek were cries of rejoicing like the cries in Latin of those who plow and drive wagons. Such cries are appropriate, Hucbald thinks (pp. 36-37), even at openings of *alleluia*s when they are cries of rejoicing. Thus, the so-called NOEANE system may have been used for the musical expression of enthusiasm and ecstasy in the *Alleluia*, the *jubilus*, or any other place whatsoever.[23]

When all is said and done, however, music and its powers are a mystery impossible to understand. In one final respect the medieval theorists differed from ancient thinkers in that the latter never said anything about the difficulties of music. For them, as we know, "practical" matters were inferior, were problems for the practical worker. Aurelian does not make anything of hidden difficulties either, but the *Musica enchiriadis* ends in a surprisingly mystical way: music is not open to understanding, we are told; we can judge whether the song follows the laws, and we can measure, among other things, the intervals of the tones; but we cannot estimate how an art can be in so great and reciprocal an association with our souls or minds. Like the Stoics, who used allegory to effect a mediation between the philosophical and the everyday consciousness through the use of the old gods and goddesses as symbols, the author of the *Musica enchiriadis* uses Orpheus as a symbolic figure of the ideal musician and his wife Eurydice as the allegorical image of the deepest secrets of harmony.

In ancient legends, Orpheus was the leader of a cult centered in the Orphic Mysteries. As a musician, he was thought to be a forerunner of modern music. With his lyre he had enchanted the Muses, and in his songs he had celebrated the creation of Earth, Sky, and Ocean. In the Middle Ages, he was legitimatized as an early monotheistic pupil of Moses. He was now a symbol of the mystery of music and was treated euhemeristically. The moral of the Orpheus story is that men cannot grasp all the mysteries of harmony with human understanding at all. Some "mixtures" are sweet, others harsh. Why? Human intellect cannot understand the secret, which must be based on reason lying behind nature in its innermost recesses (pp. 31-32). Even science, even that of numbers, is helpless before the mystery of music, whose secret is God's alone. The significance of music is rational in the transcendental sense and therefore beyond technical explanation and verbal discourse.

Regino, on the other hand, thinks Orpheus was the un-ideal music-maker and Eurydice the allegorical symbol of the deeper secrets of harmony. Only a cithara player, Orpheus did not really know the theory of music because he lacked cosmic powers. Thus his loss of Eurydice symbolizes the failure of any human being, despite all his efforts, ever to grasp with understanding all the riddles of harmony. Why should Orpheus have been so interpreted? Pseudo-Dionysius' idea that the illimitable world of God is forever closed to human understanding is surely in the background. Orpheus took hold on the human mind even among Christians who often abhorred Greek legends. Because he was a lesser pagan god, he could serve as the sign of the impenetrability of the mystery of music. God cannot so serve because nothing is beyond him. God need not master music, and Orpheus could not. Music is a difficult study, a vast study, writes Regino, and a matter so technical that few can master it (G. 1.246-47).

The theorists surveyed in this chapter to this point all stand in relation to the Carolingian renaissance, a time when closer ties developed between intellectuals--ties which also extended down in time to the post-Carolingian era. Together these writers took long steps in music aesthetics in the direction of describing current musical practice, though to be sure this was primarily ecclesiastical practice. All of them, nevertheless, copied from the writers of the sixth and seventh centuries as well as from earlier writers among themselves. However, following the time of the *Dialogus*, no really significant names in the history of the idea of music appear until the eleventh century; these names are Berno of Reichenau (d. 1048), the author of a *Prologus tonarii*, and his more famous contemporary, Guido of Arezzo.

Though there has been considerable controversy concerning the nature of mode and tetrachord (medieval writers and modern scholars alike tend to disagree about aspects of these), there is no doubting the failure of outlines such as the one presented above to transmit the experience of hearing the music itself. Nor necessarily does a modern book of chants such as the *Liber Usualis* give us a selection of this music in such a way that we can actually reconstruct its sound in earlier centuries. Anyone who has heard attempts at the "authentic" singing of Gregorian chant or of organum will have far more understanding of it (even if there are flaws in the reconstruction of the chant) and of its structure than someone who has not heard such singing. Theory is only a codified outline aimed at accurate and "permanent" description of an art already alive and undergoing change. Plainchant is not one single practice, we discover. Nevertheless, since it was used in churches, and because the Church emphasized the importance of its traditions (including its musical traditions) and its rules, it had a certain centuries-long consistency. Even modern-day interpretations of chant in actual monasteries and convents which retain its devotional purpose are able to preserve something of this ancient art, though perhaps in what for a medieval listener would certainly have been regarded as a decadent performance practice. But organum demonstrates how alteration in practice affected the forms of the music of the Church in medieval times, for this form gives evidence of the influence of human inventiveness which too would join in effecting slow changes in the musical traditions of the Church--changes with aesthetic, devotional, and musical implications which relate to the topic of the idea of music.

As with the ancient forms in rhythm, therefore, plainchant was surely much more complex in experience than we can in fact know today. It is safe to say that only a few scholar-performers in our time can begin to grasp this music in all its subtleties and complexities. Even the pale performances of ordinary or mediocre singers who do not have the advantage of being able to reconstruct early chant will present a music which is highly sophisticated up to a point. Those who allow their perceptions to be clouded by being too acclimated to the major-minor scale, to ways of using the voice which would have been unimaginable to the medieval musician, to powerful modern instruments designed for the large concert hall--that is, uninitiated modern listeners--will perhaps recognize only monotony and hear nothing of the colors or qualities of the individual intervals. Such medieval music may present immense practical and aesthetic problems for many of us, but we need to remember that it served as the musical transmitter of the sacred texts for many centuries and that its devotional function was one which found expression in different ways in various regions in Western Europe while its aesthetic implications emerged prior to being analyzed by writers on the art of music.

For plainchant has its own masterpieces, though not every listener can easily recognize or identify them. To descend into a state of reverence, mystical experience, and devotion may be beyond the spiritual abilities of many of us though at least it is necessary to imagine such a state. It seems that many of us can more easily appreciate medieval sculpture and painting as artistic forms than medieval music; their *raison d'être*, their original function as devotional images or pictures, the disappearance of the color from painted works of sculpture, and their intricate symbolism are other matters, of course. Even the music now accessible in square-note or modern notation and the documents about it presented in modern editions and translations are no more than a faint introduction to the rich musical heritage available for the people of the Middle Ages to sing and to hear.[24]

XV

Al Farabi (Alfarabius, or Muhammad ibn Muhammad ibn Tarhkan abu Nasr Al Farabi). Just as the work of Philo of Alexandria made its imprint on Christian thought only after approximately a century and a half in the writings of Clement of Alexandria, so now there emerged a major Arab philosopher, Al Farabi (c.870-950), whose influence on the West was hardly felt until the twelfth century when his work on music was noticed and translated. Chronologically, however, he belongs in the present chapter. He is one of the figures signalling a return of Greek texts into Western thought through Latin translation, but now by way of the Arab world, through Spain.

Between the eighth century, when Spain was invaded by the Arabs, and the end of the tenth century, almost all presently known Greek philosophical and scientific literature had been translated into Arabic.[25] The Aristotelian conception of man was generally accepted quite early among the Arabs, though certain scientists agreed with the atomism of Democritus or the mathematical (notably the physical-geometrical) physics of Plato. Al Farabi, like the majority of the Arabs, however, followed Aristotle because he was felt to point the way toward science--that is, induction--and to base many of his results on observation, description, and classification. Both Arabs and Jews were attracted by the rewards of discoveries in mathematics, physics, biology, astronomy, and psychology. Like Aristotle, they were concerned with the real, the material world and not with the mathematical and unsensed world of Plato.

Al Farabi was indeed a principal interpreter of both Plato and Aristotle in the Arab Middle East, working in both Baghdad and Aleppo, while his introduction to the Christian West was by Gundisalvo, the Spanish thinker of the twelfth century. In the period between Al Farabi's death and his discovery by the European writers on music, other Arabic thinkers continued to harmonize Greek with Islamic thought. Hence when the right historical moment came, Al Farabi, along with his followers--Avicenna (980-1038), the devotee of both Neoplatonism and Aristotle,[26] and Averroës (1126-98), the Spanish-Arabic philosopher who also translated Aristotle and even more deeply influenced Christian and Jewish thought--made a very great impression on Christian schools in the West. The works of these men in fact helped to inspire a new cultural renaissance in the twelfth century--a renaissance as important as that which had taken place in the time of Charlemagne.   Given passionate admiration, the ancients of Greece underwent scrutiny and were subjected to a change in perspective. Ancient music theory, aesthetics, and speculation were newly fertilized and transformed. Since Al Farabi's authority in the field of music was Ptolemy, he placed great importance on the relation of music to astronomy and number symbolism. Even though he relied on Ptolemy for mathematical-cosmic support--and thus superficially reminds us of Boethius himself--as well as of Euclid, Aristoxenus, and Aristides Quintilianus, he confined himself to non-technical philosophies and, probably for lack of interest, did nothing for the technical knowledge of music already in course. In fact, his work encouraged a purely philosophical approach. He describes a program he himself does not follow. Like the Peripatetics and Aristoxenus, he takes an empirical-scientific stance and asks for (1) a complete statement of fundamental principles, (2) a description of what follows from these principles, (3) a rejection of errors met with in the science, (4) a rejection, when necessary, of the opinions of others, (5) a judgment of what is right and what is wrong, and (6) correction of the obscure opinions of others.[27] This hardly suggests a practical approach to music or to the cumulatively technical matters of the music theorists of the West.

This program is scientific, but it hardly carries over to music theory. Al Farabi ignores organum, if he knows anything about it, and defines the science of music as an investigation of melodies, of what they are made and why, of how they are composed, and of the forms necessary for impressive and effective performance. Two sciences are relevant: the practical (or active) and the theoretical (the speculative considered as research). The practical embraces the production of melodies in instruments naturally adapted for them (the larynx, the uvula, and the nose) or artificially created (reed-pipes, lutes, and so forth)--the human and humanly made types roughly distinguished by Aurelian and Regino. The theoretical is the science of melodies, of the metaphysical reasons for everything of which they are composed. The practical covers the principles and fundamentals: it asks for the elucidation of the science and method of their application, of the rudiments of the art, of how well artificial instruments conform to the rudiments, of natural rhythms, and of the composition of melodies in general, including perfect ones (*Arabic-Latin Writings*, p. 14-16). Farmer[28] summarizes in another way: while *musica activa* embraces *acute* (high), *grave* (low), and intermediate sound and is a science of tones, *musica speculativa* has five parts: (1) the principles of the invention of music, its materials, and its method; (2) the discovery of neumes, their number and kinds, and the theory of their proportions; (3) the related proportion-theory; (4) types of natural rhythms which are the "times" of tone; (5) melodism, rhythmics, and metrics. The fourth of these parts is more Augustinian than Greek, and the fifth is clearly Isidorian. All in all, however, Al Farabi is scientific in that he asks the right questions. But he outlines a program which he does not or cannot himself carry to completion and which in part already had been executed.

    While the above, from *The Classification of the Sciences* (*De scientiis*), contains resonances of both Plato and Aristotle, a section called *Concerning the Rise of the Sciences* (*De ortu scientiarum*) is primarily Platonic because it presses on toward metaphysical causes. When substance was given motion, there resulted sound, which was divided into high, low, and medium. A science of sounds (acoustics) is therefore necessary for a knowledge of sounds, their kinds, and their relationships (ratios) to one another. Furthermore, music has a use: it can maintain the mean between extremes by tempering the characters of living beings who depart from the mean, by perfecting the fitness of those not yet perfected, and by holding in place those who appear to possess the mean and have not gone to the extremes. It is of use in bodily health too: the body adjusts to the soul and both are cured by the effectiveness of certain sounds, especially concordant ones. Here Al Farabi clearly relies on the ancient therapeutic theory. He also touches on three aspects of music: poetry (which regulates "a rational comprehension of diction"), melody (which regulates the parts of acuity and gravity in sounds), and gesture (which allows for coincident motions and their corresponding proportions with sound). If Al Farabi thinks music embraces both hearing and sight, he must have known a model resembling the ancient triune *choreia* (ibid., pp. 48-49). His whole philosophy of music leaves a "foreign" impression, perhaps as much as anything because he is treating secular music that is not European. But also he is not in touch with

Western thought on music: he does not know the work of the Christian thinkers whose writings have been the subject in the main of this chapter. Also, the effect of Al Farabi's analysis is sketchy as well. Nevertheless, because he asks good questions, his work was antecedent to some good answers, which will come later in the Middle Ages in the West. And his own clear dependence on Plato, Aristotle, and others meant that he had something to contribute to Western thought out of the philosophy of antiquity.

XV
The Middle Ages:
The Eleventh and Twelfth Centuries

Following the dissolution of the Carolingian empire, which in any case had never been very highly organized, there was an interim in which what stability Northern and Central Europe had was centered on the Germanic tribes, whose leaders were closely allied with the papacy in order to maintain a measure of peace. During this interim, as we have seen, appeared Aurelian, Rémi, and Regino of Prüm, who produced works that have been examined in the previous chapter. In 962, Otto I was crowned emperor, reigning until his death in 973. He was followed by a succession of Saxon kings, who in turn were followed after 1027 by the Franconian emperors Conrad II (d. 1039), Henry III (1046-56), Henry IV (1084-1106), Henry V (1111-25), and Lothar II (1133-37) and the Hohenstaufens Conrad III (1138-52), Frederick Barbarossa (1152-90), and Henry VI (1191-97).

In the eleventh century commerce began to flourish, cities grew larger, and the quality of city life improved on account of the increased prosperity. The famine of 1033 seemed to have a positive effect on trade, which was intensified by exchanges of luxury items. Such economic improvement in turn stimulated the political desire for conquest as well as cultural achievement. The result was the greater power of the aristocracy which would also play an important role in the rebirth of culture. The period, however, was marked by severe tensions, as we might expect. Emperor, aristocracy, and pope struggled for power at Canossa in 1077, after which Henry IV, who had been excommunicated in 1076, so humiliated himself that Pope Gregory VII removed the excommunication (though it was reinstated in 1080 for Henry's disloyal actions, including the setting up of an antipope). During the First Crusade (1096-99) and after the Norman conquest of England in 1066, there arose the question of investiture: should bishops be invested in office by the ecclesiastical hierarchy or by lay princes, as had been the practice since the time of Charlemagne? The struggle for power was somewhat resolved by the thirteenth century, when German territories were fragmented and became small lands with separate rulers. In 1273, Rudolph I of Hapsburg became emperor but renounced imperial rights in Rome, and the empire was henceforth no longer under German rule.

If the Church struggled for political power in Western Europe, it also attempted to exert its discipline in internal matters as well as in the social order. In 813, the Council of Tours had proclaimed that whatever affects or works on the eyes or ears has a weakening effect on the soul. Music was indeed to be retained in churches, but its purpose must not be pleasure. Men need not be pleased or entertained; they must serve God, and him alone, and express their love for him.   Just as the Church Fathers had considered certain rhythms and melodies dissolute--and as the ancient philosophers before them had stressed the corrupting influence of certain types of music and the dancing of corybantes--so medieval clergy would also teach that music which had gone beyond certain limits was to be looked on with suspicion.   These limits were to be established by the strictest and simplest of rational relationships.   The action of the Council of Tours was to be given philosophical support by a Neoplatonic work falsely attributed to Aristotle, the *Liber de Causis* (actually the *Institutio* of Proclus), in which it was said that God created certain instruments for realizing certain ends and gave them a power which in various ways was like his own--but of course vastly inferior to his.   These instruments, not necessarily musical ones, included the human body and its voice and with them all other creatures and creations which could do his work and sing his praises.

Yet in that time a complexity of style and even a sense of adventure calling for freedom from simply monophonic musical styles had been observed, and therefore the Church on the whole chose to ask for correctives and a return to what was seen as the purity of simplicity.   In addition to tropes--that is, interpolations into chants which might be highly ornamented or melismatic--or even ceremonies that qualified for designation as liturgical drama (for example, the *Visitatio Sepulchri* or *Visit to the Sepulchre* which appeared throughout Europe), there were the extremely elaborate chants, especially such chants as certain ones associated with the Ambrosian rite which were still influenced by Oriental forms and ornaments.   These tendencies were to be resisted.   And then organum too was to be kept under control as a form of elaboration that was frequently seen from the official point of view as an aberration.

Nevertheless, singing by the single voice or by voices joined in unison was gradually augmented by the simultaneous singing of two or more voices.   This eventually would lead through several stages of practice until after several centuries it resulted in a full-flowered and rich polyphony. This polyphony, which we can understand to have been based originally in the developments of the period 930 to 1130, would ultimately be systematized into the study and science metaphorically called harmony.   Did it arise from something latent in Gregorian chant--something which was teased into being also by the special acoustics of the buildings in which it was sung?   Or did it, as has been suggested, arise from a desire to combine religious with a secular music which, though we lack sources, we may presume was more elaborate in style and technique?   No explanation has been ingenious enough really to explain the causes of the rise of polyphony, though the theory of secular origins has not found much favor.   In any case, polyphony was an amazing achievement--"possibly the most unprecedented, original, indeed miraculous achievement of our Western civilization, not excluding science," according to a modern philosopher.[1] Singing in parallel octaves, then in parallel fifths and fourths (the three consonances of the Greeks)--all called organum--and also subsequently in the Middle Ages transposing the chant to the upper octave and harmonizing it in parallel sixths and fourths: these eventually gave way to non-parallel motion among two or more voices, the *puncta contra punctum* (note against note), with the resulting intervals still being octaves, thirds, fourths, fifths, and sixths. Polyphony thus in the end realized the potentialities of the use of a second contrasting melody more or less independent of the first, the primary or given one (*cantus firmus*), but sung with it, limited by it, and fitting with it, yet still independent, while the given first melody remained untouched and unaltered.

Music at the beginning of the eleventh century, of course, had not arrived at the kind of compositional technique described above. Secular music, whatever its state, was simply ignored in the writings on music, and ecclesiastical musical forms had not developed, though changes in such aspects as ornamentation may have taken place. A sophisticated polyphony was not yet known. Nor was there an easily decipherable written notation which might make possible the close scrutiny of what was played or sung. Consequently, there are also serious problems with regard to our interpretation of the writings on music from this period. Still, if early eleventh-century writings seem almost to return us to an earlier time, perhaps even reminding us of the state of things c.900, we need not only to remember that the period between the Carolingian period and the high Middle Ages was marked by a very active musical production of hymns, sequences, and so forth especially in monasteries, but also to recall that the twelfth century will bring some very interesting changes indeed. The men who make up the history of changing musical thought include: Berno of Reichenau (d. 1048), Hermannus Contractus (1013-54), Guido of Arezzo (c.990-c.1050), Aribo Scholasticus (d. 1079), Othloh of St. Emmeram (1032-70); of the schools of France: Hugh of St.-Victor (1096-1141), William of Conches (c.1080-1154), John of Salisbury (d. 1180), Bernard of Clairvaux (1091-1153), and Alan of Lille (c.1128-1203); and John Cotton (c.1100), Adelard of Bath (early twelfth century), and Gundisalvo (d. 1151). So international had learning become in Western Europe that these writers might be widely separated in different regions of the continent. Whereas the musical theorists among these men stayed close to the exposition of technical matters, with excursions into arithmology, the philosophers concentrated, as they always had, on eternity and the terrestrial evidences of change, of the cyclical patterns of the cosmos with its stars, seasons, regular biological changes, and the alternation of day and night. In any case, the ontology of music was of prime concern.

I

Berno of Reichenau (Berno Augiensis) and Hermannus Contractus of Reichenau (Herman the Lame). Berno and Hermannus Contractus were teacher and pupil, the former an abbot in the monastery at Reichenau in Germany who was appointed to that post in 1008 by the Emperor Henry II. Like most writers about music in the Middle Ages, Berno was a learned man, in his case including such interests as astronomy. As a writer on liturgical matters, he is said to have led a successful movement in the West to include the *Credo* (Nicene Creed) as a regular part of the Mass, itself now established as a liturgical, musical, and mystical whole. His work relevant here is a *Prologus in tonarium (Tonary with a Prologue)*.

In this work, Berno quoted generously from the *Scolica* and *Musica enchiriadis* with respect to organum, his justification for which had already been anticipated in the Pseudo-Aristotelian *Problems* (probably unknown to him) as the simultaneous singing of men's and boys' voices (G 2.64). In liturgy and musical practice, Berno believed in simplicity, in every respect a classical principle, and in clarity and good proportion as well as in a measured variety. Long or short in the tones of a song were to be as beautiful in modulation as in the declamation of a poem. All rhythmic and melodic values of notes and their connections were to be beautiful, agreeable, graceful and charming, and sung in moderate, simple, and masculine (but not weak) style (*De varia sonorum*, G 2.113). He supplies us an example of a change in the realization of the NOEANE formulae: the basic tropes now are *Primum quaerite regnum Dei, Secundum autem simile est huic*, and so forth (G 2.79-83). Like other monastics, he thought that psalmody with its limited compass and its "objectivity" was ideal for church music.

Berno was a dedicated number-symbolist and allegorist for whom number-and-music symbolism is at the core of musical reality. Numbers are truth, and no more so than in that the number 10, being the sum of $1 + 2 + 3 + 4$, justifies the existence of the ten-string psaltery as a suitable instrument for the praising of God (*Prologus in Tonarium*, G 2.66). The number 9 justifies voice factors: to the teeth belongs the number 4, to the lips 2, to the tongue 1, and to the throat and lungs 1 each (*Prol. Ton.*, G 2.64). St. Augustine had been more graphic and somewhat tasteless in his use of metaphor: in *On Christian Doctrine* (2.6.7-8, NPN1 2.537), he says that the woman's teeth which "are as flocks of sheep" in the *Song of Songs* (4.2) are holy men described as the teeth of the Church; they cut men off from their errors and soften (masticate) them so that they can be taken into the Church! Yet number is a nobler force than this. Like the ancients, Berno thinks that 4 is allied with the perfect state of the soul, for it has a double middle: $2 + 2 = 4$, and 2 has a position between 1 and 3; and though the outer sides of the perfect 3 are closely related, formative nature under God's command through a definite musical law selected the number 4 to bind reluctant elements together into an inexplicable bond with the three musics (of Boethius). Therefore, the number 4 is justified as a concomitant of harmonic music because it brings together in correct relations heaven and earth, and body and soul, and it causes animal impulses to be repressed, morals to be improved, and demonic madness to be tempered or entirely eliminated (*Prol. Ton.*, G 2.66).[2]   The importance of the allegory in elementary instructional texts is clear: 4 unites the world, and the 9 of teeth, lips, and so forth describes the natural instrument given by God to man for his singing of the *Alleluia*. Berno is not a Boethius, but he seems nevertheless to exemplify the learned and experienced master-singer.

Hermannus Contractus, his learned pupil who also wrote a history (*Chronicon*) to the year 1054, in his work on music is no more satisfied than Berno with the remarks about notation in the *Enchiriadis*. He devised a system of notation to be used for teaching intervals and used it in two well-known songs which were widely disseminated. He also was known as a writer of antiphons and sequences and additionally as a mathematician and astronomer. In his *Opuscula musica* he summarizes Boethius' ontology of music. Better yet, he seems to transform Boethius' contrast of singer and musician according to the actual conditions of medieval life.

He explains the nature of plainchant form in his remarks about his plan for tetrachords, as we have seen. Form is related to psychological effect: the *excellentes* takes its name, for example, from the high quality of its pitch. The *finales* is equal to it, however, in arrangement and its letter names. Why, then, should the *finales* of chants be assigned to the *finales* rather than to the *excellentes*? Quite simply, this is so because the flow of a song requires intensity, whereas the end requires release. Similarly, an action in its course requires intensity, its end release. Melodies therefore require an end on pitches lower than the intense *excellentes*. This end, a release, is the *finales* (*Musica* [Ellinwood], p. 40).

Himself evidently a creative artist who worked according to the techniques of his day, he gives a certain respectability to the roles of performer and composer. Heretofore, the composer frequently has been anonymous and music often a product of a practical need requiring composition in specific instances in a monastery. Without employing names, Hermannus discusses the science of the theorist who organizes the performer's art into logical systems, and then comments on the role of the critic and philosopher in music. To be able to compose a melody and to criticize and inflect (sing) it, he thinks, makes the musician. It is possible rationally not to know how to compose, but to criticize and inflect ("modulating" with the voice) are essential (ibid., p. 47). These three capacities make the true musician something more than the mere singer.

Nor is he content with the rational definitions of music of previous writers. Here his remarks about the aesthetic and logical opaqueness of definition are farsighted. The clothes of human beings, the voices of animals, the coming of the seasons--all changing things--can correctly and properly be designated in languages. But language is indirect, and we discover the nature of melodic formulas not indirectly but directly through sensuous perception or hearing. The musical professional can build a melody according to rule based on the doctrine of tropes. But for such a procedure, language with its nomenclature has no adequate expression. Meanings are multiple, even irrational, but they can be explained: (1) Modes, for example, can be rationally described through the numerical succession and order of tones according to their positions on the monochord. Hands as well as voice and sweetness of breath are the medium, tropes must be recognized and remembered, and by way of the monochord the species of fourth and fifth must be understood and recognized--and related to the modes (p. 48); (2) tropes can be designated according to the (modes of) people (nations) of whose music they are characteristic at any given time; and (3) the interpretation of their psychological-ethical characters can follow. Whereas Boethius (1.34) had said that these functions belong to three classes of people, Hermannus combines them in the really superior musician.

But all three methods, each alone or all together, are unable to explain the specific musical peculiarity of a melodic quality. The great and wonderful profundity and depth of music are therefore accessible to intellect only to a certain limited extent and can be explained only in comparatively superficial terms (p. 65).

Hermannus agrees with the *Musica enchiriadis* that for music rational understanding and explanation are helpless. He seems to look forward to the relatively modern theory that not only music but also all art must be seen as ineffable in nature and as essentially inexplicable. Such an approach is based on a direct approach to (or intuition of) art and not on language and theological dogma or metaphysical aspiration. He has the distinction, as we have seen, of having his name associated (some scholars think incorrectly) with specific antiphons (for example, *Salve regina* and *Alma redemptoris mater*) at a time when the names of most composers were not remembered. But, since he was surveying a body of music as a practical musician, he also raises a question: why, like Aribo Scholasticus, did he ignore the subject of organum, which was nevertheless treated by Guido of Arezzo, their approximate contemporary?

II

Guido of Arezzo (Guido Aretinus). Probably the most famous of all music theorists of the Middle Ages, Guido of Arezzo has been compared to Pythagoras. An advisor to Pope John XIX, he is often given credit for devising staff notation. His *Alia regulae* (c.1030) is prefatory to his antiphoner in which neumes were placed in such a way on lines and spaces that each neume on a single line or on a space between the lines always assumed the same pitch relative to the other pitches. Staffless neumes by themselves had vaguely and only approximately indicated melodic movements; they were merely guides for singers to help them to remember the pitches required by the melody of a musical tradition that was passed on from one generation to the next by memory. Because neumes by them-selves were imprecise, merely suggestive, and causes of dispute, a system was wanted which could be interpreted with absolute precision. According to Guido's supposed plan, singers now could have direct acquaintance with song from notation alone. Heretofore they had been at the whim and mercy of their memories and of the cantor or director, who taught them by rote. Aurelian long ago had described the perfect singer as one who has "implanted by memory in the sheath of his heart the melody of all the verses through all the modes, and the difference both of the modes and the verses of the antiphons, introits, and responses" (p. 46). That ideal was not always realized, however, and Guido's great purpose is in instructing singers--a purpose which tends to ignore Boethian scientific thought in the interest of a concentration on what will improve the quality of music in the churches, monasteries, cathedrals, and convents of Western Europe.

Like John Cotton later, Guido calls music a movement of tones and seems to restrict it to the limits of the purely musical. He thus in general does not repeat mystical speculations, but indeed he even finds that the teachings of the philosophers are not always useful. Aiming to make actual singers independent, he is not satisfied to repeat the traditional stereotypical stories and phrases of *virtus musicae* except in cases which serve practical designs (*Micrologus*, Epistle to Bishop Theodaldus). His aim is the cultivation of singing as such through a clear and intelligent intonation of modes and melodies as well as the correct reproducing of intervals and time-measurements. He finds that improvisation is a good teaching device. Hence though he does not fail to follow the Augustinian and Boethian theory of music as number (*Microl.* 20), he makes but little of it.

Nevertheless, numerology is not far removed, nor is it merely metaphor. He mentions ratios and applies them to values of both pitch and note-duration (*numero vocum, ratione tonorum*) (ibid. 15). The octave (diapason: "through all") is not a mere repetition of the first tone, but is like a day which returns again after a week. It is the *perfectissima similitudo*. The number is 8 for both days and notes, just as Virgil (*Aeneid* 6.646) sang of seven different notes renewed over and over in music. Not only do eight notes complete the octave, but 8 stands for modes, for beatitudes (see *Matt.* 5.3-11), for qualities among which melodic lines move, and for parts of speech and neumes so composed that we recognize the modes of the chant (*Microl.* 13). Beyond the eighth, which includes the other two perfect intervals, he sees no tone agreeing with another in so perfect a fashion.

Guido, like ancient and other medieval thinkers, makes few remarks about the reception of the hearer but concentrates largely on the composer's craft. His professional advice about composing a song or melody, naturally recalling the attempts at systematization of the ninth- and tenth-century theorists, is one of the first in the Western world to be so detailed. Here one turns to his best-known work (already cited), the *Micrologus de disciplina artis musicae* (c.1025-26) in twenty books.

Music added to the harmony of poetic language, he says, creates a double melody because the composer's knowledge begins with poetry and its divisions--letters, syllables, phrases, feet, and verses--and with speech-sounds based on syllables, which alone or combined make a neume (section of a phrase), the neume being part of the musical song. One or more of these phrases indicates a division (in performance, a place for breathing). Each division has as its final sound a "hold" or delay--slight for a syllable, longer for a phrase, longest for a division (*distinctio*). Some notes are separated from the others by a brief delay, some are twice as long as others, some are twice as short, or are a "trembling" or hold. Notes must specifically show repetitions of the same tone, combinations of two or more tones, or--and here may be the first specific reference to duration, which will be a major consideration two hundred years later--a ratio of time values. As is the poet, so is the musician. But *the musician is less rule-bound* because he can place tones with a reasonable variety.

It is notable that to the grammatical-rhetorical principles of his medieval predecessors, Guido has added considerations of verse and poetics. For the musician must be aware of the metrics of poetry--and therefore of song. The watchword is flexibility. In music as in poetry, there must be rhythmic flexibility: lyric poets make additions to poetic feet--different ones at different times--and the composer must do the same.

Like the author of the *Dialogus* formerly attributed to "Odo" before him, Guido makes good sound the purpose of music. Finding a technical analogy between poetry and music, he relies on rhetoric and rhythmics rather than on metrics, and he assumes that a knowledge of grammar and rhetoric precedes musical composition. Anything, he writes, that is spoken can be made into music, and he suggests that we should improvise. In music, melody is primary, and in poetry precise syllabification is not as important as the more loose arrangements of phrases which are similar or different as they are joined to prose. Prose phrases have balance and symmetry but not exactness and equality. The natural concerns of Cicero and Quintilian, balance and symmetry, are the responsibility of the orator and also of the musician, who in setting a sacred text should pursue them and not follow the strict rules of metrics. Vowels give a pleasant quality to words and can be the core of melody-building to effect a kind of simultaneous dual modulation of text and melody. There are five vowels which bring euphony to words; to each of them one can apply an attribute belonging to an individual tone or sound which attaches to the textual vowel in question. One may put underneath the entire scale two or three different series of vowels. From this collection of vowels, only the better should be chosen and retained (*Microl.* 17). So much for parts: the movement of the entire piece should imitate the subject of the song. Calm movement should be imitated by a tranquil melody and so forth.

In Chapter 11 of the *Micrologus* he discusses the final of a piece. It sounds longer than the others, and the others "in an amazing way" draw their color (quality) from it. Beginning, middle, and end are at one with the final note. The first note tells us nothing, but the final in retrospect tells us the mode which has preceded. The whole piece must be directed towards its end; phrases, which, as they begin and end, like verses should be in harmony with the final. A parallel in language is the dominance of final letters which tell us about cases, numbers, persons, and tenses (in an inflected language). Guido does not know the metaphor of (Aristotelian) organic form, but he implies it.

He is perhaps the first theorist on record to turn attention toward the proper way to sing (or play) the end of a long phrase or composition: he recommends a slowing of the tempo, a smooth legato between tones of an interval, and changes in dynamics. Like a horse galloping but preparing to stop running, he says, phrases (distinctions) should end with notes further apart--that is, slower--so as to prepare for the end of or a pause in the breath in singing. The impression is one of weariness before a breath-taking. Thus notes should be spaced far apart (to represent a characteristic of time) or close together, as is necessary to produce this effect. Indeed, notes can "dissolve" as can letters. The interval begins with one note and smoothly transfers to another without seeming to have a place to stop on the way. It does not matter, however, whether you make the interval more "full" or liquescent. Fullness may be more pleasing. In any case, what one does should not happen too infrequently or be too rigidly regular. Discretion and taste must be the rule. Guido's remarks bring composing and performing into a unit, and in addition combine phrasing with dynamics and possibly a sense of legato, thus to remind one of the instructional principles of theorists of oratory and rhetoric like Quintilian.

Guido is a consolidator. In discussing organum or diaphony, however, he goes somewhat beyond the *Scolica enchiriadis*. He defines organum as a practice in which "notes distinct from each other make dissonance harmoniously and harmonize in their dissonance" (*Microl.* 18). He finds that the three voices (of a triplum) blend congenially and smoothly in a "symphony." But he allows a certain freedom of movement for its own sake, and not merely as a device for avoiding the tritone. The ear (as we have heard) is judge. He does not admit the fifth in organal motion--nor the minor second (semitone), both of which are harsh. But he does allow the major second, minor and major thirds, and the fourth (here the minor third is the least desirable, and the fourth the most), and he gives examples of them in contrary, similar, or oblique motion, even to the extent of illustrating voice crossings. The aim of oblique motion is to arrive at the unison through the third or second. The explanation involves an old principle, that a tone of two must not go below a certain note of a tetrachord of the melody (ibid. 18). Thus reason seems to support the evidence of the senses. Guido's rules for organum permit intervals heretofore not allowed, add oblique motion to the conventional parallel, and serve as one great step in the direction of destroying the tyranny of the perfect consonance inherited from the Greeks.

Whatever the errors of historians about Guido's accomplishments, it is nevertheless true that he summarized mechanical rules for medieval composers, comparable to those of Quintilian, Priscian, and Aristotle on poetry (which he no doubt did not know) and those of Alcuin on rhetoric. (We may also wish to compare the establishment of rules much later in history for literature during the Enlightenment of the eighteenth century, especially in the precepts set down for tragedy in France and for literary genres by Gottsched in Germany.) Practical matters--composing in a material quite abstract and performing that material in private or public-- virtually call for such rules. Guido was presumably not writing for geniuses in any case (though masterful composers had been identified as early as Carolingian times) but rather for the everyday lesser talent.

On the philosophical level, Guido is something of a celebrant of the sense of hearing and the other senses, and, like certain other medieval writers (though this group is very likely a minority), he is enchanted by their delights. Each tone, color, and perfume has its own emotional value, its own distinctive quality; the objects of hearing, seeing, and smelling excite us, whereas the objects of the other senses depress the vital *tonus*. The ear takes delight in sound just as the eye is pleased by colors, the nose by smells, and the tongue by tastes. Guido too dwells on sweetness, a quality of delightful things which, he says, penetrate to the heart as if through a window (ibid. 14). Like the Neoplatonic followers of Pseudo-Dionysius, he is prostrate before the beauties of nature. But of course nature must remain in its place so that its sensuous beauty gives evidence not of sensuality but of the goodness of God. Artistic representations of the outside world can only be symbols and convey such moral or religious instruction as the Church can sanction. Both painter and musician are craftsmen serving the Church and its purposes. As if referring to the synaesthetic musical staff, Guido thinks sound has its visual counterpart: like silver "all chant gains in color the more it is used. After it is polished and filed, it can please though it was unpleasant at first."

The beauties of the senses which convinced Aurelian of Réôme of the harmony of the world take on a subjective, changeable, relative character in Guido's thought. Filing and polishing will change chant into something more pleasant. Yet, if there is a temporal relativity in the object, there is also a relativity of taste: what will please one person will displease another, and vice versa. The appeal of modes is varied: one man is attracted by the second authentic (Phrygian) (its "intermittent leaps"), the delightfulness of the third plagal (Hypolydian), the "volubility" of the fourth authentic (Mixolydian), or the sweetness of the fourth plagal (Hypomixolydian). Guido does not suggest that the person displeased is wrong. One person prefers regularity, another variety, and everyone prefers what suits his own mind (ibid. 14, 17).

It is clear that the Church Fathers and a number of monastics took only a mild (and literary) interest in the Greek theory of ethical effects, which were worldly and secular rather than religious. With Guido and, later, John Cotton, however, ethical-psychological symbolism was revived and reinterpreted, though the names now stand for the ecclesiastical modes, and Guido admits that their source is known only to the All-Wise (ibid. 14). Hermannus Contractus anticipated him by attempting to plumb the depths of psychological characterization, but apparently went back to the old explanation of the Greek modes. Schäfke,[3] depending on a disputed work, summarizes Guido's ethical characterizations parallel to those of the Greeks: the Dorian mode is impressive and noble; the Phrygian passionate, unsteady, and exciting; the Hypodorian sweet of tone; the Hypolydian plaintive and lamenting; the Lydian expresses cheerfulness and grace (G 2.148). Guido is more searching, and his attributions, coming two hundred years after the work attributed to Alcuin possibly defined the modes in terms of quality and quantity, are approximately these:

1. Dorian--deadly seriousness, high dignity, *gravitas*, *morositas*, solemnity, measured movement, distinguished; melodies have an epic character;
2. Hypodorian--serious and plaintive;
3. Phrygian--passionate and disconnected, impetuous, exuberant, unrestrained;
4. Hypophrygian--brilliant and glorious praise;
5. Lydian--charming and graceful, cheerful and bright, a symbol of the activity of human beings;
6. Hypolydian--erotic and plaintively sweet, the complaints of love;
7. Mixolydian--cheerful, worldly, loquacious; melody formed in short breaths; high spirited, youthful; the bliss of fleshly pleasure;
8. Hypomixolydian--sedate cheerfulness; respectable; the cheerful calm of mind of old age, eternal peace (*Microl.* 7-14).

In a sense, these characterizations are remarkable--not because they correspond with Greek descriptions of individual modes, which they do not, nor because they reveal the extent to which Greek descriptions had broken down, but because they are all secular, except possibly for the fourth one and also the last, which implies death. The modes may be ecclesiastical in origin, but Guido's list foretells the gradual liberation of music from ascetic standards and churchly ideals. Furthermore, there is a tacit recognition of the realities of social and communal life and even of individual psychology.

While Guido might have appreciated being called the Pythagoras of the Middle Ages (of "modern music") since, for him, Pythagoras with his discovery of the proportions of hammer-made sound had been the true originator of music (*Microl.* 20), Pythagorean speculation was nevertheless not his *forte*. Neither science nor cosmology was his aim, but an "imitating [of] nature" (ibid. 1) and instruction in the independent craft of making music. He furthered the separation of music and philosophy and of the philosopher-as-music-critic from the complete musician. There is an epigraph said to be by Guido which is quoted by Jerome of Moravia (c.1250) (Cou 1.2) and which in a somewhat different version is entered at the head of a *Regulae musicae rhythmicae* (G 2.25): the musician and the singer are far apart; the latter recites music but the former understands it; the singer is like a brutish animal, for, not understanding what he sings, he sings by rote and not by art; the musician's capability is not only in skill but also in doctrine. Interpretive charitability will indicate, however, that when the singer learns how to sing with notes, he will no longer be a brute, but that to be a true musician he will also need to know theory and to follow Guido's system of notation and composition. This distinction is rooted in ancient and Boethian doctrine.

It is easy to see that Guido was not much concerned with cosmic, theological, or mystical matters. His defense of organum, like that to be found in the *Musica* and *Scolica enchiriadis*, is likewise rooted in such concerns; for him, organum is a natural human creation, a new structure composed by men and not dependent on myth or divine source. Guido was a kind of great divide in music theory and thought. He put philosophical and universal structures to one side. He did not make even a tentative bow in the direction of musical therapeutics. He accepted a relativism which he seemed to think justified itself without regard for any possible cosmic or rational-intellectual contexts it may possess. He pointed toward the musician's discovery that he can earn self-respect either as composer or as performer. And from henceforth Guido was to become a greater influence among musical theorists than Augustine, Boethius, and Cassiodorus combined--especially on writers like John Cotton, who would copy him almost literally, Roger Bacon, and others who grant first place to musical structure itself in their aesthetic considerations.

III

Aribo Scholasticus.   Aribo Scholasticus of Freising (d. c.1078), having learned the methods of Guido from the master himself, wrote his own *De musica* (c.1068-78). He too concentrates on music, not on cosmology, but is more comprehensive as he describes pipe organs[4] and their construction, the tibia, and cymbals (*Musica*, G 2.221-25) in addition to the monochord. Interested in ethical and aesthetic matters, he speaks for clergy and monastics for whom symbolical relations and allegorical meaning are rightly in the foreground. Following Guido, he yet is concerned with the larger questions of transcendence as Guido was not. But he too is in the rhetorical tradition of music theory and makes some of the earliest references in his time to the anonymous *Rhetorica ad Herennium*. He seems to know Augustine's *On Music* (especially 2.8.15). Using the same backhanded phraseology as Guido, he says that the teachings of philosophers are not forever closed to the understanding of music but can be explained, as they often had been, through allegory and symbolism.[5]
This explanation, hardly a matter of arithmetic or mathematics, he gives in terms of the number 4, and he transfers the Nicomachean descriptions of numbers to the Muses: since the ancients did not originally set the

number of the (musical) Muses, whom he calls Sirens (the number 9 is first established in Homer's *Odyssey* 24.65: "a threnody of nine immortal voices"), Aribo ascends from 1 to 9, giving each number a "Musal" allegory. One Muse is the human voice, the source of all music; two Muses are the doubleness of authentic and plagal modes, of the *arsis* and *thesis* of songs, and the duple division of struck and blown instruments; three Muses are the sound-species (diatonic, chromatic, enharmonic); four Muses are four *tropi*, or four basic tetrachords, or four consonances; five Muses are the "greater" consonances, or the five vocables, or the "perishable windows of the five senses" through which the soul steps out into earthly pleasures; six Muses are the "smaller" (imperfect) consonances; the seven Muses are the Virgilian *septem discrimina vocum* of the seven planets; eight Muses are the eight modes; and nine Muses are the heavenly spheres (*Musica*, G 2.219ff).

Aribo is not yet finished with the number 4. The four Evangelists serve for a symbolic parallel with the four tetrachords. Also, *gravium* (the lowest tetrachord) is humanity, *finalium* (the next higher) is death, *superiorum* (the next) is resurrection, and *excellentium* (the highest) is the ascension. The four authentic and plagal cadences separately and the fours together are like the four phases of Christ's life: the internal relationship of the four authentic and the four plagal cadences is like four weddings. From four different bridal chambers come four wives and four husbands to perform two circular dances so that the bridal chamber is the center of the women's dance but the end-point for the men's. These symbolic "analyses" are of course attached to the *tetractys* and are expected to prove that in the tetrachordal organization the resulting fourfoldness of the finales, and ultimately of the modes coming from the number 8 (4 x 2), is a necessity based on natural as well as divine law. The 4 of the interval of the fourth plays its own decisive role; the tetrachord of *graves* relates mystically to St. Matthew's Gospel and the humanity of Christ. The sum of the numbers 4, 3, 2, and 1 equals 10, the mysterious number of the psaltery, which alone makes possible a worthy praise of God. The four authentic and four plagal modes are like the rich and the poor who, despite their diverse and opposing states in life, reach the same (heavenly) ending (*Musica*, G 2.205f). Similarly, consonances are sacred and dissonances profane.

His technical preoccupations involve the monochord and the distribution of tetrachords on its range of pitches. But more of Aribo's musical ideas are concerned with tonality: the first and fourth kinds of tetrachord (d, e, f, g; g, a, b [-flat], c) are more beautiful in song and more pleasant than the second and third (e, f, g, a; f, g, a, b [-flat]) because both the first and the fourth have the semitone in the middle, whereas the second has it in the beginning and the third has it at the end; hence, the last two produce a dull and rough impression. The tetrachord f, e, d, c is a "rural" sound. Aribo recommends a practice more protective of the ego than bold: to determine its mode, one should wait until the end of the piece; if one has named the mode in advance, he need not be refuted; nor need he regret his decision to be silent (G 2.214-15).

Aribo reveals that he is part of the rhetorical-literary tradition not only in the hidden quotations from Boethius to Martianus and Augustine, but also in his comparison of musical intervals with poetic feet: for example, tone-tone-semitone is like long-long-short in poetics. For him, spondees, trochees, and iambs are standards of compositions just as are intervals (G 2.207). He remarks also that rhythm had been an integral part of early ecclesiastical chant: "In earlier times not only the inventors of melodies but also the singers themselves used great circumspection [so] that everything should be invented and sung in proportion. This consideration perished some time ago and is now entirely buried."[6] Even, and perhaps especially in his own time, actors with their seductive exultations and celebrations had no respect for true jubilant singing (G 2.214). That the past must have had better musical taste than the present by now had become cliché often repeated (indeed, it had been a common complaint in antiquity when Plato too had claimed the superiority of past practice). Therefore, composers and singers should follow the old modal formulas so to treat music and text that the melodies will be euphonious and symmetrical (G 2.212-13).

Aribo's center of interest is aesthetic, is in beauty based on law. For him there are three kinds of musical sweetness: the lowest is physical, and the remaining two are intellectual. The lowest (1) involves agreeableness of *cantilena*, a sensuous hearing which is the basis of sweetness; the next (2) is conditioned by understanding, which grasps the beautiful relations of successive tones, ligatures (several pitches bound together in notes to be sung on one syllable), and sections; and the last (3) judges the aesthetic value of the unity in multiplicity, the blending and the modulation of the six consonances (G 2.213). These "sweetnesses" for theoretical purposes all refer to pure *sound*, though Aribo does not mention the word. Like Guido, he stresses the vocal, the tones, the consonances, and not the meanings of words, and thus he is on the verge of saying that music as sound can be an art in itself.

But we expect too much. He maintains the truth of John Scot Erigena's distinction between celestial (natural) and artificial music. The *musicus naturalis* is an untrained popular singer, but the *musicus artificialis* is a *musicus* completely versed in art and theory. Yet he retreats into the old-fashioned position that music, morality, and ethics work together (G 2.225). Again returning to sound itself (and to Guido), Aribo comments (following Guido) that certain people prefer different melodic structures. The ancients, of course, sometimes thought that modes were named after the people who preferred them because they suited different ethnic temperaments. Similarly, Aribo believes that the Lombards prefer step-wise and the Germans leap-wise progressions (G 2.212), and his method is exactly the same as ours when we contrast the music of India with Western European music on the basis of intervals, their kinds, and their common use. Aribo's distinction even here is based on sound-structures and not on moral, psychological, or literary concepts, though of course it is grounded in rhetorical parallels.

IV

Othloh of St. Emmeram. In all the variations so far mentioned on the theme of harmony, its supposed dominance of business and commercial life has not been suggested. A subject which could have been discussed without being called a sin against God or the Church, it was taken up by Othloh of the monastery of St. Emmeram at Regensburg. This monk gave up all of his humanistic interests to study music and arithmetic as sciences which, according to Otto von Simson, he could use "to convey divine secrets to his fellow monks, to prepare them for the life in a world to come."[7]

For Othloh, even the order of the heavenly hosts corresponds to the intervals of the perfect consonances (*Dialogus de tribus quaestionibus* 45, *PL* 146.123). Any number standing alone and making no consonance with another stands for sensual man, who prefers, above all, the temporal, the visible, and the fleshly. He is concerned only with what pleases him and others. But there are the numbers which please spiritual and intellectual men, who value what is foreign to them. As Paul preached and labored freely with and for others (*1 Cor.* 9), so our Savior was in correct relation and proportion (*Dialog.* 42, *PL* 146.119). Thus, the "mystical sweetness" of the consonance is numerical, and in heavenly harmony the one tone of an interval *is* the other--indeed, is in a relation of the octave, fifth, or fourth. Despite the differences in these intervals, all the saints through the harmony of love (the sound of the octave) display the same tone and the same knowledge. The Old and New Testaments are in concordance too, and, like Aribo, Othloh mentions Christ's becoming man, his Passion, Resurrection, and Ascension as symbolic of the consonance. The pure tone, which the semitone cannot reach, is not a consonance, and yet the fourth or fifth cannot be defined without one's taking the semitone into account. Beyond the octave there is nothing more because it already includes the fourth and fifth. Even the semitone, therefore, is necessary to the consonant or spiritual life, in which it offers a necessary help to married people (*Dialog.* 44, *PL* 146.122-23).

For proportions follow God's laws, but differently for the pagans and for Christians. Proportions are everywhere--for example, in the many-sided facility of the human body. They are also gloriously present in the work of professional goldsmiths, workers in iron, stone, and wood; in writers, painters, learned men, merchants, fishermen; in men experienced in war and agriculture; in weavers, doctors, tailors, sculptors, bird handlers, hunters; in cooks and bakers; and in many others who follow other skills. But no skill can be practiced if another is absent, just as everywhere there is a consonance of differentiated tones and skills (*Dialog.* 43, *PL* 146.120).

How can valuables and other (different) national products be brought into concord? Through commerce or trade. Merchants travel to distant environments or countries and take along valuable objects which are in short supply there; then they bring back objects or products which are wanted at home. The differences in these activities are mutually agreeable and entail a powerful consonance. The same is true also for the harmony between rich and poor, master and servant, master and pupil, cloistered and secular life, body and soul, man and wife. Everywhere musical consonance pervades the organization of material and social life, and all is symbolized by the monochord, which measures sounds and modes.

In Othloh the doctrine of universal harmony comes to the same end as the idea of the Great Chain of Being: whatever is, is right. Plato had described an ideal of the state in harmonious operation. This monk was sure that economic life illustrates an existing state of concord. Metaphorically speaking, the image Othloh delineates is neither horizontal nor vertical, but organic. In commercial and professional life the opposing and antithetical parts of the economy reach a reciprocal unity. He draws a picture pleasing to the freeman, the wealthy man, the master. The social, political, and commercial harmony he envisages was as purely imaginary in his own time as it would be today. In instances like this, *musica humana* and harmony are concepts pleasant to contemplate in the abstract. The concrete is and was another matter.

V

Scholastic and Humanistic Thought in the Schools of France. By the last part of the tenth century--that is, by 987, when Hugh Capet became king and founded the Capetian dynasty--France had become a recognizable kingdom separate from the rest of the European countries subordinate to the Holy Roman Emperor. Power was centered around Paris, where Scholasticism had its home, and at Cluny, where the powerful, influential, and strict Cluniac monastic order was established (in 909) and from where it spread its influence over the practice and worship of the Church throughout Europe.

After Rome, Paris now became the first genuine capital of Europe. It represented not the empire, however, but a kingdom. The Gothic style of architecture was to be its great achievement--both an urban and a royal form of art. The church itself became a work of art which would have an immediate impact on the senses. Christ and the Virgin, as Henry Adams has well told us, were the guiding religious symbols, and their veneration was sublimely expressed in the architectural structures dedicated to them and to the saints. Through Gothic architecture the philosophy of Pseudo-Dionysius was made concrete. Absolute Light, God's Radiance, was held to penetrate the cathedral for the people of the world to see, feel, and emulate. For Suger, the abbot of St.-Denis, on the day the choir of his church was consecrated, "the concordance and harmonious oneness of their exquisite singing composed a sort of symphony that was more angelic than human."[8] Liturgy, architecture, and music were practically one, and the chorus of men's voices dominating the Christian service marked the union of man and God.

Scholars refer to the twelfth-century Renaissance--a rebirth of learning, knowledge, and art. Architecture and music were only a part of this so-called rebirth, a new enlightenment to remind one of ancient Greece, of endeavors never encouraged by the Roman emperors and not equalled in their richness since the beginning of the Christian era. Charles W. Haskins has written the classical summary:

> The complete development of Romanesque art and the rise of Gothic; the full bloom of vernacular poetry, both lyric and epic; and the new learning and new literature in Latin. The century begins with the flourishing age of the cathedral schools and closes with the earliest universities already well established at Salerno, Bologna, Paris, Montpellier, and Oxford. It starts with only the bare outline of the seven liberal arts and ends in possession of the Roman and canon law, the new Euclid and Ptolemy, and the Greek and Arabic physicians, thus making possible a new philosophy and a new science. It sees a revival of the Latin classics, of Latin prose, and of Latin verse, both in the ancient style of Hildebert and the new rhymes of the Goliardi, and the formation of the liturgical drama. New activity in historical writing reflects the variety and amplitude of a richer age--biography, memoir, court annals, the vernacular history, and the city chronicle.[9]

It was in the twelfth century that the University of Paris was founded. At once the university became a center of learning throughout Europe, though its fully developed structure was not in place until the middle of the next century. While theological studies remained central, as we might expect in the case of a university that developed out of the cathedral school at Notre Dame, the arts course was in fact dominated by logic and philosophy. Grammar went into decline in the sense that, like ancient music theory, it was subordinated to logic. In the thirteenth century the University of Paris would become a battleground of the struggle between the Platonists and the Aristotelians--a struggle which centered not only on the acceptance of the Idea of the individual thing but also on ontological differences in mathematics: Plato and his Pythagorean predecessors and his followers such as St. Augustine thought number an intrinsic, ontological essence within Being. Aristotle, as we have seen, thought it an abstraction from phenomena which must undergo change and motion; for Aristotle, mathematics cannot provide knowledge of causes or substance; it can merely supply reasons, and only thus can mathematical proportions explain the facts of temporal musical harmony.

By 1100, all the known musical treatises from previous ages had been collected not only in monastic libraries but also, more significantly, in the great cathedral libraries which formed the nuclei of the early university libraries. Indeed it may be argued that the cathedral libraries at Paris and Chartres, which held more secular books and hence a greater variety of titles than the monastic libraries, provided the ground bases of the renaissance in literature and scholarship which, as we have noted, occurred in the twelfth century. Peter Abelard (1079-1142), whose Aristotelianism at first was a scandal among theologians because he stressed the individual thing and not the Platonic-Augustinian Idea, was closely associated with the University of Paris, while John of Salisbury was to study there as his student, later working at Chartres where he would be one of its greatest bishops. The end result was a humanism deeply influenced by the ancient pagan and modern Christian documents deposited in the great libraries--a humanism which in retrospect appears to be in fact the initial stage of the more widely recognized humanism of the fifteenth-century Italian Renaissance.

An important historical development in the French schools involves the embracing of both philosophy and theology in the initial stages of their separation, which occurred under the influence of Aristotelianism as well as of other ideas inherited from secular philosophy and remnants of Neoplatonic doctrine. Frequently we see the curious amalgamation of the philosophy of Pseudo-Dionysius, as it were, with that of Al Farabi and other Arabs. This mixture is already in evidence in the middle of the eleventh century in the works of Michel Psellus (1018-c.1080).

Psellus, a philosopher working in Constantinople, revived the study of Plato. In a letter to the Byzantine Emperor Constantine Monomachus (1042-55), he writes about the various forms and classes of music. They had been given to men, he says, by the Higher Powers in heaven, which, without even the possibility of dissolution, weave together eternal life, endless and unceasing movement, and creative and productive powers. To begin with, created beings were rhythmical in movement, their voices were harmonic in order, and both movement and order produced a well-composed dance. Then tuneful instruments were formed, and the power of music extended everywhere.   As scientific knowledge, music is both theoretical and practical; it embraces singing and playing in their perfection. It is also the art for training character through a mastery of what is fitting in melody and rhythm. Music leads the soul from beauty in objects on earth to the Idea of beauty. It exerts healing effects. It is related to astronomy; and since it contains relations of order, it includes chants, rhythms (dances), and divine music.   Hence, since ancient (Greek) times, it has been used in performances for the gods in hymns, odes, and dances, and similar kinds of songs and dances have been performed to celebrate the important stages in the lives of human beings. Unfortunately, Psellus adds, music is not what it was formerly, and it only faintly echoes the superior musical forms of the past.[10] In one statement, there can hardly be a more tightly knit combination of Greek (both Platonic and Aristotelian) and Arabic elements.

In the West, the importance of Aristotelianism should not be underestimated. William of Champeaux (c.1070-1121), a scholastic philosopher at Paris, taught Abelard, who became his rival in reputation. Writing about music, Abelard touches upon architecture, but he makes an initial bow to the old Pseudo-Dionysian philosophy: he sees the spheres which make music as "heavenly habitations" where angels and saints "in their ineffable sweetness of harmonic modulation render eternal praise to God" (*Theol. Christ.* 1.5).[11]   The celestial Jerusalem, like Solomon's Temple of the earthly Jerusalem, is penetrated by the same divine harmony as the celestial spheres. The proportions of the perfect consonances are the main dimensions of the Temple (*1 Kings* 6), which is the prototype of the Christian sanctuary: "symphonic perfection" made the Temple an image of heaven. Otto von Simson suggests that Abelard is the first medieval writer to think that the proportions of the Temple were those of musical consonances.[12] Perhaps. But the surprising thing is that here the individual thing is not only a symbol of the spiritual, of divine order, but also the reverse. The spiritual explains the individual, particular, material thing, which is subject of direct observation. The architectural work is not merely the symbol of divine order. Through musical concordance it actually embodies the divinity of heaven.

The aesthetic effect is structural and another evidence that in the Middle Ages beauty and mathematics were almost one. The mathematics is geometrical, and it is geometrically analogical in that it leads the mind from this world of mere appearances to a contemplation of the divine order. Classical numbers had been represented by geometrical figures; they were seen as not relatively but absolutely beautiful and had natural pleasures associated with them (Plato, *Philebus* 51). Macrobius (2.2) and Boethius (*Arith.* 2.6) followed suit, and Plato's five solids were fundamental geometric forms apparently now and forever. Gundisalvo, for example, thus insists that every artist or craftsman is a practical geometrician.[13] Since both eye and ear, according to their own capacities, take in proportions, there is a latent or suggested geometrizing also in music.

The geometrical-architectural assumption of musical structures is explained by Villard de Honnecourt, who had been trained in the Cistercian monastery of Vaucelles. In his sketch book (c.1250), which was written after such structures had been extensively used, he

> expounds not only the geometrical canons of Gothic architecture but also the Augustinian aesthetics of "musical" proportions, proportions that correspond to the intervals of the perfect musical consonances. He is our earliest theoretical witness to the proportion "according to true measure"; even more interesting, however, is one of his designs representing the ground plan of a Cistercian church drawn *ad quadratum*, i.e., the square bay of the side aisles is the basic unit or module from which all proportions of the plan are derived. And these proportions . . . correspond in each case to the ratios of the musical consonances, the same ratios that . . . were actually employed by the Cistercian builders. Thus the length of the church is related to the transept in the ratio of the fifth (2:3). The octave ratio (1:2) determines the relations between side aisle and nave, length and width of the transept, and, we may assume on the basis of Cistercian practice, of the interior elevation as well. The 3:4 ratio of the choir evokes the

musical fourth; the 4:5 ratio of nave and side aisles taken as a unit corresponds to the third; while the crossing, liturgically and aesthetically the center of the church, is based on the 1:1 ratio of unison, most perfect of consonances.[14]

Abbot Suger (c.1080-1151), in speaking of rebuilding the church of St.-Denis, mentions two aspects of medieval architectural theory, the aesthetics of harmony and that of light. In his description of the consecration of the church of St.-Denis outside Paris, he stresses the former, commenting on the disparity between things human and things divine, and concentrates on the "single, delightful concordance of one superior well-tempered harmony." The cosmos, he thinks, was created by the One "who transcends and reconciles the many." Like Bernard of Clairvaux and other Cistercians, he thinks of the universe as a symphonic composition; and like Alan of Lille, he sees God as the divine architect who followed musical laws in creating the edifice of the world. Those who build cathedrals participate in eternal reason in order to withstand evidences of the sensual, the carnal, and the mortal. They prefer the spiritual and the eternal, and they share the enduring hope of an eternal reward and the union one day with supreme reason and everlasting bliss. Clearly, Suger thinks that through the reconciliation of contraries and the differences of various parts of the universe according to the law of musical proportion (that is, by means of arithmetical and geometrical harmonic rules) the architect carries out the mandates of God.[15] For Suger, architecture and liturgical chant had one, and only one, purpose.

VI

Hugh of St.-Victor. From another locale in the vicinity of Paris, the mystically oriented School of St.-Victor, came the Scholastic Hugh (1096-1142), who perhaps had been born in Saxony. His *Didascalicon: De studio legendi* (*Lore of Teaching, or On the Study of Reading*) is a didactic work in seven books--three on the Liberal Arts, three on theology, and one on religious meditation. Like others at the Abbey of St.-Victor, he wanted to neutralize the influence of Abelard and his emphasis on the importance of the individual and of the observation of the particular object. St. Augustine and Pseudo-Dionysius (in John Scot Erigena's translation) furnished major aspects of the background of Hugh's work, as did Aristotle (by way of Boethius) and Isidore of Seville. Hugh's references, entirely religious, are frequently scriptural. On the endlessly moot question of the facts of astrology, he found that astrological predictions are the work of the devil, though there is a natural astrology when the planets affect the temperature of the human body. For him, the *Timaeus*, whose cosmogony does not conform to the teachings of Christian writers, is not a standard of Christian thought. Nor do pagan philosophical figures replace Christ and God's saints. He is the first writer to devote a full treatise (*Didasc.* 6) to beauty and literary art.   In part formalist, his aesthetic is also allegorical and symbolistic and includes a thorough-going symbolism of colors.

His theory of aesthetics is at the center of the theory of beauty of the Middle Ages.   For him, beauty is spiritual, sensible, and expressive.   It appears naturally in the visible world, where through various sensible forms it symbolizes the simple beauty of God and the soul; directly and indirectly, it turns the mind towards the infinite, the perfect, the Ideal--that is, to God. The hoped-for psychological state is mystical.   Between the ideal and the physical and psychological man there resides a metaphysical unity in which reason (but not reasoning and logic), intellect, and spirituality combine to achieve not only knowledge but also contemplation, order, harmony, movement, and aesthetic pleasure in qualities of sense.   Since the visible world is a book written by God, music, like all other arts, is not an art having its own aim and end but a lesser wisdom which, correctly used, can lead to and be illuminated by the higher divine Wisdom (ibid. 2.1), whose image a person is to find within himself and whose union with mankind is again to be realized.

The sacred Scriptures have conveyed meaning through history, allegory, and tropology.   But it is difficult to grasp the three meanings at once.   Not all parts of musical instruments like the psaltery and others of its type ring out with musical sounds; only the strings do that.   The rest is the frame to which the strings are attached and across which they are stretched so that they can produce sweet song.   The Scriptures are so arranged in their parts that God's wisdom resounds like strings but through the sweetness of spiritual understanding or through the utterance of mysteries in the histori-cal or literal text.   Certain things are supposed to be understood spiritually, others give moral conduct, and still others present a simple sense of history. Certain things can be all three.   Thus all parts of the Scriptures are so adjusted that they can give "the sweetness of spiritual understanding in the manner of strings" or show mysteries "here and there in the course of a historical narrative or in the substance of the literal context"; and as these are connected into one object, the Scriptures bind them together as does the wood of an instrument and receive the sound as a unit--a sound not of the strings alone but also as formed out of the wooden body according to its shape.   Thus the Scriptures must be so interpreted that history, allegory, and tropology each, not everywhere, but as "individual things [are] fittingly [assigned] in their own places, as reason demands."   Sometimes they are all together, the truth of history hinting at a transcendental meaning in allegory and tropologically showing "how we ought to behave" (ibid. 5.2).   In Hugh's terms, then, interpreting a holy text is also combining its various parts and functions into one metaphysical whole.

In Hugh's philosophy too, as in Augustine's, number as revealed in both what is heard and what is seen pervades the universe.   But for Hugh, light and color are more important than number, though the three together make a mystic, intellectual union.   Beauty in itself is luminosity, and the more luminous the colors (green is the most luminous) the more beautiful they are. Invisible beauty is indivisible and identical with itself; visible beauty, never simple and identical with itself, must exist in the manifold and within difference. The music of the spheres, the objective musical beauty of the world, is not separate from universal light, colors, and mathematical optics. Color seems to visualize light as the true Being, just as the inner dark spaces in churches and the outside light together represent absence in the presence of God's light.

Indeed, luminosity is the second principle (proportion is prior to it) in the aesthetics of medieval art and architecture. It is even more important than "musical" construction itself, and for twelfth- and thirteenth-century thinkers like Hugh (ibid. 7.12) and Thomas Aquinas (*Summa Theologica* I, Q. 67, 1-3) it comes first. Stained glass windows are one among the many evidences of the medieval taste for clarity and luminosity, which, no less than musical concordance, "conveyed an insight into the perfection of the cosmos, and a divination of the Creator."[16] The highest poetical expression of the medieval love of light is to be found in Dante's *Paradiso* (31.22ff).

For his theory of the arts, which include all the areas of knowledge important for man's perfection and effective in his achievement of salvation, Hugh relies on the number 4. The arts are (1) theoretical (involving truth), (2) practical (virtue), (3) mechanical (involving the relief from the difficulties of human existence), and (4) logical. (Though they supposedly characterize human life in its completeness, the aesthetic only seems to be lacking.) The categories he names mean the formal realization of the four; and the four are based on the two--theoretical (truth) and practical (action)--of Aristotle (*Topics* 7.1, *Metaph.* 2.1), Boethius, and William of Conches. By mechanical he does not mean automatic or machine-like. He means imitative: the work is human because it is not the work of nature, which in actuality produces what is hidden in the work of God; it is an imitation of nature: like John Scot Erigena's "artificial," it is an "adulterate" (*Didasc.* 1.9, 2.2); it is a relief from the "temporal, dependent, and fragile nature of bodily life."[17] The task in philosophy is to perfect man's self-knowledge through reason and the practical arts (virtue) and his knowledge of God through the theoretical arts. The (liberal) arts therefore are interchangeable with religion, though subservient to it--an opinion also of John Scot Erigena (*De divisione naturae* 1.69, *PL* 122.513) and Augustine (*Divine Providence* 2.9.26, FC 1.303-04) before his retractions. In a union with the Divine in its Wisdom, they are interdependent among themselves and necessary to man if he is to attain perfection and heaven. Following Martianus Capella Hugh believes that all intellectual activity is achieved through philosophy preceded by the Seven Liberal Arts which Philosophy had given to Mercury.

Hugh agrees also with John Scot Erigena and Pseudo-Dionysius that harmony, like the universe created by God, is the concord of many dissimilar components brought into a unity (*Didasc.* 2.1) and that music is a concord of many disparate voices brought into a unity (ibid. 2.12). He traces the term 'music' back to water (*aqua*) because no symphony ("pleasant sound") "is possible without moisture" (*Didasc.* 2.8), and the concordance and the pleasure are perceivable: he himself has felt the unity in the quality of sound. More autobiographical than most of the ancient and medieval theorists about music, he writes that he "Often . . . used to bring out [his] strings, stretched to their number on the wooden frame, both that [he] might note with [his] ear the difference among the tones and that [he] might at the same time delight [his] soul with the sweetness of the sound" (*Didasc.* 6.3).

Not only a Platonist, Hugh was also an Aristotelian classifier; to theoretical art, he thinks, correspond theology, mathematics (including music and arithmetical symbolism), and physics; to the practical arts belong the moral and normative sciences; and to the mechanical arts (seven in number) belongs poetic knowledge--as well as various crafts, architecture, and the plastic arts. To open a path to the final spiritual perfection of man, Hugh presents a comprehensive table of the sciences and the arts, outlines the entire transcendental whole of God's creation, and places music in its old Boethian and Cassiodorian positions. Music seems to have disappeared as an art, except that among the theatrics (poetry and literature) he tacitly gives music a place among poetic forms (see Appendix C). His entire system is an abstractly conceived synthesis of the traditional course which was binding later for the Dominicans Albertus Magnus (c.1193-1280) and Robert Kilwardby (d. 1279), who was to become the Archbishop of Canterbury. An unusual work to serve as a school or instruction book at any time, the *Didascalicon* serves to show that art is not an individual discipline but rather is part of a context, part of the order of knowledge in a whole. While "practical" music seems ignored, except possibly as part of song, all crafts and abilities are systematized in steps--in terms of high and low, everything finding place on the rungs of a ladder, or a chain of Being, with God (and theology) at the top. The resulting image as a whole is a pyramid.

VII

The School of Chartres: William of Conches (Gulielmus de Conches). The Platonism of the School of Chartres, founded by Fulbert (d. 1029) and further developed by Bernard of Chartres (d. 1126), was a true renaissance movement in that solutions to theological and cosmological questions were sought through a synthesizing of Platonic and Christian ideas. Again the *Timaeus* as commented upon by Chalcidius and Macrobius was the basic (though fragmentary) text. Martianus Capella's *Marriage of Philology and Mercury* was a supplementary work. The Chartres Platonists saw a single purpose in *Timaeus* and *Genesis*, which they interpreted so speculatively as to bring the two books into agreement. For example, Thierry (Theodoric) of Chartres, in his own age called the "born-again Plato," hoped in geometry combined with arithmetic to find the Divine Artist himself and in geometrical demonstration through arithmology to reveal the Trinity (*Heptateuchon*, after 1141). The aesthetic principles of the School of Chartres were the "absolute" and eternal Platonic and Pythagorean musical cosmological ratios supplemented by Augustine's measure, number, and weight coming from the book of *Wisdom*. Architectural (like musical) science was interpreted by the Scholastics as theoretical, as a knowledge of the laws of the quadrivium in general and of geometry in particular. All of this is reflected in the architecture of Chartres Cathedral. Similarly, it was supposedly reflected also in the *Consolation of Philosophy* of Boethius whose celebrations of the ancients were consistent with the thinking of the School of Chartres.

The cosmological views of William of Conches were thus identical with those of the School of Chartres--that is, of the *Timaeus* Christianized or Plato filtered through Pseudo-Dionysius. He stressed the quadrivium and placed more emphasis on the objective and less on the mystical than did Hugh of St.-Victor. God is not the craftsman but the master-builder or even the theorist.[18] He believed that the effect of the World Soul, which he identified with the Holy Spirit, is creative and that it is the source of order and harmony. Ontologically, the World Soul thus defined is a musical consonance. The current conception of architecture, artistically speaking, was musical, like Augustine's; the universe was thought to be an architectural work and God was seen as its architect. In imitation of the *Timaeus*, constructional form was Platonized. William indicates that the perfect proportions admired in musical and architectural compositions have a technical and architectural function in that they hold together cosmological elements and provide the basis for both the beauty and the stability of mundane and cosmic structures.[19]

In fact, William was a naturalist and a physicist. He believed with Democritus that the universe is made up of atoms. Yet, approaching the book of *Genesis*, he adopted the allegorical-symbolical rather than the naturalistic view. He thought that the world is three-fold in nature (in power and property): it is vegetable (in grasses and trees), sensible (in brute animals), and rational (in humans).[20] On the whole, like the School of Chartres itself, William adopted the hylomorphism of Aristotle--that is, the theory that the physical world is sufficient to explain the universe. And yet, paradoxically enough, in attempting to explain the universe in terms of natural causes, the School of Chartres relinquished complete faith in moral symbols and turned to Plato and the Scriptures. Thierry of Chartres, for example (in *De septem diebus et sex operum distinctibus*), tries to explain Creation rationally, but says he cannot do so unless the intellectual training of the quadrivium can throw light on *Genesis*. William is less progressive than Augustine or Hugh of St.-Victor in that he interprets *Genesis* not as man-centered but as a reconciliation with medieval science--that is, with the cosmology of the *Timaeus*. Beginning with natural knowledge (*scientia*), he separates things (*res*) from words (*verba*). The result is either symbolical or abstract, as we may see in his discussion of body and soul: for the soul, value lies not in the body or its qualities, but only in the ratio and harmony between them.[21]

William's interpretation of the Liberal Arts as a system follows Hugh's: the trivium is concerned with eloquence (the preparation for philosophy), the quadrivium with wisdom (the first part of philosophy, theology being the second). Among the mechanical arts, the first three--fabric making, armament, and commerce--are concerned with the extrinsic knowledges of philosophy, and the remaining four with internal remedies or foods. Dramatics (which includes practical music) is concerned with the interior human thing because it prevents mental languishing, encourages movement and play, and keeps the body from exhaustion from excessive work.[22]

His contribution to the idea of music was slight. Here he was influenced by Plato and Boethius. In his *Dialogus de substantiis physicis* and in his commentary on Plato's *Timaeus*, he follows Plato closely without making the analyses of Greek musical thought which Al Farabi supplied. Not surprisingly, he divided music into the Boethian *musica mundana*, *musica humana*, and *musica instrumentalis*, and divided the latter, probably for the first time in Latin, into *melica*, *metrica*, and *rithmica* (*PL* 172.247). It is not merely that melic poetry was song, but that the term *harmonica* (a series of tones or pitches producing a linear effect of concord), which frequently by way of convenience has been translated as "melody" (in English), now had legitimately been replaced by a new word that continued in popular use. On the other hand, 'harmony' gradually would tend to mean simultaneous concords in pleasant progressions. William of Conches was a medieval intellectual whose idea of music was derived from Boethius and hardly extended beyond the elements of chanted verse.

VII

John of Salisbury. John of Salisbury, however, illustrates the literary-humanistic character of Chartres. He deplored concentration on philosophy and science and any retreat from poetry and history. While Bede and Alcuin had commented on the technical properties of literature, he understood poetry to be an independent art though not unrelated to grammar and rhetoric. Like other Christian teachers, he enthusiastically commented on poets, fables, and history (which Hugh of St.-Victor had placed outside philosophy). He was a humanist in both taste and erudition. The Charterians in general separated the entire trivium, including literary commentary, from philosophy. Bernard of Chartres, an avid devotee of literary studies, taught grammar by means of poetry and prose, and advised students to read poems and history (see John of Salisbury, *Metalogicon* 24, pp. 65ff). John himself called William of Conches "the richest teacher of letters after Bernard of Chartres" (ibid., p. 21). His own *Metalogicon* (*Defense of the Trivium*) is a treatise moving uneasily from grammatical and literary study to logic (dialectic) and making a compromise by finding them both necessary. His *Policraticus* (translated under the title *Frivolities of*

Courtiers and Footprints of Philosophers), completed in 1159, has the non-scientific, moralistic tone of Cicero and Plutarch.   (Like the *Metalogicon*, it is dedicated to St. Thomas Becket, whom John served as secretary in 1162-70, a period which culminated in Becket's murder.) Encyclopedic in shape, it is a satire on courtiers in both Church and state and a description of the morals, philosophy, and government which should be their ideal.   In a sense, it is the religious-courtly counterpart of a later book, Castiglione's *The Courtier* (1528), a secular account of what the man of the courtly and noble life should be.   John of Salisbury draws on Quintilian, Horace, and Seneca, and does not confine his literary enthusiasm to biblical literature.   This humanistic trend is even more in evidence in the *Metalogicon* which reminds one of Bede's *De schematibus et tropis sacrae scripturae* (*PL* 90.175ff).   Here he quotes Greek, Roman, and medieval authorities without number and buttresses their opinions with biblical quotations.   Under discussion are grammar (including rhetoric), writing, spelling, composition, "speech," general literature, poetry, history, and logic as applied to theological, physiological, linguistic, and social forms of knowledge.   Logic is the science of reasoning, and the trivium is more important than the quadrivium.   In part built on Aristotle's *Organon*, the *Metalogicon* is a contribution to literary scholarship rather than to science, a guide to conduct described in Virgil and Cicero.

Though he had been a student of William of Conches as well as of Abelard, John sympathized with the Cistercian movement in its austerity. The Cistercian Order had been founded by St. Robert of Molesme in 1098 at Cîteaux, and its most famous member was St. Bernard of Clairvaux, who came to Cîteaux as a novice in 1112.   The Order spread to the founding of more than five hundred monasteries by the end of the twelfth century in Western Europe.   Such monasteries were located in rural locations rather than in cities, and their churches were austere while their liturgical music favored a more plain style which avoided unnecessary ornamentation and metrical rhythms.   Their view of the usual cathedral and Benedictine musical practice was delineated by Aelred of Rievaulx (c.1109-66) in a lengthy complaint:

> Types and figures, aside, whence, I ask, all these organs, all these cymbals in the church? To what purpose, I ask, that horrible inflating of bellows, expressing the crash of thunder rather than the smoothness of human voice? To what end that contracting and weakening of the voice? This singer harmonizes, that expresses dissonance; another divides and breaks off notes in the middle. Now the voice is strained, now it is shattered, now it swells louder, now it is broadened into a fuller sound. At one time (shame to say) it is forced into horse-like neighing; at another with its masculine vigor ignored, it is sharpened into the slenderness of the female voice; sometimes it is twisted and twisted again with a certain kind of artificial convolution. Sometimes you may see a man with his mouth open as if he were expiring, with

his wind cut off, not singing, and with a kind of ridiculous suspension of sound as if to threaten total silence; now imitating the agonies of the dying or the terror of the suffering. Meanwhile, his whole body is busy with various histrionic gestures, the lips are contorted, the arms whirl about and play wantonly; and a flexing of the fingers responds to each particular note. And this ridiculous dissoluteness is called religion; and where such things are done the more often, there the clamor is that God is the more honorably served. Meanwhile the common folk, trembling and astonished, marvel at the sounding of bellows, the clashing of cymbals, the harmony of pipes; but the lascivious gesticulations of the singers, the meretricious quavering and breaking of their voices, ought to be regarded not without merriment and laughter, as you ought to consider them suitable not to the house of prayer, but to the theater, not to praying, but to viewing.[23]

Thus they objected to what they saw as a decadent sophistication in music, to urban culture, which they saw as lacking in spirituality, and also to scholastic teaching, which they found useless. It is no wonder that they considered Paris to be the new Babylon. But as Augustinian mystics, the Order was influential at Chartres and elsewhere.

John, like the Cistercians, objected to over-elaborate church music, and his demand for simplicity may be compared to Plato's insistence on simplicity. His religious reason and Plato's secular-political one are not actually dissimilar: by nature music has affective and educational powers. Typically, John thinks music comprehends the universe and reconciles the dissident or dissonant through the law of proportion, a law harmonizing the heavenly spheres and governing both cosmos and man. Like William of Conches, he seems to be both Pythagorean and Boethian but Christianized. For him, the proper role of music is not to be an intellectual pursuit, but to educate soul and body through symphonic praise of the Lord as now sung by the Church Militant and as will also be sung by the Church Triumphant (*Frivolities* 1.6). The ghost of Boethius is materialized in the truths of music as universal fact, as mundane state, and as an instrumentality for human beings. The efforts towards betterment and improvement often miscarry, however.

With Jerome, John seems to have a relish for observing the follies of women and the sins and the madnesses of lust. This last is the child, he thinks, of the five senses, of all of which the ear seems to be closest to cleanness (and that of touch to filthiness). But there is a danger that the ear will be "charmed" by the tone of the organ and by the human voice, and the "mind's virility" will be made effeminate by them (*Frivolities* 8.6). Thus, musicians and singers show a lack of philosophical seriousness if they are too much occupied with music. Yet singing well or perfectly "without levity" is desirable if there is an incentive to be gained. Though Cato had said that "singing well" is "not the trait of a serious man," the "pleasure of the ear is [nevertheless] consonant with honor" (ibid. 8.12).

John can praise music only if it is in its proper place: it is one of the Liberal Arts; it began, according to different accounts, with Pythagoras, Moses, and Tubal (Jubal); it has great power, many forms, and harmonies which embrace the universe. Harmonious law derives from its symmetry, and heavens and the activities of the world and man are ruled by it. Its educational purpose is moral. "Its instruments form and fashion conduct and, by a kind of miracle of nature, clothe with melodies and colorful forms of rhythms and measures the tone of the voice, whether expressed in words or not, and adorn them as with a robe of beauty" (ibid. 1.6). It was praised by the Church Fathers; it controls evil and calms the soul, which, as Plato had insisted (*Tim.* 35), consists of musical harmonies. Through "concealed passages" and its own vital force, it pervades the whole universe, including sense, reason, and the soul. Tone is not spirit but conveys and is the medium of spirit--human, divine, and prophetic. It captivates with beauty and drives away gloom. Thus John of Salisbury seems to anticipate Ficino's idea that music is spirit or air which sets the soul in motion, and he comes close to allowing music the transcendence Plotinus granted. it.

The Church both Militant and Triumphant, which is a counter-weight to the corruption of political thought and power, praises music because it praises God (*Apoc.* 14.2, *Ps.* 80.2, 150.4). Is John speaking from experience or literary hearsay, however, when he says that the Phrygian mode must be avoided as leading to evil, lust, and folly? He describes florid singing in the church and thinks its climactic effect produces its own kind of pleasure. Yet "this type of music . . . carried to the extreme is more likely to stir lascivious sensations in the loins than devotion in the heart." It must, of course, be kept within "reasonable limits," and when it is, it is moral, it "frees the mind from care, banishes worry about things temporal," gives peace and joy, inspires love for God and "draws souls to association with the angels" (*Frivolities* 1.6). Singing with the spirit, with the mind, and in wisdom even without words but with rejoicings of the mind can soothe the ears of God and avert his wrath. Forbidden is a Babylonian prostitution of the voice for purposes of pandering. The Phrygian mode, "banished from the court of Greece," is indeed the villain (ibid.).

It is not unusual in the later Middle Ages that Orpheus already will receive the attention accorded him later by Renaissance thinkers such as Marsilio Ficino and Pico della Mirandola. We need only recall the *Scolica enchiriadis* and Regino of Prüm. John of Salisbury, however, scorns Orpheus as a patron of effeminate males and homosexuals (probably derived from his failure to rescue Eurydice). The "plaints" of such men, John says, "can expect for the most part no happy outcome" (ibid. 1.6). Nor does he approve of music at banquets. The Lord himself castigated the lyre, the timbrel, and the pipe at feasts (*Isaiah* 5.11-12). It was during such a feast that the king of Babylon saw the writing on the wall (*Daniel* 5.24-25).

Human bodies are vessels of the Lord, and anyone who leads them to passion and foulness should not enter God's kingdom (*Frivolities* 1.6). The contrast can be drawn between Augustus, who, being scoffed at for playing the drum, gave up such frivolity, and Nero, who sang and played for his own corruption and that of Rome (ibid. 1.7). John is of course speaking of music abused; and his horror and ostensible terror of musical corruption are more like the reactions of certain of John Calvin's followers than even of Plato himself. In spite of his association with Chartres, John nevertheless is less a humanist than William of Conches and more like the most severe, uncompromising, and demanding of Reformed clerics following the Reformation. He could have been a Cistercian, but not even Bernard of Clairvaux is so severe.

VIII

The Cistercian Reform: Bernard of Clairvaux. If music theorists like Guido of Arezzo thought that tones in music in their variety represent the wonders of God's universe, Christian theological thinkers did not always agree about polyphony. The music which best represented the multiplicity of God's world of tones was quite frequently not to their liking. Believing that chants had gotten out of hand by, among other practices, not holding strictly to the prescribed modes, the Cistercians called for musical purity. David (*Ps.* 143.9) had sung: "To thee, O God, I will sing a new canticle [song]: on the psaltery and an instrument of ten strings I will sing praises to thee." Thus, they believed, no chant should ever cover a range of more than ten tones. The result was a change in practice in keeping with modal formulae. St. Bernard (1090-1153), founder and abbot of the Cistercian abbey at Clairvaux and severe critic of Abelard, regards polyphony to be new and superficial, something to be avoided (it is the art of Paris), and a poor substitute for the old and genuine (Gregorian) music which contributes to the honor and the sacred character of the Church. Though the Augustinian idea of beauty as number, measure, and weight could justify either complexity or simplicity, the simple effect of measured words was decisive. Art does not arouse curiosity, he thinks, but calms it; it does not tire the senses, but gladdens them. Song should be dignified and neither lascivious nor coarse. It must be so sweet as not to be superficial, and it must so caress the ear that it reaches the heart. It must banish sorrow, moderate anger, and enhance the meanings of words, not empty them. But these are the limits: a serious loss of spiritual grace occurs when the superficiality of song deflects from the value of its meaning and when one listens more to the fluctuations of song than to the content (*Ad guidonam, Ep.* 393; *PL* 182.61ff). Bernard has been frequently accused of anti-intellectualism, but it is widely agreed that he is almost the ideal mystic.

As a Cistercian reacting against the alleged abuses of the Benedictines, Bernard, to whom are (doubtfully) attributed a *Tonale* and a *Tractatus cantandi* (both dated 1130), describes principles for musical reform. Thus, the true science of song belongs to those who limit themselves to the truth of law and ignore the devices of others--that is, persons who think more of the imitation of others than of nature and who separate what belongs

together and combine what does not.   Such people confuse everything.
They begin a song and end it, compose and organize it, sing up and down,
however they please, and not as they are permitted to do (*Praefatio seu
tractatus de cantu seu correctione antiphonarii, PL* 182.1121ff).   The voice
must be lively in motion so that the text is clear and well articulated, and the
singer's manner must be honest and straightforward.   Choirs must achieve a
good ensemble, according to the character and demands of the music.

On the negative side, Cistercian ideals are those expressed by Aelred
of Rievaulx in his attack on the alleged abuses of church music, as noted
above.   An Augustinian in musical matters, Bernard himself composed
music.   He thought that ecclesiastical music can radiate truth and that
sounds can radiate great Christian virtues.   Music should please the ear
enough to move the heart, though it necessarily should strike a golden mean
between the frivolous and the harsh (*Ep.* 398, *PL* 182.609ff).   For him
heavenly bliss would be an eternity of listening to choirs of angels and
saints and of joining in their singing (*Sermones in cantica, PL* 183.1130).
The highest kind of knowledge is mystical.   Dante acted justly in his
Paradiso (31-33) by giving Bernard the place of substitute for Beatrice after
she has assumed her position in the Rose of Paradise.

The Cistercian Order tried through strict asceticism and poverty to
restore the original practices of the Rule of St. Benedict.   Consequently, it
seems fitting that the abbey at Fontenay (1130-47) should have been built
according to austere Pythagorean musical principles.   Both its elevation and
ground plan were determined by Augustine's perfect ratio of 1:2 (the
octave).   The bays of the side aisles are of equal length and width, the same
dimension being marked off vertically by a string course.   Each bay, like the
central nave, is therefore a special "cube" like the "geometrical" harmony of
Boethius (*Arith.* 2.6).   The ratios of 2:3 and 3:4 (the intervals of the fifth and
fourth, respectively) are also made concrete.   Thus Augustine enters the
field of architecture in addition to that of rhetoric (poetics) and music: the
style of the Cistercian Order is more than any other type of Christian
architecture based on the "perfect" ratios which had been defined by the
medieval music theorists--and earlier by Pythagoras, Ptolemy, Boethius,
and others--prior to being taken up by Bernard and his followers.[24]

In his sermons on the *Song of Songs*, Bernard was more than ecstatic
about the effects of Cistercian architecture.   In a manner reminiscent of
Augustine himself, he exclaims:

> O truly reposeful place, which I deem worthy of being called a restful
> chamber. Here one not only sees a God who seems driven by anger or
> filled with sorrows, but his will here reveals itself as good, pleasant,
> and complete. This sight inspires no fears, but it refreshes. It does not
> stir up restless thirst for knowledge, but calms it. It does not tire the
> senses, but satisfies them. Here reigns true peace. God the silent
> quiets everything, and to contemplate all that rests is to be at peace.[25]

Such was the effect on Bernard of musical order, of a mystical number, experienced in the individual sacred architectural structure and object.

IX

Alan of Lille (Alain de Lille, or Alanus ab Insulis). Another and later Platonizer closely related to the school of Chartres was the Cistercian Alan of Lille. He was a powerfully expressive poet, a great speculative theologian, a "Universal Doctor" (like Albertus Magnus later), and by reputation an alchemist. He was not, like Adelard of Bath, a practicing physicist, but a follower of the natural science of his time, whose basic principles were embodied in the music of the spheres.

His *Anticlaudianus*, a large work with a musical section based on Martianus Capella, by title seems to signify opposition to the work of Claudianus, the Latin poet who wrote a satire against Rufinus (d. 395), the minister of Theodosius noted for his cruelty and persecutions. But Alan's work is actually a reverse imitation: Claudianus described the completely evil man; Alan describes the completely good one--the new man, both religious and courtly. *Anticlaudianus* serves as a sign of a quite new kind of secular writing in which, as by John of Salisbury, attention is turned not toward the Church at large but in the direction of the secular and political world outside, which was becoming commercially and politically powerful.

In Alan's eyes, God is a powerful and artful architect who built the universe as his royal palace and harmonized the great variety of created things by means of musical consonance (proportions) (*De planctu naturae, PL* 210.453). Nature is government, law and order, method and rule--but also light, brilliance, beauty, and form. Every science has its own superior rules not requiring further proof for the basis of its manner of demonstration. Music has its axioms as geometry has its theorems.[26] The profane sciences can be allied with the principles of theology. Faith and knowledge are two separate spheres. The Father created matter, the Son form, and the Holy Ghost their bringing together. The world's architect created form or formation, order, and harmony in that earthly forms, the species of things, imitate the divine Idea.[27]

Alan's theory corresponds to or is identical with the philosophy of the School of Chartres: here is a basic Platonism devoted to grammar and rhetoric (not, however, to music) and to the mathematical aspects of art which represent the sense-world and not Platonic forms. Number explains the parallel between music and architecture. It also explains that art by approximating the transcendent beauty of nature can realize the eternal beauty of the world--eternal, illuminative, intelligent, and beautiful because it is God's.

In the *Anticlaudianus*, a dramatic allegory of the simplest type, the Seven Liberal Arts are virgins and sisters--purified Muses--who, along with the virtues, contribute to the life of a good man. Natura calls to a council her sisters Concord, Abundance, Favor, Youth, Laughter, Modesty,

Discretion, Reason, Faith, Liberality, and Nobility. They are asked to form a new man who will be both man and God. After some disagreements (even here?), Harmonia prevails. The trivium makes up the shaft, the axeltree, and the gilt of a cart which is going to heaven. The quadrivium makes up the four wheels. Arriving in heaven, Natura can finally create a man perfect in body and soul. The allegory is clear: the Seven Liberal Arts make up the perfect man in body and soul, and nature, part of the divine order of things, can fashion the new creation, which incorporates all of the qualities (mentioned above) from concord to nobility.

When the virgins describe their disciplines, music mentions all the familiar matters: her own wonders, her cosmological significance, her place within the spheres (4.335-439), and, following Boethius, her three types. With arithmetic, geometry, and astronomy, she is one of the higher arts (*Prose Prol., PL* 210.485-86, 518-22). She is the sister of arithmetic and, like a mirror, reflects every feeling and mood. Like Orpheus and Amphion, this allegorical Virgin-as-music holds the cithara. She represents the foster-child of peace, not war, and shares the power of numbers integral to the universe, to man ("that littleness"), and to instruments. She changes (modulates) pitches to produce melody and melodies to produce laughter and tears. She interchanges the serious and the sportive and, through the diatonic, enharmonic, and chromatic species, brings about change itself. Alan thinks St. Gregory (there is, to be sure, no mention of organum or polyphony here) was the aesthetic model who steered a middle course between sweetness and noisy, ugly song (3.468; trans. Sheridan, p. 112).

On the whole, Alan of Lille contributed no insights into music beyond the now old and conventional ones attached to universal ontology and allegorized by Martianus Capella. Alan's view of this art is not entirely consistent. He sounds grudging as he assigns to music a part of universal structure: according to Kathi Meyer-Baer,[28] he thought music only fit for putting one to sleep. He obviously feels that music has a small place in any treatise on morals no matter how fundamental concordant musical relationships are to the structure of a cathedral or church in which that music is to sound. He is a literary man for whom differences among rhetorical figures and among objects in their multiplicity produce a poetic beauty resembling that of the Creation. He hardly lacks aesthetic sensibility: the creations of this world are like a book and a painting to him, like a veritable mirror of our being. But, significantly, he does attribute something more to music than sense-response when, sounding like Plotinus or Pseudo-Dionysius, he calls it a means by which men can rise from sense to reason, whereby they can be transported to a vision of the Divine Idea (*Regulae Alani de sacra theologia, PL* 210.622). And though he is said to have had the humanistic outlook of John of Salisbury and to have known the work of the Arabs and the Spaniard Gundisalvo, mostly he simply repeats accepted remarks about music which were relatively untested--but accepted nevertheless because they had for so long been part of the intellectual tradition upon which he depended.

Thinkers and architects in the Middle Ages, then, employed musical proportions in planning and realizing the structure of the Gothic church or cathedral. We are reminded of the work of Vitruvius in classical times. Yet Vitruvius discussed music in an entirely different context of aims. He thought musical relationships were universal and intrinsic to architectural planning; according to his view, the use of such relationships is not only rational and artistic, but also a guarantee that in actual practice the voice will be easily heard within the structure. Being rational in arrangement, the edifice allows sounds to be clear and beautiful and words to be distinct and readily understood. The acoustics of the Gothic place of worship differed significantly; resonance and beauty replaced clarity of the spoken word. The men of the Middle Ages who designed and built these wonderfully resonant Gothic churches also had other aims. What value is there beyond communion with God through contemplation of the symbolic material things around one? Even better, musical proportion means order, a transcendent order which has entered the church or cathedral to give evidence of the presence of God and to grant the union of the individual soul with the divine in the rites celebrated within the building. It is a mystic order beyond which human nature cannot go but which has descended from heaven to enter human experience in mind and soul. Apparently, Plato's Idea has entered space created by stone, glass, and wood and imbued with universal light in its infinite variety.

X

John Cotton (Johannes Afflighemensis). The theorist called simply John (or commonly, following Martin Gerbert, John Cotton) has been the subject of some speculation among musicologists and students of manuscripts. Probably a Benedictine monk at Afflighem near Brussels and either English or Flemish in origin, he wrote an *On Music* (*De musica cum tonario*) which, like the works on music inauthentically attributed to him, was inspired by Guido of Arezzo, whose *Micrologus* he in large part copied. If not a highly educated man, he nevertheless followed the humanistic fashion of his time in identifying authorities, including Pythagoras, Plato, Virgil, Horace, Isidore, Martianus Capella, Boethius, Odo, and the Latin writers Donatus and Prudentius, some of whom he almost certainly had not read.

He accepts the dual division of music which had become as standard as had been Boethius' three divisions. The natural is both universal (the spheres which produce harmony in the strict sense) and human, the latter not only the soul and body in general but also specific parts of the body such as windpipes. *Musica humana* is now song, or verse-and-music, and the artificial is sound produced not by nature but by instruments of handicraft. In any case, the sound must be discrete, made up of intervals consisting of tones, and not of non-discrete sounds such as dogs barking, human beings laughing and groaning, and lions roaring (*On Mus.* 4).

(According to Aristoxenus' similar distinction, non-discrete sound is continuous. John means the unmusical or non-musical, and suggests the inartistic.) He does not seem to be impressed with the idea of celestial music, and even *musica mundana* appears only to be a kind of poetic mythologizing. For him, music is "the fit progression of tones" and "one of the seven arts called liberal," a natural one, like all the arts which he defines but little. Not one of the least of the arts, music is "most necessary" to the clergy, "useful," "delightful" for its practitioners (ibid. 2). He seems to hold its classification as a science in doubt, and there may be more than what meets the eye in his avoidance, like Guido's, of mathematics. The boys he addresses, he says, would find mathematical refinement tedious (ibid. 8). Calculation always seems the least of his interests.

Natural music must be a God-given vocal activity. Otherwise, how could absolutely illiterate jongleurs and actors compose pleasant-sounding songs? Yet it must be written down and "made clear by percepts" as are grammar, dialectic, and the other arts. John analyzes the relation of music to speech and thinks its form is based on the speech-song characteristics of Gregorian chant. The three accents or "tones" of the grammarian--*grave*, *circumflex*, and *acute*--correspond to the different levels of melody (the tetrachords, *graves*, *finales*, and *acutae*). And then there is phrasing, and the three divisions or *distinctiones* (pauses) of prose are equally applicable to song: the *colon* (a member) is like the *diastema*, a point of rest, but not at the *finales*; the *comma* (*incisio*) is the point of rest at the *finales*; the *periodus* (*clausura* or *circuitus*) (the close) is the *teleusis* (the end of the song). These aesthetic as well as technical observations are partly based, as often is the case among medieval theorists, on rhetorical teachings by the Latin grammarian Donatus (ibid. 10).

He links the eight modes with the eight parts of speech. Like Hermannus Contractus and Guido, he attributes psychological-aesthetic characteristics to the modes. He speaks of the "rugged gravity" (*rauca secundo gravitas*) of the second (plagal) mode, the Hypodorian, and says of the "rambling ductus" of the third (the Phrygian) that it is an expression of seriousness, indignation, or wrath. In the fifth (Lydian) mode he finds temperate happiness which originates from a sudden change from high spirits to an unexpected return to the *finales*. The sixth mode, the Hypolydian, comes close to lamentation and crying, the Mixolydian is theatrically exuberant, and the eighth, or Hypomixolydian, is decent and respectable.

He copies Guido almost literally in holding that a musician "or even . . . a practiced singer" can identify the characters of the modes as readily as we can distinguish a Greek, a German, a Spaniard, or a Frenchman by his appearance. Furthermore, these modes attract different men, as do various foods (ibid. 16).

Following Guido, he emphasizes a lawful equilibrium of form and musical expression. Of the species, he prefers the middle (the mean) value: the enharmonic is too difficult, the chromatic too effeminate and relaxed, but the diatonic is precisely right--good and lawful--in the judgment also of history, he thinks, since it has survived (ibid. 4).   Modes take certain courses, and when singers mix them--for example, two in one melody--all they accomplish is a mongrel chant and a tickling of the ear (ibid. 12).

In any event, the expression of music and words must agree. As the poet must see to the coincidence of his words and what they describe, so the performer must so sing that the contents of the words reach full expression. Certain melodies are expressive because they take on the meaning of what they accompany: song has the power of moving the minds of hearers, and yet certain melodies are expressive in themselves. An Easter antiphon (for example, *Rex autem David*) expresses paschal joy through its sound alone, and another may cause sorrow by virtue not only of the words but also of the song (ibid. 18-19).   Even if sound alone apart from words makes its expressive mark, it is the text which is decisive. The choice of a certain voice and its limits is thus properly decided by the text: the duty of the composer is to make his song such that it has a depressing character for sad material and an exalted character for cheerful material (ibid. 18). Hence, for John music has two expressive "powers": of song with words and pitches, and of pitches alone. Like Aristides Quintilianus centuries earlier, he finds expressive qualities in individual instruments. Sound alone can be expressive, and the character of the instrument contributes to a total expressive quality.

Medieval treatises on music fall into two classes: the early ones primarily on plainchant with special attention given to organum, a duplication of plainchant, and the later ones of the thirteenth century on polyphony and the necessary notation it requires because of the element of duration. Guido and John attend primarily to the elements of plainchant with side-glances at organum.

Like Guido, John prefers plainsong to organum, but, also like Guido, he devotes a chapter to the latter, which he calls *diaphony* and describes as "the sounding of different but harmonious notes, which is carried on by at least two singers [and therefore, as an organum, probably more], so that while one holds to the original melody, another [or more] may range aptly among other tones. . . ." He claims that the term 'organum' is based on the resemblance of the method of singing to the instrument known as the organ. Organum can be a singing of note against note, but it can also be a part-writing with rhythmical embellishments.   He testifies that organum developed from a parallel structure, but recommends voice crossings or contrary motion. Always, of course, the endings must be on concords. Also, the accompanying "organal" part may have more notes than the original (tenor) part (ibid. 23). Like Guido, John is concerned with the ending of the piece, because, as he says, the wise and the stupid are identified by the degree in which they realize that all things (including business affairs) look to closure. Therefore the classification of the modes is according to the final note; in whatever way melodies may modulate, they must always return to the *finale* of the tetrachord or mode (ibid. 10-11).

"All praise is sung at the end" is a popular saying supporting the theory (ibid. 11; cf. Guido, *Microl.* 11).

John's preference for plainsong over organum may be a matter of taste or even a liking hidden behind complicated religious attitudes. Nevertheless, John displays a certain relativism which sets aside the abstractness and impersonality of Boethius. For Boethius, there is one correct taste and one judgment based on permanencies. With John, more Aristotelian than Platonic, there are social and individual differences. He thinks the selection of the appropriate mode depends on its use (he thus supplements Aristotle and anticipates Johannes of Grocheo), and he testifies to the force of the secular courtly and chivalric environment by allowing validity to courtly ceremonies, to frivolous and serious occasions, or to the tastes of the youthful or the aged (*On Music* 18). Where Aristotle corrects Plato, John corrects the whole Church by agreeing with Guido that different people are pleased by different things because the senses do not retain the same appeal for all human beings. Despite whatever expressiveness a piece may have, what is sweet to one person may be dissonant and disorganized to another (ibid. 16). The qualities of color, shape, and sound in their varieties appeal to people in different degrees, and not as abstractions. If there is a subjectivity of aesthetic impression there is also a subjectivity of taste. The immediate reality of music is sound for itself. Mathematical speculation is not favored because the basis of aesthetic impression (as Guido had insisted) is sound in all its diversity and variety, and the one end-result is a subjective judgment determined by personal leanings. Well-sounding music is preferable to any theory.

John, of course, had many precedents for distrusting the performer, whose sins he lists in various places in his work, and, like Guido and many others, he places the musician, the intellectual, who has knowledge and who always acts appropriately, above the mere singer (cantor), who, skillful as he is, only sometimes acts appropriately and then merely because he has practiced. Indeed, the singer is like a drunkard "who does indeed get home but does not in the least know by what path he returns." He succeeds through habit. The true musician knows how to judge the music he hears, to correct it if it is at fault, and to invent new pieces (ibid. 2). Should his word be questioned, the monochord, which is his superior in judgment, is available to locate precise sounds and pitches (ibid. 7). Here John's position is Guido's, as it also had been Boethius' and even Plato's, but now with a change--that the *musicus* can currently be a composer as well as a singer, aware of the science of his art.

There is yet another difference between John and his more strict contemporaries. As a church musician, he nevertheless insists on freedom and spontaneity of creation, which may involve even the inclusion of instruments in the music. In this point of view, he may be atypical for his age, though he may also be in part revealing something of actual perform-ance practice not described by other writers. In Chapter 17 he recites a whole list of "powers" of music frequently mentioned in documents from the past. He quotes Psalm 150.3-4--"Praise him with the sound of trumpet: praise him with psaltery and harp; praise him with timbrel and choir: praise him with strings and organs"--not to explain it away, as many Church Fathers had attempted to do in order to discourage or bar instruments from the Church, but to question objections to use of such instruments in the worship services. "Who would not zealously embrace it with all his heart?" he asks. Composers should be free to imitate their predecessors in the distant and immediate past. As new compositions are needed, they may be found in new musical settings of the rhythms and threnodic verses of the poets.

John, then, may be said to have had that independence of thought and even a fair disrespect for rule and limitation which is characteristically English, if English he was. He puts aside cosmic theory, says practically nothing about numbers, redefines Boethius' triad so as to emphasize the artistic humanism of "natural" human music, accepts the idea of the relativity of taste and judgment, would adopt instruments and allow poetry for Church use, accepts the Greeks and the biblical heroes but makes little of them, makes of music an art in tone (of rhythm he says little, probably assigning it to poetry), in organum finds pleasant the crossing of voices (possibly resembling the colors and smells he likes), and possibly favors chromaticism. He almost, but not quite, can serve as an example of the individualism which is said to characterize the Renaissance. It is of course possible to make too much of his additions to musical thought. He was no Augustine. But, then, in his *De musica*, Augustine was not teaching boys; and John was not writing a theory of musical perception and judgment for adults, nor was he even attempting to compose a philosophical allegory, like that of Adelard of Bath.

XI

Adelard of Bath. An English traveller of the twelfth century, Adelard of Bath, a one-time student at Laon and Tours and also at Paris, wrote chiefly about mathematics and natural science. He discovered and translated the long-lost *Elements* of Euclid, and in philosophy he differentiated between divine and natural causes for the explanation of phenomena. In his youth, before travelling widely in Italy and Sicily, he wrote *On Identity and Diversity* (*De eodem et diverso*) (1104-09), an allegory inspired by Martianus Capella which also contains many borrowings from Macrobius' *Commentary*. His other sources were Plato's *Timaeus* as translated by Chalcidius, Augustine, Boethius' *Consolation of Philosophy*, and Arabic thinkers who had taken seriously certain Greek writings which the Roman world had virtually ignored for a thousand years. Because science had lost its tight hold on scholastic thinking--rhetoric and grammar had taken its place--he used as sources certain Latin authors, including Priscian (*Institutionis grammaticae*, c.500 A.D.).

The form of Adelard's *De eodem et diverso* comes from Martianus

Capella's *Marriage* and Boethius' *Consolation*. Like Hugh of St.-Victor, Adelard was a philosopher and encyclopedist rather than a professional writer. His system carries the marks of Plato and Hugh of St.-Victor. According to this theory, the arts are liberal not because the free man pursues them, but because they liberate the soul from the body, which is enchained by worldly love (*De animae exsilio et patria, PL* 172.1241-46).

From the *Timaeus* Adelard derived his first principles of the same and the other--the former being the principle of identity, the permanent, the immobile, the invisible, the latter the principle of diversity, continual change, movement, the palpable (1.14). He gives feminine attributes and names to them: *Philocosmia* (love of the world) and *Philosophia* (love of wisdom, or the permanent). The first is not love of the cosmos; it is the love of the sensible world and everything which changes; and the second is the love of the invisible and permanent world. *Philocosmia*, unstable, always searching for new sensations, accompanies the pleasure of the senses. She includes purely practical music. But *Philosophia*'s (theoretical-practical) music is guided by a deep and intense spiritual joy unchangeable as the object from which it proceeds: philosophical (permanent) music in its functions is harmony created, appreciated, and judged by the intellect. *Musica practica mixta* is theoretical-practical. *Philocosmia* is richness, power, dignity, glory, luxuriousness (*volupta*); she symbolizes the good-earthly, the perishable, change, decay, the always-in-motion; as luxuriousness, she is epicurean. Palpable luxuriousness is connected with certain objective goods--beauty, suppleness, health, and grace--and with certain subjective states which address themselves to the senses or even to sensuous (moral) goods. Adelard of Bath therefore clearly adopts a hedonism (*Philocosmia*) which is backed up by philosophical music, and has replaced the Pythagorean ontology of the world, man, and music with the ontology of human emotion (love) and its object.

Musica instrumentalis belongs to Philosophia and is a scientific examination of the number relationships underlying all types of music whatsoever, including song and instrumental music;[29] it is intellectual, mathematical, and speculative. The stable and immaterial joys of objective harmony intellectually determined are Adelard's own preference. This is why he places philosophy among the Seven Arts and follows Hugh.

But music theoretical-practical belongs with poetry and sculpture: it is a harmony of the spirit, eternal and objective, always identical with itself, and from it emanates the agreeable and objectively consonant modulation of the human voice and of instruments strung, blown, struck. Philosophy divides into the theoretical (speculative), practical (ethical, moral), mechanical, and logical. The first is theological, mathematical, and physical, while mathematics is (the usual) arithmetic, music, geometry, and astronomy (Hugh, *Didasc.* 2.1-14). The mechanical division covers seven non-liberal arts as contrasted with the four liberal ones (ibid. 2.20-30). For Adelard, philosophy is fed and served by all of the Seven Liberal Arts, which in turn blend into a whole with it, their source and end. Nevertheless, each art develops and unfolds out of its own core. These art-sciences are (1) *vuoces* (words), the trivium, the key to the world of mind and spirit; and (2) *res* (the characteristics of things as such), the quadrivium, the key to the realm of matter.[30] The latter group of sciences liberates the soul from the fetters of earthly love, which is found within the body.[31]

Adelard rightly traces Boethius' divisions of music back to Pythagoras and at the same time emphasizes its humanistic aspect by rephrasing Boethius' advice that we look into our own depths for evidences of musical pleasure. It is a pleasure naturally based on number; for music is a science of numbers in their permanent relations to one another (cf. Boethius, *Arith.* 1.1). But what it is in itself is one thing, what it accomplishes is another. And here a love of Lucretius shows up. Its accomplishments are both intellectual and emotive or psychological: it charms men, animals, and things; like adults, infants enjoy harmony and dislike discord, and adults find it a consolation for the difficulties of life. Its form refreshes us in itself, or it proceeds to give us heartfelt joy. It makes its effects in peace and war and in all domains religious, moral, and physiological. It appeases the troubled soul and arouses religious emotions. To mature people it gives a certain calm gravity, and in medicine it heals certain maladies. But it exceeds the other arts particularly in encouraging cheerfulness and joy.[32]

A pioneer student of Arabic philosophy and science, Adelard's is the greatest name in English science before Robert Grosseteste (d. 1253), bishop of Lincoln, and Roger Bacon (c.1214-94), both also students at Paris. Almost nothing is known about his life, and the *Eodem et diverso*[33] is surely one of his earliest works. Musically he was not merely academic: it is said that in 1103 during his musical studies in France he played the harp before the queen. But he continued in the intellectual tradition in which are contrasted theory and practice, knowledge and skill, mathematical proportion and heard harmony, and the eternal laws of the universe and their application. Permanence and impermanence are the opposites with which he worked, and, though he gave approval to conventional observations about music and as a mathematician accepted the idea that music basically is number, he nevertheless found that its true place is in the love of earthly things. He may indeed have learned from the Arabs, but European theorists were locating it there on their own.

XII

The Arab Influence: Domingo Gundisalvo (Dominicus Gundissalinus). The Arabs, as noted above, were the most important link between the Greeks and Western thought. There was particular interest in the writings of the ancient astronomers, mathematicians, physicists, and physicians, especially among scholars both Islamic and Christian in Spain, which served as a convenient transfer point for knowledge. So too there was an intense interest in music and music theory from a philosophical point of view. Nevertheless, the Arabs were not merely translating and commenting on an art form of which they knew nothing. It would appear that many of the Eastern or Islamic philosophers and physicians were intimately acquainted with the art of music, even as amateur musicians. Many played, or even built, various instruments, including the lute (*'ud*), flute, harp, psaltery, and water- and wind-driven instruments. Among physicians, music was especially important because of its therapeutic effect. It was believed by the Arabs that music as medicine affects both soul and body, and whether this opinion was their own or something derived from their reading of Greek philosophy is a moot question. In the ninth century, Ibn al-Balchi had written a book *Concerning the Care of Body and Soul*, one chapter of which treats music and the health of the body while another chapter deals with music and refreshment for the soul. In Arabic medieval writings, melody and rhythm are repeatedly said to inspire sadness or joy, peace or excitement, agitation or anxiety, sleep or the arousal from sleep.

Before he died in 1151, Domingo Gundisalvo, Archdeacon of Segovia Cathedral, played an important role in the introduction of the philosophy of the Arabs to Western Europe. He wrote a *De divisione philosophiae*, an encyclopedic work in which music is treated in the tenth chapter. Aristotelianism is a predominant element, but in fact his model was Al Farabi, whom he had read in translation. Gundisalvo, rejecting the tradition of the Liberal Arts, reopened to view Aristotle's natural history,[34] his metaphysics, ethics, and politics.,

The program, noted in an earlier chapter, of translating the known Greek classics into Arabic was thus transformed into a new effort--to translate these works into the Latin that served as the international language of Western Europe. These works comprised the major Greek writings, including, in science, Hippocrates, Euclid, Aristotle, Archimedes, Apollonius of Perga, Ptolomy, and Galen. Clearly, the classical revival in the Renaissance of the fifteenth and sixteenth centuries was made possible by the earlier efforts of the allegedly benighted, dark, and ignorant Middle Ages, which revived, among other writings, Aristotle's complete works. The role of the Arabic writers in this revival, so crucial for the development of the idea of music, was very interesting indeed. Sometimes Arabic writers such as Avicenna (980-1037) and Averroës (1126-98) platonized Aristotelian philosophy and, in effect at least, made it appear to be consistent with Christian theology. When he wrote about music, Avicenna, for example, was interested in bringing the soul of the hearer into relation to the harmony of the spheres; he also believed in the therapeutic value of music and in the effect of different compositions on different moods. He agreed vaguely with Plato and Aristotle (who had, to be sure, interpreted the word 'music' in a different way) that music is the one path by which the soul can be made ready to perceive wisdom (philosophy).[35] Additional works like Porphyry's *Isagoge*, Plato's *Republic* and *Laws*, Plotinus' *Enneads*, and Proclus' miscellaneous productions--all were translated, and some of them were even erroneously attributed to Aristotle.

Gundisalvo began to treat music in quite a modern manner. He took the Aristotelian position, assumed already by Hugh of St.-Victor and Adelard, that each art has a separate status: even poetry had not been thought to be "autonomous" for a thousand years until the Arabs restored Aristotle to view. Gundisalvo's basic aesthetic, then, is right for an individual approach to the arts. But he still fosters the Pythagorean and Boethian opinion that music is a part of the vast harmony animating the universe and that modulation is an aspect of the Whole. And he reiterates Aristotle's observation that movement dominates the universe of things. In music, therefore, lines, phrases, and whole movements modulate. Indeed, modulation is a factor in both sight and hearing. Equally so is measure, which, like modulation, gives character to the whole composition, whether in the universe in human substance, or in the works produced by human beings. These are the three (Boethian) spheres of music,[36] as there are two species of instruments, the natural and the artificial. The natural belongs to both animate and inanimate beings, animals and non-animals: men make vocal sounds; so do certain animals; but certain other animals and all plants do not make them at all. Artificial music is made by objects of human construction.

Man's own natural instrument is made up of epiglottis, mouth, throat, nose, and so forth, and his artificial instruments are flutes, trumpets, strings, and others. Thus, music in the broadest sense is a science of harmonious modulation in art and nature. In its narrowest sense it is an art of sound alone. Here several sounds or several parts of compositions agree, but the material or medium is always *tone*. Think of a symphony of several voices: the harmony has quality and intensity which derives from the accent or the tenor of the voice. For, as Aristotle said, the voice characterizes both man and animal. And the character comes from the unity which results from the modulation of transient elements, whether they belong to the transient world, to body and soul, or to a sensuously perceivable *almonia* of tones.

Thus, Gundisalvo maintains that no other science has such a wealth of harmonic modulation. It is the preoccupation of two "musicians" in cooperation. The first, the theorist, the true scientific musician who follows mathematics, acoustics, and harmony, knows the rules of (the sounds and ratios of) music which must be followed by the second, the composer, who arranges pitches and harmonics (melodies), and, following art, composes melodies which touch the emotions.[37] The theorist is the artist who knows and teaches how the composer should proceed in accordance with his art. The theorist understands the science of diverse harmonies, of what and by what they are composed, how they are constructed, how they agree among themselves, and at what point they render their effect most impressively and most perfectly.

The practical composer follows the theorist's precepts for the art of melody which can move the passions. But in nature, music is both formal and expressive. Its aim (as Isidore, one of Gundisalvo's models, says) is theoretically to understand everything connected with the nature of harmony. The practical musician aims to execute intelligently what the theorist through speculation prescribes. Invented by Moses, practical music was employed by Tubalcain and then by certain Greeks (Pythagoras, following Linus and Amphion). It comes from the Muses, who invented the song which poet-musicians like the troubadours and trouvères have re-discovered. For practical music is the composition of serious songs with a rhythmical or metrical text, and it is as useful for serious songs as for happy (light) ones; it can be studied according to five subjects: (1) its principles, invention and compositional means and methods, abstract harmony and mathematics; (2) natural rhythm; (3) the principles, the musical text, the different kinds of artistic instruments, and the rules for their use; (4) the natural origins of high and low pitches, intervals, and so forth; and (5) the material called (by William of Conches) melody, rhythm, and metrics.[38] Like Al Farabi, whose outline he has assumed, Gundisalvo makes recommendations he does not himself carry out. But he is not writing about plainchant. His subject is the secular song.

Like Rémi of Auxerre in the tenth century, like Al Farabi, and like Roger Bacon in the thirteenth, Gundisalvo too sees the musical art as a synthesis, as a whole made up of music, poetry, and dance--a permanent triune *choreia*, a total music creating a total plastic and sonorous harmony. Poetic meter introduces harmony into the thought and words of a discourse of social import, melody produces agreement in a succession of low (*grave*) and high (*acute*) sounds, and the dance in gesture and movement produces measure which conforms to the meter and the melody. In an age of symbolic ingenuity, this total music must have seemed like a symbol of the universal Whole.

It inspires in Gundisalvo an ecstasy which fairly causes him to sing a hymn to all music, which tempers the customs of human beings, creates measure out of disorder, makes perfect the beauty of never-passing total (cosmic) harmony, and conserves the harmony of those who have attained uniformity and equilibrium of soul and do not lack anything excessively. It is for these moral reasons that music formerly was combined with all solemnities, sacred and profane, joyful or sad, and appeared in religious songs, hymns, wedding songs, and bacchic, funeral, and banquet songs. If all the arts are in motion, if all stir the human mind and human feeling, then music must indeed complete and supplement the other arts. It governs the spheres, influences the mind, excites the warrior, softens the heart, and so forth. Rhythm and harmony give balance to the soul, affect it ethically, and make their effects in education. Such generalizations apply not only to music in general but also to individual scales and to specific instruments of music. Music in any case behaves as a linguistic-sonorous-mimetic unity, which is the true basis of its ethical effect[39] (see Appendix D).

The narrative provided in this chapter has concluded with the restoration to historical consciousness of certain aspects of Greek thought which had been lost, sometimes having been suppressed by the Church in earlier centuries. Scientific, philosophical, and literary documents representing the culture of ancient Greece had now again been returned to public scrutiny to exert their humanizing effect on a learned society that was changing in its outlook. In one respect, the results were unfortunate, since, much to the detriment of scientific thought and investigation, Aristotle's quite dated and frequently erroneous science was given preference and even quasi-scriptural status. The now emerging art of music was nevertheless better served. For example, Gundisalvo takes note of acoustics, a pursuit which had been totally neglected for centuries. This science had been of real interest to the early Greeks, including Plato, Aristotle, and Pseudo-Aristotle, but later philosophers had simply ignored it. Yet as revived by the Arabs, great parts of Greek musical thought seem disappointing to us since, as one observes in Al Farabi and Gundisalvo, the old ideas too often merely were repeated without being re-thought or tested. Still, there are some important, even seminal changes, for the Arabs had asked good questions (which they did not always answer). Further, when they outlined methods of inquiry, they attempted to establish order within the thinking of the ancients, and, finally, when imported into Western Europe their work acted as a counter-influence against the more restrictive attitudes toward music present in the Church. Ultimately, they also tacitly encouraged some sense of respectability among secular musicians, who also had by then borrowed and adapted a considerable number of musical instruments from Arabic practice. However, when the Arabic writers encouraged an empirical approach to music theory, their work was met in the West by an irony: writers on music in the Catholic West had already made certain advances in the careful description of their living art, which had been the subject of analysis by theorists such as the author of the *Dialogus* formerly attributed to "Odo" and Guido of Arezzo. By unconscious anticipation, these astute writers on music had already entered into the kind of practical-theoretical analysis toward which the Arabs pointed.

XIII

Léonin and Pérotin. Paris continued to maintain its position as the center of European learning nevertheless. We have seen that in the twelfth century in France were erected Gothic cathedrals and churches whose construction often followed musical principles. Their beauty remains still largely unchallenged throughout the world. The great scholars, teachers, and monastic leaders of the earlier twelfth century who taught, preached, and wrote books in Paris, and spent some parts of their lives there or in surrounding monasteries and schools, may not necessarily have been fully aware of the musical developments which would emerge during the second half of the century, when polyphony came to be accepted in the services at the monastery of St. Martial of Limoges and in the Parisian school of Notre Dame. Plainchant, organum, polyphony (which, according to William G. Waite,[40] reached the peak of its development around 1225): this was the order of musical growth. In Paris, through the efforts of Léonin (Leoninus) and his successor Pérotin (Perotinus), organum became more free and more elaborate. They were true artists *antiqua* at the height of Scholastic and Catholic influence in all aspects of cultural life. Pérotin's *organa* seemed metaphorically to echo the new conception of sacred space within the walls of the ecclesiastical building of worship, in this case probably Notre Dame Cathedral at Paris, though the royal parish church of St. Germain has also been suggested. He quite deliberately provided for real echoes among the columns and vaults, so that echoing harmonies could intermingle with normal harmonies in their progress. No wonder that both architecture and polyphony represented universal harmony. Nevertheless, in their highest state of development organum and polyphony continued to follow poetic-rhetorical principles.

Léonin (fl. 1160) and Pérotin (fl. 1190) were the first in a great line of composers of polyphonic music. Unlike much of the earlier music which was often only tentatively attributed to various composers, their work is well defined on the basis of reliable medieval authority and is well preserved. They represent a type of medieval music writing which is governed by the principles of plainchant and free developments of organum in two, three, or more voices, but primarily by a new element--duration and its measurement.

Léonin wrote a cycle of polyphonic compositions entitled the *Magnus Liber*, perhaps before 1163, for the major feasts of the church year. Apparently designed for use in Paris, though the cathedral of Notre Dame was as yet under construction, it was performed and imitated throughout Europe. Pérotin shortened Léonin's work and, according to Anonymous IV, added superior compositions of his own.   From current improvisatory practice and, perhaps even more important, from St. Martial, both had inherited polyphonic techniques: the older technique according to which one note (the tenor or *cantus firmus*) held the melody while an upper part moved from note to note at the same time; and a newer practice in which the tenor again held the melody while an upper part sang a melismata above it, floridly moving over the individual sustained notes of the tenor. Léonin confined himself to two-part writing, but advanced beyond his St. Martial models by giving greater richness to the upper part. Pérotin wrote three- and four-part *organa* and *conducti* in which a *cantus firmus* (tenor) could be either an existing melody (probably a plainsong) or a newly composed melody, which might even be secular in origin and character. The *cantus firmus* usually carried the words while other voices (usually two) vocalized on the chief vowels of the words. To Léonin's corpus, Pérotin also added *clausulae*, or separate sections of an organum having rhythmically organized tenors.

The new rhythmical (and notational) nature of the "new music" (*ars nova*, as it was eventually called in France) is treated in the writings of the thirteenth century, and therefore my discussion of it will be postponed until Chapter XVII.

XVI
The Philosophers of the High Middle Ages

The twelfth and thirteenth centuries are commonly regarded as the high point of medieval culture. Vernacular literature flourished, and everywhere in Europe, as far north as Scandinavia and as far south as Spain and Sicily, the Latin language and its literature aroused a humanism latent, as we have seen, since Roman times. The Church, claiming to be universal, continued to dominate the life of Western Europe in many ways, though its influence in some sectors tended to be eroded by the end of the medieval period. It remained the great patron of music, which was still essential to its services of worship in churches including monastic and convent churches, in the chapels of the aristocratic class, and in cathedrals.

Whereas the twelfth century had been an immensely creative period, the culmination of its various contributions to culture and life came in the thirteenth century. Marked evidence of this lies in the need which was felt to draw together knowledge in encyclopedic works comparable to those of the late Latin writers such as Martianus Capella. The encyclopedic impulse revealed itself in an activity of collecting, systematizing, and collating all knowledge. Man's spiritual, moral, and intellectual accomplishments were described in a body of writing in which accepted truths and their relationships were delineated against the background of history. So Vincent of Beauvais (c.1190-1264) collected and organized material in his *Speculum majus* (*Greater Mirror*) with a completeness hitherto unknown. All literary, philosophical, and scientific knowledge was drawn into his survey. Academic knowledge emanating from all universities about every known subject was his source: law, medicine, theology, the classics analyzed, dialectics examined and employed, metaphysics, ontology, epistemology. And he codified everything which he treated in his great work.

Not surprisingly, the thirteenth century was also an age of explorers. In 1271 Marco Polo began his travels to the Far East. Gradually it was being learned that the world as a whole was less Christian than had previously been believed, and though trade with the infidels was forbidden by papal decree, business and commerce continued nevertheless with important implications for culture, which was in fact not closed to influences from the outside world. Italian merchants were already covering much of the world, except of course for the Americas, which remained unknown except in Scandinavian traditions which would culminate in the Icelandic sagas about the discovery of the region known as Vinland. The intellectual heritage from Greece, the imperial claims inherited from Rome through the political settlement of the Holy Roman Empire as established in Carolingian times, and the cultural activity of Paris under the French king were thus not isolated from the rest of the world, which had been brought to the attention of Europe through its trade with those other regions. Trade indeed proved very attractive, and in many of the cities of Europe the lawyers and politicians who had served as servants of empire were replaced by accountants needed in a business society. The arithmetic of accountants thus took its place beside that of builders of churches and cathedrals, and magnificent ecclesiastical structures began to give way to palaces elegant and worldly in show.

In spite of the pressure exerted by the crusade against the Albigenses in the early part of the century, there was a shift toward secular life, and art would now tend to be put to other purposes than the purely religious. Elaborate reliquaries containing relics of saints could now be made at the same time as secular objects such as ivory boxes carved with tournament scenes for secular use. In France, the great cathedrals and churches were of course yet to be completed in many cases, for work on Sainte-Chapelle was not done until 1248, on Notre Dame until 1250, and on Amiens until 1269. By 1260 the sculpture of Rheims Cathedral was ready to be admired, a sign of the "feverish urge to decorate"[1] which had characterized the early part of the century. This urge toward decoration had perhaps nowhere shown itself more prominently than in music, with the relatively rapid rise of the popularity of polyphony. The richness of the music is also to be seen as a correlative of the acoustics of the buildings of worship, and in England this factor may explain the continuing urge to rebuild the older Norman structures along the Gothic pattern. English rebuilding continued into the fourteenth, fifteenth, and early sixteenth centuries. Even the cathedral at Canterbury which Chaucer knew would be provided with a new nave on which work was begun in 1378.

But changes in attitude, especially on the continent, were apparent. In the court of Emperor Frederick II (1174-1250), the profane study of physics and of philosophy as natural science had fairly locked out theology, and after 1270 there was the triumph of Aristotelian logic. Astronomers at Merton College, Oxford, were the first scientists in the West deliberately to rely on experience alone, while late in the thirteenth century the philosopher William of Occam, an Oxford Franciscan and nominalist who was deeply influenced by Aristotle, insisted that conceptual knowledge was an illusion. According to his way of thinking (later characterized as the *via moderna* as opposed to the *via antiqua* or position taken by Thomas Aquinas and others), William argued that to understand the essences of things is beyond human capabilities since the mind can only grasp the sensory experience granted it. One result would be a new interest in physics, but more importantly his nominalism was a direct challenge to the so-called "realist" philosophy inherited from Augustine which linked language to essences. The importance of nominalism for the development of the idea of music has yet fully to be explored.

Yet it must be recognized that religious values and attitudes on the whole prevailed. Church art continued to be created to provide objects of devotion and edification, and the new miracle plays, especially those at Notre Dame and York, would serve a similar purpose. Albertus Magnus, in spite of his interest in natural science, commented on Pseudo-Dionysius in Cologne. St. Thomas Aquinas, whose philosophy in retrospect seems to dominate thirteenth-century theology, made an attempt to adjust Aristotelianism to Catholic thought, paradoxically serving to separate theology further from philosophy. At the same time, however, a figure like Adam de la Halle (c.1245-c.1285 [or 1306]), the trouvère--poet and composer of both monophonic and polyphonic secular works--took his place beside Pérotin and the other composers of polyphony for church services.

At the beginning of the fourteenth century, therefore, France remained the country in Europe with the highest reputation in learning, in Christian devotion and piety, and in chivalry. France was already known for elegant and courteous living, and that kingdom was given credit for Gothic architecture, the remarkable development in ecclesiastical building to which attention has been given above. The University of Paris retained its place as the leading university in the world for theology and philosophy, in the latter of which Aristotle came to be the leading object of study. In spite of an attempt to prohibit the study of Aristotle's works (except for his *Logic*), the change had come about as philosophers took up the study of his *Natural Philosophy*, *On the Soul*, and other writings. The university's influence thus was international, and, for example, it had its own "English" college to which belonged a number of famous individuals from England including Adelard of Bath, Robert of Kilwardby, Roger Bacon, and Robert Grosseteste as well as later figures. Not all of those associated with Paris were convinced of the value of Aristotelianism, of course; the Franciscans Alexander of Hales and St. Bonaventure remained cool to this aspect of Greek philosophy. On the other hand, Albertus Magnus and his pupil Thomas Aquinas accepted it, the former in part and the latter more completely so long as it could be absorbed into Christian thinking. Curiously, Aquinas like Bonaventure was regarded in his time as an enemy of Aristotelianism.

Among the students at the University of Paris was the translator, Scholastic, and, according to reputation, wizard Michael Scot (c.1175-c.1234), who would be given a place by Dante in his *Inferno* (20.116-17). This scholar learned Arabic in Toledo, translated Aristotle from Arabic into Latin, and is sometimes thought to have been a major force in the revival of Aristotle and of European learning in general. Reputed to have been an astrologer at the court of the Emperor Frederick II, he wrote a *Physionomia de secretis naturae*, a compendium of occult sciences in which he compared music and astronomy by symbolizing the former as Mars and the latter as Jupiter. Apparently aware of the music of his time and knowing both music and letters, Scot expanded the conventional theory of the music of the spheres. Citing the traditional, cultural, and legendary stories related to music, and, furthermore, adding definitions and classifications, he draws the usual analogies: there are seven rules of the world, he thinks, seven planets, seven metals, arts, and colors, and all are like the seven days of the week, seven notes of music, and seven letters of the alphabet. He describes organum, notational systems, and the classical idea of world harmony.[2] He names the degrees and steps of the scale--and was probably the only scholastic academician to do so. He also lists the modes, taken from a passage in Guido who was rapidly replacing Boethius in reputation among the theorists, and he follows Cassiodorus' division of harmonics, rhythmics, and metrics. In his *Liber introductorius* he attempts to adjust Boethius to contemporary developments, while, using Isidore as a model, he treats music as a philosophical art.

Elsewhere, Neoplatonism continued to have its adherents, although, as one would expect, at this time it was often blended with Aristotelian elements. In the thirteenth and fourteenth centuries in southern Germany there was an entire Neoplatonic school led by Ulrich von Strassburg, Dietrich von Freiburg, and Meister (Johannes) Eckhart. The combination of the Platonism and Aristotelianism in musical writings came to a climax in the work of Jacob of Liège (early fourteenth century), who seems to have combined all streams of musical thought into a single system.

It is thus important to recall that the history of the idea of music reflects the international character of medieval artistic and intellectual developments. Indeed, discussions about music speculation and about music itself were not again to be so international until the twentieth century. Yet, while a few Pythagorean principles had widely been accepted as law, the philosopher and musician in the thirteenth century began to take divergent paths. The secular musical works of the troubadours, who had been suppressed at the time of the crusade against the Albigenses, the trouvères, the Minnesingers, and, later, Meistersingers could no longer be entirely ignored, and among musicians technique became very important for its own sake. In the Church, the liturgy and its music continued to change with the addition of more and more polyphony despite common complaints about the failure to uphold liturgical standards. For example, Pope John XXII in his decretal *Docta Sanctorum Patrum* (1324-25) warned against innovation in church music and insisted that it should not be too elaborate and that the vernacular must be avoided. Always it must be remembered that music is for the church service: a complex music, including the new school of polyphony, is one which threatens to become a thing in itself. Since such practices are contemptuous of devotion and only serve to delight the ear, they are not to be tolerated. Instead, music is to preserve its traditional peaceful dignity with clearly differentiated notes. In the universe of things, nothing is for itself because everything remains subordinate to God and his Church. Nevertheless, John did not intend to prohibit less complex forms of organum or polyphony which would not obscure the melody or the words.

Few philosophers between the beginning of the thirteenth and the end of the fifteenth centuries had the breadth of interest we have observed above in Michael Scot, however, and none was an architectural-musical theorist like certain of the individuals centered in Paris in the eleventh and twelfth centuries. Robert Grosseteste placed music in a tight context of cosmic, aesthetic, and number theory, while Albertus Magnus' thought was a throwback to earlier medieval symbolism. Thomas Aquinas, in large part on the basis of what he had read, placed music within an aesthetic but restrictive religious context, and Roger Bacon returned to describing the interdependence of music and rhetoric. These men represent the last philosophers of the Middle Ages to take music seriously--the last, in fact, until Nicholas of Cusa (1401-64).

I

Robert Grosseteste.   Robert Grosseteste (c.1170-1253), one-time student at the University of Paris, was chancellor of Oxford and eventually bishop of Lincoln. As a philosopher he was primarily Augustinian in sympathy, a man who associated himself with the Franciscan Order, and one who was opposed to Aristotelianism, which he nevertheless encouraged by translating and commenting on Aristotle's work.[3] He was also opposed to certain aspects of Scholasticism as taught at Paris. Like other Franciscans, he especially deplored the exaggerated emphasis on logic. In his view, neither logic nor speculation had anywhere to go since they had no actual subject matter. The Aristotelian syllogism was irrelevant, he felt, and even Peter Lombard's *Sentences*, which were made up of passages from the Scriptures and the Church Fathers, were inadequate. Improper translations were also a problem. Accurate versions of the Bible and of Aristotle were needed, and to achieve these ends it was necessary to obtain a knowledge of Hebrew, Greek, and Arabic grammar as well as to employ accurate methods of translation.[4] Like Roger Bacon after him, Grosseteste tried to observe nature and to apply mathematics to his observations, but here again the aim was not Aristotelian: he expected mathematics to reveal the essences of things.

Grosseteste is best known perhaps for a series of small works on physiological, cosmological, and astronomical problems, on questions about color, the rainbow, tides, heat, sound, and on the reform of the calendar, always an important subject to the Church for the determination of Easter and other moveable feasts of the church year. In *De artibus liberalibus* he combines in one statement all the "kinds" of music so far mentioned here except the mathematical, which seems to be implicit in the rest; music is the harmony of the human voice and movements, the harmony of instruments, the harmony of everything which through sound or movement gives pleasure, and the harmony of both heavenly and non-heavenly things. Beauty is based on number, "musical" proportion, and light, and if mathematics, with the help of astronomy, is the universal means of explaining a knowledge of nature, music too shares in mathematical power. For music, not arithmetic, is at the top of the mathematical sciences and resides close to geometry, whose principles govern all forms of natural bodies. It is the harmony of the astronomical world, and the Pythagoreans and Plato are in the background. Like Augustine and Hugh of St.-Victor, he interprets Boethius' *musica mundana* as: number, weight, and measure in the elements; as *situ*, *motu*, and *natura* in plants; and finally as the seasons. Music is related to the body on the one hand and to the soul on the other, but in epistemology it is absolutely necessary because without it there is no proportion and no knowledge. It is a study of proportion in all of its phases, either successive or simultaneous, in both song and dance.

From Aristotle or Al Farabi, Grosseteste learned that music establishes relations of motion or movement because it is intrinsic to time, space, and vibration (acoustics). This follows from the fact that not continuous (non-discrete) but discontinuous (discrete) tones are subject to number. Since its significance is universal, music is also a science of human relations and, too, of all the ratios of physical movement. As Al Farabi recalls Greek thought, so Grosseteste thinks that music governs all harmonies--not only those of human voices and gestures (vocal music and dance) and of instruments, but of heavenly bodies as well and even of the creation of earthly human bodies out of the four elements.

As harmony, mathematical proportions are the foundations of the musical sense-arts of music, dance, and poetry. The beauty of the world consists of unifying measures which harmonize things among themselves, the measures following from proportions from which emanate proportionalities: the concord of multiple forms in the universe, the harmony of the principles of every thing, and the co-adaptation of each form to other determinate ones (*In div. nom.*, p. 195; Bruyne 3.137). All composition depends on four principles: form, matter, reciprocal adaptation, and composition. Form, in principle the simplest of these, is represented by the number 1; matter, endowed with passivity and density, by 2; the composition, in which matter is informed and form materialized, by 3; the resulting compound by 4. The highest of luminous bodies, the heavens, is governed by the perfect number 10, the sum of the first four numbers (*On Light*, p. 17). All, of course, are the numbers of Pythagorean mathematics interpreted symbolically in the Nicomachean fashion but now applied to aesthetic structures.

In the thirteenth century the preoccupation with light led to the study of optics as well as of geometry and even of astronomy (steps were taken towards accurate measurements of the stars). Though geometry attempted to measure real things, the essential rather than the individual was the goal. More than any other Scholastic, Grosseteste blends luminosity and musicality into a unified whole. In keeping with the musical conception of the universe, however, Grosseteste sees that these two qualities are metaphysical in nature. A symbolism of spiritual and physical light qualifies an aesthetics of light: here St. Basil and St. Ambrose as well as

Plotinus agree, not to mention Plato, who describes the Forms or Ideas as radiant, splendid, and brilliant (*Phaedr*. 250). In Grosseteste's aesthetics of light, color is deduced mathematically from light and results from its quality and quantity, or intensity. Like Aristotle, he lists seven tones or colors (white, yellow, purple, green, blue, and black), and, like certain of his twelfth-century predecessors, he thinks the world is both a vast painting and a magnificent song. Luminous beauty, tonal beauty, and plastic beauty are integral parts of this total aesthetic system.

For a theory specifically of music, he takes the indirect approach; he knits the "mystical" book of St. Augustine's *On Music* into a piece of psychological and idealistic fabric and speaks less of music than of the apprehension and judgment of it. His naturalism rests on a universal idealism. About rhythm in sound and in the soul, he says that the sensation of objective sound implies the existence of number in the physical and phenomenal world of the exciting or stimulating thing; furthermore, a physiological rhythm which is spontaneous and active exists in the structure of perception itself. Sonal rhythm is produced by the most subtle movements of light in air, vibrant with the most simple proportions; the rhythm of the soul is the expression of the soul's own activity. The movement of air courts the ear and calls up a reaction proportional to the movement of the soul: we call this sensation. The rhythm of the physical world acts on the life of consciousness. If he were to add the idea of breath, Grosseteste would be close to anticipating Marsilio Ficino.

Yet, to grasp a melodic phrase is to do more than experience sensation. The sounds must have a coherent form, a simulated total, and memory must de-materialize the sound. As the mind synthesizes impressions, it is entirely aroused; it goes beyond the immediate tone and compares it with other tones, all of which create an interior harmony residing in the memory; without reflecting or judging rationally, it is delighted by the melody, which corresponds naturally to its own harmony; or it takes offense if anything discordant should occur. After spontaneous pleasure comes judgment: now the mind compares its impressions with the intelligible ideal. "Descending" to the physical man, Grosseteste observes that the organ of hearing is in a definite and measurable number-relation to the tone. Like Augustine (*On Mus.* 6.5-8), he thinks that when a tone presses on the ear, the soul with its interwoven number encounters the sounding number, perceives it, preserves it, and assimilates it to find a corresponding term between the tone in the soul and that tone outside, which of course has long ago ceased to sound. Judgment through understanding has not yet been made, however. The number calling up a feeling is the *numeris sensualis*. Superior to it is the *numeris judicilis*, by which the soul is put in a position to judge the other tones (that is, their relations). Thus the soul proceeds, in order, from the sounding (physical) number, to the outgoing or encountered number, and then to recorded (remembered), felt, and judicial numbers. And from these observations about numbers and music Grosseteste proceeds to the other sciences. It is Augustine's psychological system literally given once more but placed in a preferred spot ahead of the other mathematical sciences.

Because psychological effects depend on the agreement of the proportionality of the soul with that of nature, ethical effects too depend on the proportions of music. The formal structures are the determinants, no matter how the elements differ. The wise man in the natural sciences and medicine knows the correct proportions of the elements, of the fundamental harmonies of physical-psychical life, and of the ideal proportions necessary to human equilibrium. The proportions in sound-rhythms and soul-rhythms alike meet in sensation: when rhythms of the soul correspond with those of the body, minds expand in joy or contract in sorrow. Rhythms in tone produced on instruments also correspond with soul-rhythms and can change the listener's state of mind--almost exactly as the rhythm-producer wishes. The final result is the composition, the synthetic action of the mind through the energy of transfer rather than in a spatial order only. Though he employs Augustine almost literally, Grosseteste does not associate the psychological-ethical effects of music with rhetoric. His is a formalistic aesthetic. In place of the rhetorical orientation of Augustine he seems to be substituting the ancient theory of musical affects almost arbitrarily created and administered. But the affects are only vague and general, and not specific according to ancient expectations.[5]

II

Albertus Magnus (Albert von Bollstädt). Albertus Magnus (c.1193-1280), who taught at the Dominican school in Cologne, is credited with ushering in the great and final age of Scholasticism. As noted above, this Dominican thinker tried to achieve a reconciliation of Christianity and Aristotle: he is thus sometimes called the Christian Peripatetic. The Jews knew God, he thought, by the Scriptures, but the Greeks supplied to the world the natural wisdom of reason, the most sublime reason the world has ever seen. He was a theologian, philosopher, and natural scientist who studied insects, birds, and mammals (including polar bears and whales). For his scientific efforts he received a reputation as a magician,[6] but in fact he may have been the most serious naturalist to have worked since Pliny the Younger. Yet his interests were hardly only scientific, for he wrote a commentary on Pseudo-Dionysius. With regard to music, his points of contact are Augustine and Aristotle, and it is from the latter's *On the Soul* that he derives his ideas about the production of sound and hearing (acoustics) and its source in nature. His commentary on Aristotle's *Politics* provides more paraphrase than analysis, but nevertheless he recognizes Aristotle's skepticism about world (musical) harmony, based, as he thinks, on the concept of harmony as soul (rather than body). In connection with the reciprocal harmony of body and soul, he mentions that David played the harp first to release Saul from evil demons and then again before God to please him. Albertus quotes Aristotle about music as a civilizing force; as an entertainment for mature, old, and wise men; as useful for relaxation, the elimination of care, and mental insight; for its ability to build character and produce good affects and states of mind; and as a necessity in education. For Albertus, however, a choir of singers is a symbol of a harmonious state of mind (*Comm. on Arist.* 8.3-4)--clearly an Augustinian remark made in opposition to Aristotle.[7]

Whereas Grosseteste in part outlined a formalistic aesthetics and yet was a psychological theorist in the Augustinian manner, Albertus, associated with the *via antiqua* as we have seen, tends to remind us of the concerns of the Church Fathers. His primary concern remains practical: how music is to be used in the Church. Singing must conform with thinking, he says, and thinking with action or good works (*Comm. on the Psalms: Ps.* 88.2, 134.3). The psalms exist for the praise and honor of God (*Comm. on St. Dionysius the Areopagite* 2.11b). In church singing, the rising of voices symbolizes the soul's excitement at seeing the works of God, their descent its realization of its own insufficiency. Thus symphony, like singing itself, is a harmony occurring when a Christian congregation or an exultant Christian choir praises God in song (*Comm. to the Gospel according to St. Luke* 15.25-27). Yet both symphony and song, as Albertus discusses them, are less musical than symbolical. The psalms are vessels containing the truth of faith; at the same time they are like musical instruments embracing spiritual harmony (*Ps.* 70.22). He returns to terminology as old as Clement of Alexandria: the new song (the hymn) has symbolic connections with the New Testament in that it inclines man toward renewal through the mercy of God. To sing to God in the new song means through word and deed to fulfill in one's own life the precepts given in the new Testament. The singing of the unrenewed person cannot be called new, or a song, at all; it resembles the grunting of pigs before a feeding-trough (*Ps.* 95.1). When he lauds the *jubilus*, he resembles Hippolitus and Augustine (*Ps.* 65.2). And, like Hippolitus, he distinguishes the song of the psalms from the psalmic song: the first is primarily instrumental and then vocal (ibid.), and the second is first vocal and then instrumental (*Ps.* 67.5-26). Tradition is his servant and guide: the Church makes a distinction between Old Testament praise of God accompanied by instruments (*Ps.* 150-3-5) and New Testament praise of God through sheer vocality (*Col.* 3.16).

It is obvious that symbolism is Albertus' abiding interest and that a musical instrument, though a servant of religion, is chiefly a physical reminder of spiritual matters. The harp is the mortification of the flesh (*Ps.* 32.2), the wood and the strings being the body of Christ and the bodies of the saints, respectively. The tension of the strings represents the punishment of the body during repentance. As differently tensed strings ultimately come together in a melody, so the different paths to death (crucifixion or decapitation) bring together the saints within the Christian faith (*Luc. expos. in apocal. Beati Joan. Apost.* 5.8-10). The sound of the trumpet is comparable to the singing and exultation of the angels (*Ps.* 46.6) or to the sermon of the first apostle (*Ps.* 150.3). The brass trumpet is like the purification of martyrs through peril and persecution; the hard-skinned (leather-covered) trumpet or cornett is like people who profess their religion; and the trumpet in general is a symbol of the preacher (*Ps.* 97.6). The organ is like the Church Fathers: the pipes of different size produce beautiful music, just as the various sermons of the Fathers about different Scriptural works ultimately reach a harmonious agreement in Christian faith (*Ps.* 150.4).

In his commentary on a passage in the Gospel according to St. Luke, he asks about the value of instrumental playing in the lives of human beings in general. Here he turns to Aristotle's *Politics*. There are two general kinds of playing and passing the time, the profitable and useful (but more or less devoid of ideas), and the disgraceful and injudicious. Among the first belong riding-contests, which advance military service and national defense; to the second belong theatrical exhibitions, which do not lack for the lascivious or obscene, and dice-playing, which is equally dishonorable. But the philosophers have discovered and demonstrated that the playing of instruments valued by freemen is able to effect refinement, goodness of soul, and gentleness and meekness of heart, though it also exists for its own sake.

Albertus Magnus, then, allows music an important but secondary place in the scheme of things religious. As we would expect, he is less an original thinker than an eclectic who is able to combine different schools of thought. Augustine and Aristotle are for him the great authorities who have defined aesthetic truth about music for all time. His way of proceeding is to bring together quotations,[8] a method which would then produce significant insights. It is a method of which Thomas Aquinas, his pupil, eventually would become the special master.

III

Thomas Aquinas.   Neither Albertus Magnus nor any other philosopher of his period valued innovation *per se*, and in fact the Scholastic method itself militated against change in thought and practice. Tacitly, then, Albertus seemed to stand against novelties, among which we may include polyphony. So too did the learned Italian, St. Thomas Aquinas (c.1125-74), who, however, followed the Scholastic method to discover a theory of art and beauty which had been latent in the writings of the past. He depended on the great thinkers ancient and medieval, in alphabetical order: Al Farabi, Algazel, Anaxagoros, Aristotle, Boethius, Epicurus, Euclid, Heraclitus, Homer, Macrobius, Maimonides, Ovid, Plato, Plotinus, Porphyry, Proclus, Diogenes the Areopagite, Ptolemy, Pythagoras, the Sophists, the Stoics, Theophrastus, and Virgil.   Termed the "Angelic Doctor" and "Prince of Scholastics," Aquinas, in continuing the work of his teacher Albertus Magnus toward the reconciliation of theology and Aristotelianism, additionally systematized Catholic theology, which in his *Summa theologica* became separated from philosophy, the knowledge of things and of their ultimate causes.

For Aquinas, the recognition of good and evil begins with seeing and hearing, and hence both sight and sound administer to cognition and reason.

Knowledge begins with sense experience but does not stop there. Like many of his predecessors, he thinks that light and number are a unity creating beauty. A sign of a lower science, however, is that it depends on a higher. Thus music depends on arithmetic (*ST* I, Q. 1, Art. 2.5), and the metaphysically ontological basis of music lies in its number-governed sound because harmony is a mathematical-ontological reality occupying a place alongside acoustical phenomena (*On Aristotle's Metaphysics* 1.16.242, 1.3.412) and because number is the foundation of all music. Furthermore, there is a connection between "debita harmonia" and the delight aroused in the hearer (*Comm. on Arist. De Anima* 1.3., Lectio 7.97), a delight which can be spiritual as well as sensuous (*On the Nic. Ethics* 2.1986).

Thomas explains the terms *proportio* (a harmonizing relation between two quantities or relations), *consonata* (audible, musical sound-qualities of tones), and *harmonia* (in the true musical sense) as a synonymous sounding together (*Comm. De an.* 1.4, Lectio 7.93ff). Proportion is applicable to music in the arithmetic sense. Thus number is the cause (*On Aristotle's Physics* 2.179). Musical consonance depends on definite number relations both horizontal (melodic) and vertical ("harmonic") (*The Heavens and the Earth* 14.422). Hence harmony is intrinsic to simultaneous or successive intervals. Actual tone, of course, is tone heard; tone as possibility is latent in a physical body which can produce tone as actuality. Its medium is air set in motion by a physical body. Higher and lower tones eventuate from the faster and slower movements of air which a living being produces with its voice; lifeless beings have no voices except by analogy--an analogy based on duration, melody, and expressive ability (*Comm. De an.* 2.8, Lectio 18.467).

The numerical in actuality is harmony and perfection, and perfection pertains to both the beautiful and the good. The aesthetic is distinguished from the moral (which is action) by the formal matters of clarity (unity), order, simplicity, and a reconciliation of forces; its opposites are confusion and chaos (progressively worse as a departure from unity increases), and the unformed, the uncontrolled, the destructive; and it is recognized only in sight and hearing--both human capacities for understanding the real and actual material world (and not the Imperium). While tones and objects of sight create beauty, taste and smell do not (*ST* II-I, Q. 27, Art. 1, repl. 3). Thus St. Thomas makes distinctions between the higher and the lower senses and among harmony, the beautiful, and the good, which go back at least as far as Plato and are also very important for Aristotle, Alcuin, Ptolemy, and Hugh of St.-Victor. All suggest that sweet melodies (as well as beautiful forms and pleasant tastes) are associated with infinite beauty and tenderness. But the pleasures even of sight and hearing can be physical and therefore self-seeking and low; or they can be disinterested and higher. On the other hand, the senses of taste, smell, and feeling grant only a lower pleasure. St. Thomas' classification of the senses has been fairly universally accepted throughout the history of aesthetics, and his separation of the biological from the aesthetic pleasures, already tacitly understood by music theorists, has also become a staple of modern thought. Furthermore, he supplies no special transcendental or mythical explanation for either.

The Church had thought beauty to be vain, but St. Thomas led the way to its acceptance as a proper, legitimate, and good human experience. Having distinguished "low" physical pleasures from the higher one of beauty, he also makes a distinction between the good and the beautiful, which under the term *kalokagathia* had been united in ancient theory. He illustrates the difference in the relation of a lion to a stag. When a lion meets a stag, he is happy at seeing his prey. He is pleased not by the sight, however, but by the biological satisfaction it promises him. Biological satisfaction--for example, eating, drinking, and reproduction, all allied with and dominated by pleasures of touch--are common to all animals, and the lion cannot see the stag indifferently as a beautiful object. But man has a spiritual nature which allows him to find joy and pleasure when he disregards physically fundamental needs and seeks knowledge for its own sake (as mentioned by Aristotle [*Poetics* 1448b], for example). Man can delight "in the beauty of physical objects in and for itself"; setting biological utility aside, he can enjoy the harmony of physical objects and of sounds for their own sake (*ST* II-II, Q. 141, Art. 4, repl. 3). Yet, beauty "cannot be defined without a certain relationship to knowledge: the beautiful is that which is pleasing to the sight, that which gratifies our desire to perceive or to know." A thing is beautiful if it is in harmony with reason (*ST* II-II, Q. 142, Art. 2). Furthermore, "by nature, sight and hearing serve the mind. In contrast, we do not call tastes and odors 'beautiful'" (*ST* I-II, Q. 27, Art. 1, repl. 3).

Beauty has completeness, proportion or harmony, and perfection (including brightness, or clarity) (*ST* I, Q. 39, Art. 8, obj. 5). Perfection is transcendental, a formal distinction by which an object is declared beautiful. The ugly is the imperfect. Beauty is both divine and human, and when it is created by man, it includes both physical and spiritual-moral beauty. Mere acquaintance is the mode and manner by which beautiful things are experienced as pleasant (*ST* I, Q. 5, Art. 4, repl. 1) and satisfying to our perceptions (*ST* II-I, Q. 27, Art. 3): a formal cause is grasped through reason and sense. Therefore beauty concerns the objective aspect, the quality of the thing; and qualities make up the entirety, the complete, the perfect thing. What is incomplete or spoiled is ugly. Ultimately, perfection or completeness is the same as goodness.

Proportion in music, as we have seen, applies to melody-building, harmony, and rhythm, but physical clarity (*claritas*) and light are not the same as non-physical nature, though both have the power of manifestation in common (*ST* II-II, Q. 145, Art. 2). Spiritual light is more like the intellect than the will (*ST* II-I, Q. 1, Art. 4, repl. 1-3), and clarity is the quality of a musical thing (thus, possibly, the reflection of the artist's idea) which allows its own nature as music to be clearly discernible. An example is an approach to the grandeur of God through the clear singing of praises along with the spirit, which is the knowledge of the holy.

The subjective aspect of musical beauty (which was suggested in Augustine's *On Music*) involves the recognition of aesthetic pleasure in musically beautiful things. Experiencing sensuous musical beauty, the hearer arrives at a knowledge of it, though he cannot possess beauty itself as such. Like aesthetic objectivity, sensuous perception, which is subjective, includes perfection, proportion, and clarity--and these turn perception towards the super-sensuous. The organs of perception cannot grasp the causality-factor or the form itself. Man knows things (which animals too can perceive) as beautiful (which animals do not) and does so through his intellect (*Comm. De an.*, liber 7.9, *ST* I, Q. 5, Art. 4, repl. 1). Though beauty includes aesthetic pleasure, it is also associated with a spiritual knowing (*ST* II-I, Q. 27, Art. 1, repl. 3). Aesthetic pleasure and satisfaction, then, are both sensuous and spiritual in their disinterestedness, as contrasted with (extraneous, purposeful) interest in the experience of the good. Aesthetic pleasure and satisfaction seem not unrelated to contemplation, which St. Thomas defines as a high kind of play or game having no end but itself. An artist can work for sheer sensual pleasure, but he is under control. So acrobats, dancers, and comic actors (those foils for the early Church Fathers) achieve pleasure which is not immoral because play is a necessity--but a temperate necessity--to the rhythm of human life (*ST* II-II, Q. 168, Art. 3, repl. 3). However related to the soul and to spiritual things, then, music like all art is a matter of feelings given order and of human perceptions in activities related to the real world of physical things. Its secret lies in its audible motion, which is a direct correlation with the soul itself.

Repeating the familiar anecdote of Pythagoras' re-directing a young man's frenzy of love, St. Thomas gives it a Christian interpretation: music is a strengthening of spirit as one turns to the devotion of God (*In Ps.* 32). Praising God in his eternal perfection and thanking him for his welcome gifts of grace and salvation (*Ps.* 12.4f), we employ music to perfect ourselves, and both vocal and instrumental music are capable of turning the soul towards God.

But the man who sings and plays must be potentially musical, and his teacher must be actually musical. The latter is the mover, the former the moved (*On Aristotle's Metaphysics* 9.1848, 1851). Someone with a good voice who has technical skill, keeps in practice, and can sing with authority must have a joyful heart faithful to and filled with the Divine. It is with the novice that one sings the psalms, whose prophecies are the most noble of all prophecies. The psalmist is a precentor, and since he recites with a chant, he calls for the participation of a choir (*ST* Suppl. 37.2.5, repl. 5).

Thomas seldom mentions instruments. He refers to the tibia, organ, trumpet, drum, and fistula when necessary, but the technique of playing these instruments calls up no remarks. Like his forebears, he makes mention of the symbolism of instruments. The psaltery because of its ten strings is like the Ten Commandments and is symbolical of spiritual teaching, and thus it is related to the celestial and heavenly. The harp is an artificial instrument as compared with natural ones like the voice. Whereas the psaltery is heavenly and points to eternal things, the harp is earthly. The psaltery, played with the hand, is like good works, but the harp too corresponds with doing right. For praising God, the harp is inferior, and, like Aristotle (*Pol.* 1341a), St. Thomas calls it an artificial instrument designed for the professional. The tibia corresponds with the Dorian mode and can put the very strife of mankind on a certain right course directed toward constancy of soul. The fistula (like the Greek aulos) too is an artificial instrument. The trumpet makes a powerful sound (it brought down the walls of Jericho, as noted in *Joshua* 6.4-5) (Burbach, pp. 92-99).

It was the scholastic practice to employ what seems today to be quotations in the excess. Thus we again read that the Dorian, Phrygian, Hypolydian, and Mixolydian modes all have different affects--and here St. Thomas is probably relying on the Greeks (and possibly Cassiodorus) (Burbach, pp. 54-58). Ultimately, however, all judgment depends on the extent to which music can serve the Church: Church tradition says that music is justified only as it serves in the Mass and Offices and creates a good inner state of mind (*ST* II-II, Q. 91, Art. 2, repl. 3-4). In effect instruments are (with a certain ambiguity) banished from the Church. And it seems to be assumed that Gregorian chant untouched by polyphony is the only church music and that it is so composed that through it one can give himself up to the devotion of and submission to God, whom one must praise, thank, and implore.

In one section of the *Summa* (II-II, Q. 91, Art. 2), St. Thomas treats the question "Whether God should not be pleased with song?" in the scholastic manner. He describes five denials (derived from more than five sources) which must be satisfactorily answered: (1) God should not be praised in song because St. Paul in speaking to the Colossians (3.16) says that the teaching and admonishing of the faithful can be accomplished through psalms, hymns, and spiritual canticles, but not through "corporeal canticles"--that is, those which are not Scriptural in origin. Also, (2) St. Jerome in commenting on the *Ephesians* (5.19) says that only the music of the heart, not that of the voice, nor that of play-actors with their theatrical "measures and airs," can be used in the praise of God. Furthermore, (3) great (important) persons, according to St. Gregory, should not sing in church, and neither should little persons, according to the *Apocalypse* (14). (4) Instruments must be banned from the Church because, though it is said in Psalm 32.2-3 that the Lord should be praised with the harp and the psaltery of ten strings, the Church ought not to use musical instruments "for fear of imitating the Jews" (of the Old Testament). Consequently, (5) music should not be employed in the divine service when it calls up praise from the lips and not from the heart, when the singers are distracted from what they are singing, and when the congregation is less able to understand what is sung than what otherwise would be recited.

These negatives are denied so that positives can emerge. Thomas points out that St. Ambrose, as St. Augustine testifies (*Conf.* 9), established singing in the church at Milan. Also, the voice expressing praise is needed if man's devotion to God is to be aroused. The human soul is moved in various ways according to the melodies it hears; so say Aristotle (*Pol.* 1340a) and Boethius (Prologue, *Of Music*). Thus the use of music in the praise of the divine is salutary: again, Augustine says as much (*Conf.* 9.6, 10.33). Therefore the five denials call for these five answers:

1. If canticles sung inwardly in spirit and those sung outwardly with the lips arouse spiritual devotion, both can be called spiritual canticles.

2. Jerome condemns people who are exhibitionists and who arouse pleasure, but he does not condemn singing itself: as Augustine says (*Conf.* 10.33), in the Church one should be moved by the words, not the voice.

3. It is indeed better to arouse men to devotion by teaching and preaching than by singing because through the latter people are "withdrawn from greater things."

4. Also, as Aristotle said (*Pol.* 1340a-b), teachers who employ instruments give pleasure. They do not, as they should, effect a change of disposition through imitation; but men of the Old Testament needed instruments because they themselves were "coarse and carnal" (more than those of the present) and needed to be aroused by instruments, which were "figures of something else."

5. If chanting is to encourage devotion, the singer must note the words of the text, linger upon them, and achieve "an affection of . . . spirit according to its variety" and according to its "appropriate measure in the voice." Singing must stir "a hidden correspondence" in the spirit (Augustine, *Conf.* 10.33). But even if the hearer does not understand what is sung, he nevertheless understands why it is sung--that is, to arouse his devotion to God and to celebrate God's glory.

Thus Thomas dwells on the words-and-music aspect of the liturgy and the chanting which accompanied it. For him, music is instrumental in the broadest metaphorical sense. True, he seems to follow Augustine in thinking that the *Alleluia* is a spiritual song of jubilation, a spiritual sigh (Burbach, p. 120).[9] For the rest, the word predominates. And yet he does not apply his aesthetic principles to church music. The strife for the eternal through beauty seems to have little to do with singing or, when permissible, with instrument playing during the service. Nor does musical symbolism play a part except as it is a medium for holy words. It is not described in mystical, intellectual, or transcendental terms. It is almost a naturalistic phenomenon, a pleasant contributory accompaniment. Aesthetically considered, it appeals to the human mind through its clarity, simplicity, and form. It leads to the spirit and divine truth. Its aims are not the excitement of the ego but an order and calm suggested by the text. In this respect it reminds one of the mental state of Bernard of Clairvaux when he meditated in the setting of his Cistercian abbey. But Thomas is less mystical, and his aim in theory is the more or less visible spiritual and mental state of the faithful.

For Bernard of Clairvaux, however, the religious experience is personal and mystical. Thomas, like most of his Scholastic and non-Scholastic predecessors, is thinking of the religious experiences of groups of people, learned and ignorant, who make up the Christian community. And thirteenth-century men and women were obviously different from those of ancient Israel. The instruments of the Old Testament, for example, had always been a problem for the Church Fathers. Legitimate or not in the church service, they now were held to have been figures foreshadowing the Passion and the work of salvation of Christ, an element of physical worship which had been eventually subsumed into the spiritual. The purpose of the Church, which is the praise of the pure Spirit, requires song, not instruments, and never more than now. The text is liturgical and the words holy, and human beings as they sing them are praising, thinking, and praying. And this is not a private matter; it is a communal experience for holy people attending Mass or participating in the Offices, for people who love God with all their hearts, souls, and minds, and with all the strength they have. St. Thomas' own *Lauda Sion, Pange lingua, Adoro devote*, and *Martyr Dei*, like the hymns of Peter Abelard and Hildegard of Bingen, remain as distillations of the best in medieval liturgical poetry, where, ontologically speaking, music and art exist in the realm of human sense and feeling--and their best use is religious. Thus for St. Thomas aesthetic theory appears in the end to be of less consequence than the devotional act itself.[10]

IV

Roger Bacon. A student of Grosseteste at Oxford and then in attendance at the University of Paris with which he was also later associated, Roger Bacon (c.1214-52) was a prominent scholar who, like his teacher, found himself in opposition to the current Scholasticism and its emphasis on logic. In place of the Scholastic method, he believed in the value of empirical science, though he never reached the point of seeing the weaknesses of Aristotelian physics. His remarks on music suggest a respect for music as a science and a devaluation of metaphysical speculation concerning it. Typical among late medieval philosophers, Bacon preferred Gregorian chant to polyphony and its complexities, and he also condemned performance practices such as singing in falsetto. His models included Augustine, Cassiodorus, Isidore, Boethius, Al Farabi, and Avicenna, among others.

Called the "Admirable Doctor," Bacon was both scientist and

Franciscan friar; like Grosseteste, he had an interest in revising the calendar; cited today as the first person in the West to mention gunpowder, he was also very controversial in his own time, having his works condemned for heresy at Paris in 1277. Again like Grosseteste, he had a keen interest in Aristotle, though he in general tended to find his translators weak and misleading. At the request of Pope Clement IV (d.1268), he had written an encyclopedic work, the *Opus majus*.

His scientific work seems in some sense to anticipate the Renaissance thinker and essayist Francis Bacon (1561-1626) since he first lists the causes of error, then doubts authority and the reliability of the human mind, and finally favors experiment in pursuit of learning. Roger Bacon's interests were wide-ranging in any case. Following Grosseteste, he was interested in such topics as optics--the offshoot of the mystical preoccupation with light--and meteorology. Like Albertus Magnus, Bartholomeo Anglicus,[11] and Vincent of Beauvais, he was called a magician and alchemist because he speculated on the origins of things. All academic men rather than practicing alchemists, none of these individuals influenced alchemy itself, yet the works of Roger Bacon and the others had a wide appeal in the late Middle Ages, and author-imposters even assumed their names. Bacon himself remains well known among knowledgeable people today as someone mentioned along with Albertus in Marlowe's *Doctor Faustus* (i.153). Bacon strongly maintained that there is a difference between white magic (or the investigation of nature) and black. All of this sets him off from his Scholastic contemporaries, who concentrated on recognized authority. As one might expect, he thought music a positive science. Yet he abjured Pythagorean universalism for music and adopted the Aristotelian position that it is sound made by air stimulated by the striking of a resisting object. In this he resembled music theorists like Guido. He was ready to rely on the evidence of the senses, to which he added the data of spiritual conscience. Nevertheless, he was noted for his extreme enthusiasm for the clarity and certitude of mathematics, without which, he taught, no science, pure or applied, is possible, including even theology, to which music is highly important (*Opus Majus* 4.16).

For Roger Bacon, music is the basic art without which it is not possible for one to understand grammar or the arts of the trivium (ibid. 4.2) It is an independent discipline. Yet it and harmony are not, at least metaphorically, limited to the world of sound; harmony is a consonant and reciprocal adaptation (or a regular variation following a unique *modulus*) of diverse things. Like Cassiodorus, whom he quotes (ibid. 4.16), Martianus Capella, Rémi of Auxerre, and Robert Grosseteste, he sees a rhythmic parallel between music and the dance, including other human movements and bendings of the body. Dance is the visible parallel to the kind of music which is audible; both are pleasures of the senses brought about by movement in song, in the sounds of instruments, and even in punctuation, rhythm, and meter (ibid.).

With Bacon, music becomes a full member of the trivium. This is in keeping with the anti-scientific and the pro-language arts attitude of French schools and universities, which extends to all education of the time. Grammar and rhetoric, Bacon thinks, give children the facts of speech and its properties in prose, meter, and rhythm, but music gives reasons for these things: the nature of tones (which alone are music) has varieties and parts, one dealing with prose, another with meter, another with rhythm, and a fourth with singing. Prose-teaching considers the rise and fall of the voice according to accents and prose-punctuation; the teaching of meter is concerned with the measures of feet and meters; and rhythm-teaching covers all modulations and sweet relations: all of these are related to singing, which is taught separately. "Accent," as it were, is song, and grammar depends on the divisions of music--as does logic, which, like everything else having its aim and its noblest part, is subject to the power of music (ibid. 4.2). Even children should understand numbers before they sing (ibid. 4.3).

As a mathematician, however, Bacon inevitably explains phenomena by referring to numbers as found in the quadrivium, to the numerical ratios in which are found all musical relationships (ibid.). From Augustine he has learned that one should not read writings aloud without a "knowledge of the potency of numbers" because an ignorance of numbers bars the way to understanding and because mutable numbers lead to immutable ones. From Augustine's theology of numbers he turns to Cassiodorus' use of symbolism: numbers are essential to doctrine and to the avoidance of carnal things since they apply to common speech, music, sound, and gesticulation. Furthermore, the science of numbers opens the way to the commands of the Lord, to morals, to the Scriptures, and to all created things: melody charms us because knowledge which lifts our minds to things above is pleasing and useful (ibid. 4.16).

To grammar, rhetoric, and music as a complex of sound and words, Bacon adds acts (mimicry or dancing), and thus makes a theoretical return to Greek practice. It was a position taken by others, even though the Church discouraged dancing, expressed contempt for instrumental music, and preferred the requirements of rhetoric or oratory to any others because their preaching, they thought, demanded rhetoric. But Bacon unashamedly accepts the complex and analyzes it: sensible sound-music separates into the forms or the harmony it concretizes--that is, into sonorous and plastic music. All sonorous music is occupied with harmonies which are a source of delight for the ear. Instrumental music is made by percussive, blown (wind), or tensed (stretched) instruments, all often mentioned in the Scriptures. This music is acceptable in its own right. Yet, sonorous music is also that of the human voice. Vocal music contains the melody of language as found in the numbers of oratory, in the meter of classical verse, and in the accents and rhythms of modern rhythmic poetry (the music of prose, meter, and free rhythm) (ibid. 4.2). Here Bacon describes the differences between musical and linguistic motion implicit in the thought of rhetoricians like Quintilian and the young Augustine, the first five books of whose *On Music* he finds necessary for an understanding of meters and rhythms--and of the Scriptures.

Alongside this sonorous music, vocal and instrumental, is the plastic, which governs visible forms.   Though he is clearly indifferent to the practicalities of the dance, Bacon thinks that this art is a science, and that the two arts of music and dance together form a complete art and a total aesthetic pleasure in that the music of song and instrument, of dance, and of poetry form a true dramatic art.[12]   He is able to say that the leaps and bendings of the body in the dance are indeed proper (ibid. 3.3).   All of music is a part of nature, a copy in miniature of the structure of the world, and a creation of God; it pleases the good man because it can bring him into sympathy with the divine order from which it has descended.

It was Bacon's chief objection to the Scholastics that they ignored the physical and mathematical sciences--*pace* Albertus Magnus and Thomas Aquinas.   St. Thomas' classification of music in a place below arithmetic was no contribution to thought at all.   His predecessors in Church thought had said as much, but even music theorists had added certain analyses to the idea.   In Bacon's view, the physical and mathematical sciences were the basis of true philosophy.

For Bacon and other non-Scholastic thinkers, number exists: it is universal and *a priori*.   Its essence is ratio, which governs everything animate and inanimate.   Music, the prime science of number, occupies both space and time.   It represents space metaphorically in highs and lows and time by movements of high and low.   All combinations of space and time are measured according to ratio, the simpler the better.   The relationships of space can be measured by sight.   One can count the columns of an architectural work.   The relationships of time are calculated according to the temporal relationships of sounds and silences, which can be metaphorically recorded in space: thus the relations of long and short (indicated by beats of the hand or foot or interpreted in writing) and their punctuations (accents and rest-signals, and equivalent lengths in sound).   The numbers of seen objects are external, those of heard numbers (in music) are internal, not observable by the eye but nevertheless capable of being represented metaphorically in space.   Their representations (like notation, for instance) are not symbolical, however.   They are spatial recordings of temporal phenomena which are not seen but are sensed only by the ear. (One is able, of course, to see and hear numbers simultaneously.)   Therefore, musical notes, written schemes of qualitative or quantitative divisions of sound in poetry and their counterparts in the art of music--rhythm and meter visualized--written punctuation marks, rest-indications, and so forth, are external signs of an internal numerical reality.   Music, then, embraces number in all things, movements in sound and silence, and movement and equilibrium in the heights and depths of space.   It is the dance of internal numbers externalized; it is the grammar of internal and external numbers of words.   Number is external, as Aristotle thought, but its internality is Platonic, and therefore Bacon's (and others') use of it in experience is both external and scientific and internal and mystical.

In the end, Bacon must admit that musical theory (like mathematical subjects) must serve theological science. Practical music--at least as realized in speech, the poem and the song--can influence the moral and even the devotional life. A complete delight in it arouses a kind of subtle and unexpected transport which, springing from the beauty of meter and rhythms--from sensual "numbers"--suddenly invades the soul and carries it into the pure region of truth and eternal satisfaction (ibid. 4.16). Rhetoric is brought over to music, all beauty reduces itself to harmony and proportion, and the trivium--prose and poetry--derives from a quadrivial music.

XVII
Music Theories and Theorists
of the High Middle Ages

Very little that was absolutely new was to be said in the writings of the theorists of the thirteenth century, though they continued to develop musical thought in the directions suggested by the Arabs and required by the musical practice of the time. The author of another *Ars musica*, the Spanish Franciscan Gil of Zamora, draws the conventional contrast between the mere singer and the true musician who theoretically and rationally evaluates songs, all varieties of melody, and heavenly harmony itself (G 2.376). In his thinking, the scales of music--that is, the modes--control ethical states. Nevertheless, his work signals the virtual end of the Greek idea that *specific* affects can be attributed to each mode.

The first tonus (Dorian), he says, for example, has motive power and is useful for the expression of all feelings. The third (Phrygian) is a general and instructive example of unrestraint. He speaks of its fiery character and sudden changes and of its healthy effects as well. Making reference to the story of Pythagoras and the love-sick youth, he anachronistically adds that through the use of the Phrygian mode, the youth was cured of his madness and restored to good temper. (It will be remembered that the designation of modes in antiquity differed from the labels applied in the practice of the Church in the Middle Ages.) In medieval tradition, the fifth or Lydian mode (which, like Mixolydian, is said to be the basis for the modern major scale) was indicative of cheerfulness and grace; for Gil it is suited to drive off grief and anxiety and to cheer up the depressed and despairing. Other modes are lachrymose (the sixth mode) and high-spirited and pleasant (the seventh mode) so that, with its many changes, the latter is able to stimulate the power of motion and the vigor of young manhood (G 2.387).

As a devout man of his order, Gil conventionally thinks that *musica caelestis* is in a superior position to the *musica mundana*. Furthermore, both singing and instrumental music[1] are artificial (as they were for John Scot Erigena and Boethius, who called them merely instrumental); so are all arts which imitate human beings (Hugh of St.-Victor's mechanical arts); by contrast, God created three kinds of non-instrumental music: *caelestis*, *mundana*, and *humana*[2] (G 2.377).

Gil's information is patently out of date, for he is merely repeating what he had learned rather than observing and analyzing the music of his day. As we have seen, the older writings assumed the ancient system of long and short syllables. But the longs and shorts, regardless of the firmness of the theory, were not perfectly predictable since they always had depended to some extent on the reciter. Even in chant, there was not any need for absolute standardization of duration, though the change in hymns to texts which were accentual would have tended to level out the durations. Thus in the early medieval period a beginning was made toward the establishment of rhythmic orders of long and short according to strict time. A dependable rhythmic structure was also important for early organum since as the number of voices or parts increased, accompaniment to the melody of the chant became more complicated. Plainchant was definitely not repudiated: it continued to be used across Western Europe. Indeed, it was extended and developed.[3] And with organum, followed by polyphony, it needed technological change in the development of notation for its full flowering.

In the music of the Church in the twelfth century, then, monophony and organum had existed side by side. The latter therefore illustrated a tendency to move away from note-for-note singing in cathedrals, major churches, large monasteries, and perhaps convents. Léonin and Pérotin lived and worked, as we have seen, at a crucial time for the development of polyphony and for the codification of rhythm. An exception seems to have been the Cistercian tradition, which even regarded measured chant as an unsatisfactory development. But in the great cathedrals and some Benedictine monasteries, music apparently arrived at a point where a new discipline was felt necessary. The new type of music of which John XXII had complained was utilizing voice crossing, parallel and contrary motion, and greater use of melisma. In such music, exactness of duration would now be essential.

There were also other characteristics which later would be seen to be imperfections. Sometimes one had to break the parallelism of the voices, and this breaking gradually led to greater freedom of voice-leading. Varieties of intervals, which were themselves imperfect, proceeded to perfect intervals as directly as possible. Such a compositional technique could integrate oblique motion, contrary motion, and voice crossing, as we have seen.

I

How may three, four, or even more voices be kept together?[4] The answer came, as suggested above, through a new look at the question of time and its divisions. Notation, which had previously involved a number of systems only some of which even gave definite indication of pitch and failed to notate precise rhythms, was to be improved through a standardized system that delivered the precision needed for the complexities of polyphonic music. From another point of view, we may say that the music now peeled itself away from the domineering text and took on its own characteristics and laws. Such laws could, of course, be more exact than they had been with regard to rhythmic and harmonic practice. The theorists who now took up matters of this kind said little about chant except when they were writing merely another digest of its properties, while they instead concentrated on complications of sound governed by time and motion, on the mathematics of measurement of rhythm. While they failed to provide a grammar of polyphonic structures (an approach which would have been as unsatisfactory as it would have been limiting), they rather explained such structures in terms of duration.

The men who attempted to discern order in a prevailing diversity of musical practice included the following:

1. John of Garland (c.1195-c.1273) wrote a *De mensurabili musica*. Believed by some scholars to have been born in England (a theory strongly rejected by others), he may with some certainty be associated with the University of Paris. He seems to have been a mathematician, theologian, and alchemist. He is probably also the grammarian who wrote a *Poetria exempla vitae honestae* in the middle of the thirteenth century. It is a book replete with rhetorical figures and their analysis. Here the progress of events in time is analyzed, poetic forms being divided between the natural (events happen in sequence--that is, chronologically) and the artificial (events occur in some other arrangement--as *in medias res*). In an appended section on rhythm, he analyzes numerous stanza forms. His work on the rhythmic modes was crucial in the late Middle Ages for understanding this aspect of music.

2. Franco of Cologne (thirteenth century), a central figure among medieval theorists, may have been himself a composer. To him is attributed, probably falsely, an *Ars cantus mensurabilis* (c.1260) in which mensurable music is explained according to what it is, just as Boethius and Guido of Arezzo from different perspectives had explained plainsong. "Mensurable music," the author of this treatise writes, "is melody measured by long and short time intervals. . . . Measure is an attribute showing the length and brevity of any mensurable melody"; it is absent in plainsong. "Time is the measure of actual sound as well as of the opposite, its omission, commonly called rest." Some music, like discant, is wholly measurable; some, like organum, is only partly so; and in all polyphony measure is a basic element (Strunk, pp. 140-41). Franco is also called the originator of the opinion that the third should be admitted as a consonance, which may have been used, though in theory not accepted, for a considerable time. More importantly, his name is associated with the extremely complicated system of rhythmic values and their alterations known as Franconian notation, which he summarized and codified.

3. The "new" mensural art of music was often called the *ars nova* (contrasted with the *ars antiqua* of Léonin and Pérotin). Marchetto of Padua (fourteenth century) was one of the first and most important exponents of this art. The apparent audience of his *Lucidarium* [*Giver of Light*] *in arte musicae planae* of c.1317-18, about plainchant, and *Pomerium* [*Fruit-bearing Tree*] *artis musicae mensurabilis* (c.1318-19) seems to have been aristocratic and courtly rather than academic. His aim was also less scientific (though he attempts that too) than to give musicians

(the judges of music, the men who perceive, select, and order) and singers (who are only messengers to the heralds who are the musicians) a means of approaching and a rational understanding of the structure and practice of music--the former as they listen, the latter as they perform (*Lucid.* 1.7.3).

For Marchetto music is harmonic, organic, and rhythmic (ibid. 1.7). The harmonic comes from the voice (the natural instrument) of man or animal which sets sound in vibration to be perceived by the ear. Voice-instruments are lungs, throat, palate, tongue, front teeth, and lips. But only articulate and literate voices can produce harmonic music, which can be understood and written down (1.8-9, 11).

Organic music is made up of sounds made not by the human voice but by human breath or by air (e.g., trumpets, pipes, reeds, organs, etc.). The sound produced without natural instruments (that is, by artificial ones) is a sort of breath (ibid. 1.12-13). On the other hand, rhythmic music is produced without voice or air. Here vibration is due to percussion, as in the monochord, the psaltery, etc. (ibid. 1.14).

4. Philippe de Vitry (1291-1361), bishop of Meaux during the last decade of his life, was not actually a professional in the modern sense. He was, however, highly admired, an all-round literate man of the Renaissance type. Nevertheless, his view of classical literature was in many ways negative, and, writing as a mathematician, he even speculated that certain aspects of the works of poets, historians, and orators of ancient times might be inappropriate for study in a university. For him, as for many rhetoricians and grammarians, literature served only to illustrate the rules of grammar and usage. Thus he stands in sharp contrast to Alan of Lille and others of the Charterian school and to John of Garland. Yet he himself wrote poetry, composed music, and theorized about the latter, which he treated in his treatise *Ars nova* (after c.1319). Though he was a diplomat, he was known among singers and musicians as the "flower" of them all.[5] He extended the church modes into secular composition. His motets have complicated isorhythmic structures and in quite an original way represent experimentation with the expression of feeling. For him music is the knowledge of accurate singing, while he notes that its very name derives (as had been said previously) from the Greek *moys* = water and *ycos* = knowledge, a derivation that indicates music to have been invented according to water (which flows).

In a sense, Philippe de Vitry was the prototypical churchman-writer and humanist of his day. He belonged, for example, in the stream of writers who allegorized and moralized the classics in order to rescue them for Christian readers, and, like the Church Fathers and, for example, Rabanus Maurus, his approach to the Bible also heavily depended on allegorical methodology. The stories of the Old Testament, it was thought, typologically anticipated Christian truth, as did certain of the ancient pagan stories and gods of Greece and Rome. If *Ovide moralise* was indeed by Vitry, he explained how Ovid had anticipated all of Christian morality: Actaeon became a symbol for Jesus, Phaeton revealed aspects of Lucifer, and so forth.

5. His great admirer and follower was Jean de Muris (Jehan des Murs) (c.1290-c.1351), sometimes erroneously called the first secular theorist and aesthetician.   His writings include not only the *Ars novae musicae* (1319-21) but also works which treat Boethian theory, mathematics, astronomy, and astrology in addition to two further books on music (*Libellus cantus mensurabilis* and *Ars contrapuncti*) that may not be his. (His *Questiones super partes musicae* is merely a condensation of Book 2 of the *Ars novae musicae*.)   His little *Ars novae musicae* is filled with discussion of the mathematical determinations of pitches and the signs for them.   Hoping to free music from the old rhythmic models and rules, he defends the use of chromatic tones (*musica falsa*) and of duple rhythm.   He was enough aware of form as such to make perhaps the first theoretical description of syncopation (Strunk, p. 178n), which he may have accepted from Philippe de Vitry, who in this context employs not the term 'syncopation' but a kind of omnibus term--'color.'   But *ars nova* obviously means not a new art in the modern sense but rather a new craft.   Jean, like Vitry, says nothing about the aesthetic characteristics of polyphony but much about the process of writing it.   Like other attempts to set up rules for counterpoint as it probably existed, his book represents another phase of the quarrel of the ancients and the moderns (clearly revealed by Jacob of Liège)--this phase having to do with structural technique and aesthetic change.

Jean de Muris would appear to have been unusually progressive for a man of his time since, like the author of the *Musica enchiriadis* and John Cotton, he indicates that there is still much to know about the art of music. His reason is that no man, unless he has the intellect of an angel, can "comprehend the whole truth of any science."   The ancients thought they "held the end" (comprehended the final purpose) of music. They of course were wrong.   And so shall we be proved to be: we have not (consciously) "concealed the state of music or its immutable end."   Freely and involuntarily, God has created and segregated everything in the world, and each of us must speak according to his place on the circle of knowledge and opinion (Strunk, p. 179).

6. Johannes of Grocheo was an older contemporary of Philippe de Vitry and Jean de Muris.   In c.1300 he wrote a *Theoria* (sometimes called *De musica* but identified as *Ars musicae* in a manuscript in the British Library) in which he summarized many of the technical innovations of the new music.   He differed substantially from Vitry and Jean de Muris, however, since he was something of a social scientist of music.   Because his extant work shows a genuine (and unique) interest in secular music, he merits separate treatment. He was familiar with John of Garland and Franco of Cologne, though he took his own unique methodological direction in his survey of music.

Duration and Perfection. According to Johannes of Grocheo (p. 25), the universal rules for musical art should be stated, just as those for medicine were given by Galen. He proves to be Aristotelian in his assumptions that the law of measurement is governed by the virtue of the thing, its intrinsic worth or value, and "everything moving is governed by virtue of a prime mover." How is motion measured? First, there is the *tempus*, the object moved or thought of. It is the first moved, the first mover, "of anything else." It is a time-interval of a note or pause. It is the basic measure of the whole song like the measure of one revolution of one day and like the canon of Polyclitus (p. 22), the Greek sculptor and architect whose work was said to illustrate perfect proportions. The consequence of the use of the *tempus* for the setting up of a system of mensurable music is a new set of modes.

The fundamental question is: how many *tempora* make up a basic combining or combined unit? One by itself would of course not do because, according to ancient theory, 1 is not a number. The first number is 2, and 3 is the sum of 1 and 2. Now the number 3 and therefore also triple meter are symbols of perfection. Since 3 is everywhere and perfect, however, at the very beginning of the process of mensuration, there was a "problem." If 3 is perfect, 2 is imperfect; and though Franco of Cologne makes the distinction (Strunk, p. 142), he leaves its philosophical discussion to Marchetto of Padua, who explains it in his *Pomerium*.

Perhaps relying on Aristotle's opinion that time is the measure of motion (*Phys*. 218a-220a) and possibly also on the idea (*Metaph*. 1021b) that the thing perfect or complete is something which lacks no part in its "natural magnitude" with respect to the "form of its proper excellence," Marchetto calls a perfect thing that which lacks nothing. Imperfect (duple) time, on the other hand, lacks something. Perfect time has "fulness of voice," which the imperfect lacks. The science of perfect time apprehended by the intellect or the senses comes first (imperfect is so only when it is compared with the perfect); subtraction from the perfect by the intellect causes recognition of imperfection and is understood to be imperfect. The composer "who understands the science of music thoroughly" (Strunk, p. 163) should, after he makes a decision about the perfection or imperfection of his piece, place a sign at its beginning to indicate which is used. (There was no difference in the notation used in the two cases, a ♩ serving for both perfect and imperfect lengths of sounds. But an O indicated the perfection of something having a beginning, middle, and end, and the ⊂ indicated something imperfect.) The designation is for the "harmony," a manner of singing, and not for the nature of the music itself. For perfect and imperfect time are contradictory, and there is no mean between them; they are distinct and separate, as Aristotle said: contraries admit and sometimes have an intermediate term, contradictories do not (Aristotle, *Metaph*. 1057a). Duple time suffers from deprivation or privation; something is lacking; and according to Aristotle (ibid. 1046a, 1.32), privation is a determinate capacity, a lack of what naturally belongs to the subject.

Something is not what it is going to be as a result of change.

Jean de Muris makes it seem as though music takes its origin from the number 3. It is the quality of God (three persons in one); numbers (1 = separate, 2 = concrete, 3 = composite); celestial bodies (1 = the thing moving, 2 = the thing moved, and 3 = time); the stars and the sun: heat, light, splendor; and so on through the elements, individuals, finite time (beginning, middle, end), curable disease, intellectual operations, the syllogism (three terms), argument, and so forth. After 1, 3 is the first odd number. Multiplied by 3, it becomes the first cubic number. Three lines enclose a surface, the triangle is the source of polygonic figures, the first rectilinear figure is a triangle--and every object has these dimensions (Strunk, p. 173). The number 3 is clearly the number for the permanently divine order of things, and the basic unit to be perfect had to be made up of three *tempora*.

But there is here a philosophical problem involving limitation. For Jean de Muris, music as sound "generated by motion" belongs to the "class of successive things." Echoing Augustine, he declares that "while it exists when it is made, it no longer exists once it has been made" (Strunk, p. 172). Motion produces succession, and time "unites motion" and is the measure of both motion and sound. It has two forms--the natural and the mathematical. Though sound is divisible to infinity, nature sets limits, a maximum and a minimum, to sound, as to all things--limits which are humanly physical and psychological. Sound is a natural form to which we have attributed quantity. Employing reason, we want to apprehend the quantitative limits which we attribute to natural sounds. Sound when it is prolonged must be seen as measured by definite time. Formed in air, it is calculated, not like a point, a line, or a surface, but, rather, like a cone or sphere, just "as light is formed in free space" in the likeness of a sphere. Since a finite individual strikes a finite object, however, the duration and continuation of a tone are of necessity limited (ibid., p. 174). And it is this limitation which must be recorded on the page.

With tonal perfection and imperfection, Marchetto makes one of the first comparisons of national characteristics in medieval musical thought. French and Italian practices differ, he says, thus: the Italians put the "imperfection" at the beginning, the final and more perfect note at the end.[6] The French say that this is acceptable for perfect time, but in imperfect time the final tone is less perfect. Which is the more rational? The French, Marchetto answers: the perfect thing is perfect at its end and the imperfect imperfect at its end. Yet the Italians, as far as they can, imitate perfection by changing the imperfect to the perfect. Marchetto asks that the music of his own time shine not with artificial brilliance, but with the light of reason and order (*Pomer.* G 3.175-76), and the latter of course means perfection in time, or deprivation denied.

Number and the Rhythmic Modes. That music is a science made up of and dealing with numbers, of proportions, of intervals and especially consonances in sound, and based on quantities--this was understood for centuries. From early times it had been observed that sound is continuous or discrete. Probably depending on Nicomachus, Marchetto translates this into quantity, which can be either continuous or discrete. Continuous quantity is reflected in magnitude of sound. But music moves, and thus is impermanent and quantitatively discrete. Multitude, not magnitude is its characteristic, and number its essence. The numerical proportions of music are arithmetical, and its motional impermanence makes it like astronomy, or the moving stars, and like geometry, or the impermanent but immobile earth. The movements of music can, like all impermanent things, be measured.

Rhythmic modes are now applied to musical structures and textures; these are not ecclesiastical modes, registering the progress of sounds, but modes of duration measuring lengths. Number is intrinsic to the distinction between duple and triple time. Just as in the past sounds had been regarded as spatial only metaphorically yet subject to number, now impulses metaphorically dividing sounds--indeed, sounds crystallized in imagination--are organized or interpreted according to mathematical calculations.

Thus Marchetto finds that irrational (uneven) numbers have great power. It is an opinion going back to Nichomachus, Aristides Quintilianus, and finally the early Greeks. For Marchetto irrational (uneven) numbers have a greater masculine inner power than the rational (even) ones, which are assigned to the weaker feminine species. The even numbers are changeable and divisible, but the uneven are indivisible because their center is the number 1, which resists division (*Lucid.* 6.2.13-14). Odd numbers are authentic, then, and the even are plagal. Hence Marchetto prefers the unequal (authentic) church modes to the even (plagal) ones (ibid. 11.2.8-9).

Again Aristotle is the clue or model: number, he had insisted in his *Physics* (207b), is a plurality of "ones," 2 and 3 merely being derivative terms (as are other numbers). Here is the root of the division of time: 1 is the *tempus*, and 2 and 3 are multiples. The ratio of 1:3 is perfect, 1:2 imperfect. Therefore the six rhythmic modes, as now used, are ultimately based on Latin poetic feet (numbers) and are constructed in terms of perfection. A sound of two *tempora* is long, and of one *tempus* is short. A long is therefore equal to two shorts. A total of three makes a foot; a minimum of two feet makes an *ordo* or basic unit. Latin poetic feet and their names are relevant because composers have tried to follow the natural accents of words, as seen in the chart at the top of page 401.[7]

The explanation of notation[8] in terms of numbers by Jean de Muris is complicated but instructive: all music, and especially the mensurable, takes its origin from the number 3: $3 \times 3 = 9$, which in a sense includes every number; $3 \times 9 = 27$; $3 \times 27 = 81$. The maximum limits of a whole sound are 1 to 81, its length being embraced by the extremes between 1 and 81. Now, there are four degrees of perfection, and a perfection can be divided into three equal parts or two unequal ones (if the larger is two times larger than the smaller). Unity, naturally, is indivisible (see chart following).

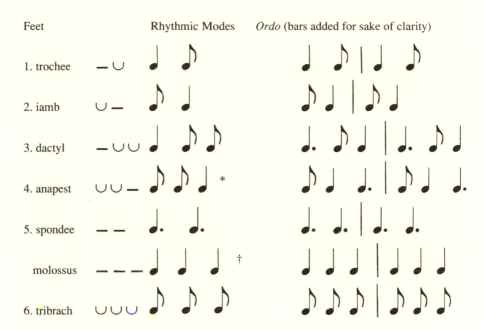

Feet		Rhythmic Modes	*Ordo* (bars added for sake of clarity)

* Seldom used in practical music.

† Could be ♩ ♩ ♩ as employed by the tenor in motets, the other voices moving more rapidly.

Whatever seems illogical in the chart below is due to the use of notes common to perfection and imperfection. Notes perfect and imperfect are combined--three ternary note values in perfect time and two of the same note values in imperfect. Perfect is played off against imperfect, and in a composition perfect and imperfect feet may alternate as being of "equal" proportion. Furthermore, with Jean de Muris and Philippe de Vitry the (French) system is set, and a new term, *prolation*, is introduced: the long

First degree
(major mode)

81 is ternary and perfect (*triplex long*)

54 corresponds and is imperfect (*duplex long*)

27 corresponds and is imperfect (*simplex long*):
    makes perfect imperfect and imperfect perfect

Second degree   ■   27 perfect long
(mode)

                   ■   18 imperfect long

                   ■   9 breve (1/3 in perfect time; 1/2 in imperfect)

Third degree   ■   9 perfect breve
(time, tempus)

                   ■   6 imperfect breve

                   ◆   3 minor breve

Fourth degree   ◆   3 perfect semibreve
(prolation)

                   ◆   2 imperfect semibreve

                   ↓   10 minim semibreve[9]
                   ◆

serves two purposes--the perfect (▜ = 3 ■) and the imperfect (▜ = 2 ■);
time (*tempus*) divides into perfect 3 (■ = 3 ◆) and 2 (■ = 2 ◆), and
prolation similarly divides into 3 and 2 (◆ = 3 ↓ or 2 ↓).[10]
    Though in the Middle Ages there were several systems for notation,
Jean explains his own and gives a rationale for it. As "the wiser ancients
long ago agreed," he says, "geometrical figures should be the signs of
musical sounds," and now the quadrilateral, because it can be made with "a
single stroke of the [fourteenth-century] pen," is like a genus, and all
musical notes have their origin in it. It is a figure of nine virtues (a
rectangularity, equilaterality, the tail, the dot," etc.) arbitrarily representing
"numbered sound measured by time" (Strunk, p. 175). (In his calculations
Jean de Muris ignores both numbers 11 and 12--a not uncommon practice
because 11 was often called the number for sins since it is 1 over 10, and 12
was sometimes given as the number for opposites.)

    Rests. The idea of perfection and imperfection was applied to rests as
well as to sounds. As has been shown above, two or more patterns are an
ordo, and two at least are necessary. This is so because one cannot
recognize a foot until it is repeated. Individual foot following individual
foot means chaos. According to Augustine, a foot must have two times and
a verse at least four times (two times as a unit repeated) (*On Music* 3.9.21).
(Augustine himself counted 568 meters and excluded permissible exceptions!) The distinction was a rhetorician's and came from Latin. Cicero
(*Orator* 47.183-84) had found that there are three kinds of rhythm--the
regular schemes of recited verse, the patterns of rhythmic prose, and,
between them, the rhythms of the lyric poets. And Quintilian (9.4.45-54)
had divided verse into two kinds--that for recitation employing basic feet
without much variation or change (*metrum*), and that for song, in which
different feet are combined in various ways (*numerus*). It is the latter which

Augustine and late medieval theorists have in mind.

The rule is that when an *ordo* is complete (and this could occur after two feet) the foot could be changed by the intervention of a rest. There must be two feet of any meter, said Augustine, or a foot plus a partial foot completed with a rest, a silence--two completed feet--and then a new meter may be begun (*On Music* 3.9.19) (yet a silence of more than half a foot is disallowed [ibid. 4.8.9]). When an *ordo* is complete, the rest says so, but the rest must be at the second part of the pattern (according to modern notation: ♩ ♩ | ♩ 𝄾) if the result is to be perfect. Should a rest occur on a final foot (♩ ♩| ♩ ♩| 𝄾), the effect is imperfect, and a different mode will follow.

Rests now create a new feeling of variety in rhythm, and in diagram the basic minimum of types of *ordo* are those which appear below:

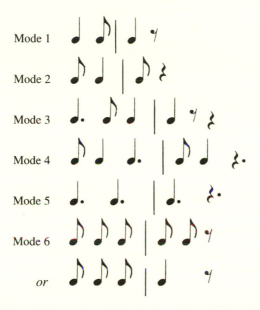

Mode 1

Mode 2

Mode 3

Mode 4

Mode 5

Mode 6

or

For Franco, rests have "a marvelous power" because they can cause a change from one mode to another (Strunk, pp. 149-50). He explains thus: the rest is the "omission of actual sound in the quantity proper to some [rhythmic] mode." Actual sound must precede its omission as "habit" precedes "privation," the habit of music being sound and its privation or rest. Here Franco is either Aristotelian or Augustinian. Habit comes from *habitus*, meaning a condition, habit, character, a quality adhering permanently and aiding in the operation to which it is proper. Aristotle had made all of this clear in his *Categories* (8b): "Habit differs from disposition in being more lasting and more firmly established." Disposition is a condition easily changed. Privatives, which presuppose a predeterminate subject, are the absences of positives (ibid. 12b). Privation (*Metaph*. 1046a) is precisely what occurs, according to Marchetto, in imperfection. For Augustine, both good and bad (imperfection) are necessary, and evil is nothing but the privation of something; it does not exist anywhere except as part of a good thing (*Div. Prov*. 1.7, FC 1.256-58). Furthermore, Aristides Quintilianus too had seen that a rest fills a poetic foot. And Aristotle in his *Physics* (253a-b) again had said that when a quality is given logically as the opposite of a sense form (as silence is the opposite of sound), there is a form of privation, like motionlessness in a context of motion. In the habit-privation distinction, Franco finds philosophical justification for the aesthetic character of an abstract and technical form, a state of affairs which has been elegantly described as the presence of absence.

In plainchant, as in prose, an unspecified silence means a breath taken because the singer needs it or has come to the end of a thought or a smaller part of it. Orators, of course, had always breathed when they needed to, when statements of thought required punctuation or when they used "pregnant" silences by design. Franco and his followers are speaking about a measured, calculated rest, however, even one recorded in manuscript. Singers sang together, and they had to keep together; in polyphonic music this was difficult without measurements as a guide. They had (and still have) to maintain a regular meter or rhythm, mixed, as Marchetto might say, in order to realize the composer's intentions. Hence measurement of lengths of time, of duration, took on an importance it had never had before. And thus was established the importance of meter and, in it, the rest, whether privative or positive in character.

The music of the *ars nova* is often highly complex and requires the modern performer and listener to be alert to its complicated rhythms and melodies. The shift to a music dependent on the rhythmization of tone based not on accents but on lengths, on duration, was not only significant for subsequent polyphony, but also it created a highly sophisticated art in its time. Furthermore, this new music as described by Marchetto, Jean de Muris, and the others is far more intense than one would guess without practical experience with the music. The rhythmic modes, for example, were frequently mixed. As Waite points out,[11] pieces of organum of some length undergo a change of modes, even within one of the voices. Compositions may have an opening section in the first mode, followed by another extended section in the third mode, and then perhaps another section once more in the first mode. But how can the feet of the *modi recti* which contain three *tempora* be combined with the feet of the *modi in ultra mensuram* which contain six *tempora*? Obviously a foot of the third mode cannot be equated with a foot of the first mode, because the former has a time value precisely twice that of the latter. On the other hand, the first mode and the second mode seem to be equivalent since they both contain three *tempora*, but nevertheless these modes are never combined in practice.

These seeming discrepancies are explicable only through a phenomenon which belongs properly to the art of metrics. And Waite is writing about an organal form far simpler than the motet, in which rhythmic variety was marvelously intense.

The Usable and the Perfect Intervals. The insistence on quantity makes it possible to interpret intervals in terms of quality. Thus the perfect intervals of the octave, fifth, and fourth were still regarded as consonances, as perfect in quality. In the late Middle Ages, which often share an inconsistency of definition with all preceding ages, the term 'concord' seems to be the more inclusive term, recalling the 'harmony' and the 'symphony' of the ancients, and 'consonance' is the narrower. The preservation and use of consonances is the aim, and Boethius is frequently its textual authority.

Franco defines concord as two or more sounds occurring at one time and perceived by the ear as an agreement. Discords are the opposites, sounds perceived as dissonances. By Franco's time the number of recognized concords had increased. They are: (1) perfect, in which differences could scarcely be perceived: the octave and the unison (sung by two or more voices); (2) imperfect, in which there are considerable differences not conceived as discords: the ditone (major third) and semiditone (the minor third); and (3) those superior in perception to the imperfect but not superior to the perfect: the fourth and the fifth. Discords are also subdivided. They are (1) perfect when they appear in perception to disagree: the semitone, tritone, ditone with the addition of a fifth (major seventh), and semitone with the addition of a fifth (minor sixth); and (2) imperfect, when two tones are perceived to disagree to a certain extent and are still discordant: the tone, the tone with the addition of a fifth (major sixth), and a minor third with the addition of a fifth (minor sixth). It will be observed that the thirds are now acceptable though they are imperfect. In fact, as Franco indicates, they sound well when they are placed before concords (Strunk, pp. 152-53). Though by 1260 thirds and sixths had been admitted among consonant intervals, they were often only tolerated as dissonances.

The almost haunting question of the quantities of the whole tone and semitones continued to be argued. In the tenth century, the author of the *Dialogus* formerly attributed to "Odo" had said that the greater space is the tone, that the semitone may never be equal to the tone, but that on the monochord a nine-fold division will produce the proper intervals, the proper proportion for the semitone being 256/243, the Pythagorean division (Strunk, p. 106n). This does not satisfy Marchetto, though he too is a Pythagorean in part and also (as we have seen) accepts the number 9 (one of the perfect numbers). It is a compound of the perfect number 3, and the highest in the series of 1 to 9. Thus the whole tone with its proportion of 9:8, already calculated by the Pythagoreans, is the greatest and most perfect of all intervals, and it represents the measured distance of one sound to the next. Now, its half is a *hemitone*. In Greek times half of a semitone (or a usable quarter tone) was a *diesis* used in the enharmonic and chromatic *genera*, but Marchetto would divide the tone into three *dieses*: 1/4, 1/2, and 3/8. The whole tone (which had the perfect number 9) could not of course be divided into two, though common folklore called for two even halves; and now Marchetto divides it into five equal parts. How this was to be he did not illustrate mathematically. But he did hold that *diesis* is one-fifth of a tone, and an interval of two *dieses* (Plato's *leimma*) is an enharmonic semitone, of three *dieses* a diatonic semitone (the major *apotome*), and of four *dieses* a chromatic semitone. Thus there are nine *dieses* in the tone. Though he compromised by allowing only two divisions actually to occur (the enharmonic and the diatonic semitones, and the chromatic and *diesis*) and indicated separate uses for them--the first in both mensurable and non-mensurable music alone--for facilitating movement from dissonances to consonances, and while his division seemed to have a certain mathematical rationality, the major question concerning the tuning of the instruments was not taken up. Vitry (p. 212) declared that the semitone derives not from "half" because it is usually less than a half tone according to the monochord, but from *semus*, meaning imperfect, an interpretation with which Johannes of Grocheo agrees.

For Johannes of Grocheo too the concord is the more inclusive interval, and the more restricted number of 7 is its base: a few principles are better, he says in the manner of William of Occam, than a plurality of them, like infinity or 13. There are parallels in the Seven Gifts of the Spirit, the seven planets, the seven days of the week. Man the microcosm should imitate divine law as much as possible. Thus seven stars govern the "diversity of generating and corrupting forces of all the universe," and hence reason says that there are seven principles in human arts which cause all the diversities of sound (p. 8). Like Philippe de Vitry, he thinks the semitone not a true half-tone, and the other intervals are the unison, the tone, the ditone, the semitritone (the fourth), the fifth, and the octave.

But most marked was the advance in respectability of the third and the sixth. Why the long delay in recognizing the third? It is the first (to our ears) of the pleasant consonances. Why was it not accepted from the beginning? The Pythagoreans, who had laid down the original musical laws, had omitted it from their musical canon. The third did (and does) conform to the *a priori* rule that the best intervals or ratios are the simplest--that is, exist in various relations employing the numbers of 1 to 4. Perhaps the third is too "complex." According to Pythagorean belief, the octave (like the fifth, fourth, and whole tone) could not be halved. Furthermore, the interval of the third had not appeared in Plato's *Timaeus*, and Boethius had merely accepted the scale as the Greeks had described it and had passed it on to the Middle Ages. Thus the third, ostracized from intervallic perfection, remained unrecognized long after it was used with pleasurable practical effect, its rejection being based on abstract, cosmic speculation. Its theoretical acceptance did not come easily. The reasons were intellectual and rational, and even the fact that the third was expressed by the first real and perfect number, that triple time was thought perfect, that the number 3 is the sum of the first two numbers, that it reflected the Trinity and the perfection of the Godhead, and so forth--these reasons carried no weight. In Franco's day it was time to legitimize what the senses had made familiar to the mind, and thus the third was admitted to the canon of consonances. Franco (Strunk, p. 153) dares to call it imperfect but a concord. And Marchetto points to the tendency (according to current thought) of both thirds and sixths, which he terms dissonances, to move into perfect consonances "compatible to the ear" (5.2.7).

Color and Coloration. Though quantities mathematically measured were not characterless and tacitly explained or embodied quality, there were several other aspects of writing music which created "color," an omnibus term indicating devices of change arousing aesthetic pleasure (as compared with rational understanding alone).   The flatting of the b-note for the purpose of avoiding the tritone has already been mentioned as a practice, and Vitry labels it a *musica falsa* or *ficta*[12] necessary to achieve good sounds and to avoid bad ones. It is an example of qualitative change--of color--for reasons of law as well as aesthetic effect. And thus the semitone, called by Aristoxenus the soul of music, is allowed to be both imperfect and the sugar and spice of all music without which song is "corrupted, altered, and destroyed" (p. 212).   And Marchetto, recalling Martianus Capella, speaks in the *Lucidarium* (1.2.4) of the mathematical relations of music, the branches of whose wonder-working tree allow numbers to be in a beautiful relation to one another, their blossoms being different kinds of consonances and their fruits being the sweet harmonies the consonances bring about. The image stands for the perfect consonances, which he later holds in mind for contrasts made by "colored" semitones (the Greek word *chroma* is defined as "color" or colored dissonances [9.1.24], whose beauty allows composers to arrive at more perfect and more satisfying consonances-- meaning that chromatic tones enhance the usual consonances to make them more perfect and satisfying by contrast. The characteristic interval of the color of beauty is the semitone, which brings elegance along with dis- sonance. Like the imperfect consonances of the third, the sixth, and the tenth, the four-*diesis* semitone proceeds towards a consonance. The part of the whole tone thus divided will be larger if the melody ascends (and thus similar to the leading tone as played by a modern violin). Marchetto is less sure about a descending smaller division; he calls it a "feigned color," less appropriate, and bound to bounce back after the descent (ibid. 5.6.27). Since chromaticism had been employed in Italian music before his time, Marchetto once more demonstrates that theory follows practice, and he serves as another theorizer illustrating the medieval principle of color, of sense-effect, through number.

Among the musical mathematicians, color was not always tone-color, however. It was not a matter of aesthetic perception based on sense-color, visual or aural. It was perception meaning knowledge of structure: to grasp a unitary form, one must experience its repetition at least once.   This repetition is a musical fundamental. It is a matter of structure, the form of an abstract outline, of mathematical relationships (whether identified as such or not).

The author of the *Dialogus* formerly attributed to "Odo" had his reservations about the repetition of a single note as a coloristic device (and in John of Moravia [G 3.238] there is doubt about the coloristic use of intervallic repetition). But John of Garland praises repetition in the same voice because an unknown by this means is made known: in abstract music a single statement takes on significance when it is repeated, and the more its significance (color), the more it is repeated (to the point of monotony, of course). Aristotle in his *Poetics* (1448a), which Garland could not have known, says that to be learning something is the greatest of pleasures for philosophers and men of small capacity alike. The learning principle is one of repetition, and John of Garland assumes that the coloristic principle (of significance, recognition, and hearing) can be applied to both plainsong (monophony) and polyphony. Though he allows the quality of color to all beauty of sound giving pleasure through hearing, three special devices can achieve it. And they involve repetition.

Aristotle had little to say about color except that it is governed by light and dark, white and black, and that there are seven colors appearing in different proportions (*De sensu* 439b). For Plotinus the beauty of color (or its "sweetness") was also form (*Enneads* 1.6.3), and in general throughout the Middle Ages colors were proportions of parts taking their significance from their ability to reflect the light of God. Augustine allied "a certain agreeableness of color" with beauty as proportion. But the scientific thinkers about music no doubt took their ideal of color from language and speech.

The idea of color in music thus seems to have been derived from or at least ostensibly supported by principles of grammar or rhetoric. According to such principles, figures of speech (or images) are often thought to be "easy ornament" and are thus called colors of rhetoric (as by Geoffrey of Vinsauf in *Summa de coloris rhetoricis* [c.1213], drawing illustrations from the anonymous *Ad Herennium*); it is a term sometimes applied to figures as a whole. Not surprisingly, there followed the development of a very ornate kind of expression.[13]   Colors were ingenuities (anagrams, patterns like crosses or diamonds, *words repeated*, macaronic verses, etc.).[14] Hence John of Garland uses the word *colores* for ornaments of the upper voices, like those in Pérotin's three-voiced organa: there are (1) repetitions of an initial note alternating with other notes making a sequential pattern downward to a fifth, (2) a "flowering of voice" (repeating of single notes in a scale), and (3) the exchange of parts, one voice taking over from another (pp. 53-54).

In late medieval music theory the terms 'color' and *talea* ("cuttings") were used for purposes of comparison.[15] The latter was applied to *iso*- ("the same")-*rhythms*, a device used in his music by Philippe de Vitry, who adopted red and black notes to designate pitches. The device utilized the repetition of a series of notes and rests of certain rhythmic values which were imposed on the melodic structure of the composition. In Jean de Muris' *Libellus cantus mensurabilis* (mid-fourteenth-century), color is "one series of similar note values repeated several times [and] placed in the same melody," color residing in the repetition of pitches, *talea* in that of the repetition of similar note values "in such a way that the note values are associated with different pitches" (Cou 3.58)[16] The result could be an overlapping of melody and pitch, or their coincidence; or the rhythm could be exactly repeated, speeded up or slowed down.

The summarizer of opinions about color is Prosdocimus de Baldemandis, who attacked Marchetto's mathematics but praised his performances of chant. He finds two definitions in Jean and supplies a third set forth by "some modern people": (1) color is the repetition several times of similar note values in the same order in the same melody; (2) it is only a series of several pitches (a melody) repeated in the same order several times, but *talea* is a separate matter: the repetition of similar note values alone repeated several times in the same order in a certain melody; (3) color and *talea* are distinguishable from one another: color then is "a series of similar note values and similar pitches repeated several times in the middle of any melody, in the same order," and *talea* is the repetition of similar note values alone (Cou 3.225-27).[17]

Forms. The forms of medieval music are usually indistinguishable from their techniques, and the art of precisely measurable song, as Johannes of Grocheo (p. 21) terms it, could be roughly divided into these parts:

1. *Organum*: is generally agreed to be an ambiguous word. John of Garland (p. 1) says measured music is organum in the generic sense, and is divided into *discant*, *copula*, and *organum*. Franco of Cologne describes organum as, properly, *organum duplum* (or *purum*), in general acceptance designated as "any ecclesiastical chant measured by time," but not so measured in all its parts (Strunk, pp. 140-41). There were two organa--a new and an old. The new is not the old note-against-note variety, but a flexible type in which the tenor sustains long single notes in the example of Léonin and Pérotin. Rhythmical modes alternate. Should the tenor take a number of notes in a row, a discant results (Strunk, p. 158).

2. *Discant*: is wholly measured, is a "consonant combination of different melodies proportionately accommodated to one another by [perfect and imperfect] long, short [perfect and imperfect breve], or still shorter [semibreve and prolation] sounds" (ibid., p. 141) according to the (rhythmical both perfect and imperfect) modes. Of discant, there are three types:

    a. *Simple*: sound and sound alone, with or without words; if with words, it may have a single text (in *purum*), as in the secular cantilena or rondellus or in any sacred chant.

    Or *Complex*: written with several texts in the motet, which has a "triplum or a tenor, for the tenor is the equivalent of some text." In all of these forms the (already existing) tenor (or cantus *prius factus*) comes first and is the support of the other voices (ibid., p. 153). Thus a *discantus* is sung by several persons and is based on a *cantus* (*vox principalis*).

b. The *Conductus* (with or without words): here the entire piece is written by one person who himself first invents a "beautiful" melody which he uses as the tenor and supplies with a discant. If he writes a *triplum*, he should employ concords, but the third voice should be in concord up or down with one voice (the tenor) and then with the other (the discant) (ibid., p. 155). A similar rule governs the quadruplum and quintuplum (ibid., p. 156). The conductus may be embellished with elaborate melismatic *caudae* (tails), which may appear at the beginning, middle, or end, or all in one piece.

c. The *Copula*: a binding or connection, a "rapid, connected discant, either bound or unbound" (ibid., p. 156), never used with words--a vocalization against the word-carrying tenor.

3. The *Hocket* ("hiccough"), made up of sound and silences: based on a *cantus firmus*, the other voices sing sounds and admit silences in strict measurement with the *cantus firmus*, the silences alternating with the sounds of the third voice; there is hence a dove-tailing of alternating short groups of notes and rests. Consonances are required at cuttings-off. (Johannes of Grocheo [p. 26] indicates that it is good for hot-tempered and young men because it moves with speed.)

4. The *Clausula*: a section of the organum, an interpolation, an interpretation of the text, the tenor singing along with the other voices, sometimes having the same text as the other parts; often a different trope (melodic formula) for each part, the trope being usually in Latin, other parts occasionally being in the vernacular. Sometimes serving as an independent piece, it led to the motet.

5. The *Motet*: an outgrowth of the conductus, it replaced organum and had a greater contrapuntal freedom than the organal conductus. In it, different sacred (and sometimes secular) melodies were combined into two, three, or four voices. The same rhythmical mode was often used. It was common for the tenor, who, according to Johannes of Grocheo (p. 28), is the heart, liver, and brain of the piece, to sing a chant item or other melody with two higher voices singing more rapid notes above it. (Sometimes the upper voices explained the meaning of the Latin text.) The different parts usually carried different words (for example, French words in the upper voices need not explain the Latin text), but all voices were in "harmony." Occasionally the tenor voice was performed by instruments. And in the ecclesiastical motet, used in the Mass and especially for processions, only the trained choir (not the congregation) could sing.

The *Secular Motet*: an offshoot of the ecclesiastical motet, using both Latin and vernacular text, it became musically independent to take a prominent part in chamber music for clerical, monastic, and courtly audiences. Tenors (remnants of plainchant) may have been played by instruments. The tenor began to take on the free rhythm of other voices (the *cantus firmus* lost its dominant position). The motet was mostly an unaccompanied composition, all voices being "equal."[18]

By 1300, polyphonic music had triumphed in the cathedrals, larger churches, and chapels of the aristocratic class and royalty. It was to retain its place as the most glorious kind of music until the seventeenth century. Yet, there remains some mystery about its origins, and some accounts of its beginnings have been met with scepticism. Late in the twelfth century, for example, Giraldus Cambrensis[19] wrote of the singers of Wales that they already as a matter of long habit had sung in parts. "There are as many different parts and voices," he said, "as there are performers, who all at length unite, with organic melody, in one consonance and the sweet softness of B flat." In Britain, north of the Humber, singing was said to have been only in two parts. In both Wales and Britain, such singing was so old as to seem natural and familiar. In fact, Giraldus says, it is unusual to hear a well-sung simple melody. Even children sing in parts. In the rest of England this type of singing is absent. The practice must have come, then, he conjectures, from Denmark or Norway.

After 1260 there began to appear religious music quite different from the Gregorian chant and its melismata. The works connected with Notre Dame were widely disseminated as models for motet practices, because they were "set," could be notated, and need not be especially altered or modified by cantors or their singers. The breve as duration was divided, sometimes as often as seven times, in motets of three voices, while tenors sang longs and even double longs. The triplum (the third voice) was supported by two lower, slower voices, and the quadruplum sang doublings as demanded. Virtuosity entered into the whole, with a kind of declamation which began to obscure the more rhetorically inspired tenor, which became shapeless and was almost obliterated by a barrage of notes sung by other voices.

Originally the basis of the composition, the tenor now served only as a technical device. By 1300, the polyphonic structure was so all-embracing that a song was composed freely for its own sake and not for that of the text--for the music and not for the doctrine of the Church or the presentation of its liturgy for the direct edification of the congregation. The tenor had almost become an accompaniment to the song, and even in Machaut (1300-77), the greatest poet and composer of his day who has even been claimed as the last poet-musician of the Western world, the song was no longer monodic but polyphonic.

The musical texture of course differed from that of modern "harmony." While the voices seemed to proceed independently, they were still largely centered on the "permanent" consonances of the unison, the fourth, fifth, and octave. There were no special restrictions related to these or other intervals. There were gradual changes, however: the fourth was used frequently between a lower and an upper voice, though it continued between upper voices, and the fifth and octave above the lowest note tended to predominate. Thirds were often found within phrases, but not at crucial beginnings or conclusions, and dissonances began to appear at telling points--probably more frequently during improvisations than the notation in the manuscripts will show.

But the more free handling of metrics and rhythm in polyphony inevitably made church music a target for the charge that it was not religious. The new music especially adopted features which offended against ecclesiastical aims as perceived by more ascetic or rigid clergy. The holy, reverential character of early church singing was being replaced in the major centers of religious worship, and singers who loved the new fashions and took advantage of them were accused of worldliness. Furthermore, the introduction into church services of secular melodies, often as the basis for a polyphonic composition such as a segment of a Mass setting, and even of secular texts, however disguised, seemed offensive. Earthly words, even erotic poetry, upon occasion sounded through the musical texture along with the sacred words. The ecclesiastical modes, normally avoided in secular music, were bypassed, and reforming clergy and the hierarchy alike finally objected and insisted, as the Cistercians had done earlier, on a return to the church modes and practices or at least to a less modern polyphony. With the change from Latin as the language of the people, the congregational or communal spirit, so highly valued in the time of St. Ambrose and the basis of the congregational singing of psalms, hymns, and so forth, had long disappeared except in the monasteries; now the singing of the services in the greater churches, cathedrals, and chapels was being delegated to trained musicians in a further erosion of the communal spirit. Composers so much cherished their abstract and beautiful polyphony, which seemed perfectly designed for the new Gothic buildings in which it was sung, perhaps sometimes with instrumental accompaniment, that they seemed to offend against a Church founded to spread the teachings of Jesus who saw his ministry in terms of the simple shepherd feeding his simple sheep--a Church which was designed to represent the drama of Christ's death and resurrection for Everyman.

For some of these reasons, then, Pope John XXII, who was known as combative and jealous for papal authority, issued from Avignon the decretal *Docta sanctorum Patrum* to which reference has been made above. The new school of composers of which Jean de Muris and Vitry had spoken was also the object of his writing, though as we have seen he took an opposing stance against the emergence of certain aspects of this music. He objected to the "divisions" of notes into small values, the use of hockets, discants, and sometimes secular songs, the frequent obscuring of the ecclesiastical modes (which those listening could neither recognize nor distinguish), and the use of gestures in singing. Originality of invention he deplored: it "encourages effeminacy in the discant, a rushing on without rest, and an intoxication of the ear without a healing of the soul. It sins against moral, religious, political matters, but also against universal canonical church music whose beauty it threatens."[20]   Allowed, however, was the use of the perfect consonance and more simple forms of organum to enhance melodic beauty, provided that the *cantus* is not obscured, especially on important feasts and during solemn celebrations of the Mass. Nevertheless, we know that at Avignon itself polyphonic music was not in fact suppressed, and indeed was allowed except during penitential seasons.[21]

The strictures of John XXII against discant were, as one might expect, given a broad interpretation, and were widely circumvented by the introduction of a technical device called *faux bourdon* (English: *faburden*) or false bass. Assuming a variety of shapes, it was initially made up of combinations of sixths and thirds. The recipe might have read: take a two-part organum of thirds, add a third below the two voices and thus write a fifth (b - d, for example, and an added lower g), or a perfect triad; then sing the lowest note an octave higher (to produce b - d - g) to make a sixth. The lowest voice g is the *cantus firmus* but it is now the highest voice, and a true discant has been avoided. Written, it is a discant; sung it is not. This, like other similar devices, involved florid singing and was most popular around 1400 but began to lose its popularity around 1600.[22]

However we understand the strictures of John XXII, the polyphonic music of the time, in contrast to humble plainsong, had a discernible place in the Church Militant and (in the worldly sense) triumphant, the Church of worldly power. It was a Church which in many respects could not have been envisioned by Christ himself. The Gothic cathedrals and greater churches, vast and flamboyant, with their stained glass windows colored with red, blue, and yellow in designs and iconography infinitely varied, as well as the older romanesque buildings were theaters for the enactment of the mystic drama of Christ, the Savior of the Church Universal. The sanctity and beauty of the worship and the transformation of the individual soul remained the object of the Church powerful beyond all original expectations. The rich vestments which varied in color according to the liturgical season or the feast day, the sequences, antiphons, and hymns, and the incense overwhelmed all of the senses and acted to accompany the music. John's restrictions on music early in the fourteenth century were indeed not different from those of earlier popes or those which St. Bernard of Clairvaux, two centuries earlier, had directed against the splendors of the Church: "O vanity of vanities, yet no more vain than insane!"[23]

II

Johannes of Grocheo. The fourteenth century had already seen the beginning of a division between philosophy and faith. As philosophy tended to turn more toward secular matters, writing about music also found a new emphasis, though this new emphasis was nowhere else as pronounced as in Johannes of Grocheo. Generally it may now be said that neither philosophy nor music any longer seemed entirely a servant to the Church. Encouragement for change came from current secular music and its practice,

emancipated from the old theory of the tetrachord and symphonic concord
to its own more unrestricted way. The process seems to have taken almost a
millenium, during which official clerical opinion practically smothered it
with neglect and villification. In pointing out that the ecclesiastical modes
are not those of secular music, Johannes of Grocheo in a sense was a
pioneer in a new study which now is called musicology. If one may use the
term 'revolutionary' in a cavalier fashion, Johannes was a revolutionary
because he was almost alone in recording observations about music of his
own day in both Church and Court.

In the France of Johannes' time (possibly in the days of Philip IV), the
long winter evenings at court were filled with various entertainments.
People listened to long verse epics and romances, stories of Roland and
Arthur and Tristan, and singers sang to the accompaniment of instruments.
Prior to the arrival of the bubonic plague but continuing thereafter, secular
music in Court and castles flourished. As Jeremy Montagu notes, the
"instruments of the central Middle Ages" had been "mainly those imported
from non-European sources. In the later Middle Ages [and beginning in the
fourteenth century], they were adapted and modified to such an extent that
they became clearly and recognisably European and wholly distinct from
their Moorish origins."[24] Not only are keyboard instruments developed
(e.g., the clavichord), but also the various families of percussion, string, and
wind instruments, many of them used only for secular music and hardly
appropriate for church music at all. We have only very limited record,
however, of the performance practice associated with the use of these
instruments. No collection of popular instrumental works survives from
earlier times, and indeed the earliest popular tunes date from the twelfth
century. It may be assumed that as people in courts and castles became
more affluent and powerful, they turned to popular music for recreation as
well as to church music for devotion, though with regard to the latter they
tended more and more to be audiences rather than participants. Secular
poetry with musical settings has been in some part preserved, as the work of
the troubadours and trouvères demonstrates. Among the Germans, Minnesingers such as Walther von der Vogelweide are still classics. It would
seem that in many quarters by the later Middle Ages a boy's training for
knighthood included instruction in dance and music, including instrumental
music and perhaps in some instances composition.

The history of secular-popular music goes back to the tenth century
and earlier, of course. Though John Cotton in approximately the eleventh
century had bracketed the early troubadours with ignorant actors, they were
already part of the civilization of Court and castle, the first great secular
civilization following those of ancient Greece and Rome. A combination of
Germanic tribal culture, Christianity, and art, literature, and the thought of
the Normans and Celts, and influences coming from the Orient and Islamic
countries by way of the crusades, this civilization had its own festivals and
even its courts of love, its personal ideals of gallantry, including the worship
of women (of high social status), and a concentration less on the teachings

of the Church than on social and military behavior in earthly life. It was a civilization that in fact functioned under the aegis of the rules of social-secular life.   Even nobles and princes themselves could be poets or musicians, sometimes both at once.

Their efforts were social and communal: the secular (feudal) order was parallel with the ecclesiastical order. Clerical musicians, especially in the monasteries, were probably most often indifferent to (and sometimes hostile to) the knights and their arts, though we cannot be certain that courtly entertainment did not invade these institutions also. Secular music involved poetic and musical traditions that were in part and in some cases wholly oral, with notation even of the troubadour melodies being so incomplete with regard to rhythm that any modern-day performance can only be conjectural. Already in Charlemagne's time there had been court poets, just as the poet-musician known as the *scop* had been present in the mead halls of the Anglo-Saxons. Carolingian prohibitions against nuns singing *Frauenlieder* or women's songs[25] suggest another popular strain, the content of which we can only guess from later examples of romantic and erotic song. But there were many later types of popular entertainers, including the goliards or wandering students who sang throughout Europe, the jongleurs who not only wrote and sang songs but also trained and exhibited bears and did various tricks of their own (perhaps like the ignorant actors mentioned by John Cotton), and the more courtly troubadours and trouvères already mentioned. Flourishing in various degrees through the Middle Ages, secular musicians were, however, not given full treatment until Johannes of Grocheo, though to be sure the court or castle and the music designed for performance in such settings had already been not entirely ignored by Gundisalvo, John of Salisbury, and Marchetto of Padua.

Just as some clergy thought polyphony a form of blasphemy, so many also believed that secular music encouraged sinful behavior and corruption. The secular text, the very delivery of wandering musicians and jongleurs, the harmony of the emotions of people living as part of the world--the Earthly City as described by St. Augustine--as well as the different dance rhythms, the use of melodies not belonging to the accepted church modes, the individual invention of melody not Church-sanctioned, and the character of troubadour or trouvère in general--all were deficiencies which called for denunciation or prohibition.   But secular musicians continued more frequently than not to make their own rules and to ignore accepted or traditional ones.

Johannes of Grocheo, less a theorist than what is loosely called a social critic, wrote his *De musica* (*Concerning Music*), "something about musical concepts," at the request of "certain young men" who had given him "the greatest support for the needs of [his] life." He is to be scientific (that is, like John Cotton, empirical): music is interpreted as based on "a complete understanding of bodies that are moving and are moved"; it is sound taken in by the senses and apprehended by human beings; there results a practical good of correcting and improving "the customs of men" when it is used properly. Thus it is superior to other arts because it is "more immediately and completely designed for the praise and glory of our Creator" (Preface, p. 1). It is both secular and ecclesiastical, and its principles are both sensory and analytical, as taught by Aristotle[26] in his *Physics*, and embrace its nature or substance, its quantity, quality, and its resulting characteristics (see Aristotle, *Physics* 184a-185a). Grocheo will bear in mind diversities of opinion as reflected in the mechanical arts of architecture and the clothes of men. For change means improvement, and improvement comes from the continual efforts, whose success is never complete, of trying to be the equal of nature or divine art. For these reasons speculation about music has given ground to practical considerations (*De Musica*, p. 2).

Conventionally, however, like Philipp de Vitry, Johannes of Grocheo recalls that music was discovered by the Muses living near water and derives its name from this "fact"; but he calls it a fable.[27] He rushes quickly over the musical discoveries of holy men and prophets, and repeats with a certain approval Pythagoras' musical and proportional discoveries as perpetuated by Boethius and others: it is "the efficient force in natural things [which] is called its principle rather than its material" or substance; but in contrived non-natural things "the material is its principle" because the material has no will and the form of art is "given [it] by accident"--that is, something not belonging to the thing, but caused by outside agents (ibid., p. 4)--and here Johannes again probably recalls Aristotle (*Physics* 193 a-b), as he does frequently.

What are these principles for music? His distinction between (1) the concord as one sound continued (like motion) harmonically by another and (2) a consonance as two or more tones united in perfect harmony recalls John of Garland, though Johannes is more precise. Consonances are prior in classification to concords. There is no infinite number of consonances. For the theory of consonances according to number, he refers to Pythagoras, Nicomachus, Plato (especially the *Timaeus*), and Boethius, but comments that the foundations are not certain and that the pupils of Aristotle, not sure of this theory, think of proportion (ratio) as "the first among qualities and natural forms . . ."--as Johannes must have learned from the *Metaphysics* itself. Why had Boethius followed the reasoning that there are only five kinds of proportion or inequality? Johannes is no hero worshipper: Boethius in understanding Aristotle "perhaps understands something else by proportion, wishing to conceal by it occult causes and things unnamed" (*De Musica*, p. 5). There should obviously be no mysteries or unnaturalness about art.

In any case, though certain animals are naturally attracted by sounds, it is only man who delights in music and the three consonances, which are three perfections in sound like the Trinity, for in them God has revealed his goodness and through them is praised (as by David) in his own name. To characterize the three perfect consonances, he draws a matriarchal-allegorical comparison in which the male is completely ignored. Basic harmony is like a mother, the octave, in whom is contained a daughter, the fifth, and a third person (granddaughter?), the fourth, derived from the other two: the conscious soul of man perceives this triple perfection in sounds (as in the triple image of the Creator), while imperfect animals do not (ibid., pp. 6-7). He agrees with the almost universal opinion that music is an art or science "concerning numbered sound taken harmonically [and] designed for singing easily." As a science it is a knowledge of principles; as an art it rules the practical intellect in performance; harmonic sound is its basic material; number is its form (ibid., p. 10). Like Boethius and John of Garland, he divides music into the types *mundana, humana*, and *instrumentalis* (natural and artificial) only to doubt the entire enterprise. He finds unacceptable, or at least puzzling, the idea that *musica instrumentalis* divides into the diatonic, used for most melodies, the chromatic, used by the planets, and the enharmonic, called the sweetest of these because it is used by angels (ibid., pp. 10-11). Almost everything he says is about the natural music produced by the human voice, and one is aware that since the time of John Scot Erigena the term 'natural music' has undergone redefinition.

As with the above-mentioned triple symbols, one can be sure Johannes is ambiguously both serious and ironical when he outlines arguments for the fixing of the number of concords, which by some are said to be seven (in the Perfect System) because there are Seven Gifts of the Spirit, seven planets, seven days in the week (ibid., p. 7). In connection with the conjectural determination of concords, he impatiently mentions John of Garland, though he seems to agree that the laws of the world should and do imitate the laws of the universe as completely as possible (ibid., p. 8). For him harmony is an allegory. Yet he is no Othloh of St. Emmeram, assuming universal harmony in the competitive world of business and commerce. Nor is he easily taken in by fantasy. For him, the many definitions of tone (its rise and fall, for example, and its place at the end of the song) are like the snow on the mountains. The diversity of music--a diversity of use, idiom, language--in differing cities or regions cannot be exaggerated.

Music may be a science of sound related to number (ibid., pp. 8-9), but he prefers to stress experience with it and to call it an art. His method in exploring the subject is, first, to employ the "universal" knowledge of definition and description, then to describe the parts of music as a "mechanical" art, and finally to consider the whole composition. Musical composition, according to Johannes (ibid., p. 15), is like simple bodies (fire, air, water, earth), or mixed or mineral (stones, metals), or animate (plants, animals), which are delineated in these ways, as had Aristotle in his *Concerning Animals, Concerning the Parts of Animals*, and the *Generation of Animals*. The tripartite Boethian division of music is either invented or a surrender to authorities like Pythagoras. It is not a matter of truth, of nature, or of logic. Aristotle was right: planets do not make sounds or "divide their rotation" (*On the Heavens* 2.9). Like Walter of Odington (*De speculatione musices*, early fourteenth century), he does not think music is found in the human constitution. And only theologians and prophets in divine inspiration can possibly hear the angels.

He thinks he has the correct definition of music: it is a tool (a knowledge of principles, a science of number related to sound harmonically considered) and an art of singing (ibid., pp. 9-10). Boethius', Cassiodorus', and Isidore's classifications are as if transformed and even compressed into one: it is an art governed by taste--the taste of social groups. He means secular groups. The history of music designed for such groups begins in fact with the troubadours, of whom Guillaume IX, Count of Poitiers, is reputed to have been the first. Vernacular poetry, written in Provençal, including a great deal of praise for one's lady according to conventions that modern scholars have dubbed "courtly love," arose and spread in the aftermath of the First Crusade, though this poetry, which retains a substantial body of items that retain their musical notation, was to be suppressed at the time of the crusade against the Albigenses in the thirteenth century. There was even a woman troubadour, the Countess of Dia, whose verse and music are extant. Unfortunately, the notation used by the troubadours does not give sufficient information about the rhythmic values, and hence modern performances can only be conjectural attempts at authenticity. But the Provençal music designed for the courts and castles of the region which is now located in southern France is hardly unique, and some of the music--that of the jongleurs, for example, who travelled widely--tended to cross international boundaries. Thus were certain types of compositions-- e.g., the *chanson de geste*, which was based on a form that largely dictated the singing of the same music to verses strung together--popular across Europe and even among audiences in different social classes.

In contrast to Plato, who had chided Athens for allowing its music to deteriorate, Johannes does not look back with any such nostalgia: the Paris of his day provides justification for his theory and his classification. Music has, we are told (p. 12), three kinds of living form:

1. *Civil or simple*: vulgar, simple music (that of the common people) (single voiced).
2. *Measured music*, composed according to rule (ordinarily discantus, organum duplum, the hocket, motets).
3. *Ecclesiastical music* (for church services), made up from the first two, and measured to the extent that it is measured by the rules of art.

All are performed by the human voice, which serves not only courtly purposes but also those of all branches of society, not only in the country towns but also in the city.[28]

How are these songs composed? Words are prepared "on the level of the raw material"; then a melody is adapted in an appropriate way to the formed material--that is, as a gestual, coronate, or *versiculate cantus* (ibid., pp. 18-19). These categories are described in the chart on page 419.

1. *cantus*

2. *cantilena*

a. **GESTUAL (heroic)**:
the deeds of heroes and saints in their
battles for faith and belief. For old men,
workers, average citizens; lifts burdens,
consoles workers, is support for the whole
state. Many stanzas ending on same poetic
rhyme; occasionally *cantus* may close on
an unrhyming line. Same melody in all
stanzas, their number not being fixed but
dependent on material and composer's
wishes.

a. **ROUND**, or *rondellus*:
a dance with refrain in strict rhythm:
turns back on itself like a circle, begins and
ends with same refrain; in each strophe
melody stays the same and rhymes with
refrain; sung in the West by girls and
young men at festivals, at feasts of
common people.

b. **CORONATE or simple *cantus***:
(a category of song) excellent text and
melody accompanied by instruments;
composed by kings and nobles and
performed for kings and princes to move
souls to bravery and magnanimity; about
delightful and serious subjects like
friendship and charity; many *puncta*
(phrases, melodic fragments) and
concords: 7 verses because there are 7
concords; the *puncta* join the concords
together as they ascend and descend.

b. **STANTIPES** (*Estampie*):
diversity of (vocal or instrumental) parts
(in both rhymed words and melody) and
refrain: "causes souls of young men and
women to concentrate because of its
difficulty and turns them from improper
thinking."

c. **VERSICULATE**:
also called a *cantilena*; lacks excellence of
coronate text and concord, should be
performed for the young, "lest they fall
completely into idleness"; verse much like
coronate *cantus*; number of verses not set;
depends on material and will of the
composer.

c. *DUCTIA*:
light *cantilena*: rapid in ascent and descent,
sung in chorus by young men and girls:
influences their hearts, keeps them from
vanity, is a force against passion of love.[29]

What about instruments--that is, artificial ones? Here designations are
vague, empirically speaking, probably because vocal and instrumental
music were often interchangeable. Now Johannes most clearly reveals his
abandonment of mathematical and allegorical principles and his adoption of
the purely artistic. All instrumental sounds, he says, are made through
percussion. The sound of strings (psaltery, cithara, lyre, Saracen guitar,
vielle or fidel) is subtler and more various than that of breath-instruments
(trumpets, reed instruments, organs, flutes) (p. 19). Like Philippe de Vitry
(p. 205), he confirms that instruments now played a more than secondary

role in early fourteenth-century music, and in discussing the *neupma* (pp. 37-38) he reminds us of the NOEANE formula of Aurelian (pp. 24-25) and of the *Commentario brevis*, a series of formulaic phrases to be remembered easily and used with their void-of-meaning phrases for various modes. Johannes of Grocheo now makes a comparison which would have been unthinkable in Aurelian's time: the *neupma* behaves "like a coda or ending proper for each mode following the antiphon and resembles and is like the ending to a secular piece played by the vielle after a coronate song or *stantipes*."[30]

Philippe de Vitry had mentioned the vielle (fidel) as almost identical with the monochord (p. 205) and apparently had tuning in mind. Johannes of Grocheo has in mind its place in musical composition: of string instruments, it takes first place. Just "as the intellective soul" contains "virtually all the natural forms, as a tetragon includes the triangle, and as a large number includes the smaller, so the vielle includes virtually all the others" (p. 19). All musical forms shaped by it are understood more thoroughly than by other instruments, including the trumpet and the drum, used in war games and tournaments.[31]

Johannes of Grocheo, in an effort to educate the young man who approached him, makes some very interesting observations. He recalls to us Aristotle's delineation of music proper for young and old, workmen and freemen. He identifies artistic simplicity with the common people, with the "folk," who need music to cope with the difficulties of daily life. A motet, which is complicated, he thinks should not be "propagated among the vulgar, since they do not understand its subtlety, nor do they delight in hearing it; but it should be performed for the learned and those who seek after the subtleties of the arts" (p. 26). The forms best performed before the wealthy, he believes, are the *coronate cantus*, the *stantipes*, and the *ductia*. The *stantipes* is an untexted piece with complicated succession of concords determined by *puncta* (sections), and a complicated succession of concords causes the souls of performer and listener to pay close attention "and frequently turns aside the souls of the wealthy from depraved thinking." It lacks the percussive beat or measure of the *ductia*, which too is untexted, though it may also be performed unworded by the human voice; in it, beats serve to measure the music and the movements of the performer: it excites the soul of men "to moving ornately according to that art they call dancing" (p. 19).

Johannes, less interested in ecclesiastical music than in the secular, does not describe the former in so much detail, presumably because his young friends needed only to be reminded of the context of religious music--music with which they already were familiar. Even so, he provides mostly commentary: frail fleshly man, inferior to the angels in their nobility, must give special praise to the Creator in the daily Offices and the Mass and in the rules (not unlike those of grammar) followed in their music. He mentions ecclesiastical song while, Aristotle-like, he refers to the organic structure of three parts--beginning, middle, and the end--and indicates that there is a different formula for each of the eight modes (four authentic, four plagal) (resembling the eight Beatitudes and, according to logic and mathematics, the first of the cubes). Furthermore, the end varies according to the mode, according to the beginning of the accompanying antiphon, and according to the practice of individual parishes or monasteries (pp. 33, 37). The mode or the tone is the center of judgment of beginning, middle, and end--but only in ecclesiastical music. Neither popular song nor measured music is judged in this way because they do not always "obey the rules of tones" (p. 32). Indeed, mensurable music calls for different comparisons.

In mensurable music the structure of the parts to the whole resembles architectural form. The tenor is the part on which other parts are based, just as the foundation of an architectural structure supports the other parts of the building. It regulates the other parts, and gives them their quantities just as bones do the other parts of the body (p. 27). The whole is numerical, and like the church or cathedral, music is a quadrivial art. Number is the common term of the audible and observable. One song is built on another as are roofs and covers of houses--and thus a continuous "cutting-up" (as in the hocket) can be made (p. 29) as in doors and windows. For Johannes, then, music is quadrivial as number and architecture, trivial as parallel with grammar and rhetoric.

Mentioning most of the Seven Liberal Arts, Johannes thinks that the most important arts for the praising of God are the triad of grammar (writing, speaking, pleading), astronomy (the distinctions of the seasons and their computation), and music (song and the manner of singing) (p. 30). And all of these are human inventions, close to the human frame and makeup. Yet sound is not a part of the human constitution itself. Not even celestial bodies make sounds as they go through their rotations; and no one has ever experienced the song of angels, thought to be the sweetest of all songs (pp. 10-11). Though Johannes carefully describes the parts of the Mass and the music which attaches itself to them, he does so again not for the clergy but for laymen. His real interest, then, is in the sociology of secular forms, which he correctly says are not held to the requirements of the ecclesiastical modes (pp. 31-32). Nevertheless, he sometimes discusses aspects of music relevant to both the Church and the secular group, including of course the Court. His treatment of mensuration illustrates why it was made necessary--namely, to keep together several or more voices singing at the same time for people capable of grasping complexities. Therefore mensuration involves organa, and the motet, and hockets--all many-voiced (p. 26). He writes about living forms and discards the old popular theories if they no longer apply. His (social) class-conscious point of view is a new thing in the history of the idea of music, and it would not be until Nicola Vicentino (1511-72) and his *L'antica musica ridotta alla moderna* (Rome, 1555) that a further sharp occasional distinction would be made, in this instance between chamber, church, and popular music.

To Johannes' mind, music remains a craft or art and is not a "creative" or "original" activity. Assuming a non-modern position, he says that the composer of music for the Mass should take a traditional or approved text and then give the music the shape the text requires. The role of the poet and writer of verse for use in the liturgy is distinct from that of the composer. His use of the word *componere* has been likened to a quite free invention, like the *conductus* (p. 26), and, indeed, in rhetorical teachings, invention was the first of creative abilities. The mechanical arts (painting, sculpture, and so forth) assist one another, as is illustrated by the preparation of leather made in one workshop for shoes which will be made in another workshop, that of the shoemaker (p. 42). The composer should therefore artfully and in a calculating way fashion his music to suit someone else's text as well as to the occasion and social class for which it is appropriate.

By the end of the thirteenth century, then, on advice garnered from Aristotle as translated into Latin, theorists began to limit music, vocal and instrumental, to its own province. New interpretations of old concepts promised to be the result. Johannes of Grocheo largely discusses music as it was used for pleasure and entertainment; he makes little of its possible moral and devotional effects. From the point of view of the Church, he could be said to have submitted to the tastes of the rich and courtly, of the powerful in secular life. His little book introduces into the philosophy of music something new, a sociology of taste, though he uses neither term, of course. His knowledge of Aristotle encourages him to adopt a cultural method in criticism. He ignores the old speculations about cosmic music and its possible magical effects, even as reflected in the nature of the modes. He seems to have had no followers among subsequent theorists of the Middle Ages.

III

Jacob of Liège. The move of the papacy to Avignon in 1309 marked the beginning of the loss of its power and the decline in the stability of the Roman Catholic Church. This period was called the Babylonian Captivity of the Western Church, followed by the Schism which began in 1378 and did not end until 1417. Because of these factors, the institution which had been the source of undoubting authority began to disintegrate. During the same period, the political situation, especially in France, again became disorganized. France and England were to engage in the Hundred Years' War--a tremendous strain on social, political, and economic institutions and ultimately the cause of the civil war in England known as the War of the Roses. Social and political structures were falling, and in the East the Turks became a threat to Christendom, culminating with the fall of Byzantium (Constantinople) in 1453. The fourteenth century also had been the time of the beginning of the epidemics of the bubonic plague that continued to haunt Europe through the Renaissance, while the uprising of the peasants against the nobles also was a threat to the order of things. France and

England failed to achieve the desired stability indeed until nearly the last decade of the fifteenth century.

In France, kings followed one another in rapid succession.   If Johannes of Grocheo lived during the reign of Philip IV, Jacob of Liège probably lived in the time of Philip VI (1328-50)--five kings later.   As might be expected, the strife of the times dampened the production of literature and thought in France, though not its music, which flourished even in forms of which the Church at the time did not officially approve. Even in the French royal chapel, religious music began to mean an art *per se*, and traditionalist pressure for the rejection of polyphony was widely rejected.   However, later in the fourteenth century, under the reigns of Charles V (1364-80) and Charles VI (1380-1422), not only musicians but also philosophers and all types of artists were encouraged in their work.

In certain universities (e.g., Prague) Boethius was supplanted in the fourteenth century by one of the greatest encyclopedists of the Middle Ages, Jacob of Liège, whose *speculum musicae* (*Mirror of Music*), designed for the musical expert, was at one time curiously attributed to Jean de Muris in spite of the fact that its chief burden is an attack on Jean's *Ars novae musicae*.   Yet Jacob and Boethius must be regarded as alike in one important way, since both are savants whose tendentiousness causes us once again to be offered the musical theories of the past.   Unlike Cassiodorus, they did not appeal for attention to schools of grammar and rhetoric.   Jacob's book has been continually regarded as a most authoritative source, a veritable anthology of opinions in and of medieval music theory.   Divided into seven books, not all even now translated into English, it is a compendium unexcelled in its completeness for medieval music studies.

The first book is an omnibus recounting of past theory, based on Boethius' *Consolation* and *Musica*, Aristotle's *Metaphysics* and *Nicomachean Ethics*, Plato's *Timaeus*, Guido, Franco, and, more unusual among music theorists, Seneca the Younger (c.4 B.C.-65 A.D.) and his letters to his friend Lucilius.   From the last Jacob receives support for ideas of the best quality of soul in men who prefer the noble, reject the low and mean, are uplifted by visions of greatness, and seek the open instead of the dim and dismal in order to find repose in the contemplation of nature and philosophy (*Epistles* 39: 1.259-60; 58.17: 1.397; 82: 2.241-45).   He brings into the net of his thought past considerations of motion, time, sound, sense and intellect, numbers and proportion, and of the latter the arithmetical, the geometric, and the harmonic.

"What is music?" he asks, like most of the theorists he is summarizing. What is its utility, who invented it, and what are its types? He divides music into theoretical and practical, the Aristotelian division applied by Aristides Quintilianus and revived by the Arabs, and finds practical music to be pure and mixed.   In all of his considerations, Jacob finds authority in Boethius: quadrivial music is not dead; it is only sleeping (even though writers from Aurelian to Marchetto of Padua hardly used Boethius except in polite reference or occasionally for number and consonance theory).   Jacob records all the theories of which Johannes of Grocheo had been skeptical and ignores the social legitimacy of which he had approved.

The second book concerns intervals, especially the permanent or consonant ones, which are (and always have been) the core of music, and the always problematic semitone and the Pythagorean comma. Here his authorities are the expected Boethius, Ptolemy, and Nicomachus. The third book, relying on Archytas and Boethius, is a further examination of mathematical proportion which governs all art, and especially music; the fourth is on perfection and imperfection; the fifth is on tetrachords and the monochord with support from Boethius, "Pythagoras," Philolaus, and Guido. The sixth seems miscellaneous but is directed towards singing by way of considerations of Greek notation (based on the Greek alphabet), of tetrachord, monochord, and the modes (with references to Berno and Ptolemy) and of Guido's theory of identifying finales while emphasis is placed on intoning the various modes in chant. The final book embraces mensurable music, consonances, duration or time (perfection and imperfection), and musical figures. The entire work is replete with specific and admirable musical examples.

In the incessant quarrel between the ancients and the moderns, Jacob defends the old art[32] and castigates the new. He himself calls his work satirical and controversial, and he finds frequent philosophical support in Aristotle. He knows both ancient musical theory (*musica speculativa*) and the practical music (*musica theorica*) of his own time. His anti-modernistic sermonizing is of course only a small part of his great work, but is placed in a context of the entire field of music. His targets are the *ars nova* (a term which after his time gradually disappeared from French writing) and polyphony, and he defends the *ars* or *musica antiqua* (discant, or "double song," as well as organum) based on the conjunction of perfect consonances (with the allowance of contrary motion) in two (and also additional) parts.

He says that contemporary attacks on the ancients, who for him are indeed the early medieval writers, are the work of young people. Jacob quotes from Aristotle on the ancients to defend the old art of plainchant. The ancients, he insists, should be imitated, approved of, and commended, and new music should not be so praised that the old is sent into oblivion. For the old teachings persist while the new sometimes do not last long (*Deut.* 19.14: "Thou shalt not take or remove thy neighbour's landmark, which thy predecessors have set in thy possession"). Jacob specifically refers to Tubal Cain (Jubal) who lived before the Flood, to Franco of Cologne (*Teutonicus*), and to Pseudo-Aristotle (Magister Lambert), all of whom have written about plainsong and also mensurable music. But there are men "in our day," he says, who write about mensurable music without reverence for the ancients. In contrast, his own first aim is to write about mensurable music in "defense of the ancients," and his second is to discuss plainsong (which should not exceed an octave in extent) and theoretical and practical music (Strunk, p. 181). "Reason follows the law of nature," he thinks, following a classical mode of thought, "which God has implanted in rational creatures"; hence reason enables him to compare ancient and modern modes of mensuration (ibid., p. 182). He recognizes that practice and custom disregard theory; and while he claims not to be hostile to modern practice or to the persons who perform music in his time, ancient theory is more compelling. Like Jean de Muris, he adopts perfection as his major criterion for judgment; though for Jean it refers to the *tempus* times 3 for dividing duration, for Jacob it is a universal Platonic principle.

The new art, he finds, has many imperfections. Using the terminology commonly accepted, he shows that moderns take perfect notes, modes, and measures and make them imperfect. Imperfect time (two *tempora* to the verse) illustrates an imperfection which has been compounded in modern music. Modern composers want to give it equal place with perfect time. If speculative imperfection is defensible, practical imperfection is not: it has all the weaknesses of subtlety, and subtlety has "no place" in perfection or completeness (see Aristotle, *Metaph.* 1021b). The greater difficulty of modern art does not make for perfection, but even difficult art is devoted to the good and useful; it has "a virtue perfecting the soul through the medium of the intellect" (Strunk, p. 184). The moderns, however, need to acquire charity: the old art and the singers who performed it were not, as people sometimes claim, rude, idiotic, undiscerning, foolish, and ignorant. The greater subtlety of the new art only means greater imperfection: and why are the ancients thought rude if they employed perfections?

Jacob scorns the exclusive use by the moderns of motets, with the addition of hockets, and the practice of *cantilena*. He scoffs at the modern failure to follow the example of the ancients in the use of proper forms, of measured organa, of organa not measured throughout, and of organa *pura* and *dupla*, as well as beautiful and delightful *conducti* of all types, all used in rotation and as foundations by older singers and written by composers now thought to be rustic, rude, and ignorant. They had not confined themselves to motets and chansons. The arguments against ancient art are contrary to reason, and when the moderns themselves add to the store of perfect ancient ("organic") art, they fail to demonstrate that it is rude.

Boethius, who laid the foundations of music, and others of the early medieval period--are they really rude and irrational? (ibid., p. 186). Sarcastically Jacob contrasts liberty and servitude and, employing a Boethian image, says that the new art seems to be the mistress and the old art the servant. Compared with the new law, the old law of measured music had few but clear principles or rules. The new law is complicated, and its proponents cannot even agree among themselves. The many burdens of modern art have caused it to lose liberty and take on bondage. The old art was free of such burdens; finally, as Aristotle in his *Politics* had maintained, a free man cannot be subject to one unfree (ibid., pp. 186-88).

Although this sounds as though Jacob had adopted a practical approach to music in contrast to Boethius' theoretical one, such is not the case. His approach does not have the predominantly grammatical bias of theorists from Aurelian to John Cotton but supports the quadrivial system of the arts. Thus for him, as for Boethius, a *musicus* is a musical thinker (one who "muses"), and theory is superior to and more complete than its dependent, which is practice. Such a musical thinker will deplore merely ignorant singers, for example, who make horrible noises as if they were novelties or sing discants too wantonly and floridly so that, in their undisciplined reliance on inappropriate vocal display, they sound like dogs or lunatics (Cou 2.394). On the other hand, the old art of measured music, cherishing concord and shunning discord, will be recognized to have been more perfect, rational, seemly--that is, freer, simpler, plainer--than the new. Originally discreet, masculine, and morally good, music now has been rendered lascivious--that is, words are lost (not able to be understood by listeners in modern motets), the harmony of consonances is reduced, the values of notes changed, perfection decried, imperfection praised, and measure confused. Moderns reject the rational approach to music through number. They are offensive now as was Thales (of Crete? or Timotheus?) to the Spartans and Lacedaemonians. Every layman prefers the ancient music to the new. Why does lasciviousness please? Clearly, the old music should be restored and brought back.

The ancient truths are reiterated, and for the Scholastics, we know, motion manifests itself in three ways: in quantity (growth and decrease), quality (alteration), and "whereness" (local motion). But now Augustine seems to hover over Jacob: motion is an act of potency[33] involving an agent and a receiver. Once its end is achieved, it ceases to exist. Its motion is imperfect, while its arrival at its end is perfect (but no longer existent). Time is a motion according to a "before" and an "after"; since numbering is done by reason, time gets its actual movement from the mind: if there is no mind to grasp number, there is no time. Eternity is timeless, but time itself is consequently a corruption or imperfection. Motion and time are thus a unity, and unity is either formal (that is, Platonically speaking, real and intrinsic) or material (that is, virtual and extrinsic). The form of number is a unity, itself divided discretely into unities. Number is an absolute but related to concretenesses. Proportion is a relation of two terms to each other, and mixed proportion involves more than two terms or is a proportionality of the mean. Music, in the terms just given, is a mixing, uniting, and proportioning arising from and resulting in sound so that there are produced distinct tones "coming together in the medium and diffusing themselves in the faculty of hearing according to a certain proportion which is reducible to numbers."[34] It is the mixture of sounds which produces modulation. Consonance is sound, number, form; it is the subject or substance of music, and it pleases in accordance with reasoned proportions. Considered objectively, then, music includes the knowledge of harmonic "modulation," of many kinds of things which are related to the transcendental and the divine, the heavenly and the human, the spiritual and the physical, each pair organized in relation to one another. God, as Augustine said long ago, means number, measure, and weight, and his (celestial) music is superior to all other musics because it is more complete and perfect than they, just as its object is more perfect;[35] but it is divorced from movement and sensual matter, the elements of the sound-music of the world. *Musica caelestis*, *mundana*, and *humana* are theoretical and not further divisible; graspable by the intellect, they differ from sonorous music, which, graspable by the senses, divides into the theoretical and the practical, but is only a subdivision of *musica caelestis*. Thus to summarize Jacob's ideas is to summarize the idea of music in the Middle Ages. And to note them carefully is to see the application of Scholastic argument to musical thought.

He too relies on the monochord to support his systems of tetrachords and their three *genera* and the church modes. He denies the validity of Aristoxenus' reliance on the senses and compromises with Ptolemy's "adjustment" of Aristoxenus and the Pythagoreans. What is in the intellect or *anima* is in the senses, he thinks, and not the reverse. The judgment of the senses is of individual things. But for him music of the transcendental type is the true object of contemplation, an eternal beyond the limits of time; such music is not the object of hearing: we can see that it is the old music of the spheres transformed into a purely spiritual harmony. Basically, music is intelligibility (not sound). A perfect musician is a savant; he can be a composer or a singer who realizes harmony in sound and voice, but he must also apply his abstract science to sound and judge sound-music on the basis of abstract, perfect principles. Sound itself is nothing--only a striking thing (a plectrum), a struck object (a string), and a medium (air). In the end, like Sextus Empiricus, whose ideas would have horrified him, Jacob doubts the reality of sound. It is number-sound which is the seat of judgment.

For Jacob, as for countless of his predecessors, music is in general an objective thing. As a term, it applies to everything--to God and all of his works, spiritual and physical, celestial and earthly, to the scientifically theoretical, and to the practical. It is number, measure, and weight. Music is numbered sound, as Augustine thought. But it is internal to man, because it is the harmony everywhere in the world. Music of voice and instrument, in the end, are produced only by men, but harmony and music as a One are fixed by God in nature once and for all. Thus celestial music must be superior to all other kinds, which can act only as its symbols. Musical laws are those of a well-regulated world construction, of spiritual and pure harmony, existing there. He accepts the old "laws" and contradicts Roger Bacon and Johannes of Grocheo, who reject a "harmonic" world-structure ruled by musical principles. And he admirably summarizes much of the idea of music from the past though much of it already is evidently passé. He describes a whole cosmology of music which Hugo Leichtentritt[36] has compared with Dante's *Divine Comedy*. Others have compared it as an encyclopedia with a compendium of the cathedral. It is a symbol of the thought which contemplates spiritual music. His stance is purely intellectual.

In 1905, Hermann Abert published his pioneering *Die Musik-anschauung des Mittelalters*, which treats the philosophy of music in the Middle Ages. In it (p. 191), he charted what he thought was Jean de Muris' symbolical scheme for music, religion, and the parallels between them. He did not know that the *Speculum musicae* was Jacob's, and thus his sources were really two. His chart, which I have revised and supplemented on the following page, provides a useful summary.

IV

Ugolino of Orvieto: The Italian Summary of Medieval Music Theory. In a sense, Ugolino of Orvieto (c.1375-c.1455) may be considered a lesser Jacob of Liège. Also a comprehensive writer, Ugolino in his *Declaratio musicae disciplinae* combined and related to one another all the elements or departments of music instruction pursued during the Middle Ages. However, unlike Jacob, his preference was for "complicated" music rather than plainchant. In Italy, Francesco Landini (b. c.1325) had already written *ballati*, madrigals, and *cacce*, the latter involving two voices singing in canon, all representing the new style. In France, Machaut also had already written motets for four voices as well as a complete polyphonic setting of the Mass, while the Englishman John Dunstable (c.1370-1453), who was Ugolino's contemporary, left behind a body of songs, hymns, and motets in three parts.

The context of musical practice with regard to composition in the "complicated" style may perhaps best be judged by reference to Machaut, whose application of polyphonic techniques to secular music rivaled his ecclesiastical compositions. He wrote *lais, rondeaux, virelais*, and *ballades*. Of these, to be sure, all of the *lais*, a majority of the *virelais*, and one of the *ballades* are monodic. For the works with more than one voice, however, Machaut composed his own tenors in a texture more complex than Philippe de Vitry's isorhythmic motets. Further, his *ballades* and *rondeaux* were highly ornamented, with long passages of florid counterpoint on a single syllable occurring at the beginning and close of the composition. The *ballade* was simpler, more syllabic, more like a song, and was usually based on imperfect (duple) time and mensural rhythm. In Machaut's compositions there was a strong virtuosic tendency, and in addition there were technically startling devices and the employment of prolation and syncopation.

It seems relevant also to mention here the late medieval literary accomplishments in Italy, particularly the work of Dante, who illustrates the extent to which the thinking of his time was ingrained with the idea of poetry and music as a union. He had himself employed the *canzona*, the typically Italian form which he called a fiction expressed in rhetoric and music: here we have pure craftsmanship, serious poetry as an imaginative invention involving both words and music. It is a true *cantio* just as a *lectio* is a reading, and it comes in two forms: as an action, an author's composition; and as a *passio*, an utterance by the author or someone else--that is, by a third person--of a created work with or without modulation in sound. The subject matter of the canzona is of the highest worth, and this is joined to a tragic style of equal stanzas without refrain. *Cantilena*, on the other hand, is

Both rooted in unity and perfection:

Numbers	MUSIC	CHU
1	music itself two voices singing the same tone	one church ecclesiastical matters a congregation

2	cosmic (macrocosm)--human
	    (microcosm)
	music natural--instrumental
	song authentic--plagal
		the two Testaments
		life contemplative--active
		the love of God--love of
		    neighbor

3	song: low, medium, high
	instruments: blown,
	    percussive, plucked
	beginning, middle, end
	pitch: high, medium, low
		contrite heart, oral confes-
		    sion, penance
		faith, hope, charity
		Father, Son, Holy Spirit (the
		    Trinity)

4	world structure
	tones (in tetrachord) 1, 2, 3, 4
	4 final notes of authentic
	    modes
	4 note-lines
	4 temperaments
	4 seasons
	4 weeks in the month
	4 elements (earth, water, fire,
	    air)
		modesty, temperance,
		    fortitude, justice (the 4
		    virtues)
		4 Evangelists

7	final notes
	letters of notes
	spoken words of the high
	    voice
		official religious hours,
		    sacraments
		Gifts of the Holy Spirit

8	modes (from the 4 finals)	the 8 Beatitudes (from the 4 virtues)

9	intervals
	interval-spaces (between
	    note-lines on staff)
		angelic orders teaching
		    Church dogma
		readings, responses, psalms

10	note-lines on staff	the Ten Commandments
19	divisions ("distinctions")	different degrees of the Christian faithful

a comic joining together (*On Vulgar Poetry* 2.4). Thus Dante provides a description of the tradition exemplified by the lyrics of his own *Vita Nuova* and *Convivio*.

Music and song interpreted metaphorically, symbolically, and mystically have a superior place in the *Paradiso* of Dante's *Divine Comedy* (begun 1307). In the immovable Empyrean live the spirits who appear in the nine heavens that encircle the earth. Graded according to merit and their degrees of beatitude, the spheres are given their ancient names (different from those adopted in Pseudo-Dionysius) from Mercury, Venus, the Sun, Mars, Jupiter, Saturn, the Fixed Stars to one not previously noted, the Crystalline Heavens (the *primum mobile*). In the Heavens of the Fixed Stars is the triumph of Christ, in the *primum mobile* the triumph of the angels, and in the empyrean the Vision of God. Light in its gradations reflects different degrees of beatitude and permeates Paradise, just as aspects of earthly nature reflect those of heavenly perfection. Here love is a lyrical musical state found in melody and song, not in poetry alone. Music fills the songs of the blessed souls. Dante celebrates the harmony of the universe, the intellectual harmony of God's creation.

In the heaven of the sun there are, among others, certain theologians who have been treated or mentioned above: St. Thomas Aquinas, Albertus Magnus, Dionysius the Areopagite, Boethius, Isidore of Seville, and Bede. St. Bernard of Clairvaux, noted for his devotion to the Virgin Mary, invites Dante to contemplate her beauty. Among the many songs of the *Divine Comedy*, St. Anne, the mother of Mary, sings *Hosanna* (*Parad.* 32.133-34). At the beginning of Canto 29 of the *Purgatorio*, during the Mystic Procession in Earthly Paradise, the beautiful Lady Matilda sings as if in love and forces to Dante's attention the surrounding brightness permeated by sweet melody; in Canto 30.83ff, the angels sing from Psalm 30 (31). And in *Paradiso* 31, angels flit back and forth singing in the radiance of the White Rose of Paradise, while in Canto 28.92ff *Hosanna* is sung antiphonally from choir to choir by Seraphim and Cherubim.

The Dantean ascription of music to a favored place in heaven runs parallel to the persistence of Jacob and Ugolino of Orvieto to treat music philosophically. Intellect and theory come first in any philosophy of art: in his treatise on painting (*Craftsman's Handbook*), Cennino Cennini (1370-c.1440) declared that theory is superior to other important considerations in painting, like skill of hand and imagination.[37] Thus, Ugolino also, though himself a practicing composer, seems in his discursive prose to be primarily interested in theory and not in the music of his own time. His mind, like Jacob's, is pervaded by the inherited tradition of Pythagoras, Boethius, and Aristotle. Music here retains its place in the quadrivium. Practical music is treated in a universal context, and the quadrivial tradition of Boethius in part supplies explanation of the practices of Ugolino's day. In Book I, he discusses the power of the intellect according to Aristotle, the human hand, the consecutive intervals of music according to Boethius, hexachords according to Guido, and the chant of the Roman Church; and he adds a *tonarius*. In Book 2 he discusses the simple counterpoint of simultaneous intervals, in Book 3 measured music (according to Jean de Muris), in Book 4 proportions based on number. These first four books embrace *musica activa* or *practica*, and Book 5 is devoted to *musica speculativa* (including discussion of the perennial semitone and the tuning of the monochord).

Written at the request of certain musical students, Ugolino's work purports to describe the perfect musician, including the composer of counterpoint. His foundations are more than familiar: everything in the world is organized and moving, and everything includes music. Speculation about God, the world, the soul, and all types of music are necessary considerations, though ultimately the nature of terrestrial music of man's devising and its rules are a primary subject, as they had been for Aristoxenus in antiquity. The practical interest is in musical technique (*ars*), notation, the rules for counterpoint, that which is improvised and that which is written down (and thereby recorded), and the sensuous and affective qualities of sounding music.

Ugolino begins with a discussion of the meaning of *anima intellecta*, the noblest part of the soul which, ruled by reason, comprehends God and benefits the will. Then he turns to a review of the various kinds of music, and ends with a demonstration that music, part of the quadrivium, is a science. It is active and speculative in the sense described by Al Farabi (Jacob of Liège had still followed the Boethian notion that theory is superior to practice). But active music, sensuous and practical in appeal, is now almost the equal of the philosophical-theoretical.

As Jean de Muris and Jacob had found their philosophical support in the idea of perfection, so Ugolino finds his in the dichotomy between sense and reason--a distinction as old as Plato and Boethius. Both men and beasts have senses; only man has reason, and reason allows him to separate the true from the false. When the senses perceive objects, they serve reason; and it is reason which judges.

A true man of the Church, Ugolino allies reason and God. Reason was given to man so that he can know God, and, consequently, music study is necessary because reason understands the numerical relations of sound, which is an object of the hearing faculty. It can recognize musical truth, which is the music of the heavens, not the sensory impression that can mislead. Reason is the beginning and foundation of all nature. Here St. Augustine seems to be recalled, but it is Boethius who is mentioned as though his classifications had included only heavenly or celestial music. The result must be that in music, speculation and ethics are inseparable--and that men of all ages are moved by music and the beauty of the correct proportion of sound it embodies.[38]

Thus it is logical to justify the existence of singers and instrumentalists by their performance, which exists *not* to delight the senses but to liberate reason from their domination. In this way, music becomes a Liberal Art delighting the mind. Any judgment of it must come from one who knows music and its causes, so that the result is a pure delight which is conjointly musical and ethical. Speculation is mandatory because sense-impressions are not enough. First things--proportion and mathematical ratio--must come first. Indeed, without proportion and the consonance it causes there can be no music. Speculative music, which is superior to the active-practical kind, strives for truth; the latter misleads the senses, which look towards a (false) truth conforming with physical appetite. Truth is above and beyond sound, physical and sensual, and, prefacing his remarks with a reference to Aristotle (*Physics* 1) on learning, Ugolino describes plainchant, simple counterpoint, and mensurable music preliminary to reaching his final goal of divorcing sound from sense experience. Ugolino, a priest of the late Middle Ages, unites human reason with a recognition of the Divine to justify his having written a musical-theoretical handbook for the education of his readers, who, learning how to handle sound, were expected to recognize that sound is only an avenue to a transcendent numerical truth.

As we have seen, Ugolino is in sharp contrast to Jacob of Liège since, while the latter had asked for a return to the principles of the early medieval "ancients," the former clearly accepts polyphony, which he prefers over monophony though he rejects neither. Polyphonic music appeals to one's sense of number or ratio and order. The true effects of music reside not in the single melody but in many voices sounding together according to contrapuntal laws, and they thereby please the soul (*anima*) of the hearer (p. 123). Ugolino does not choose an either-or (monophony or polyphony) when both are legitimate.

Ugolino influenced Franchinus Gaffurius (1451-1522), Adam of Fulda (c.1445-1505), John Hothby (c.1415-87), an English theorist who taught and wrote during much of his life in Italy, and other theorists who helped set Renaissance ideals for theorist and composer. More than anyone before him, Ugolino stresses the perception of sounds, especially those of many-voiced music. By this time, it had become technically acceptable to recognize diminished fifths, octaves, and twelfths, which, however, must be made perfect by being enlarged a semitone. Only major thirds could be expanded by steps to a fifth and only major sixths to an octave. Minor thirds were required if the third was to be compressed to a unison.[39] These were rules recognizing chromaticism and yet preserving perfection. They represent the acceptance of practices which would have been forbidden a thousand years earlier.

Ugolino was nevertheless attached to the old ideas. Though the Pythagorean music of the spheres in its original form seems almost to have disappeared from speculation, Ugolino, true to his time and Church, still reflects the thought of pseudo-Dionysius when he thinks heavenly music (of the angels) in its *interminabilis altitudo* and incredible sweetness is superior to all three of the traditional (Boethian) types of music. He seems philosophically to be out of step with his time despite his praise of polyphony, and Book 3 of his work is only a gloss on Jean de Muris, his predecessor by almost a century.

As has been pointed out above, monastic chant and the ecclesiastical music of cathedral and church were now being supplemented by a rich music of court and town. Singers and instrumentalists supported by the aristocracy not only were associated with their private chapels, but also performed in their halls, which in effect were converted to private concert salons. Townspeople employed waits, who were essentially instrumentalists, to perform at ceremonial occasions such as the installation of a mayor, at civic processions, and in plays such as the great Corpus Christi cycles of England. It is also true that the universalism of medieval chant, always influenced to be sure by regional practices, was exchanged for a new and increasing nationalism in music French, German, English, and Italian.

Greater attention was being given to the structure of both vocal and instrumental music, marking the controversial nature of the new developments in compositional technique. While some saw the older traditions of plainsong as rigid and less interesting, others objected to polyphony in church music. Acoustics gradually came into its own as a science. And the music of the Church in the end had to go its own way, eventually to be confronted with the Reformation and the Council of Trent, which would set different geographical regions in Europe upon separate paths. Secular music, which like church music had a communal function, had to go its own way also. And the two kinds of music, sacred and secular, influenced each other more than could have been realized by either tradition-minded clergy or pope on the one hand, or the theorists on the other.

In the two centuries which followed the fourteenth, there were, of course, new and rich cultural-intellectual developments. Not so encouraging, perhaps, was the continued Latin preference for rhetoric over philosophy--a preference which would merge into the work of Peter Ramus, whose influence on the Puritan movement in England was indeed strong. But there were also other trends in which music played a share. Albrecht Dürer and Leonardo da Vinci outlined theories of painting which included music, and the musical ratios applied to architecture were not entirely forgotten. There was something of a revival, too, of the theme of music and magic, as D. P. Walker has reminded us.[40] For example, Marsilio Ficino, inspired by Plotinus and other early Neoplatonists, revived the idea of music and magic in terms of a universal sympathy recalling the ideas of the Pythagoreans. And eventually, as noted above, religious differences played a role in the practice of music, with Martin Luther and the bishops of the Church of England looking with favor on choral music performed by choirs, and John Calvin and his Puritan followers in England preferring congregational singing limited to vernacular settings of the psalms. In the area of secular music, there was throughout the years following the Middle Ages an intense discussion of a subject which had been stressed by Guido of Arezzo--namely, music and poetry.

Historians have often stressed the significance of military and political events, in some instances even dividing one period (the Middle Ages) from another (the Renaissance) by such an event as the fall of

Byzantium in 1453. But to those interested in the idea of music, a more important event at about this time was the invention of moveable type, the ingenious advance over woodblock printing for which Johann Gutenberg of Mainz was responsible. Already by the 1460's, presses were established in Rome, Berlin, Florence, and Naples, and in the next decade printers were already working in England (at Westminster, where William Caxton had set up his shop), Paris, Lyon, Bruges, and Valencia. In 1476, the first successful square-note music printing by Ulrich Hahn was issued, a Missal which has been described as "outstanding" in comparison with the pioneering Constance Gradual of three years earlier. But the truly revolutionary development in music printing came in 1501 with the invention of a way to print music from type and with the issue of Ottaviano dei Petrucci's *Harmonice musices odhecaton A*. With the wide availability of printed music, musical literacy increased dramatically and with it immense possibilities for the further development of the idea of music.

Appendix A
Diagrammatic Scheme of Ptolemy's Psychology Relating to Music

There are two basic powers of the soul:

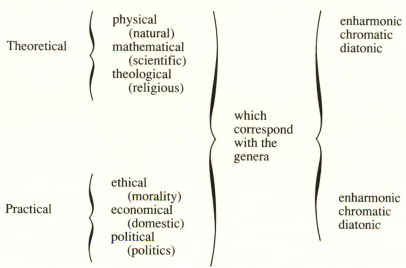

Theoretical
- physical (natural)
- mathematical (scientific)
- theological (religious)

Practical
- ethical (morality)
- economical (domestic)
- political (politics)

which correspond with the genera

- enharmonic
- chromatic
- diatonic

- enharmonic
- chromatic
- diatonic

There are also three powers of the individual psyche or soul (see following page):

435

Powers	Symphonic Intervals		Virtues
1. to think (thought) a. simplicity b. uniformity c. the syn-onymity	the octave (the seven intervals of the octave)*	Reason	sagacity dexterity presence of mind insight wisdom discretion knowledge to live simply
2. to perceive (perception) a. seeing b. hearing c. smelling d. tasting	the fifth (four intervals)	Feeling	gentleness fearlessness courage constancy
3. to live (life) a. growing b. blossoming c. withering away	the fourth (three intervals)	Desiring	prudence control modesty

---

*Aso like the seven intervals of the octave: Powers for the treatment of the perceived are:

1. imagination for the assessment of the perceived
2. understanding for the formation of the perceived
3. reflection for the retaining and the easy remembrance of formed things
4. reconsideration for repetition and investigation
5. opinion for superficial conjecture
6. reason for critical judgment
7. knowledge for clear comprehension in accordance with truth

(3.5-6)

Appendix B
The Roman Rite

The Roman rite, imposed throughout his territories by Charlemagne and eventually the rite used throughout Western Europe (with modifications, as in the case of the Sarum, or Salisbury, rite in England), has as its central ceremony the Mass, the development of which is thoroughly discussed by Josef A. Jungmann in *The Mass of the Roman Rite* (New York: Benziger Brothers, 1951), 2 vols. Certain chants associated with the various Mass ceremonies became traditional:

A. The (unchangeable) Ordinary (Congregation and Schola)

1. *Kyrie eleison*
2. *Gloria*
3. *Credo* (Nicene Creed)
4. *Sanctus* (including *Benedictus*) (precedes the Canon of the Mass)
5. *Agnus Dei*

B. The (changeable) Propers

1. Introit† - processional psalm: antiphon and verse from psalm
2. Gradual* - antiphon or responsory with schola
3. Epistle - reading
4. Alleluia* - responsorial: a verse-psalm in whole or in part
   (omitted during Lent, and Tract substituted)
5. Gospel - reading
6. Offertory† - offering of bread and wine
7. Communion (Eucharist)† - sung during Communion and ablutions

    * The Soloist
    † The Schola

In addition to the above parts of the Mass, the following should be noted: (1) the *Jubilus*, which is a florid, melodic, and wordless extension of the Alleluia; (2) the sequence, following the Alleluia, after approximately 1000 A.D. becoming metrical and even rhymed; (3) the trope, or insertion in a liturgical piece, such as the Introit, of a new set of words and ornamental vocalizations; and (4) liturgical drama or ceremonies such as the *Visitatio*

Sepulchri (*Visit to the Sepulchre*) presented in many major monasteries, cathedrals, and churches on Easter morning. For the sequence, see especially Richard Crocker, "Sequence," *The New Grove Dictionary of Music and Musicians*, ed. Stanley Sadie (1980), XVII, 141-51. Texts of tropes have been collected by the Corpus Troporum, and are in the process of being published by Almqvist & Wiksell (Stockholm, 1975-). Their music is conveniently surveyed by Ruth Steiner, "Trope," *The New Grove*, XIX, 172-87. For the liturgical drama, see especially Karl Young, *The Drama of the Medieval Church* (Oxford: Clarendon Press, 1933), 2 vols.

The Mass, however, was never the only service of the Church, and special notice needs also to be taken of the Canonical Hours or Offices, which are services of prayer maintained in monastic churches from very early times. These include: (1) the Greater: Matins, Lauds (at sunrise), Vespers (at sundown), Compline (at nightfall); and (2) the Lesser: Prime (6 a.m.), Terce (9 a.m.), Sext (at noon), and None (3 p.m.). These services are characterized by the use of chanted psalms, antiphons, hymns, and canticles.

Appendix C

Hugh of St.-Victor's Classification of the Arts and Sciences (All learning pursued for the knowledge and love of God)

PHILOSOPHY
(The pursuit of all the Divine Wisdom one can achieve in this life)

I. Theory (Wisdom)
(Philosophical: the pursuit of Divine Wisdom)

1. Theology (The Christian science of God) (invisible substances)

2. Physics (the science of nature) (invisible causes of visible things)

3. Mathematics (visible forms of visible things) (the quadrivium)

   a. Arithmetic (number: discrete quantity in itself; first element: 1)

   b. Music (proportion: discrete quality in relation to something else; its first element: the single tone)
   1. world: (1) elemental; (2) planetary; (3) temporal
   2. human: (1) body, (2) soul, (3) the two together
   3. instrumental: (1) struck, (2) blown, (3) vocal

   } MUSIC AS SCIENCE (Boethian and Cassiodorian)

   c. Geometry (space, or immobile continuous quantity; its first element: the point)

   d. Astronomy (motion, or mobile continuous quantity; its first element: the moment in time)

439

II. Practice (Virtue, Morals)

1. Ethics: Individual or solitary: moral science (the individual life with its habits and virtues)

2. Economy: domestic or private (heads of families): economy (regulation of domestics and relatives)

3. Politics: public (rulers): science of citizenship (the governing of a whole people or nation by its rulers)

III. Mechanics (Men's Needs)
(A lower knowledge turning man back to divine Wisdom)
(The seven non-liberal arts: the occupations of men)

Protective:
external covering
for nature:
like the trivium
(in that words are
external things)

1. Weaving
2. Construction,
   crafts, armaments,
   forging and
   casting (sculpture,
   architecture,
   drawing)
3. Commerce

Nature's methods of
feeding and nourishing
herself: like the
trivium: concepts are
internally conceived:
all activities

4. Agriculture
5. Hunting
6. Medicine
7. Theatrics
   (poetry and
   literature)
   (performed on
   porches of
   buildings, in
   gymnasia,
   amphitheaters)
Epics
   a. recited
   b. acted
   c. puppets and
      masks
Dances
Wrestling
Racing
Songs to the gods

Purpose: to temper
motion and stimulate
natural heat in the
body and, through
enjoyment, to refresh
the mind

servants of
eloquence
wed to wisdom

a. Poetical song
   1. tragedy
   2. comedy
   3. satire
   4. heroic form
   5. lyric form
   6. iambic form
   7. didactic poems
b. Fables and fiction
c. History
d. The elaborate
   writing now called
   philosophy

MUSIC AS
SERVANT
TO
LITERARY
FORMS

IV. Logic[1]

1. Grammar (words: their origin, formation, etc.)

2. Theory of argument (conceptual content of words)
   a. demonstrative or necessary argument (of philosophers)
   b. probable argument
      1. dialectic
      2. rhetoric
   c. disputatious or sophistical argument of sophists[2]

---

[1] To be studied first (though invented last): these studies precede the others in experience and open the way for the first three.

[2] Derived from *Didascalicon* 2.4ff, pp. 64ff and 152-54, as adapted from Charles Henry Buttiner, ed., *Hugonis de Sancto Victore Didascalicon de studio legendi: A Critical Text* (Washington, D.C.: Catholic Univ. Press, 1939), pp. xv-xvi.

Appendix D
Gundisalvo's System of the Arts and Sciences

It must be remembered that I have given only a one-sided view of the encyclopedic writers I have been discussing. For many of them, music, if not initially, perhaps eventually (I think of Adelard whose *De eodem et diverso* is a youthful work) became part of a system. The place of music in Gundisalvo's thought, based on that of Al Farabi, should be clear from this diagram (reduced from *De divisione philosophae*, for which Gundisalvo copies almost literally from Al Farabi, *De scientis*).

Theoretical	Practical
Physics	Politics
Mathematics[1]	Art of civil government
Metaphysics	Art of family government:
	Instruction in:
	1. Liberal Arts
	(music: science)
	2. Mechanical Arts
	(music: art)
	3. Ethics
	(the art of self-government)

Mechanical Arts

	Theoretical	Practical
	Arithmetic (the theory of numbers)	Use of the abacus (in commerce)
Something useful to man made out of matter from living things (wood, wool, linen, bones, or dead things: gold, silver, lead, iron, etc.)	Music[2] (speculative and contemplative: the theory of proportions and harmonics)	(Practical productive) Harmonies of voices and instruments
	Geometry (the theory of lines, surfaces, and volumes)	Measuring bodies Surveying

443

Astrology and astronomy (position and motions of heavenly bodies)

Use of astrolobe and other astronomical instruments

Weights (theory of balance)

Balance and lever: instruments for lifting and carrying heavy things

Mathematical devices (principles of its outer mathematical sciences)

Stone masonry
Instruments for
   measuring and
   lifting bodies
Musical instruments
Optical instruments
Carpentry

---

[1] Mathematics: science of abstract quantity (lines, surfaces, circles, triangles) found in material things not themselves quantity. Abstraction is the form of things, however apprehended, a universal science containing the seven arts of arithmetic, geometry, music, astronomy, optics, weights, mathematical devices. See A. C. Crombie, *Medieval and Early Modern Science* (Garden City, NY: Doubleday, 1959), I, 179.

[2] The musical division is from Al Farabi, of course, but it can be traced back to Aristides Quintilianus and even to Pseudo-Aristotle's *Problems*. The division, like the idea of mathematics above, is Aristotelian, and even Plato makes it: the speculative is scientific, the practical is not.

Notes

Part I

CHAPTER I
From Apollo to Damon

¹ Orpheus and Musaeus too were musico-medical gods, and sometimes Aesculapius was called Apollo's son (Pausanius [second century B.C.] 2.26.4-5). All musician-physicians were supposed to represent natural, or magical, not supernatural, powers. Today we think of their reputed effects as in large part psychological in nature, since ecstasy and self-forgetfulness are aspects of the correction of a disharmony between body and mind. Orpheus is said by Pausanius (9.20.4) to have excelled his predecessors in the healing of disease and in the discovery of mystic rites leading to purification from unholy deeds--that is, in achieving therapeutic effects through music. Important as a figure of the magical-mystical-musical-religious rites of ancient Greece, Orpheus loses reputation (though he is not forgotten) during the Middle Ages but regains high renown at the hands of Marsilio Ficino during the Italian Renaissance.

² Kathleen Freeman, *Ancilla to the Pre-Socratic Philosophers* (Cambridge, Mass.: Harvard Univ. Press, 1957), p. 65. All citations to this volume will be identified as *Ancilla* hereafter.

³ Forty-one musical fragments containing music with notation according to the two systems prevalent in ancient Greece are extant; see Thomas J. Mathiesen, "New Fragments of Ancient Greek Music," *Acta Musicologica*, 53 (1981), 14-32. For a study of the notation, see J. Murray Barbour, "The Principles of Greek Notation," *Journal of the American Musicological Society*, 13 (1960), 1-17. For a recording, by the Atrium Musicae de Madrid under the direction of Gregorio Paniagua, see *Musique de la Gréce antique* (Harmonia Mundi HM 1015), which provides a conjectural reconstruction of fourteen examples from the extant fragments.

It should be noted that I have used the term 'the Greeks' only as a kind of shorthand. There were no Greeks in the unified sense of the term as used today. Plato and Aristotle and even Pythagoras are included under the term, as are all writers of classical Greece. Ancient Greece was, of course, made up of many races, languages, and city-states.

⁴ The Muses were invoked by Homer, Hesiod, and Pindar, but they had no marked personalities, seemed to be unknown as individuals, and apparently represented pure intellect. Associated with Apollo, they were vague of image from the earliest times. Yet they were always patronesses

of poetry, philosophy, and music. Pythagoras, Plato, and their followers fairly made a cult of them. Later, the Christians rejected them in favor of the Heavenly Choirs.

⁵ For convenience I have provided line numbers for the works of Homer from the translation by Robert Fitzgerald; it should be noted that these do not correspond with the line numbers of the original Greek text.

⁶ Werner Jaeger, *Paideia: The Ideals of Greek Culture*, trans. Gilbert Highet (New York: Oxford Univ. Press, 1943-45), I, 143.

⁷ W. B. Stanford, *The Sound of Greek* (Berkeley and Los Angeles: Univ. of California Press, 1967), pp. 7-8.

⁸ The term 'polyphonal' signifies "many sounds," not polyphony. 'Flutes' are obviously *auloi*; the next two lines speak of the instruments imitating the "wailing clamor" coming from the jaws of Euryala, a sound said to describe that of the aulos. For a brief review of Greek musical instruments, see the article by R. P. Winnington-Ingram on the music of classical Greece in the *New Grove Dictionary of Music and Musicians*, ed. Stanley Sadie (1980), VII, 661-63.

⁹ I shall not discuss the validity or invalidity of certain documents and the extent to which they establish or fail to establish who Pythagoras was and what he taught. On the one hand, scholars say that there exist no genuine documents concerning Pythagoras himself; on the other, more recent scholars find that often certain supposedly spurious documents are authentic and that others hitherto ignored, or only recently made known, can paint an authentic picture of Pythagoras and his cosmical, political, scientific, and religious thought. The controversy is well documented in C. J. de Vogel, *Pythagoras and Early Pythagoreanism* (Assen: Van Gorcum, 1966), pp. 3-19, 245-46.

¹⁰ I am indebted in large part to Edward A. Lippman, *Musical Thought in Ancient Greece* (New York: Columbia Univ. Press, 1964), for my discussion of Pythagoras.

¹¹ John Burnet, *Greek Philosophy, I: Thales to Plato* (London: Macmillan, 1914), pp. 4ff.

¹² Prominent groups of Greek cities and the closely related dialects their inhabitants spoke were: Dorians (Sparta, Syracuse, Argos, Corinth, the cities of Crete), Aeolians (Boeotia, Lesbos), Ionians (Athens, most of the Aegean islands, cities of the Aegian coast of Asia Minor).

¹³ These calculations are based on the strings of the lyre, of which there were four, though later there were seven or possibly eight. All of the strings were of equal length and tuned entirely by ear to the required pitch to produce intervals of the octave, the fifth, and the fourth, all thought to be "permanent" or "stationary." Any other intervals were "moveable."

Pythagoras is said to have divided the monochord, a single string with a moveable bridge, so as to establish the numerical ratios of concords. But there is another story, repeated frequently in musical discussions throughout the centuries, that Pythagoras one day passed a forge and was fascinated by the harmonious sounds produced by four hammers struck one after the other on the anvil. Weighing each hammer, he discovered their respective weights to be 12, 9, 8, and 6. A 12 followed by a 6 produced an octave; a 12 followed by an 8, or a 9 by a 6, produced the fifth; a 12 followed by a 9, or an 8 by a 6 produced the fourth; 8 followed by 9 produced the whole tone. That the story is legendary is almost certain; that it is scientifically inaccurate has often been demonstrated. It is based on the false assumption that the vibrations and sounds of a metallic body are in proportion to its volume and weight.

[14] For an excellent short account of Greek musico-mathematical theory, see Richard L. Crocker, "Pythagorean Mathematics and Music," *Journal of Aesthetics and Art Criticism*, 22 (1963-64), 189-98, 325-35.

[15] In *Timaeus* 55-56, by a geometical process, five "regular" solids were discovered, four of which were the tetrahedron, the octahedron, the icosahedron, and the cube. These Plato related to the four elements, fire, air, water, and earth, respectively. The fifth solid, the dodecahedron, with twelve faces, was used to "embroider the universe with constellations" (cf. also Euclid, *Elements* 13). Plato's solids were still an element in the musical theory of Johannes Kepler (1571-1630) and his *Harmonices Mundi* (1619).

[16] The Greek terms for the perfect intervals (employed throughout the Middle Ages and thereafter) were diapason (1:2), the octave ("through all"); diapente (3:2), the fifth ("five" notes); and diatessaron (4:3), the fourth ("four" notes).

[17] Cf. Lippman, p. 35.

[18] For a detailed study of the concept of number, see ibid., pp. 34-35.

[19] See also Iamblichus, *Mysteries* 3.9n.

[20] In another connection, Iamblichus tells a story, later so often repeated as to seem more than a legend: Pythagoras once calmed a young man who, having feasted all night, was determined to burn the vestibule of the house of his mistress, whom he had seen coming home from the house of his rival. A Phrygian song had inflamed him and excited him to do the deed. But Pythagoras, who was astronomizing at that time, happened to meet the piper of the Phrygian song and persuaded him to substitute a spondaic song for it. Upon doing so, the young man found his fury suppressed, and he returned home in an orderly manner (*Life of Pythag.*, p. 60). See also Iamblichus, *Mysteries* 3.9n.

[21] Aristides Quintilianus 62. Though this present history concentrates on the Western world, there are certain similarities between occidental and oriental thought; however, there is little, if any, evidence that Greek music and music theory had connections throughout the inhabited world of that time. The same cultural theories were nevertheless current in China, Egypt, and India. In Hermann Pfrogner, *Musik: Geschichte ihrer Deutung* (Freiburg and Munich: Karl Alber, 1964), pp. 2-11, 14-21, there are passages from the Chinese, Indian, and Egyptian, Scandinavian, and Finnish about music and magic. Again, Greece was not alone in teaching the cosmological basis for the principle of harmony and music, which is also

found in Chinese, Indian, and Egyptian literature (ibid., pp. 25-28).

    [22] See Lippman, pp. 1-44.

    [23] When 6 - 4 = 2, then 4 - 3 = 1, and 2:6 = 1:3. The harmonic mean was so called because its terms give the principal musical intervals: 6:3 = 2:1 (the octave); 6:4 = 3:2 (the fifth); 4:3 (the fourth). See Kathleen Freeman, *Pre-Socratic Philosophers*, 2nd ed. (Oxford: Blackwell, 1949), p. 235.

    [24] The attribrution of pitch to rapidity of movement has often been cited as a forerunner of the vibration theory because a stroke or hitting is involved. The first enunciation of the vibration theory is often held to have come from Heracl(e)ides Ponticus (fourth century B.C.), a geometer and disciple of Plato, who is reputed to have said that: "according to certain Pythagoreans, musical intervals cannot exist without . . . movement, which too cannot exist without number, as number cannot exist without quantity. There are two movements, then--one in place and the other in modification (change). The first is circular, a movement from point to point, like the movements of sun, moon, and stars around the earth; or it is in a straight line, as when ninepins and balls turn on their own axes. Of straight motion there are many kinds. Now, tone is spatial movement from point to point which leads directly to the perceptual part of hearing. A striking occurring outside the ear is carried to the perceptual part of the ear. The sense of hearing is now set in motion and a perception is achieved. The striking takes no time, but occurs in a division between past and future time. The striking occurs at neither the moment it is initiated nor when it ceases, but between the coming and the past time. The striking, so to speak, is a boundary dividing time. . . ."

    The explanation continues: "Certain tones are rough (*ekmelic*) and unbalanced, and others smooth (*emmelic*) and pleasant. All tones vibrate according to certain numbers, according to ratios, the *ekmelic* and *emmelic* having different (sub)movements of number. Nothing is in such accord with numbers as the calculable ratios which vibrate to achieve the *emmelic*. Thus the difference between symphony and diaphony (dissonance), between *emmelic* and *ekmelic,* is based on the effect of number relations" (Ingemar Düring, *Ptolemaios und Porphyrios über die Musik* [Göteborg: Erlander, 1934], pp. 152-54).

    This fragment, its authenticity, and the authenticity of its origins have for long been matters of dispute. It may even be a forgery. See ibid., pp. 154-55; Düring shows that Porphyry (third century B.C.) quotes it, probably from Didymus (b. 63 B.C.).

    [25] See Freeman, *Ancilla*, pp. 238-39.

    [26] A translation of Euclid's *Section of the Canon* is available in Charles Davy, *Letters upon Subjects of Literature* (Bury St. Edmunds, 1787), 2 vols. More accessible is Thomas J. Mathiesen's "An Annotated Translation of Euclid's *Division of the Monochord,*" *Journal of Music Theory*, 19 (1975), 236-58.

    [27] *De institutione musica*, in Oliver Strunk, ed., *Source Readings in*

Music History (New York: Norton, 1950), p. 83.

[28] See Schäfke's edition of Aristides Quintilianus, p. 63, and also the "reconstruction" by H. Ryfell, *"Eukosmia*: Ein Beitrag zur Wiederherstellung des Areopagitikos des Damon," *Museum Helveticum*, 4 (1947).

[29] For an excellent influence study, see Warren Anderson, "Damonian Theory in Plato's Thought," *American Philosophical Association Transactions*, 86 (1955), 88-102.

CHAPTER II
Plato

[1] The ancient Greeks knew only five major planets: Mercury, Venus, Mars, Jupiter, Saturn.   To these they added the spherical sun, moon, and fixed stars.   The last shone with a steady light and furnished a stable background against which the other spheres moved back and forth.

[2] Ernest G. McClain, *The Pythagorean Plato: Prelude to the Song Itself* (Stony Brook, N.Y.: N. Hays, 1978), pp. 51-52.   There have been differences of opinion about the "musical" scale.   Musicians are concerned with the various degrees and quantities of tones and how they are and can be performed and heard.   Plato and Archytas were thinking of the nature of things, of universal harmonies, of Harmonia, which includes the infinitude of Being, seen and not seen, heard and not heard, the perceptible and the imperceptible.   See J. Handschin, "The 'Timaeus' Scale," *Musica Disciplina*, 4 (1950), 3-42: Plato's scale is not a scale, but the principle of a scale.   Even more interesting, though probably incorrect, is the opinion of Paul Shorey that the *Timaeus* requires to be studied "as a great scientific poem, rather than as a masterpiece of metaphysical exposition," no doubt because in it the cosmos is treated as a living organism; see his "The Interpretation of the *Timaeus*," *American Journal of Philology*, 3 (1888), 400, 402.   But McClain disagrees with both ("Plato's Musical Cosmology," *Main Currents in Modern Thought*, 30 [1973], 34-42; *The Myth of Invariance: The Origin of the Gods, Mathematics, and Music from the Rig Veda to Plato* [Stony Brook, N.Y.: N. Hays, 1976]; and *The Pythagorean Plato*).   McClain usefully finds many examples of musical analysis and application in Plato.   Hidden in the marriage allegory (*Rep.* 546), for instance, is "just" tuning, in the tyrant's allegory (*Rep.* 587-88) is Pythagorean tuning, and in the myth of Er is tempered tuning.   In his musical investigations, McClain makes some refreshing and challenging observations.   For long thought to be philosopher, poet, writer of dialogues, fascist, ironist, and fantasist, Plato is now also a punster and allegorist.   He has also been called "the notorious Athenian philosopher."

Nevertheless, he is the father of Western philosophy. It should be remarked that cosmic harmony is still with us: Joseph Matthias Hauer, a modern twelve-tone composer, in the *Begleitwort zu dem Zwölftonspiel für Klavier* of 1946, calls twelve-tone music a cosmic playing with twelve even-tempered semitones!

3 Freeman, *Pre-Socratic Philosophers*, p. 113n.

4 See *Republic*, Book 7, for the whole argument between Socrates and his disputants about the nature of the soul.

5 See John Burnet on the Socratic Doctrine of the Soul, in *Essays and Addresses* (London: Macmillan, 1929), pp. 126-62. Plato, Aristotle, and (later) Plotinus and Porphyry allowed some form of the soul even to plants, a notion denied by Iamblichus, the Roman historian Sallust (80-34 B.C.), and the Emperor Julian the Apostate (331-63 A.D.).

6 There were two kinds of letter-notation, one for the song and one for the instrument. The aulos played the melody along with the singer, but played alone when the singer arrived at a pause. The relationship of singer to aulos was like Homer's to his *phorminx*.

7 For discussions of this theory, see Lippman, pp. 44-86, and Warren Anderson, *Ethos and Education in Ancient Greece* (Cambridge, Mass.: Harvard Univ. Press, 1966), *passim*.

8 Heraclides Ponticus is credited by Athenaeus (624) with having thought the Phrygian and Lydian modes not to be separate harmonies because there were really only three harmonies corresponding with only the three kinds of Greeks--Dorians, Aeolians, and Ionians. The ethical character of the music is the result of the ethical and national characteristics of the people. He is also said, because of observations in his *On Music*, now lost, to have been the first person to say that the rotation of the heavens is caused by the rotation of the earth on its axis.

9 For commentary on the Greek modes, see R. P. Winnington-Ingram, *Mode in Ancient Greek Music* (Cambridge: Cambridge Univ. Press, 1936), and the same author's article on the music of ancient Greece in the *New Grove*, VII, 667-68. See also Otto Gombosi, "Key, Mode, Species," *Journal of the American Musicological Society*, 4 (1951), 20-26.

10 See, for comparison, Aristides Quintilianus 21-22; Aristotle, *Politics* 1340-42; and Pseudo-Plutarch 1136-37.

11 Eric A. Havelock, *A Preface to Plato* (Cambridge, Mass.: Harvard Univ. Press, 1963), pp. 45, 57-60n.

12 Gerard F. Else, "Imitation in the Fifth Century," *Classical Philology*, 53 (1952), 87.

13 Havelock, p. 151. On ancient word-music subtleties, see Warren Anderson, "Word-Accent and Melody in Ancient Greek Musical Texts," *Journal of Music Theory*, 17 (1973), 186-202.

14 For an account of the education of boys in military Arcadia and of young men up to the age of thirty, see Polybius 4.20-21.

The battle between the art-directed and those devoted to the "manly" sports is one "form" Plato did not mention. In Euripides' fragmentary *Antiope,* Amphion praises music and song. He is answering his brother Zethos, a farmer and warrior, who scoffs at music and musicians; Amphion, according to Zethos, represents the womanish in appearance and is unable to defend himself with a shield or to defend others through manly counsel. A musician can achieve nothing for his family, city, or friends, and his inborn qualities are lost because he delights in pleasure. But Amphion thinks that for saving a city, a brain is better than brawn. Greek literature itself, like judgments of its music, is often divided between energetic work, athletics, or military training and artistic or intellectual pursuits (Kenneth James Dover, *Greek Popular Morality in the Time of Plato and Aristotle* [Berkeley, Calif.: Univ. of California Press, 1974], pp. 163ff).

[15] McClain, *Pythagorean Plato*, p. 5.

CHAPTER III
Aristotle

[1] Movement or motion is more important in Aristotle's thinking than is apparent in his writing on music. It is basic to everything in the world: space would reach perfection if each point in it were identical with all points at once. Motion is the way in which space attempts to reach this goal. The Primum Mobile, the highest physical sphere of fixed stars, moves rapidly, with all its own parts, to touch each and every part of the Empyrean at once, to make perfect contact with the perfect Empyrean. As motion increases, the contacts are closer and closer together in time and approach the perfect contact. Infinity is therefore the cause of this motion. The whole theory is yet another example of the importance in ancient thought, not of the individual parts, but of their relations, the perfect relation being a reposeful identity in and of the Whole.

[2] Aristotle discusses voices from the naturalistic standpoint in *On the Generation of Animals*. He finds them deep in some animals, high in others, and well-pitched with due proportion in between extremes in yet others. Generally, he shows, in all animals voices are high in the young, low in the older; in females high, in males low. But man alone has speech, and voice is the substance of speech. The physical explanation of differences in pitch is that low voices depend on a slow amount of air in motion, high ones on a swift amount--but not always: one can speak softly and deep, and loud and high (8.786b). In human beings too there are exceptions: old men's voices often become high-pitched. But Aristotle indulges in false science when he says that heat or cold gives some animals deep or high voices, hot breath being thick and causing depth, cold being thin and causing high sounds. So in pipe-playing: if the breath of the performer is hot, the note is deep. Roughness, smoothness, flexibility are based on the roughness, smoothness, or softness of the physical mechanism (ibid. 788a).

[3] Rhetoricians, some of them Sophists (whom Gregory of Nazianzen [c.329-89 A.D.] later called oratorical acrobats), were numerous in the fifth century B.C.; the prominent ones included Gorgias, Protagoras, Hippias, and Prodicus (the last being Damon's friend) as well as Thrasymachus of Chalcedon, who according to Plato (*Phaedrus* 269-70) did not partake of the nature of philosophy but nevertheless possessed the art of a finished

orator (that is, he had a natural power added to knowledge and practice). The Greeks thought of Homer as oratory's creator: formal addresses in the *Iliad* and *Odyssey* served as sources for didactic and hortatory speeches. In the time of Pericles after the Persian Wars, rhetoric was a basic discipline and an Ionian legacy to all of Greece. Demosthenes (384-322 B.C.) brought rhetoric into the legal tradition and made it the ornament of legal speech.

CHAPTER IV:
Post-Aristotelian Theory

[1] Like many of the ancients, Speusippus is remembered chiefly for what others said about him. Thus, what he probably thought about music is to be found in Sextus Empiricus, who lived five or six centuries after him. In his *Adversus Mathematicus* (*Against the Mathematicians*) (7.145), Sextus says that Speusippus believed perception to be dual, including that received by the senses and that by the mind, the former being judged as educated impressions, the latter as educated thought.   For Speusippus educated impressions partake of reasoned truth: flute and string players perform with mental activity, and, by contrast, any musician who decides what is and what is not harmonious does so not naturally but after thought. If a person has learned accomplishments, educated impression is benefited in a natural way.   Educated thought is different; it is based on reason and achieves a faultless knowledge of an object.

[2] McClain believes that modern classical scholars have done a grave injustice to Aristotle and Aristoxenus (and, also, to Plato and Plutarch) by their indifference to (and ignorance of) the role in ancient thought of mathematical harmonics.   Both Aristotle and Aristoxenus were fallen-away Pythagoreans,   as   it   were,   and   though   they   vigorously   criticized Pythagoreanism from within, they are a proper study in their own early thought of Pythagoreanism itself and of the history of Greek abstract reasoning (*Invariance*, p. 200n).   See also "Musical 'Marriages' in Plato's *Republic*," *Journal of Music Theory*, 18 (1974), 242-72.

[3] For a comprehensive treatise, see Louis Laloy, *Aristozène de Tarente . . . a la musique de l'antiquité* (Paris: Societé française d'impremerie et de librairie, 1904), esp. pp. 54-61.   Norman Cazden, in his article "Pythagoras and Aristoxenus Reconciled," *Journal of the American Musicological Society*, 11 (1958), 5-105, finds that Pythagoras stands for *before* and Aristoxenus for *after*: music in relation to nature, and in relation to man, respectively.   Pythagoras stands for what "is," Aristoxenus for what is humanly possible and acceptable.   Aristoxenus makes music theory *per se* possible.

[4] Aristokenus von Tarent, *Melik und Rhythmik des classischen Altertums,* ed. P. Saren (1883; rpt. Hildesheim: Georg Olms, 1965), I, 219.

[5] The Greeks from Pythagoras to Ptolemy devoted a great deal of their thinking to acoustics; we may mention, besides these, only Archytas and

Eratosthenes (third century B.C.)--and, much later, Claudius Didymus (b. 63 B.C.).

6 The word 'shades' introduces the subject of ancient terminology for the various arts. We of course use it for the definition of color, which in turn is a word specifically ruled out by Plato in descriptions of melodies (*Laws* 655); we may also apply the word *tonos* (tone) for any mode or scale to color. Harmony in music is symmetry in the visual arts. At the same time, we use the term 'color' for tonal variations, though Aristoxenus used it for variations (shades) within a given scale (24). The rhetorician Apollodorus of Pergamon (c.104-22 B.C.) developed a ratio of contrasts between lights, highlights, and shades, probably by relying on analogies with music.

J. J. Pollitt in *The Ancient World of Greek Art* (New Haven and London: Yale Univ. Press, 1974), p. 23, lists terms used for ancient art which had a common quality or entity in music: *rhythma* (shape, composition), *metra* (measurements), and *rhythmoi* (shapes) were sometimes arranged so as to form spatial equivalents of "perfect numbers" (*teleia*) which caused the whole work to express truth (*aletheia*). See also Silvio Ferri, *Tedenza unitaria delle arti nella Grecia antica,* Atti R. Accademia di Polermo, Ser. 4, No. 2 (1942), 531-60.

7 According to Henry S. Macran in his translation of Aristoxenus' *Harmonics*, p. 73.

I have already noted that Greek melody was unlike conventional modern melody in that it was not based on a closed "vertical" harmonic system. But the desire for unity, which is an aesthetic universal, called for a definition of the law or the relation of all tones of a scale to a central point. In modern compositions of the last two centuries written according to conventional harmonic structures, the tonic or central point is at the beginning of the scale and is usually heard at the beginning of the composition. In Greek music, however, the tonic had merely to appear frequently to establish itself. The scale or mode was determined not by the absolute position of the tonic, but by the relation of the tonic to the other notes in the mode; and the established tonic was then judged to be high or low, or higher and lower than other tonics. In modern harmony, the tonic is at the beginning of the scale; in the Greek modes, it was in the middle. From this middle point, the piece derived its unity, its pitch-character, and its name. Thus:

MODE	PLACE IN SCALE OF OF TONIC (OR *MĒSE*)	INTERVAL OF TONIC FROM TOP	INTERVAL OF TONIC TONIC FROM BOTTOM
Lydian	3 from top, 6 from bottom	1 1/2 tones	4 1/2 tones
Phrygian	4 from top, 5 from bottom	2 1/2 tones	3 1/2 tones
Dorian	5 from top, 4 from bottom	3 1/2 tones	2 1/2 tones

The Lydian mode was one tone higher than the Phrygian and two tones higher than the Dorian, and therefore the ethical characteristics of the three were presumably different. Assuming that Aristotle is right, that the Platonic (or Socratic) laws against the Lydian deny the proper mode to old men's failing voices (*Politics* 1342b), then Socrates (Plato?) was prejudiced not only against the unmanly and "relaxed" or "soft and drinking" modes but also against the enjoyments of old age.

[8] An enlightening account is to be found in Richard L. Crocker's "Aristoxenus and Greek Mathematics," in *Aspects of Medieval and Renaissance Music*, ed. Jan LaRue (New York: Pendragon Press, 1966), pp. 96-110.

Paul Marquardt, who translated into German and edited Aristoxenus' works, has diagrammed the knowledge they reveal of the accomplishments of the ancients, a knowledge theoretical (scientific and technical) and practical (educational and productive). The following chart is adapted from Marquardt, *Die harmonischen Elementen des Aristoxenus* (Berlin, 1868), with modifications.

KNOWLEDGE OF MUSIC

THEORY	PRACTICE	
Scientific Foundations	Technical Application	(Educational, Productive)
Arithmetic Physics	Harmonics Metrics Eurythmics	(Composition, vocal, bodily motion)

[9] See Rudolf Westphal, *Die Fragmente und Lehrsatze der griechischen Rhythmiker* (Leipzig: Teubner, 1861). Also helpful is Lewis Rowell's "Aristoxenus on Rhythm," *Journal of Music Theory*, 21 (1977), 61-79. I have used Ruth Halle Rowan, *Music Through Sources and Documents* (Englewood Cliffs, N.J.: Prentice-Hall, 1979), and also the more "popular" but highly useful work of C. F. Abdy-Williams, *The Aristoxenian Theory of Musical Rhythm* (Cambridge: Cambridge Univ. Press, 1911).

[10] *About the Ends of Goods and Evils* 5.50. Besides Cleonides, followers of Aristoxenus were Gaudentius, who wrote an abridgement of Aristoxenus in one "book"; Bacchus the Elder (*circa* first century A.D.), who wrote an *Introduction to Music*.

[11] Westphal, *Aristoxenus von Tarent*, II, cxl-liii, devised the following diagram and added his own nineteenth-century analyses which conform to Aristoxenian thought:

I. "APOTELESTIC" OR PLASTIC ARTS OF REPOSE AND SPACE	II. PRACTICAL, OR ARTS OF MOTION OR PERFORMANCE
	A. Subjective
Architecture	Music
	B. Subjective-Objective
Painting	Poetry
	C. Objective
Sculpture	Dancing
	General Formal Law: Regularity, Proportion
of space: symmetry	of time: rhythm

Reduced to Aristotle's doctrine of imitation, sculpture and dance are imitations of the natural, sculpture being an idealized imitation of the human body in a rigid, continuing material and dancing an idealization of the motions of the human body realized by human beings themselves. Both arts are therefore objective. Architecture and music, on the other hand, are subjective arts not because they are imitations or idealizations of something in nature, but because in them the ideal of beauty is immanent in the artistic spirit. But painting and poetry are both subjective and objective. Like the poet, the painter partakes of the beauty by which he presents the inner part of his soul as well as the outer world which is the model for his artwork.

[12] Williams, p. 7; see also p. 25.

[13] Westphal, *Fragments*, p. 28.

[14] Williams, p. 31.

[15] Ibid., p. 44.

[16] Ibid., p. 69.

[17] Ibid., pp. 95-99.

[18] George Malcolm Stratton, *Theophrastus and the Greek Physiological Psychology before Aristotle* (1917; rpt. Chicago: Argonaut, 1967), p. 35.

[19] Ibid., p. 50.

[20] The following material is summarized in and from Theophrastus, *Metaphysics*, trans. W. D. Ross and F. H. Fobes (1929; rpt. Hildesheim: Georg Olms, 1967), pp. xi-xvii.

[21] Ibid, pp. 15-17.

[22] See Düring, *Ptolemaos und Porphyrios*, pp. 160ff, and also Lippman, pp. 157-61.

[23] This is a doctrine derived from Aristotle in his comparisons of habit and potentiality with privation (*Categories* 10, 12a, 26ff; *Metaph.* 1046a).

In the later Middle Ages this theory was used by Franco of Cologne and Marchetto of Padua to characterize the musical rest and rhythmic perfection (or imperfection), respectively.

[24] Philodemus, *De musica*, ed. J. Kemke (Leipzig, 1884), p. 37.

[25] Düring, *Ptolemaos und Porphyrios*, p. 168.

CHAPTER V
The Hellenistic Dispersal of Greek Musical Theory: Epicureans and Stoics

[1] In the above paragraph, I am indebted to Gunther Wille, *Musica Romana* (Amsterdam: Schippers, 1967), pp. 716-23.

[2] According to Plutarch ("Reply to Colotes," *Moralia* 1109), Epicurus taught that all experiences reaching us through the senses are true, but that every perceptible thing is a blend, which means that there must be a difference of opinion about objects. But Plutarch, like Cicero, chastises him for allowing no place for discussions about music or for inquiries of critics and scholars "even over wine" ("A Pleasant Life Impossible," *Moralia* 1095). Does Epicurus not care, it is asked, to hear Theophrastus on concords, Aristoxenus on modulation, and Aristotle on Homer?

[3] For Philodemus, I have relied, in part, on Wladyslaw Tatarkiewicz, *History of Aesthetics* (The Hague: Mouton, 1970-74), 3 vols.; Hermann Abert, *Die Lehre vom Ethos in der griecheischen Musik* (Leipzig: Breitkopf und Härtel, 1899); and Hermann Pfrogner, *Musik: Geschichte ihrer Deutung*, pp. 54-58.

[4] Sometimes called of Seleucia (of the Middle Stoa). He wrote an *On Music* lost until 1783, when the thirty-six treatises attributed to Philodemus were discovered at Herculaneum.

[5] See L. P. Wilkinson, "Philodemus on Ethos in Music," *Classical Quarterly*, 32 (1938), 174-81.

[6] Cicero's *Scipio's Dream* eventually almost became a substitute for the *Timaeus* itself. The most famous commentary on it was by Macrobius (fourth and fifth centuries A.D.), but other commentaries were written by a contemporary and pupil of St. Augustine, called Favonius Eulogius. And the political interpretation of the music of the spheres was adopted in the seventeenth century by Jean Bodin and Athanasius Kircher, both of whom of course knew their Cicero.

CHAPTER VI
The Hellenistic Dispersal of Greek Music Theory

[1] Ernst Holzer, *Varronia*, Programm des Gymnasiums Ulm (1890).

[2] My summary depends on Holzer and on Wille, *Musica Romana*, pp.

414-20, both of whom give detailed evidence for the details of Varro's *Disciplines.*

3 See Francis W. Galpin, *The Music of the Sumerians* (Strasbourg: Strasbourg Univ. Press, 1955), Pl. vii.2.

4 See H. J. Zingel, "Die Harfe als Symbol und allegorisches Attribut," *Musikforschung,* 10 (1957). See also Boethius, *Consolation of Philosophy* 1, Prose 4, which supposedly provides the source of the popularity of the ass symbol in the Middle Ages. Reinhold Hammerstein, *Diabolus in Musica* (Bern and Munich: Francke, 1974), adds St. Jerome, Clement of Alexandria, and (considerably later) Hugh of St.-Victor (see *PL* 177.127) to the list of persons citing the legend.

The earliest account of the ass-harp or ass-lyre story is a fable of Phaedrus (*Babrius and Phaedrus,* trans. and ed. Ben Edwin Perry, Loeb Classical Library [Cambridge, Mass.: Harvard Univ. Press, 1965], p. 391), but here the ass simply says he is ignorant and that someone more skillful will have to be charmed by the lyre's divine music. William Stauder in "Asinus ad lyram," in *Helmuth Osthoff zum seinem siebzigsten Geburtstag* (Tutzig: H. Schneider, 1969), pp. 25-32, traces the story to the Sumerians and lists, with eight photographs, examples of the ass-lyre theme in Roman sculpture. The story also is found in medieval bestiaries. In medieval façades, portals, capitals, and other obvious places, the ass represents ignorance and evil in turn.

The ape is not given high place until Robert Fludd in the late Renaissance made man the ape of Nature. In satires and parodies of the Middle Ages, the ape (and monkey) often mimicked human behavior and appears as the player of an instrument, usually the vielle or fidel. See H. W. Janson, *Apes and Ape Lore in the Middle Ages and the Renaissance* (London: Warburg Institute, 1952), pp. 54-55, 70, figs. 117-19.

5 See also the aforementioned work by Holzer and also Hellfried Dahlmann, "Art: Varro," Pauly's *Real encyclopädie der classischen Altertumswissenschaft,* ed. Pauly-Wissowa (Stuttgart: Metzler, 1935), VI, 1172-1277; and D. Ribbeck, "Über Varronische Satiren," *Rheinisches Museum,* 14 (1859), 102-30.

6 Vitruvius may have known the Pseudo-Aristotelian chapter on voices in the *Problems,* where there are questions and remarks about the resonance of materials (plaster, in this case), the qualities of and the impressions caused by "thrown" voices, and the resonance of hollow vessels used in Greek theaters (899b-900a).

CHAPTER VII
Hebraism and Hellenism

1 Düring, *Ptolemaios und Porphyrios,* pp. 201-15.

2 Martianus Capella (fifth century A.D.) and Cassiodorus (fl. 520 A.D.) again mention fifteen modes.

³ See Matthew Shirlaw, "Claudius Ptolemy as Music Theorist," *Music Review*, 16 (1955), 181-90. Shirlaw shows how the manner of thinking about the modes changed sometime during the first century after Christ. Earlier, the Dorian was the dominating basic scale and the downward movement of the scales was the practice, just as the upward movement is modern practice. Through an enigmatic kind of transition in development, the reverse manner of perceiving the progression of tones within the scale took over. Possibly because of the higher tones of stringed instruments, the Lydian became the leading scale and then, later, the Hypolydian. But here Ptolemy is regressive. At the time when the Lydian scale was favored, he still held the Dorian to be the basic scale from which the others were derived. His calculations overrode the facts. See Ingemar Düring, *Porphyrios Kommentar zu Harmonielehre des Ptolemaos* (Göteborg: Erlander, 1932), pp. 5-6.

⁴ G. Junge, *Die Sphären-Harmonie und die Pythagorische-Platonische Zahlenlehre*, Classica et Mediaevalia, 9 (Copenhagen: Gyldendal, 1947).

CHAPTER VIII
Aristides Quintilianus

¹ John Hawkins, *A General History of the Science and Practice of Music*, introd. Charles Cudworth (1853; rpt. New York: Dover, 1963), I, 82-83. This work was originally published in five volumes in 1776.

² The numbers refer to the Meibom edition (Vol. II), but I use the Schäfke edition, recognizable in page numbers. The translation by Thomas J. Mathiesen (1983) was not available to me at the time when I wrote this chapter.

³ Thus Aristides Quintilianus divides the universe of elements into the sublunary regions and, in addition, that of ether. This is a division adopted by the Neoplatonists, but it derives from Xenocrates (396-314 B.C.), who added ether to the traditional four elements. A disciple of Plato, Xenocrates from 339 to 314 B.C. succeeded Speusippus, Plato's successor and heir, as president of the Academy. Ether also appears in Orphic philosophy (see *Ancilla*, pp. 3-4). It is additionally found in Anaxagoras (ibid., p. 83), and may possibly derive even from Philolaus. For Plotinus the Forms of Plato were ether eternally. See also Parmenides, in *Ancilla*, p. 45, and Aristotle, *On the Heavens* 1.2-3.

⁴ See Plato, *Republic* 428ff, *Laws* 963, and *Euthydemus* 279.

⁵ See Schäfke, in his translation of Aristides Quintilianus (p. 263), for geographical identifications.

CHAPTER IX
The Fruits of Hellenism: Plotinus and Neoplatonism

[1] My account of Plotinus' system is indebted to Stephen MacKenna's translation of the Enneads, 2nd ed. (London: 1962), pp. xxv-xxxi.

[2] For the analysis which follows, I am indebted to Hermann Abert, *Die Musikanschauung,* pp. 52-55.

[3] Laurence Jay Rosán, *The Philosophy of Proclus: The Final Phase of Ancient Thought* (New York: Cosmos, 1949), pp. 23-24, 27-28.

[4] There is an excellent discussion of Proclus in his intellectual and religious context (and also of the historical evidences in philosophical texts which lead up to him) in Thomas Witaker, *The Neoplatonists: A Study in the History of Hellenism,* 4th ed. (1918; rpt. Hildsheim: Georg Olms, 1961). Like Rosán, Whitaker confines himself to philosophy and avoids discussion of music. For Proclus' ideas about music and thus for the citations which follow, I am indebted to Abert, *Musikanschauung,* pp. 61-63.

CHAPTER X
The Decline of Hellenism

[1] Horace refers to the *tibia,* which is a term often translated as "flute":
sonante mixtus tibiis carmen lyra
hac Dorium, illis barberum . . . .
The confusion comes from the translation of different terms as "flute," a word that is used by translators as a kind of generic term for a wind instrument, including the Greek *aulos* and the Roman or Latin *tibia.* Only the scholar with an interest in music seems to wince when the terminology of instruments is inaccurate.

[2] See Stahl's Introduction, pp. 34-35.

[3] For Chalcidius, I am indebted to Wille, *Musica Romana,* pp. 599-601, and also to Bronislaw Switalski, *Chalcidius Kommentar zu Platos Timaeus,* Beiträge zur Geschichte der Philosophie des Mittelalters, 3, No. 6 (1902).

[4] From Iamblichus' *Theologoumena arithmeticae* Macrobius translates a paragraph about the number 7 and the stages of the development of the human embryo. Both Strato the Peripatetic, who was head of the Lyceum after Theophrastus, and Diocles of Carystus (third century B.C. or earlier) describe these stages according to seven-day periods. During the first period, the seed is surrounded with a sack; in the second period, drops of blood appear on the sack; in the third, the drops of blood work their way into the "humor" within; in the fourth, the humor in coagulating causes a "curdling intermediate between flesh and blood," liquid and solid; in the fifth (occasionally), the human shape is formed in the substance of the humor--no larger than a bee, it takes on the limits and contour of the body. If the limits are determined in the fifth period, the child is born in the

seventh month; if in the seventh (for a boy) or the sixth (for a girl), the child is born in the ninth month (1.6.65).

5 See Wille, *Musica Romana*, pp. 595-96.

Part II

CHAPTER XI
The Early Fathers

1 Robert Nisbet, *History of the Idea of Progress* (New York: Basic Books, 1978).

2 It has been conjectured that the repression of the dance and its exclusion from synagogue and church forced people to think about rhythm in the abstract apart, if not from music, at least from words. As an abstract phenomenon, it could appeal to ear, mind, and imagination and not precisely or especially to the more "sensuous" sense of sight. The result was an encouragement of the higher development of dance as an independent art.

3 For a concise description of types of antiphons and their role in the early liturgy, see the article by Michel Huglo in the *New Grove Dictionary of Music and Musicians*, I, 471-81. In its earliest use, the term defined matter sung along with a psalm; later, the antiphon would be an integral part of psalmody. Antiphons can also exist as separate chants, as in the case of the Marian antiphon *Alma redemptoris mater*, which is the song sung by the "litel clergeon" in Chaucer's Prioress' Tale.

4 The early form of worship, as described by Hippolytus, is conveniently summarized by Theodor Klausner, *A Short History of the Western Liturgy*, trans. John Halliburton, 2nd ed. (Oxford: Oxford Univ. Press, 1979), pp. 14-15.

5 There were cloister schools (with schola), episcopal schools (c.500-700) for second degree clerics, parochial schools, and palace schools (from the time of Charlemagne and later).

6 Abert, *Die Musikanschauung des Mittelalters*, p. 77.

7 Ibid., pp. 77-78.

8 D. W. Robertson, Jr., *A Preface to Chaucer: Studies in Medieval Perspectives* (Princeton, N.J.: Princeton Univ. Press, 1962), pp. 29-38. This work contains an excellent summary of the two "songs" in medieval visual art.

9 Hippolitus' contribution to instrumental allegory or symbolism strikes one as a copy of Clement. He finds that the psaltery is straight on all sides and hence symbolizes the even pathway to God, and that the cithara has a curved sound-box symbolizing the tortuous way to God. Since its sounds come from the upper part of the box and are sent upwards, the psaltery symbolizes the spirit. The cithara, whose tone goes downward, however, symbolizes the flesh, but the flesh of Christ made incarnate

because its sound-box and strings form the sign of the cross (*On the Psalms* [dubious fragments], *PG* 10.715).

[10] See Klausner, *Short History*, pp. 14-15.

[11] Charles Sears Baldwin, *Medieval Rhetoric and Poetic (to 1400)* (New York: Macmillan, 1928), p. x.

[12] Demons are an inheritance in Patristic writings from Neoplatonism. They are not to be confused with the Devil of the Hebrew scriptures, but rather are to be seen as lesser evil spirits, sometimes categorized as belonging to a rank higher than man but lower than the angels. Often demons were interpreted to be gods of the pagan cults.

[13] To anticipate: Ambrosian melodies apparently did not employ the eight modes, which in any case were probably not yet defined. They had a wider range than the melodies of Roman chant, which tended to dwell around the tetrachord. Probably free of codified rule and system, they were not required to follow the Roman model, and at least one modern scholar, Jean Hur, finds Ambrosian melodies more satisfying than the Gregorian (*Saint Augustin musicien* [M. Senart, 1924], p. 133n).

[14] There was a tendency in the early Church to attempt to suppress the hymn since it did not have a text derived directly from scripture; so the fourth-century Council of Laodicea objected to this form. The objection was not withdrawn until 633, when the fourth Council of Toledo approved this kind of composition. However, the form had already found an important place in the liturgy of the Mass and the Offices, being given a place in worship by the Rule of St. Benedict (c.530). See the convenient article by Ruth Steiner on the monophonic Latin hymn in the *New Grove Dictionary of Music and Musicians*, VIII, 838-41. Hymn texts are collected in *Analecta hymnica medii aevi*, ed. C. Blume and G. M. Dreves (Leipzig, 1886-1911), 55 vols.

[15] I have deliberately used the words "is said to have" in this sentence to indicate one degree of historical conjecture with which many statements in the rather uncertain history of Gregorian chant--and, to be sure, not of chant alone--must be characterized. On the accuracy or inaccuracy of dates, assertions, and interpretations of the "facts" in this history, see especially Willi Apel, *Gregorian Chant* (Bloomington: Indiana Univ. Press, 1958), pp. 38-42. About St. Jerome's probable role in the inclusion of the *alleluia* in the Mass and about its use elsewhere see ibid., pp. 376-77.

CHAPTER XII
St. Augustine

[1] Augustine saw only architecture of all the arts as an equal of music in arousing enjoyment. Number is their common ground (and thus music can be a fluid architecture, as Schelling claimed). Rules of number (the "perfect" ratios) must be applied to a beautiful edifice. Mathematical law, not feeling or sensibility (which can only uncertainly arrive at cosmic

harmony), is a metaphysical reality: the universal musical concords expressed in ratios partake of the ultimate sacred concord in architecture, and their contemplation can lead one to God. Religious art is a real art, the real being universal harmony. And thus the medieval architect followed and probably even benefited by the Augustinian theories of musical perception. See Otto von Simson, *The Gothic Cathedral* (1962; rpt. New York: Harper and Row, 1965), pp. 4-25.

2 Ibid., pp. 23, 507.

3 F. J. Thonnard, *Notes to [Augustine's] De Musica*, Oeuvres Bibliothèque Augustinienne, Ser. 1, No. 7, Pt. 4 (Paris, 1936), pp. 513-14, analyzes the difficulties of translating the Latin word *numerous*. He arrives at four possibilities: (1) as it is found in mathematics, (2) as rhythm, (3) as harmony among the parts of a physical movement, or as sensible, intellectual, or moral harmony in man, (4) as God in his supreme unity, a unity itself producing mathematical law, unity, rhythm, and harmonic forms in the activities of man and nature.

Augustine uses the number ratio 1:2 (the octave) to stand for the concord between the inferior nature of man and Christ himself (*On the Trinity* 4.2; FC 45.134): God was made flesh and died once, while man dies twice; Christ died and was resurrected, just as we die to our sins and are resurrected at baptism but shall die finally at the end of our lives. Christ and man are therefore as 1:2.

4 Augustine has numbered the Psalms according to an African Bible used in his day. The numbers in brackets, which I have supplied, are equivalents in the Vulgate and Douay-Rheims Bibles when the numbering systems differ.

5 The early Church Fathers tended to be rhetoricians, orators, and, sometimes, students of classical literature. In some cases they were ambiguous about the ancient gods and goddesses except as they could be interpreted as symbols. Augustine was not alone in subscribing to the euhemeristic theory of their origin (*City* 7.18, 8.26). Like Cassiodorus and Isidore of Seville later, he accepts the minor Greek gods (e.g., Orpheus) as legendary musicians and places David beside them (*City* 18.14). He is more censorious about the heathen gods who received pagan acceptance as if they constituted a religion based on astrology (he decries "the lying divinations and impious nonsense of the astrologers" [*Conf.* 7.6.8]). The heathen gods, he thinks, really exist as demons and relish the filthy stories told about them which cause injury to men (*City* 2.14).

Thus astrology is false and wicked. Thinkers of the past were right about God and wrong about the gods. The Stoics thought Fate was connected with astrology: they were wrong, because men and angels have free will. Because Plato denied materialism, he was superior to the philosophers Thales, Anaximenes, the Stoics, and Epicurus (*City* 8.5). For God is immanent, and the Platonists who followed God were of all men the nearest in logic and ethics to Christianity; and of all the Platonists, Plotinus understood God the best.

CHAPTER XIII
The Latin Textbook Pioneers

[1] Apuleius was known by his contemporaries and thereafter as a Platonist and encyclopedic savant. Martianus Capella was more likely under the influence of Neoplatonism than himself a Neoplatonist, and he was also influenced by Gellius. See the introduction by William Harris Stahl *et al.* in *Martianus Capella and the Seven Liberal Arts*, Records of Civilization, 84 (New York: Columbia Univ. Press, 1971), pp. 26-27.

[2] Latin compilers (the term is from *compilatio*--that is, plundering or pillaging) had no scruples about using any authority at all and even about listing authorities they had not in fact ever used. Copyright did not exist to protect the former, and honesty did not concern the latter. Stahl *et al.* (ibid., p. 41) call the compiler "a *poseur*, an encyclopedist pretending to a mastery of his subjects while skimming the surface." Martianus actually concealed his sources and often copied them verbatim. Orpheus, Pythagoras, Fabius Cunctator (the list is that of Stahl *et al.*), Cato, Thales, Democritus, Eratosthenes, Archimedes, Ptolemy were cited as a matter of convention whether they were actual references or not--and how could some of them be?

Citations from Martianus' text are from Stahl *et al.* and Gunther Wille, *Musica Romana* (Amsterdam, 1967), esp. pp. 634-54, 761-62.

[3] The corresponding Aristides Quintilianus references are for the *Harmonics* 1.1-12 and for the *Rhythmics* 1.13-19. In his commentary on Macrobius' *Commentary on the Dream of Scipio* (New York: Columbia Univ. Press, 1925), pp. 208-18, the translator William Harris Stahl gives a detailed analysis.

[4] Alexander Pope, *Essay on Criticism*, ll. 298 and 88, respectively.

[5] It must by now be clear that in a study such as this one it is literally impossible to record all instances of the mention of even a single aspect of the idea of music or its variations, to say nothing about all similarities and identities. For example, the story of Pythagoras' discovery of the numeral ratios of the concords from the blacksmith's hammers hardly undergoes change until Galileo Galilei (1564-1642) and Johannes Kepler (1571-1630) denied its validity. There is therefore general agreement about this story in the work of Nicomachus, Iamblichus, Macrobius, and Boethius. All also agree that music is "regulated" by divine reason and is therefore intellectual--a point on which Pliny (2.84), Chalcidius (73), and Censorius (11.3-5) also agree. Instances of quotation and misinterpretation (especially of the *Timaeus*) are legion.

[6] Which Albinus this was is not known with certainty. He is also mentioned by Cassiodorus. See J. Freudenthal, "Der Platoniker Albinos und der falsche Alkinos," *Hellenistic Studien*, 3 (1895), 275ff, 322. Wille, *Musica Romana*, p. 597, says that he flourished c.335 but that his work is lost.

[7] Boethius was perhaps the first person to introduce the term *quad-*

rivium, which appeared in his *De institutione arithmetica* 1.1, where it was applied to the mathematical disciplines.

[8] Of course Boethius is referring to the modes as defined in Greek antiquity and hence as known to him only by report. The ecclesiastical modes of the Middle Ages were not yet defined. As a presenter in Latin of the Greek modal system, including also the two-octave (Greater Perfect) System, in ancient theory, Boethius was highly influential until the tenth century. Unfortunately, the anonymous author of an *Alia musica* (wrongly identified as Hucbald in G 1.125) misinterpreted the system, whether as outlined by Ptolemy or Boethius is not known, and gave the ecclesiastical modes the names of the ancient ones. The ecclesiastical modes, unnamed but numbered, seem to have been referred to by the author of an anonymous treatise formerly attributed to Alcuin, as we shall see, and the general confusion betweeen ancient and medieval modes and their names is now well known.

[9] "Instrumental music" here means *practical* and includes vocal music in that it imitates world and human music. It was once thought that Boethius had ignored vocal music, but the term 'instrumental' here signifies part of what later was called "natural" and all of "artificial" music.

[10] Cf. Aristotle, *On the Soul* 420b, *Historia Animalum* 505a, 535a-536b, *On the Generation of Animals* 786b-788a.

[11] Hawkins, *General History*, p. 124.

[12] *The Letters of Cassiodorus*, trans. Thomas Hodgkin (London: Frowde, 1886), p. 169.

[13] Ibid., pp. 193-94.

[14] The actual early identification of Orpheus with Christ in early catacomb paintings is well known.

[15] All references are to the section of Book 2 entitled "Secular Letters," in Cassiodorus' *Divine and Human Readings*, beginning on p. 189 of the edition I have used.

[16] Oliver Strunk (*Source Readings in Music History*) rightly notes that this passage comes from Augustine (*Divine Providence* 2.14). Isidore calls for an effective notation to help the memories of singers, and writes in his *Etymologies* (2.15.2) as if notation does not exist at this time. Lawrence Gushee ("Questions of Genre in Medieval Treatises on Music," in *Gattungen der Musik in Einzelderstellungen: Gedankskrift Leo Schrade*, ed. Leo Wulf Arnlt *et al.* [Berne: Francke, 1973], pp. 583-86) thinks, however, that he regrets that music is made up of sound "inarticulata et illiterata" and thus belongs at the bottom of a list of types of sounds cited by the Latin grammarian Priscian (*Institutiones grammaticae* 1.1-2). The locus of Isidore's remarks is grammar, a "trivial" subject, and not either quadrivially scientific or "practical." But he cannot mean more than that sounds disappear as soon as they are made and that there is no exact mode of writing them down.

[17] The numerical indications correspond with the edition of Isidore's *Etymologies* which I have used, and are supplemented by Wille, *Musica Romana*, esp. pp. 711-15, 757-58.

18 The first epics, he thinks, were composed not by Homer or Pherecydes (fifth century B.C.), who were contemporaries of Saul, but by Moses as he sang his song of triumph after crossing the Red Sea. David preceded Timothy in singing before God, Solomon's song antedated the first epithalamia of the Greeks, and Jeremiah's lamentations preceded Simonides' laments. Writing was a Jewish invention, not a Phoenician one. The first poets were Jewish. Tubal (Jubal), not Apollo, composed the first instrumental melody.   Abraham contemplated the stars and founded astronomy long before Atlas (1.39).

19 Not Apollo but Jubal is credited with inventing the cithara and psaltery. The invention of the cithara by Apollo is merely a Greek tradition. The ancient cithara had seven strings because that number filled the range of human voice and because the heavens make sound with seven motions. The psaltery also had seven strings, but the Hebrew psaltery had ten because of the Ten Commandments.   Isidore, treating other instruments in similar fashion, describes accepted tradition, true to fact or not. All this of course he derives directly from his sources; for example he copies Cassiodorus' pun that strings (*chordae*) were so called from *cor/cordis* (heart), the striking of strings being like the beating of the heart.

20 In the post-classical era, astronomical authors were supposed to be Abraham, Moses, and Promethius; see *Martianus Capella and the Seven Liberal Arts*, introd. Stahl *et al.*, p. 242.

21 *Organ*, Isidore explains, "is the generic name of all musical vessels"; he adds that the Greeks had another kind of organ, an instrument so-called, activated by bellows (*Etymologies* 3.22.2). Cassiodorus speaks of *organum musicum* as a type (*Ps.* 4, Pref.; *PL* 70.47).

22 For Isidore's influence on the qualities of good singing, see Audrey Ekdahl Davidson, "High, Sweet, and Clear: Singing Early Music," in *Sacra/Profana: Studies in Sacred and Secular Music for Johannes Riedel*, ed. Audrey Ekdahl Davidson and Clifford Davidson (Minneapolis: Friends of Minnesota Music, 1985), pp. 217-26.

23 *Music, History, and Ideas* (Cambridge, Mass.: Harvard Univ. Press, 1941), p. 48.

CHAPTER XIV
The Carolingian and Post-Carolingian Age

1 Bede was symptomatic of the successful effort to keep learning alive in Britain at a time when Western Europe was suffering a decline. Sometimes called the outstanding scholar of the early Middle Ages, he in some ways continued Isidore's work. Like Isidore, he wrote a *De natura rerum*. Both were less concerned with philosophical speculation than with useful learning and with serving the needs of the Church. Bede wrote a highly regarded ecclesiastical history of England (731) which remains a principal source of information about Anglo-Saxon times, and as an analytical writer,

according to the fashion of the time, he stressed versification and grammar rather than literature. He is also credited with having written an *Ars metrica*, a text-book based on his knowledge of Latin, Greek, and Hebrew. He applies the term 'rhythmics' to either quantitative or accentual poetry. Of the more than one hundred different measures usually described in texts like his, he analyzes chiefly the dactylic (or the heroic) hexameter and other Latin meters, including the measures of certain Christian poets. He compares rhythmic with metric verse, both being a harmonized pattern of words, and recalls Cicero, Quintilian, and Augustine.

Bede admires the verse of Virgil, and like St. Jerome he thinks that metrical verse is present in the Bible; for him, sacred and profane writers are equally valid as models, but the word-forms of the Scriptures are authoritative. Rhythm is a harmonious proportional order of words achieved by a recurrence of syllables satisfactory to the ear. Meter is a system resulting in harmony; ratio is its base; rhythm, on the other hand, is based on temporal proportion and is harmony without regular system (*De arte metrica* 14, *De rhythmo* 173-74). There are therefore verse-forms based both on quantity (rhythm: number in syllables) and quality (meter: accent), and aesthetic quality adheres to both. For Bede, an example of a third kind of rhythm was found in the Ambrosian hymn, which according to classical rules was deficient. Thus the Ambrosian hymn serves as an example of the influence of music on verse itself. His sources included a long list of grammarians and scholiasts. See Richard Crocker, "*Musica Rhythmica* and *Musica Metrica* in Antique and Medieval Theory," *Journal of Music Theory*, 2 (1958), 8-15.

For the rest (and if other writings are actually his), Bede continues to be fairly conventional. He says that music is both heavenly and earthly and that it has a mathematical base (*Musica theorica*, PL 90.910ff). Music is a free science--a liberal art--dealing with the art of singing. Its sub-species are instrumental, human, and rhythmical. A good singer who is also a musician exercises the art or singing, but is also a theorist. The true musician can explain music, the mere singer can only perform it.

While the *De arte metrica* is undoubtedly by Bede, the *Musica theorica* cited in the previous paragraph and also the *Musica quadrata seu mensurata* are probably not his. The last two are also attributed to a thirteenth-century Pseudo-Aristotle, an Englishman who went by the name of Magister Lambert. The confusion is compounded by the printing of Lambert's work as Bede's by Migne (in *PL* 90) and by Coussemaker (in Cou 1).

[2] Denes Zoltai, *Ethos und Affekt,* trans. Bela Weingarten (Berlin: Academie Verlag, 1970), p. 74.

[3] Tartarkiewicz, *History of Aesthetics,* II, 100.

[4] Rudolf Schäfke, *Geschichte der Musikästhetik im Umrissen,* 2nd ed. (Tutzing: Hans Schneider, 1964), pp. 212-13.

⁵ These points are conveniently summarized in Bertrand Russell, *A History of Western Philosophy* (New York: Simon and Shuster, 1945), pp. 303-04.

⁶ Rosán, p. 10.

⁷ Ibid., pp. 138, 223.

⁸ Kathi Meyer-Baer, *The Music of the Spheres and the Dance of Death* (Princeton, N.J.: Princeton Univ. Press, 1970), p. 51.

⁹ Erigena (John the Scot) has been called the first Scholastic, though Alcuin and Rabanus Maurus in certain ways anticipated him and, along with Boethius, are sometimes said to have a place ahead of him. First applied to a teacher in ecclesiastical schools of the Seven Liberal Arts, the term 'Doctor Scholasticus' later designated thinkers who specialized in dialectic or logic and in the philosophical problems related to those subjects. Scholasticism may thus be described as a trend extending from the ninth century to the fifteenth. Logic and theology, reason and authority or faith, universals, and eventually nominalism (or conceptualism) as opposed to realism (as interpreted variously in the light of Plato and Aristotle)--all of these were the staples of scholastic discussion. Until translations into Latin through the Arabs of the basic works of Aristotle were disseminated in the West in the twelfth and thirteenth centuries, the texts often discussed were those referred to in this book: Chalcidius on the *Timaeus*, Boethius' translations of Aristotle as well as his translation of Porphyry, the works of Macrobius, St. Augustine, Martianus Capella, Cassiodorus, and Isidore of Seville--in other words, secondary works which only reflect certain Greek ideas of antiquity.

Among Scholastics in general there was less interest in art than in the beautiful (though later Scholastics made much of specific sense impressions, and especially of light as symbolizing the luminosity of science or knowledge) and specifically in beauty as it could be identified with the good. And this is why music, like each of the other arts and sciences, should have been only a small (though important) part of the philosophical and aesthetic thought of the ecclesiastical writers of the Middle Ages. The constant aim and objective was not the parts, but the whole which is ideal, permanent, annd universal.

¹⁰ Two virtually complete lists of works embracing music theory in medieval Europe are to be found in J. Smits van Waesberghe, *Musikerziehung: Lehre und Theorie den Musik im Mittelalter* (Leipzig: Deutscher Verlag für Musik, 1968), pp. 195-98.

¹¹ Unfortunately, prior to the ninth century there is little evidence concerning the actual practice of chant in the West; for a list of relevant documents, see Apel, *Gregorian Chant*, pp. 38-42.

¹² For the history of the medieval tonary, see the description in Michel Huglo, *Les Tonaires: Inventaire, Analyse, Compa*rison (Paris: Societé français de musicologie, 1971).

¹³ For a discussion of Hucbald, see Rembert Weakland, "Hucbald as Musician and Theorist," *Musical Quarterly*, 42 (1956), esp. 84. The *Musica*

enchiriadis was also at various times attributed to Otiger (d. 940), a shadowy figure who was once Abbot of St. Pons de Tomieres, and to Hoger (d. 902), an abbot of Werden. The work today is generally regarded as anonymous, though all students of its text are not in agreement (see Strunk, p. 126).

[14] Adapted from Gustave Reese, *Music in the Middle Ages* (New York: Norton, 1940), p. 115.

[15] The first example is from G 1.119, and the second is from *Hucbald, Guido, and John on Music*, trans. Warren Babb, ed. Claude V. Palisca (New Haven: Yale Univ. Press, 1978), p. 98.

[16] Zoltai, pp. 87-88, points out that ecclesiastics conveniently forgot the Aeolian and Hypoaeolian and the Ionian and Hypoionian modes which later played a part in the development of the major-minor system. These modes are to be found in medieval secular (especially folk and dance) music. The eight-mode system as described in work formerly attributed to Alcuin was restricted to church music, but allowed secular music, not limited to rules devised by the Church, to go its own way.

[17] Calvin Bower, "The Modes of Boethius," *Journal of Musicology*, 3 (1984), 252-63.

[18] See also Harold S. Powers in *The New Grove Dictionary of Music and Musicians*, XII, 377-96, and (on tonality) Apel, *Gregorian Chant*, pp. 137-44.

[19] This grammatico-literary device of distinction making, valuable for the singer, who had to control his voice, and necessary for the listener, who wanted to understand what was sung, was variously described. The medieval theorist's efforts to make this technical matter clear are excellently summarized in Frederick Baron Crane, "A Study of Theoretical Writings on Musical Form to ca. 1460," unpubl. Ph.D. diss. (State Univ. of Iowa, 1960), *passim.*

[20] *Die Lehre vom Ethos in der griechischen Musik* (Leipzig: Breitkopf und Härtel, 1899), pp. 69ff.

[21] Schäfke, *Geschichte der Musikästhetik*, p. 268.

[22] François Gevaert, *La mélopée antique dans le chant de l'Église latine* (Paris: Gand, 1895-96), p. 125.

[23] The authoritative work on the NOEANE system is Terence Bailey, *The Intonation Formulas of Western Chant* (Toronto: Pontifical Institute of Mediaeval Studies, 1974).

[24] Since my discussion focuses on the intellectual background of music in the ninth to the eleventh centuries, it may be useful to remind readers that my analysis cannot serve as a substitute for the music itself, even if the music is primarily inherent in the words of the texts. I have not appended a discography here, but I am able to recommend Derrick Henry, *A Listener's Guide to Medieval and Renaissance Music* (New York: Facts on File, 1983), pp. 4ff and, for recordings of church music discussed here, pp. 13-17.

[25] A succinct and comprehensive account of Arabic scholarship

during this period is conveniently given in Frederick Charles Copleston, *History of Philosophy* (rpt. Garden City, N.Y.: Doubleday, 1962), II, 213-19.

26 Avicenna was an outstanding physician. As such he knew of Galen (second century A.D.), who formulated the medical canon accepted for centuries and explained in detail the relation of musical rhythm to pulse-beat. Avicenna asserted that Galen divided pulse-beat by these ratios: double time is 3:4, "common" time is 4:5, time 5:6. He also reported that persons with a sensitive touch, a keen sense of rhythm, and training in music can correlate such minutiae of observation in the mind. See Cameron Gruner, *A Treatise on the Canon of Medicine of Avicenna,* incorporating a translation of the first book (London: Luzac, 1930), pp. 292-93.

27 Henry George Farmer, *Historical Facts for the Arabian Musical Influence* (London: W. Reeves, 1930), pp. 67-68, 286-88.

28 Ibid., p. 326.

CHAPTER XV
The Middle Ages: The Eleventh and Twelfth Centuries

1 Karl Popper, *Unended Quest: An Intellectual Autobiography* (1974; rpt. LaSalle, Illinois: Open Court, 1976), p. 56.

2 Berno was not alone among theorists, of course, in giving prominence and even predominance to the number 4. William of Hirsau (d. 1091) in his dialogue *De musica et tonis* confines himself to purely technical structural matters, but exhibits a pronounced love of the number 4 and is convinced that everything related to it takes precedence and has a higher rank from the very beginning (G 2.157). When a certain tonality has been selected for a melody, he says, its chief tone (that is, the tetrachord) must have first place throughout the duration of the song. They claim the control of the entire monochord and are superior to the other tones, which willingly serve them (G 2.171). He thinks the lowest tone of the tetrachord is the source of all the others and has a preferred place in the tonal system. He arrives at this conclusion through mathematical calculation (G 2.156). Like many of his predecessors, he is struggling for a definition of form and finds that the *finale* governs, organizes, and furnishes a standard of judgment of the whole (G 2.157).

3 Schäfke, *Geschichte der Musikästhetik*, p. 202.

4 In mentioning the organ, Aribo was anticipated by a writer, possibly Notker Labeo (d. 1022) of St. Gall, who wrote a treatise in Old High German which included a section entitled *Mensura fistularum organicorum,* about pipe organs, as one of its four chapters (G 1.101-02). This instrument was widely used for church music already by this time.

5 Medieval symbolism was part of a system of linguistic interpretation in which the poet reveals divine truth in human terms. This system has been long thought to have been outlined fully first in Dante's Letter to Can

Grande Scala in 1319 as an introduction to the *Paradiso* (see also *Convivio* 2 [c.1304-08]), but it appears very much earlier in explanations of the theological effort to relate the literal sense of the scriptures to the superior truths of Christianity. Origen mentions somatic, psychical, and penumatic (spiritual) meanings; Cassian (Johannes Cassianus) (c.360-c.435) in his *Collationes* 14 (*De spirituali scientia* 8; *PL* 49.963-64), Bede, and Rabanus Maurus refer to historical, tropological, allegorical, and anagogical meanings (*PL* 125.513). St. Jerome uses different terminology (*PL* 22.1005), as does Thomas Aquinas, but they are almost synonymous with Cassian's. The literal level is obvious, and Hugh of St.-Victor (*Didasc.* 6.3) specifically defends it as "history" against its critics. Cassian names the historical level as literal, and the typological level as that on which the Old Testament anticipates the New in a prophetic way. He adds that the tropological or moral level appeals to the individual soul, and that the final--the analogical level--refers to the Heavenly City. These classifications are of course more relevant to literature than to music, but since music accompanied the psalms and induced Christians through the hymn to worship through literary texts, it must also have shared in the symbolical levels of meaning attributed to spoken poetry.

For an excellent treatment of literary and linguistic interpretation from the aesthetic point of view, see Monroe C. Beardsley, *Aesthetics from Classical Greece to the Present* (New York: Harcourt Brace, 1966), pp. 105-14. See also H. Flanders Dunbar, *Symbolism in Medieval Thought* (New Haven: Yale Univ. Press, 1929), though I can find only one reference to music in the text and none in the index.

6 Quoted in Willi Apel, *The Notation of Polyphonic Music 900-1600* (Cambridge, Mass.: Harvard Univ. Press, 1949), p. 132; and also Hugo Riemann, *History of Music Theory*, I-II, trans. Raymond H. Haggh (Lincoln: Univ. of Nebraska Press, 1962), p. 374, on rhythm and hymn singing.

7 Simson, *The Gothic Cathedral*, p. 41.

8 Georges Duby, *The Age of the Cathedral: Art and Society, 980-1420*, trans. Eleanor Levieux and Barbara Thompson (Chicago: Univ. of Chicago Press, 1981), p. 101.

9 Charles W. Haskins, *The Renaissance of the Twelfth Century* (Cambridge, Mass.: Harvard Univ. Press, 1939), p. 7.

10 Egon Wellesz, *History of Byzantine Music and Hymnography*, 2nd ed. (Oxford: Clarendon Press, 1961), pp. 60-62.

11 Pierre Abailard, *Opera*, ed. V. Cousin (Paris: Imprimerie royale, 1849-59), II, 384, as cited by Simson, *The Gothic Cathedral*, p. 37. For examples of Abelard's own compositions, see Peter Dronke, *Poetic Individuality in the Middle Ages* (Oxford: Clarendon Press, 1970), pp. 114-49.

12 Simson, *The Gothic Cathedral*, p. 38.

13 Ludwig Baur, *Dominic Gundissalinus, Le Divisione Philosophie*, Beiträge zur Philosophie des Mittelalters, 4, Pts. 2-3 (1903), pp. 102ff.

14 Simson, *The Gothic Cathedral*, p. 199.

[15] Ibid., pp. 124-26, 132; *Abbot Suger on the Abbey Church of St. Denis and Its Art Treasures*, ed. and trans. Erwin Panofsky, 2nd ed. (Princeton: Princeton Univ. Press, 1979), pp. 82-85.

[16] Simson, *The Gothic Cathedral*, p. 51.

[17] Jerome Taylor, ed. and trans.: Hugh of St. Victor, *Didascalicon* (New York and London: Columbia Univ. Press, 1962), p. 10.

[18] Ibid., p. 31.

[19] See Simson, *The Gothic Cathedral*, pp. 29-30.

[20] Taylor, ed. and trans.: Hugh of St. Victor, *Didascalicon*, p. 169n.

[21] Heinrich Oster, *Die Psychologie des Hugo von St. Viktor*, BGPM (Münster: Aschendorf, 1906), p. 20.

[22] See also Taylor, ed. and trans.: Hugh of St. Victor, *Didascalicon*, pp. 205n, 206n.

[23] Aelred of Rievaulx, *Speculum Charitatis* 2.33, as quoted by Karl Young, *The Drama of the Medieval Church* (Oxford: Clarendon Press, 1933), I, 548; see also *PL* 195.571.

[24] Simson, *The Gothic Cathedral*, pp. 48-50.

[25] *Super cantica canticorum* 23.16, as quoted by Rosario Assunto, *Die Theorie des Schönen im Mittelalter*, trans. Christa Baumgarten (Cologne: Dumont Schauberg, 1963), p. 154.

[26] M. Baumgarten, *Die Philosophie des Alanus des Insulis*, Beiträge zur Geschichte des Philosophie des Mittelalters, 2, Pt. 4 (1896), pp. 28-29.

[27] Ibid., pp. 32, 71-73.

[28] Meyer-Baer, *The Music of the Spheres and the Dance of Death*, p. 125.

[29] Gerhard Pietzsch, *Die Klassification der Musik von Boethius bis Ugolino von Orvieto* (1829; rpt. Darmstadt, 1968), p. 73.

[30] H. Willner, *Des Adelard von Bath Traktat De eodem et diverso*, Beiträge zur Geschichte des Philosophie des Mittelalters, 4, Pt. 3 (1903), pp. 23, 89-90.

[31] Ibid., p. 16.

[32] Ibid., pp. 25-29, 99.

[33] He is supposed also to have written a *De septem artibus liber* which may have been identical with the *De eodem*.

[34] A. C. Crombie, *Medieval and Early Modern Science* (Garden City, N.Y.: Doubleday, n.d.), I, 37-47, has a list of the principal sources of science in the West from 500 to 1300 A.D.

[35] Farmer, *Historical Facts*, pp. 11, 23.

[36] Baur, *Dominic Gundissalinus*, pp. 2-3.

[37] Ibid., p. 100.

[38] Ibid., p. 98.

[39] Ibid., pp. 247-48. In his eclecticism Gundisalvo reminds one of the Arabic-Jewish scholars of his century.   For example, Maimonides (1135-1204), who studied under Arabic scholars, tried to reconcile Judaism with Arabic Aristotelianism, admits that exceptional people can reach a higher wisdom through music, but holds that the majority (for whom the

laws of the Torah were recorded) under musical influence are often only inspired to lust because linguistic content is the real inciting (and therefore controlling) factor in music: thus it is best used for religious and not secular purposes, though it can produce therapeutic results. Like Aristotle and Al Farabi, Maimonides regarded the idea of music of the spheres with skepticism. For a comparison of Arabic-Jewish music theory with Greek and medieval theories, see Eric Werner and Isaiah Sonne, "The Philosophy and Theory of Music in Judaeo-Arabic Literature," *Hebrew College Annual*, 16 (1941), 251-319; 17 (1942-43), 253-72.

40 William G. Waite, *The Rhythm of Twelfth-Century Polyphony: Its Theory and Practice* (New Haven: Yale Univ. Press, 1954), p. 45.

CHAPTER XVI
The Philosophers of the High Middle Ages

1 Duby, *Age of Cathedrals*, p. 162.

2 Alberto F. Gallo, "Astronomy and Music in the Middle Ages: The *Liber Introductorius* by Michael Scott," *Musica Disciplina*, 27 (1973), 5-9.

3 For the thought of Robert Grosseteste, I am indebted to Ludwig Baur, "Die Philosophie des Robert Grosseteste, Bischofs von Lincoln," *BGPM*, 18 (1917), and A. C. Crombie, *Robert Grosseteste and the Origins of Experimental Science, 1100-1700* (Oxford: Oxford Univ. Press, 1953).

4 J. W. H. Atkins, *Literary Criticism: The Medieval Phase* (Cambridge: Cambridge Univ. Press, 1943), p. 124.

5 Possibly a pupil of Robert Grosseteste but surely an acquaintance and colleague, Thomas of York (d. 1260), lecturer at Oxford and Cambridge, wrote a *Sapientale* (*Wisdom of the World or Universe* [1250-60]) which has been said to be the first autonomous metaphysical work in the West. His citations are "universal": the *Timaeus*, Aristotle, Trismegistus, Cicero, Seneca, Macrobius, Augustine, William of Auvergne, Pseudo-Dionysius, Avicenna, and Algazel. What is good, he asks, what is one, true, beautiful, and ordered, what has the transcendental properties which can cause one to ascend to God and praise beauty, goodness, unity, truth, and reason? Clearly, it is a universal music, a reflection of an immense concert of incomparable sweetness finding its source in divine melody unfolding itself. God is beauty itself, and the world is the most perfect and best possible work. Nothing exists which is better than the world; nothing is superior to it; not only is nothing more beautiful, but something better cannot even be conceived. What is beauty itself? It is number. Thus Thomas of York bases his aesthetic on music and form. See Edgar de Bruyne, *Études d'esthétique médiévale* (Bruges: De Tempel, 1946), III, 227ff.

6 Fortunately for Michel Scot, Hugh of St.-Victor, Roger Bacon, and Albertus Magnus, the term 'magician' or 'magus' usually carried a scientific connotation: a magus could be a savant who was trying to discover the

(chemical, alchemical, physical, "electrical") secret of the earth (which God had placed there). But the medieval Church in general frowned on magic, and its pursuit had to go underground. The term 'magician' generally was used only surreptitiously because magic itself was thought to be "black," furtive in action, and evil. As it had appeared in Iamblichus and Porphyry, however, it was not thought to indicate ignorance, inferiority, or profound evil. Orphic hymns, said to date from the second or third centuries A.D. and believed to have originated with Orpheus himself who was known as the second among the *prisci theologi* (Hermes being usually the first), were eventually allowed, and an acceptable "white" magic came to the fore in the Renaissance.

Alchemy was based on the supposition that all matter is unified and that any element of it can be transformed within the principle of differentiation. Unities in the physical world could be changed into other unities. Also, opposites could be combined to bring about new unities in constructions and substances. Basic to the enterprise also was the idea of universal correspondences. Alchemy was the most popular of all the applied sciences. It was thought that in no other way could the influences of the planets be explained. Astronomy was the noblest science and astrology the greatest determinant of men's affairs--except, of course, for God alone. Tubalcain (not Jubal) was often allied with alchemy.

⁷ For the thought of Albertus Magnus, I am indebted to Heinrich Hüschen, "Albertus Magnus und seine Musikanschauung," in *Speculum Musicae Artis*, ed. Heinz Becker and Reinhard Gerlach (Munich: Fink, 1870), pp. 206-18.

⁸ It has been assumed that opposites dynamically lead to a synthesis and that conflicts could be and were resolved even in argument. The method of Albertus Magnus and Thomas Aquinas was to give the two sides of a question, to choose one side, and then to raise objections against the rejected one. The two sides often did not merge into one. The modern idea (as in Hegel) is that the two opposing sides are dramatically reconciled to make something new, a progress or a "creation." Thus Coleridge, like Hegel, differs from the medieval thinker and also even from the Pythagoreans. In the Middle Ages, the aim was to find a point of repose within a hierarchical system. The modern desire is through a restless search to make an "advance" over the past. In personal terms, the former offers satisfaction to the individual in his being absorbed into his context; the latter assumes that the individual will go forward (or "express himself") to establish his uniqueness. The first creates a situation which calms and quiets, the second (the "romantic") a situation in which one creates something "new" and disturbing. See Robertson, *Preface to Chaucer*, pp. 11-13, 17-18.

⁹ See also Apel, *Gregorian Chant*, p. 267.

¹⁰ Pfrogner, *Musik*, pp. 132-33, quotes from a (probably spurious) Thomasian *De arte musica* in a manuscript at Turin, Italy; this treatise is based on the *Tractatus de musica* (c.1240-50) of Pseudo-Aristotle (not the

anonymous Peripatetic philosopher, but Magister Aristotle Lambert). God, in his mercy, it is said, gave man the ability to cultivate the arts in order to procure wisdom, virtue, and eloquence. In them man's pleasures are raised to a high plane, and among the Seven Liberal Arts music alone can resound pleasantly in the Church triumphant and Militant. It is the music the angels sound in their prayers, through which mercy is asked for the remission of sins, the mourning are given strength, the mentally disturbed can find release, and those in battle are given courage. The author cites Isidore's *Etymologies*: it is as much of a shame not to be able to sing as to know nothing of science because every day the Angels and Archangels, the Thrones and Dominions, with all the heavenly hosts, sing "Holy, holy, holy" unceasingly. Like the Venerable Bede, he declares that music alone of the sciences dares to enter the Church. All of this is so derivative that one suspects it could be Thomas Aquinas' work after all.

11 (Fl. 1230-50), *De proprietatibus rerum*: an encyclopedic effort in which are drawn illustrations of a perfect heaven, an imperfect earth, Christ as Plato's demiurge creating the four elements, the tetrad for the explaining of time, the shepherd's calendar, the occupations of the months, the tetrad of Evangelists in support of God's throne. There are three worlds: (1) the non-corporeal archetypal world, (2) the sense-perceptible world made up of the four elements and the quintessential ether, and (3) the human world or microcosm. All of this is allied with music.

The work was translated into English by John Trevisa in 1398, and the text alone without illustrations was published in 1495 by Wynkyn de Worde at Westminster. Stephen Bateman in 1582 translated and commented on it under the title *Batman uppon Bartholome his booke De proprietatibus rerum*.

12 H. Müller in "Zur Musikauffassung des 13. Jahrhundert," *Archiv für Musikwissenschaft*, 4 (1922), 407, holds that the theory of total composition as found in Bacon, Al Farabi, and others is a preview of Wagner's total work of art (*Gesamtkunstwerk*). But they suggested no such thing and spoke in terms of collection or concretion, of simultaneous procedure in time. The addition seems less cohesive, "organic," or completely one than a combination, an adding together. They do not describe a mystic unity. They are not at one with the Idea (close as Plotinus comes to thinking music so). Medieval art was not nineteenth-century art.

CHAPTER XVII
Music Theories and Theorists of the High Middle Ages

1 He also lists instruments: conical and straight trumpets (*buccina, tuba*), shawm (*calamo*), organistrum (*symphonia*), cittern (*sistra*), pipe (*tibia*), *sambuca* (variously defined in the Middle Ages as a stringed or woodwind instrument), psaltery, harp (*cithara*), lyre, harmonica, drum (*tympanon*), cymbal, and bell (*tintinnabulo*). The enumeration is taken over

by one of Zamora's imitators and followers, Batholomaeus Anglicus, who studied or taught at Oxford, Paris, and Magdeburg (see also Chap. XVI, n. 11).

[2] An entirely different kind of classification of music, one which never received acceptance, was that of Absolom (twelfth and thirteenth centuries), an abbot of Springiersbach, near Trier. In his twentieth sermon on the Annunciation in his *Sermones festivales*, he speaks of God as the supreme musician who has created animalic music (the interval of the fifth: the outer senses do not demand anything superfluous and do not deviate from the path of reason, so that the eye sees nothing vain, the ear hears no slander, smell searches for nothing delightful and taste for nothing in excess, and the hand grabs nothing forbidden: these are the five tones of animalic music that result in the five steps of harmony, which proceed from the five sense organs regulated by order). There also are spiritual music (the interval of the fourth: the growth in virtue, the spiritual joy and mildness of custom, the fear of God, and the love of neighbor deriving from the four virtues of bravery, justice, moderation, and prudence so that in all things well done bravery brings support, justice shows the way to judgment, measure brings comfort, and prudence dispenses advice); and heavenly music (the interval is the octave: its existence is in the contemplation of God, a longing for the eternal, serenity of mind, and immortality of the flesh; here is a harmony of eight steps produced by eight kinds of bliss or blessing when the heavenly kingdom is given to the poor, the earth of the living to the meek, comfort to the sad, nourishment to the hungry, and so forth, delineating the Corporal Acts of Mercy as set forth in *Matthew* 25). All represent, of course, the harmony of morals more than of voices (*PL* 211.121ff). These musics are all allegorical; all literary, they can be discovered in various writings but in not so concentrated a form; as combined here, they have no connection with music proper--except as an elaborate, ornamental, Christian "cosmic" music.

[3] Though the development outlined here has been previously described in terms of evolution, it is important not to imply that such development is subject to the biological principles originally set forth by Charles Darwin.

[4] In 1274, in his *Tractate de musica,* the French theorist Elias Salomonis describes the conducting of groups of musicians, of singers singing in parts, in free organum. One of the group sings from a large book with notation in front of it, and the three others sing along in parallel octaves, fifths, or fourths. The conductor, himself one of the singers, must be well trained: he beats time with his hand on the book and signals the cues and rests to the singers. If one singer is wrong, the conductor whispers a warning and correction in his ear so that none of the other singers can hear him; or in emergencies he gives support with his own voice if the singers are lost (G 3.59, 88). Salomonis also sketched a solmization of syllables of Guido and gave them a mysterious hidden meaning through symbolization. The eight church modes, he thought, came from a primal *tonus*, the first

mode being a "son," the others being brothers, companions, grandsons, etc.

[5] Theodore de Campo (c.1450), in Cou 3.191, and Simon Tunsted (d. 1369), in Cou 4.257.

[6] Marchetto is brother in this respect to Prosdocimus de Beldemandis (*Tractatus practice cantus mensurabilis ad modum Ytalicarum*, 1412) who thinks Italian notation superior to the French.

[7] As with early plainchant, the implication is that rhythm is qualitative, in keeping with ancient, inherited prosody. Leo Treitler, however, makes a case for the emergence of accentual rhythm in the *ars antiqua* ("Regarding Meter and Rhythm in the Ars Antiqua," *Musical Quarterly*, 65 [1974], 524-58): the initial (long) element of the modal foot was consonantal and accented, especially in perfections. This raises questions not only about the durational organization of late medieval polyphonic music, but also about the possibly accentual character of Greek and Latin poetry as advanced by John Addington Symonds (*Blank Verse* [1895]) and others.

[8] In the last section of the *Pomerium musicae mensuratae*, Marchetto lists four "imperfect" modes to be added to the traditional perfect five and seems to suggest that a composition be "mixed," perfect and imperfect intermingling, as it were. (Modes 1, 2, and 6 were proper [*modus rectus*] because they were set in ancient versification. On the other hand, 3, 4, and 5 are "beyond measure" [*ultra mensuram*] because mathematical elements were less than 1 or more than 2.)

[9] Adapted from Strunk, *Source Readings*, p. 177.

[10] A more detailed account of mensuration can be found in the work of 1412 by Prodocimus de Baldemandis, who, admitting a dependence on Marchetto, in discursive prose lists the notes, their measurements and alterations, and the corresponding rests--all against a background of French and Italian practice.

[11] Waite, *Rhythm of Twelfth-Century Polyphony*, p. 44.

[12] Nino Pirrotta, "Marchettus de Padua and the Italian Ars Nova," *Musica Disciplina*, 9 (1955), 66, suggests that chromaticism was the result of the freedom felt by ecclesiastical musicians to express themselves in secular music when they left the monasteries.

Philippe de Vitry refers to *musica falsa* as chromatic alterations in pitches required by the old modal rules. The first such alteration, dated at least as early as the tenth century, is, as I have mentioned, the substitution of b-flat for b so that the augmented fourth of f--F could be avoided (or b--f-sharp so that the b--f diminished fifth could be avoided). Other alterations as Marchetto describes them were the raising of the seventh so that the interval between the seventh and the eighth was a half-step rather than a whole-step. The alterations were often singers' changes not always incorporated in the written text or score. A description of the practice is found later also in Ugolino of Orvietto and Prosdocimus de Beldemandis.

[13] Atkins, *Literary Criticism: The Medieval Phase*, pp. 108-09.

[14] Ibid., p. 167.

[15] Crane, "A Study of the Theoretical Writings on Musical Form to c.

1460," pp. 201ff.

[16] Translated in ibid., p. 206.

[17] See also ibid., pp. 217-20, and the chart showing different opinions on p. 226.

Among the theorists one should not forget Jean Ciconia (1335-1411), a Walloon who was born in Liège but died in Italy. He was both composer and theorist. His *Nova musica* is a general musical instruction book about plainchant. Its sources seem almost universal: Jerome, Augustine, Boethius, Isidore, Hucbald, Guido, Rémi, Marchetto, and others. Especially to be noted is the book-section, *De proportionibus musicae*, in which Ciconia goes beyond plainchant to discuss the French isorhythmic style and canonic imitation as well as rhythmic and voice-leading styles which look forward to usage occurring much later.

[18] For a convenient discography of polyphonic works available on recordings, see Henry, *Listener's Guide*, pp. 53-55.

[19] *Itinerary through Wales and the Description of Wales*, trans. Richard C. Hoare and Thomas Wright, in Giraldus Cambrensis, *The Historical Works* (London: Bohn, 1913), p. 498.

[20] Tatarkiewicz, *History of Aesthetics*, II, 130-31.

[21] Andrew Tomasello, *Music and Ritual at Papal Avignon, 1309-1403* (Ann Arbor: UMI Research Press, 1983), pp. 6-9, 116-17.

[22] Anselm Hughes, ed., *Early Medieval Music Up to 1300*, rev. ed., New Oxford History of Music, 2 (London: Oxford Univ. Press, 1955), pp. 350-52. There is also a convenient description in H. E. Woodbridge, *The Oxford History of Music*, rev. ed., 2nd ed., rev. by Percy C. Buck (1929), I, Pt. 1, 299.

[23] G. G. Coulton, ed., *Life in the Middle Ages*, revised ed. (Cambridge: Cambridge Univ. Press, 1967), IV, 173.

[24] Jeremy Montagu, *The World of Medieval and Renaissance Musical Instruments* (Newton Abbot and London: David and Charles, 1976), p. 51.

[25] See Peter Dronke, *The Medieval Lyric* (New York: Harper and Row, 1968), p. 91.

[26] For an excellent account of Johannes' Aristotelianism, see Patricia DeWitt, "A New Perspective on de Grocheo's *Ars Musicae*," unpublished Ph.D. diss. (Univ. of Michigan, 1973), pp. 43-46.

[27] See ibid., pp. 94-102, for a fine summary of medieval definitions of music.

[28] Eustache Deschamps (d. 1391), in a section called *De musique* of his *L'art de dictier*, says that it is not music as such which pleases men, but rather its courtly or polite forms (*Ouvres complètes,* ed. G. Raymond [Paris: Didot, 1878-1903], VIII, 269ff). He of course in some degree reminds one of Johannes de Grocheo. But there are differences: he contrasts polyphony with natural music. Artificial music is polyphonic, but natural music is poetic and cannot be learned if one has no disposition for it. This is hardly Erigena's and Regino's distinction. Though both musical and poetic arts can be performed for themselves alone, both benefit by being combined

(ibid., pp. 269-72). Thus Deschamps is concerned not with the musical work of art or with national or popular and artistic music (as is Johannes of Grocheo), but with artistic forms of expression appealing to the sense of hearing. Among these forms he includes instrumental music. Courtly, polite forms seem to have their own autonomy.

29 Johannes de Grocheo, pp. 16-17, and Crane, "A Study," p. 131.

30 For a searching textual analysis of the use of the two terms considered here, see Crane, "A Study," *passim*, according to his listing of "neume, neupna," p. 306. Since 'neume' may be a corruption of the Greek 'pneuma,' or breath, the neume and neupna are related to the distinction, another breath-related term.

31 For a convenient treatment of homophonic secular music, not treated at any length in medieval theory except by Johannes of Grocheo, see *Early Medieval Music*, ed. Hughes, pp. 220-69.

32 Engelbert of Admont (d. 1331) did not: in his *De musica*, not a comprehensive work but an introduction for a specific audience, he shows himself to be conventional and a repeater of accepted theories. His work is like an index to Part II of the present book because he quotes directly from Boethius, Plato's *Timaeus*, Macrobius, Rémi, Martianus Capella, Aristotle, Galen, Avicenna, Algazel, Aribo, "Odo," Aurelian, Guido, and others. He is especially fond of referring to Pseudo-Aristotle. He himself composed poems and various kinds of writings in prose. His *De musica* was written for the monks at Admont, but also was designed as a corrective for the corrupting influences of wandering students (the Goliards, presumably). He uses the term *melodicus* with reference to Boethius (G 2.289) and reminds one of William of Conches' use of the term *melica*. He finds the use of distinctions especially appropriate for the convenience of the singer and for the recognition by the listeners of effortful rises, quiet descents, and final repose (G 2.368).

33 Joseph Smith, "Ars Nova--A Re-Definition?" *Musica Disciplina*, 18 (1964), 27.

34 Ibid., Pt. II, *Musica Disciplina*, 19 (1965), 92.

35 Walter Grossman, *Die Einleitenden Kapital des Speculum Musicae von J. Muris [Jacob of Liège]* (Leipzig: Breitkopf und Härtel, 1924), p. 76.

36 Leichtentritt, *Music, History, and Ideas*, p. 56.

37 In Elizabeth Gilmore Holt, *Literary Sources of Art History* (Princeton: Princeton Univ. Press, 1947), p. 71.

38 The above is indebted to Albert Seay, "Ugolino of Orvietto, Theorist and Composer," *Musica Disciplina*, 9 (1955), 111-66; 11 (1957), 126-33.

39 Reese, *Music in the Middle Ages*, p. 381.

40 D. P. Walker, *Spiritual and Demonic Magic from Ficino to Campanella* (London: Warburg Institute, 1958), *passim*.

41 H. Edmund Poole, "Printing and Publishing Music (I)," *New Grove Dictionary of Music and Musicians*, XV, 233.

Select Bibliography

ABBREVIATIONS

ACW Ancient Christian Writers: The Works of the Fathers in Translation. Westminster, Maryland: Newman Press, 1946-65. 35 vols.

Ancilla Freeman, Kathleen. *Ancilla to the Pre-Socratic Philosophers.* Cambridge: Harvard Univ. Press, 1957.

ANF Ante-Nicene Fathers: The Translations of the Writings of the Fathers down to A.D. 325, ed. Alexander Roberts and James Donaldson. 1917-25; rpt. Grand Rapids, Mich.: Eerdmans, 1951-53. 10 vols.

Aspects *Aspects of Medieval and Renaissance Music*, ed. Jan LaRue. New York: Pendragon Press, 1966.

BGPM Beiträge zur Geschichte der Philosophie des Mittelalters.

Cou Coussemaker, C. E., ed. *Scriptores de musica medii aevi series.* 1864-76; rpt. Milan: Bolletino Bibliografico musicale, 1931. 4 vols.

FC The Fathers of the Church: A New Translation. New York and Washington, D.C.: Catholic Univ. of America Press, 1947- . 73 vols.

G Gerbert, Martin, ed. *Scriptores ecclesiastici de musica sacra potissimum.* 1784; rpt. Hildesheim: Georg Olms, 1963.

JAMS *Journal of the American Musicological Society.*

JMT *Journal of Music Theory.*

LCL Loeb Classical Library. Cambridge, Mass.: Harvard Univ. Press.

Meibom   Meibom, Martin. *Antiquae musicae auctores septem,*
                  graece et latine. Amsterdam, 1652. 2 vols.

MD   *Musica Disciplina*

NPN1   Nicene and Post-Nicene Fathers of the Christian Church,
                  1st ser., ed. Philip Schaff.   1886; rpt: Grand Rapids,
                  Mich.: Eerdmans, 1956. 14 vols.

NPN2   Nicene and and Post-Nicene Fathers of the Christian
                  Church, 2nd ser., ed. Philip Schaff and Henry Wace.
                  1890; rpt. Grand Rapids, Mich.: Eerdmans, 1925-56. 14
                  vols.

Pfrogner   Pfrogner, Herman. *Musik: Geschichte ihrer Deutung.*
                  Freiburg and Munich: Karl Alber, 1964.

PG   *Patrologia Graeca,* ed. Jacques Paul Migne.   Paris,
                  1857-86. 162 vols.

PL   *Patrologia Latina,* ed. Jacques Paul Migne.   Paris,
                  1844-55. 221 vols.

Strunk   Strunk, Oliver. *Source Readings in Music History: From*
                  Classical Antiquity through the Romantic Era.   New
                  York: W. W. Norton, 1950.

Tatar.   Tatarkiewicz, Wladyslaw. *History of Aesthetics.*   The
                  Hague: Mouton, 1970-74. 3 vols.

Wille   Wille, Gunther. *Musica Romana.* Amsterdam: Schippers,
                  1967.

SOURCES CITED IN TEXT
AND OTHER PRINCIPAL WORKS

Adelard of Bath

Haskins, Charles H. "Adelard of Bath," *English Historical Review*, 26 (1910), 491-98.
Willner, Hans. *Des Adelard von Bath Traktat De eodem et diverso.* BGPM, 4. 1903.

Alan of Lille

Alan of Lille. *Anticlaudianus, or the Good and Perfect Man*, trans. James J. Sheridan. Toronto: Pontifical Institute of Mediaeval Studies, 1973.
Baumgarten, M. *Die Philosophie des Alanus de Insulis.* BGPM 2, No. 4. 1896.

Albertus Magnus

Hüschen, Heinrich.   "Albertus Magnus und seine Musikanschauung," *Speculum musicae artis: Festgabe für Heinrich Husmann*, ed. Heinz Becker and Reinhard Gerloch.   Munich: Wilhelm Fink, 1970.   Pp. 205-18.

Alcuin (formerly attributed to)

Alcuin. *Musica.* G 1.26-27.

Al Farabi

Al Farabi. *Arabic-Latin Writings on Music*, trans. and ed. Henry George Farmer. Glasgow: Civic Press, 1934.
Farmer, Henry George. *Historical Facts for the Arabian Musical Influence.* London: W. Reeves, 1930.
Randel, Don M. "Al Farabi and the Role of Arabic Music Theory in the Latin Middle Ages," *JAMS*, 29 (1976), 173-88.

Ambrose

Ambrose. *Concerning Virgins*, trans. E. de Ronastin. NPN2 10. Rpt. 1955.
_____. *De Abraham. PL* 14.
_____. *De Eliaet et Jujunic. PL* 14.
_____. *De Noe et Arca. PL* 14.
_____. *Explanation of the Twelve Psalms of David. PL* 14.
_____. *Jacob and the Happy Life*, trans. Michael P. McHugh.   FC 65. 1972.

_____. *Letters*, trans. Sister Mary Melchior Beyenka. FC 26. 1954.
_____. *Homilies on the Hexaemeron and Various Psalms*, trans. John J. Savage. FC 42. 1961.
_____. *The Prayer of Job and David*, trans. Michael P. McHugh. FC 65. 1972.
_____. *Select Works and Letters*, trans. H. de Romestin. NPN2 10. Rpt. 1955.

Ammianus Marcellinus

Ammianus Marcellinus. [*Works*], trans. J. C. Rolfe. LCL. 1950-52. 3 vols.

Aribo Scholasticus

Aribo Scholasticus. *De musica*. G 2.197-230.

Aristides Quintilianus

Aristeides Quintilianus. *Von der Musik*, trans. (German) Rudolf Schäfke. Berlin: Hesse, 1937.

Aristotle

Aristotle. *The Basic Works*, ed. Richard McKeon. New York: Random House, 1941.
_____. *Works*, ed. F. A. Smith and W. D. Ross. Oxford: Clarendon Press, 1908-52. 12 vols.
See also Pseudo-Aristotle.

Aristoxenus

Aristoxenus. *The Harmonics*, trans. and ed. Henry S. Macran. Oxford: Clarendon Press, 1902.
Abdy-Williams, C. F. *The Aristoxenian Theory of Musical Rhythm*. Cambridge: Cambridge Univ. Press, 1911.

Athenaeus

Athenaeus. *The Deipnosophists*, trans. Charles Burton Gulick. LCL. 1927-41. 7 vols.

Athanasius the Great

Athanasius the Great. *Epistola ad Marcellinum, De titulus in psalmorum*. *PG* 27.

Augustine, Bishop of Hippo

Augustine. *The City of God*, trans. John Healey. New York: Dutton, 1945. 2 vols.

_____. *Confessions*, trans. William Watts. LCL. 1960-61. 2 vols.

_____. *Divine Providence and the Problem of Evil*, trans. Robert F. Russell. FC 5 [1]. 1948.

_____. *Expositions of the Psalms*, trans. J. E. Tweed. NPN1 8. 1888; rpt. 1956.

_____. *Letters*, trans. Sister Winifred Parsons. FC 12, 18, 20, 30, 32. 1951-56.

_____. *On Christian Doctrine*, trans. D. W. Robertson, Jr. Indianapolis: Bobbs-Merrill, 1981.

_____. *On Christian Doctrine*, trans. J. F. Shaw. NPN1 2. 1886; rpt. 1956.

_____. *On Music*, trans. Robert Catesby Taliaferro. FC 4. 1949.

_____. *On the Psalms (1-37)*, trans. Scholastica Hebgin and Felicitas Corrigan. ACW 29-30. 1960-61. 2 vols.

_____. *On the Trinity (De Trinitatis)*, trans. A. W. Hadden. NPN1 3. 1887; rpt. 1956.

_____. *The Retractions*, trans. M. I. Bogan. FC 60. 1968.

_____. *Sermons on the Liturgical Seasons*, trans. Mary Sarah Mudowney. FC 38. 1959.

_____. *The Teacher, The Free Choice of the Will, Grace and Free Will*, trans. Robert P. Russell. FC 59. 1968.

_____. *The Way of the Manicheans*, trans. I. Gallagher. FC 56. 1966.

Knight, W. F. Jackson. *St. Augustine's* De Musica*: A Synopsis*. 1946; rpt. London: Orthological Institute, 1949.

Aurelian of Réôme

Aurelian of Réôme. *The Discipline of Music (Musica Disciplina)*, trans. Joseph Ponte. Colorado Springs, Colorado: Colorado College Music Press, 1968.

_____. *Musica disciplina*, ed. Lawrence Gushee. American Institute of Musicology, 1975.

Aurelianus, Caelius

Aurelianus, Caelius. *On Acute Diseases and Chronic Diseases*, trans. and ed. I. E. Drabkin. Chicago: Univ. of Chicago Press, 1950.

Bacon, Roger

Bacon, Roger. *Opus Maius*, trans. and ed. Robert Belle Burke. Philadelphia: Univ. of Pennsylvania Press, 1928. 2 vols.

Basil the Great

Basil the Great. *De titulis in psalmorum 150. PG* 27.
_____. *Epistola ad Marcellinum. PG* 27.
_____. *Exegetic Homilies (on the Hexaemeron and Select Psalms)*, trans. Sister Agnes Clare Way. FC 46. 1963.
_____. *Expos. in Psalmorum. PG* 27.
_____. *Letters*, II (186-368), trans. Sister Agnes Clare Way. FC 28. 1955.

Bede (attributed to)

Bede, the Venerable. *Musica Theorica. PL* 90.
_____. *Musica quadrata, mensurata, seu practica. PL* 90.

Bernard of Clairvaux

Bernard of Clairvaux. *Epistles. PL* 182.
_____. *Praefatio seu tractatus de cantu seu correctione antiphonarii. PL* 183.
_____. *Sermones in Cantica. PL* 183.

Berno of Reichenau

Berno of Reichenau. *Prologus in Tonarium.* G 2.62-91.
_____. *De varia psalmorum.* G 2.91-114.

Boethius

Boethius. *Arithmetica. PL* 63.
_____. *Consolation of Philosophy*, trans. of 1609 revised and ed. H. F. Stewart. LCL. 1962.
_____. *Fünf Bücher über die Musik*, trans. (German) Oskar Paul. 1872; rpt. Hildesheim: Georg Olms, 1973.
_____. *The Principles of Music*, ed. and trans. Calvin Bower. Ph.D. diss., George Peabody College, 1969.
Chamberlain, David S. "Philosophy of Music in the *Consolatio* of Boethius," *Speculum*, 45 (1970), 80-97.

Cassiodorus

Cassiodorus. *De artibus et disciplinis liberalium litterarum. PL* 70
_____. *Exposito* in *Psalterium. PL* 70.
_____. *Institutiones.* Trans. in Strunk, pp. 87-92.
_____. *Letters,* trans. Thomas Hodgkin. London: H. Frowde, 1886.
_____. *Senator: An Introduction to Divine and Human Readings
[Institutiones],* trans. Leslie Webber Jones.   1946; rpt. New York:
Octagon Books, 1966.

Censorinus

Censorinus. *De die natale,* ed. F. Hultsch. Leipzig: Teubner, 1867.
Wille, pp. 595-601.

Chalcidius

Switalski, Bronislaw W. *Des Chalcidius Kommentar zu Platos* Timaeus.
BGPM, 3, No. 6. 1902.

Cicero

Cicero. *Brutus, On the Nature of Gods, On Divination, On Duties,* trans.
Hubert M. Poteat, introd. Richard McKeon. Chicago: Univ. of Chicago
Press, 1950.
_____. *Brutus, Orator,* trans. G. L. Henderson and H. M. Hubbell.
LCL. 1962.
_____. *De Finibus Bonorum et Malorium [On the Ends of Goods
and Evils],* trans. H. Rackham. LCL. 1951.
_____. *De Natura Deorum, Academica,* trans. H. Rackham. LCL.
1961.
_____. *De Officiis [On Moral Duties],* trans. Walter Miller. LCL.
1968.
_____. *De Oratore [The Making of an Orator], Books I and II,* trans.
E. W. Sutton and H. Rackham. LCL. 1959.
_____. *De Oratore, Book III, De Fato, Paradoxa Stoicorum, De
Partitione Oratoria [The Parts of Oratory],* trans. H. Rackham. LCL.
1960.
_____. *De Senectute, De Amicitia, De Diviniatione,* trans. William
Armistead Falconer. LCL. 1971.
_____. *Letters to His Friends (including Letters to Quintus),* trans.
W. Glynn Williams *et al.* LCL. 1927-28. 4 vols.
_____. *On the Laws: De Re Publica, De Legibus,* trans. Clinton
Walker Keyes. LCL. 1961.
_____. *Tuscalan Disputations,* trans. J. E. King. LCL. New York:
Putnam, 1927.

Clement of Alexandria

Clement of Alexandria. *Christ the Educator*, trans. Simon P. Wood. FC 23. 1951.

_____. *Exhortation to the Heathen*, trans. Mr. Wilson. ANF 2. Rpt. 1951.

_____. *The Instructor*, trans. Mr. Wilson. ANF 2. Rpt. 1951.

_____. *Miscellanies (Stromata)*, trans. Mr. Wilson. ANF 2. Rpt. 1951.

Cleonides

Cleonides. *Harmonic Introduction*. Trans. in Strunk, pp. 34-46.

Cotton, John

See John Cotton.

Dante Alighieri

Dante Alighieri. *The Banquet (Convivio)*, trans. W. W. Jackson. Oxford: Clarendon Press, 1909.

_____. *The Divine Comedy*, trans. John Ciardi. New York: New American Library, 1954-61. 3 vols.

_____. *On Eloquence in the Vernacular*. In *Literary Criticism of Dante Alighieri*, trans. Robert S. Haller. Lincoln: Univ. of Nebraska Press, 1973.

Diogenes Laertius

Diogenes Laertius. *Lives of the Eminent Philosophers*, trans. R. D. Hicks. LCL. 1942. 2 vols.

Dionysius of Halicarnasus

Dionysius of Halicarnasus. *The Critical Essays*, trans. Stephen Usher. LCL. 1976.

_____. *On Literary Composition*, trans. W. Rhys Roberts. 1910; rpt. New York: AMS Press, 1976.

_____. *Roman Antiquities*, trans. Ernest Carey. LCL. 1937-50.

Dionysius, the (Pseudo) Areopagite

Dionysius, the Areopagite. *Celestial Hierarchies*. *PL* 122.

_____. *The Divine Names and the Mystical Theology*, trans. C. E. Rolt. New York: Macmillan, 1957.

Engelbert of Admont

Engelbert of Admont. *De musica*. G 2.287-369.
Fowler, George Bingham. *The Intellectual Interests of Engelbert of Admont*. New York: Columbia Univ. Press, 1947.

Euclid

Davy, Charles. *Letters . . . upon Subjects of Literature*. Bury St. Edmunds, 1787. Vol. II.

Eusebius Pamphili of Caesaria

Eusebius. *Commentary on the Psalms*. *PG* 23.
_____. *Ecclesiastical History*. NPN2 1. Rpt. 1952.

Franco of Cologne

Franco of Cologne. *Ars cantus mensurabilis*. Trans. in Strunk, pp. 139-59.

Gellius, Aulus

Gellius, Aulus. *The Attic Nights*, trans. John C. Rolfe. LCL. 1927. 3 vols.

Gil of Zamora
See John (Gil) of Zamora.

Gregory of Nyssa

Gregory of Nyssa. *On the Soul and Resurrection*. In *Ascetical Works*, trans. Virginia Woods Callahan. FC 58. 1967.

Gregory the Great

Gregory the Great. *Dialogues*, trans. Odo John Zimmerman. FC 39. 1959.

Grosseteste, Robert

Baur, Ludwig. *Die Philosophie des Robert Grosseteste, Bischofs von Lincoln*. BGPM, 9 (1912); 18 (1917). 2 vols.
Grosseteste, Robert. *On Light*, trans. Clare C. Riedl. Milwaukee: Marquette Univ. Press, 1942.

Guido of Arezzo

Guido of Arrezo. *Micrologus*. In *Hucbald, Guido, and John on Music,* trans. Warren Babb, ed. Claude Palisca. New Haven: Yale Univ. Press, 1978. Pp. 57-100.

Gundisalvo

Gundissalinus, Domenicus. *De divisione philosophie*, ed. Ludwig Bauer. BGPM, 4, Pts. 2-3. 1903.

Hermanus Contractus

Hermanus Contractus. *Musica*, trans. and ed. Leonard Ellinwood. Rochester, N.Y.: Eastman School of Music, 1936.

Hesiod

Hesiod. *The Works and Days, Theogony, The Shield of Heracles*, trans. Richard Lattimore. Ann Arbor: Univ. of Michigan Press, 1959.

Hibeh Papyri

The Hibeh Papyri, Pt. I, trans. and ed. Bernard P. Grenfell and Arthur S. Hunt. London and Boston: Egypt Exploration Fund, 1906.

Hilary of Poitiers

Hilary of Poitiers. *Prologue to the Book of Psalms*. PL 9.

Hippolytus

Hippolytus. *Fragments from Commentaries on the Psalms.* ANF 5. Rpt. 1951.

Homer

Homer. *The Iliad,* trans. Robert Fitzgerald. Garden City, N.Y.: Doubleday, 1975.
_____. *The Odyssey*, trans. Robert Fizgerald. Garden City, N.Y.: Doubleday, 1963.

Horace

Horace. *The Complete Works*, trans. various hands, ed. Casper J. Kraemer, Jr. New York: Random House, 1936.

_____. *Opera*, ed. Edward C. Wickham. 1901; rpt. Oxford: Clarendon Press, 1952.

Hucbald

Hucbald. *Melodic Instruction*. In *Hucbald, Guido, and John on Music*, trans. Warren Babb, ed. Claude V. Palisca. New Haven: Yale Univ. Press, 1978. Pp. 13-46.

Hugh of St.-Victor

Hugh of St. Victor. *Didascalicon*, trans. Jerome Taylor. New York: Columbia Univ. Press, 1962.
Ostler, Heinrich. *Die Psychologie des Hugo von St. Viktor*. BGPM, 6 Münster, 1906.

Iamblichus

Iamblichus of Chalcis. *The Life of Pythagoras, or Pythagorean Life*, trans. Thomas Taylor. London, 1818.
_____. *The Mysteries of the Egyptians, Chaldeans, and Assyrians*, trans. Thomas Taylor, 2nd ed. London: Dobell Reeves and Turner, 1895.

Isidore of Seville

Brahaut, Ernest. *Isidore of Seville: An Encyclopedist of the Middle Ages*. New York: Columbia Univ. Press, 1912.
Isidore of Seville. *Etymologiarum*. Trans. in Strunk, pp. 93-100.

Jacob of Liège

Grossmann, Walter. *Die einleitenden Kapital des Speculum Musicae von J. Muris [Jacob of Liège]*. Leipzig: Breitkopf und Härtel, 1924.
Jacob of Liège. *Speculum musicae*, ed. Roger Brogard. Rome: American Institute of Musicology, 1955-73. 7 vols.
_____. *Speculum musicae*. Trans. in Strunk, pp. 180-90.

Jean de Muris

Jean de Muris. *Ars novae musicae*. Trans. in Strunk, pp. 172-79.
_____. *Libellus cantus mensurabilis*. Cou 3.

Jerome

Jerome. *Commentary on the Epistle of St. Paul to the Ephesians*. PL 26. Trans. in Strunk, pp. 71-72.

_____. *Letters and Select Works*, trans. W. H. Fremantle. NPN2 6. Rpt. 1955.

_____. *Select Letters*, trans. F. A. Wright. LCL. 1963.

Johannes of Grocheo

Johannes de Grocheo. *Concerning Music (De musica)*, trans. Albert Seay, 2nd ed. Colorado Springs: Colorado College Music Press, 1974.

John Chrysostom

John Chrysostom. [*Works.*] *PG* 48, 55, 57.

Jerome. *Exposition of Psalm XLI*. Trans. in Strunk, pp. 67-70.

John Cotton

John. *On Music*. In *Hucbald, Guido, and John on Music*, trans. Warren Babb, ed. Claude V. Palisca. New Haven: Yale Univ. Press, 1978. Pp. 101-87.

John of Garland

Johannes de Garlandia. *Concerning Measured Music (De mensurabili musica)*, trans. Stanley H. Birnbaum. Colorado Springs: Colorado College Music Press, 1978.

Paetow, Louis John. "The Crusading Ardor of John of Garland," in *Essays Presented to Dana C. Munro*, ed. L. J. Paetow. New York: Crofts, 1928. Pp. 207-22.

_____. *The Intellectual Interests of John of Garland*. Memoirs of the University of California, 4. 1914.

John (Gil) of Zamora

Joannes Aegidii Zamorensis. *Ars musica*. G 2.369-93.

John of Salisbury

John of Salisbury. *Frivolities of Courtiers and Footprints of Philosophers (Policraticus, Books I, I, III, and Parts of VII and VIII)*, trans. Joseph B. Pike. Minneapolis: Univ. of Minnesota Press, 1958.

_____. *The Metalogicon*, trans. Daniel D. McGarry. Berkeley and Los Angeles: Univ. of California Press, 1955.

John Scot Erigena

Handschin, Jacques. "Die Musikanschauung der Ioh. Scotus," *Deutsche*

Vierteljahrsschrift für Literaturwissenschaft und Geistesgeschichte, 5 (1927), 316-41.
John Scot Erigena. *De divisione naturae*. *PL* 122.

Lactantius

Lactantius. *The Divine Institutes*, trans. Mary Francis McDonald. Books I-VIII. FC 49. 1964.

Lucretius

Lucretius. *On Nature*, trans. Russel M. Geer. New York: Bobbs-Merrill, 1965.

Macrobius

Macrobius. *Commentary on the Dream of Scipio*, trans. William Harris Stahl. New York: Columbia Univ. Press, 1952.

Marchetto of Padua

Marchetto of Padua. *The Lucidarium*, trans. Jan W. Herlinger. Chicago: Univ. of Chicago Press, 1985.
_____. *Pomerium artis musicae mensurabilis*. G3.121-88. Trans. in Strunk, pp. 160-71.
Herlinger, Jan W. "Marchetto's Division of the Whole Tone," *JAMS*, 34 (1981), 193-216.

Martianus Capella

Martianus Capella. *The Marriage of Philology and Mercury*. See *Martianus Capella and the Seven Liberal Arts*, I: *The Quadrivium of Martianus Capella*, trans. William Harris Stahl, Richard Johnson, and E. L. Burge. New York: Columbia Univ. Press, 1971.
Wille, pp. 634-54, 761-62.

Michael Scot

Gallo, Alberto F. "Astronomy and Music in the Middle Ages: The *Liber Introductorius* by Michael Scott," *MD*, 27 (1973), 5-9.

Musica Enchiriadis

Musica Enchiriadis. Music Handbook, trans. Léonie Rosenstiel. Colorado Springs: Colorado College Music Press, 1976.

Nicomachus of Gerasa

Nicomachus of Gerasa. *Introduction to Arithmetic*, trans. Martin Luther d'Ooge. 1926; rpt. New York: Macmillan, 1936.
_____. *Harmonices manuales*. Meibom 2.1-60.

Odo of Cluny (formerly attributed to)

Odo. *Dialogus de musica*. G1.251-303.
_____. *Enchiridion musices*. Trans. in Strunk, pp. 103-16.

Origen

Origen. *Homily on Jeremiah*. PG 13.
_____. *Against Celsus*, trans. Frederick Crombie. ANF 4. 1951.
_____. *On Psalm 150*. PG 12.

Othlo of St. Emmeram

Othlo of St. Emmeram. *Dialogus de tribus quaestionibus*. PL 146.

Ovid

Ovid. *The Art of Love and Other Poems*, trans. J. H. Mozley. LCL. 1929.
_____. *Metamorphoses*, trans. F. J. Miller. LCL. 1916. 2 vols.
_____. *Tristia, Ex Ponto*, trans. A. L. Wheeler. LCL. 1924.

Pausanias

Pausanias. *Description of Greece*, trans. J. G. Frazer. New York: Macmillan, 1898. 6 vols.

Philippe de Vitry

Philippe de Vitry. "Ars Nova," trans. Leon Plantinga, *JMT*, 5 (1961), 204-23.
Bohn, Peter. "Philipp von Vitry," *Monatshefte für Musikgeschichte*, 22 (1890), 141-79.
Werner, Eric. "The Mathematical Foundation of Philippe de Vitry's *Ars Nova*," *JAMS*, 9 (1956), 128-32.

Philodemus

Philodemus. *De musica*, ed. J. Kemke. Leipzig: Teubner, 1884.
Gomperz, Theodor. *Zu Philodemus Bücher von der Musik*. Vienna: A. Hölden, 1885.

Wilkinson, L. P. "Philodemus on Ethos in Music," *Classical Quarterly*, 32 (1938), 174-81.

Philo Judaeus

Philo of Alexandria. [*Works*,] trans. and ed. F. H. Colson and G. H. Whitaker. LCL. 1929-62. 10 vols.

Philostratus

Philostratus. *The Life of Apollonius of Tyana*, trans. F. C. Conybeare. LCL. 1926. 2 vols.

Photius

Photius. *Bibliothèque*. Paris: Les Belles Lettres, 1959-62. 3 vols.

Pindar

Pindar. *The Odes*, trans. Richard Lattimore.   Chicago: Univ. of Chicago Press, 1947.

Plato

Plato. *The Dialogues*, trans. Benjamin Jowett.   New York: Random House, 1937. 2 vols.

Pliny, the Elder

Pliny, the Elder. *Natural History*, trans. H. Rackham, W. H. Jones, and D. E. Eichholz. LCL. 1938-63. 10 vols.

Pliny , the Younger

Pliny, the Younger. *Letters*, trans. William Melmoth. LCL. 1923-24. 2 vols.

Plotinus

Plotinus. *The Enneads*, trans. Stephen Mackenna, 3rd ed., revised by B. S. Page. London: Faber and Faber, 1962.

Plutarch

Plutarch. *Moralia*. LCL. 1926-76. 15 vols.
_____. *On Moral Virtue*, trans. W. C. Helmhold. *Moralia*, Vol. XIII.

_____. *On the Generation of the Soul in the* Timaeus, trans. Harold Cherniss. *Moralia,* Vol. XIII.

_____. *The Parallel Lives,* trans. B. Perrin. LCL. 1914-26. 11 vols.

_____. *A Pleasant Life Impossible,* trans. B. Einarson and P. H. DeLacey. *Moralia,* Vol. VII.

_____. *Table Talk,* trans. Paul A. Clement and Herbert B. Hoffleit. *Moralia,* Vol. VIII.

See also Pseudo-Plutarch.

Polybius

Polybius. *The Histories,* trans. W. R. Paton. LCL. 1954. 6 vols.

Porphyry

Düring, Ingemar, ed. *Ptolemaios und Porphyrios über die Musik.* Göteborg: Elander, 1934.

_____. *Porphyrios Kommentar zu Harmonielehre des Ptolemaios.* Göteborg: Elander, 1932.

Porphyry. *On Abstinence from Animal Food,* trans. Thomas Taylor, ed. Esme Wynne-Tyson. New York: Barnes and Noble, 1965.

Proclus

Proclus Diadochus. *The Commentaries of Proclus on the* Timaeus *of Plato,* trans. Thomas Taylor. London, 1820.

Rosán, Laurence Jay. *The Philosophy of Proclus.* New York: Cosmos, 1949.

Prosdocimus de Beldemandis

Prosdocimus de Beldemandis. *A Treatise on the Practice of Mensural Music in the Italian Manner (Tractatus pratice cantus mensurabilis ad modam ytalicorum),* trans. and ed. Jay A. Huff. American Institute of Musicology, 1972.

Psellus, Michael

Psellus, Michael. *Chronographia,* trans. E. R. A. Sewter. London: Routledge and Kegan Paul, 1953.

Pseudo-Aristotle

[Pseudo-] Aristotle. *Problemata,* trans. under editorship of E. S. Forster. In Aristotle, *Works,* ed. F. A. Smith and W. D. Ross. Oxford: Clarendon Press, 1927. Vol. VII.

Pseudo-Dionysius

See Dionysius, the [Pseudo-] Areopagite.

Pseudo-Plutarch

[Pseudo-Plutarch.]   *On Music*, trans. Benedict Einarson and Philip H. DeLacey. In Plutarch, *Moralia*, Vol. XIV. LCL. 1967.

Ptolemy, Claudius

Düring, Ingemar.   *Porphyrios Kommentar zu Harmonielehre des Ptolemaios*. Göteborg: Elander, 1932.
_____, ed.   *Ptolemaios und Porphyrios über die Musik*. Göteborg: Elander, 1934.
Shirlaw, Matthew. "Claudius Ptolemy as Musical Theorist," *Music Review*, 16 (1955), 181-90.

Quintilian

Quintilian. *Institutio Oratoria,* trans. H. E. Butler. LCL. 1953-60. 4 vols.

Rabanus Maurus

Rabanus Maurus. *Commentarium in Ecclesiasticum*. *PL* 109.
_____. *Commentaria in Libros II in Paralipomenon*. *PL* 109.
_____. *De Clericorum Institutiones*. *PL* 107.
_____. *De Universo*. *PL* 111.

Regino of Prüm

Regino of Prüm. *De harmonica institutione*. G1.230-47.

Rémi of Auxerre

Remigii Atissiodorensis. *Musica*. G1.63-94.

Scolica Enchiriadis

Scholia Enchiriadis. Trans. in Strunk, pp. 126-38.

Seneca

Seneca. *Epistulae Morales to Lucilius*, trans. Richard M. Gummere. LCL. 1920. 3 vols.

Sextus Empiricus

McMahon, A. Philip. "Sextus Empiricus and the Arts," *Harvard Studies in Classical Philology*, 42 (1931), 79-137.
Sextus Empiricus. *Outlines of Pyrrhonism, Against the Logicians, Physicists, Ethicists, Professors*, trans. R. G. Bury. LCL. 1935-76. 4 vols.

Solon

Freeman, Kathleen. *The Life and Work of Solon, with a Translation of His Poems*. London: Oxford Univ. Press, 1926.

Strabo

Strabo. *Geography*, trans. Horace Leonard Jones. LCL. New York: Putnam, 1917-32. 8 vols.

Suetonius

Suetonius. [*Works,*] trans. C. Rolfe. LCL. 1924. 2 vols.

Tertullian

Tertullian. *On Prayer*. ANF 3. 1887; rpt. 1951.

Theodoret

Theodoret. *Comm. on Isaiah*. PG 81.
_____. *Comm. on Ps. 150*. PG 80.
_____. *De Providentia*. PG 83.

Theon of Smyrna

Theon of Smyrna. *Mathematics Useful for Understanding Plato*, trans. Robert and Deborah Lawlor. San Diego: Wizards Bookshelf, 1979.

Theophrastus

Theophrastus. *Metaphysics*, trans. W. D. Ross and F. H. Forbes. 1929; rpt. Hildesheim: Georg Olms, 1967.
Regenbogen, Otto. "Theophrast," *Real Encyclopedie Suppl.*, VII (1950), 1354-62.

Thomas Aquinas

Burbach, Hermann-Joseph. *Studien zur Musikanschauung des Thomas von Aquin.* Regensburg: Gustav Bosse, 1966.

Thomas Aquinas. *Commentary of Thomas Aquinas in Aristotle's* De Anima *in the Version of William of Moerbeke*, trans. Kenelm Foster and Silvester Humphries. 1951; rpt. New Haven: Yale Univ. Press, 1965.

_____. *Commentary on Aristotle's* Physics, trans. Richard J. Blackwell, Richard J. Spaeth, W. Edmund Thirkel. New Haven: Yale Univ. Press, 1963.

_____. *Commentary on the* Metaphysics *of Aristotle*, trans. John P. Rowan. Chicago: Henry Regnery, 1961. 2 vols.

_____. *Commentary on the* Nicomachian Ethics, trans. C. I. Litzinger. Chicago: Henry Regnery, 1964. 2 vols.

_____. *Summa Theologica*, trans. the Fathers of the English Dominican Province. New York: Benziger Brothers, 1947-48. 3 vols.

Ugolino of Orvieto

Seay, Albert. "Ugolino of Orvietto, Theorist and Composer," *MD*, 9 (1955), 111-66; 11 (1957), 126-33.

Virgil

Virgil. *The Aeneid*, trans. Robert Fitzgerald. New York: Random House, 1981.

_____. *The Poems,* trans. James Rhoades. London: Oxford Univ. Press, 1921.

Vitruvius

Vitruvius. *De Architectura*, trans. F. Granger. LCL. New York: Putnam, 1931-34. 2 vols.

William of Conches

William of Conches. *Commentarius in Timaeum Platonis. PL* 172.

_____. *De philosophia mundi. PL* 172.

GENERAL REFERENCES

See also the sources cited in the endnotes to the text of this book.

Armstrong, Arthur H. *An Introduction to Ancient Philosophy*, 3rd ed. London: Methuen, 1957.

Bailey, Cyril. *The Greek Atomists and Epicureans.* Oxford: Clarendon Press, 1928.

Borinski, Karl. *Die Antike in Poetik und Kunst-theorie.* Leipzig: Dietrich, 1914-24. 2 vols.

Bower, Calvin M. "Natural and Artificial Music: The Origins and Development of an Aesthetic Concept," *MD*, 25 (1971), 17-33.

Bragard, R. "L'harmonie des spheres selon Boèce," *Speculum*, 4 (1949), 206-13.

Bruyne, Edgar de. *The Esthetics of the Middle Ages*, trans. Eileen B. Hennessy. New York: Ungar, 1969.

Bukofzer, Manfred F. "Speculative Thinking in Medieval Music," *Speculum*, 17 (1942), 165-80.

Burgh, W. G. de. *The Legacy of the Ancient World.* Harmondsworth: Penguin, 1953. 2 vols.

Burkert, Walter. *Lore and Science in Ancient Pythagoreanism*, trans. Edwin L. Miner, Jr. Cambridge, Mass.: Harvard Univ. Press, 1972.

Burnet, John. *Greek Philosophy, I: Thales to Plato.* London: Macmillan, 1914.

Cantor, Norman F. *Medieval History: The Life and Death of a Civilization,* 2nd ed. New York: Macmillan, 1963.

Carpenter, Nan Cooke. *Music in Medieval and Renaissance Universities.* Norman: Univ. of Oklahoma Press, 1958.

Cazden, Norman. "Pythagoras and Aristoxenos Reconciled," *JAMS*, 11 (1958), 75-105.

Collingwood, Robin George. *An Essay on Metaphysics.* London: Oxford Univ. Press, 1940.

Cornford, Francis M. *Plato's Cosmology.* London: Routledge and Kegan Paul, 1966.

Crocker, Richard L. *The Early Medieval Sequence.* Berkeley and Los Angeles: Univ. of California Press, 1977.

_____. "Hermann's Major Sixth," *JAMS*, 25 (1972), 19-37.

_____. "Some Ninth-Century Sequences," *JAMS*, 20 (1967), 367-402.

Crombie, A. C. "Medieval Scientific Tradition." In *Avicenna: Scientist and Philosopher*, ed. George M. Wickens. London: Luzac, 1952.

Curtius, Ernst Robert. *European Literature and the Latin Middle Ages*, trans. Willard R. Trask. New York: Pantheon Books, 1953.

Dillon, John M. *The Middle Platonists (80 B.C.-A.D. 220).* London: Duckworth, 1977.

Dörrie, Heinrich. "Porphyrios als Mittler zwischen Plotin und Augustine." In *Antike und Orient im Mittelalter*, ed. Paul Wilpert. Miscellanea Mediaevalia, 1. Berlin: Walter de Gruyter, 1962. Pp. 26-47.

Dunbar, H. Flanders. *Symbolism in Medieval Thought*. New Haven: Yale Univ. Press, 1929.

Ellinwood, Leonard. "Ars Musica," *Speculum*, 20 (1945), 290-99.

Finley, M. T. *The World of Odysseus*. New York: Viking, 1977.

Friedman, John Block. *Orpheus in the Middle Ages*. Cambridge, Mass.: Harvard Univ. Press, 1970.

Gérold, Theodor. *Les Péres de l'Église et la musique*. Paris: Hirsch, 1931.

Gibbon, Edward. *The Decline and Fall of the Roman Empire*. New York: Random House, n.d. 3 vols.

Gilbert, Katharine Everett, and Helmut Kuhn. *A History of Esthetics*. New York: Macmillan, 1939.

Gombosi, Otto. "Key, Mode, Species," *JAMS*, 4 (1951), 20-26.

Goodenough, E. R. "A Neo-Pythagorean Source in Philo Judaeus," *Yale Classical Studies*, 3 (1932), 117-64.

Grabman, Martin. *Die Geschichte der scholastischen Methode*. Berlin: Akademie-Verlag, 1956. 2 vols.

Gushee, Lawrence. "Questions of Genre in Medieval Treatises on Music." In *Gattungen der Musik in Einzeldarstellungen: Gedankschrift Leo Schrade*, ed. Wulf Ardt *et al*. Berne: Francke, 1973. Pp. 365-433.

Haase, Rudolf. *Geschichte der Harmonikalen Pythagoreismus*. Vienna: Lafite, 1969.

Hammerstein, Reinhold. *Die Musik der Engel*. Berne and Munich: Francke, 1962.

Handschin, Jacques. "The 'Timaeus' Scale," *MD*, 4 (1950), 3-42.

Henderson, Isobel. "Ancient Greek Music." In *The New Oxford History of Music*, I, ed. Egon Wellesz. London: Oxford Univ. Press, 1957. Pp. 336-403.

_____. "The Growth of Ancient Greek Music," *Music Review*, 4 (1943), 4-13.

Hipkins, A. J. "Dorian and Phrygian," *Sammelbände der Internationalen Musikgesellschaft*, 4 (1903), 371-78.

Hopper, V. F. *Medieval Number Symbolism: Its Sources, Meaning, and Influence on Thought and Expression*. New York: Columbia Univ. Press, 1938.

Hoppin, Richard H. *Medieval Music*. New York: Norton, 1978.

Hucke, Helmut. "Toward a New Historical View of Gregorian Chant," *JAMS*, 33 (1980), 438-67.

Hüschen, Heinrich. "Antike Einflüsse in der mittelalterischen Musikanschauung." In *Antike und Orient im Mittelalter*, ed. Paul Wilpert, Miscellanea Mediaevilia, 1. Berlin: Walter de Gruyter, 1962.

Hughes, Andrew. *Medieval Music: The Sixth Liberal Art*. Toronto: Univ. of Toronto Press, 1974.

Hughes, Anselm, ed. *Early Medieval Music.* New Oxford History of Music, II. 1954; rpt. London: Oxford Univ. Press, 1969.

Jones, L. W. "The Influence of Cassiodorus on Medieval Culture," *Speculum,* 20 (1945), 433-42.

Jungmann, Josef. *The Mass of the Roman Rite,* trans. Francis A. Brunner. New York: Benziger, 1951. 2 vols.

Kirk, Geoffrey S. *Homer and the Oral Tradition.* Cambridge: Cambridge Univ. Press, 1976.

Lang, Paul Henry. *Music in Western Civilization.* New York: Norton, 1941.

Liber Usualis, ed. by the Benedictines of Solesmes. Tournai: Desclee, 1960.

Lippman, Edward A. "Hellenic Conceptions of Harmony," *JAMS,* 16 (1963), 3-85.

Marcuse, Sibyl. *Musical Instruments: A Comprehensive Dictionary.* 1964; rpt. New York: Norton, 1975.

McKeon, Richard. "Rhetoric in the Middle Ages," *Speculum,* 17 (1942), 1-32.

_____, ed. *Selections from Medieval Philosophers.* New York and Boston: Scribner's, 1929-30. 2 vols.

Meyer, Kathi. "Music in Dante's *Divina Commedia.*" In *Aspects,* pp. 614-27.

_____. "Psychologic and Ontologic Ideas in Augustine's *De Musica,*" *Journal of Aesthetics and Art Criticism,* 11 (1952-53), 224-30.

Mountford, James Frederick. "The Harmonics of Ptolemy and the Lacuna in II, 14," *Transactions and Proceedings of the American Philological Association,* 57 (1926), 71-95.

Müller, Hermann. "Zur Musikauffassung des Mittelalters." In *Festscrift Hermann Kretzschmar zum 70. Geburstag.* Leipzig: Hinsch, 1918. Pp. 96-100.

Münxelhaus, Barbara. *Pythagoras Musicus.* Bonn: Verlag für Systematische Musikwissenschaft, 1976.

Neubecker, Annemarie Jeanette. *Die Bewertung der Musik bei Stoikern und Epikurean.* Berlin: Institut für griechisch-römische Altertumskunst der Deutschen Akademie der Wissenschaft, 1956.

Olson, Clair C. "Chaucer and the Music of the Fourteenth Century," *Speculum,* 16 (1941), 64-91.

Perl, Carl Johann. "Augustine and Music," *Musical Quarterly,* 41 (1955), 496-510.

Pfaff, R. W. *Medieval Latin Liturgy: A Select Bibliography.* Toronto: Univ. of Toronto Press, 1982.

Pietzsch, Gerhard. *Die Musik in Erziehungs und Bildungsideal des ausgehenden Altertums und Frühen Mittelalters.* Halle: Niemeyer, 1932.

Pirenne, Henri. *Mahomet and Charlemagne*, trans. Bernard Mirall. London: Allen and Unwin, 1939.

Reaney, Gilbert. "The Question of Authorship in the Medieval Treatises on Music," *MD*, 18 (1964), 7-17.

Rist, John M, ed. *The Stoics*. Berkeley and Los Angeles: Univ. of California Press, 1978.

Sadie, Stanley, ed. *The New Grove Dictionary of Music and Musicians*. London: Macmillan, 1980. 20 vols.

Sanders, Ernest H. "Consonance and Rhythm in the Organum of the 12th and 13th Centuries," *JAMS*, 33 (1980), 264-86.

Schering, Arnold. "Über Musikhören und Musikempfinden in Mittelalter," *Jahrbuch der Musikbibliothek Peters*, 28 (1922), 41-56.

Schipper, Edith. "*Mimesis* in the Arts in Plato's *Laws*," *Journal of Aesthetics and Art Criticism*, 22 (1963-64), 199-202.

Schlesinger, Kathleen. *The Greek Aulos*. Groningen: Bouma, 1970.

Schmitt-Görg, Joseph. "Zur Musikanschauung in den Schriften der Hl. Hildegard." In *Der Mensch und die Künste: Festschrift für Heinrich Lützeler um 60. Geburtstag*. Düsseldorf: L. Schwann, 1962. Pp. 230-37.

Schneider, Marius. "Die historischen Grundlagen der musikalischen Symbolik," *Musikforschung*, 4 (1951), 113-45.

Scott, J. E. "Roman Music." In Egon Wellesz, ed. *Ancient and Oriental Music*, The New Oxford History of Music, I, London: Oxford Univ. Press, 1957. Pp. 404-20.

Seay, Albert. *Music in the Medieval World*, 2nd ed. Engelwood Cliffs, N.J.: Prentice-Hall, 1975.

Snell, Bruno. *The Discovery of the Mind: The Greek Origins of European Thought*, trans. T. G. Rosenmeyer. Cambridge, Mass.: Harvard Univ. Press, 1953.

Sternfeld, Frederick William, ed. *Music from the Middle Ages to the Renaissance*. New York: Praeger, 1973.

Thomson, George D. *Aeschylus and Athens*, 2nd ed. New York: International Publishers, 1950.

Walker, D. P. "Orpheus the Renaissance Theologian and Renaissance Platonist," *Journal of the Warburg and Courtauld Institutes*, 16 (1953), 100-20.

Whittaker, Thomas. *The Neoplatonists: A Study in the History of Hellenism*, 4th ed. 1918; rpt. Hildesheim: Georg Olms, 1961.

Wiener, Philip P. *Dictionary of the History of Ideas*. New York: Scribner, 1968-73. 5 vols.

Winnington-Ingram, R. P. *Mode in Ancient Greek Music*. Cambridge: Cambridge Univ. Press, 1936.

Wolf, Johannes. "Early English Musical Theorists: From 1200 to the Death of Henry Purcell," *Musical Quarterly*, 25 (1939), 420-29.

Zitzmann, Rudolf. "Wort und Weise in Ordo des Mittelalters," *Deutsche Vierteljahrsschrift für Literaturwissenschaft und Geitesgeschichte*, 21 (1943), 437-61.

INDEX

503